Toward a Just
and Caring Society

Toward a Just and Caring Society

Christian Responses to Poverty in America

Edited by David P. Gushee

Baker Books

A Division of Baker Book House Co
Grand Rapids, Michigan 49516

© 1999 by David P. Gushee

Published by Baker Books
a division of Baker Book House Company
P.O. Box 6287, Grand Rapids, MI 49516-6287

Printed in the United States of America

Library of Congress Cataloging-in-Publication Data

Toward a just and caring society : Christian responses to poverty in America /
  edited by David P. Gushee.
      p.   cm.
  Includes bibliographical references.
  ISBN 0-8010-2220-7 (pbk.)
    1. Church work with the poor—United States. 2. Poverty—Religious
  aspects—Christianity. 3. Poverty—United States. I. Gushee, David P., 1962– .
  BV639.P6T73   1999
  261.8'325'0973—dc21   99-41933

For current information about all releases from Baker Book House, visit our web site:
http://www.bakerbooks.com

Contents

Acknowledgments

This work emerged as the result of a collaborative scholarly initiative over a two-year period from 1996 to 1998. The project involved periodic meetings of the volume's contributors, who worked together at every stage of writing to sharpen and refine one another's work.

Funding for this process was generously provided by the Bauman Foundation of Washington, D.C. The editor wishes to thank Patricia Bauman, co-director of the Bauman Foundation, for her foundation's steadfast support of our efforts to craft a significant evangelical response to the problem of poverty in America.

The Bauman Foundation provided its grant to Evangelicals for Social Action (ESA), which provided sponsorship, organizational leadership, and a home for this project throughout its life. ESA contracted with me in the summer of 1997 to assume leadership as project director and editor of the final volume. At that time, the Center for Christian Leadership of Union University, my own institutional home, joined ESA as a co-sponsor of what internally came to be called "the Bauman project." I am grateful to Ron Sider, President of ESA, and to his staff team, for their invitation to take leadership of the project and their partnership in seeing it through to completion.

I offer particular thanks—and congratulations—to each contributor. Reviewers will have the final word as to whether we have done good work here. But I am deeply impressed with the seriousness of purpose and the prodigious scholarship represented by this project's contributors. Mark Noll, among others, has called in recent years for the significant advance of evangelical scholarship. I hope and dare to believe that this interdisciplinary work represents the kind of scholarship needed at this moment in the life of the church and the nation—both in its substance and in its spirit.

I am grateful to David Dockery, Union University's president, and to our provost, Carla Sanderson, for their willingness to invest in the life of evangelical scholarship by releasing me from certain teaching obligations in order to complete work on this volume. More broadly, I am grateful to Union for its unequivocal support of my service on projects such as these, and its appreciation of the place of such efforts within the mission of the university.

My wonderful mother-in-law, Earlynn Grant, deserves thanks for reviewing this manuscript with her careful editor's eye.

I am also grateful to Maria denBoer, senior editor at Baker, for her excellent work in preparing this lengthy manuscript for publication.

I wish to thank my precious family—my wife, Jeanie, and my children, Holly, David, and Marie—for their sacrifice in once again sharing me with a publishing project.

Finally, I thank God, who has graciously seen fit to involve me and other brothers and sisters in Christ in the kingdom work of empowering the poor. Find us worthy servants, O Lord.

Introduction

Christian thinking about the problem of poverty needs to reach a new level of sophistication.

We need to get beyond debates about whether or not poverty really is a problem in this nation; about whether any poverty that might exist can be blamed more readily on conservatives or liberals, Democrats or Republicans; about whether it is the responsibility of the church or the government to address poverty; about whether poverty is rooted in personal irresponsibility or structural injustice, and so on.

We also need to move beyond rhetoric. While cries of anguish on behalf of the poor are altogether appropriate, and prophetic denunciations of poverty in the midst of abundance are also more than legitimate, such expressions of concern mark a beginning to Christian response to the needs of the poor rather than the substance of an anti-poverty agenda.

This project represents an effort to take Christian reflection on poverty to the next level. In this volume, fifteen evangelical Christian scholars of a variety of denominational and professional affiliations tackle various aspects of the problem of poverty as it exists in the United States at the turn of the millennium. The first part of this book explores the relevant biblical, historical, political, and economic foundations both of our poverty problem and of Christian engagement with poverty. Part II addresses a range of specific responses—by churches, other agencies of civil society, and policymakers—that could contribute to the empowerment of the poor.

That term, "empowerment," is significant, and it is carefully chosen. It reflects much about the convictions and spirit animating this work. Let me explain what I mean.

Every contributor to this volume, it is fair to say, is moved deeply by the plight of the poor in the richest nation on earth. We share a passionate desire to see the poor of our nation empowered to enjoy successful participation in the bounty of American economic life.

The foundation of this passion is our shared understanding of the biblical witness, in which God is depicted as profoundly and intimately concerned with economic opportunity for all who are able to work and as compassionate toward those who cannot care for themselves. Prosperity and abundance are good gifts from God, who desires—and demands—that provision be made so such blessings can be universally enjoyed. That provision begins with personal and family responsibility, but extends outward to broader community obligations to establish structures of justice facilitating economic opportunity and offering compassionate relief to those who through no fault of their own cannot participate in them. Various aspects of biblical thought concerning economic life are sketched in various essays included here, but they are the focus of the opening chapter by Ron Sider and Steven Mott. All biblical reflection in this book shares the conviction that empowerment—equipping persons and families for maximum participation in the abundance of economic life—lies at the heart of the biblical economic ethic.

Any honest treatment of the contrast between this biblical norm and contemporary American economic realities reveals an intolerable gulf, and one that cannot be tolerated by people of biblical conviction. The causes, nature, and extent of that gulf between biblical norms and contemporary poverty are very carefully discussed in several chapters. In particular, the contribution by George Monsma (ch. 6), documents the extent of economic inequality in our nation and the way in which the problem is worsening rather than improving. In a restrained but nonetheless devastating presentation, Monsma describes some of the major causes and consequences of poverty today. He makes abundantly clear that despite the overall flourishing of the American economy, many millions are being left behind.

If we are to take poverty seriously it will require some significant intellectual reconfigurations. This is the strand that unites several of the other chapters in part I of the book. Steve Monsma (ch. 2) discusses the need for us to move beyond either/or toward both/and thinking when it comes to both the causes of poverty and ways to address its effects. In particular, he highlights the need for a strong church and civil society aspect to our response to poverty, while not letting government off the hook for its appropriate contribution. Kurt Schaeffer's critical yet appreciative review of Marvin Olasky's influential *Tragedy of American Compassion* (ch. 5) also helps to redress the anti-government imbalance that has developed in conservative Christian economic thought concerning the empowerment of the poor. James Halteman (ch. 3) takes the reader inside the structures of economic theory in search of the place of the poor in that work. Ashley Woodiwiss (ch. 4) examines contemporary political theory in quest of an emphasis on economic justice there, and Tim Slaper (ch. 7) assesses the subtle but still negative impact that the use of current indicators of economic progress has on national concern for (or even consciousness of) the poor.

Building on the groundwork laid in part I, in part II another group of scholars takes aim at various dimensions of the poverty problem and how it might be addressed. A particular value of this section is a reminder that poverty, like the environment, is an inherently multidimensional problem, profoundly interconnected with a host of related social ills and policy problems. Clarke Cochran, for example, leads off this section with a discussion of health care policy as it relates to the poor (ch. 8). His proposals for what can be done reflect the mix of individual, church, civil society, and governmental responses that will be required to adequately address any dimension of a problem as deep as poverty in America. The economist John Anderson next takes on the complex issue of tax policy, indicating both its promise and its limits as a tool for empowering the poor (ch. 9). Charles Glenn, one of our nation's leading experts on education policy, reviews both current educational realities and reform proposals with a keen eye toward their impact on the poor (ch. 10). In a very rich and reflective piece, John Mason follows Glenn with an examination of the health and well-being of our nation's cities, how they got to be the way they are, and what metropolitan responsibility might look like in biblical perspective (ch. 11). Helene Slessarev's contribution (ch. 12) picks up where Mason leaves off, looking closely at community organization efforts, particularly in our nation's cities, with an eye to opportunities for Christian participation in this form of economic empowerment effort. Joe Macariello (ch. 13) takes the discussion in an entirely new direction with an examination of several successful corporations "with a heart for the poor." This chapter highlights the critical role of business in providing opportunity and training for those who are seeking to make the transition from unemployment and/or welfare to work. The final two chapters of the book include Stanley Carlson-Thies's thorough examination of federal welfare and anti-poverty programs after the watershed 1996 welfare reform law (ch. 14), and my own discussion of the relationship between family breakdown and poverty (ch. 15).

The work that results from these disparate contributions is substantive rather than rhetorical, pragmatic rather than utopian, non-ideological rather than partisan, hard headed yet softhearted, and characterized by both/and rather than either/or thinking. It hews closely to the best available data from the relevant social scientific research while always being driven by the foundational biblical concern for—no, commitment to—the poor. It acknowledges market capitalism in a democratic society as the best available economic system in terms of the generation of wealth but seeks ways to involve the maximum number of people in its benefits and to guard the rest from privation and hunger. It includes rich biblical reflection as well as numerous clear and concrete recommendations for action.

While it cannot be denied that this work is of an academic and scholarly nature, it is generally accessible to the informed nonspecialist. The general reader should feel free to peruse this work in ways that are most helpful: skipping the footnotes, jumping around between chapters, scanning the charts, etc. The specialist, on the other hand, will find much rich material here for the advance of her or his thinking about particular matters in economics, political science and public policy, business, social work, education, medicine, urban studies, Bible, and ethics.

As I conclude work on this volume, the House of Representatives has just voted to impeach the President of the United States. Of all the many things one could say about this extraordinary moment in American history, one can certainly say at least this: *every day spent arguing about who will lead the nation is another day spent failing actually to provide that leadership.* As a nation, we—both the people and our representatives—are tempted these days to forget that the reason we have government and elect people to fill its posts is in order to address the pressing problems that face the nation. Very near the top of the list of those problems is the fact that millions of American children live in fractured families, are inadequately nourished, lack access to decent health care, attend miserable schools, dwell in substandard housing, and struggle to survive the dangerous neighborhoods in which they live. While every Christian is called upon to take the most meaningful individual and church-based initiatives available to address poverty, surely we also should work and pray for the time when government itself will have energy once again to address the problems of the miserable ones among us.

David P. Gushee
Union University, Christmas 1998

Note: Public policy is an ever-changing thing, as is social research. Contributors finished their work in the summer of 1998. They cannot be held responsible for data or policy changes that have occurred since then.

Part I

Empowering
the Poor

Foundational Reflections

~ 1 ~

Economic Justice: A Biblical Paradigm

Stephen Mott, Cochesett United Methodist Church
and
Ronald J. Sider, Evangelicals for Social Action

Introduction[1]

Values shape economics. Economic thinking combines empirical analysis and normative beliefs. Whether or not persons realize it, some normative system of values partially determines every economic decision.

Economic thinking, in fact, combines three components: normative beliefs, empirical analysis, and a political philosophy.[2] Fundamental beliefs about things like the nature of persons, history, the creation of wealth, and the nature of just distribution, guide economic decisions. So do complex analyses of economic data and economic history. Each time one wants to make a specific economic decision, however, one cannot stop and rethink all one's normative beliefs on the one hand and undertake elaborate socioeconomic analyses on the other. One needs a road map, a handy guide, so one can make quick but responsible decisions about economics and politics. Such a road map, often called an ideology or a political philosophy, is "a pattern of beliefs and concepts (both factual and normative) which purports to explain complex social phenomena with a view to directing and simplifying socio-political choices facing individuals and groups."[3] Marxist communism and democratic capitalism, of course, have been the two dominant political philosophies of the twentieth century.

Christians, like everyone else, require a political philosophy or ideology. But they dare not adopt an ideology uncritically or they risk violating their most basic confession that Jesus is Lord of all—including economics and politics. That means that Christian truth must determine the shape of a Christian's ideology. Since analysis of the world and normative beliefs are the two essential components that shape any ideology or political philosophy, a Christian must construct his or her political philosophy by combining the most accurate, factual analysis that is available with normative Christian truths.

Where should Christians go for these normative principles and ideas that guide their thinking about economics? The fall has not destroyed all knowledge of truth and goodness given by the Creator to all persons made in God's image (e.g., Rom. 1:18–25); therefore, some Christians look to natural law as a source for the norms needed to guide economic and political life.[4] Sin, however, has profoundly distorted our total being, including our minds. Therefore, in this study we turn to the revealed truth of the Bible as the primary source for our normative framework.

The Bible provides norms for thinking about economics in two basic ways: the biblical story and the biblical paradigm on economic justice.

The biblical story is the long history of God's engagement with our world that stretches from creation through the fall and the history of redemption to the culmination of history when Christ returns. This biblical story offers decisive insight into the nature of the material world, the dignity and character of persons, and the significance and limitations of history. For example, since every person is a body-soul unity made by God for community, no one will ultimately be satisfied with material abundance alone or with material abundance kept only for oneself. Since every person is so important that God became flesh to die for her sins and invite her to live forever with the living God, economic life must be ordered in a way that respects this God-given dignity. We need to explore systematically these and other implications of the biblical story for economic life.

The Bible also provides norms in a second way. It is true that there is no biblical passage with a detailed systematic treatise on the nature of economic justice. But throughout the Bible, we find materials—commands, laws, proverbs, parables, stories, theological propositions—that relate to all the normative questions that economic decisions require. For example, should everyone own productive capital or should just a few? Is justice only concerned with fair procedures or does it include a fair distribution of wealth? In what sense is equality a central goal? What about the creation of wealth? Should we care for those unable to provide for themselves? Every book of the Bible offers material relevant to these kinds of questions.

The same is true of the various types of justice that different thinkers over the years have sought to define. Some of the most important are:

- procedural justice, which specifies fair legal processes for deciding disputes between people
- commutative justice, which defines fair means of exchange of goods (e.g., honest weights and measures)
- distributive justice, which specifies a fair allocation of a society's wealth, resources and power
- retributive justice, which defines fair punishment for wrongs committed
- restorative justice, which is an aspect of distributive justice and specifies fair ways to correct injustice and restore socioeconomic wholeness for persons and communities.

Here, too, of course, there are no lengthy systematic discourses on these topics. But there is much relevant biblical material.

Since there is no detailed systematic treatise on economic justice, we must construct a biblical paradigm on economic justice by looking carefully at all the relevant canonical texts that stretch from Genesis to Revelation. These texts represent many different literary genres, from history to poetry to prophetic declaration. They were written over many hundreds of years and addressed to people in dramatically different cultures, all of which differ from our own complex civilization at the beginning of the third millennium A.D. In order to develop a faithful biblical paradigm on economic justice, we must in principle first examine every relevant biblical text using the best exegetical tools to understand its original meaning and then, secondly, construct an integrated, systematic summary of all this diverse material in a way that faithfully reflects the balance of canonical teaching. In this short chapter, unfortunately, space does not permit examination of every relevant passage. But we seek to include important, representative texts. Mistakes, of course, are possible at any point, either in our specific exegesis or our overall summary. But our aim is fidelity to the text and to the balance of canonical teaching. To the extent that critics—friendly or hostile—can help us approach closer to that goal, we will be grateful.

The interpretative task, of course, does not end when one completes even the most faithful biblical paradigm. We should not take biblical mechanisms like the return of the land every fifty years (Leviticus 25) and apply them mechanically to our very different culture and economy. A literal, mechanical application would neither fit our different settings nor even speak to many of our urgent questions. There is not a word in Scripture about the merits of a flat tax, the activity of the International Monetary Fund, or the Earned Income Tax Credit. We must apply the biblical framework paradigmatically, allowing the biblical worldview, principles, and norms to provide the normative framework for shaping economic life today.

Our goal in this essay is to present a faithful biblical paradigm on economic justice. We offer this summary of biblical teaching in the hope that all Christians, starting with ourselves, will allow biblical revelation rather than secular ideas of left or right to provide the decisive normative framework for their thinking about economics. We also hope the biblical paradigm on economic justice will even prove attractive to those who do not claim to be Christians.

The Biblical Story

The biblical story of creation, fall, redemption, and eschaton teaches us many things about the world, persons, and society that are foundational for Christian economic thought.

The World

Because it is created out of nothing *(ex nihilo)* by a loving, almighty Creator, the material world is both finite and good.

The material world is not divine. The trees and rivers are not, as animists believe, divinities to be worshiped and left as unchanged as possible. Biblical faith desacralizes the world, permitting stewardly use of the material world for wise human purposes.

Nor is the material world an illusion to be escaped, as some Eastern monists claim. It is so good in its finitude (Genesis 1) that the Creator of the galaxies becomes flesh and even promises to restore the groaning creation to wholeness at his Second Coming (Rom. 8:19–23). Although not as important as persons, who alone are created in the image of God, the non-human creation has its own independent worth and dignity (Gen. 9:8–11). Persons therefore exercise their unique role in creation as caring stewards who watch over the rest of the created order (Gen. 2:15).

The biblical vision of the world calls human beings to revel in the goodness of the material world, rather than seek to escape it. It invites persons to use the non-human world to create wealth and construct complex civilizations—always, of course, in a way that does not destroy the rest of creation and thereby prevent it from offering its own independent hymn of praise to the Creator.

The Nature of Persons

Created in the image of God, made as body-soul unities formed for community, and called to faithful stewardship of the rest of creation, persons possess an inestimable dignity and value that transcends any economic process or system.

Because our bodies are a fundamental part of our created goodness, a generous sufficiency of material things is essential to human goodness. Any economic structure that prevents persons from producing and enjoying material well-being violates their God-given dignity. Because our spiritual nature and destiny are so important that it is better to lose even the entire material world than lose one's relationship with God, any economic system that tries to explain persons only as economic actors or that offers material abundance as the exclusive or primary way to human fulfillment contradicts the essence of human nature. Any economic structure that subordinates labor to capital thereby subordinates spiritual reality to material reality in contradiction to the biblical view of persons.[5] For persons invited to live forever with the living God, no material abundance, however splendid, can satisfy the human heart. Because human beings are body-soul unities, definitions of human rights should include both freedom rights and socioeconomic rights.

People are made both for personal freedom and communal solidarity. The God who cares so much about each person that the incarnate Creator died for the sins of the whole world and invites every person to respond in freedom to the gift of salvation, demands that human economic and political systems acknowledge and protect the dignity and freedom of each individual. Any economic order that denies economic freedom to individuals or reduces them to a factor of production subordinated to mere economic goals, violates their individual dignity and freedom.

Since persons are free, their choices have consequences. Obedient, diligent use of our gifts normally produces sufficiency of material things (unless powerful people oppress us). Disobedient, lazy neglect of our responsibilities normally increases the danger of poverty. Totally equal economic outcomes are not compatible with human freedom.

The first few chapters of Genesis underline the fact that we are also created for community. Until Eve arrived, Adam was restless. Mutual fulfillment resulted when the two became one flesh.[6] God punished Cain for violating community by killing his brother Abel, but then allowed Cain to enjoy the human community of family and city (Genesis 4).[7] As social beings, we are physically, emotionally, and rationally interdependent and have inherent duties of care and responsibility for each other. Authority, corporate responsibility, and collective decision-making are essential to every form of human life.[8] Therefore, economic and political institutions are not merely a consequence of the fall.

Because our communal nature demands attention to the common good, individual rights, whether of freedom of speech or private property, cannot be absolute. The right to private property dare not undermine the general welfare. Only God is an absolute owner. We are merely stewards of our property, called to balance personal rights with the common good.[9]

Our communal nature is grounded in God. Since persons are created in the image of the triune personal God who is Father, Son and Holy Spirit, "being a person means being united to other persons in mutual love."[10] Any economic system that emphasizes the freedom of individuals without an equal concern for mutual love, cooperation and responsibility neglects the complex balance of the biblical picture of persons. Any economic system that exaggerates the individual right of private property in a way that undermines mutual responsibility for the common good defies the Creator's design for human beings.

The biblical view of persons means that economic injustice is a family problem. Since we are all "God's offspring" (Acts 17:29; cf. all of vv. 24–29), we all have the same Father. Therefore all human beings are sisters and brothers. "Exploitation is a brother or sister treating another brother or sister as a mere object."[11] That is not to overlook differentiation in human society.[12] We do not have exactly the same obligations to all children everywhere that we have to those in our immediate biological family. But a mutual obligation for the common good of all people follows from the fact that all persons are sisters and brothers created in the image of our Heavenly Father.

Human rights specify minimal demands for how we should treat people to whom God has given such dignity and worth. Human institutions cannot create human rights. They can only recognize and protect the inestimable value of every person which flows from the central truths of the biblical story: every person is made in the image of God; every person is a child of the Heavenly Father; every person is loved so much by God that the eternal Son suffers crucifixion because God does not desire that any should perish (2 Peter 3:9); every person who accepts Christ, regardless of race, gender or class, is justified on exactly the same basis: unmerited grace offered through the cross. Since that is the way God views people, that is the way we should treat each other.

Statements of human rights spell out for individuals and communities the fixed duties which implement love for neighbor in typical situations of competing claims. Rights extend the gaze of love from spontaneous responses to individual needs to structured patterns of fair treatment for everyone. Vigorous commitment to human rights for all helps societies respect the immeasurable dignity and worth that the Creator has bestowed on every person.

Stewardship of the Earth

Persons alone are created in the divine image. Persons alone have been given the awesome responsibility of exercising dominion over the non-human creation (Gen. 1:28). This stewardly dominion, to be sure, must be that of the loving gardener who thoughtfully cares for, and in a sense serves, the garden (Gen. 2:15). It dare not be a destructive violation of the independent worth of the rest of creation. But God's earthly stewards rightly cultivate and shape the earth placed in our care in order to produce new beauty, more complex civilizations, and greater wealth.

Creation of Wealth

The ability to create wealth is a gift from God. The One in whose image we are made creates astounding abundance and variety. Unlike God, we cannot create *ex nihilo;* we can only retrace the divine design. But by giving us minds that can study and imitate his handiwork, God has blessed human beings with awesome power not only to reshape the earth, but to produce things that have never been.

The Creator could have directly created poetry, plays, sonatas, cities and computers. Instead, God assigned that task to us, expecting us to cultivate the earth (Gen. 2:15), create new things, and expand human possibilities and wealth. Adam and Eve surely enjoyed a generous sufficiency. Just as surely, the Creator intended their descendants to probe and use the astoundingly intricate earth placed in their care to acquire the knowledge, power, and wealth necessary, for example, to build vast telescopes that we can use to scan the billions of galaxies about which Adam and Eve knew nothing. In a real sense, God purposely created human beings with very little so that they could imitate and glorify their Creator by producing vast knowledge and wealth. Indeed, Jesus' parable of the talents sharply rebukes those who fail to use their skills to multiply their resources.[13] Just, responsible creation of wealth is one important way persons obey and honor the Creator.

The Glory of Work

God works (Gen. 2:1–2). God Incarnate was a carpenter. St. Paul mended tents. Even before the fall, God summoned Adam to cultivate the earth and name the animals (Gen. 2:15–20). Work is not only the way we meet our basic needs. In addition, it is both the way we express our basic nature as co-workers with God and also a crucial avenue for loving our neighbors. Meaningful work by which persons express their creative ability is essential for human dignity. Any able person who fails to work disgraces and corrodes his very being. Any system that could but does not offer every person the opportunity for meaningful work violates and crushes human dignity.

The Lord of Economics

There is only one God who is Lord of all. God is the only absolute owner (Lev. 25:23). We are merely stewards summoned to use the wealth God allows us to enjoy for the glory of God and the good of our neighbor. We cannot worship God and Mammon. Excessive preoccupation with material abundance is idolatry. No economic task, however grand, dare claim our full allegiance. That belongs to God alone who consequently relativizes the claims of all human systems. God's righteous demands for justice judge every economic system. As the Lord of history, God works now with and through human co-workers to replace economic injustice with more wholesome economies that respect and nurture the dignity and worth of every human being.

The Importance of History

Modern secular thinkers absolutize the historical process even while they say it is meaningless. Even if life is absurd, our time here is all we have. Medieval thinkers sometimes belittled history, viewing earthly existence merely as a preparation for eternity. The biblical story affirms the importance of history while insisting that persons are also made for life eternal. It is in history that the Redeemer chooses to turn back the invading powers of evil by launching the Messianic kingdom in the midst of history's sin. It is in history that persons not only respond to God's call to eternal life, but also join the Lord's long march toward justice and righteousness. And it is because we know where history is going and are assured that the Redeemer will return to complete the victory over every evil and injustice that we do not despair even when evil achieves sweeping, temporary triumphs. So we work for better economic systems knowing that sin precludes any earthly utopia now, but rejoicing in the assurance that the kingdom of *shalom* that the Messiah has already begun will one day prevail, and the kingdoms of this world will become the kingdom of our Lord.

The Tragedy of Sin

Nothing on God's good earth has escaped sin's marauding presence. Sin has twisted both individual persons and the ideas and institutions they create. Rebelling against their Creator's instructions, people either exaggerate or belittle the significance of history and the material world. Exaggerating their own importance, they regularly create economic institutions—complete with sophisticated rationalizations—that oppress their neighbors. Workable economic systems must both appeal to persons' better instincts which sin has not quite managed to obliterate, and also hold in check and turn to positive use the pervasive selfishness which corrupts every act.

Sin, Power, and Justice

One of the important ways that God has chosen to restrain and correct evil, including economic injustice, is through the use of power by human beings.[14]

Power is the ability to realize one's own will in a communal action even against the resistance of others.[15] Power itself is not evil. It is essential to human life and precedes the fall. It is God's gift to each person so that they can act in freedom as a co-worker with God to shape their own life and that of their community and world. By using power, we make actual our possibilities of being, which God presents as a particular gift designed for each life.[16] God wants persons to have power to control the material necessities of life. God gives power over wealth and property for human enjoyment (Eccles. 5:19).

The special attention which Scripture gives to the plight of the widow, the orphan, the poor, and the resident alien reflects the awareness in Scripture that when persons lack basic power, evil frequently follows. Thus, in the center of Job's declaration of the injustices to these groups is the statement: "The powerful possess the land" (Job 22:8, NRSV; cf. Job 35:9; Eccles. 4:1). In the real world since the fall, sinful actions against others pervert the intention of the Creator. Sinful persons and evil forces which thwart the divine intention greatly restrict the ability to act in accordance with one's created being. This fallen use of power to impede the Creator's intentions for the lives of others is *exploitative power*. Exploitative power allows lust to work its will.[17] "Alas for those who devise wickedness and evil deeds upon their beds! When the morning dawns, they perform it, because it is in their power. They covet . . . they oppress . . ." (Micah 2:1–2, NRSV). Unequal power leads to exploitation.

The biblical understanding of human nature also warns us about the potential for evil afforded by sharp differences in power among individuals and groups in society. John Calvin described a "rough equality" in the Mosaic Law. In commenting upon the canceling of debts in the sabbatical year, he wrote,

> In as much as God had given them the use of the franchise, the best way to preserve their liberty was by maintaining a condition of rough equality [*mediocrem statum*], lest a few persons of immense wealth oppress the general body. Since, therefore, the rich if they had been permitted constantly to increase their wealth, would have tyrannized over the rest, God put a restraint on immoderate power by means of this law.[18]

A Christian political philosophy and economic theory accordingly must be based on a realism about human nature in light of the universality of sin. Powerful forces prey upon the weak. Human selfishness resists the full costs of communal obligations. Individual egoism is heightened in group conflict, and sin is disguised and justified as victims are blamed for their own plight.

An *intervening power* is necessary to limit exploitative power.[19] Power can demand and enforce political and economic change that corrects exploitation. Power produces changes which guarantee basic human needs and resist the forces that deny them. Intervening power is creative as it defeats exploitative power and reestablishes the creative power God wills for each person.

The source and model is God, who in common grace and in special grace restores persons' creative power by overcoming the forces which pervert the creation. God exerts power as the defender of the poor. Yahweh does "justice for the orphan and the oppressed" (Ps. 10:18, NRSV) by "break[ing] the arm [i.e., power] of the wicked" (v. 15) "so that those from earth may strike terror no more" (v. 18).

God's normal way of exerting power is through human creatures, who are God's lieutenants on the earth. Sometimes, when human justice fails and there is "no one to intervene," God acts in more direct and extraordinary ways (Isa. 59:15–18). But God's intention is for human institutions, including government, to be the normal channels of God's intervening power.

Justice determines the proper limits and applications of intervening power. Justice provides the right structure of power. Without justice, power becomes destructive.[20]

Power, on the other hand, provides fiber and grit for justice. "I put on justice. . . . I championed the cause of the stranger. I broke the fangs of the unrighteous, and made them drop their prey from their teeth" (Job 29:14, 16–17).

Biblical justice relates to both power (see Ps. 71:18–19) and love (Ezek. 34:16, 23–24; Ps. 146:7). As Martin Luther King stated, "Power without love is reckless and abusive and . . . love without power is sentimental and anemic. Power at its best is love implementing the demands of justice."[21]

One criterion of the legitimacy of power is whether it is being used for justice. The deliverance from Egypt was carried out by power ("outstretched arm") with great acts of justice (*sepatim*, Exod. 6:6–7; 7:4). As in the stories of the judges, so in the exodus God "is acting in history as the one who uses his power to see that justice is done."[22] Power is used against power.[23] God upholds the poor and needy (Isa. 41:17) by His "just power" (vv. 10, 20). God works "justice to the fatherless and oppressed" by breaking the arm (power) of the evildoer to eliminate the source of oppression (Ps. 10:15–18). In our sinful world, intervening power is essential to correct exploitative power.

Thus far, we have seen how the biblical story provides important insight into the nature of the world, persons, history, the creation of wealth, sin and power. All this offers important elements of a biblical framework for thinking about economics. But we need more. We need a more detailed understanding of justice, equity (and equality), God's attitude toward the poor, and the role of government in fostering economic justice. For that we turn to a more detailed analysis in order to develop a biblical paradigm on economic justice.

A Biblical Paradigm

Justice identifies what is essential for life together in community and specifies the rights and responsibilities of individuals and institutions in society. What does the Bible tell us about the nature of justice?

Earlier, we noted several different types of justice. It is clear from biblical material that procedural justice is important. Legal institutions should not be biased either toward the rich or the poor (Deut. 10:17–18; Lev. 19:15; Exod. 23:3). Everyone should have equal access to honest, unbiased courts. Similarly, scriptural teaching on honest weights and measures (Lev. 19:35–36; Amos 8:5; Prov. 11:1) underlines the importance of commutative justice in order that fair, honest exchange of goods and services is possible.

Distributive Justice

There is less agreement, however, about the nature of distributive justice. Are the resources of society justly distributed, even if some are very poor and others very rich, as long as procedural and commutative justice are present? Or does a biblically informed understanding of distributive justice demand some reasonable standard of material well-being for all?

Calvin Beisner is typical of those who define economic justice in a minimal, procedural way:

> Justice in economic relationships requires that people be permitted to exchange and use what they own—including their own time and energy and intellect as well as material objects—freely so long as in so doing they do not violate others' rights. Such things as minimum wage laws, legally mandated racial quotas in employment, legal restrictions on import and export, laws requiring "equal pay for equal work," and all other regulations of economic activity other than those necessary to prohibit, prevent, and punish fraud, theft, and violence are therefore unjust.[24]

Carl Henry provides another example. In a fascinating chapter on the nature of God and social ethics, he argues that modern theological liberalism's submerging of God's wrath in God's love has led to a parallel disaster in society. Both in God and society, love and justice are very different and should never be confused. The state should be responsible for procedural justice, not love. In dire emergencies (the Great Depression, for example), it may be proper for the government to assist the poor and jobless, but normally, voluntary agencies like the church should perform such acts of love or benevolence. "In the New Testament view," Henry argues, "the coercive role of the State is limited to its punitive function."[25]

Henry is surely right that the biblical God is both searing holiness and amazing love. The one dare not be collapsed into the other. But does that mean that love is not connected with economic justice? Does it mean that economic justice exists, as Beisner argues, as long as procedural justice prevents fraud, theft, and violence?

Others argue that the biblical materials point to a much closer relationship between justice and love. If justice is understood to be in continuity with love, it takes on the dynamic, community-building character of love. Rather than having primarily a minimal, punitive and restraining function, justice in the biblical perspective has a crucial restorative character, identifying and correcting areas of material need. The debate over whether human rights includes economic rights is an extension of the debate over the continuity of love and justice. Are human rights essentially procedural (freedom of speech, religion, etc.) or do they include the right to basic material necessities?

To treat people equally, this second view argues, justice looks for barriers which interfere with the opportunity for access to productive resources needed to acquire the basic goods of society or to be dignified, participating members in the community. Justice takes into consideration certain handicaps which are hindrances to pursuing the opportunities for life in society. The handicaps which justice considers go beyond individual physical disabilities and personal tragedies. Significant handicaps can be found in poverty or prejudice. A just society removes any discrimination which prevents equality of opportunity. Distributive justice demands special consideration to disadvantaged groups by providing basic social and economic opportunities and resources.[26]

Is there biblical data to help us decide how to define distributive justice? Again, there is no systematic treatise on this topic anywhere in the Scriptures. But there is considerable relevant material. This is especially true in the Old Testament which, unlike the New Testament, usually addresses a setting where God's people make up the whole society, not just a tiny minority. (Therefore it is strange for Carl Henry to make his case for a minimal, procedural definition of justice on the basis of the New Testament alone, rather than the full canonical revelation.)

Several aspects of biblical teaching point to the broader—rather than the narrower, exclusively procedural—understanding of justice.[27] Frequently the words for *love* and *justice* appear together in close relationship. Biblical justice has a dynamic, restorative character. The special concern for the poor running throughout the Scriptures moves beyond a concern for unbiased procedures. Restoration to community—including the benefit rights that dignified participation in community require—is a central feature of biblical thinking about justice.

Love and Justice Together

In many texts we discover the words for love and justice in close association. "Sow for yourselves justice, reap the fruit of steadfast love" (Hos. 10:12).[28] Sometimes, love and justice are interchangeable: ". . . [It is the Lord] who executes *justice* [*mišpāt*] for the orphan and the widow, and who *loves* the strangers, providing them food and clothing" (Deut. 10:18, NRSV; see Isa. 30:18).[29]

Justice's Dynamic, Restorative Character

In the Bible, justice is not a mere *mitigation* of suffering in oppression, it is a *deliverance*. Justice involves rectifying the gross social inequities of the disadvantaged. The terms for *justice* are frequently associated with *yasaᶜ, yᵉšûᶜâ* the most important Hebrew word for deliverance and salvation: "... God arose to establish justice [*mišpāṭ*] to save [*hôšîaᶜ*] all the oppressed of the earth" (Ps. 76:9; see Isa. 63:1).[30] "Give justice to the weak" and "maintain the right of the lowly" are parallel to "rescue the weak and the needy and snatch them out of the power of the wicked" (Ps. 82:3–4).[31]

Justice describes the deliverance of the people from political and economic oppressors (Judg. 5:11),[32] from slavery (1 Sam. 12:7–8; Micah 6:4), and from captivity (Isa. 41:1–11 [cf. v. 2 for *sedeq*]; Jer. 51:10). Providing for the needy means ending their oppression, setting them back on their feet, giving them a home, and leading them to prosperity and restoration (Pss. 68:5–10; 10:15–18).[33] Justice does not merely help victims cope with oppression; it removes it. Because of this dynamic, restorative emphasis, distributive justice requires not primarily that we maintain a stable society, but rather that we advance the well-being of the disadvantaged.

God's Special Concern for the Poor

Hundreds[34] of biblical verses show that God is especially attentive to the poor and needy. God is not biased. Because of unequal needs, however, equal provision of basic rights requires justice to be partial in order to be impartial. (Good firefighters do not spend equal time at every house; they are "partial" to people with fires.) Partiality to the weak is the most striking characteristic of biblical justice.[35] In the raging social struggles in which the poor are perennially victims of injustice, God and God's people take up the cause of the weak.[36] Rulers and leaders have a special obligation to do justice for the weak and powerless.[37] This partiality to the poor provides strong evidence that in biblical thought, justice is concerned with more than fair procedures.

The Scriptures speak of God's special concern for the poor in at least four different ways.[38]

1. Repeatedly, the Bible says that the Sovereign of history works to lift up the poor and oppressed. Consider the exodus. Certainly God acted there to keep the promise to Abraham and to call out the chosen people of Israel. But again and again the texts say God also intervened because God hated the oppression of the poor Israelites (Exod. 3:7–8; 6:5–7). Annually, at the harvest festival, the people of Israel repeated this confession: "The Egyptians mistreated us. . . . Then we cried out to the Lord, the God of our fathers, and the Lord heard our voice and saw our misery, toil and oppression. So the Lord brought us out of Egypt" (Deut. 26:6–8). Or consider the Psalms: "But the Lord

says, 'I will now rise up because the poor are being hurt'" (12:5). "I know the Lord will get justice for the poor and will defend the needy in court" (140:12). God acts in history to lift up the poor and oppressed.

2. Sometimes, the Lord of history tears down rich and powerful people. Mary's song is shocking: "My soul glorifies the Lord. . . . He has filled the hungry with good things but has sent the rich away empty" (Luke 1:46, 53). James is even more blunt: "Now listen, you rich people, weep and wail because of the misery that is coming upon you" (James 5:1).

Since God calls us to create wealth and is not biased against the rich, why do the Scriptures warn again and again that God sometimes works in history to destroy the rich? The Bible has a simple answer. It is because the rich sometimes get rich by oppressing the poor. Or because they have plenty and neglect the needy. In either case, God is furious.

James warned the rich so harshly because they had hoarded wealth and refused to pay their workers (5:2–6). Repeatedly, the prophets said the same thing (Ps. 10; Jer. 22:13–19; Isa. 3:14–25). "Among my people are wicked men who lie in wait like men who snare birds and like those who set traps to catch men. Like cages full of birds, their houses are full of deceit; they have become rich and powerful and have grown fat and sleek. . . . They do not defend the rights of the poor. Should I not punish them for this?" (Jer. 5:26–29).

Repeatedly, the prophets warned that God was so outraged that he would destroy the nations of Israel and Judah. Because of the way they "trample on the heads of the poor . . . and deny justice to the oppressed," Amos predicted terrible captivity (2:7; 5:11; 6:4, 7; 7:11, 17). So did Isaiah and Micah (Isa. 10:1–3; Mic. 2:2; 3:12). And it happened just as they foretold. According to both the Old and New Testaments, God destroys people and societies that get rich by oppressing the poor.

But what if we work hard and create wealth in just ways? That is good—as long as we do not forget to share. No matter how justly we have acquired our wealth, God demands that we act generously toward the poor. When we do not, God treats us in a similar way to those who oppress the poor. There is not a hint in Jesus' story of the rich man and Lazarus that the rich man exploited Lazarus to acquire wealth. He simply neglected to share. So God punished him (Luke 16:19–31).

Ezekiel contains a striking explanation for the destruction of Sodom: "Now this was the sin of your sister Sodom: She and her daughters were arrogant, overfed and unconcerned; they did not help the poor and needy. . . . Therefore I did away with them as you have seen" (16:49–50). Again, the text does not charge them with gaining wealth by oppression. It was because they refused to share their abundance that God destroyed the city.

The Bible is clear. If we get rich by oppressing the poor, or if we have wealth and do not reach out generously to the needy, the Lord of history moves against us. God judges societies by what they do to the people at the bottom.

3. God identifies with the poor so strongly that caring for them is almost like helping God. "He who is kind to the poor lends to the Lord" (Prov. 19:17). On the other hand, one "who oppresses the poor shows contempt for their Maker" (14:31).

Jesus' parable of the sheep and goats is the ultimate commentary on these two proverbs. Jesus surprises those on the right with his insistence that they had fed and clothed him when he was cold and hungry. When they protested that they could not remember ever doing that, Jesus replied: "Whatever you did for one of the least of these brothers of mine, you did for me" (Matt. 25:40). If we believe his words, we look on the poor and neglected with entirely new eyes.

4. Finally, God demands that his people share his special concern for the poor. God commanded Israel not to treat widows, orphans, and foreigners the way the Egyptians had treated them (Exod. 22:21–24). Instead, they should love the poor just as God cared for them at the exodus (Exod. 22:21–24; Deut. 15:13–15). When Jesus' disciples throw parties, they should especially invite the poor and disabled (Luke 14:12–14; Heb. 13:1–3). Paul held up Jesus' model of becoming poor to show how generously the Corinthians should contribute to the poor in Jerusalem (2 Cor. 8:9).

The Bible, however, goes one shocking step further. God insists that if we do not imitate God's concern for the poor we are not really God's people—no matter how frequent our worship or how orthodox our creeds. Because Israel failed to correct oppression and defend poor widows, Isaiah insisted that Israel was really the pagan people of Gomorrah (1:10–17). God despised their fasting because they tried to worship God and oppress their workers at the same time (Isa. 58:3–7). Through Amos, the Lord shouted in fury that the very religious festivals God had ordained made God angry and sick. Why? Because the rich and powerful were mixing worship and oppression of the poor (5:21–24). Jesus was even more harsh. At the last judgment, some who expect to enter heaven will learn that their failure to feed the hungry condemns them to hell (Matthew 25). If we do not care for the needy brother or sister, God's love does not abide in us (1 John 3:17).

Jeremiah 22:13–19 describes good king Josiah and his wicked son Jehoiakim. When Jehoiakim became king, he built a fabulous palace by oppressing his workers. God sent the prophet Jeremiah to announce a terrible punishment. The most interesting part of the passage, however, is a short aside on this evil king's good father: "He defended the cause of the poor and needy, and so all went well. *'Is that not what it means to know me?'* declares the Lord" (v. 16; our italics). Knowing God is *inseparable* from caring for the poor. Of course, we dare not reduce knowing God only to a concern for the needy as some radical theologians do. We meet God in prayer, Bible study, worship—in many ways. But if we do not share God's passion to strengthen the poor, we simply do not know God in a biblical way.

All this biblical material clearly demonstrates that God and God's faithful people have a great concern for the poor. Earlier, we argued that God is partial to the poor, but not biased. God does not love the poor any more than the rich. God has an equal concern for the well-being of every single person. Most rich and powerful people, however, are genuinely biased; they care a lot more about themselves than about their poor neighbors. By contrast with the genuine bias of most people, God's lack of bias makes God appear biased. God cares equally for everyone.

How then is God "partial" to the poor? Because in concrete historical situations, equal concern for everyone requires special attention to specific people. In a family, loving parents do not provide equal tutorial time to a son struggling hard to scrape by with "D's" and a daughter easily making "A's." Precisely in order to be "impartial" and love both equally, they devote extra time to helping the more needy child. In historical situations (e.g., apartheid) where some people oppress others, God's lack of bias does not mean neutrality. Precisely because God loves all equally, God works against oppressors and actively sides with the oppressed.

We see this connection precisely in the texts that declare God's lack of bias: "For the Lord your God is God of gods and Lord of lords, the great, the almighty, the terrible God, who is not partial and takes no bribe. He executes justice for the fatherless and the widow, and loves the sojourner, giving him food and clothing" (Deut. 10:17–18). Justice and love are virtual synonyms in this passage. There is no suggestion that loving the sojourner is a benevolent, voluntary act different from a legal demand to do justice to the fatherless. Furthermore, there is no indication in the text that those needing food and clothing are poor because of some violation of due process such as fraud or robbery. The text simply says they are poor and therefore God, who is not biased, pays special attention to them.

Leviticus 19 is similar. In verse 15, the text condemns partiality: "You shall not be partial to the poor or defer to the great." The preceding verses refer to several of the Ten Commandments (stealing, lying, blasphemy [v. 11]). But special references to the poor are in the same passage. When harvesting their crops, God's people must leave the grain at the edge of the field and not pick up the grapes which fall in the vineyard: "You shall leave them for the poor and the alien" (v. 10). This is a divine command, not a suggestion for voluntary charity, and it is part of the same passage that declares God's lack of bias.[39]

Precisely because God is not biased he pays special attention to the poor. Consequently, an understanding of justice that reflects this biblical teaching must be concerned with more than procedural justice. Distributive justice which insists on special attention to the poor so they have opportunity to enjoy material well-being is also crucial.

Justice as Restoration to Community

Justice is restoration to community—and to the benefit rights necessary for dignified participation in community. Since persons are created for community, the Scriptures understand the good life as sharing in the essential aspects of social life. Therefore justice includes restoration to community. Justice includes helping people return to the kind of life in community which God intends for them. Leviticus 25:35–36 describes the poor as being on the verge of falling out of the community because of their economic distress. "If members of your community become poor in that their power slips *with you,* you shall make them strong . . . that they may live *with you*" (Lev. 25:35–36 [our translation]). The word translated as "power" here is "hand" in the Hebrew. "Hand" (*yad*) metaphorically means "power."[40] The solution is for those who are able to correct the situation to do so and thereby restore the poor to community. The poor in fact are their own flesh or kin (Isa. 58:7). Poverty is a family affair.

In order to restore the weak to participation in community, the community's responsibility to its diminished members is "to make them strong" again (Lev. 25:35). This translation is a literal rendering of the Hebrew, which is the word "to be strong" and is found here in the causative (Hiphil) conjugation and therefore means "cause him to be strong." The purpose of this empowerment is "that they may live *beside you*" (v. 35, emphasis added). According to Psalm 107, God's steadfast love leads God to care for the hungry so they are able to "establish a town to live in; they sow fields and plant vineyards. . . . By his blessing they multiply greatly" (vv. 36–38, NRSV). Once more the hungry can be active, participating members of a community. The concern is for the whole person in community and what it takes to maintain persons in that relationship.

Community membership means the ability to share fully, within one's capacity and potential, in each essential aspect of community.[41] Participation in community has multiple dimensions. It includes participation in decision-making, social life, economic production, education, culture, and religion. Also essential are physical life itself and the material resources necessary for a decent life.

Providing the conditions for participation in community demands a focus on what are the basic needs for life in community. Achieving such justice includes access to the material essentials of life, such as food and shelter. It is God "who executes justice for the oppressed; who gives food to the hungry" (Ps. 146:7 NRSV). "The Lord . . . executes justice for the orphan and the widow, and loves the strangers, providing them food and clothing" (Deut. 10:18, NRSV). "Food and clothing" is a Hebrism for what is indispensable.[42]

Job 24, one of the most powerful pictures of poverty in the Bible, describes the economic benefits that injustice takes away. Injustice starts with assault on the land, the basis of economic power (v. 2). It moves then to secondary means of production, the donkey and the ox (v. 3). As a result the victims experience powerlessness and indignity: "They thrust the needy off the road; the poor of the earth all hide themselves" (v. 4, NRSV). The poor are separated from the bonds of community, wandering like wild donkeys in the desert (v. 5). They are denied basic needs of food (vv. 6, 10), drink (v. 11), clothing, and shelter (vv. 7, 10). Elsewhere in Job, failure to provide food for the needy is condemned as injustice.[43] Opportunity for everyone to have access to the material resources necessary for life in community is basic to the biblical concept of justice.

As we shall see at greater length in the following section, enjoying the benefit rights crucial to participation in community goes well beyond "welfare" or "charity." People in distress are to be empowered at the point where their participation in community has been undercut. That means restoring their productive capability. Therefore restoration of the land, the basic productive resource, is the way that Leviticus 25 commands the people to fulfill the call to "make them strong again" so "they may live beside you" in the land (v. 35). As the poor return to their land, they receive a new power and dignity that restores their participation in the community.

Other provisions in the Law also provide access to the means of production.[44] In the sabbatical laws, the lands remain fallow and unharvested so that "the poor may eat" (Exod. 23:10–11). The means of production were to be given over to the poor in entirety every seven years, recognizing, as Walter Rauschenbusch correctly noted,[45] that the entire community had rights in the land. We also see this general right of all the people to be fed from the land in the laws which allow people to eat grain or fruit as they walk through someone else's field or orchard (Deut. 23:24f.). Similarly, the farmer was not to go back over the first run of harvesting or to harvest to the very corners of the field, so that the poor could provide for themselves (Deut. 24:19–22; Lev. 19:9–10).

There are also restrictions on the processes which tear people down so that their "power slips" and they cannot support themselves. Interest on loans was prohibited; food to the poor was not to be provided at profit (Lev. 25:36f.). A means of production like a millstone was not to be taken as collateral on a loan because that would be "taking a life in pledge" (Deut. 24:6, RSV). If a poor person gave an essential item of clothing as a pledge, the creditor had to return it before night came (Exod. 22:26). All these provisions are restrictions on individual economic freedom that go well beyond merely preventing fraud, theft, and violence. The Law did, of course, support the rights of owners to benefit from their property, but the Law placed limits on the owners' control of property and on the quest for profit. The common good of the community outweighed unrestricted economic freedom.

The fact that justice in the Scriptures includes benefit rights[46] means that we must reject the concept of the purely negative state, which merely protects property, person, and equal access to the procedures of the community. That is by no means to deny that procedural justice is important. A person who is denied these protections is cut off from the political and civil community and is not only open to abuse, but is diminished in his or her ability to affect the life of the community. Procedural justice is essential to protect people from fraud, theft and violence.

Biblical justice, however, also *includes positive rights,* which are the responsibility of the community to guarantee. Biblical justice has both an economic and a legal focus. The goal of justice is not primarily the recovery of the integrity of the legal system. It is the restoration of the community as a place where all live together in wholeness.

The wrong to which justice responds is not merely an illegitimate process (like stealing). What is wrong is also an end result in which people are deprived of basic needs. Leviticus 19:13 condemns both stealing *and* withholding a poor person's salary for a day: "You shall not defraud your neighbor; you shall not steal; and you shall not keep for yourself the wages of a laborer until morning." Isaiah 5:8–10 condemns those who buy up field after field until only the rich person is left dwelling alone in his big, beautiful house. Significantly, however, the prophet here does not denounce the acquisition of the land as illegal. Through legal foreclosing of mortgages or through debt bondage, the property could be taken within the law.[47] Isaiah nevertheless condemns the rulers for permitting this injustice to the weak. He appeals to social justice above the technicalities of current law. Restoration to community is central to justice.

From the biblical perspective, justice is both procedural and distributive. It demands both fair courts and fair economic structures. It includes both freedom rights and benefit rights. Precisely because of its equal concern for wholeness for everyone, it pays special attention to the needs of the weak and marginalized.

None of the above claims, however, offers a norm that describes the actual content of distributive justice. The next two sections seek to develop such a norm.

Equity as Adequate Access to Productive Resources

Equality has been one of the most powerful slogans of our century. But what does it mean? Does it mean equality before the law? One person, one vote? Equality of opportunity in education? Identical income shares? Or absolute identity as described in the satirical novel, *Facial Justice?*[48]

As we saw earlier, equality of economic results is not compatible with human freedom and responsibility. Free choices have consequences; therefore, when immoral decisions reduce someone's earning power, we should, other things being equal, consider the result just. Even absolute equality of opportunity is impossible unless we prevent parents from passing on any of their knowledge or other capital to their children.

So what definition of equality—or better, equity—do the biblical materials suggest?

Capital in an Agricultural Society

The biblical material on Israel and the land offers important clues about what a biblical understanding of equity would look like. The contrast between early Israel and surrounding societies was striking.[49] In Egypt, most of the land belonged to the Pharaoh or the temples. In most other Near-Eastern contexts a feudal system of landholding prevailed. The king granted large tracts of land, worked by landless laborers, to a small number of elite royal vassals. Only at the theological level did this feudal system exist in early Israel. Yahweh the King owned all the land and made important demands on those to whom he gave it to use. Under Yahweh, however, each family had their own land. Israel's ideal was decentralized family "ownership" understood as stewardship under Yahweh's absolute ownership. In the period of the judges, the pattern in Israel was, according to one scholar, "free peasants on small land holdings of equal size and apportioned by the clans."[50]

Land was the basic capital in early Israel's agricultural economy, and the Law says the land was divided in such a way that each extended family had the resources to produce the things needed for a decent life.

Joshua 18 and Numbers 26 contain the two most important accounts of the division of the land.[51] They represent Israel's social ideal with regard to the land. Originally, the land was divided among the clans of the tribes so that a relatively similar amount of land was available to all the family units. The larger tribes got a larger portion and the smaller tribes a smaller portion (Num. 26:54). By lot the land was further subdivided among the protective association of families, and then (Joshua 18–19) among the extended families. The criterion of the division was thus equality, as is stated directly in Ezekiel's vision of a future time of justice. In this redistribution of the land, it is said to be divided "equally" (NRSV, literally, "each according to his brother," Ezek. 47:14). The concern, however, was not the implementation of an abstract ideal of equality but the empowerment of all the people. Elie Munk, a French, Jewish Old Testament scholar, has summarized the situation this way: "The point of departure of the system of social economy of Judaism is the equal distribution of land among all its inhabitants."[52]

The concern for empowerment was not merely for the first generation but for all subsequent generations. Several institutions had the purpose of preserving a just distribution of the land. The *law of levirate* served to prevent the land from going out of the family line (Deut. 25:5). The provision for a *kinship redeemer* meant that when poverty forced someone to sell his land, a relative was to step in to purchase it for him (Lev. 25:25).

The picture of land ownership in the time of the judges suggests some approximation of equality of land ownership—at least up to the point where every family had enough to enjoy a decent, dignified life in the community if they acted responsibly. Albrecht Alt, a prominent Old Testament scholar, goes so far as to say that the prophets understood Yahweh's ancient regulation on property to be "one man—one house—one allotment of land."[53] Decentralized land ownership by extended families was the economic base for a relatively egalitarian society of small landowners and vinedressers in the time of the judges.[54]

The story of Naboth's vineyard (1 Kings 21) demonstrates the importance of each family's ancestral land. Frequent Old Testament references about not moving ancient boundary markers (e.g., Deut. 19:14; 27:17; Job 24:2; Prov. 22:28; Hos. 5:10) support the concept that Israel's ideal called for each family to have enough land so that they had the opportunity to acquire life's necessities.

"Necessities" is not to be understood as the minimum necessary to keep from starving. In the nonhierarchical, relatively egalitarian society of small farmers depicted above, families possessed resources to earn a living that would have been considered reasonable and acceptable, not embarrassingly minimal. That is not to suggest that every family had exactly the same income. It does mean, however, that every family had an equality of economic opportunity up to the point that they had the resources to earn a living that would enable them not only to meet minimal needs of food, clothing, and housing, but also to be respected participants in the community. Possessing their own land enabled each extended family to acquire the necessities for a decent life through responsible work.

The Year of Jubilee

Two astonishing biblical texts—Leviticus 25 and Deuteronomy 15—show how important this basic equality of opportunity was to God. The Jubilee text in Leviticus demanded that the land return to the original owners every fifty years. And Deuteronomy 15 called for the release of debts every seven years.

Leviticus 25 is one of the most radical texts in all of Scripture,[55] at least it seems that way to people committed either to communism or to unrestricted capitalism. Every fifty years, God said, the land was to return to the original owners. Physical handicaps, death of a breadwinner, or lack of natural ability may lead some families to become poorer than others. But God does not want such disadvantages to lead to ever-increasing extremes of wealth and poverty, with the result that the poor eventually lack the basic resources to earn a decent livelihood. God therefore gave his people a law to guarantee that no family would permanently lose its land. Every fifty years, the land returned to the original owners so that every family had enough productive resources to function as dignified, participating members of the community (Lev. 25:10–24). Private property was not abolished. Regularly, however, the means of producing wealth was to be equalized—up to the point of every family having the resources to earn a decent living.

What is the theological basis for this startling command? Yahweh's ownership of everything is the presupposition. The land cannot be sold permanently because Yahweh owns it: "The land shall not be sold in perpetuity, for the land is mine; for you are strangers and sojourners with me" (Lev. 25:23).

God, the landowner, permits his people to sojourn on his good earth, cultivate it, eat its produce, and enjoy its beauty. But we are only stewards. Stewardship is one of the central theological categories of any biblical understanding of our relationship to the land and economic resources.[56]

Before and after the year of Jubilee, land could be "bought" or "sold." Actually, the buyer purchased a specific number of harvests, not the land itself (Lev. 25:16). And woe to the person who tried to get more than a just price for the intervening harvests from the date of purchase to the next Jubilee!

> If the years are many you shall increase the price, and if the years are few you shall diminish the price, for it is the number of the crops that he is selling to you. You shall not wrong one another, but you shall fear your God; for I am the Lord your God (Lev. 25:16–17, RSV).

Yahweh is Lord of all, even of economics. There is no hint here of a sacred law of supply and demand that operates independently of biblical ethics and the Lordship of Yahweh. The people of God should submit to God, and God demands economic justice among his people.

The assumption in this text that people must suffer the consequences of wrong choices is also striking. A whole generation or more could suffer the loss of ancestral land, but every fifty years the basic source of wealth would be returned so that each family had the opportunity to provide for its basic needs.

Verses 25–28 imply that this equality of opportunity is a higher value than that of absolute property rights. If a person became poor and sold his land to a more prosperous neighbor but then recovered enough to buy back his land before the Jubilee, the new owner was obligated to return it. The original owner's right to have his ancestral land to earn his own way is a higher right than that of the second owner to maximize profits.

This passage prescribes justice in a way that haphazard handouts by wealthy philanthropists never will. The year of Jubilee was an institutionalized structure that affected all Israelites automatically. It was the poor family's right to recover their inherited land at the Jubilee. Returning the land was not a charitable courtesy that the wealthy might extend if they pleased.[57]

Interestingly, the principles of Jubilee challenge both unrestricted capitalism and communism in a fundamental way. Only God is an absolute owner. No one else has absolute property rights. The right of each family to have the means to earn a living takes priority over a purchaser's "property rights" or a totally unrestricted market economy. At the same time, Jubilee affirms not only the right but the importance of property managed by families who understand that they are stewards responsible to God. This text does not point us in the direction of the communist model where the state owns all the land. God wants each family to have the resources to produce its own livelihood. Why? To strengthen the family (this is a very important "pro-family" text!); to give people the freedom to participate in shaping history; and to prevent the centralization of power—and the totalitarianism which almost always accompanies centralized ownership of land or capital by either the state or small elites.

One final aspect of Leviticus 25 is striking. It is more than coincidental that the trumpet blast announcing Jubilee sounded on the Day of Atonement (Lev. 25:9). Reconciliation with God is the precondition for reconciliation with brothers and sisters.[58] Conversely, genuine reconciliation with God leads inevitably to a transformation of all other relationships. Reconciled with God by the sacrifice on the Day of Atonement, the more prosperous Israelites were summoned to liberate the poor by freeing Hebrew slaves and by returning all land to the original owners.[59]

It is not clear from the historical books how much the people of Israel implemented the Jubilee.[60] Regardless of its antiquity or possible lack of implementation, however, Leviticus 25 remains a part of God's authoritative Word.

The teaching of the prophets about the land underlines the principles of Leviticus 25. In the tenth to the eighth centuries B.C. major centralization of landholding occurred. Poorer farmers lost their land, becoming landless laborers or slaves. The prophets regularly denounced the bribery, political assassination, and economic oppression that destroyed the earlier decentralized economy described above. Elijah condemned Ahab's seizure of Naboth's vineyard (1 Kings 21). Isaiah attacked rich landowners for adding field to field until they dwelt alone in the countryside because the smaller farmers had been destroyed (Isa. 5:8–9).

The prophets, however, did not merely condemn. They also expressed a powerful eschatological hope for a future day of justice when all would have their own land again. In the "latter days," the future day of justice and wholeness, "they shall all sit under their own vines and under their own fig trees" (Mic. 4:4; cf. also Zech. 3:10). No longer will the leaders oppress the people; instead they will guarantee that all people again enjoy their ancestral land (Ezek. 45:1–9, especially vv. 8–9).

In the giving of the land, the denunciation of oppressors who seized the land of the poor, and the vision of a new day when once again all will delight in the fruits of their own land and labor, we see a social ideal in which families are to have the economic means to earn their own way. A basic equality of economic opportunity up to the point that all can at least provide for their own basic needs through responsible work is the norm. Failure to act responsibly has economic consequences, so there is no assumption of equality. Central, however, is the demand that each family have the necessary capital (land) so that responsible stewardship will result in an economically decent life.[61]

The Sabbatical Year

God's law also provides for liberation of soil, slaves, and debtors every seven years. Again the concern is justice for the poor and disadvantaged (as well as the well-being of the land). A central goal is to protect people against processes that would result in their losing their productive resources, or to restore productive resources after a time of loss.

Every seven years the land is to lie fallow (Exod. 23:10–11; Lev. 25:2–7).[62] The purpose, apparently, is both ecological and humanitarian. Not planting any crops every seventh year helps preserve the fertility of the soil. It also was God's way of showing his concern for the poor: "For six years you shall sow your land and gather in its yield; but the seventh year you shall let it rest and lie fallow, so that the poor of your people may eat" (Exod. 23:10–11). In the seventh year the poor were free to gather for themselves whatever grew spontaneously in the fields and vineyards.

Hebrew slaves also received their freedom in the sabbatical year (Deut. 15:12–18). Poverty sometimes forced Israelites to sell themselves as slaves to more prosperous neighbors (Lev. 25:39–40).[63] But this inequality and lack of property, God decrees, is not to be permanent. At the end of six years Hebrew slaves are to be set free. When they leave, masters are to share the proceeds of their joint labors with departing male slaves:

> And when you let him go free from you, you shall not let him go empty handed; you shall furnish him liberally out of your flock, out of your threshing floor, and out of your wine press; as the Lord your God has blessed you, you shall give to him (Deut. 15:13–14; see also Exod. 21:2–6).

As a consequence, the freed slave would again have some productive resources so he could earn his own way.[64]

The sabbatical provision on loans is even more surprising (Deut. 15:1–6) if, as some scholars think, the text calls for cancellation of debts every seventh year.[65] Yahweh even adds a footnote for those with a sharp eye for loopholes: it is sinful to refuse a loan to a poor person just because it is the sixth year and financial loss might occur in twelve months.

> Be careful that you do not entertain a mean thought, thinking, "The seventh year, the year of remission, is near," and therefore view your needy neighbor with hostility and give nothing; your neighbor might cry to the Lord against you, and you would incur guilt. Give liberally and be ungrudging when you do so, for on this account the Lord your God will bless you in all your work and in all that you undertake (vv. 9–10, NRSV).

If followed, this provision would have protected small landowners from the exorbitant interest of moneylenders and thereby helped prevent them from losing their productive resources.

As in the case of the year of Jubilee, this passage involves structured justice rather than mere charity. The sabbatical release of debts was an institutionalized mechanism to prevent the kind of economic divisions where a few people would possess all the capital while others had no productive resources.

Deuteronomy 15 is both an idealistic statement of God's demand and also a realistic reference to Israel's sinful performance. Verse 4 promises that there will be no poor in Israel—*if* they obey all of God's commands! If the more wealthy had followed Deuteronomy 15, small landowners would have been far less likely to lose their productive resources. But God knew they would not attain that standard. Hence the recognition that poor people will always exist (v. 11). The conclusion, however, is not permission to ignore the needy because hordes of paupers will always exceed available resources. God commands precisely the opposite: "Since there will never cease to be some in need on the earth, I therefore command you, 'Open your hand to the poor and needy neighbor in your land'" (v. 11).

Jesus knew, and Deuteronomy implies, that sinful persons and societies will always produce poor people (Matt. 26:11). Rather than justifying neglect, however, God intends that this knowledge will be used by God's people as a reminder to show concern and to create structural mechanisms that promote justice.

The sabbatical year, unfortunately, was practiced only sporadically. Some texts suggest that failure to obey this law was one reason for the Babylonian exile (2 Chron. 36:20–21; Lev. 26:34–36).[66] Disobedience, however, does not negate God's demand. Institutionalized structures to prevent poverty are central to God's will for his people.

Does the biblical material offer a norm for distributive justice today? Some would argue that the biblical material on the land in Israel only applies to God's covenant community. But that is to ignore the fact that the biblical writers did not hesitate to apply revealed standards to persons and societies outside Israel. Amos announced divine punishment on the surrounding nations for their evil and injustice (Amos 1–2). Isaiah condemned Assyria for its pride and injustice (Isa. 10:12–19). The book of Daniel shows that God removed pagan kings like Nebuchadnezzar in the same way he destroyed Israel's rulers when they failed to show mercy to the oppressed (Daniel 4:27). God obliterated Sodom and Gomorrah no less than Israel and Judah because they neglected to aid the poor and feed the hungry. The Lord of history applies the same standards of social justice to all nations.

That does not mean, however, that we should try to apply the specific mechanisms of the Jubilee and the Sabbatical release to late-twentieth-century global market economies. It is the basic paradigm that is normative for us today.

It would be silly to try to apply the specific mechanisms of the Jubilee and Sabbatical release of debts in today's world. Land, for example, has a very different function in an industrial economy. Appropriate application of these texts requires that we ask how their specific mechanisms functioned in Israelite culture, and then determine what specific measures would fulfill a similar function in our very different society. Since land in Israelite society represented productive power, we must identify the forms of productive power in modern societies. In an industrial society the primary productive power is the factory, and in an information society it is knowledge. Faithful application of these biblical texts in such societies means finding mechanisms that offer everyone the opportunity to share in the ownership of these productive resources. If we start with the Jubilee's call for everyone to enjoy access to productive power, we must criticize all socioeconomic arrangements where productive power is owned or controlled by only one class or group (whether bourgeois, aristocratic, or proletarian), or by a state or party oligarchy. Indeed, we saw that the prophets protested the development of a different economic system in which land ownership was shifted to a small group within society. And we must develop appropriate *intervening processes* in society to restore access to productive resources to everyone.

The central normative principle that emerges from the biblical material on the land and the sabbatical release of debts is this: *Justice demands that every person or family has access to the productive resources (land, money, knowledge) so they have the opportunity to earn a generous sufficiency of material necessities and be dignified participating members of their community.* This norm offers significant guidance for how to shape the economy so that people normally have the opportunity to earn their own way.

But what should be done for those—whether the able-bodied who experience an emergency or dependents such as orphans, widows, or the disabled—who for shorter or longer periods simply cannot provide basic necessities through their own efforts alone?

Generous Care for Those Who Cannot Care for Themselves

Again the biblical material is very helpful. Both in the Old Testament and the New Testament, we discover explicit teaching on the community's obligation to support those who cannot support themselves.

The Pentateuch commands at least five important provisions designed to help those who could not help themselves:[67]

1) The third year tithe goes to poor widows, orphans and sojourners as well as to the Levites (Deut. 14:28–29; 26:12).
2) Laws on gleaning stipulated that the corners of the grain fields and the sheaves and grapes that dropped were to be left for the poor, especially widows, orphans, and sojourners (Lev. 19:9–10; Deut. 24:19–21).
3) Every seventh year, fields must remain fallow and the poor may reap the natural growth (Exod. 23:10–11; Lev. 25:1–7).
4) A zero-interest loan must be available to the poor and if the balance is not repaid by the sabbatical year, it is forgiven (Exod. 22:25; Lev. 25:35–38; Deut. 15:1–11).
5) Israelites who become slaves to repay debts go free in the seventh year (Lev. 25:47–53; Exod. 21:1–11; Deut. 15:12–18). And when the freed slaves

leave, their temporary "master" must provide liberally, giving the former slaves cattle, grain and wine (Deut. 15:14) so they can again earn their own way.

In his masterful essay on this topic, John Mason argues that the primary assistance to the able-bodied person was probably the no-interest loan. This would maintain the family unit, avoid stigmatizing people unnecessarily, and require work so that long-term dependency did not result.

Dependent poor, such as widows and orphans, received direct "transfer payments" through the third-year tithe. But other provisions, such as those on gleaning, required the poor to work for the "free" produce they gleaned. The widow Ruth, for example, labored in the fields to feed herself and her mother-in-law (Ruth 2:1–23).

It is important to note the ways that the provisions for helping the needy point to what we now call "civil society." Not only did Ruth and other poor folk have to glean in the fields; more wealthy landowners had responsibilities to leave the corners of the fields and the grapes that dropped. And in the story of Ruth, Boaz, as the next of kin, took responsibility for her well-being (chapters 3, 4).

The texts seem to assume a level of assistance best described as "sufficiency for need"—"with a fairly liberal interpretation of need."[68] Deuteronomy 15:8 specifies that the poor brother receive a loan "large enough to meet the need." Frequently, God commands those with resources to treat their poor fellow Israelites with the same liberality that God showed them at the exodus, in the wilderness, and in giving them their own land (Exod. 22:21; Lev. 25:38; Deut. 24:18, 22). God wanted those who could not care for themselves to receive a liberal sufficiency for need offered in a way that encouraged work and responsibility, strengthened the family, and helped the poor return to self-sufficiency.

Were those "welfare provisions" part of the law to be enforced by the community? Or were they merely suggestions for voluntary charity?[69] The third-year tithe was gathered in a central location (Deut. 14:28) and then shared with the needy. Community leaders would have to act together to carry out such a centralized operation. In the Talmud, there is evidence that the proper community leaders had the right to demand contributions.[70] Nehemiah 5 deals explicitly with violations of these provisions on loans to the poor. The political leader calls an assembly, brings "charges against the nobles," and commands that the situation be corrected (Neh. 5: 7; cf. all of 1–13). Old Testament texts often speak of the "rights" or "cause" of the poor. Since these terms have clear legal significance,[71] they support the view that the provisions we have explored for assisting the poor would have been legally enforceable. "The clear fact is that the provisions for the impoverished were part of the Mosaic legislation, as much as other laws such as those dealing with murder and theft. Since nothing in the text allows us to consider them as different, they must be presumed to have been legally enforceable."[72]

The sociopolitical situation is dramatically different in the New Testament. The early church is a tiny religious minority with very few political rights in a vast pagan Roman empire. But within the church, the standard is the same. Acts 2:43–47 and 4:32–37 record dramatic economic sharing in order to respond to those who could not care for themselves. The norm? "Distribution was made to each as any had need" (Acts 4:35). As a result, "there was not a needy person among them" (v. 34).

The great evangelist Paul spent much of his time over several years collecting an international offering for the impoverished Christians in Jerusalem (2 Cor. 8–9). For his work, he found a norm (2 Cor. 8:13–15)—equality of basic necessities—articulated in the exodus story of the manna where every person ended up with "as much as each of them needed" (Exod. 16:18; NRSV).[73]

Throughout the Scriptures we see the same standard. When people cannot care for themselves, their community must provide a liberal sufficiency so that their needs are met.

A Role for Government

Thus far we have seen that the biblical paradigm calls for an economic order where all who are able to work enjoy access to appropriate productive resources so they can be creative co-workers with God, create wealth to bless their family and neighbors, and be dignified participating members of their community. For those who cannot care for themselves, the biblical framework demands generous assistance so that everyone has a liberal sufficiency of basic necessities.

But what role should government play?[74] Certainly government does not have sole responsibility. Other institutions, including the family, the church, the schools, and business, have crucial obligations.

At different points in the biblical text it is clear that the family has the first obligation to help needy members. In the great text on the Jubilee in Leviticus 25, the first responsibility to help the poor person forced by poverty to sell land belongs to the next of kin in the extended family (Lev. 25:25, 35). But the poor person's help does not end with the family. Even if there are no family members to help, the poor person has the legal right to get his land back at the next Jubilee (25:28). Similarly, 1 Timothy 5:16 insists that a Christian widow's relatives should be her first means of support. Only when the family cannot, should the church step in. Any policy or political philosophy that immediately seeks governmental solutions for problems that could be solved just as well or better at the level of the family violates the biblical framework which stresses the central societal role of the family.

But is there a biblical basis for those who seek to exclude government almost completely from the field of the economy? Not at all. The state is not some evil to be endured like an appendectomy.[75] According to Romans 13, the state is a gift from God designed for our good. Hence John Calvin denounced those who regarded magistrates "only as a kind of necessary evil." Calvin called civil authority "the most honorable of all callings in the whole life" of mortal human beings; its function among human beings is "no less than that of bread, water, sun, and air."[76]

Government is an aspect of community and is inherent in human life as an expression of our created social nature. This perspective is contrary to the social contract theory at the base of liberal political philosophy, in which warring individuals put aside their independent existence by contracting to have a society to whose government, when formed, they transfer their individual rights. Governmental action to empower the poor is one way we implement the truth that economic justice is a family affair.

Sin also makes government intervention in the economy necessary. When selfish, powerful people deprive others of their rightful access to productive resources, the state rightly steps in with intervening power to correct the injustice. When other individuals and institutions in the community do not or cannot provide basic necessities for the needy, government rightly helps.

Frequently, of course, the state contributes to social cohesion by encouraging and enabling other institutions in the community—whether family, church, non-governmental social agencies, guilds, or unions[77]—to carry out their responsibilities to care for the economically dependent. Sometimes, however, the depth of social need exceeds the capacity of non-governmental institutions. When indirect approaches are not effective in restraining economic injustice or in providing care for those who cannot care for themselves, the state must act directly to demand patterns of justice and provide vital services.

The objective of the state is not merely to maintain an equilibrium of power in society. Its purpose is not merely to enable other groups in the society to carry out their tasks. The state has a positive responsibility to foster justice. The nature of justice defines the work of government so fundamentally that any statement of the purpose of government must depend upon a proper definition of justice.

That is why our whole discussion of the biblical paradigm on the economic components of justice is so important. "The Lord has made you king to execute justice and righteousness" (1 Kings 10:9; cf. Jer. 22:15–16). These two key words (*justice* and *righteousness*), as we have seen, refer not only to fair legal systems but also to just economic structures.

The positive role of government in advancing economic justice is seen in the biblical materials which present the ideal monarch. Both the royal psalms and the Messianic prophecies develop the picture of this ideal ruler.

Psalm 72 (a royal psalm) gives the following purpose for the ruler: "May he defend the cause of the poor of the people, give deliverance to the needy, and crush the oppressor" (v. 4, NRSV). This task is identified as the work of justice (vv. 1–3, 7), and, in this passage, justice includes using power to deliver the needy and oppressed.

According to Psalm 72, there are oppressors of the poor, separate from the state, who need to be crushed. State power, despite its dangers, is necessary for society because of the evil power of such exploiting groups. "On the side of the oppressors there was power," Ecclesiastes 4:1 declares. Without governmental force to counter such oppressive power there is "no one to comfort" (Eccles. 4:1). Whether it is the monarch or the village elders (Amos 5:12, 15), governmental power should deliver the economically weak and guarantee the "rights of the poor" (Jer. 22:15–16; also Pss. 45:4–5; 101:8; Jer. 21:12).

Prophecies about the coming Messianic ruler also develop the picture of the ideal ruler. "With righteousness he shall judge the poor, and decide with equity for the meek of the earth; he shall smite the earth with the rod of his mouth, and with the breath of his lips he shall kill the wicked" (Isa. 11:4, NRSV).

This ideal ruler will take responsibility for the needs of the people as a shepherd: "He shall feed them and be their shepherd" (Ezek. 34:23). Ezekiel 34:4 denounces the failure of the shepherds (i.e., the rulers) of Israel to "feed" the people. Then in verses 15–16, the same phrases are repeated to describe God's promise of justice:

> ". . . I will make them lie down," says the Lord God. "I will seek the lost, and I will bring back the strayed, and I will bind up the injured, and I will strengthen the weak, but the fat and the strong I will destroy. I will feed them in justice" (NRSV).

This promise will be fulfilled by the coming Davidic ruler (vv. 23–24). Similarly in Isaiah 32:1–8, the promised just and wise monarch is contrasted to the fool who leaves the hungry unsatisfied (v. 6).

This teaching on the role of government applies not just to Israel but to government everywhere. The ideal monarch was to be a channel of God's justice (Ps. 72:1), and God's justice extends to the whole world (e.g., Ps. 9:7–9). All legitimate rulers are instituted by God and are God's servants for human good (Rom. 13:1, 4). In this passage, Paul states a positive reason for government (government acts "for your good" [v. 4]) before he specifies its negative function ("to execute wrath on the wrongdoer" [v. 4]). Romans 13 is structurally similar to Psalm 72:1 in viewing the ruler as a channel of God's authority. All people everywhere can pray with the Israelites: "Give the king thy justice, O God" (Ps. 72:1).

Daniel 4:27 shows that the ideal of the monarch as the protector of the weak has universal application. God summons the Babylonian monarch no less than the Israelite king to bring "justice and . . . mercy to the oppressed." Similarly in Proverbs 31:9, King Lemuel (generally considered to be a northern Arabian monarch) is to "defend the rights of the poor and needy" (NRSV). "The general obligation of the Israelite king to see that persons otherwise not adequately protected or provided for should enjoy fair treatment in judicial proceedings and should receive the daily necessities of life is evidently understood as the duty of all kings."[78]

The teaching on the ideal just monarch of Israel, whether in royal psalms or Messianic prophecies, cannot be restricted to some future Messianic reign. God demanded that the kings of Israel provide in their own time what the Messianic ruler would eventually bring more completely: namely, that justice which delivers the needy from oppression. God's concern in the present and in the future, within Israel and outside of Israel, is that there be a community in which the weak are strengthened and protected from their foes.

Conclusion

The traditional criterion of distributive justice which comes closest to the biblical paradigm is distribution according to needs.[79] Guaranteeing basic needs for life in community becomes more important than the criteria which are central in many worldly systems: worth, birth, social contribution, might and ability, or contract.

Some of the other criteria of distributive justice are at least assumed in the biblical approach. Achievement (e.g., ability in the market so stressed in Western culture) has a legitimate role. It must be subordinate, however, to the central criterion of distribution according to needs for the sake of inclusion in community.

The biblical material provides at least two norms pertaining to distribution of resources to meet basic needs.

1) Normally, all people who can work should have access to the productive resources so that, if they act responsibly, they can produce or purchase an abundant sufficiency of all that is needed to enjoy a dignified, healthy life in community.
2) Those who cannot care for themselves should receive from their community a liberal sufficiency of the necessities of life provided in ways that preserve dignity, encourage responsibility and strengthen the family.

Those two norms are modest in comparison with some ideals presented in the name of equality. A successful effort to implement them, however, would require dramatic change, both in the U.S. and in every nation on earth.

～2～

Poverty, Civil Society and the Public Policy Impasse

Stephen V. Monsma, Pepperdine University

Each generation of Christians needs to struggle anew with how it ought to interpret and apply God's ancient command to the Hebrews: "There will always be poor people in the land. Therefore I command you to be openhanded toward your brothers and toward the poor and needy in your land" (Deut. 15:11). This brief command is only one of a great cloud of witnesses from the Old and New Testaments testifying to God's concern for the poor and to all believers' God-imposed duty to live out that concern. Taking note of this God-imposed duty is the easy part. The difficult task is determining the actions to which that concern should lead in the end-of-the-twentieth-century United States. Christians equally convinced of their duty to act with concern and love toward the poor among us will differ on the theoretical positions and concrete actions to which that concern and love should lead. Especially as it relates to governmental action and public policies, there are wide differences of opinion and position.

This essay is an attempt to bring greater clarity to this issue. It does not propose specific, concrete policies and programs; rather it seeks to think through some of the fundamental issues facing all thoughtful Christians desiring to respond with obedience and effectiveness to our Lord's command to exhibit a genuine concern for the poor. Its basic thesis is that a caring, effective response to the continuing tragedy of poverty in the midst of affluence necessarily involves strengthening the sense of personal responsibility of individuals, engaging civil society in the struggle against poverty, and developing appropriate governmental actions. All three are important. One should not be emphasized to the exclusion of the other two; each must take into account the other two. This essay seeks to develop this basic thesis in four sections. The first section briefly seeks greater clarity on the causes of continuing poverty in what is one of the wealthiest societies in the history of the human race, and the following section focuses attention on civil society and how weaknesses in American civil society are contributing to poverty today. Next, in light of these causes of poverty, this essay argues that the traditional policy prescriptions of neither the political left nor the political right are adequate, and that greater attention must be paid to strengthening civil society and the values and virtues engendered by it. The fourth section considers possible strategies to be pursued if the civil-society route to combating poverty is to be followed.

Causes of Poverty

Other essays in this book go into greater detail on the causes of poverty, but our discussion here will be helped by briefly noting that most explanations for the existence of poverty can be grouped under three headings. One heading includes causes rooted in cyclical economic changes. National economies historically have been marked by cycles of boom and bust—or at least growth and recession—and by other cycles such as those of high inflation or, less frequently, rapid deflation. Persons at the lower end of the economic ladder are especially vulnerable to such cycles. Rapid inflation, even brief periods of unemployment due to a stagnating economy, and other cyclical economic problems can push many persons into the ranks of the poor. A second group of causes for poverty relate to structural changes in the economy. These are distinguished from the cyclical changes in that they concern the basic structure of the economy and are long term trends that emerge gradually and become permanent features of the economy. The shift from a rural, agriculture-based economy to an urban, industrial based economy in the late nineteenth and early twentieth centuries is an example. Today, the United States is in the midst of a long-term trend involving the loss of low-skill, high-pay manufacturing jobs as corporations look overseas to take advantage of cheaper labor in other areas of the world. Structural trends can result in major dislocations, and persons caught in the negative backwash of such trends can be thrown into poverty, which they may find impossible to overcome on their own. Yet other causes of poverty can be grouped under a third heading, that of causes related to the circumstances and characteristics peculiar to the individuals experiencing poverty. The death of a spouse or an incapacitating illness are two clear examples. Also, one thinks of divorce and the birth of out-of-wedlock children, as well as substance abuse problems, a lack of self-discipline, and other self-destructive behaviors.

Structural changes in the economy and circumstances peculiar to the individuals suffering poverty are receiving renewed attention today, due in part to the persistence of poverty in the United States despite the absence of sharply negative cyclical forces in recent years. Some scholars, such as William Julius Wilson, have placed a prime emphasis on structural changes as a cause of poverty in the United States today.[1] Two trends are frequently mentioned in this context. One is the shift of many low-skill, high-paying manufacturing jobs overseas. It used to be that a Detroit young person could go right from high school—even without completing high school—to one of the automobile assembly plants and, thanks to strong unions, make good, solid, middle-class wages. Those opportunities have diminished as manufacturing jobs that require no special education or technical skills either are being automated, so no human labor is required, or are going overseas where unskilled labor can be obtained for a fraction of what unionized American workers are paid. A second major structural trend is the movement of many jobs from the central cities to the suburbs. As retail stores relocate from downtown or neighborhood shopping streets to suburban malls, as office complexes move to suburban locations closer to many of their workers' homes and with convenient parking and aesthetically pleasing settings, and as suburban industrial parks replace crowded, multi-story factories, jobs are becoming scarcer in the old central cities and more abundant in the surrounding suburban fringes. This makes it increasingly difficult for employees to depend on public transportation and requires dependable, private automobiles. This is no problem for most of the population; it is often an almost insurmountable challenge for the poor.

The third group of causes of poverty—that of circumstances and characteristics peculiar to the persons suffering poverty themselves—is receiving even more attention today in public policy circles. Empirical data linking much of present-day poverty to certain circumstances surrounding those individuals experiencing poverty and to certain negative behavior patterns and practices is rapidly accumulating. Census data reveal that the median family income of two-parent families was $52,000 in 1996, while for mother-only families it was $18,000.[2] In the same year one-third of all mother-only families were below the poverty line—27 percent of white mother-only families, 43 percent of African-American mother-only families, and 51 percent of Hispanic mother-only families.[3] Also, in 1995, 24 percent of the families in which the head had not graduated from high school were in poverty, while only 10 percent of families whose head had a high school diploma, even without any college, were in poverty.[4]

Ronald Brownstein has pointed out that while 14 percent of Americans fall under the official poverty line, only 6 percent of families headed by a married couple are poor and almost one-third of families headed by a single woman are poor.[5] These figures mean that the entire increase in poverty since 1976 among families can be explained by the increase in the percentage of families headed by a single woman—the poverty rate for married couples has remained unchanged. The discouragingly high poverty rates among African-American families can be explained largely in terms of the prevalence of female-headed families among African-Americans. The median income of African-American families is only 59 percent that of white families, but African-American families headed by a married couple earn 84 percent as much as white families headed by a married couple. The problem is that only 45 percent of African-American families are headed by a married couple. If one could wave a magic wand, the two most significant changes one could effect to reduce poverty would be to replace all mother-only families with two-parent families and assure that all persons completed high school.

One must be careful, however, in interpreting the public policy implications of the above cited statistics. One could interpret them to mean that government and the broader society have little responsibility when it comes to poverty. After all, if poverty is largely the result of persons' individual choices and behaviors relating to such factors as marriage, childbearing, and education, perhaps there is little government can do. Barring a totalitarian government that regulates its citizens' sexual practices, bans all divorce, and forces all to complete high school, what is there to be done? There is much, however, that government can and should do, and there is much the concerned Christian can do through his or her role as a citizen.

First, it is wrong to assume that the whole problem of poverty is simply one of individual character flaws. This is too simple. The fact that much higher percentages of African-American and Hispanic mother-only households fall below the poverty line than is the case for white mother-only households, by itself indicates that more is at play than two-parent versus one-parent families. Also, as noted earlier and as noted elsewhere in this book, structural changes in today's economy no doubt are also contributing to poverty. In addition, some have claimed that governmental policies and programs have encouraged the very forms of behavior and attitudes—especially out-of-wedlock births and easy divorce—that result in poverty. Examples often cited are the no-fault divorce laws passed by most states in the 1970s, the Aid to Families with Dependent Children (AFDC) program that (it is claimed) encouraged out-of-wedlock births and discouraged marriage, and the imposition of the concept of judicially enforced due process rights and entitlements that sought to protect the poor from arbitrary actions of government officials but resulted in making it nearly impossible to enforce obligations onto those receiving public assistance in its various forms.[6] Although these claims are far from proven, the possibility that public policies—including even certain anti-poverty policies—may actually be contributing to poverty remains.

This very brief consideration of the causes of poverty indicates that to understand the continued persistence of poverty one certainly needs to take into account individual persons' choices, attitudes, and patterns of behavior. But one also needs to take into account how these individual factors interact with public policies that do much to structure the environment that helps mold these individual factors and within which these individual factors operate.

This analysis, however, leaves out a third key ingredient needed to understand poverty and how the Christian citizen should react to it. It is the one most frequently missed by analyses of poverty. It may also be the most important one. This ingredient is the concept of civil society, which is crucial in giving us perspective on the causes of, and possible answers to, poverty. It is much too simple to think in terms of only the individual and the government. Such thinking assumes that the only two moving forces in society are the individual, who wills and acts as an autonomous entity, and the government, which is the agent through which society as a whole wills and acts. But increasing numbers of scholars and other observers are pointing to civil society as a major force in society, and Christian social thought has long emphasized the importance of society's intermediate social structures. Especially once one understands that poverty is more than purely an economic problem or a problem for government to solve purely by its initiatives, it becomes important to understand civil society: its nature, its function, and its relevance to the problem of poverty in the United States. That is what the following section seeks to do.

Civil Society

Definitions

The first difficulty in using the concept of civil society to understand poverty more fully and to formulate proper responses to it is that there is no consensus on a precise definition. Jean Bethke Elshtain has defined civil society as "the many forms of community and association that dot the landscape of a democratic culture, from families to churches to neighborhood groups to self-help movements to volunteer assistance to the needy."[7] Gertrude Himmelfarb sees civil society as consisting "of those mediating institutions (families, friends, neighbors, communities, churches, civic organizations, and informal institutions) that intervened between the individual and the state and that served as a corrective both to excessive individualism and to an overweening state."[8] Alan Wolfe has defined civil society as "those forms of communal and associational life which are organized neither by the self-interest of the market nor by the coercive potential of the state."[9] These conceptualizations of civil society, taken together, offer a broad, somewhat ambiguous definition of civil society. They include almost all societal associations outside of for-profit businesses and government, and include everything from informal friendship groups and families to more structured religious congregations and voluntary associations such as civic clubs and nonprofit social service agencies. There is an intermediate or mediating quality to civil society, since its structures lie between government (and other large bureaucratic structures) and the indi-

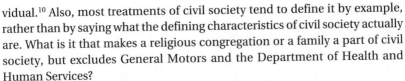

vidual.[10] Also, most treatments of civil society tend to define it by example, rather than by saying what the defining characteristics of civil society actually are. What is it that makes a religious congregation or a family a part of civil society, but excludes General Motors and the Department of Health and Human Services?

At the heart of the concept of civil society—even though it is often not clearly articulated—is the insistence that we do not live our lives as discrete, autonomous individuals, nor do we simply live them as a part of large, impersonal, modern bureaucratic structures, such as corporations or political units. Instead, all of us are woven into a larger fabric of human relationships—families, friends, clubs, neighborhoods, and more. Persons are united into social units by way of regular, repeated contacts of one type or another. These contacts may be face-to-face, as in a family or a local service club, or they may be somewhat more impersonal, as with a large religious congregation that meets periodically for worship and celebration, engages in joint projects, and receives a common newsletter or bulletin, even though all its members rarely meet together in one place and many of its members do not even know each other personally. Thus, the key characteristic of civil society is that its various entities include members who—to a greater or lesser extent—are personally aware of each other and interact with each other, thereby giving their members a meaningful sense of belonging to, or identity with, the larger entity. These qualities come close to being the defining characteristics of those structures that make up civil society.

Thus families, neighborhood groups, local religious congregations, local service clubs, hospital guilds, and other service organizations are the archetypal structures of civil society. One could argue that a neighborhood public school that serves the children of the area and also serves as a center for community contact and interaction is a part of civil society, even though it formally is part of the governmental structure. Also a small township government, serving a rural area and composed of friends and neighbors, would be a part of civil society, even though it is also part of the governing structures. A small neighborhood store that provides needed products but also serves as a neighborhood center, providing social contact and a sense of belonging, should be considered a part of civil society even though it is a part of the economic marketplace. On the other hand, there are non-governmental and non-marketplace social structures that cannot truly be considered a part of civil society. Although individual religious congregations are clearly within the scope of civil society, it is hard to conceive of the national, impersonal, bureaucratic structures of the Presbyterian or Roman Catholic churches as parts of civil society. More important than the formal composition of an association in determining whether or not it is a part of civil society is its members being aware of each other, interacting with each other, and having a sense of belonging or identity that emerges from their relationship with the association.

Christian social thought has long insisted that the structures of what is now called civil society are an integral part of God's will for humankind. Franz

Mueller has pointed out that Thomas Aquinas insisted "that society is not regarded as a homogenous mass" but that its "individual members are conceived as being incorporated into the large social bodies not directly, but through the medium of intermediate associations. Therefore, society is, properly speaking, not a mere aggregation of single human beings, but an ordered unity of associations . . ."[11] The French Catholic social thinker, Jacques Maritain, wrote: "But the body politic also contains in its superior unity the family units . . . and a multiplicity of other particular societies which proceed from the free initiative of citizens and should be as autonomous as possible."[12] And the British Anglican, John Figgis, has written: "What do we find as a fact? Not, surely, a sandheap of individuals, all equal and undifferentiated, unrelated except to the State, but an ascending hierarchy of groups, family, school, town, county, union, Church, &c., &c."[13] Kenneth Woodward of *Newsweek* magazine has summarized Christian social thought on this point well:

> Unlike the individualisms of the secular left and right, Catholic doctrine [and, one can add, much of Christian thought more generally] conceived society as an interdependent organism rather than a social contract between isolated individuals. Rights and duties flow from the sacredness of every human person, justice seeks the common good, the state ensures public order. In this view, persons are inherently social and proper human development requires civic space for a range of institutions: family, neighborhood, religious and other voluntary associations like labor unions and political parties.[14]

A Christian conception of society, public policy, and poverty needs to take into account the nature of human society, including the dimension of civil society, as established by God.

Many observers have claimed that the United States has an especially vibrant civil society. This was affirmed by Alexis de Tocqueville in an often-quoted passage:

> Americans of all ages, all conditions, and all dispositions constantly form associations. They have not only commercial and manufacturing companies, in which all take part, but associations of a thousand other kinds, religious, moral, serious, futile, general or restricted, enormous or diminutive. The Americans make associations to give entertainments, to found seminaries, to build inns, to construct churches, to diffuse books, to send missionaries to the antipodes; in this manner they found hospitals, prisons, and schools. If it is proposed to inculcate some truth or to foster some feeling by the encouragement of a great example, they form a society.[15]

Two Roles of Civil Society

The growing literature on civil society assigns it two fundamental roles that are crucial for public policy purposes in relation to the problem of poverty. It is important to look at both roles carefully. One is that the structures of civil society themselves provide the support and help all of us need as we live our lives. Children receive physical sustenance and emotional support in their families, adults find structure and meaning for life in their religious congregations, persons are able to pursue avocational interests within civil society organizations, and in times of need such as unemployment, ill health, and death, persons can find support and help from family, church or synagogue, and other civil society organizations. If it were not for civil society, all of us would live in a cold, barren, inhospitable world, and government would be called upon to provide a staggering array of additional services.

As important as is this first role of civil society, most would argue that a second role is the more important one. This role is to inculcate the values, attitudes, and norms of behavior essential to a democratic regime. David Blankenhorn has written that the structures of civil society, and especially the family, are "the foundational sources of competence, character, and citizenship in free societies."[16] Later he writes, "Liberal politics presuppose these virtues and depend upon these institutions [of civil society] in order to create the good citizens without which self-government is impossible."[17] Mary Ann Glendon has asked the penetrating question:

> What is it that causes individual men and women to keep their promises, to limit consumption, to stick with a spouse in sickness and health, to care for their children, to answer their country's call for service, to reach out to the poor, to respect the rights of others, and to moderate their own demands on loved ones, neighbors, and the body politic? More particularly, how do children first learn to empathize with others and to acquire self-restraint along with self-confidence?[18]

Her answer is that if these virtues are to be learned at all they are to be learned in civil society, and in families in particular. Similarly, over fifty years ago Clinton Rossiter wrote:

> It takes more than a perfect plan of government to preserve ordered liberty. Something else is needed, some moral principle diffused among the people to strengthen the urge to peaceful obedience and hold the community on an even keel. . . . [Free] government rests on a definite moral basis: a virtuous people. Men [and women] who are virtuous may aspire to liberty, prosperity, and happiness; men [and women] who are corrupt may expect slavery, adversity, and sorrow. In addition to such recognized virtues as wisdom, justice, temperance, courage, honesty, and sincerity, these may be singled out as attitudes or traits of special consequences for a free republic: the willingness to act morally without compulsion, love of liberty, public spirit and patriotism, official incorruptibility, and industry and frugality. Men [and women] who display these qualities are the raw material of free government.[19]

Later we will consider how qualities such as those Blankenhorn, Glendon, and Rossiter cite are crucial not only for free democratic government but also for overcoming poverty.

Is Civil Society Declining?

Given this picture of civil society as crucial for a healthy, democratic society, it is cause for deep concern that a growing number of scholars have reached the conclusion that civil society in the United States is in deep trouble today. Most of these observers are writing from a concern over the negative impact the decline of civil society will have for the health of democracy, but such a decline, if it is occurring, could also be having highly negative results in terms of fostering attitudes and behaviors likely to lead to poverty. In addition, the decline of civil society may lead to attitudes that undercut any recognition on the part of the more affluent segment of the population that they have an obligation to help those mired in poverty. It is worth our while to look carefully at the alleged decline of civil society.

That civil society in the United States is in decline was a central contention of Robert Putnam in his famous article, "Bowling Alone: America's Declining Social Capital."[20] He pointed out, for example, that membership in parent-teacher organizations is down by 42 percent since 1964, in the League of Women Voters by 59 percent since 1964, in the Boy Scouts by 26 percent since 1970, and in the Red Cross by 61 percent since 1970.[21] He writes, "After expanding steadily throughout most of this century, many major civic organizations have experienced a sudden, substantial, and nearly simultaneous decline in membership over the last decade or two."[22] Michael Sandel has concluded, "From families and neighborhoods to cities and towns to schools, congregations and trade unions, the institutions that traditionally provided people with moral anchors and a sense of belonging are under siege."[23] William J. Bennett has pointed to rising crime rates, lower educational achievement, and the near epidemic use of illegal drugs as further evidence that something has gone profoundly wrong in American society.[24]

As we will shortly see, whether or not civil society is in decline is subject to debate, yet there is no doubt that families—the most important of all the structures in civil society—are in deep trouble. Illegitimacy and divorce—both of which lead to single-female-headed families—have sharply increased in the United States in the past 40 years. William J. Bennett, among others, has chronicled the depressing statistics.[25] From 1960 to 1991 the percentage of out-of-wedlock births among all births increased from 5 percent to 30 percent. Among whites it has increased from 2 percent to 22 percent and among African-Americans it has increased from 23 percent to an astounding 68 percent. In the following ten major cities over half of all births are out-of-wedlock births: Detroit, Washington, St. Louis, Newark, Atlanta, Cleveland, Baltimore, Philadelphia, Chicago, and Pittsburgh.

Similarly, divorce is up sharply from the 1960s. In 1960 there were 2.2 divorces for every 1,000 persons; by 1980 that rate had increase by 140%, to 5.3 divorces for every 1,000 persons. Since then the rate of divorce has improved somewhat, with the Census Bureau estimating there were 4.1 divorces in 1995 for every 1,000 persons—still almost twice the 1960 level.[26] It is estimated that every year over 1 million children experience the divorce of their parents.[27] High rates of divorce and out-of-wedlock births resulted, as of 1996, in 31 percent of all children under eighteen years of age living with only one parent.[28]

Gertrude Himmelfarb has pointed out that one of the key reasons for the importance of the family in civil society—apart from its intimate, continuing ties—is its non-voluntary nature. One cannot join and resign from one's family at will, nor can one expel members one finds a burden or inconvenient. As a result the family traditionally was a support for the very young, the very old, and others who have been left vulnerable (such as the very poor) by life's tragedies. "But in the last few decades," Himmelfarb goes on, "the family has become 'voluntarized.' . . . we will to go in and out of the family, just as we like. That is the meaning of divorce, serial marriage, cohabitation, single-parent families, single-sex parenting."[29]

On the other hand, many are arguing that the decline of civil society is—outside of the impossible-to-deny figures related to the problems faced by the family—grossly exaggerated, and perhaps not accurate at all. Alan Wolfe, who himself has suggested civil society is in decline, has written, "There seems little doubt that some of the more alarmist accounts of civil society's decline, including my own, were exaggerated."[30] Particularly striking is the continued health and growth of churches and other religious congregations. Nancy Ammerman made this point in a lecture she gave in direct refutation of Robert Putnam. After a careful study of 300 congregations in nine different communities she concluded: "Both suburban growth and the influx of non-U.S. immigrants has resulted in congregational growth, adaptation, and—especially—entrepreneurship. . . . When we consider the religious ecology as a whole, adaptation and innovation are at least as visible as decline and death. As older forms of congregational life are suffering, new forms are thriving."[31] The most recent statistics bear out Ammerman's contention. A recent study found that church membership is holding steady, as is church attendance.[32] It also found 76 percent of adult Americans believe "God is a heavenly father who can be reached by prayers" and 80 percent believe the Bible is either "the actual word of God to be taken literally, word for word" or "is the inspired word of God, but not everything in it can be taken literally." The authors of this study concluded that "the religious tapestry of America today shows a country that by external measures is at least as religious as it has always been."[33] Sociologist Robert Wuthnow has concluded: "Judging from the wider range of information available about religious trends, then, one would have to conclude that Robert Putnam is wrong as far as the decline of religion is concerned."[34]

Other forms of religious involvement and interaction, such as church-organized small groups, have grown dramatically in recent years. Wuthnow estimates there are as many as two million such groups.[35] John DiIulio has pointed to the recent movement of church-based coalitions that have successfully worked to stem crime, neighborhood deterioration, and irresponsible sexual behavior in Boston, Philadelphia, and other major cities.[36] William Galston and Peter Levine have termed church-affiliated groups "the backbone of civil society in America."[37] Sidney Verba and his associates have argued that religious groups make an especially valuable contribution to civil society because they tend to attract not only the well educated and wealthy—who are often tied in to other associations—but also those with little income or education, who are unlikely to be members of other formal associations.[38]

In short, the picture with regard to the decline of civil society is mixed. Many civil society organizations seem to be suffering falling memberships; others—and especially religious congregations—are holding steady or strengthening. Families, as evidenced by very high divorce rates and out-of-wedlock births, are suffering severe strains. There are enough negative signs to raise concerns; there are enough positive signs to give hope.

Civil Society and Poverty

The state of civil society in our nation has huge implications for poverty. Three are particularly important. First, as seen earlier, the high levels of divorce, out-of-wedlock births, and single-parent, female-headed families have enormously negative implications for poverty in the United States. At least one-third of female-headed, single-parent families are poor. Also, the evidence gathered by social science research documenting the negative impact on children of growing up in a single-parent family is growing into an avalanche. As is discussed at greater length elsewhere in this book, children growing up in single-parent families, as compared to children growing up in two-parent families, are more likely to have lower SAT scores, to drop out of high school and not to attend college, are more likely to experience divorce in their own marriages, and are more likely to have children out of wedlock.[39] In addition, children coming from single-parent families are much more likely to be involved in criminal behavior and to use illicit drugs, both of which are indicators of and causes of poverty. Barbara Whitehead has pointed out that the relationship between growing up in a father-absent family and crime "is so strong that controlling for family configuration erases the relationship between race and crime and between low income and crime. This conclusion shows up time and again in the literature."[40] Richard Gill summarized much of the research when he wrote: "If one had to select the single most important factor responsible for the disturbing condition of many of today's younger generation—a condition that almost everyone now views with alarm—the breakdown of the intact biological-parent family would almost certainly be at or near the top of the list."[41]

All this is not to say that some single parents are not highly dedicated and skilled in raising children under often extremely difficult circumstances—and some raise children who have well integrated personalities, with strong self-discipline, high self-esteem, and other values and attitudes conducive to useful, productive lives. And some children coming from intact, two-parent families are the exact opposite. Also, the often negative consequences of single-parent families mentioned above may in part result from public policies that do not give adequate support to single-parent families. I am thinking here of inadequate systems to enforce child support payments and sometimes very weak public schools. I am only saying that in the United Sates today, statistically, children with the qualities of mind and character associated with avoiding poverty are more likely to come from intact, two-parent families than one-parent families.

Although the family is the backbone of civil society and the preeminent institution for teaching values and patterns of behavior that lead to habits and attitudes conducive to avoiding poverty, other structures of civil society—churches, neighborhoods, circles of friends, and voluntary associations—can both help prevent poverty directly and teach the attitudes of heart and mind that succeed in staving off poverty. They constitute the second reason for the importance of civil society for understanding poverty and potential responses to it. The structures of civil society are the structures that often have provided help in time of need, support and paths back to self-sufficiency in times of dislocations, and the moral fortitude and courage one needs to overcome the difficulties life sometimes throws in one's path. Religious congregations have an especially strong potential to play a leading role in halting the disintegration of civil society and encouraging the habits of heart and mind that families and other civil society structures are no longer teaching as well as they should. I say this, first, because religious congregations are still successfully incorporating large numbers of persons into them, including congregations in some of the worst neighborhoods of our large cities. In fact, in some of the most depressed inner city neighborhoods, churches are the only functioning structures of civil society. As Eugene Rivers of the Azusa Christian Community in Boston has said, "The only thing that stands between this community and nihilism is the black church."[42]

Also, research shows that religion has an enormous potential to teach the habits of virtue and character helpful in overcoming poverty. Psychologist Allen Bergin, after a survey of published studies, concluded that religious involvement reduces "such problems as sexual permissiveness, teen pregnancy, suicide, drug abuse, alcoholism, and to some extent deviant and delinquent acts, and increases self-esteem, family cohesiveness, and general well-being. . . . More generally, social scientists are discovering the continuing power of religion to protect the family from the forces that would tear it down."[43] In central city Boston, where a group of African-American pastors and churches have been actively working with at-risk youths, there had not been, as of the fall of 1997, a gun-related youth homicide since July, 1995![44] A Boston police officer told a group of Philadelphia clergy: "With the churches, with cooperation, we can turn our neighborhoods around. Without them, without cooperation, we can't."[45] As John DiIulio has pointed out, "When you look at the gutbucket stuff, the everyday, in-your-face working with troubled kids in these neighborhoods across the country, almost all of it is being done by people who are churched."[46]

A third reason civil society is important for understanding poverty and responses to it is that civil society is crucial for the development of a sense of shared, communal responsibility. As Sandel has written, "Above all, the institutions of civil society draw us out of our private, self-interested concerns and get us in the habit of attending to the common good."[47] For government to act with understanding, compassion, and justice towards the poor—whether that is the national government or a state or local government—it must be supported by citizens who see themselves and the poor as part of one body or community. Without this view there is no reason for the whole to be concerned with the poverty of the few. With large numbers of Americans—including Christian Americans—living in affluent suburbs and even in gated communities where the poor are never allowed to trespass, the danger is great of a society so fragmented that a sense of shared responsibility is lost. It is in the institutions of civil society—from Little League to churches, from Neighborhood Watch to school groups—that we often meet persons beyond our immediate circle of friends, gain new perspectives, and develop a broader sense of responsibility and community.

Again, it is the church that may offer the most hope; surely it should. Churches are active, alive, growing, located in both the worst neighborhoods of the inner city and the most affluent of suburbs, and can speak with authority concerning the importance of a God-imposed obligation towards the poor. Promise Keepers, with its emphasis on the reconciliation among different racial and ethnic groups, stands as a symbol of what the church can do—and is called to do—in a society fragmented by race, ethnicity, and economic status.

Answering the Problem of Poverty Today: Ending the Public Policy Impasse

Is there a public policy impasse when it comes to formulating effective, humane responses to the question of poverty in our society today? Have both the political left and the political right led us up dead end roads with no path to better policies clearly visible? Up until very recently the answer to these questions clearly would have been "yes," but there are signs that the impasse is breaking up. At the very least a way towards breaking it is becoming more evident. In this section I explore the impasse that until very recently was in place, the reasons we as a society became caught in it, and the emerging way out of it.

To understand the recent impasse it is helpful to go back to the three causes of poverty discussed earlier in this essay. It is clear that in regard to the first type of cause—cyclical economic changes—liberals and conservatives, Democrats and Republicans, are, and have been, largely in agreement that government-sponsored fiscal and monetary policies ought to be pursued so as to maintain a stable economy marked by moderate growth, low inflation, and high employment. There may at times be somewhat different emphases by liberals and conservatives, such as liberals tending to favor lower unemployment rates even at the risk of some greater inflation, and conservatives leaning in the opposite direction, but the differences are on the margins. There is basic consensus. In the past ten years or so, the United States has largely escaped negative economic cycles, and certainly at the end of the 1990s—with low inflation and high employment—the current economic cycle is not a cause of poverty. Yet poverty persists. Thus there has been a search for other causes for poverty and it is among them that a public policy impasse has been present.

The second cause of poverty discussed earlier consists of structural changes in the economy and society. As seen earlier, some scholars, such as William Julius Wilson, have placed a strong emphasis on structural changes in society and the economy as a cause of poverty in the United States today. Structural barriers to escaping poverty have tended to be ignored by political conservatives and emphasized by political liberals. Up until very recently liberals tended to see structural change—along with education, training, and child care—as *the* key to overcoming poverty. Thus liberals emphasized government programs designed to block or slow down the movement of manufacturing jobs overseas, to increase jobs in the central cities and to slow down the growth of suburbs, to improve public transportation, and to provide education, training, and subsidized child care. The implicit assumption was that it is a combination of structural changes in the economy and society, a lack of educational and training opportunities, and the lack of readily available, affordable transportation and child care that lie at the root of poverty.

The third set of causes of poverty outlined earlier relates to circumstances peculiar to the poor themselves. Single parenthood, not completing high school, poor spending habits, substance abuse, low self-esteem, and poor work habits are frequently cited causes falling into this third category. These causes have tended to be seized upon by conservatives and ignored by liberals. Conservatives pointed to the figures cited earlier to show that those who complete high school and do not have children out of wedlock are unlikely to be poor. Given the conservatives' distrust of large centralized government programs, they put forward two interrelated approaches to meeting the problem of poverty. One emphasized the importance of a healthy, expanding economy, which, in turn, they saw as depending upon a free market liberated from rigid regulations and overly high rates of taxation. If government, so the reasoning went, would only reduce regulation and taxation levels, economic growth that would lift most of the poor out of poverty would result. A second, related approach saw large welfare programs as encouraging the very attitudes and patterns of behavior that tend to create poverty. The encouraging of single-parent families, out-of-wedlock births, divorce, and sloth were seen as the inevitable consequences of welfare programs that offered benefits without

imposing obligations. The answer was to reduce benefits and even to eliminate whole programs.

These two approaches to reducing poverty complement each other. As welfare programs would be reduced or eliminated, taxes could be cut further. Thus
the economy would be stimulated, creating more jobs at the same time that
persons were being forced to become more self-reliant. This was the libertarian approach. Less government is the answer to poverty.

Liberals saw this conservative approach to poverty as replacing a responsible, caring approach that offers help and hope to the weakest and most vulnerable in society with an uncaring abdication of society's responsibilities. The
conservative claim was that one does good by doing well (one reduces poverty
by cutting taxes and jettisoning expensive programs of help and assistance).
Liberals argued that such an approach had more to do with selfishness and the
quest for political advantage than a genuine, realistic concern for the poor.
They insisted that government welfare efforts—composed of such programs
as job training and education, child care, cash payments, and health care—
were essential. They viewed claims that welfare programs encourage attitudes
and behaviors that work to perpetuate poverty as "blaming the victims." Conservatives, meanwhile, saw liberals as naive and in love with big, centralized
government programs that were fostering the very habits and attitudes that
led to more poverty. They saw the high taxes that were needed to sustain the
liberals' programs as stifling the economic growth needed to provide jobs for
the poor.

It was these contrasting public policy positions of the left and right and their
underlying assumptions that led to an impasse in anti-poverty policies. But in
the past four or five years there seems to have been a break in the impasse. To
understand both the nature of the impasse and signs of its breaking up it is
helpful to understand a crucial point Robert Bellah has made, namely, that
both conservatives and liberals at heart are strong individualists. Conservatives "think free competition is the best context for individual self-realization."[48]
Liberals "seldom believe in government as such. They simply see it as the most
effective provider of those opportunities that will allow individuals to have a
fair chance at making something of themselves."[49] Liberals are "pro-choice"
(that is, pro-individual choice) when it comes to abortion and pornography;
conservatives are "pro-choice" when it comes to economic issues. Neither have
a well-defined, or well-thought-out view of communities. As Bellah puts it,
"This ideological world [of liberals and conservatives] is a world without families. It is also a world without neighborhoods, ethnic communities, churches,
cities and towns, even nations (as opposed to states)."[50] Conservatives have
traditionally felt the free market was the way to fight poverty, with individuals
being encouraged (or forced) by the market to act responsibly. Once they did
so, they would escape poverty. What was needed was for government to stop
rewarding or accommodating irresponsible behavior. Liberals traditionally felt
that with the needed help from government (education and training, child

care, transportation) individuals would be able to get their lives in order and escape poverty. Both, Bellah is saying, were individualist strategies. One saw only the individual and the free market, the other saw only the individual and government.

As a result both liberals and conservatives have usually overlooked what may be the most important, most effective approaches to overcoming poverty. David Blankenhorn has recommended a "civil society strategy."[51] Such a strategy could do much to attack poverty on an underlying, causative level. It would seek to strengthen and make use of families, churches, neighborhood groups, nonprofit social service agencies, and a host of other structures of civil society lying between the individual on the one hand, and the impersonal market and government on the other. If such a strategy would be followed, the structures of civil society—and especially religious congregations and other religiously based associations—would be encouraged and empowered to do more to combat poverty and its related pathologies. They would be enabled both to do more to respond to poverty directly and to help overcome attitudes and patterns of behavior in individuals that are self-defeating.

There are indications that both liberals and conservatives are beginning to pay greater attention to civil society as a key element in the struggle against poverty. Their doing so gives hope of breaking the public policy impasse. Conservative think tanks such as the Heritage Foundation and the American Enterprise Institute are paying renewed attention to issues of civil society. Leading Republican spokespersons such as George Bush, Jr., Steve Forbes, Dan Coats, J. C. Watts, and Jack Kemp are calling for a renewed recognition of, and reliance on, the institutions of civil society, and, most importantly, are not assuming that a healthy civil society will appear automatically if government simply shrinks. Senator Dan Coats has written: "The retreat of government does not automatically result in the rebirth of civil society."[52] A task force appointed by Governor George Bush, Jr., of Texas concluded: "In our view, Texas's social institutions have shared responsibilities. Government cannot divest itself of all responsibility, but neither should it cling to the statist belief that it has exclusive jurisdiction for the poor."[53] William J. Bennett has written that he wants "to be clear and unequivocal in my belief that we need to reduce government's overall size and reach. . . . That said, I am under no illusion that relimiting government alone is sufficient to the task of American renewal." He goes on to argue that "the conservative fallacy could easily become an abiding faith in the all-sufficiency of non-government."[54] These and other conservatives are calling for specific government initiatives that will enable, strengthen, and affirm the institutions of civil society.

Meanwhile, liberals are also beginning to recognize the importance of civil society. The fact that the Brookings Institution—probably the foremost liberal think tank in Washington—devoted almost its entire fall 1997 issue of *The Brookings Review* to civil society, is itself revealing. President Clinton has sometimes gone out of his way to affirm the importance of civil society, especially the family and religious congregations. There are reports that he has shown much interest in Senator Coats's Project for American Renewal, a civil-society-based initiative for meeting many social needs.[55] William Galston, former aide in the Clinton White House, has acknowledged that "addiction, dependency, and other weaknesses of character disempower individuals just as much as do the absence of material resources and social order."[56] Former Democratic Senator Bill Bradley has written: "Any prescription for America must understand the advantages and limits of both the market and government . . . [and] how neither is equipped to solve America's central problems: the deterioration of our civil society and the need to revitalize our democratic process."[57] More liberals, in government and academia alike, are coming to acknowledge that divorce, bearing children out of wedlock, and substance abuse are factors in the stubborn persistence of poverty.

The passage of the 1996 federal welfare act through the joint action of a Republican Congress and a Democratic President in itself indicates that the public policy impasse between liberals and conservatives may be starting to break up. That law contains a "charitable choice" provision that one observer has termed "potentially earthshaking."[58] It provides that when states contract for the provision of social services they must allow religiously based agencies to compete for those contracts on the same basis as secularly based agencies, and when services are provided by religiously based agencies it protects their freedom to pursue their religiously based practices.[59] It thereby seeks to allow faith-based agencies—which have historically been a key element in civil society—to play a greater role in combating poverty and its related pathologies. Liberals and conservatives in Congress worked out acceptable language, and it was passed by the Congress and signed by President Clinton, who has indicated his support of it.[60] "Charitable choice" remains subject to court challenges and may ultimately be overturned in its current form, but the momentum that created it continues unabated.

Noting these signs that the political left and right are finding some common ground in combating poverty in the concept of civil society does not mean that the political spectrum is now united in recognizing civil society as having a crucial role to play in overcoming poverty in the United States. Many liberals remain suspicious that any talk of civil society is a way for government to avoid its responsibilities towards the poor and probably is a harbinger of a time when the personal choices of the poor will be dictated by others. They are especially wary of bringing religious congregations and religiously based schools and social service agencies into the picture, out of an innate suspicion of religion and out of a fear that doing so will violate (their concept of) appropriate church-state separation. They fear a revival of an intolerance they associate with religion.

Most conservatives do not need to be convinced of the importance of civil society, but many seem to believe that civil society will flourish if only taxes are reduced and government programs and regulations eliminated. Many of them fear that any attempt by government and the structures of civil society to work together will inevitably lead to the government making the structures of civil society into arms of the government, marked by all the pathologies of big, impersonal government.[61]

In short, the left and the right are open to civil society discussions in a way they were not open even five years ago, and thus there is a basis for dialogue and a quest for common ground that was not present earlier. But this is only an opening, a beginning; much work needs to be done if that opening or beginning is to be made into a solid foundation for renewed anti-poverty efforts resting on a broad consensus.

Christians may have a special role to play in that work. Christians are especially well situated to have something of importance to say and can offer actual, concrete, remedial programs in revitalizing civil society and using it to overcome poverty. This is true for two underlying reasons. First, there is the size, vitality, and pervasive presence of churches in American society. As noted earlier, civil society may in some respects be declining in the United States; religious associations are not. In many high poverty areas, churches are the only form of associational life that is flourishing. Second, religion can speak with a moral authority and force that most other associations in civil society cannot even approach. Churches can draw on a spiritual power that has proven successful in overcoming addictions, inspiring renewed commitments to personal integrity, and in other ways changing lives in dramatic fashion.

Families in particular are in trouble, and the church is uniquely positioned to speak to and bolster that all-important, God-created institution. Marriage and the family have traditionally been closely associated with the church, with the church sanctioning and blessing most marriages. Thus churches are in a strategic position to reemphasize the solemnity of entering into marriage, to insist on premarital counseling, to offer support and help to troubled marriages, and to resist divorce as an easy option when a marriage begins to fail. There are movements within several Christian denominations encouraging progress in these directions. The church and parachurch associations are also in a strategic position to emphasize the traditional Christian position of "abstinence outside of marriage and faithfulness in marriage." Many individual congregations, the parachurch Promise Keepers, and church-based organizations that encourage young people to promise not to engage in premarital sex, are already effective in preventing out-of-wedlock births. More such efforts are needed. The moral authority of religion and the biblical basis for moral standards give individual churches and parachurch groups a strong moral basis that more pragmatic, secularly based efforts can never possess. If the churches and parachurch organizations could be successful in such efforts, the number of two-parent families would increase and one-parent families—due either to divorce or out-of-wedlock births—would decrease. Just this change would do more to reduce poverty in the United States than any other step one could imagine.

Meanwhile, when families fail—when out-of-wedlock births or divorce occur, resulting in mothers-only families, or when other crises hit families—

the church can partially meet the needs thereby created. To some degree the church can give children and single parents the encouragement, material support, and direction they need. Churches can focus not only on families, but also on schools, neighborhoods, crime reduction efforts, and a wide variety of religiously based service agencies. Doing so would mean schools would be improved, youths would have alternatives to drug-infested gangs, child care services for working parents would be more readily available, hope and self-esteem would be reinforced, habits of work and discipline would be encouraged, substance dependency would be reduced, and support would be available in times of crisis. All this would help reduce poverty.

There is, of course, a yawning gap between wishing for the revitalization of civil society, with churches leading the way, and actually seeing it happen. No one should underestimate the difficulty of achieving this, nor the number of setbacks and disappointments that will accompany such efforts. There are no grounds for triumphalism. In this world human efforts are always accompanied by failures and imperfection; they ultimately are totally dependent on God's grace and favor for any success at all.

Strategies

This section does not presume to present a full-blown strategy for the revitalization of civil society in order that it become a more effective means for combating poverty. What it does seek to do is to present some basic principles and perspectives on that revitalization and put forward some examples of the types of steps that need to be taken. Several of the other essays in this book develop more fully the actual and potential role of civil society in responding to the problem of poverty. In thinking through the impasse out of which we are only beginning to emerge, it is important to avoid simply looking to government—liberal fashion—for the key leadership and the needed policy changes; neither is it appropriate—conservative fashion—to ignore government and assume it has no role to play in revitalizing civil society other than cutting taxes and reducing its programs. In this section I offer some thoughts on the complementary roles that need to be played by civil society and government. Both have a role to play. Both are important. At the end of this section I also briefly consider the role that needs to be played by societal opinion leaders if the civil society sector is to play its vital role in overcoming poverty.

Civil Society's Role

The institutions and structures of civil society—and especially religious congregations and parachurch groups—need to take the lead in teaching family responsibility; counseling against divorce and premarital sex; creating support groups for families in difficulty; and in providing a myriad of services such as housing, drug awareness and treatment for addiction, financial counseling, child care, transportation, and more. An article in a national news magazine recently asked, "What's the surest guarantee that an African-American urban youth will not fall to drugs or crime? Regular church attendance turns out to be a better predictor than family structure or income."[62] This is an amazing finding, given the frequently documented significance of family structure on behavior. It is also a source of great hope. The institutions of civil society and churches in particular are in a position to do much to step into the breach where the family has faltered and the government has failed.

An increasing number of inner-city churches and their allied ministries are already achieving much. This has been one of the great untold success stories of the past fifteen years. John DiIulio tells the story of how "a group of black inner-city ministers in Boston organized themselves around a plan for cutting juvenile violence, reclaiming parks and sidewalks, educating at-risk children, promoting local economic development, strengthening families, and resurrecting the civil life of their jobless drug-and-crime-infested neighborhoods."[63] The success of this effort has been recognized by the local Boston authorities and now a national group has formed that is seeking to mobilize one thousand inner-city churches to put in place similar efforts in the nation's twenty-five largest cities. Glenn Loury has reported: "The reports of successful efforts at reconstruction in ghetto communities invariably reveal a religious institution, or a set of devout believers, at the center of the effort."[64] Each year the Christian Community Development Association, composed of more than two hundred inner-city churches and agencies devoted to combating the problems of poverty and urban alienation, attracts three thousand to four thousand attendees from around the nation to its annual convention. Urban Concern in Columbus, Ohio, World Impact in Los Angeles, and the Pittsburgh Project are all examples of its member organizations. As is typical of these Christian community development associations, the Pittsburgh Project has described itself in a brochure it has put out as "a neighborhood-based Christian community development ministry that seeks to restore the city by developing the local community, rejuvenating its residents, developing leaders for its future, serving the poor, and building the kingdom of God." Such organizations are already effective both in rebuilding civil society and in providing direct assistance to those who continue to be in need in spite of all of our best efforts. As Senator Paul Wellstone of Minnesota has said, "Some of the best antipoverty work I've seen has come from faith-based agencies."[65] These efforts need to be multiplied and expanded.

Christian schools—whether sponsored by a church or by an independent organization—are an aspect of civil society that already is playing a large role in combating poverty and has the potential to play a much larger role. The track record of Catholic schools located in inner-city neighborhoods is well documented and no less than astounding. One reporter has written of a Catholic school in the Bronx, "in one of the nation's poorest urban communities," that "despite the surrounding threats of violence and their own humble beginnings, students at St. Angela's—like many of the archdiocese's inner-city schools—do remarkably well. Test scores for St. Angela's 489 students show a pattern of *exceeding state standards* for reading, writing and especially math."[66] The principal of the integrated Capitol Christian Academy outside Washington, D.C., reports that nearly all of their graduates go on to two-year or four-year colleges.[67] Two organizations of Christian schools report that the standardized Stanford Achievement Tests show their students at all grade levels an average of one year and eight months above national norms.[68] More formal studies confirm observations such as these. James Coleman and Thomas Hoffer of Harvard University, after a major study of inner-city Catholic schools, concluded: "The achievement growth benefits of Catholic school attendance are especially strong for students who are in one way or another disadvantaged: lower socioeconomic status, black or Hispanic."[69] The differences in the educational achievements of minority and low income children in nonpublic, usually Christian schools are not minor or at the margins; they are large and substantial.

As a result, low income and racial minority parents often strive to enroll their children in Catholic or Protestant schools. "Black private school enrollment is now growing at a faster rate than that of the overall private school enrollment and that of white private school enrollment. The overwhelmingly largest share of the growth is in the Christian school population. . . . The number of African-Americans attending conservative Christian schools nearly doubled from 1991 to 1994."[70] Voucher plans that would make it financially feasible for parents to send their children to nonpublic schools are especially popular among black and Hispanic parents.[71] In New York City, when a program of privately funded scholarships for low-income children to attend religiously based and other private schools was initiated, some forty thousand applied for the 2,200 scholarships that were available.[72] When Ohio created a program of vouchers for low-income Cleveland children, a lottery had to be held to determine which of the six thousand applicants would receive one of the coveted two thousand vouchers.[73]

In short, churches, other religious congregations, parachurch associations, and religiously-based K–12 schools have proven their value as crucial facets of civil society and have demonstrated their ability to inculcate the values, habits, and commitments crucial to avoiding and escaping poverty. Any strategy Christians develop for reducing poverty in the United States must look to the structures of civil society by working through and strengthening their churches, parachurch groups, and schools.

Government's Role

It is a central contention of this chapter that we must look to civil society for answers to the problem of poverty more fully than we as a society have been doing. But this does not mean that government has no role to play. What is needed is a strategy that does not focus on government to the exclusion of civil society, nor civil society to the exclusion of government. That sort of thinking led to the impasse in public policy discussed earlier and does much to explain the continued persistence of poverty in the midst of a highly affluent society. What is needed is a cooperative relationship between the institutions of civil society and government. Government must seek neither to dominate nor to ignore civil society. Rather, it must seek to deal with civil society in justice—to recognize its institutions for what they are and to respect and protect the roles they have to play in society. Doing so will involve sometimes leaving them alone, sometimes helping or assisting them, and sometimes curbing or correcting them. There are three basic principles I believe government should follow in seeking to know what kind of response is needed.

The first of these principles is to follow the millennia-old injunction Hippocrates laid down for the medical profession: First do no harm. Every governmental policy and action needs to be scrutinized from the perspective of what impact it will have on the structures of civil society, and especially on families, churches, parachurch organizations, and religiously based service organizations. As Peter Berger and Richard John Neuhaus wrote in 1977, "Minimally, public policy should cease and desist from damaging mediating structures."[74]

As is discussed more fully in David Gushee's essay, the second principle government needs to follow is to do what it can to protect marriage, nurture intact, two-parent families, and discourage divorce and out-of-wedlock births. The family is the bedrock of civil society and society's first line of defense against poverty. Thus the general principle of "do no harm" needs to be applied with special vigilance in regard to the family. We need to acknowledge that the movement to no-fault divorce in the 1960s and 1970s has been a disaster. New approaches to protecting marriage legally, while still recognizing the need in some circumstances to dissolve a marriage, should be developed. Any responsible measure aimed at signaling that marriage is not something to be lightly entered into nor easily exited needs to be explored.

Much more can and needs to be done to protect the family. Family-leave legislation, as good as it is now, needs to be strengthened and broadened. The recent move to increase personal income tax exemptions for dependents was a good step forward. If money for further tax cuts is available, further increases in tax exemptions and credits would be advisable. This is a better way to deal with the issue of child care than increasing child care subsidies of one type or another. Child care subsidies give a financial incentive for both parents to work outside the home, since those subsidies only become available when both parents hold paid jobs. When child tax credits or deductions are made available, this important lifestyle choice will be made by parents based on their circumstances and beliefs, without government tilting the decision in one direction or the other.

Other initiatives to strengthen the family and childrearing should be explored. George F. Will has suggested a "GI Bill for Mothers" that would grant tuition vouchers to women who stay home as full-time mothers when their children are young, and could be used to gain the education needed to reenter the world of paid employment once the children are older.[75] Careful study and creative reflection would result in other policy proposals that would encourage the formation and survival of intact, two-parent families and discourage—or at least no longer encourage—divorce and single parenthood.

A third principle is that when government undertakes to provide certain educational or social services itself or subsidizes their provision by secularly based agents, it should provide the means by which religiously based schools and agencies can qualify for public support on equal terms. Right now, the generally most effective structures of civil society are placed at an enormous disadvantage as government itself provides certain educational or social services out of tax funds rather than helping to fund private, often religiously based organizations providing parallel or similar educational or social services in a much more effective manner. Think of K–12 schools in their massive public school systems in contrast with the small, often struggling Christian schools. I am not saying that religiously based schools should be favored over public schools, or that the schools of one religious tradition should be favored over those of another. I am only asking for a level playing field. As Senator Bob Kerrey of Nebraska once said, "If I were running a public-school system, I'd sign a contract with the parochial schools—as Mayor Giuliani wanted to do in New York—and have them educate some of the poorest kids. I don't see the First Amendment as so rigid that it prevents us from contracting with people who are getting the job done right."[76]

This third principle also means that when government provides certain social services to the poor, it should at least at times work with and through religiously based social service organizations in providing social services to the poor.[77] Again, I am not saying religious agencies should be favored over government agencies or secular agencies; but neither should government agencies and secular agencies be favored over religious ones. Thus the "charitable choice" provision included in the 1996 welfare act is highly desirable. The most important aspect of "charitable choice" is its effort to protect the religious integrity of religiously based agencies that do take part in government-funded programs. This is essential, both in terms of justice for the agencies and also in the interest of effective services for the poor. If government would insist that the religious elements of religious service organizations must be removed before they can receive government funds, many organizations would refuse to participate and the expanded services they could offer would be lost. Other religious agencies, if they would give up important aspects of their programs in order to qualify for government funds, would lose the very characteristics that now often make them effective. It is the ability to speak with a sense of religious-moral authority and to attract dedicated workers from one's religious tradition that make these agencies so effective now. Remove that religious component and one is back to an agency that looks very much like a government or secular agency.

Opinion Leaders

If civil society is to be renewed and freed to play a robust role—on its own or in partnership with government—there is also a role that needs to be played by opinion leaders. I am thinking here especially of analysts and advocates in academic and research institutions and leaders in the media, both in their news reporting and their entertainment. Opinion leaders such as these do much to set the public policy agenda, mold attitudes and opinions, and shape long-term trends in values and culture.

Researchers from think tanks and research universities, for example, regularly fail to study civil society, and when they do they usually ignore its religious dimension. John DiIulio of Princeton University once said, "You can go through thousands and thousands of studies, and people don't even look at the religion variable."[78] Religion is simply not on the radar scopes of much of the academic and public policy community. As a result the religious aspect of civil society is a void in too much of academia, and it thus tends not to figure into the theories and policy prescriptions flowing from academic and public policy centers. If these centers ignore the religious dimension, the news media also tend to ignore it, and if the news media ignore it, public officials tend to ignore it. Churches and other religiously based structures working to help persons out of poverty and to defeat the values and behavior patterns that lead to poverty need to be studied and understood. They need to be respected, acknowledged, taken seriously, studied by the academic community and reported on by the news media.

There may be signs of hope on this score. In articles cited earlier, *Newsweek* magazine recently carried a cover story with the headlines: "God vs. Gangs. What's the Hottest Idea in Crime Fighting? The Power of Religion."[79] *The New Yorker* recently carried an article by Joe Klein on the power of religion and churches in overcoming inner city problems.[80] Sidney Verba and his colleagues give appropriate emphasis to religion as a factor in citizen participation in their academic study of political participation.[81] But these are more the exceptions than the norm.

There are even fewer signs of hope with regard to the popular entertainment industry. Bill Bradley has made a telling point:

> We need a more civic-minded media. At a time when harassed parents spend less time with their children, they have ceded to TV more and more of the all-important role of storytelling which is essential for the moral education that sustains civil society. But too often TV producers and music executives and video game manufacturers feed young people a menu of violence without context and sex without attachment, and both with no consequences or judgment. . . . Too

often those who trash government as an enemy of freedom and a destroyer of families are strangely silent about the market's corrosive effect on those very same values in civil society.[82]

Anyone who has taken note of the lyrics of "gangsta rap," has viewed many of the movies emerging from Hollywood with an eye to the values implicitly or explicitly fostered by them, or has noted the sexually explicit material now available on the internet, has to raise questions concerning what the entertainment industry is doing to the values and attitudes of our society. Also sobering is the thought that these forms of entertainment are especially popular among youth, who are at an impressionable age. Solid, empirical evidence is hard to come by in this area, but one would have to be extraordinarily naive to assume that this steady flow of violence, marital infidelity, premarital sex, and disrespect for authority figures simply has no effect. Especially among those who come from single-parent families or families where there is little adult guidance and no strong sense of values, the reasonable assumption is that the entertainment industry is having a major impact, and one that is largely negative in nature.

If this is true, and given the pervasiveness of the various forms of entertainment media, strengthening civil society and enabling it to play a major role in overcoming poverty will be made more difficult if the entertainment media do not pull back from their more egregious forms of sex, violence, and disrespect for the basic values of a healthy civil society. Otherwise civil society, in its attempt to teach and model attitudes and patterns of behavior conducive to avoiding poverty, will be on a collision course with the entertainment industry. This is an area where government regulation, beyond restricting the access of minors to much of this material and regulating hard-core pornography, is not the answer. Too many civil liberties and effectiveness questions arise. Strengthened families can help by controlling the access children have to the more offensive forms of entertainment. As well, families vote with their consumer decisions. Every time one attends a movie, rents a video, buys a CD, or logs onto an internet site, one is voting to have more of that type of movie, video, CD, or internet site.

In our lifetime there has been a major shift in our society's attitudes toward smoking—from glamorous and sophisticated to dirty and stupid. In the old movies it was the heroes who were seen smoking, while today it is normally the villains. Similarly, one can observe the beginnings of a shift in attitudes towards single parenthood and divorce, as evidence accumulates of the problems children experience in such situations. If these sorts of shifts can be made with regard to these practices, is it too much to hope they can also be made in relation to violence, gratuitous sex, and other attitudes and behaviors that degrade human beings and undercut the values of a healthy civil society?

Conclusion

Just as the causes of poverty are not unidimensional, so the answer to poverty cannot be unidimensional. At the beginning of this essay I mentioned personal responsibility on the part of individuals, a strong, healthy civil society, and appropriate government policies—all three—as somehow needing to be a part of the mix. It would be easier if the answer were purely governmental. Then all we would have to do to meet the challenge of poverty in the midst of affluence would be to mold the right government policies. Christians could live out their Lord's command to care for the poor and needy simply by advocating the needed public policies.

As is often the case in real life, however, things are not this simple. Surely, certain government actions are needed. But those actions must not ignore the potential of civil society in averting poverty and helping those in poverty to escape it. As this essay has stressed at several points, what is needed today is for government and civil society to work together. The structures of civil society should seek to strengthen themselves and expand their efforts—both direct and indirect—to help those caught in the web of poverty to overcome it. Government policies should protect and strengthen civil society and should work through, and take advantage of, the strengths of civil society. The many structures of civil society that have a religious nature appear to be especially effective and relevant to helping the poor overcome their poverty. Thus they need to be especially active in struggling against poverty and its underlying causes; government policies need to take into account, protect, and utilize the religious dimension of civil society. As civil society is allowed and even empowered to play a more fulsome role in combating poverty, the needed qualities of hope, personal responsibility, and self-discipline essential to escaping poverty will be affirmed and encouraged. The strategies for overcoming poverty that incorporate this basic approach are complex and often difficult to articulate and implement; yet they are also essential. They are more realistic and more likely to result in positive results than the unidimensional approaches too often undertaken in the past.

~3~

The Market System, the Poor, and Economic Theory

James Halteman, Wheaton College

Introduction

The call for social justice is an ancient one. It was expressed by Moses and his laws of moral behavior and care for one's neighbor, based on the veneration of God the Creator. Even the stranger in our midst is to be cared for. Throughout the Old Testament the prophets pointed to the injustices that the rich and powerful wrought on the poor and neglected. Isaiah projected a society of justice where behavior was based on care and faith, not on economic value and profits.[1]

Capitalism and democracy are uneasy partners and a balance between them must be struck in any nation that tries to live by both creeds. The driving force behind capitalism is inequality—the dream of making more money than other people. The driving force behind democracy is equality—one person, one vote. If a democrat is born equal, a capitalist intends to die as unequal as possible. In the balance between these two great strivings lies the health of nations.[2]

We Christians would find our mission to and within the world perplexed if we were confronted by a worldview that proclaimed capitalistic individualism morally satisfactory. But the world is under God's judgment, and therefore it is right that the worldview of present-day capitalism agrees that it must be judged by standards that transcend individualistic calculations of interests.

Thus, the opening in today's capitalism to consider a higher standard of justice gives the biblical norm of social justice more opportunity for a future than many suppose: biblical social justice can speak meaningfully to the post–Cold War West. There is a pervasive societal awareness that the "moral high ground" does not in fact belong to capitalism, and therefore biblical norms of social justice are not necessarily prevented from gaining a broad public audience in the foreseeable future.[3]

Capitalism, by most accounts, has in fact won the day as the twentieth century draws to a close. But capitalism can have many faces as one moves from the general theory of resource allocation by prices toward a market economy as it is practiced in the Western world. The United States has marched so triumphantly forward as a leader in promoting markets that conservative William Bennett now expresses concern. "What I am concerned about is the idolatry of the market. . . . Unbridled capitalism . . . may not be a problem for production and expansion of the economic pie, but it's a problem for human beings. It's a problem for . . . the realm of values and human relationships because it distorts things."[4]

This paper will explore how the biblical concern for the poor may get distorted when markets become idolized. At the outset it is important to recognize that both the theory of markets and the United States application of that theory, often called capitalism, provide the context for the analysis. In other words, the general theory of resource allocation will be examined with the cultural and institutional framework of American market capitalism as the reference point for applications. It must be recognized that this is somewhat problematic because capitalism involves much more than the fundamentals of resource allocation theory. In fact, economic theory comes with an entire package of political, social, and geographical components that will vary from one market economy to another. However, whatever complication this causes is more than outweighed by the need to contextualize pure theory to make it relevant.

This chapter consists of six parts. The first section is a short discussion of the hermeneutical problems that arise in addressing the issue of integrating faith and economics. The second section attempts to lay the philosophical foundation upon which economics was built using the writings of Adam Smith as the primary source material. Third, working from these philosophical foundations, a general description of neoclassical market theory is spelled out and critiqued. The fourth section explores how people build on philosophy and theory to develop a worldview that governs their understanding of policy formation. Liberal and conservative approaches are explored to illustrate how economic opinions are often based on non-economic values and beliefs. It should become clear in this section that one's Christian faith should provide a distinctive perspective on economic life, particularly in the area of income distribution. In the fifth part, the Austrian-libertarian and institutional critiques of mainstream neoclassical theory are presented as examples of heterodox views from opposite sides of the political-economic spectrum. The final section explores what unique additions Christianity can make to our under-standing of economic theory and policy.

Some Hermeneutical Concerns in Doing Economics

The ancient world did not see social arrangements as natural systems that were part of creation. They did not think of economic relationships as some-thing scientific to be discovered through careful analysis. Rather they looked to the sages and philosophers and prophets for advice on how to live. People were responsible to create their social arrangements and relationships in ways that worked for them. Thus Jesus never taught comparative economic systems. Instead, he advocated a revolutionary approach to social organization that called into judgment the social norms of his day. Efficiency was not defined outside of a completely radical value system that recognized the highly inter-dependent nature of all people. There was no natural mechanistic order with an internal consistency to which people and social structures must conform. Consequently, the teachings of Jesus focus on both process and outcomes, on people's motives, their behavior and on a view of fairness that did not permit debilitating poverty. Jesus taught as if the preferences of people could be changed.

On the other hand, pure market theory focuses heavily on process with min-imal attention to outcomes. It assumes self-interest as the main human moti-vation and accepts that motivation as appropriate. It elevates efficiency above other values such as fairness because it sees fairness as a normative concept outside of the realm of economics. For these reasons there is a big gap between modern economic analysis and ancient economic teaching. Bridging the gap requires far more than gleaning some generalized principles from the biblical texts and grafting them on to modern economic institutions.

At the core of such a bridging process is the question of whether the mech-anistic Enlightenment worldview under which markets operate is compatible enough with the ancient worldview to make straightforward applications of biblical material meaningful. Two kinds of problems present themselves. First, some modern economic understandings and technological opportunities open possibilities unknown to the biblical world. If these possibilities involve a rein-terpretation of some biblical teaching, then the Christian is required to exer-cise very careful discernment. For example, if savings from someone can be invested by someone else in machinery that generates large profits, is it not appropriate for the lenders of the funds to receive interest from the borrower who makes the profit? If, as is true in ancient culture, most loans were made for the consumption needs of the poor, then interest seems morally offensive. In this case the technological context determines the moral teaching. It is not helpful to forbid usury today as a direct application from Scripture. Many bib-lical practices are subject to similar hermeneutical problems.

A second problem in interpretation is that some modern economic institutions that seem to be supported in Scripture might have new trappings that negate the apparent biblical blessing. For example, the modern view of private property has far fewer constraining social norms than a biblical understanding of private property. In 1 Kings 21, Naboth felt highly constrained when he had the option to sell his land to the king for a better piece of land. He did not feel free to do it because of established religious and social norms that seem strange to us now. Thus the biblical support for a highly individualistic concept of private property is weaker than it seems to someone who does not explore the range of constraint possible in a private property based system. This is not an argument against private property, but it does raise questions about the possibility for constraints on certain types of ownership and it does qualify the claim that the Bible supports private property as we understand the term.

In light of these and other hermeneutical issues, it is precarious to derive economic norms from a simple, straightforward application of biblical texts. Sensing this dilemma, Christians frequently despair of any application effort and simply accept the norms of whatever economic system prevails in the culture. For example, a piecemeal after-the-fact justification of Western capitalism unfortunately has often been a substitute for the hard task of integrating biblical teachings and economic life. Many people have become pro-capitalist Christians without seeking to understand the underlying philosophy or the human dynamics of the system. At the same time, they often do not articulate the first principles of the Christian faith most germane to economic life. These are put forth in various ways in several chapters of this book. The primary principles are listed below but are not developed here because they are explored more completely in other chapters.

1. Human dignity is bestowed upon all people from God. Debilitating poverty is unacceptable.
2. God is the Creator and ultimate owner of everything.
3. Human sinfulness precludes an ideal social order.
4. Humans are to steward resources in ways that glorify God.
5. Government is God-ordained for the good of all people.

Any view of efficiency or fairness must be consistent with these principles. If maximum efficiency results in a segment of the population living with less than basic human needs, then efficiency must be questioned. Likewise, any definition of fairness that results in irresponsible waste must also be examined anew.

The Philosophy of Market Capitalism

From the beginning of recorded history humans have tried to design a social order that could function smoothly and effectively. Successful systems have found ways to nurture the good passions in people while controlling the bad passions that are always present. In fact, the types of systems that are used to deal with human passions often define the entire flow of history. The medieval system of authority, obligation and moral duty dealt with human passions very differently than the freedom and competition mode of the modern era.

Two primary, but very different, traditions stand out as options around which a social order can organize. The civic republican tradition began with the Greek philosophers and was built upon by the church fathers from the early church through the Middle Ages. Commerce was suspect and the answer to the question "what is the good life" was found in the pursuit of virtue in the context of community. In the civic republican tradition the social glue of society came from a shared vision of the public good. Virtuous behavior, including care for the poor and helpless, was generally part of that vision even though the average standard of living was not far in excess of subsistence. Liberty meant the right to help form the shared vision. Individual material accumulation was considered destructive of the shared vision.

But shared vision turned out to be a precarious social glue. Indeed coming to a shared vision was becoming more difficult and social harmony more elusive as the Middle Ages gave way to increased commerce, material accumulation, and religious fragmentation.

When the unity of western Christendom was shattered in the sixteenth century, a period of religiously motivated civil and international war set in which was to last for well over a century. The great historical fact which served as the moral backdrop for thinking about capitalism was not the factory or the mill, but war between men with rival views of salvation, men who were so sure of their own view of salvation that they were prepared to shed the blood of their fellow man in order to save his soul.[5]

Unfortunately, this "ungluing" of a shared social vision destroyed the safety net of the poor in society. The parish paternalism that provided for those in need was heavily based on religious teaching and was part of the shared vision that became a casualty of the disintegrating feudal worldview.

Slowly the search began for a theory of social organization that would allow for social harmony without a shared vision of the social order. What was required for this option to work was enough control of human passion to make diversity possible without conflict. The Roman civil law tradition provided an alternative to the civic republican tradition. Thinkers like Hugo Grotius, a seventeenth-century jurist, abandoned the idea that a just polity could control human passion and create a social order dependent on virtuous people. For writers like Samuel Pufendorf and John Locke, the structure of law and contracts became important as rules of a game governing human behavior. These rules could sufficiently curb negative behavior and people could then play the game with only their own interest in mind. Philosophers Spinoza, Hobbes, Pascal, and Rousseau all sought a system that would deal with people as they are rather than as they ought to be, and argued that what seemed like virtue on the surface was little more than disguised self-love or self-preservation. "Philosophy considers man as he ought to be and is therefore useful only to the very few who want to live in Plato's Republic and do not throw themselves into the dregs of Romulus. Legislation considers man as he is and attempts to put him to good uses in human society."[6]

But exactly how could the civil law tradition be applied in the post-medieval world? If people really are slaves to their passions, and if religious and philosophical appeals to social harmony are ineffective, then there seemed to be only three options available around which to focus the new law. First, coercion and repression by the state was one option. Second, the passions might be harnessed using social institutions designed to soften the bad passions. For example, military force gave vent to random ferocity; organized commerce was an outlet for greed and avarice; and politics substituted for the worst aspects of ambition. Finally, countervailing or competing passions could be mobilized to offset the undesirable passions. The appeal of this third view was strong. Over time the notion of competing passions evolved to interests and interests became identified with a narrow sense of material well being called self-interest. The bad passions could be tamed by competing, less harmful, passions. People would give up revenge for money, or jealousy for social approval. By the mid-eighteenth century the metamorphosis was complete. Operating out of self-interest was considered to be sinful a century earlier, but now it became the positive force that controlled the unsocial and selfish passions. The pursuit of self-interest had become the backbone of the civilizing project of humanity. The redemption of humanity came, not through self-sacrifice and self-denial and a glorified life in the world to come, but rather in the pursuit of one's own interest in the present world. For many, this metamorphosis reached fruition when the pursuit of self-interest became highly individualistic, bounded only by the appropriate rules of the game.

Unfortunately, this glorification of self-interest as the new social glue did not offer much to those who were losers in the game of production and accumulation that proceeded vigorously in the late eighteenth and early nineteenth centuries. "Throughout the period of the Industrial Revolution, there is no doubt that the standard of living of the poor fell precipitously in relative terms. . . . There can be no doubt about which class paid the social costs in terms of the sacrificed consumption that was necessary for industrialization."[7] Following the Industrial Revolution, the idea that it was virtuous to help the poor all but disappeared as a systemic value. In its place came the notion that people should help the poor if it is in their self-interest to do so.

But this individualistic and self-centered approach to economic activity was not the vision of Adam Smith, who closely observed the events of the late 1700s. Smith is often called the father of economics but few have read beyond his most famous book. By the time he wrote *The Wealth of Nations* he had already developed an elaborate theory of human behavior in *The Theory of Moral Sentiments*. Among the most prominent components of behavior to Smith were interdependency, a moral base grounded in natural law, and self-control which conditions the excesses of selfish and unsocial passions. Because of Smith's insights into human behavior and his belief that virtue still oiled the gears of the social system, it is instructive to examine his views more closely.

To Adam Smith, people are motivated primarily by passions and sentiments rather than reason. These passions are natural and innate rather than disguised self-interest. In contrast to some readings of Hobbes and Mandeville, Smith depicted humanity as a bundle of socially constructive and socially destructive passions. One of the constructive passions was the desire to be approved of by others, a quality that he called approbation. Generosity, compassion and esteem are also innate qualities that Smith saw as central to understanding persons as they really are. These social passions, or constructive passions as I will call them, are only part of the complex picture of humanity.

The socially destructive passions—hate, revenge, and envy—are also part of the fabric of being human. They compete with the constructive passions, and a third category of passion called the selfish passions (grief, joy, self-preservation, and selfishness). Somehow, the civilizing project of society must blend the interests that derive from the passions in such a manner that social harmony can result. Here Smith parts ways with some of his contemporaries who see the selfish passions as primary in human behavior. Unlike Smith, they see all other passions as merely disguised selfishness, from which it follows that behavior is little more than the pursuit of a personal agenda. This psychological egoism is far from what Smith has in mind in either of these two books. On the contrary, Smith focuses on the human desire to be what one desires to see in others. The approbation of other people is only fulfilling when that approval comes from behavior that ought to be approved of by them. Thus a bank robber who receives approval from his peers will not find satisfaction in his actions because, although he has experienced sympathy from his friends, he has not met the measure of moral sympathy toward which the social passions point.

Another fundamental premise of Smith's view of behavior involves the principle of sympathy. People are created with the ability to project themselves into the experiences of others in order to gain perspective on their action. This fellow-feeling of the passions is then conditioned by the moral input from an impartial spectator, the final component of Smith's understanding of human behavior. While some ambiguity exists about Smith's impartial spectator, it clearly is a metaphor for an unbiased and detached assessment of what is appropriate in a given circumstance with all angles considered and all biases removed. One receives the approbation (approval) of others by behaving in ways that others see as right from a position of unbiased sympathy (a projection of themselves into the situation with the guidance of the impartial spectator). This process is not devoid of moral input so, according to Smith, moral judgments do impact individual behavior. In the end, the accumulated wisdom of the impartial spectator over time comes to constitute the social norms and societal mores so that behavior is not destructive of the social order no matter what passions are being exercised. Figure 1 below illustrates this system of moral sympathy which Smith felt could lead to social harmony.

There is no room in this system for a highly individualistic expression of preferences that are devoid of moral input. However, Smith parts ways with his mentor, Hutcheson, who believed in a moral sense theory of ethics, because Smith did not believe religion or innate morality was the source of moral behavior. His understanding of morality was derived from the innate social passions, the search for approbation, the ability to sympathize, and the desire to respect the judgments of the impartial spectator. Smith spent his life seeking ways to structure social institutions that could interact effectively with the passions to form a workable social system. He was convinced that the virtues of benevolence and self-control were necessary for the system to work, but he was skeptical about the ability of the masses to appropriate those virtues in everyday life. Consequently prudence (looking after oneself effectively) and justice (establishing rules of the game) become all-important in making society work. What is significant in this analysis is that people are not autonomous preference-islands who are independent of others. We live in relationships where benevolence is one of the two highest virtues and all segments of society must be provisioned so that both commutative and distributive justice can be achieved.

Figure 1

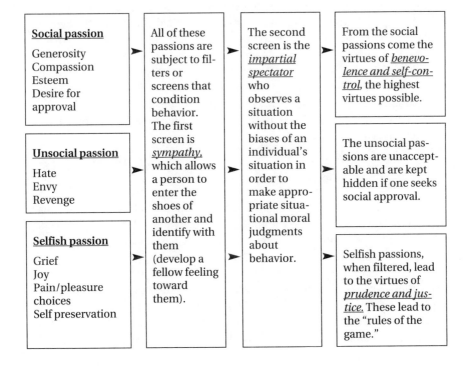

Smith's specific view of distributive justice is complex and can only be understood in the context of all of his writing. A superficial reading of Smith's work leads some to believe that he relegated acts of charity to those capable of true benevolence and that the government was not charged with solving income distribution problems. A more careful reading suggests that Smith had what might be labeled an "optimal degree of inequality" in mind for the system of natural liberty. In this system there is no room for debilitating poverty. Government does have a role in seeing that such poverty does not happen. At the same time, some variation in income stimulates industry, encourages the arts and commerce, and fosters social mobility across the rungs of the social ladder. Smith's optimism about his system of natural liberty, in contrast to the mercantilism of his day, led him to believe that the opulence generated by such a system would benefit the poor and give them an escape from poverty. Smith's obvious compassion for the poor, suspicion of the rich, and acceptance of a public role for benevolence would surely make him an advocate of efforts to help those caught in a web of poverty and hopelessness.[8]

Some claim that Smith began what we now call the positive-normative dichotomy with his dualistic view of the virtues. Benevolence and self-control are the ideals or normative standards toward which we should strive. Prudence and justice are the basis for the way the world really must work. This view sees his *Moral Sentiments* as dealing with the normative area of life and *Wealth of Nations* as constructing the positive framework around which economic life must function. The problem with this view is that Smith himself articulated no such dichotomy. For him the entire system sketched above was intertwined with and conditioned by the Creator so that morality pervaded the whole behavioral enterprise as a natural system. While benevolence and self-control were relatively rare and while the impartial spectator was somewhat ambiguous, the behavioral package was not split into a positive and normative dichotomy. Unfortunately, in modern economics there is little if any concern given to benevolence and self-control as virtues integrated into models of how the world works.

Neoclassical Economic Theory Today

From these philosophical issues which concerned the classical economists, modern-day neoclassical economics has evolved into a highly mechanistic tool which seeks to predict behavior rather than to explain it. Economics has become so convinced that it is a positive science that the positive and normative dimensions of economic behavior are now easily separated. What follows is a four-part description of what neoclassical economics is all about. First a general model of the economic problem of scarcity is explored so that the categories of economic analysis can be dissected. Second, the rational choice mode of thinking that has become the method of neoclassical economics will be explored. Third, a short history of how economic theory moved from Adam Smith to the present mainstream is presented. Finally, a listing of the strengths and weaknesses of the neoclassical market theory is discussed. Along the way attention will be given to the implications of the theory for those who are poor and at risk in the system.

To explore neoclassical economic theory systematically, it is helpful to establish the categories of discussion by using a sketch model (figure 2 below) of its components. The triangle illustrates how the key economic questions are connected. First, it is important to note that human wants exceed the resources available if all resources were free. Second, the right side of the triangle represents the economic interactions of the production process. The left side deals with distribution issues once the goods are produced. Between the two sides, an arrow points out the important connection between them. At the heart of most debates about economic systems is some implied notion about what motivates people to behave as they do. Political pressures, moral responsibility, fear of starvation, or individual material gain have all been driving forces in production throughout history. Some drive production better than others, but each one comes with some package of complementary cultural, philosophical, moral, and social qualities. In short, the context of economic activity is an essential part of understanding and evaluating the performance of any economy. These factors must be carefully understood when transporting a biblical economic message across the ages to our time.

Figure 2

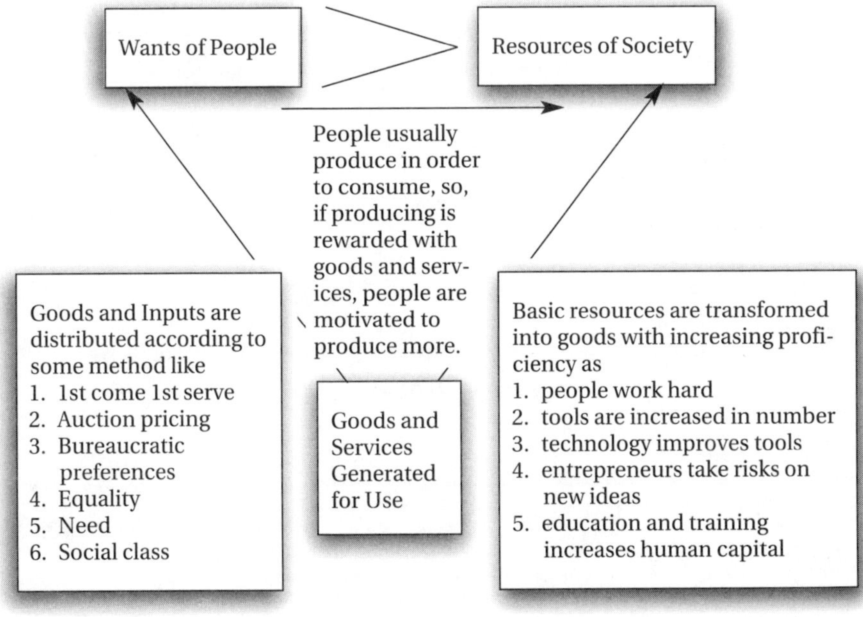

Wants of People — Resources of Society

People usually produce in order to consume, so, if producing is rewarded with goods and services, people are motivated to produce more.

Goods and Services Generated for Use

Goods and Inputs are distributed according to some method like
1. 1st come 1st serve
2. Auction pricing
3. Bureaucratic preferences
4. Equality
5. Need
6. Social class

Basic resources are transformed into goods with increasing proficiency as
1. people work hard
2. tools are increased in number
3. technology improves tools
4. entrepreneurs take risks on new ideas
5. education and training increases human capital

The triangle above poses the three basic questions that economics must answer about resource use. 1) What is to be produced? 2) How will the production be accomplished? 3) Who will get the production? The first question is answered in the interplay of forces across the top of the triangle. People express their wants in some fashion. In a free enterprise economy this is accomplished when consumers attempt to purchase goods and services in a market. Producers answer the second question as they interact with the issues highlighted in the right side box. In a market economy the entrepreneur combines the five inputs listed in the box in ways that maximize profits which implies that the proper quantities are produced at the lowest possible cost. The third question is answered by relying on one of the methods listed in the left side box. A market economy relies on a modified auction pricing mechanism where the highest bidder gets the goods.

For many, there is something offensive about a system that distributes the goods to those that have the money. Some of the other methods of allocation listed in the left side box seem to command a higher moral ground than the price system, but none seem to motivate production as well as the price mechanism. Since a person must have money to acquire goods and since the way to get money is to work, it follows that the person who produces the most will get a larger share of the product. Of course there are exceptions to this general principle because some receive money from inheritance, chance, or the manipulation of economic power that does not lead to additional production. Nevertheless, if a market economy is thriving, it is likely that these exceptions are limited in the economy at large.

For the market system to answer the three questions effectively, human behavior must be motivated by a desire to improve oneself. The motivational theory that economics relies on in its analysis is referred to as rational choice theory. Figure 3 shows various elements that motivate human behavior. While Smith's explorations ranged widely over all the categories, neoclassical economics focuses primarily on the rational choice area and relates to the others if they can be interpreted in a self-interest-maximizing fashion.

Five assumptions of the model interact to form a behavioral model that is then used to predict actions.

1. More is better than less of any good thing where more is measured in terms of an individual's assessment of what is good.
2. People have objectives common to most. Where atypical objectives are exhibited, the rational choice model will not predict effectively.

Figure 3

Other	Emotion & feeling	Social norms	Biology & genes	Values & ethics	Rational choice

3. People are independent and free to choose and human preferences are built into one's being and therefore are consistently stable.
4. People are risk-averse.
5. People maximize their own self-interest.

From these assumptions behavior is analyzed using a cost-benefit approach which maximizes individual welfare. Firms seek to maximize stockholder wealth and individuals maximize personal utility even in committed relationships like a marriage. In fact, any relationship is a commitment designed for the gain of the individuals who would do well to terminate the relationship if the benefits and costs of the relationship change. While we may design contractual deterrents to reneging or shirking, and while institutional relationships may prohibit blatant opportunism, the notion that the individual is in business for himself is predominant. The market becomes the institutional form in which autonomous individuals make their exchanges and maximize their welfare.

Defenders of this pure neoclassical market model will argue that the construct is purely an instrumentalist device to predict behavior, and that it works better than other models at performing the predictive task. They will contend that social norms, emotions, and other forms of behavioral motivation are woven into some models (particularly the theories of the firm) since those motivations can be understood as derivative of rational behavior. The new institutionalists have attempted to enrich rational choice analysis in this way.[9]

In a critique of rational choice the important question involves the manner in which this method of analysis deals with the disadvantaged and the poor. The first possibility that rational choice presents is that the poor are poor by choice. They choose leisure over work and thereby select poverty over a higher income as a rational preference that we should accept. Enabling that sort of choice by welfare payments is not the way to eliminate poverty. Instead we need to make poverty more onerous so that people will choose against it. Some of the provisions of the present welfare reform reflect this kind of thinking.

In conjunction with this "pull yourself up by your bootstraps" individualist mentality is a recognition that when one chooses to be poor the consequences impact others negatively in ways that they cannot escape. Poor beggars make richer people feel guilty. Rundown property devalues neighborhood property and worn out cars are a danger on the highways. Thus the well-being of the masses is enhanced when those who will not choose work over leisure or are unable to do so are cared for enough to keep them out of sight. This kind of thinking has led to concentrations of poverty in sections of cities from which escape seems improbable at best. The minimization of social disruption is more the goal than a comprehensive effort to help the poor escape from poverty.

What response is needed to these champions of self-sufficiency? Barend A. de Vries writes that

> Believers in the self-sufficiency of the market see little role for government in the economy. They are apt to overlook the fact that to function well markets need, in Thurow's phrasing, "supportive physical, social, mental, educational and organizational infrastructure." And, as both Adam Smith and today's Evangelicals emphasize, the market system needs operators with moral strength and fiber.[10]

The infrastructure that Thurow suggests is necessary for the market to work is, in many cases, almost totally missing from the lives of the poor and so the self-sufficiency market solutions that many might hope for are little more than an idealistic dream. In short, the hope for the poor is not likely to be found in the economic theories of the rational choice, free market advocates.

From the philosophy and method of market economics come schools of thought which specify how the world works and what questions about economics are the most important to address. Adam Smith and his followers are considered as the founders of economics as a discipline and they began the classical school of economics. These classical economists focused more on the long term issues of growth as described on the right side of the economic triangle (see Fig. 2). They did not concern themselves much with short-term changes in relative prices. Rather they wanted to uncover the underlying forces that led to a strong, growing economy. They saw prices always tending toward the long-term cost of production of the commodity where cost was measured primarily in terms of labor inputs. Competitive markets would successfully keep resource flows in line with the underlying fundamentals of the economy. Over time the economy would be self-correcting if recessions or excessive expansion took place for some reason in the short run.

Adam Smith was optimistic that the marvelous engines of growth would ultimately solve the worst aspects of the scarcity problem faced by society. "It is the great multiplication of the productions of all the different arts, in consequence of the division of labour, which occasions, in a well governed society, that universal opulence which extends itself to the lowest ranks of the people."[11] Smith was concerned about the poor, but he believed the best way to solve the problem in the long run was to let the market economy do its magic and generate the universal opulence. Years later, after a half century of poverty and hardship of the working class, some of Smith's followers were not so optimistic.

Thomas Malthus (1766–1834) was more inclined to see spurts of progress as leading to population growth and low wages and a future in which the poor were destined to a life of misery and disease. David Ricardo (1772–1823) saw little chance of the laborer's welfare being improved by economic growth, and Karl Marx followed classical wage doctrine to hypothesize a comprehensive revolution which would overthrow capitalism. With two hundred years of hindsight it appears as if Smith was overly optimistic and Malthus, Ricardo, and Marx were too pessimistic.

By 1860 the big questions of economic growth and progress had given way to a new set of questions. Whereas Smith and the classicists focused on how much could be produced, most economists of the last half of the nineteenth century and beyond took full employment production as a given and then sought to make sure each resource ended up in its best possible use. Efficiency became the dominant concern and markets were explored for how they might contribute to this efficiency. The relative prices of goods and services now took center stage because it is these prices that provide the signals for resource flows. By 1860 several theorists developed the notion that the exchange value of a commodity was determined by the pleasure the consumer received from the product being bought. This notion that value is determined by the utility or pleasure that the buyer receives rather than the cost of production to the seller opened the door to a host of subjective considerations that had not been apparent before.

By 1890 the utility side of price had become a demand curve and the older cost of production idea of price had been formalized into a supply curve. Together supply and demand formed the market and price was then jointly determined by both cost and utility. Now nearly every issue relating to the welfare of people became an issue for economic discussion and supply and demand became the vehicle by which the value of everything was measured. At the same time, economics was becoming more closely tied to the Newtonian mechanistic understanding of how the world worked, so all parts of economic life were viewed as part of an interrelated system. This led to a formalized mathematical treatment of many issues and an aura of scientific inquiry that became known as neoclassical economics. Today neoclassical microeconomics is the mainstream school of thought in the economics discipline and the chief player is the individual, sometimes called "Homo economicus," who instantly calculates costs and benefits as the various stimuli of life come across his stage. For such a person opportunism is the mode of operation and emotions, values, and social norms are secondary motivating forces. "*Homo economicus* is woefully ill-suited to the demands of social existence as we know it. Each of us probably knows people who more or less fit the *Homo economicus* caricature. And our first priority most of the time, is to steer clear of them."[12]

The highly mechanistic nature of neoclassical analysis fit with the positivism in the scientific world so that economics became a science where moral values and ethical considerations were irrelevant to the theory. Neoclassical economists studied the world as it is, not as it should be. During the latter part of the nineteenth and earlier part of the twentieth centuries the rational choice framework for economic analysis became the workhorse of the discipline. Economic actors are maximizers of utility and profits, they pursue their own interests, they have freedom of choice in an environment where transaction costs are minimal, they have low cost information, and they are risk averse. A consumer will buy a good or service as long as the benefits from the last unit purchased are greater than what it cost to purchase the item. A firm will produce an item as long as the increase in total revenue is greater than the increase in total costs. This incremental evaluation of behavior takes both the consumer and producer to the point where consumer pleasure and producer profit are maximized for a given set of circumstances. This process of maximizing is referred to as marginal analysis because the focus of analysis is always on the margin or cutting edge of a decision situation. Any policy arrangement will need to focus on the impact generated at the margin.

The following example shows the concept of neoclassical market efficiency in contrast to the other resource allocative mechanisms listed in Figure 2. Consider the case where people seek education that requires labor and capital resources as inputs into production. Since there is not enough education for everyone at zero price, a method of allocating the scarce resource is required. Assume that there are five people in the economy who receive benefits from education according to the following table. Also assume that they all have the qualities of *Homo economicus* and seek their own self-interest throughout the process.

Table 1

Benefits Table for Education
Units of Education

	1	2	3	4	5	6
Carl	5	9	12	14	15	15
Sue	4	7	9	10	10	10
Fred	3	5	6	6	6	6
Sara	2	3	3	3	3	3
Pete	1	1	1	1	1	1

Each cell represents the total benefit received from the number of units of education shown in the top row. For example, Sue will get 9 units of benefit if she has three units of education. Suppose that the system has produced ten units of education and must allocate them to the five people. First consider the situation where a first-come-first-serve method is used. If the various schedules result in a queue of Sara, Sue, Fred, Pete, and Carl in that order, Sara would take two units of education and get her maximum possible benefit of three. Sue takes four units and benefits ten. Fred consumes three units for a total benefit of six, Peter uses one unit of education and receives one unit of benefit, and Carl would get no education because the ten units would be allocated by the time his turn came around. The total benefit from all four educated people is twenty. Of course, this total will vary depending on how the people queue up, but twenty-seven benefits is the maximum benefit that could be achieved and that is possible only if Carl, Sue, and Fred are first, second, and third in line.

Next, if everyone is given equal education each will get two units. The total benefits of the second column in the chart show that in this case the overall sum of the benefits equals twenty-five. The auction price allocative mechanism can be understood by having each unit offered to the highest bidder in a sequential sale process. Clearly Carl buys the first unit because he is willing to bid as high as five which is more than anyone else. Since Carl's total benefit rises from five to nine for the second unit of education, he is willing to bid four for the second unit. However, Sue would also be willing to bid four for her first unit of education, so whichever one bids four first gets the second unit of education. As each successive unit comes up for auction, each person is willing to bid up to the point where the bid equals the value received. In the final analysis, Carl gets four units, Sue three, Fred two, and Sara one. The last unit sells for two and Pete never bids more than one, so he remains uneducated. Now the sum of the benefit is thirty which is the highest maximum amount of education benefit available when ten units are produced. Economists will note that if the auction is not sequential (no price discrimination among education units exists), the bidding will rise only to two and the units are allocated in the same amounts as described above because people will pay an amount equal to their marginal benefit.

To summarize, the auction market pricing mechanism of the neoclassical school is the preferred mechanism if optimal market net utility is the goal. Of course, in order to bid on education, the people have to possess money, so they must produce something to earn the money. This allocative connection with production is perhaps the auction, or price mechanism's, strongest advantage over the alternative allocation methods. As this system works itself out, the consumer gets maximum benefit and production is more vigorously pursued.

When this same mechanism is applied to the right side of the triangle of resource flows, the efficient placement of production inputs results. In this case the inputs of labor, capital, and technology are allocated across all the production processes by a bidding process where entrepreneurs are willing to bid according to the value of those inputs to their business. Now, as in the education example, the inputs flow to their best use, which is the point where production is done at least cost. Efficiency is achieved and, because many desire to improve themselves, some measure of economic growth occurs as the flows around the triangle expand.

So far the case for allocation by a neoclassical market price mechanism is compelling if efficiency is the key goal. Below is a review of six of the market's strong points.

1. People are free to engage in the balance of work and leisure that best suits their preferences and interests.

2. People are free to seek involvement in any business venture where they can make a living and their search is rewarded according to their ability and preparation.
3. Resources are all employed in their best possible use given the various preferences of the population. This means production efficiency is reached.
4. Information is processed in the market interactions that would be hidden from anyone trying to program the optimal resource flows on their own. This helps consumers engage in voluntary exchange of goods and services until all the gains from trade are exhausted. Thus exchange efficiency is reached.
5. The incentives to produce and to care for property are built into the system since one's own level of resource use will depend upon how well these production activities are carried out.
6. The market interactions can go on in a spontaneous fashion without extensive supervision except for the definition and enforcement of property rights.

If the story of markets achieved all its ideals its critics would be little more than a friendly nuisance. These critics might point out that such a decentralized set of interactions makes it impossible to have a shared vision among the citizens. Without some shared vision there is no consensus in the area of values and social norms, so it is difficult to make moral judgments or set standards of right and wrong. In other words, it is possible to have technical efficiency but no moral solidarity. Market capitalism can answer the little questions of resource allocation, but in so doing it fosters a structure that makes the big questions of purpose, values, and meaning hard to address in any way apart from the purely private setting of the individual. Any common standards of truth, beauty, and moral behavior are elusive. The heavily decentralized nature of the process makes purposeful group action difficult, so the moral conscience of Christians in the area of income distribution cannot easily be addressed.

The pro-market counter to these critics is that a pluralistic approach to values need not be fatal as long as we agree on basic rules of the game designed, not as moral precepts, but as functional guidelines. For this a minimal government is needed to define and enforce property and personal rights. In such a diverse world a shared vision is inconsistent with freedom and unnecessary for material and social well-being. High individual moral standards, however, will reduce the costs of enforcing the rights defined in the system.

But the beauty of the market model is tarnished by more than the nagging concern that it detracts from shared vision and social and moral solidarity. There are real-world complications that limit some of the desired outcomes listed above. Some of these complications are inherent in the nature of a market system. Some are simply universal shortcomings of temporal life experience and some are problems related to human nature. The following list summarizes some of these difficulties.

1. Those incapable of competing effectively in the markets become losers dependent only on the benevolence of others with no guarantee that help will be available.
2. Positive and negative neighborhood effects (externalities) in both production and consumption can substantially distort the costs and benefits being evaluated in the market. Positional externalities also create distortions in resource use.
3. Market efficiency depends on free or low cost information. Frequently information is high cost and allocated through the market process itself to those able to pay.
4. Oligopoly or monopoly power can distort the efficiency process. This is true if market concentration results from benign technological or demographic considerations, or from more malicious efforts to control market pricing.
5. The market has no means of claiming the moral superiority of basic need over luxury goods or of socially desirable goods over "sin" products. It fosters the attitude that all preferences are morally equal.
6. Markets move toward efficiency via the entry and exit method. One expresses approval or disapproval of products or employers by leaving the market or the job. This negates the valuable concept of voice where people try to change something that is wrong rather than run away from the problem.

What follows is a more extended discussion of each of the items listed here with attention given to how they impact the poor and disadvantaged in society.

The Concern for Those Incapable of Market Participation

The neoclassical theory of labor markets is referred to as the marginal productivity theory of income distribution. In its simplest form, this theory means that every worker is paid a wage equal to the market value of what the last worker on the job produces. Consequently, a worker we shall call "Scott" receives wages which depend on two things. First, the number of workers seeking the kind of work Scott is doing will determine how much output Scott can generate. (Production theory tells us that the more congested the production environment, the less the output will be of the last person hired.) Second, the market price of the output will determine how much Scott is worth to his employer.

Unfortunately for Scott, he does not have control over either of these two variables that determine his pay. If his type of work is unskilled and there are unemployed people looking for jobs, Scott will probably not get a raise and he may have his wages cut. If the market in which his output is sold is falling in demand, he is likely to lose income or even his job.

Unfortunately, most poor people are not prepared to work in highly skilled jobs where the marginal product of the labor force is high and the output is highly valued in the marketplace. Instead they tend to be pawns in the unskilled, low-paid labor markets. Job security is low, the work is undesirable, and there is little opportunity to get ahead. If one has physical or psychological impairments the market can be a very hostile place to make ends meet and to recover from unfortunate circumstances. The labor market is not a place where compassion can be expected and competition will make it hard for most employers to hire more people or pay higher wages than the labor market would dictate. In short, poor people usually are less equipped to face the labor market than are their richer peers. Thus, if markets are given free play, the balance between the equality of democracy and the inequality of capitalism spoken of earlier is likely to swing heavily in favor of inequality. The U.S. economy has swung in this direction more than that of most developed nations.

Since the market makes no provision for the losers in the labor markets or for those who are unable to enter the labor markets, these people have no way of buying basic necessities. Apart from intervention from family or other sources, such a person would be doomed to starvation. In pre-market times the family or the parish was expected to provide for the poor. With markets came geographic mobility, cities which were more impersonal than towns, and specialization of labor which made in-kind provision of the poor more difficult. To avoid a social crisis, all market economies provide some form of income transfer by the government, and it is generally true that most non-poor citizens support these programs.

While the need for income transfers in a market economy may be clear, it is less obvious that government transfers will have the general support of the population. Some argue that private charities and religious people should solve the problem, leaving government out of the picture. But there are compelling theoretical reasons why this can only be a partial solution. If Sam is starving on the street, his condition affects more than his own well-being. Carl, observing the plight of Sam, is appalled by his circumstances and feels morally obligated to contribute. Of course every other passerby is also negatively impacted and experiences the same obligation to help. However, if one person does solve the problem with his own resources, everyone else receives a benefit because they no longer need to watch Sam suffer. In other words, there are positive externalities to any one person's efforts to help Sam. What inevitably happens is that everyone waits on the other person to solve the problem and the poor person never is adequately helped. This effort to let someone else solve the problem is what dooms the private effort to solve the externality problem. So we are left with the problem and a society where everyone is willing to do their part if others will do theirs. The only way to ensure that everyone will do his or her part is to require everyone to pay in the form of a tax. Consequently, of the three choices—walking past suffering people, helping them by yourself, joining together with everyone in a tax commitment to pay a fair share—most people enthusiastically support the third option. This is why we will always have public welfare programs of some sort. Of course we will constantly debate about the best way to help the poor. Having the government collect taxes which then are paid to private agencies and churches who provide care for the poor is one way that is presently being touted. Other creative ideas will likely be forthcoming, but it is theoretically untenable to argue that the private market on its own can solve the poverty problem.

The Externality Problems of Production and Consumption

This externality problem of markets is much broader in the system than the case of the poor who will need transfers of income. In fact the problem exists wherever the behavior of one person impacts another against the other's will, and the world is full of such behavior in both the production process and consumption activity. A person or a factory smoking irritates another's breathing. Airplanes disturb the sleep of those living near airports. A beehive operator enhances a neighbor's apple yield when the bees pollinate the apple trees, but he does not charge for this service. The list could go on forever because so much of what we do imposes costs or benefits on others who neither pay nor receive payment for the external effects.

Because of the way we are interrelated in our feelings, positional externalities also exist. If we are friends in similar circumstances it may be disruptive to the relationship if one becomes increasingly wealthy relative to the other. Therefore, the added income of the one enhances his position with respect to the other person and this imposes a negative positional externality on the poorer party. While this may sound like trivial jealousy, it is common for people to work more overtime than they would prefer simply to keep up with another person who is working long hours simply to keep up with them. While neither worker would cut back unilaterally they both would support a new working rule that limited overtime. This logic is why race drivers prefer horsepower limitations on race cars and high school football teams prefer rules that forbid practicing before August. Without these rules, competition will accelerate horsepower to dangerous levels and football teams will be practicing all summer and all parties will be worse off. In short, externalities distort the market signals and misallocate resources unless they are somehow corrected.

The economist Arthur Pigou (1877–1959) proposed that the best way to correct the externality problem was to tax the offenders and subsidize those injured by the negative externalities. If done properly the inefficiencies would be addressed, assuming that the tax and subsidy officials had complete information about the externality problem. Since this is never possible, others follow

Ronald Coase, who argued that properly specified property rights could solve the problem. If pollution is the concern, simply identify the amount of discharge that is scientifically acceptable and then auction off the rights to discharge that level of pollution. Those with the most difficult time cleaning up the pollution will bid the highest and the others will install clean up processes. One of the bidders could be a group of community people organized to purchase the rights to pollute. By not exercising that right they can reduce the pollution level that they must live with in the community.

In this case, as in all market transactions, bidding in the marketplace requires both the desire for something and the money to bid for it. Poor people with the identical preference pattern of rich people are much less influential in the marketplace than are those rich people. Consequently if market solutions to negative externalities like pollution are used, the poor, who are unable to register effective demand, will end up in the most polluted and unhealthy areas of town. In short, without some supra-market standard of justice in a social order that is enforced by collective action of the people, the poor will absorb a disproportionate share of the negative externalities.

The Information-Cost Problem

High cost information may create real distortions in market situations where niche information markets are impractical. Consider a barber and a surgeon. If the barber is incompetent, others will see the customers walking around for a week or two with strange haircuts. While this is a short term cost to the unfortunate skinned heads, the problem will soon be solved with the bankruptcy of the barber. Contrast this to the surgeon whose incompetence is made public when patients perish under his knife. Now the costs are so high for doctor competency information that it would have been cheaper to have mandatory training and licensing for the doctor. Some will argue that a niche business will spring up providing information on the quality of doctors. While there would be a market for such information, the customer base might be very thin because when one buys the information and finds the best doctor, others will be observing that behavior and seek out the same doctor without paying for the information. In other words, there are positive externalities in this information market that make it a difficult market in which to succeed. The licensing of doctors is a common result. Indeed, the acquisition and processing of information in an economy is rarely as simple as the basic "free information" models suggest.

What is particularly disturbing about the information problem is that poor people have a special disadvantage in this area. Information is becoming increasingly a technological matter. Those with the technical training and computer know-how are able to acquire information more effectively than the technological have-nots and those with low education. Since income and wealth often separate the educational and technological haves from the have-nots, it is reasonable to assume that the gap between the rich and the poor will widen as the poor are left behind in the technological race.

The Market Power Problem

The market power problem for market economies is probably overrated by the non-economist. It is common for people to talk about near monopoly power which leads firms to deliberately hold production back in order to receive a high profit maximizing price. To do this the firm must be sure that no other existing firm or possible new upstart firm will enter the market with prices slightly less than the monopoly profit-maximizing firm. For one firm to corner a market in an environment where the world is interconnected and where technology is constantly on the move is no simple matter. For the same reasons it is hard to establish cartels of cooperating firms for price-fixing purposes because the incentive is very high for one of the firms in the cartel to cheat on the agreement.

Despite all these obstacles to monopoly power it is true that the high volume of domestic mergers, the proliferation of international joint ventures, and the inherent weakness of national and international monitoring devices, all indicate that the potential for monopoly pricing power still exists. Where legal, technological, and geographical factors act as barriers to meaningful competition, monopoly power is certainly possible. In fact there are many investigations of monopoly power underway constantly at the Justice Department and a considerable number of regulatory orders are issued against such action annually. In the present case against Microsoft the government is challenging the monopoly power of one firm which has over 80 percent of computer operating system sales.

In the current rush toward a global presence by many companies there is a distinct possibility that companies will evolve toward independent status, uncontrolled by any one government. As massive entities playing off one country against another for special privilege and monetary advantage, these companies will have little or no commitment to any given location or labor group. Workers, particularly the unskilled and low income groups, are likely to become pawns in the process and become more marginalized and powerless.

The Moral Discernment Problem

The sixth problem with which markets must deal involves the inability of the market to prioritize consumer preferences according to any hierarchy of values or ethical norms except that of human freedom. Since human preferences are fixed and since individual autonomy and freedom is held in such high regard, there is great resistance to the imposition of values which might restrict one's choices. Consequently, there is no moral case preventing resources from flowing to luxury goods and "sin" products, such as liquor and tobacco, while basic housing, food or other basic human needs go unmet. Increasingly, poor people are unable to find housing near their work. Many in my town feel morally offended by the demolition of a small house and the building of a luxury home in its place. The poor must move out because the market value of the land under their house exceeds their ability to pay. Like-wise, the small farmers in France and Italy are under pressure to close down if the common agricultural policy of the European Union is dismantled in favor of the advancing global agricultural markets. Of course special provisions can be made to accommodate these moral concerns, as is happening in European agriculture, but the market itself is incapable of dealing with these moral trade-offs. If the market ideology becomes idolized and the political efforts to deal with the moral tradeoffs are viewed as unforgivable heresy, then the losers will be those who cannot vote with money in the marketplace. Indeed, a *Wall Street Journal* article raises this concern in the following way. "In California, high-ways that charge higher rush-hour tolls are attacked as 'Lexus lanes' for the impatient affluent, turning the poor into second-class drivers."[13]

The Exit Over Voice Problem

The final qualifier of market efficiency listed here comes from the recogni-tion that the auction market involves an impersonal take-it-or-leave-it men-tality. Arthur Okun, Graham Dawson and others contrast this with what they call the customer market. In the customer markets, relationships are personal and voice, not exit, is the way information on goods and services is received by the producer. Dawson asks whether there are worthwhile values and ideals which flourish under a voice system that are missing in an exit-based system. Since a voice system involves the positive characteristics of dialogue and inter-personal interaction, a case can be made that the exit method of signaling in markets leaves something to be desired. In many ways, the exit option is sym-bolic of the impersonal nature of neoclassical market theory in general. This claim may appear odd to those who see market models as purely theoretical constructs designed to predict as simply as possible rather than to describe reality. However, when negotiation, persuasion, personal relationships, and other features of voice are present, the market outcomes vary from the pure, impersonal market predictions.

It is one thing to discuss the weaknesses of the market allocative mecha-nism and another to offer solutions to the difficulties. The most obvious sug-gestion that usually surfaces puts forth government policy options as the best way to solve the problems. Consequently we have many programs which try to alleviate the problems we have named, including welfare transfer payments, externality taxes and regulations, information data bases sponsored by government, an antitrust wing of the Justice Department, and all sorts of tax incentives, credits and information sources to enhance entry and exit activity.

The obvious question underlying all of these policy solutions is, do they work? Are the resource allocation inefficiencies being alleviated and is human welfare increased when governments influence the allocation mechanisms? Researchers have come at this question in two ways. At one level the question seems to be an empirical one. Does government enhance the welfare of those it tries to help? The second level of analysis, posed by the public choice proponents, is more theoretical and tends to be critical of collective action. They assume public servants are as self-maximizing as the rest of the citizens are assumed to be, and so they doubt that policy will reflect any social sense of justice. They argue that the public interest will be replaced by the private interests of those in power.

The empirical considerations are mixed, primarily because data is often less objective than it might at first appear. For example, observe the public welfare programs that currently exist. While it is easy to point to certain negative outcomes with government action, it is less easy to compare that action with the counter-factual outcomes that can never be observed. In other words, we can observe how many poor people have become hard-core poor and we can surmise that the welfare policy was the cause of these dismal conditions, but we cannot compare the existing circumstances with what would have happened in the absence of the programs or with some alternative programs. It is possible to compare people in one setting under a certain policy regime with those in a similar setting without the policy in place. This cross sectional attempt to understand the impact of policy offers some insight into the question being pursued, but the inability to control all other variables affecting the situation leaves enough ambiguity so that the biases and preferences of the researcher come into play. Time series efforts also suffer from changing contexts that are not easy to adjust for.

Even if the statistical work is definitive, interpretations regarding its meaning may vary widely. Suppose that ten out of each one hundred in the population are shown to be in poverty year after year. Also, assume that the data is clear that two of the ten never get out of the poor category. The other eight escape poverty each year but others fall into poverty as marriages fail, jobs disappear, or illness occurs. Each year a different eight are impoverished so that the total of ten remains constant. Charles Murray observed such a circumstance and concluded that the welfare programs have not reduced poverty, and they should therefore be disbanded. Others observed that eight people had been helped out of poverty because of public assistance. In fact, there is no way to prove either viewpoint correct because the viewpoint is formed by some composite of fact and opinion. A policy regime depends on both facts and a policy perspective, a circumstance that is often overlooked by proponents of one side or another in policy controversies.

The public choice contention that policy makers are self-maximizers leads to the view that any gains from public policy will be lost in the policymaking process. Take an example where a business would save $100 if it could discharge hot water into the river. This, however, reduces the value of fishing downstream for five hundred fisherman by $.25 each. Efficiency would require that the water be cooled before discharge at a cost of $100, thereby saving the community $125 in fishing value. The net savings would be $25. A public servant, knowing this data, would make sure that the river rights went to the fisherman or that some anti-pollution regulation protected the $25 public net gain. However, a self-maximizing government official would seek ways to acquire personal benefit from the situation. The fishermen individually lose less than the cost of a stamp, so they are not inclined to lobby the official, and organizing with a group of five hundred is costly as well. On the other hand, the firm has much to gain if it can convince the official to ignore the water discharge. It would be worth lobbying expenses and campaign contributions totaling $99 if the firm were certain of success. In the end, the fishermen lose and the firm gains only the difference between the lobbying expense and the benefit received from the water rights. The government official has benefited by the amount of the lobbying. Efficiency has not been served.

Consequently, public choice proponents adopt a conservative, minimalist view of government. Their critics are less pessimistic. A free press is a constant thorn in the side of self-serving political behavior and information does spread over time at lower cost. The fishermen will eventually blame the firm and the government for the poor fish catches. If, in elections, information and a candidate's record are more important that a candidate's campaign money and TV presence, then competition in the political arena can help to move political action toward more efficient outcomes than would exist if no public policy was enacted. Public choice proponents are skeptical of these checks because they do not believe that there will be enough of a shared social justice vision or enough people willing to hold officials accountable to make a positive difference.

There is increasing evidence that government mandated activities that are privately run tend to operate at lower cost than operations run by the government. In exclusive contracting arrangements, government sets the specifications for a good or service and contracts the work out to the lowest bidder. Local garbage hauling is frequently done in this fashion. Pickup days are specified, recycling services listed, and quantity limitations are identified. Then various companies bid for the job, knowing that the winner will be the sole garbage collector. Each company has an incentive to price near their lowest cost for fear that a competitor will come in with a lower bid. Performance standards are reviewed regularly and a new bidding process is done at specified intervals. In one study of garbage collection in 260 cities, the exclusive contracting method led to an average savings of 50 percent.[14] It is likely that many government functions could be handled by the private sector in this fashion if some creative possibilities were tried.

In the final analysis, the balance between the public and private sector in an economy often hinges on political philosophy rather than technical analysis of costs, benefits and welfare maximization. Some will trade away potential increases in standard of living for a less unequal income distribution if that is the choice. These folks tend to see family economic well-being in relative rather than absolute terms. Some people are more willing to absorb environmental risk than others and no one has exactly the same concept of freedom and bondage. Pro-family advocates may lament the high labor mobility and the desire for a lifestyle that mandates two full-time jobs per household. When all of this is considered, the notion of economic efficiency and appropriate public policy becomes more subjective and values-based than it might at first appear. Consequently, alternate schools of economic thought are not accepted by people on the basis of which one is right and which one is wrong. Rather, one gravitates toward the viewpoint that is most consistent with their worldview, value system, and social and economic position.

Because of the subjective nature of economic viewpoints and because economic conditions are constantly changing, there will always be heterodox views that challenge the accepted orthodoxy. They serve as a fringe nuisance forcing the mainstream to constantly mend its flaws or run the risk of being replaced. The modern era of neoclassical economics is still young by historical standards and its overall impact cannot be definitively judged. It specializes in the small questions of technique and efficiency and largely ignores the larger questions of purpose, values and meaning. More than any other, it has delivered high levels of production and provided higher material standards of living for the masses. Robert Heilbroner is concerned that neoclassical economics has no great vision, no understanding of its relationship to the other social sciences and no ambitious goals to capture the hearts of people. He asserts that "the chapter we call modern economics, compared with earlier chapters of our discipline, is shallow and poor rather than deep and rich, and that the intellectual puzzle of some future time will be to account for the failure rather than the success of the period in which we have lived."[15]

Indeed, successful economic systems must have an ethical and moral dimension which contributes to social cohesion and well-being. Without this dimension there can be no vision, no cause, and ultimately no fulfillment for people. "The popular notion is that modernization has overthrown religion. The notion is mistaken, though secular intellectuals from Voltaire to the average reader of the *New York Times* have believed it fervently."[16] In biblical times the vision of *shalom* inspired the prophets and, in good times, the people. Central to that concept of *shalom* was the proper treatment of the poor and the disadvantaged. There is reason to believe that the same is true in modern times. Believers need to examine whether the existing mainstream economic ideology has enough vision and purpose and concern for the poor so that *shalom* can be a meaningful goal to put forth. If neoclassical markets lack such vision we must be qualified in our endorsement of them. Christians often overlook

the degree to which they ascribe legitimacy to a system in which they participate. Therefore, it is important that such legitimacy is not extended based on
one's own personal comfort, but rather on the moral appropriateness and
social justice of the system. If a system does not have a mechanism to help the
poor escape poverty it is important that Christians become the heterodox conscience of the system rather than a mouthpiece proclaiming its legitimacy.

To summarize, in the last two sections we have examined the philosophy
of our market allocation system, what the system does well, what shortcomings it has, and how it has become an accepted school of thought. Also, it has
been suggested that the technical and the philosophical are conditioned by
the overarching worldview that one brings to the discussion. For example, a
Christian worldview that posits a preferential option for the poor will see economic theory and philosophy in a different way than worldview that believes
only that poor people have an obligation to pull themselves up by their own
initiative because of the opportunities available in market economies. Next we
explore a bit more about what a worldview is and how it becomes the glasses
through which we understand reality.

From Theory and Philosophy to a Worldview
that Conditions Policy Formation

A worldview starts with presuppositions about reality and then puts the
parts of that reality into relationships that make life coherent. For Christians,
God is what is really real and from that base comes an understanding of what
it means to be human, how one relates to nature and all of creation, and what
is the purpose of life. Part of one's worldview is an understanding of how the
world works and what role a person should play in the social order. Any pronouncements on policy must fit into the larger framework of belief. Consequently it is important to have an economics component in one's worldview
that is integrated into the overall belief system.

Included in this economic component of a worldview will be perspectives
on the following questions.

1. What is the overarching purpose of economic activity?
2. Are economic relationships part of nature or do people consciously form
   those relationships in some manner?
3. What is the relationship of the individual to the group in social organization?
4. How are things valued or what determines real worth?

While there are no simple answers to these questions, people answer them
every day in some fashion as they go about their economic activity. In most
cases the answers are packaged in ways that can be identified with a label for

simplicity. In economics, people frequently refer to themselves as conservatives or liberals. Sometimes they use labels like "Marxist" or "Keynesian" or "Chicago School." Any school of thought will pull together some of the issues involved in a worldview. Later in this paper the Austrian school and the Institutionalists will be examined as alternatives to the neoclassical approach which has already been described. The last part of the paper entertains the question of whether or not there is a uniquely Christian economic approach. While labels never completely encompass a worldview, they are useful as shorthand for certain similarities in the way the worldview questions are answered.

The Conservative Economic Framework

There is an internal logic to conservative economics. It fits within the modern worldview of mechanistic, orderly behavior that tends toward a desirable equilibrium. It has the appeal of being "natural." Schematically, the following flow chart (figure 4) illustrates the logic of the system.

The conservative worldview sees human welfare as a function of freedom and freedom as a function of the degree of individual choice a person has. From

Figure 4

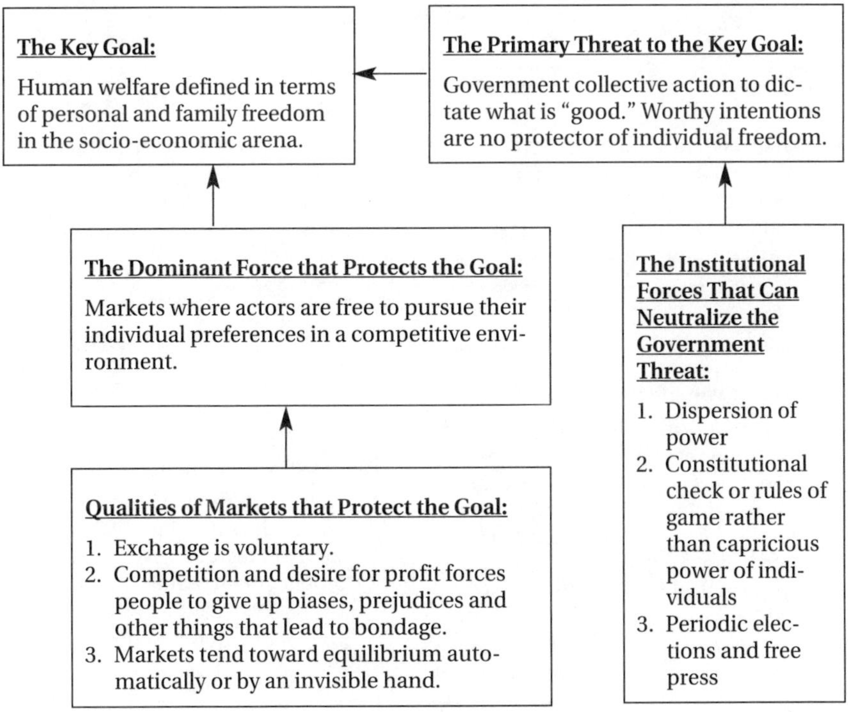

The Key Goal:

Human welfare defined in terms of personal and family freedom in the socio-economic arena.

The Primary Threat to the Key Goal:

Government collective action to dictate what is "good." Worthy intentions are no protector of individual freedom.

The Dominant Force that Protects the Goal:

Markets where actors are free to pursue their individual preferences in a competitive environment.

The Institutional Forces That Can Neutralize the Government Threat:

1. Dispersion of power
2. Constitutional check or rules of game rather than capricious power of individuals
3. Periodic elections and free press

Qualities of Markets that Protect the Goal:

1. Exchange is voluntary.
2. Competition and desire for profit forces people to give up biases, prejudices and other things that lead to bondage.
3. Markets tend toward equilibrium automatically or by an invisible hand.

freedom flow all other good things. The key words of this viewpoint for economic purposes are natural, equilibrium, self-adjustment, and liberty. The idea that protecting the processes of the system is more important than guaranteeing specific outcomes leads to a "let the chips fall where they will" approach to outcomes.

In many ways this system fits with Adam Smith's understanding of how the world works, except that Smith added the selfish passions as potential threats to the goal of natural liberty. He also added the much more socially interdependent force of moral sympathy as a countervailing check on the selfish passions. The fact that modern conservative economics has lost this concern for the excess of the selfish passions has weakened its ability to speak to the morality of human behavior. The loss of sensitivity to the interdependence of people makes it hard for the committed conservative to enter actively into the life of poor people in a society without feeling that poor people are somehow less worthy of the things that the wealthy enjoy.

The Liberal Economic Framework

The schematic below (figure 5) depicts the liberal framework of thought about economic relationships.

Figure 5

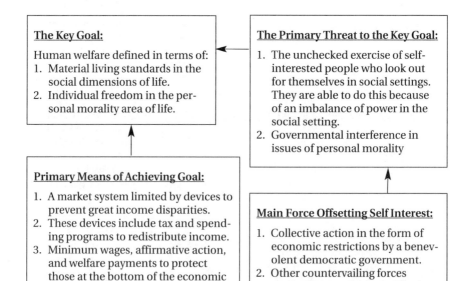

The Key Goal:

Human welfare defined in terms of:
1. Material living standards in the social dimensions of life.
2. Individual freedom in the personal morality area of life.

The Primary Threat to the Key Goal:

1. The unchecked exercise of self-interested people who look out for themselves in social settings. They are able to do this because of an imbalance of power in the social setting.
2. Governmental interference in issues of personal morality

Primary Means of Achieving Goal:

1. A market system limited by devices to prevent great income disparities.
2. These devices include tax and spending programs to redistribute income.
3. Minimum wages, affirmative action, and welfare payments to protect those at the bottom of the economic ladder.
4. No legislation regarding personal morality.

Main Force Offsetting Self Interest:

1. Collective action in the form of economic restrictions by a benevolent democratic government.
2. Other countervailing forces against economic power like the press, labor unions, and consumer co-ops.

The liberal sees sufficiency in standard of living as more important than complete individual freedom. A social order with high poverty levels is bad for everyone and lowers overall welfare. As may be apparent from the sketches above, the liberal worldview is not a natural system with a self-correcting mechanism or a sense of systemic organization. It is rather a human creation with institutions formed by people to arrive at certain stipulated goals. From within the constraints imposed by the key goal, free market interaction is the accepted system. Liberals tend to be outcome-oriented rather than process-oriented and they assume that people can have social and personal goals toward which they can work simultaneously.

In one sense, the conservative approach tends to focus on the positive aspects of a market economy (listed in section III above) while the liberal approach is concerned with its potential problems. The contemporary American scene couples a strong market rhetoric with a significant amount of public policy intervention in the markets so that we have a system sometimes referred to as a mixed economy where both conservative and liberal ideas are in constant tension.

At this point it is interesting to observe the manner in which conservative and liberal Christians position themselves in terms of the issues considered here. Those in the conservative camp tend to see public social welfare policy as ineffective and conceptually flawed because it downplays individual responsibility and the ability of markets to solve the problems of the poor. Thus, on this and other socio-economic matters, like health care and the minimum wage, they are not likely to favor governmental action. However on private morality issues they want the government to take up their causes. They see abortion as an issue of the individual rights of the child and therefore seek government protection of the fetus. They see homosexual practice as sinful and do not want the government to grant equal rights in all matters to gay and lesbian people.

By contrast, liberal Christians tend to seek government involvement in socio-economic matters. They believe the government has a responsibility to find ways to solve poverty and urban blight. They generally support higher minimum wages and universal health care. On the other hand they tend to oppose government intervention in the areas of personal morality. Liberals tend to permit limited abortion options and equal rights for the homosexual community. They do not want legislation against what they see as personal behavioral choices.

This curious contrast begs for an integration where either a non-interventionist position is taken on both social and private issues or an interventionist position is taken on both kinds of issues. If Christians have a message for the world in both social justice and private morality, then they should not be apologetic about finding creative solutions to poverty and insisting that the government do its part to make the solutions work. Private morality and social justice are each part of the biblical message and the liberal or conservative worldviews of the secular society should not be the ground on which believers stand to make pronouncements.

For Christians to speak effectively to issues of economic justice it is important to move beyond the general labels of conservative or liberal. What follows is a look at two schools of thought that challenge the neoclassical mainstream on numerous key points. They provide very different challenges to the mainstream and in so doing provide additional perspectives to consider in the final section of the paper.

Two Schools of Thought as Creative Qualifiers of Mainstream Economic Theory

The Austrian challenge is an example of a critique of the mainstream from the right side of the ideological perspective. This will be followed by the institutionalist critique as an example of a left side challenge to neoclassical orthodoxy. What is interesting is the way in which both have the same concerns but differing solutions.

It is not hard to see why neoclassical theory tends to favor a conservative worldview. Government involvement should be limited to prescribing and enforcing the rules of the game, particularly those relating to property rights and the provisions of contracts. In addition, freedom of choice for all buyers and sellers is essential for efficient markets and no one should impose their moral judgments on others. However, libertarians and the Austrian school do not think that mainstream neoclassical economics is on the right track. A modern Austrian, Israel Kirzner, is very supportive of the individualistic presuppositions of neoclassical theory, but concerned that its abstract equilibrium focus makes it irrelevant to the life of people. He writes:

> Despite our remarks on the healthy roots of modern neoclassical economics, there should be no doubt about the gulf which separates the mainstream view of market capitalism from that with which Austrian economics proposes to replace it. In the Austrian view, a thorough training in neoclassical economics simply does not equip one with a sensitive understanding of how the market economy works.[17]

Kirzner goes on to list several areas where Austrian economics alters economic analysis. "This perspective is that which particularly emphasizes the purposefulness of individual action rather than collective planning; the role of knowledge in economic choice; the subjectivity of the phenomena that interest economists; the competitive-entrepreneurial character of the market process, and the *ex-ante* role in which time affects economic activity."[18] What is interesting about this approach is that it leads toward a system where the individual is unfettered and supreme in economic activity.

F. A. Hayek, a twentieth-century pillar of Austrian thought, speaks of the world as being composed of three types of structure. There are the natural forces which, like the weather, are not within our control. We accept these forces as part of the givens to which we must adjust. A second category of organization is the planned and managed areas of life where people are the architects of a structured and invented order. Since they are in control of these areas it is possible to reinvent the social forms into whatever structures are desired. According to Hayek, social scientists all too often stop with these two categories of social structure. They miss the in-between category where social institutions are formed by the purposeful action of individuals that in no way were attempting to create something permanent in the social order. Hayek refers to human language, beehives, and footpaths as examples of social institutions that formed through no specific plan or design by thinkers seeking to solve a problem. Rather, they exist because, over time, individuals acting in their own interest came upon patterns that worked to solve a particular problem. Behavior was coordinated in an unconscious way to achieve results that improve the life of the community. Any conscious collective effort to design a language, beehive, or footpath would have led to far less social cohesion. Consequently, any collective effort is counterproductive.

The primary reason why designed social action fails is that information is far too complex to organize into systematic models. This concern strikes at the heart of neoclassical equilibrium models that assume perfect information. Hayek argues:

> What is the problem we wish to solve when we try to construct a rational economic order? On certain familiar assumptions the answer is simple enough. If we possess all the relevant information, if we can start out from a given system of preferences, and if we command complete knowledge of available means, the problem which remains is purely one of logic. That is, the answer to the question what is the best use of the available means is implicit in our assumptions. . . . This, however, is emphatically not the economic problem which society faces.[19]

For Hayek, the economic problem involves the stimulation of innumerable economic actors who pursue their individual interests through ventures that may or may not succeed. The consumer-worker buys and sells in a search to find the best deals. The entrepreneur takes risks and through trial and error muddles along hopefully toward success in profit-making.

According to the Austrians, what should be of interest to economists is the dynamics of the searching processes. Competition in this view is intense rivalry among the actors to outdo each other to ensure success, not the equilibrium state of the neoclassical models where all parties are price takers with perfect information mechanically equating marginal cost and price. Indeed the entire focus of neoclassical economics on equilibrium states rather than on the dynamics of individual opportunities is misguided because it is these dynamics that form the social institutions around which life is organized. These institutions evolve spontaneously and could never be planned by intentional planners no matter how noble were their intentions. If planners tried to design workable social institutions a host of unintended consequences would result which could lead to undesirable results.

One reason information is so difficult to get is because it is inherently subjective in nature. Commenting on Hayek's view of information, Norman Barry observes that

> The sum total of knowledge existing in any society will be fragmented and dispersed throughout the members of that society and neither economic knowledge or any other kind of knowledge can be centralized in any one mind or institution . . . . Since no observer can get inside the minds of those he observes, and since so much of our knowledge consists not in fact about the world but in what individuals think about the world, his ability to make accurate, quantitative predictions of future single events will be non-existent.[20]

It is clear that the Austrians approach facts far differently than neoclassical economists. If most knowledge consists of what we think about the world rather than in facts about the world, then the economic enterprise is subjective and values oriented. This makes it even more precarious for any one person to make choices for another. It does, however, open the door to a discussion of values among economic players even though each individual ultimately makes his own choices. The Austrian system is definitely not the value-free project that neoclassical economics has become.

Finally, economic activity moves over time in a perpetual unfolding of new information and changing perspectives. Economic consumers and producers learn and change over time, which complicates any effort to aggregate data or systematize choices into predictive models. For the Austrian economist, the interesting agenda is to understand as much as possible the process of change and to promote the kind of rules of the social game that best free up the individual to engage in the pursuit of his best interest. Property rights are essential to a smoothly functioning market environment. Therefore intentionally designed and clearly defined rules of the economic game, like property rights, are appropriate government activity. There are very few other rules of the game that Austrians believe should be intentionally planned lest damaging, unintended consequences result. Regulation toward specific ends is generally not acceptable because outcomes are not the concern of the Austrian policy agenda. Efficiency is ultimately defined by the degree to which individuals achieve their own goals, not the degree to which a society has achieved long run equilibrium in a perfectly competitive market structure.

Austrian economics has a certain appeal to Christians. It offers a critique of the value-free notion that mainstream economists espouse and it suggests that there is more to economics than predicting outcomes from data that is given.

Because process is important and subject to normative analysis, the door is open for rhetoric and persuasion in economic discourse. Even its methodological individualism feels less objectionable than the individual freedom goals of free market, neoclassical types like Milton Friedman. The Austrians are individualists because they believe that a viable social order forms without planning in an individually oriented, evolutionary process. Hayek called this process of resource organization a catallaxy. This word comes from the Greek verb *katallassein,* which means "to bring into the community" or "to change from an enemy to a friend." Clearly this is a richer view of individual freedom in markets than the "freedom because it feels good" approach so common to most neoclassical, free market advocates.

What makes a Christian uncomfortable with the Austrian variant of free market economics is the contention that only the individual can act purposefully, without a concern for negative, unintended consequences, and those acts can only be focused toward individual purposes. As soon as an individual or a group of individuals begin to plan activity that is intended for the larger social welfare, there is little chance of success and considerable chance of making things worse since such action would necessarily be done with only fragmented and distorted information. A Christian coming from the Austrian perspective would not be inclined to propose any income redistribution policies, any affirmative action legislation, or any antitrust laws. This is not because they do not have a heart for the poor, but because they do not believe they have the information to work toward a genuine solution. On the other hand, an Austrian sympathizer would find it far easier to partner with those who focus on the individual and on defining the process that protects individual liberty without regard for the outcomes that result. While wearing Austrian and libertarian glasses one sees in scripture the individual side of the salvation story and tends to spiritualize or individualize the passages that speak to social justice as something that society can purpose to achieve.

In my opinion, this is a serious misreading of the Bible. While we ultimately stand before God with only the merits of Jesus as our claim to salvation, we come to that point because we have been nurtured by a community of faith. That community exists because of a covenant among believers who recognize that self-aggrandizement does not lead to meaning and contentment. They see in scripture evidence that purposeful group action influenced by Kingdom values can have better results than the alternatives. One does not get the sense from the biblical story that the best results in life evolve spontaneously from the actions of individuals focusing primarily on their own wishes.

While the Austrians object to the neoclassical school's quantitative search for equilibrium, and while they promote the study of dynamic processes rather than efficient outcomes, they still retain the methodological individualism of the neoclassical theorists. Their system still has its primary roots in the individual economic person, that individual who is the lightning calculator of costs and benefits which are defined from built-in, stable preference patterns. The

Austrian critique does not attack the foundation of the neoclassical house, it rather hopes to rebuild the upper floors to make economic theorists less vulnerable to calls for purposeful social action.

The same cannot be said of the institutionalists. Their protest against the mainstream begins with the belief that individuals are social beings who need groups to survive and therefore cannot be defined in terms of individual wants and fixed personal preferences. For institutionalists, the social grouping is not simply the summation of autonomous individuals. Solomon Asch, speaking about the basic building unit of economic theory, put it this way: "the unit is not an individual but a social individual, one who has a place in the social order . . . to understand the individual we must study him in his group setting; to understand the group we must study the individuals whose interrelated actions constitute it."[21] Clarence Ayers stated the critique more stridently in a lecture to the American Economics Association several decades ago.

> [T]he object of dissent is the conception of the market as the guiding mechanism of the economy or, more broadly, the conception of the economy as organized and guided by the market. It simply is not true that scarce resources are allocated among alternative uses by the market. The real determinant of whatever allocation occurs in any society is the organizational structure of that society—in short, its institutions. At most, the market only gives effect to prevailing institutions. By focusing attention on the market mechanism, economists have ignored the real allocative mechanism. Hence the hiatus between economics and the other social sciences, all of which are concerned with various aspects of the institutional structure of society. Economics is more advanced than those others—in the wrong direction.[22]

These critiques represent what is sometimes called the older institutionalist approach which traces its roots back to Thorstein Veblen and the Wisconsin school of Commons, Mitchell, and Ayers. The "old institutionalists" argue that if institutional life in society is given its proper place in economic theory, the mechanistic "economic man" of the neoclassical modeling process will be destroyed. In contrast a more recent group of writers has recognized that institutions play a vital role in economic life but they have sought to analyze institutions as collections of individuals operating in the self-maximizing way of the neoclassical model. For example, Richard Posner considers the legal structure of society as an institution to help individuals and groups overcome the information and transaction cost problems that are inherent in conflictual situations. Likewise, other writers such as Oliver Williamson, Mancur Olson, Douglas North, and Andrew Schotter seek to apply neoclassical modeling methods to social institutions in an effort to broaden economic analysis without giving up the "economic man." Needless to say the old and new institutionalists are clearly in different camps, and it is the old institutionalists that are referred to in the following pages because they represent a substantive critique of the neoclassical mainstream.

Perhaps the starting point in understanding the institutional critique is the rejection of the neoclassical contention that the formation of tastes and preferences of individuals is beyond the scope of economics. To say that tastes and preferences of individuals are given and essentially fixed is to take the person away from all the external influences that might impact behavior. Gone is the possibility that social norms, legal doctrines, emotional experiences, educational processes, and religious experiences form and change the person's deepest commitments and desires. Consequently there is no point in attempting to alter any of these influences toward some social goal. In fact the idea of a social goal or shared vision by the group is contrary to the individual freedom that is the highest value of the neoclassical worldview.

Of course, the methodological individualists agree that forces outside an individual might impact his thinking, but for purposes of simplicity they are ignored. Gary Becker argues as much in the following selection:

> Just as many noneconomic variables are necessary for understanding human behavior, so too are the contributions of sociologists, psychologists, sociobiologists, historians, anthropologists, political scientists, lawyers, and others. Although I am arguing that the economic approach provides a useful framework for understanding all human behavior, I am not trying to downgrade the contributions of other social scientists, nor even to suggest that the economist's are more important.[23]

This recognition is stating the obvious, but Becker goes on to claim that, despite this complexity of human behavior, the rational choice approach provides an overarching model for understanding behavior and it is the most successful at predicting behavior. Methodologically this approach boils down to the instrumentalist position taken by Milton Friedman. If the model predicts better than any other, then it should be the model of choice whether its assumptions fit reality or not. The problem with this instrumentalist stance is that it does not offer much if behavioral change is an objective. The best that can be done is to alter the price of behavior in hopes that the individual will substitute toward or away from certain behavior. Of course this conclusion fits well with the notion that the individual is supreme and, apart from destructive behavior, should not be changed by the will of the group.

Institutionalists are more inclined to examine motives and causes of why people do what they do. They see, as did Adam Smith, the social and the unsocial passions. Veblen divided human behavior into instincts that are socially helpful or socially destructive. The parental instinct is the concern for family and nation. The workmanship instinct is the creative element in everyone that brings satisfaction from our productive work. Idle curiosity is the instinct of the inquisitive mind that seeks answers to problems and makes people have a philosophic bent. Finally, the acquisitive instinct is the self-serving drive to dominate and conquer. To Veblen it is the opposite of the parental instinct and is a destructive quality that detracts from the social good. He put much of the competitive drive for economic dominance in this category and sought to promote the first three instincts as necessary for the enhancement of life processes. At all points in his thinking Veblen fought the neoclassical tendency to pull economic analysis out of the social fabric of society. While he was not a proponent of government intervention, he believed that education and the promotion of social norms could make life more meaningful.

While Veblen himself was a social misfit in many ways, he did stimulate a line of thought that has become a significant challenge to the methodological individualism of the mainstream. At least four prominent themes should be highlighted in the evolutionary, institutional approach.

1. Economic behavior should be analyzed in such a way that the relevant institutions are central to the understanding of behavior. Social norms, legal practices, psychological boundaries, customs and political forms must all be part of the exploration of economic behavior.

2. The movement of society over time is evolutionary in nature. The economic order is in constant process where becoming rather than being is the relevant concept. The preferred exemplar in the sciences would be something organic like zoology rather than physics or mechanics. Accordingly, the notion of long-run equilibrium is not helpful. The dynamics that move the system are important. In this regard the Austrian critique and the institutionalist critique are similar. However, the institutionalists have a more integrated view of social evolution than do the Austrians because they see both people and systems in a constant evolutionary mode where both are involved in mutual change. The Austrians see individual preferences as independent of the structures for purposes of analysis.

3. There are diverse goals present in economic life. Utility maximization is only one of many goals that people consider important. Some trade away utility for security of all kinds. For others, relative standing in the community is far more important than absolute standing. Still others seek acceptance and belonging above all else. Any model that focuses on one narrow goal is bound to miss much of what needs to be understood and analyzed. While Austrians and neoclassicals admit this is true, they rarely extend their analysis into these areas.

4. Because of the nature of the economic system described in the three points above, there is no way to avoid normative considerations and value judgments. A society without some shared vision and common understanding of key values will eventually fragment and lose its way. It is hard to agree on even the appropriate basic rules of the game if the social order is understood as a machine that is value-free when it really is value-laden. For the institutionalist, the search for the grand, mechanistic social theory is folly.

In the final analysis the institutionalist is a philosophical pragmatist who seeks through inductive means to find relationships that can lead to problem solving. Reality is not found in some deductive, abstract model that assumes the hedonistic economic man. Rather, it is found in the empirical data that springs from a myriad of special cases, and economic theory should evolve from this data with the full help of all the academic disciplines. Only then will Clarence Ayers be able to say that economics is headed in the right direction.

What can the Christian say about the institutionalist option? The institutional focus on the solution of social problems is consistent with the biblical calling to be salt and light in the world. Whether the philosophical pragmatism of institutionalism is inconsistent with a revealed faith is open to interpretation. Charles Saunders Peirce, an originator of pragmatism, felt that there was compatibility between religion and his philosophy even though philosophical pragmatism did not require a belief in a final cause. He argued that it did not preclude a belief in a final cause and it did not require the stringent verification test for truth that the positivists required. In Peirce's view, religion and positivism were incompatible because no religious doctrines or dogmas could pass the verifiability tests.

In a paper on institutionalism and pragmatism Lewis E. Hill concludes that religion and pragmatism are compatible.

> Explicitly, pragmatists have nothing to do with Final Cause; their philosophy neither requires nor prohibits an explicit belief in Final Cause. Implicitly, it is my judgement that pragmatism implies an acceptance of Final Cause. The pragmatic method always requires that normative value judgments be made; and it is my belief that all normative value theory is either based on some (explicit or implicit) concept of Final Cause or it is meaningless. Final Cause can be interpreted either in secular or in religious terms. A religious interpretation of Final Cause is entirely consistent with almost any belief in revealed religion.[24]

Thus Hill sees the institutionalist option as preferred on religious grounds over the neoclassical option because the neoclassical methodology requires strict verification requirements before something can be declared to be true. The fact that institutionalism provides opportunity for the infusion of values and beliefs into policy is another feature that makes it appealing to Christians.

Conclusion: Elements of a Christian Economic Theory

Evangelical Christianity is spread all across the economic ideological spectrum. Some are Austrian or even libertarian in orientation in that they put high value on individual freedom and are skeptical of most efforts to manage the system in the direction of some Christian view of fairness or justice. Others come from an institutionalist perspective claiming that the Austrian and neoclassical approaches are a sellout to the individualistic thinking of the Enlightenment. They see this as being a rejection of the biblical call to structure a system that deals effectively with the needs of the poor and the oppressed. Most tend toward the middle ground and follow a modified neoclassical approach which allows for limited market adjustments in cases of market failure or market distribution patterns that are felt to be unfair. While this kind of diversity may be the best we can achieve given the fragmented nature of the church universal, it is helpful to trace out a vision of what might be.

To dream about what ought to be requires one to look through the lens of a Christian worldview. This worldview must come from what God has revealed to us in Scripture, church history, and his Spirit, properly discerned in the community of faith. While it is true that much of this revelation came before a market system was dreamed of, we still can grasp the broad themes from which present day applications must be made. Several of these themes are enumerated here—I link them to the four economic worldview questions raised above (p. 98).

1. *What is the overarching purpose of economic activity?* The *shalom* dream of God's people envisioned a world the way it was supposed to be. Sufficiency for all and harmony in all relationships were not optional. They defined the dream.

2. *Are relationships part of nature or do people consciously form those relationships in some manner?* All people are created in God's image. This presents a set of qualities chief of which is the human desire to create. People need to create not just goods and services, but social environments, life plans, institutions and programs. We are not cogs in the wheel of nature submitting to exogenous forces while being deluded into thinking we are free.

3. *What is the relationship of the individual to the group in social organization?* Sharing relationships of trust with others that provide security and support is the purpose for which we were created. The creating activity listed above is not an individual enterprise, but rather a shared venture where people contribute to one another and feel valued and honored. The output from production at all levels is consumed both according to need and to effort.

4. *How are things valued or what determines real worth?* Things are valued in terms of their contribution to *shalom*, not in terms of short-run personal pleasure. The commodification of items that are ideally shared in committed relationships should not occur. The most obvious and offensive commodification exchange is prostituting one's body, but in a *shalom* environment food, basic shelter and basic health care would not be commodified to the extent that they are in a market economy. Surely the poor would fare better if they were brought into relationships that were upbuilding rather than competitive.

By this time most readers will declare this dreaming as a futile exercise. It certainly appears to be when viewed through the eyes of a neoclassical economist or an advocate of Austrian economics. Even institutionalists will question the usefulness of such dreaming. Most Christians will relegate such visions to the coming kingdom of God or to Marxist fantasy. Of what use can this vision possibly be in light of the realities of this world and the sinful nature of people?

I suggest it is important to keep this vision before us for two reasons. First, if we think enough about what things should be like, we will begin to practice our thoughts where they might have the best chance of working. After all, the church is to give some foretaste of what the coming *shalom* might be, so occasionally some of this dream can break through in our communities of faith. There may even be more opportunities for Christians to practice these thoughts in everyday life in their communities of faith and in the larger society than we even realize now.

Second, a vision of what ought to be can help us see how far reality is from the dream. This should help us be more humble when we adopt a theory of second best and accept lower standards. Most Christian economists have taken a second best approach to market capitalism. Since *shalom* does not appear to be possible, we are forced to accept a system that is not simply a watered-down attempt at *shalom,* but rather a system with values that seem opposed to *shalom* values. In so doing we are tempted to buy into market values and convince ourselves that its Enlightenment philosophy really is biblical and its practice really is Christian. Some have yielded to this temptation, but most have stayed with the second best viewpoint. What we all need is a constant reminder of the contrasts between what should be and what is the best we can do in this world. Sometimes, if the dream is focused clearly enough, the best we can do in this world may get better. Perhaps the place where this is most likely to be true is in the relationships between the rich and the poor.

4

Christian Economic Justice and the Impasse in Political Theory

Ashley Woodiwiss, Wheaton College

Federal welfare policy as we have known it has now largely passed into history. The fifty American states now face an uncertain future in terms of just how they will settle the inevitable problem of the poor who "will always be with you." It is both a daunting and yet potentially vibrant time for those concerned with matters of economic justice, and especially for Christians committed to heeding the cry of the poor. In this chapter I am concerned with how Christians should think about matters of economic justice. To that end I attempt to answer the following questions: 1) What is the status of contemporary, secular, political theory about such matters? 2) Do such theories assist Christians in developing a theory of economic justice? and 3) What resources indigenous to the Christian tradition ought to be mined for such a theoretical effort? My ultimate aim is to identify and describe our (Christian) best prospects as we seek to hear the cry of the poor in the late twentieth-century, American context.

This essay is set up in five parts. In the Introduction, I use the recent work of political philosopher Michael Sandel to help set out a historical sketch of the contemporary U.S. political situation in which liberalism, the dominant theoretical framework for our discussions of political and economic justice, is shown to have reached an impasse and is thus considered no longer workable. In contemporary, liberal America, political decisions and actions institutionally ensure that shared public agreements on matters of substantive economic justice in fact *cannot* be arrived at. Too many actors on all sides of the political-theoretical spectrum have profited by the structural creation of conflict for there to be the hope of attaining what in the traditional parlance of politics was called the "common good." Our politics of interest-group pluralism (and the language it is couched in) ensures the continuation of this condition for the long, foreseeable future.

If this condition characterizes contemporary liberalism, perhaps that means the problem is only a contemporary problem. May it not be possible that there resides something within liberalism as a tradition, which, if recovered and refurbished for our day, could provide a way out of the present liberal impasse? In part II, I trace out the history of liberalism as a tradition, from its origins in the sixteenth and seventeenth centuries to the threshold of the twentieth century. While I am concerned to identify some of the key ideas associated with the liberal tradition, I am chiefly preoccupied with showing how exclusivism of a certain kind characterizes the tradition; an exclusivism that prohibits the Christian account of the poor from entering the public discussion, and thus ensures that full justice for the poor *cannot* be secured. From a Christian theoretical perspective, the tradition of liberalism rests upon a mistake.

But liberals have always defended their project. In part III, I analyze the two leading approaches to liberal justification in the quarter-century after Watergate and Vietnam. In this period of time, the "crisis of liberalism" has intensified. Both the criticisms and the defenses of liberalism have come into sharper focus and carry more significant political and theoretical import. Since the 1970s there have been two major approaches to defending liberalism. The first, appearing with the 1971 publication of John Rawls's *A Theory of Justice*, attempts to overcome the critics of liberalism by refashioning an account of liberalism employing the traditional resources at hand (Kant, imaginative thought experiments, the appeal to reason, etc.). Its chief theoretical claim regarding public policy is that the state must remain neutral concerning the support or advocacy of any particular account of the Human Good Life. More recently, there has emerged an effort to extend or reconceive the tradition of liberalism by employing new resources (e.g., Aristotle, virtues, the community, Human Good, etc.). This latter development appears, arguably, to be the dominant method of defense in our day. But this development, which I call a Neo-Aristotelian form of liberalism, explicitly rejects the neutrality thesis of the earlier liberals. Rather, it argues that liberalism *is itself* a particularly explicit account of the Human Good. I conclude this section with the argument that despite their differences, both versions of liberalism (neutralist and Aristotelian) carry with them into the contemporary moment versions of the exclusivism that haunts the entirety of the liberal tradition. Even liberalism in its most sophisticated contemporary formulations cannot provide Christians with the theoretical resources necessary for an adequate theory of economic justice.

If liberalism is judged wanting, does its chief theoretical challenger, communitarianism, answer the need for Christian economic justice? In part IV, I move to consider the communitarian critique of liberalism. Communitarianism is an inelegant label for a broad philosophical and political development that has occurred in the past two decades. The term both embraces and yet misses much. Widespread disaffection with liberalism has triggered the search for a new way of talking about economic justice; away from the individual with her rights toward that of the community and its interests. In order to make some sense of this disparate situation I limit myself, in part IV, to discussion of just those philosophic and political sources that most directly impinge on the topic of economic justice. As will be seen, the literature of communitarianism replaces liberalism's emphasis on rights with its own concern for civic responsibility. But while this shift of emphasis may be salutary at some levels, is it sufficient for the specifically Christian concern for the poor? Does it help us to get any closer to our goal? I conclude this section with the pessimistic assessment that communitarianism simply replaces the disfiguring discourse of liberalism with its own. By neglecting the deep structural problems that pervade our contemporary pluralist context, and by a studied silence on the situation of the poor, communitarians would distract Christian theoretical concerns away from those matters which ought to be central to Christian economic justice. The poor and the powerless have no voice in the communitarian literature.

If neither liberalism nor communitarianism should be the basis for Christian political reflection, does secular theory have anything to offer Christian theoretical reflection at all? In my final section, I answer both yes and no. Recent developments within secular theory have produced a salutary "chastening" of theory and its ambitions. We live in a day when grand theorizing and its assumptions are on the retreat. Rather, the move is toward a recovery of our practical ability to make good judgments concerning political matters. I identify this "recovery of political judgment" as beneficial for Christians because it frees them from captivity to theory, allowing them to cultivate their own particular ("peculiar") judgments about the poor and what is needed. While political philosophy (as grand theorizing) has reached an impasse, Christians can cultivate their own account of economic justice in thought, word, and deed.

Introduction: Political Theory at an Impasse

Political theory is a peculiar academic enterprise. It straddles two different intellectual efforts: the theoretical reflection upon matters of "first principles" traditionally associated with philosophy on the one hand, and the practical concern for the stuff of everyday politics on the other. Thus the impulse for political theorists (or political philosophers as they sometimes dub themselves) to "get political" always lurks at the door. As Ronald Beiner notes, especially in the Anglo-American tradition with its built-in pragmatic concerns, there always exists within this academic enterprise called political theory "an insistence on offering a guide to practical affairs—cutting theoretical speculation down to the need for practical decisions on the immediate questions of daily life."[1] This insistence has inserted the philosopher into the maelstrom of contemporary policy debates with "the function of the philosopher to supply clever arguments for favoring one set of policies rather than another."[2] A recent and notable example of this occurred in the spring of 1997 when six of America's leading political philosophers penned an amicus brief to the U.S. Supreme Court arguing in support of declaring a constitutionally protected right to doctor-assisted suicide.[3]

Given this insistence, this urge to be "relevant" that resides within and, in part, drives the Anglo-American tradition of political philosophy, it would not be surprising to discover that as issues of political economy and economic justice have come to the fore in post–World War II America, political philosophers have been in the lead in shaping our language and ideas concerning justice. Indeed, if we are to accept Michael Sandel's account of it (Sandel is himself a political philosopher in the Department of Government at Harvard University)—many of the pathologies we associate with the contemporary American political and social context are directly attributable to the work of philosophers. In his recent, well-known and influential book, *Democracy's Discontent,* Sandel writes of how America's current predicaments can be traced to our public philosophy, by which he means "the political theory implicit in our practice, the assumptions about citizenship and freedom that inform our public life."[4] I want to use Sandel's book to illustrate the problems that afflict all political theorizing when done under the horizon of contemporary liberalism.

Sandel's large volume is divided into two unequal sections. The first four chapters (about a third of the text) survey the constitutional basis for our current political regime. In a discussion deeply steeped in the interpretive work of the Supreme Court, Sandel argues that this institution has been central to the creation of "the procedural republic," a term which, for him, signals the practical thrust of a deleterious contemporary public philosophy.

In the next five chapters (the remaining two-thirds of the text), Sandel shifts his focus from Constitution to political economy. Here his concern is to point out how the changing nature of the American political economy, from a rural, local economy to that of our present-day postindustrial global corporate structure has sapped the vitality and resources of democratic self-government. Taken together the two parts of the book set out his case for why "the public philosophy of contemporary liberalism fails to answer democracy's discontent." Throughout, Sandel's argument is clear: the United States has been suffering under the *wrong* public philosophy and needs a better philosophy to replace it. Since public philosophy has in some way damaged the American soul, it also can (and should) be part of the cure.

Given the concern of this chapter I want to focus particular attention on the second half of Sandel's book, because it is here that we get an insight into why political theorists have reached an impasse concerning economic justice.

In detailing what he calls "the political economy of citizenship," Sandel traces historically how from a nation of craftsmen and artisans schooled in the practices of local self-government we have become a mass society of passive consumers more concerned with our private lives and pleasures than the common good. The result: today, our economic debates have shifted from a concern about how "public policy should cultivate the qualities of character self-government requires" (the Jeffersonian notion that certain forms of economic work should be privileged for the direct contribution they make to good citizenship) to our contemporary preoccupation with "prosperity and fairness" (the modern debate between conservatives and liberals as to who should get how much of the national product and why). As he notes, "So familiar are the terms of our economic debates—about prosperity and fairness, employment and inflation, taxes and spending, budget deficits and interest rates—that they seem natural, even timeless. If economic policy is not about the size and distribution of national wealth, what else could it be about?"(250).

But his survey of the history of these debates over economic policy reveals a startling shift: from the beginning of American history up through the age of the progressive reformers, political economy was chiefly a debate about citizenship, and about which policy would best serve the needs of democratic citizenship. So, for example, as late as the great presidential contest of 1912 between Woodrow ("New Freedom") Wilson and Theodore ("New Nationalism") Roosevelt, one thing was held in common—they agreed despite their differences that economic and political institutions should be assessed for their tendency to promote or erode the moral qualities self-government requires. Like Jefferson before them, they worried about the sort of citizens the economic arrangements of their day were likely to produce. They argued, in different ways, for a political economy of citizenship (221).

Sandel identifies the Keynesian revolution in fiscal policy, which surfaced in the 1930s, as signaling the disengagement of political economy from its traditional concern for citizenship. Keynesianism soon attained intellectual dominance in the public debates. Whether Republican or Democratic, liberal or conservative, in the half-century following the New Deal the economic policy of all administrations was tilted towards the stimulation of consumption over production, deficit spending and the consequent rejection of the republican concern with forming particular habits and virtues of citizenship. Once-republican, yeoman farmers have now become liberal couch potatoes. "The Keynesian revolution can thus be seen as the counterpart in political economy of the liberalism that emerged in constitutional law after World War II, as the economic expression of the procedural republic" (262). Thus, by the 1930s, the twin forces of proceduralist constitutional interpretation and Keynesian economic policy had laid the foundation for the dominant postwar philosophy of liberalism.

In reviewing the performance of recent administrations, Sandel records the baneful effect which this liberal public philosophy has had upon the democratic faith of Americans. Citing "confidence gap" research and National Election Survey polling data, Sandel tells a grim tale indeed. One example: in 1964 more than three-quarters of Americans believed they could trust the government in Washington to do what is right most of the time, but by the 1990s this rate had dropped to 20 percent (297). Not surprisingly, in reaction millions of American citizens have restlessly sought their salvation in sometimes exotic political figures who have felt their pain and promised them relief: a George Wallace in 1968 or Ross Perot in 1992. But where most presidential candidates (and all the eventual electoral winners) were tied to the twin evils of the liberal public philosophy, the 1980 campaign of Ronald Reagan offered the first real prospect of a major-party candidate who was "unbound by the strictures of the procedural republic, and [whose] rhetoric resonated with the ideals of self-government and community" (308). But once in office, Reagan was ultimately unable to hold together the strands of libertarian and communal conservatism which informed his campaign rhetoric. Implacable foe of big government (and its threat to self-government) though he was, Reagan nevertheless was a champion of big business (and its threat to community). At this point, Sandel invokes the late social critic Christopher Lasch's assessment: "Reagan's rhetorical defense of 'family and neighborhood' could not be reconciled with his championship of unregulated business enterprise, which has replaced neighborhoods with shopping malls and superhighways" (313).

After 300 pages detailing the failure of modern liberal theory and economic practice, Sandel concludes by setting out "in search of a public philosophy" to replace that of bankrupt liberalism. His own description of, and call for, a revitalized republicanism, I will assess in the later section dealing with the communitarian critique of liberalism. For now I want to draw out the lessons which Sandel's text provides.

Democracy's Discontent is a helpful way to identify the conditions whereby the American public discourse has reached an impasse on economic justice. Sandel employs a classical republican critique of liberalism.[5] This means that he is concerned to show how liberalism either neglects, distorts or frustrates such classical republican concerns as the moral character of the citizen (known as civic virtue), citizens' active political participation in decision-making, and the language of the common good as pointing toward the object of political deliberation (see his discussion, 25–28). He distinguishes the two this way:

> In virtue of their contrasting accounts of liberty, the two traditions assess political institutions by asking different questions. The liberal begins by asking how government should treat its citizens, and seeks principles of justice that treat per-

sons fairly as they pursue their various interests and ends. The republican begins
by asking how citizens can be capable of self-government, and seeks political
forms and social conditions that promote its meaningful exercise (27).

Sandel's classical republicanism helps us to identify some of the problems
with the liberal way of handling the poor. First, structural economic changes
have occurred which have largely been accepted uncritically and which bring
into being historically novel ways of either ignoring or displacing primary questions of economic justice in favor of a shared commitment to growth and prosperity. In this context, the poor, rather than being treated as full members of
the community, become marginalized (in both thought and action) and as a
result come to be patronized as "victims" of, or discounted as the necessary
result of, economic development. Next, when justice issues do emerge, the
conceptual and linguistic resources of the dominant tradition, liberalism, are
found to be inadequate to address the situation. *Under liberalism our political imagination and linguistic resources have become stunted.* We are unable
to envision any other way to see and feel the poor than to describe them in
largely socioeconomic terms, reducing them to units of calculation and statistical description. By its focus on the individual and his rights, liberalism has
cast poverty almost exclusively as an issue of material wealth and conditions.
Liberalism has effectively shut us off from any other way of hearing the poor.
As Sandel describes it, "The priority of individual rights, the ideal of neutrality, and the conception of persons as freely choosing selves, taken together
form the public philosophy of the procedural republic" (28). From the classical republican tradition, contemporary liberalism is not *capable* of articulating a full account of economic justice for the poor, for its conceptual range is
too limited and too limiting. Thus, not surprisingly, the search for an alternative tradition becomes imperative for those who reject the liberal vision. For
Sandel, the impasse in political theory can be overcome only by the replacement of one public philosophy with another.

But does this indictment of contemporary, liberal political theory extend to
liberalism, *per se?* Perhaps the tradition of liberalism possesses the resources
sufficient to amend its present disfigurement? Before rejecting liberalism out
of hand, what is needed is an account of the conceptual resources which the
tradition possesses. Perhaps Christian efforts on behalf of the poor might be
aided by some other version of liberalism.

Liberalism: Taking the Long View

Scholars debate the finer points of historical precision as to just when the
modern tradition of liberalism emerged (with some claiming that liberalism
actually possesses an ancient pedigree which we moderns have simply recovered). For our purposes I think it is most important to recall that liberalism

emerged as a coherent, political, philosophic project in the sixteenth and seventeenth centuries in the contentious European context. But at its origins it stood for liberty in a most important sense. As Pierre Manent describes it in his brief but elegant *An Intellectual History of Liberalism:*

> The point must be stressed: the political development of Europe is understandable only as the history of answers to problems posed by the Church, which was a human association of a completely new kind. Each institutional response created in turn new problems and called for the invention of new responses. The key to European development is what might be called, in scholarly terms, the *theologico-political problem.*[6]

Manent reminds us that liberalism emerged explicitly and publicly as a project to redefine and re-imagine the public order and matters of justice separated from the grounding in the traditional Christian terms, categories, etc., that these matters once had. One way to view liberalism, then, is as a project to recast the understanding of politics and justice as distinguishable from the historic Christian understanding of these practices. That is, justice became a domain of thought and reflection autonomous from the control of the Christian narrative. Following Manent's lead, I think it important to stress that how we understand contemporary problems of economic justice must be seen in its historical context by placing our present debates within the tradition of liberalism—which has served as the dominant way of structuring our ideas, language, institutions, and even our political imagination of what is possible and what is not. In what follows, I want to give a brief overview of the emergence of liberalism. My point in doing so is to help situate the later consideration of contemporary liberalism and just why it cannot supply Christians with the necessary theoretical framework for thinking about economic justice.

By the beginning of the seventeenth century there developed an increasing tendency for political philosophers to replace Christian theology as the starting point for reflection with a new authority, the natural sciences. The impetus for this move must be seen in light of the intellectual reaction to the years of religious civil war on the Continent coupled with the promising developments within the natural sciences themselves. The social and political thought of this period was chiefly concerned with science and the social contract. But as both intention and outcome, the result was the eviction of the church as the starting point for thinking about our obligations to each other.

One gets a sense of this liberation in Francis Bacon's *The New Organon* (1620). In the *Organon,* Bacon, an Englishman of politics as well as science, claimed: "We must begin anew from the very foundations, unless we would revolve forever in a circle with mean and contemptible progress." In the crisis of authority, which the so-called "Wars of Religion"[7] had precipitated, intellectuals in England and on the Continent rejected the traditional reliance on theology and cast about for a new public authority by which to undergird political society. The twin ideas of *material progress* as the goal and *science* as the means of public administration were bannered throughout the age as a suitable replacement. Consider Thomas Hobbes' aphorism in his masterpiece, *Leviathan* (1651): "Reason is the pace; increase of science the way; and the benefit of mankind the end." Science seemed to offer the promise of a sure and secure foundation for human affairs, political and economic. The "new learning" was rapidly extended to cover not only the mechanics of the material universe but the affairs of the human *polis*. But what was necessary for early liberalism to succeed was the *hermeneutical* effort to re-read and re-interpret the Scriptures so that the new sciences might have their life free from ecclesiastical domination. John Milbank has described this hermeneutical effort as the liberal "capturing of the Biblical text." In setting out the logic of this new thinking, he argues:

> [O]ne use of the Bible had to be prohibited. This was its truly Catholic use, which accorded interpretative authority to a *tradition* of reading, to readers whose power preceded not from arms, property, or contract, but rather from their socially-made-available time for reading. It was therefore necessary for the new political science to "capture" from Catholic Christianity the text of the Bible: to produce a new Biblical hermeneutic. That is the reason why both Hobbes's *Leviathan* and Spinoza's *Tractatus Theologico-Politicus* comprise a political science and a Biblical hermeneutics bound together in one volume.[8]

The major form this new learning took in political thought was that of the social contract. Between 1651 and 1762 a number of major thinkers associated with social-contract thought were active. Hobbes, in his *Leviathan,* applies the new learning to the political situation in England, whose foundations had been rocked by the English Civil War. He employs the Biblical metaphor of the Leviathan ("upon the earth there is not his like"; Job 41:33) to argue that man's security can only rest under an absolute political sovereign who also controls theological matters. (In his little known work on the Civil War itself, *Behemoth,* Hobbes explicitly states that a primary reason for the disturbances was the fantastical and unregulated preachments of Presbyterian clergy.) In this massive volume Hobbes deconstructs both the classical natural law tradition (Parts I & II) and traditional Christian theology (Parts III & IV). Positively, he contends for a commonwealth which would preserve man in his basic human need: self-preservation. Hobbes rejected the classical concern for "the good life" with an account of "mere life." Thus *liberalism* commences with a shifting of the focal concern from Man's spiritual condition to his basic material needs. That is, liberalism lays the foundation for justice not on Divine Authority but on fragile social agreement, which in its primary focus takes into cognizance only Man's basic needs. On the Continent, Spinoza extended Hobbes's argument for a natural right of self-preservation to that of a natural right to do all that one can do to preserve oneself. He offered his *Theological Political Treatise*

(1670) as an encouragement to those "who would philosophize more freely if they were not prevented by this one thought: that reason must be the handmaid of theology." John Locke, in his *Two Treatises of Government* (1690), modifies Hobbes's gloomy account by employing the language (though not the substance) of traditional natural law, casting men as more reasonable and more able to cooperate socially. Hence, the heavy power of the state so present in Hobbes recedes in Locke. Yet in one area, the control of religion, Locke and Hobbes are in full agreement. For all social contract theorists, society is the realm of a fragile social agreement. The one thing that needs to be controlled is the disruptive power of religion. In his brief *A Letter Concerning Toleration* (1690) Locke puts the matter more succinctly: "[T]here is absolutely no such thing under the Gospel as a Christian commonwealth." Rather, he argues, the commonwealth can only be defined materialistically:

> The commonwealth seems to me to be a society of men constituted only for the procuring, preserving and advancing their own civil interests. Civil interests I call life, liberty, health and indolency of body; and the possessions of outward things, such as money, lands, houses, furniture and the like.

Presaging the liberal tone of our day, Locke asserts that the "chief characteristic mark of the Church is toleration." Thus liberalism, even as it is concerned with securing individuals with rights and the liberty to enjoy those rights, sets up an exclusionary wall (indeed the very language of walls and separation can be found in Locke's *Letter*) to seal off a thorough Christian account of how public life ought to be ordered. From its inception then, the dominant language of our tradition has been handicapped by its inability (stronger: refusal) to allow Christian categories into its thinking about matters of justice.

The secularizing tendencies of social-contract theory increased in the eighteenth century. Well-known are Jefferson's claims that a healthy polity must rid itself of every trace of "priestcraft." But the anti-Christian animus of social-contract thought reached its most explicit eighteenth century expression in the work of Jean-Jacques Rousseau. In *The Social Contract* (1762), Rousseau argues that justice and morality cannot have reference to traditional Christian understandings. Indeed, as Rousseau claims, Christianity is antithetical to the just order because with its deference to authority, its humility, and its hope for salvation beyond history, it is simply a doctrine for slaves, not citizens. Rather, Rousseau stresses the autonomy of Man's will to create for himself the values by which he would live. Where earlier forms of social-contract thought argued that the presence of the church was a problem for human emancipation and liberty, the eighteenth century witnessed a deepening of the critique: the church is a positive danger to justice.

This "policing of Christianity" continued in the nineteenth century as liberalism. J.S. Mill makes a moving appeal for the maximization of individual

freedom in his *On Liberty* (1859). Here he pushes for the idea of absolute freedom still within the bounds of a constitutional order: "the sole end for which
mankind are warranted, individually or collectively, in interfering with the liberty of action of any of their number, is self-protection." Again in the mid-nine-
teenth century we encounter the emphasis which liberalism places upon the
body and its needs for maximum space and freedom of motion. Striking a
rhetorical posture familiar to us in our day, Mill claims:

> The only part of the conduct of any one, for which he is amenable, is that which
> concerns others. In any part which merely concerns himself, his independence
> is, of right, absolute. Over himself, over his own body and mind, the individual is
> sovereign.

It is not surprising then, that Mill privileges what he calls "pagan self-asser-
tion" over "Christian self-denial," looking to Pericles as the embodiment of liberal self-development.

While this account of the history of liberalism is admittedly cursory, I do
think it gives a fair indication of the tone and temperament of the tradition
when it comes to just how the Christian narrative and the public institution of
the Church ought to be regarded when it comes to political matters. Setting
aside the Christian conception of economic justice (which had situated justice within the divine horizon), *liberalism* emerged as the dominant narrative
of our political way of life, articulating a conception of economic justice limited to the temporal and material conditions of life. As such the liberal tradition has been *exclusionary*.[9] What this means for economic justice in the context of late-twentieth-century-American liberalism is the focus of the next
section.

Liberalism at Century's End: a Way of Life in Crisis

As Sandel documents, liberalism in America reached its fullest and most
complete articulation in the decades following the Second World War. This is
what he refers to as "the triumph of the procedural republic." Soon after the
war, as E.J. Dionne reminds us in his popular *Why Americans Hate Politics*, the
shared consensus between Democrats and Republicans on matters of political economy had a name. In 1949 Arthur Schlesinger coined the phrase, "the
vital center." Because both political parties agreed with the main thrust of the
public philosophy, their disagreements were carried out at the margins, thus
rendering substantive political judgments innocuous. Indeed, Dionne comments how Schlesinger himself, in his pamphlet concerning the 1960 Presidential campaign, "Kennedy or Nixon: Does it make a Difference?" while ultimately siding with Kennedy, argued in effect that the difference was not all
that great.[10]

The Neutrality Thesis

However, the classic articulation of the postwar liberal theory of justice was set forth in 1971 with the publication of John Rawls's *A Theory of Justice*. Rawls brought into theoretical clarity what the practical political center was all about. It was both an articulation and a championing of the postwar liberal arrangement. At the center of his effort is the argument that the liberal arrangement (which comports with our shared intuitions about justice, according to Rawls) is predicated upon and requires a right-prior-to-good argument. That is, the success of liberalism historically, and its future success, must be seen in its principle that no discussion of the Human Good (way of life) can come before shared principles of right are first established. Justice, then, as a necessary part of any discussion of the Human Good, emerges in the liberal state by discovering those principles which all reasonable persons would agree to if they were not burdened or prejudiced by their particular accounts of the Human Good. Consequently, this manner of theorizing forbids any substantive or "thick" accounts of the Human Good from being present in liberal theorizing. So *public* in this account requires *neutrality;* the claim that the state must not privilege any specific account of the Good. Relegated to, and cordoned off to, the private realm was any project which Rawls damningly refers to as "perfectionism." In the literature that sprang up around *A Theory of Justice*, exponents of Rawlsian liberalism extended this into a full-blown *neutrality thesis:* the public square is to be seen as the realm of the universally rational, unencumbered by the particular claims or voices of "perfectionist" communities. Liberalism provides a framework of basic rights and liberties "that even the welfare of society as a whole cannot override"[11] and its principled neutrality means that the state is not involved in soul-crafting (or the forming of certain traits of character deemed necessary for the health of the polity), but rather permits individuals to pursue their own particular conception of the good. This is the neutrality thesis which is chiefly identified with the work of Rawls, and as Sandel puts it, "it is this claim that defines the liberalism of the procedural republic."[12]

But events conspired to lead some liberals to the conviction that, in fact, Rawlsian neutrality was a mistaken way to describe and defend what liberalism was really all about. Beginning in the early 1980s a new generation of liberal political philosophers began to argue for the rejection of the neutrality thesis.

From Neutrality to Virtue: Liberalism in the '80s and '90s

Signs that the old orthodoxy was losing its grip surfaced in the early 1980s when William Galston, a political theorist with a history of activism in Democratic party politics, took the neutrality thesis head-on in his article, "Defending Liberalism."[13] There he claimed the standard Rawlsian description and defense of liberalism was "fundamentally misguided." Such a defense, when applied in public discourse, judicial proceedings, administrative guidelines, etc., fueled the widespread public perception of "liberalism as morally empty." In light of this (and the subsequent electoral success of the Republican Party), Galston argued for the reconstruction along different lines of liberal theory as necessary for the future electoral success of liberal politics and the maintenance of the liberal regime.

A new generation of liberal scholars has emerged that is quite willing now to talk about virtue, religion, community, and other items which the neutrality thesis had banished from liberal public concern. Michael Perry, in one of his earlier works, described his own project as a kind of "Neo-Aristotelian liberalism."[14] I use Perry's apt phrase to describe this literature in general. While certain differences surely separate these Neo-Aristotelians (differences both in tone and content), what unites them is a shared rejection of defending liberalism in the way it had been done for the previous two decades. Where the neutrality thesis took substantive discussion of virtue, religion and community off the table, the Neo-Aristotelian thesis puts it back on. For Neo-Aristotelians, the conclusion was simple: "Neutrality cannot be achieved because neutrality itself requires justification."[15] In short, liberalism does itself contain a particular account of the Human Good. It is the liberal Human Good. As Galston puts it: "Aristotle was right: core political principles shape the character of every aspect of the community. Like every other form of political community, liberalism is a regime."[16]

If Rawlsian liberalism makes a public Christian account of economic justice impossible due to its exclusionary nature, does this newer Neo-Aristotelian version of liberalism include an inclusionary element which perhaps might free up the Christian voice?

At first glance, things look promising. The newer liberals in fact pointedly fault the neutralists for this discounting of the religious voice in the public square. Galston faults Rawls for his misreading of classically liberal sources like Locke on toleration: "Locke's argument is not only less sweeping than, but actually contradicts, the contemporary conception of neutrality."[17] Not only do neutralists misread the liberal tradition, they also misunderstand the ineliminable place which religion has in American life. Sounding like de Tocqueville, Galston speaks of how "the level of religious commitment among Americans is demonstrably higher than is the case for all other Western countries." Consequently, the juridical version of the neutrality thesis which underlies most of the controversial twentieth-century Supreme Court cases on religious practice, while accepted by many elites, "was not firmly rooted in a popular consensus."[18] The disastrous political conclusion of the neutrality thesis was the view (held by academic, judicial, policy and administrative elites) that religion was dispensable when thinking about and defending liberalism. The neutralists had misconceived the relationship between religion and the liberal regime. For the Neo-Aristotelians (some more than others, it must be acknowledged), religion and liberalism have a necessary relationship to each other. So, again Galston: "[R]eligion and liberal politics need each other. Religion can undergird key liberal values and practices; liberal practices can protect—and substantially accommodate—-the free exercise of religion."[19] And Perry posits a model of "ecumenical politics" which recognizes that the fundamental standards of American political morality "derive from the religious traditions of American society, in particular the biblical heritage."[20] Obviously then, Neo-Aristotelian liberalism is committed in some way to the inclusion of the Christian voice.

But a careful analysis of their literature reveals that while an element of inclusion is present, it is narrowly drawn. There still lurks an exclusionary dimension to their project which would, in effect, seek to chasten, discipline, police and ultimately control the Christian voice when in the public square.

This quality in their thought stands out whenever the Neo-Aristotelians discuss traditionalist religious communities and the public language such communities are disposed to use. Neo-Aristotelians consider such arguments to be based on non-liberal principles. They hold that the forms of discourse or kinds of arguments which such communities regularly employ within their shared life are invalid for the public square. In the Neo-Aristotelian literature there lurks a politically correct form of religion suitable for the ends of the liberal state. Galston states that neither "juridicalism [i.e., the neutrality thesis] nor fundamentalism can serve as an adequate basis for a liberal society." But he gives a rather broad account of fundamentalism for he later claims "ways of life that require self-restraint, hierarchy, or cultural integrity are likely to find themselves on the defensive, threatened with a loss of both cohesion and authority." And later, when he celebrates the liberal regime's inculcation of a sense of critical self-reflection, he acknowledges that such liberal civic virtues are "bound to have an effect on our ability to maintain those commitments, especially the ones resting on tradition, unquestioned authority, and faith."[21] It is obvious then (at least in Galston's account of it), that in Neo-Aristotelian liberalism, some Christian voices will be privileged, others excluded.

The same theme can be seen in Stephen Macedo's celebration of the citizenship, virtue and community he identifies as resident in liberal constitutionalism. He considers the distinguishing characteristic of the liberal polity to be its aspiration to public reasonableness, which requires that appeals to inner conviction or faith be ruled out in public justification for one's policy claims. While this may lead to public positions "that religious fanatics will find deeply objectionable," nevertheless such is the nature of the liberal way of life. For unfettered liberalism produces a way of life in which "nuns criticize their bishops and even the Pope; authorities of all kinds come into question. Certain types will find the liberal culture hospitable (artist, entrepreneur, arguer, and playboy) and others (devout and simple) will find the going tough."[22] More recently he has acknowledged: "liberal civic education is bound to have an effect of favoring some ways of life or religious convictions over others. So be it." He is clear on just whom he has in mind when later in the same article he declares, "we must remind fundamentalists and others that they must pay a price for living in a free, pluralistic society."[23]

A review of the Neo-Aristotelian literature thus gives grounds for the conclusion that liberalism simply cannot serve as an adequate basis for a Christian account of economic justice. While open to the view that religion has something to say and to offer the modern liberal regime, the Neo-Aristotelians are nevertheless committed to the marginalizing and silencing of traditionalist voices. Religion is either helpful to the ends of the liberal state (and is thus to be included) or it is not (and is thus to be excluded). For liberalism, the Christian narrative is viewed as politically necessary (for the time being, while there are still so many Americans who are both Christian and vote), but theoretically irrelevant. For a liberal theory of justice (whether Rawlsian or Aristotelian), there is no need of Christian theoretical insight in its basic formulation. Liberalism is sufficient unto itself.

Prior to my discussion of communitarianism, and serving as a transition to it, I want to give some concluding reflections on what the ineliminably exclusionary nature of liberalism should mean for Christians concerned for economic justice and the cry of the poor.

I think some recent ways of viewing liberalism provide Christians with the necessary perspective whereby to size up the possibilities for Christians concerned for economic justice to work within the horizon of liberal categories of thought. For instance, Margaret Moore, in her analysis of liberalism, is concerned to show how liberalism

> is itself a conception of the good, on all fours with other conceptions of the good, and deeply antithetical to many moral and religious conceptions. It is committed to the value of autonomy and its principles presuppose the importance of protecting individual autonomy above all else.[24]

Ronald Beiner, too, sounds a similar note when he says that liberalism "no less than socialism, feudalism, or any other social order, is a global dispensation—that is, a way of life that excludes other ways of life." Liberalism, and the liberal way of life, are about securing a particular human good. So, Beiner argues, liberalism "recognizes one particular vision of the good, that choice itself is the highest good." That is to say, "choice is the essence of personhood."[25]

Over and against the liberal narrative of sovereignly choosing individuals is the Christian narrative of the covenanted body of believers. One's account of justice (which includes an account of what the poor need and deserve) is clearly bound up with whether we see the world through the liberal or the Christian description. Moore's own conclusion may well serve as a starting point for Christian theoretical reflection. As she notes, real Christian communities in the United States and Canada find such emphasis militantly opposed to their own long-term survival. She concludes: "Their cultural survival depends on . . . devaluing the exercise of autonomy and emphasizing instead living according to the word of God."[26]Against the liberal self-image of the liberal regime as the realm of full human emancipation, reason and the human good, is arrayed the Christian counterimage of the liberal regime as police state. As Barry Harvey puts it, "the notions of confinement, surveillance, and utilization accurately describes the fate, not only of certain individuals, but also of non-liberal traditions and communities within the disciplinary configurations of liberal cultures and institutions."[27]

Christians seeking to do justice to and for the poor should not expect liberalism to provide the way. The question now becomes, as unease with liberalism has grown in the last decades of our century, whether the emerging communitarian alternative promises better for Christians.

The Communitarian Critique of Liberalism

What is communitarianism?

As mentioned at the beginning of this chapter, what generally falls under the umbrella term, *communitarianism,* is really a fairly inchoate collection of philosophic arguments, political positions, cobbled together policy proposals, initiatives, journals, etc. There is no precise definition for the term. Rather it might be thought of more as a sensibility, a persuasion, or a conviction. And if we adopt the latter term, it is precisely the conviction that liberalism (both in its philosophic and political expressions) has caused the crises that plague our contemporary society and is itself unable to lead us out of them. An alternative way of thought and action is required. Originally, this conviction made itself felt in the academy, but it has now reached policy, political and pragmatic fruition in the public space.

Beginning in the early 1980s, what might be called *philosophic* communitarianism (associated, somewhat problematically, with the work of Alasdair MacIntyre, Michael Sandel, Michael Walzer and Charles Taylor)[28] succeeded in putting "community" on the theoretical agenda. As Beiner points out, it did so by "addressing questions both to liberalism as a social philosophy and to the kind of society we think of as a liberal society."[29] That is, philosophic communitarianism criticized, at a theoretical level, not just the principles of political organization which liberalism (at the hands of its philosophic apologists like Rawls, Ronald Dworkin, Bruce Ackerman, Charles Larmore, Amy Gutmann, etc.) set forth, but also probed the liberal psyche; or put differently, the liberal soul. This earlier philosophic critique of liberalism undertaken in the 1980s set the stage for the more programmatic communitarian efforts of the 1990s. While none of the (so-called) philosophic communitarians mentioned above offered specific prescriptions for how to resolve this crisis, the programmatic communitarians have taken it as their task to do precisely this.

Because my discussion of Sandel set out, I think, in fairly clear terms what the philosophic discontent with liberalism is all about, I want to turn my attention in the next section to the programmatic communitarians. After that discussion, I will turn to a consideration of the limits of "the communitarian movement" as a whole.

Responsive communitarians

Even as the liberalism vs. communitarianism philosophic debate of the 1980s appears to be winding down, there has emerged, and continues to be, a practical effort to give communitarianism a political and programmatic thrust. While not singularly linked to the arrival of the journal *Responsive Community* (which debuted in 1990), that journal has served as an excellent location for the articulation and expression of these programmatic communitarian efforts. Thus while a full consideration of recent communitarian efforts in a host of policy issue areas would be too much for this essay, a consideration of the journal, its aspirations and intentions, can be taken as a good starting point to assess this political communitarian project in general. I turn then to an analysis of *Responsive Community*.

The journal, edited by Amitai Etzioni, has been a clearinghouse for communitarian ideas and policies from an eclectic array of academics, policy-makers, think-tank policy advocates, practitioners and consultants. In its first years it was chiefly concerned with setting out the theory of communitarianism and addressing national topics such as family issues, welfare, national health, etc. But since 1995 the journal has increasingly shifted its attention away from theory and Washington, and towards local communities, their efforts and their accomplishments (for example, those of taxpayers in Missoula, Montana, of welfare reform in Milwaukee, and of the community-building efforts of New York's 4th Street Basketball League). A regular feature, called "Community News," serves as an inspirational bulletin board for such local stories. In its first issue, the editors (who are all academics) set out their position as *beyond* the categories associated with typical national politics; that is, the politics of liberalism: they are "as a group, neither right nor left, liberal nor conservative, but dedicated to providing a voice to address and articulate issues we believe concern us all." Indeed, communitarians reject such ideological labels because they see this typical way of seeing politics and political differences as part of liberalism's entrapment of American politics and dialogue in false bipolar oppositions. For communitarians, the public good is identifiable, achievable and ultimately publicly realizable. It is beyond conservative and/or liberal. What stands in the way of America attaining the public good is liberalism's false description of the world. What is necessary to attain the common good is the rejection of liberalism's description of politics (as the inevitable group struggle for power) and its bipolar language (right/left, conservative/liberal). In its place is the recovery of the (now dormant) language of community, public good, and the linking of rights and responsibilities. (The last phrase serves as the journal's subtitle.) Etzioni, in the introduction to his edited volume, *The Essential Communitarian Reader,* describes how he and some fellow academics met in late 1989 and found "a surprising amount of consensus on the need for a new position and on its main outlines."[30]

This main outline came to light in 1991 in the widely publicized release of "The Responsive Communitarian Platform." The platform is a thirteen-page document that sets out the communitarian vision and contains about eight pages of policy discussion. Its fifty-eight signatories, while drawn disproportionately from the academy, nevertheless also include individuals with practical policy, public administration and political experience. (Since that time the journal has claimed to have enlisted both President and Mrs. Clinton, Vice-President Gore, as well as such foreign politicos as Prime Minister Tony Blair of Great Britain and Rudolf Scharping, former head of Germany's second largest political party, the Social Democrats, in some of its causes.) In its preamble, the platform sets out the kind of middle ground or balancing that typifies communitarian thought. For example, we read of how "a communitarian perspective recognizes both individual human dignity and the social dimension of human existence" (xxv). Key to reviving the necessary sense of civic responsibility, communitarians argue, are those "moral voices" that persuade and educate citizens in their duties but which have been "much neglected" by liberal thought, word and deed.

Where are such moral voices to be found? In "starting with the family" communitarians show their difference from liberal bipolarity by emphasizing moral and personal responsibility, a theme which appears initially to imitate the claims associated with conservative traditional-family advocates. The platform speaks out against materialism and consumerism and underscores the social seriousness of child-rearing, pointing to how "the weight of the historical, sociological, and psychological evidence suggests that on average *two-parent families are better able to discharge their child-raising duties*" than other domestic arrangements (xxviii—emphasis in the original). But the communitarian perspective on the family possesses a social responsibility dimension largely absent from conservative thought. The platform here goes beyond conservative thought and appears to include liberal concerns as well: "It follows, that *work places should provide* maximum flexible opportunities to parents to preserve an important part of their time and energy" to attend to this most socially vital task. Paid and unpaid parental leave, flextime, job sharing, etc., are some of the policies the platform encourages. At the same time, legislation ought to discourage—not eliminate—divorce and adopt a "children first" perspective that would be fundamental to property settlements and support awards.

The other elements of the platform follow the same basic formula: a move away from exclusive reliance on either statist or market-driven solutions to

America's social ills, and towards fresh civic solutions. Thus public education ought to reduce the emphasis on students as consumers and rights-bearers, but should rather stress "those values Americans share" (xxix), a project of moral-civic character formation. Public service (whether national, local or volunteer) is to be encouraged as a way of bringing Americans out of their reclusive privacy and into the experience of shared work which builds community and fosters "mutual respect and toleration" (xxxi). When the platform moves to the area of social justice, a new term is introduced: "At the heart of the communitarian understanding of social justice is the idea of *reciprocity:* each member of the community owes something to all the rest, and the community owes something to each of its members" (xxxiv—my emphasis). Seeking to reconcile the liberal concern for protection with the conservative concern for personal responsibility, the platform claims that "communitarian social justice is alive to both the equal moral dignity of all individuals and to the ways in which they differentiate themselves from one another through their personal decisions" (xxxiv). Thus reciprocity underscores how members of communities have the responsibility of providing for themselves and their families, but at the same time the community "is responsible for protecting each of us against catastrophe, natural or man-made; [and] for ensuring the basic needs of all who genuinely cannot provide for themselves" (xxxiv).

The platform is, in the nature of such things, long on inspiration and short on specific policy proposals. Especially when it comes to social justice and the "moral voice" of the poor, the platform offers little more than the ideas cited. So what do the communitarians propose? To get at this we need to move beyond the text of the platform and to consider some specific proposals which have been set forth in the journal.

And here, curiously, we find only scant attention given to matters of economic justice and a concern for the poor. Indeed this has led one contributor, Philip Selznick, to take his fellow communitarians to task. In a fall 1996 article, he chastises the journal for not balancing a concern for social justice and social responsibility along with its emphasis on personal responsibility. To redirect the journal's attention he claims: "Communitarians need to appreciate the close connection between personal and collective responsibility. *Personal responsibility is most likely to flourish where there is genuine opportunity to participate in communal life*" (62—emphasis in the original). To this end, he sets out an initial description of a communitarian social justice which is founded upon the four principles of equality, mutuality, stewardship and inclusion. In each principle there is mention (albeit slight and passing) of how communitarians ought to consider the plight of the poor and the powerless.

Communitarian equality, Selznick maintains, emphasizes the moral equality of all members of the community even as it acknowledges the inevitable inequalities that will characterize any human association. A strong emphasis on the moral equality of members will help to offset what Selznick recognizes is the inevitable tug which such social inequality has toward social subordination. "Social justice requires eternal vigilance against this caste principle, and against the invidious discrimination it breeds" (63). The vindication of moral equality may in fact require that certain forms of mandated affirmative actions should be taken to "remedy the most important effects of domination and impoverishment" (63). Thus, even as communitarians seek to address the personal responsibility which adheres to each member of the community to carry out their civic and personal duties and obligations, they should nevertheless maintain that certain material and civic preconditions are necessary for the project of personal responsibility to be carried out successfully: "Social justice requires a regime in which everyone's basic needs for life, health, liberty and hope are respected and addressed. Therefore we must be committed to a baseline equality of condition, that is, a social minimum of nurture and opportunity" (63).

The communitarian principle of mutuality points to the way in which rational self-interest can be promoted to serve long-term and community (rather than immediate and private) ends. Mutuality thus reigns in the free play of the market (and market logic as it is applied in non-economic domains) by restraining domination, serving to "protect the weak against the strong" (66). It creates a "more robust view of equal opportunity" which would allocate "special resources to children of poor families and provide a variety of programs to encourage and sustain hope and self-respect" (67). Communitarian stewardship moves beyond the familiar environmental context for that term and extends into corporate economic life what Selznick describes as "an expanded conception of fiduciary responsibility." Finally, the communitarian principle of inclusion rests on the assumption that in a healthy community people "aspire to full membership" (69). Selznick points to work as a key facet of an individual's sense of being a part of the community. Central to the life of responsibility must be the guarantee of a decent and steady job: "Therefore full employment must be a lodestar of communitarian policy. A jobless underclass is wholly unacceptable, and the poor need more than money. They need effective participation in social life. They need jobs, education, and opportunities for service" (69).

With Selznick we can perceive the outlines of a communitarian social justice, one that stresses the civic dimension of poverty and powerlessness. Unlike liberal social justice, which focuses on the poor as individuals (to be treated as such by the state or the market), communitarian justice focuses on the poor as members of a community. Communitarians thus take a more contextual approach to matters of poverty and powerlessness. It is not surprising then that their prescriptions (even when as faintly set out as in Selznick's article) tend to cut across both traditional conservative and liberal positions. Those positions tend to frame the issue around the question, "What do poor people need?" And the traditional answers are either state intervention or conservative market-oriented policies. Communitarians, on the other hand, ask a different question: "What does the existence of poverty, of poor members in our community, mean for the kind of community we want to be—and how do we help our poor members realize full and meaningful membership?" This rephrasing of the question, I suggest, may be closer to a Christian articulation of a theory of economic justice (committed to hearing the voice of the poor) due to the similarity of the communitarian recognition of the individual in the context of her community and the Christian recognition of the saint in the context of the ecclesial community. However, similarity does not imply identity. And I think it most important for future Christian reflection on the matter to distinguish between communitarianism's "thin" understanding of the community and the Christians' "thick" understanding of the church. This kind of distinction is what has led Stanley Hauerwas (whose work is often considered an example of Christian communitarianism) to assert: "I must be more emphatic in my rejection of the description of being a communitarian. Community is far too weak a description for that body we call church."[31] In the following section I want to assess whether a Christian theory of justice can be developed from the communitarian literature.

The prospects for communitarianism

Beyond Selznick's brief outline, the *Responsive Community* has had little to say about the situation of the poor. Indeed one critic has taken the journal to task at this very point. Steven Lukes suggests that the journal's editorial stance of being neither left nor right, etc., has significant theoretical and practical effects. For, he suggests, "it drastically limits the topics addressed." He goes on to argue that "the major absentee is the economy" and because of this there is in its pages "virtually nothing about the ramifications of economic inequality."[32] Unfortunately, this neglect through silence seems to characterize the communitarian literature writ large. Even in the earlier philosophic literature of the 1980s, communitarian critics of modern liberal society were strikingly reluctant to address economic theory or practice except to lament, in broad strokes, the increasing materialism of society and its unreflective, uncritical commitment to economic growth, and to call for some forms of economic democracy (in which workers could more fully participate in the decision-making of their business or corporation). Sandel, to be sure, in his *Democracy's Discontent* discusses at length, as we have seen, the "political economy of citizenship." He points to the economic conditions of the late '80s and early '90s in which the income gap between the wealthy and poor increased, and he distinguishes between the liberal argument for more income equality on the principle of distributive justice or fairness, and the newer civic argument which argues against such extreme inequalities because it "undermines freedom by corrupting the character of both rich and poor and destroying the commonality necessary to self-government" (330). In addition, Sandel faults both conservatives and liberals for failing to recognize the civic effects of growing economic inequality with its consequent diminution of the number of shared public spaces (like schools, parks, playgrounds, etc.) which, when in healthy order, serve as loci for civic education by bringing together the different faces of the community. And finally, he calls for a policy to recover the sense of the public as shared space by addressing inequality and seeking "communal provision less for the sake of distributive justice than for the sake of affirming membership and forming the civic identity of rich and poor alike" (333). But such points (insightful though they may be) certainly do not constitute a theory of economic justice. At best, they simply are pointers to where a communitarianism would have to begin. *To date communitarianism has been silent on the matter of economic justice and the condition of the poor.* Such silence is unacceptable for Christians concerned with economic justice as it pertains to the poor.

The key question for Christian theoretical reflection is whether such silence is, in fact, a necessary part of contemporary communitarian thought, or whether the situation is remediable? I suggest the situation for communitarian thought is indeed the former.

Interestingly, the reasons for such a conclusion may emerge from the pages of *The Responsive Community* itself. In the summer 1995 issue, one reads Ralf Dahrendorf's sobering account of the contemporary global political and economic situation. After describing (and even defending) the achievements of the First World which have made the United States and Western Europe "the happy few" of political societies worldwide, able to enjoy economic opportunity, civil society and political liberty, Dahrendorf goes on to analyze the contemporary condition of globalization in which "all economies are interrelated in one competitive marketplace, and everywhere the entire economy is engaged in the cruel games played on the stage."[33] In brief, "the effect of globalization is felt in all areas of social life" (78). Given this condition, the key economic imperative is what he terms "flexibility" (79–81). Flexibility is an umbrella term which justifies any number of policies such as downsizing, deregulation, the changing nature of the workforce, the technologizing of the workplace, the increased mobility of capital and production, and, borrowing a phrase from theorist Joseph Schumpeter, the tapping of the entrepreneur's "creative destructiveness." All of this is done for the sake of what Dahrendorf describes as "seemingly unending increases in productivity" and the narrowing of the language of public economics to the obsession with economic growth, measured only in terms of wealth, measured as per capita GNP. While good for economic competition and growth, however, the logic of flexibility poses a great threat to particular communities and especially to the losers in the global Darwinian struggle.

Dahrendorf describes in chilling detail the effect of globalization on civil society. He identifies globalization as associated with the creation of a new kind of inequality. The new kind of inequality would better be described as inequalization, the opposite of leveling. It builds paths to the top for some and digs holes for others, creating cleavages. The incomes of the top 10 or 20 percent are rising significantly, whereas the bottom 20 to 40 percent are watching their earnings decline (82).

But the creation of such cleavages is only part of the problem. Added to this condition, and intensifying it as a central problem for the future, is the permanent or fixed nature of this situation. In short, globalization with its demand for constant technological innovation is creating the structural condition in which, as Dahrendorf describes it, "some people are—awful as it is even to put this on paper—simply not needed. The economy can grow without their contribution. Whichever way you look at them, they are a cost to the rest, not a benefit." The effect on civil society then becomes strikingly clear: "Poverty and unemployment threaten the very fabric of civil society." And this will only intensify as the opportunities for meaningful participation in the workplace continue to decrease. Dahrendorf concludes, "once these are lost by a growing number of people, civil society goes with them" (83).

Indeed, an additional structural development added to the condition of a permanent (and growing) underclass makes the communitarian prospect even bleaker: the powerlessness of the poor. As Dahrendorf describes it, the underclass is also politically marginalized "because they do not represent a new productive force, nor even a force to be reckoned with at present. The rich can get richer without them; governments can even be reelected without their votes; and GNP can rise and rise" (85). The problem of course, is that the consequent pathologies that emerge from the permanent underclass—drugs, violence, antisocial behavior, etc.—unleash the cry for order and authority from among the secure who find the presence and proximity of such behavior threatening to their comfort and convenience. Dahrendorf thus describes how globalization carries with it the temptation to authoritarianism. In the name of protecting our standard of living and the material benefits of our civil society, we begin to permit encroachments into that society by a growing police power (private and public). Dahrendorf's self-confessedly modest proposals include "reaching out to the underclass." Here his focus is prospective rather than remedial. That is, given the fact of the underclass, "we may not be able to do enough for those already excluded, but we must prevent another generation from having the same dismal experience" (91).

Dahrendorf's analysis provides some brilliant insights for communitarianism's prospects. His picture is of the world divided (and dividing) along deep structural lines. Conflict, not consensus, characterizes the modern polity. This will continue into the third millennium. And, most troubling of all, there seems to be the irresistible conclusion that the fate of the poor will be even bleaker than at present. But in the face of these deep and troubling systemic developments, communitarians blink. That is, their positive and uplifting language simply ignores the conditions which Dahrendorf sets out. The condition is one of deep, pervasive and permanent conflict. Globalization is throwing the world into a Darwinian struggle, but communitarians such as Etzioni, as Lukes points out, "hang on to the hope of a society-wide community while remaining systematically ambiguous about where precisely 'community' is located, and [are] evasive about conflicts between communities that compete for resources and allegiances."[34] It is this situation, I think, that also indicates why the communitarians have been so silent regarding the poor. To take the poor seriously is to acknowledge their essential, and perhaps permanently fixed, condition of powerlessness. It is, in short, to give the lie to the very idea of communitarianism. In fact, in the world of "flexible" globalization, a full civic life may be impossible for a particular group or class in the community. Unable to accept this brutal reality, communitarians turn away from it and retreat into a kind of conceptual softness where conflict, if even present, is nevertheless resolvable through civic persuasion. The concrete relations of power and dependency for communitarians seem "best ignored, since attending to them threatens to undermine the very moral consensus that their perspective promises.... Thus the terms in which communitarians typically frame issues optimistically assume social actors potentially open to moral persuasion rather than intractably divided by conflicting interests and values."[35]

I view such silence as a theoretical necessity for communitarian thought. Communitarians are like their liberal counterparts when they believe that "the various values of a 'pluralistic community' are all jointly realizable without too much strain—that wealth creation, social cohesion, individual freedom, and the various goals of all kinds of different 'communities' can all be fitted together and 'optimized.'"[36] The silence of the poor, then, stands as the great indictment of communitarian thought and practice.

That both liberalism and communitarianism contain "silencing" qualities repugnant to a Christian theory of economic justice may have something to do with the recognition that for all the apparent heat generated between communitarians and liberals, they are in effect conceptually related. That is, communitarianism at its heart is but a version or expression of liberalism and not its theoretical opposite. This condition has been acknowledged by communitarian supporters and critics alike. Mary Ann Glendon, one of the co-editors of *Responsive Community,* in a 1994 essay considers the American polity as facing "the great dilemma of how to hold together the two halves of the divided soul of liberalism—our love of individual liberty and our sense of community for which we accept common responsibility."[37] Does liberalism in the late twentieth century tend to overemphasize individual liberty? Then communitarianism is to be understood merely as a corrective to that imbalance. As such, it is not truly a real theoretical alternative to liberalism. Ronald Beiner wonders "whether the very character of the communitarian 'solution,' far from resolving the discontents of liberalism, perhaps confirms at a more fundamental level the really intractable dilemma at the heart of the liberal dispensation."[38] Indeed it is a frequent criticism of communitarian thought that it does not provide the resources whereby to establish the criteria for what is a just or unjust community. States Beiner:

What is absent here is any independent, external standard that sheds light on whether identity-constituting communities confer worth upon their members beyond the bare fact of possessing something shared. The mere presence of community furnishes no such standard, and therefore fails to make good the default of liberalism.[39]

Beiner's own conclusion points out "how deeply implicated the liberal and the communitarian are in each other's dilemma."[40]

We have thus reached the following impasse: neither liberalism nor communitarianism can provide the theoretical resources sufficient for a Christian theory of economic justice. Liberal thought "silences" the church up front. Communitarianism is conceptually vacuous, politically simplistic and when it comes to the poor, is itself inescapably silent.[41] Neither of the leading theoretical alternatives, liberalism or communitarianism, can provide the basis for a Christian theory of economic justice. In the final section of the paper I want to address the question, where ought Christian theoretical reflection to go?

The Church and the Poor

The limits of theory (and, by extension, theology)

The impasse at which theoretical thought has arrived has not escaped the notice of philosophers themselves. Indeed, at the end of the second millennium of the Christian era there has developed a crisis of theoretical thought; a crisis in which the belief has come to be widely held that there is simply no way to provide an account of reality apart from greatly distorting reality itself.[42] What is commonly called *post-modernism* is the effort to give philosophic articulation to this widely held view. I suggest that we see post-modernism not as a cause of this crisis but rather as a result of it. That is, post-modernism is but the reflection in philosophic language of the felt incoherence which most citizens in contemporary advanced democracies feel in their everyday lives, lives which increasingly seem to make no sense. With the rise of European postmodern thought (and its American derivative, pragmatism, identified chiefly with the work of Richard Rorty), there has come to be the settled conviction that the great project of the modern age—i.e., to give a fully rational philosophic account of human behavior and justice and to provide a blueprint for the "fully rational society"—has failed, and further, *ought not to be recovered*.

As we have seen *both* liberalism and communitarianism try to tell a story about who we are and how we ought to live which greatly distorts reality. In post-modern terms, they do violence to reality, because in their articulation they close off voices, marginalize communities and disempower particular groups of peoples. In liberalism, as we have seen, voices which are silenced include those of small rural communities, traditional communities, and people of faith.[43] Meanwhile communitarianism, insofar as it articulates a vision of a national community of communities, ignores the unequal distribution of power and the voice of the poor. As such, both do violence to the complex reality of life in the United States. But the question becomes, can any theory hope to capture the fullness of reality, and in such a way as to be translatable into concrete policies that will respect and honor the voices of those most in danger of being silenced?

Indeed, the increasing conclusion is that such is in fact not possible. We have entered upon an age in which the limits of theory have come to be accepted. For the foreseeable future, we can expect less grand theorizing on the scale of a Rawlsian *Theory of Justice* and more limited, careful and localized theoretical efforts. Ronald Beiner concludes his volume on liberalism with this call:

> It is time that theorists adopted a more modest conception of their calling. Theories alone cannot tell us how to reorder the world. At best they can alert us to some of the dangers of a bad unity of theory and practice, in the form of a technocratic understanding of politics. Theory can teach us to limit the intrusions of itself into the practical sphere.[44]

Secular political theory has been humbled, its reach and explanatory power chastened, its policy pay-off questioned. But a similar impulse is under way within Christian theological circles. In the last decade there has developed a consistent internal critique by some Christian thinkers who question the historical linkages between theology and the liberal public square. With a suspicion towards public theology similar to that held by post-modern philosophers toward liberal public philosophy, these Christian critics argue that theologies which uphold the liberal public square actually contribute to the public crises which beset the American society, and unwittingly lead to the silencing of the church.[45] So Hauerwas:

> In effect the praise of democracy by protestant Christians in the past has been but a justification for why we should rule. It now functions primarily to give Christians the illusion that we continue to rule long after the *practices* of liberal societies have rendered our convictions as Christians puerile. In the name of supporting democracy, Christians police their own convictions to insure that none of those convictions might cause difficulty in making democracy successful.[46]

At the end of the twentieth century, both political theory and public theology stand indicted. As Beiner notes, since the seventeenth century, philosophers from Bacon to Rawls "have advanced a succession of theories that, if applied, were supposed to lead to practical salvation. The experience of modernity, if nothing else, has taught us what to expect of such promises."[47] But does this mean that we Christians, along with our fellow citizens, are bereft of guidance? If theory/theology cannot provide a blueprint solution to our problems (including that of poverty), does this mean we are simply cast upon the tumultuous sea of power and interest? Has justice been evacuated?

If not theory (or public theology), then what?

In his *Rethinking Modern Political Theory,* John Dunn speaks directly to this point: "What a political philosophy for the turbulent world of today and tomorrow needs at its center is a theory of prudence—a theory adequate to the historical world in which we have to live."[48] Prudence refers to the exercise of certain kinds of intellectual capabilities in the practice of decision-making, the making of judgments, the understanding of situations, and all with reference to the choosing of the best course of action. In the political context it refers specifically to the practice whereby citizens understand politics in a certain kind of way and make judgments about the particular political cases, issues, and situations which confront them. Prudence (Aristotle's *phronesis,* Aquinas's *prudentia*) as an intellectual virtue concerned with practical wisdom in decision-making is thus linked to the exercise of political judgment. In light of the collapse of (grand) theory, political judgment has come to primacy in contemporary political theory.[49] Although the world can no longer be made coherent and orderly by philosophy/theory, we are still left with the resources to be able to order our collective lives well.

What is meant by this term, "political judgment"? Beiner, in his slim 1983 volume, sets out the basic outline of political judgment, underscoring first its reflective quality. Modern science has a more deliberative nature because the rule, the principle or the law is given in advance and the matter in question is to be simply applied to the relevant rule, etc. But politics is an open-ended practice, more like chess if you will, in which multiple possibilities of understanding and/or action present themselves. So, for example, in chess there is no single "good move," but rather a plurality of good moves exist, and the choosing of one reconfigures the game, opening up new possibilities. So in politics, political judgment seeks to discern and understand what good move is appropriate in what context and with what beneficial results. Policymaking then is more game than science.

A second quality of political judgment is its communal context. When political judgments are made, implicit within those judgments are statements about what kind of community we are. As such, political judgments are exercises of communal self-understanding which involve meaning and tradition. But more. Linked closely to this dimension of communal self-understanding, political judgments also carry with them a normative concern of what kind of community we *ought to be.* Following Beiner, we may conclude that political judgment is the reflexive deliberation over concrete political issues informed by a sense of communal self-understanding and oriented by the normative sense of what the community ought to be.[50] When we do politics over matters of justice we are aware that such issues are not and cannot be "solved" by some kind of abstract policy algorithm. Rather, deliberation, consideration and reflection upon the kind of community we claim to be and aspire to be are essential constituent parts of all such debates. This is the exercise of political judgment.

What emerges from the literature of political judgment is a recognition that politics is not a science but a practice of ongoing judgments, reflected upon, debated, decided upon and (usually) revised in the light of experience. It thus becomes necessary to recognize the inherently contestable nature of politics. Policies adopted in response to, or to promote, certain social-political conditions are at best good guesswork. There is not a science of politics. This last point is the strongest claim that emanates from the literature of political judgment. As such it is an effort to reestablish the priority of *phronesis* (practical wisdom) over *theoria* (science).

A politics better informed by the cultivation of political judgment becomes at the same time a politics better shielded from those unhealthy substitutes for judgment: science and ideology. The former seeks to banish the need for judgment behind the specious pretense of expert knowledge (located in the academy, schools of public administration, policy sciences, and governmental bureaucracies), while the latter deforms the practice of judgment by means of gross oversimplification, a reductionism of reality as carried out by populists, pamphleteers, politicians, and politically minded pastors whether liberal or conservative. Neither science nor ideology contributes to the flourishing of the whole community but inevitably sets one part of it against the other. In this condition, the "poor" too frequently become abstracted, the material for power politics. They tend to be treated either as a "social problem" in need of rational, policy science solutions, thus increasing the power of "experts," or as a "political problem" to be embraced by liberal politicians or demonized by market-frenzied conservatives. But in either case, they serve as the *means* for the advancement of particular group interests. What is lost is what might be called the *face* of the poor. Neither science nor ideology can retain the image of God in the poor. They cannot envision the poor as the locus of love and respect—as equals! That is, what is lost by the substitution of science and ideology for political judgment is the person of the poor. Political judgment, on the other hand, rejects the pretenses of science and the seductiveness of ideology, seeking to retain the person and the dignity of poor citizens by deliberating in concrete terms about their situation and the alternatives open to addressing their condition.

It will not be surprising then to find that the literature of political judgment carries with it a strong inclination to pragmatism. Rather than subscribing to theories or ideologies with their simplifying logics, political judgment recognizes the complexity of reality and the fact that what serves as good law or policy in one place or time may in fact not work in another. Thus, when it comes to the poor, an exponent of political judgment is inclined to neither accept nor reject in whole either liberalism or communitarianism. Rather, one might be inclined to suggest that while neither a liberal nor a communitarian way of looking at the poor can be solely sufficient, it might be possible to cobble together insights from each to form a workable, practicable approach on an *ad hoc* basis. This is a current development in secular political theory which, given the complexity of contemporary pluralist reality, will probably be the approach that will most characterize public policymaking for the foreseeable future.

A political judgment approach to the poor will resist both the traditional, liberal, statist/bureaucratic, and the communitarian, rhetorical/simplistic depictions of reality. This permits an openness to competing viewpoints and an orientation to the various voices which are present within the community. This means, however, that the political judgment approach ultimately carries with it a good news/bad news message. The good news is that after the rejection of liberalism and communitarianism, after the rejection of philosophy/theory's claims about truth, there does remain a way to do politics that is not simply an exercise of meaningless nihilism. The bad news is that after the rejection of simplicity, there does in fact remain the reality of political complexity. Political judgment exponents do not promise easy, quick-fix solutions. Politics, like the poor, will be with us always. And for the poor, as for the rest of us, that means our fates and fortunes are thus subject to the play of politics. Their fate and our fate are left up to unknown and indeterminate factors. The best we have is our considered judgments. And truth to tell, sometimes that simply might not be good enough. While restoring dignity to politics, political-judgment exponents also recognize its danger. Sandel, against whose brand of civic republicanism I have sought to raise strong suspicions, nevertheless gets this point right. For he, too, recognizes that in our contemporary, complex, pluralist society, citizens are tempted to abdicate their judgments in preference for various fundamentalisms which banish the ambiguity and complexities of modern life, or for various forms of post-modern thought and cultural expression which celebrate the absurdity and meaninglessness of all things. He concludes:

> Self-government today . . . requires a politics that plays itself out in a multiplicity of settings, from neighborhoods to nations to the world as a whole. Such a politics requires citizens who can think and act as multiply-situated selves. The civic virtue distinctive to our time is the capacity to negotiate our way among the sometimes overlapping, sometimes conflicting obligations that claim us, and to live with the tension to which multiple loyalties give rise.[51]

This capacity, this civic virtue, is part of what I have here identified as political judgment. And, in the section below, I trace out how this literature of political judgment may in fact provide some promising insights for Christian reflection.

Christians and the Poor

The importance of the political-judgment literature for Christians concerned with the poor is evident in the way it returns a number of heretofore absent concepts to the mainstream of theoretical literature. For the proponents of *phronesis,* even as they reject *theoria* as a sufficient guide for practical political affairs, recover such ideas as *ethos,* or the particular ethical condition of a society which serves as the ground for the possibility and limits of political judgments; *virtue,* or those qualities of character necessary for the citizen to possess in order to make sound and good political judgments; *tradition,* or the shared meanings, beliefs, rituals, etc., by which a society has been held together over time and which centrally forms their identity; and *exemplars,* or the identification of particular individuals in the history of the community who have embodied, demonstrated, and exercised political judgment in its highest and best form and thus are deserving of public honor.[52]

With each of these ideas or concepts the Christian community is vitally familiar. And indeed, there has commenced a reconfiguring of Christian thought by Christian scholars concerned that too much of Christian thinking about politics and justice is informed more by modern assumptions and categories than by original Christian inspiration. They argue that Christians ought to be less concerned with getting the machinery of the state to embody one theory of justice or another, for that way is doomed to failure along with all other efforts to conceive of, and solve our problems, by means of a science, or by technologizing the problem. The problem of the poor simply evades a scientific-policy solution. Finding the right policy is inevitably elusive because ultimately it is an illusion. The issue is not to get government working better (though we might harbor slight hopes that such might, by the grace of God, actually occur); rather, the issue becomes what kind of community do we need to be in order that God's will for the poor be realized by us and through us, thus serving as a witness that God's kingdom has indeed broken into human history?

Let us make the following claim: After three hundred years of Enlightenment progress, scientific and technological advances, the glory of the market economy, and the determination of policymakers, human poverty has not only not been eliminated, but arguably has actually grown worse. Let us conclude: the poor stand as a permanent aspect of the human condition, ineradicable by human means or ingenuity. This means that the church of Christ exists not as the institution for the eradication of poverty, but rather as God's emblematic institution for how the poor are to be treated, welcomed, cared for, and respected.

What does this require? Let me summarize much of the literature which I have described elsewhere as "ecclesiocentric"[53] in the following terms. Ecclesiocentrics argue that too much of Christian thought and action has been concerned with supporting a modern regime which not only systematically excludes the Christian narrative from its public deliberation, but *must do so* in order to secure its own project: the formation of citizens who think of themselves essentially as individuals, consumers, and as autonomous. Ecclesiocentrics conclude that modernity is itself a narrative of violence and thus cannot but create continuously destructive and injurious conditions of life.

Ecclesiocentrics take to task Christian philosophers and theologians who do not see this condition but rather, by means of their "public theologies," actually contribute to the maintenance of this system. So what is necessary? Christians must recover the original critique of "the principalities and powers" embodied in their story. It is, to use John Milbank's phrase, to recover the Christian narrative as "an ontology of peace." Milbank's *Theology and Social Theory* is the central theoretical text in the ecclesiocentric literature. In it he argues that St. Augustine's *City of God* exemplifies the kind of Christian thinking needed for our own day:

> In my view, a true Christian meta-narrative realism must attempt to retrieve and elaborate the account of history given by Augustine in the *Civitas Dei*. . . . A re-reading of the *Civitas Dei* will allow us to realize that political theology can take its critique, both of secular society and of the Church, directly out of the developing Biblical tradition, without recourse to any external supplementation. For with Augustine's text we discover the *original* possibility of critique that marks the Western tradition . . . .[54]

Simply put, ecclesiocentrics argue that the church must be seen as the location of God's work in the world. In terms of political philosophy this means rejecting the nation-state (and its vocabularies, grammars, concepts, etc.) as the starting place for political thought and concern. Rather, the church is to occupy this position, for "all 'political' theory, in the antique sense, is relocated by Christianity as thought about the Church."[55]

The privileging of the Church comes with an important claim: "to be able to read, criticize, say what is going on in other human societies, is absolutely integral to the Christian Church, which itself claims to exhibit an exemplary form of human community."[56] Here Milbank's point underscores my comments above. There exists a conceptual language, as a resource, which belongs to the Christian church (and it alone) and that sets it apart from the modern state and its descriptions of the human condition. Our language, our practices, our worship and liturgy, make us a peculiar people in the world.[57] As such it is not surprising that a Christian approach to the poor will be different from the dominant perspectives and methods of secular society.

This is where the political judgment literature is applicable. For the emphasis on virtue in Christian theological ethics involves the appropriation of many of the same concepts we see among the exponents of political judgment. So, for instance, the idea of *ethos*, or the ethical condition of the community, appears among ecclesiocentrics as a concern for the presence of the proper sense of discipline and understanding among Christians. So Stanley Hauerwas:

> My claim "that the church does not *have* a social ethic, but rather *is* a social ethic" cannot help but sound, in some contexts, like a call for group narcissism. Yet I make such a claim in the hope of reminding Christians in America that we too are an imperialistic polity that must challenge the imperialistic pretensions

of that entity called "The United States of America." The question for me, then, is how does the description "the body of Christ," help Christians better understand what we must be in order to face the challenges of being the church in the United States.[58]

Central to the ecclesiocentric reconfiguring of a Christian approach to politics (and the poor) is the recovery of the proper *ethos* of the church.

The same can be seen in the contemporary Christian recovery of those other elements of political judgment: virtue, tradition and exemplars. Taken together, this ecclesiocentric perspective argues that as Christians we can only see the poor for who they are as we are shaped and informed by our participation in the church, with its storied practices, traditions, liturgies, worship and saints. That is, our vision must and can only be shaped by means of a deep immersion in our Christian narrative. Such an intentionality in our lives will wash away the accumulated distortions which inevitably accrue as we live in the world.

It is with these claims that ecclesiocentrics offer to American Christians a way out of the impasse we witness in the theoretical literature and the practical political life. It is a way out that does not guarantee a solution to the problem. Rather, it is a way for American Christians to recover their primary allegiance to the church, and in so doing become a peculiar people who approach the poor not by means of science or ideology, but by means of judgment informed by Christian vision.

I seek, therefore, not for the church to be a community, but rather to be a body constituted by the disciplines that create the capacity to resist the disciplines of the body associated with the modern nation-state and, in particular, the economic habits that support the state. For the church to *be* a social ethic, rather than to *have* a social ethic, means the church must be (is) a body polity.[59]

Does this way offer local churches a blueprint? Of course not. The life of judgment accepts that each situation in its concrete particulars, in its locality, and in its specific time, presents alternatives for good work. There simply cannot be a Christian *theory* of justice. There can only be local, particular, ecclesial efforts to be the church, and in so doing to love, serve, respect and embrace the poor whom God has placed in our midst, and we in theirs. The preferential option for the poor will find its practical embodiment in America when American Christians exercise a preferential option for the church. The need in our day is not for more theory, but good diplomacy.

~5~

The Privatizing of Compassion: A Critical Engagement with Marvin Olasky

Kurt C. Schaefer, Calvin College

Introduction

My assigned task was to survey contemporary Christian opinion on matters of economic justice. Of course, a chapter aiming to survey the entire terrain of evangelical Christian opinion about what kind of economic culture best serves economic justice would be an enormous tract indeed. Even if we limited our attention to contemporary work in the United States, we would have too large a task.

Fortunately, our options quickly diminish if we limit ourselves to recent, influential and fresh efforts. Craig Gay's excellent review[1] covers the waterfront of evangelical opinion before this decade. And there can be little doubt that the most energetic recent evangelical discussions of economics have emerged from those who are economically, politically, and socially conservative.

Thus we are in need of a review that pays particular attention to this decade's evangelicals who are skeptical of government activism and generously disposed toward other means of promoting justice. I have chosen to review the major work of one leading conservative thinker whose approach has been particularly influential: Marvin Olasky's *The Tragedy of American Compassion.*[2] The book has been widely cited, within evangelical circles and well beyond, and apparently played a significant role in the recent overhaul of the American welfare system. Like many other evangelical authors, Olasky emphasizes the proper independence of non-governmental institutions, the value of limited governance, and the legitimate responsibilities and rights of individuals. We will want to consider whether he may have overstated the case against the possibilities for legitimate, constructive governmental engagement with economic culture.

This review is important because there is probably no other facet of American culture that is more contentious, or changing more rapidly and unpredictably, than our views of the proper role of the state in our economic culture. Just ten years ago a conservative president could speak of merely reducing the growth rate of welfare programs and be greeted with a declaration that his budget was dead-on-arrival at Capitol Hill. Now a Democratic president vows to end welfare as we know it and garners no effective opposition. In such times the church must maintain a prophetic distance from the ebb and flow of culture, because in the midst of these fundamental changes in public opinion, the church's faithfulness to God's revelation and God's concern for the poor are at issue. The ideas of evangelicals in positions of influence must be sifted, in as dispassionate and generous a way as possible, in the interest of maintaining a clear and faithful biblical vision.

Marvin Olasky and the Virtues of Volunteerism

Marvin Olasky is an academic and a journalist. Like several other relatively young evangelicals engaged in similar work, he has "been there and back" when it comes to the ideas of the left. Before his conversion from atheism in his mid-twenties, he was a Marxist.

Nearly twenty years later, in *The Tragedy of American Compassion,* he places before us a new telling of American history, ambitious in a way that might make even a Marxist blush. Here is an account of how poverty and "underclass" are to be defined, what has worked and not worked in addressing the problems of the underclass, and how poverty and the human spirit are interrelated. The core of the argument runs as follows: Poverty was more severe, yet social breakdown more rare, in an era when human needs were met voluntarily and holistically by other human beings. The *way* in which one is helped affects one's spirit and behavior; and spirit, not poverty, is the core cause of modern social disintegration. Bureaucratic solutions involving government spending exacerbate such problems, because this approach is fundamentally out of touch with the needs of the human spirit that drive social dysfunction. Authors who argue that the free market itself can solve the problems of poverty also fail to appreciate the crucial place of genuinely compassionate persons and groups in fighting poverty.[3] Both sides neglect pre-twentieth-century moral understandings of what is required for a well-functioning social order. As a result, American cities are now in cultural, economic and moral crisis, and our political discussion of welfare is at an impasse, primarily because of the public hijacking of compassion.

In a sense we are a little late in evaluating Olasky's 1992 work. His position has, in broad strokes if not in all details, become the political mainstream. The United States has "ended welfare as we knew it," imposed work requirements, essentially ended general relief for able-bodied males, and imposed lifetime limits on the length of support one can receive. As a result welfare rolls have shrunk dramatically. If Olasky's analysis of the harm done by the welfare system is correct, we should soon expect to see a dramatic revitalization of the American work ethic, marriage and philanthropy. And yet, while we wait, it is worthwhile reviewing the book that then House Speaker Newt Gingrich waved before the television cameras at the beginning of the process, because this book is representative of the thinking that has shaped both conservative Christian opinion and general federal policy in the 1990s.

The Early History of Organized American Compassion

Olasky makes his case by discussing the exercise of American compassion chronologically, beginning with his interpretation of the early American model of compassion. The earliest colonial approaches to generosity stressed personal aid to the sick, home-opening hospitality to those suffering from disaster, and denial of benefits to those who were judged openly indecent or unwilling to work when work was available. In fact, the English approach of granting benefits to all, without regard to cause of poverty, was sometimes viewed as resulting in "stingy" benefits (as resources were spread quite thinly to all who were poor), whereas it was believed that the worthy poor (such as widows and orphans) should be relieved "amply."[4]

While most support for the poor came in-kind or in the form of time, some caregivers were compensated by town councils or other community organizations. The disorderly or idle could find support in strict workhouses, in which punishment for refusal to work was viewed as a way of treating all humans as members of a community in which all have responsibilities, rather than as animals.[5] "Charity schools" were founded to teach the young good work habits and fear of God, and in the Northwest Territory justices of the peace were appointed "overseers of the poor," setting up poorhouses maintained by the work of their inhabitants and withholding benefits from all who did not lodge and work in the poorhouse. Families were viewed as the central means of support for the poor, and "nothing that could contribute to the breakup of families, or to the loss of the family's central role as support of its members, was encouraged."[6] Immediate relatives who did not offer support to needy family members were fined heavily.

Olasky believes that this model of compassion, like other models, was directly related to the general cultural theology:

> Cultures build systems of charity in the image of the god they worship, whether distant deist, bumbling bon vivant, or "whatever goes" gopher. In colonial America, emphasis on a theistic God of both justice and mercy led to an understanding of compassion that was hard headed but warm-hearted. Since justice meant punishment for wrongdoing, it was right for the slothful to suffer. And since mercy meant rapid response when people turned away from past practice, malign neglect of those willing to shape up also was wrong.[7]

These theological understandings led to other subthemes in early American compassion. God's personal involvement in the creation implied that God's people should go beyond "clockwork charity" to give their hearts and love to the needy; the better-off should know the poor as individuals with distinct characters, backing the mistreated but chastising the indolent. In fact, charity should be withheld when it would lead to a descent into idleness and dependence, with some relief societies agreeing that families of drunkards, who "may be without food . . . and wholly innocent in respect to the causes of their destitution," should not receive money. Instead they should be given aid in kind, and only to cover "the demands of unquestionable necessity."[8] This seeming hardheartedness was based on the belief that some needed to suffer in order to be willing to change,[9] though no one was left to starve without any means of support. The belief that God's good law informed all of life meant that the most important need of the poor who were unfaithful was to know of God's expectations; material help would fall flat without spiritual formation and God's gracious alteration of the direction of human lives. Shaming and stigmatizing the voluntarily poor seemed appropriate.

Olasky acknowledges that there are some flies in this colonial-and-early-American pudding. Reinforced by sermons and other spiritual admonitions to those able to help, this model was appropriate in part because "in practice, since work was readily available, there was no talk of structural unemployment . . . the major type of poverty . . . was caused by a calamity . . . or crippling accident or early death (often by disease)."[10] An expanding border provided growing opportunities for able-bodied workers, at least those of European extraction. More organization of relief efforts did become necessary as cities grew. Yet they were generally still compact, with rich and poor living near each other and worshiping together; thoroughgoing economic segregation was rare.[11] Orphanages were established (sometimes with state support), groups provided small monthly allowances for working widows (often after checking the applicant's means and character, and the availability of relatives who could help), and aid was generally given in kind rather than cash. In summary, through the nineteenth century, most support for the poor was offered voluntarily, given in kind and with personal involvement, and aimed at those in difficult situations not of their own making, who were cooperating in trying to change things. This is the picture that Olasky paints.

The Challenge of Urbanization

But the country stood in need of a new model by the end of the nineteenth century: "American social conditions of the past seemed almost paradisaical to charity leaders slouching through crowded urban slums" by the end of the century.[12] One is left wondering why Olasky has been singing the praises of the early American model of charity if it was such a flop at solving the problems of the emerging urban nation—the kind of nation we now live in. No doubt the difference in population density partly explains not only changes in the American approach to poverty since the last century, but also the difference between the early American model and its contemporary European state-centered counterpart.

Olasky indicates that the future-minded who saw the emerging cities' problems looked to Great Britain's experience, and there observed the detrimental effects of "outdoor relief"—aid given to individuals who continued to live in their homes rather than poorhouses. They worried that this practice would lead—in fact had led—to dependence, support of those not truly in need, a concomitant reduction in aid to the truly deserving, and donor fatigue at seeing resources used unwisely. The relief work of Thomas Chalmers in Glasgow in the early 1820s is championed as a counter example. Receiving permission to experiment in a ten thousand-person district, he limited aid to those judged deserving (not poor through their own unaltered behavior, willing to work and save and live an upright life), and stressed small-scale personal involvement of the better-off by dividing the area into twenty-five districts under deacons' leadership. In doing so, voluntary collections increased and costs fell so much that a parish school could be staffed with the surplus. This theme—restricted access, adjudicated by small-scale volunteers—pervades Olasky's entire analysis of the needs of America's emerging cities, and in fact, of organized compassion generally. Impersonal, indiscriminate, "promiscuous" charity is, for Olasky, the villain that reduces benefits to the deserving, reduces the incentive for personal saving and insurance, and cuts everyone off from the potential benefits of personal contact and moral development. Aid should be restricted to those whom it might physically and morally elevate, and given by persons who suffer alongside the recipients, in whom they have a personal interest; those who are idle or intemperate should be left to suffer the consequences.[13]

By the 1840s and 1850s societies organized roughly along Chalmers's principles were being founded in every major American city, often providing aid in kind rather than cash. The goal was "to make city relations as much as pos-

sible like those of the countryside."[14] Olasky argues that the possibility of religious conversion was the motive that called forth sacrifice on the part of the
volunteers, and that the need for religious renovation was the underlying cause
of poverty of the recipients. Professionals could be facilitators of aid, bringing
giver and receiver together, but should not become major suppliers.

Acknowledging that this approach often failed—in cases of recessions that
caused urban jobs to dry up, or for the hundreds of orphaned and abandoned
children roaming urban centers—Olasky cheerily suggests that the nineteenth-
century response was to bring the city to the country.[15] One wonders how "large
cities became centers of anonymity" and "hundreds of homeless children . . .
roamed the slum areas of . . . cities during the 1850s"[16] if the traditional American model of charity was really such an effective thing. But not to worry—
these conditions existed "until Charles Brace and other charity leaders found
a way to send the city into the country."[17] Private organizations subsidized
mobility for adults and arranged for children to be sent westward, working on
farms in return for room, board and education—in the best case, arranged by
a local board that supervised the child's treatment; or established residential
schools ("lodging houses") for abandoned children.

Aside from documenting the formation of these aid societies, Olasky essentially offers nothing to support an evaluation of their work—no description of
the social conditions of the nineteenth century, no before-and-after analysis,
no meaningful direct comparison of this approach with the so-called "outdoor
relief" approach's actual results. The vast, overwhelming majority of the book's
analysis consists of quoting various persons making pronouncements about
the (then) contemporary state of affairs. Though one must acknowledge that
there are some data difficulties, in this area Olasky commits the same error he
identifies in defenders of the welfare state: merely initiating a program does
not necessarily cause anything to change, and merely quoting well-known historical figures asserting that public assistance ruins the work ethic does not
establish the point, at least not for those who are disposed toward the benefits of relieving poverty directly rather than through indirect incentives. Would
Olasky be persuaded by a book that endlessly quotes Ted Kennedy and Jesse
Jackson giving lists of public programs that have been established and pronouncing them good? If not, why should skeptics be impressed with quotations from colonial sermons and Victorian newspaper essays? And the Victorian state poverty board studies that *are* quoted as more substantial evidence
of the ill effects of indiscriminate relief[18] tend, as they are written by state
boards, to deny the thesis that poverty relief is fueled by the opportunism of
bureaucracies of the state. We need some hard-headed evaluation of which
approaches actually do the greatest good, especially now that "taking the city
to the country" is simply not an option. It is certainly thinkable that personal
involvement and restrictive access to aid cause ennoblement, but many of us
know plenty of well-meaning, non-professional volunteers who are inefficient
and demeaning to those who "need their help," and plenty of children who

would have had a much more miserable life if they were denied support because of their parents' habits.

Later in this essay we will survey some current research evidence concerning the alleged work disincentives of the contemporary American welfare system; suffice it to say for now that, while I do not naturally warm to the American welfare system, even I have trouble being convinced that the disincentives are anything close to those claimed by Olasky.

The emphasis on reducing population density and bringing the city to the country also seems misplaced, at least as to modern implications. Many nations, with a population density much greater than that of the United States, can boast urban areas that are, by comparison, pristine. And the rural population of the United States is, by size, economic future and location, essentially irrelevant to urban problems. Even in Iowa, which produces roughly one-fourth of the nation's hogs and corn, only 5 percent of the state's population lives on farms. What might we expect to accomplish via a massive relocation of urban youth to Iowa? Surely our contemporary emphasis should fall on helping children have normal and healthy families, not on where this family lives or how many other families live nearby. I expect Olasky would respond that the best way to "normalize" a family is through personal engagement and limited access to aid. But he acknowledges that this approach resulted in severe urban problems already in the last century.

This brings us to Olasky's chronicle of objections and threats to the nineteenth-century consensus about charity. The first threat, apparently imported in part from England, was a demand for the provision of "outdoor relief," that is, relief not tied to the performance of work or life in a poorhouse. These calls began to surface in journalism of the 1840s. The earlier consensus had been that such an approach would create a disincentive to work and saving which creates more paupers even as one tries to reduce their number; that a rationalized government approach would be unable to adjust support standards to the nuances that should make an individual eligible or not, and that such aid was unable to touch the personal causes of poverty (most often intemperance in this era) in the way that personal, voluntary aid might. Turning a matter of love into one of litigation might also result in donor fatigue and harm the character of the well-off via jealousy and cynicism. Thus indiscriminate public aid might actually reduce, not increase, the amount of help going to the worthy poor.

But some mid-century journalists, beginning with Horace Greeley, challenged this consensus. Olasky ties Greeley's support of relief for able-bodied persons who do not work to Greeley's universalism and belief in the natural goodness of all people. For Greeley, salvation and prosperity are the right of every person, and the corrupting influences of capitalist society should be overturned by communal associations, including redistribution through collective agencies—an "unimpeded, unpurchased enjoyment" of each person's natural right to an equal part of the world's wealth.[19] In contrast to the earlier empha-

sis on the personal, moral transformation of individuals as a necessary requirement of fighting poverty, Greeley promoted an early social gospel: the centerpiece of Christianity is communal living and material redistribution, to be
accomplished not by churches and their members but by changing the economic environment along socialist lines to abolish the causes of poverty.
Human desires, being good in themselves, must be given full scope. The result
will be "universal happiness . . . a perfect Society . . . the Kingdom of Heaven."[20]

Thus Greeley set out the moral case for universal redistribution to a large
audience in the northeastern United States. Justifications for public welfare
multiplied in the 1850s, due partly to his influence. Olasky cites published
reports that, by the late 1850s, outdoor and poorhouse relief were rising, primarily due to changes in donor attitudes and, particularly after the Civil War,
to opportunistic legislators who benefited politically from offering handouts.

This upsurge in indiscriminate relief is very weakly documented by Olasky,
and we are left wondering about its extent and the plausibility of the argument
that it was responsible for the increasing incidence of miserable poverty in
American cities from the 1870s onward. Greeley had certainly recanted his
socialist position by 1869, denouncing the "thriftless vagabonds" who should
be given the choice to "work or starve."[21] If he and his cadre of journalists indeed
carried so much weight in public culture just twenty years earlier, one wonders why this change of heart did not lead to changes in outdoor relief, if it was
indeed to be blamed for urban problems.

Olasky argues that immigration and growing urbanization after the Civil
War also resulted in economic segregation—sharply defined areas of rich and
poor, with the rich riding from home to work rather than walking through
diverse neighborhoods. The wealthy, and their churches, were less likely to
meet the needy personally, instead, learning of them through the press. Voluntary aid became less attuned to the poor's actual needs. Without personal
contact, social "help" became less realistic or even destructively indiscriminate. Compassion fatigue set in.

This was a context ripe for Social Darwinism, a movement arguing that the
economically unfit must be eliminated, not "artificially" preserved. And spread
it did, throughout the 1870s into the 1880s. Olasky presents orthodox Christian believers as engaged in beating back both Social Darwinism and the "stingy
relief" of indiscriminate outdoor aid. Evangelicals sought to respond with new
forms of charity that removed government's indiscriminate, dependency-
forming relief while applying to harsher urban conditions the lessons taken
from earlier in the century. Olasky grants the emergence of involuntary unemployment and other sources of poverty which came about through no fault of
one's own; but Olasky maintains that open-handed charity without a work
requirement was likely to worsen the problem by creating willing paupers.
Evangelicals continued to insist that compassion should consist of suffering
with the marginalized, with donors becoming personal workers meeting more
than physical needs. This became especially important in anonymous urban

settings, where the character of recipients would be otherwise uncertain. Aid sometimes went as an interest-free loan as a further incentive to good faith, and recipients were linked to a church or individual whose work it was to move the applicant toward self-sufficiency.

By the mid-1880s the new evangelical approach had gained the upper hand in bookstores, but required an outpouring of volunteers to become effective. Denying that the next decade's events are too distant to be relevant to modern realities, Olasky lists dozens of urban organizations, quotes from their charters, and relates numbers of recipients to whom some form of aid was dispensed, in order to demonstrate that the outpouring of volunteerism was significant enough to constitute a sufficient response to urban poverty. Some cities saw engagements between the needy and volunteers numbering in the tens of thousands per year.

While one can't help but be moved by the many acts of compassion and initiative in these descriptions, this method of documenting impact has serious limitations. It does not account for actual effect on the poor; it measures "impact" in terms of inputs rather than effects. It also does not measure impact relative to other, potentially more effective alternatives, and it does not measure impact relative to the need of the population, the crucial question at this juncture of the argument. For example, tens of thousands of personal acts of kindness spread over a decade in New York must be measured relative to a population density of two hundred thousand per square mile. We would no doubt be unimpressed by a defense of the modern welfare state if it relied on the same approach to data. And this sudden flurry of activity, in an ironic way, documents one of the disadvantages of voluntary approaches: they may lack the staying power that we should expect of poverty programs, something that bureaucracies by their nature do well. Olasky acknowledges that his evaluation at this point is weak; he argues that the paucity of general statistics for the period forces one to rely on eyewitness reports and journalistic assessments. He ultimately appears to stake his argument on a single set of comments by Jacob Riis in 1890, pointing to New York's unprecedented recent growth and crowding and claiming that, whatever problems remained, the previous decade had brought dramatic improvement due to personal charity, and that charity would one day catch up with the emerging problems.

From this evidence, Olasky argues that late-nineteenth-century charity was marked by upward movement among the deserving poor (which he contrasts with intergenerational dependency today). He asserts that this was no anti-statist spirit, that all acknowledged that private agencies could be as bad as government ones; although the force of his argument seems to cut against this claim. And he gives seven general attributes that fueled and characterized the works of compassion: *affiliation* (fighting the tendency of men and other family members to abandon their families; rebonding the marginalized to the community), *bonding* (with volunteers, when no other natural tie to community could be reinforced), *categorization* (ensuring that charity goes to the willing-to-work or otherwise worthy, including children with one parent unable to support them), *discernment* (which allows categorization through personal knowledge of the poor and "the benign suspicion that came naturally to charity workers who had grown up reading the Bible"),[22] *employment* (eventually, if not immediately, for all able-bodied heads of households, though this emphasis "would have been savage had jobs not been available"[23] and if "alternatives to begging did not exist during short-lived periods of unemployment"),[24] *freedom* (defined by Olasky as the opportunity to work and worship without governmental restriction, bribery, or restrictive licensing requirements),[25] and *God* (accounting for spiritual needs and sources of problems, the possibility of conversion and change, and emphasizing "suffering with" on the part of donors). These seven attributes form the framework for asking what has gone wrong with American compassion in our own time.

Olasky, the Social Gospel, and the Poor

For Olasky, the beginning of the great descent (near the turn of the century) was the desire "to do more." Despite contributions by volunteers, much of urban life remained stubbornly dysfunctional at the turn of the century. Olasky argues that the call for public initiatives was precipitated by a universalist, social gospel theology, with its denial of the fallenness of real human beings and their need for personal conversion and moral regeneration:

> Underlying this demand for mass transformation was the belief that man was naturally good and productive unless an oppressive system got in the way . . . . Ignoring the experience of the 1860s and 1870s, and harkening back to the commune spirit of the 1840s and the Greeleyite message of that era, their faith was clear: the only reason some people did not work was that they were kept from working.[26]

Hence the social gospelers called for universalistic and unconditional aid, and were embarrassed by the evangelical emphasis on personal regeneration. This approach "became the inspiration of governmental social work programs of the 1930s and community action programs of the 1960s."[27]

This is certainly a key juncture in Olasky's argument, and deserves richer support. It might appear to be an ace-in-the-hole argument: volunteers had supplied all the legitimate needs, and those remaining poor were marginal by choice due to personal sloth that should be judged and excluded from aid. An alternative reading would be that terrible social conditions persisted because voluntary aid was minuscule relative to the problems, as well as inefficient in delivery. Even Olasky acknowledges that by the 1890s the lack of coordination among voluntary agencies led to calls *from the voluntary organizations themselves* for government to be the hub that would force organizations to use careful methods, to limit relief by districts to avoid overlapping and fraud, and to keep accurate statistics.[28] Olasky also concedes that sectarian warfare over the funding of social programs had seriously eroded volunteerism's ability to respond effectively, or even to give a consistent story about whether governmental or voluntary responses to need were preferred.[29]

Most of the question of the proper approach to poverty hangs on this issue, and the related questions of how much poverty is induced by "outdoor" relief and how much impersonal financial aid erodes the condition of the soul. These are not satisfactorily documented in the book, and we shall see that the research evidence concerning welfare's work disincentive effects tends to contradict Olasky. Civil servants and non-evangelistic workers are presumed to be less caring and personally involved; spiritual causes of poverty are presumed to dominate; contrary readings of history are simply dismissed as "conventional" or "liberal." When forced to acknowledge that horrible social conditions persisted under voluntary relief, the argument ultimately becomes a statement that things were improving, however slowly, and that public assistance, by its nature, creates more poverty and undermines the human spirit.[30] The question deserves a dispassionate study.

Having failed to establish these points, it may border on bad faith to claim that people who sought to supplement volunteerism's successes with other approaches were motivated by social-gospel universalism. Surely this is not the only possibility, nor the most obvious explanation. Many people, including those directly involved in volunteerism, apparently did not think it was working very well in this era and these circumstances. Seeking the involvement of government when things are not working well is not necessarily a sign of bad theology. In fact, it can be a sign of good theology, which has correctly rejected a pure libertarianism as inconsistent with the Christian tradition.

Moving into the Twentieth Century

Beginning with the Theodore Roosevelt administration, Olasky documents the slow development of a federal presence in welfare policy, and the growing emphasis on professionalism (and the displacement of volunteerism) in social work. Olasky again associates this professionalization of social work with liberal theological commitments.[31] Donors distanced themselves from recipients, both geographically and empathically; boards of charities became fund-raising bodies; bonding was reduced to photos of grateful clients; discernment was lost in self-satisfying reports to donors. The more secularized social relief movements (such as the settlement house movement) tended to lose their initial stress on personal contact. Large-scale social change was stressed over personal involvement and conversion. Many religious programs had become functionally secularized; there seemed no reason but "conservative stinginess" to oppose massive new governmental systems,[32] especially when private agencies had difficulties responding personally to the mass needs and reduced donations of the 1930s. Thus, through theological liberalization and the long-term depersonalization of charity, the stage was set for large-scale change under the New Deal.

One wonders about Olasky's emphasis on the necessity of relief involving personal conversion and moral renewal. Of course conversion and renewal are of terrific importance, and no doubt they are the ultimate answer to many of the problems of the poor. But do we require the same emphasis in the other social institutions by which we live each day? Does anyone criticize the local grocery chain for not emphasizing the fact that we do not eat by bread alone? Perhaps if they did we would have less obesity. Do we fret that gas stations do not lobby their patrons to quit speeding? Perhaps we would have a lower highway mortality rate. Or would we champion a human resources department of a major corporation if it withheld salaries of employees until there was evidence that the employee is tithing?

In all cases we should answer "no." Isn't this because there is a difference between the "common grace" institutions that make civilization possible among persons who are not redeemed, and the "special grace" institutions that press forward the gospel into lives and cultures? If this distinction is a legitimate one, which I think it is, we would need a careful argument from Olasky that the institutions by which we care for each other when marginalized should by nature be considered special grace institutions; otherwise I suspect we could construct a diatribe against any organization of society that does not preach while it works—groceries, gas stations, government, anything. No doubt each might "work better" if it considered spiritual sources of dysfunction, at least if it did so well. But experience shows that even well-intentioned practitioners often get it wrong, hence, the human tendency toward pluralism and our reliance on common grace institutions for daily-bread-items, surrounded by special-grace institutions to help us advance the gospel.

The presumption that public charity always displaces private compassion and erodes the moral sensibilities of the recipients is also arguable. It is not enough, for Olasky, to say that this happened in the particular historical circumstance of the United States in the twentieth century. Olasky is claiming more: that this is a universal truth and that we must choose one approach or the other. Why should this be so?

Why, for example, can't the two be complementary? I think of driving around my medium-sized city. Safe and efficient travel depends absolutely on hundreds of small voluntary acts of charity, self-discipline, and empathy on the part of the drivers surrounding me. But does it somehow displace this private philanthropy to have posted speed limits, enforcement police, weather advisories, and road repair crews? We could just rely on the innate, voluntary goodness of drivers to patch up their own roads, voluntarily limit speeds to safe levels, and so forth. But that would be foolish. (It would also be an instance of the kind of naive utopian theology that believes in the innate goodness of all persons, a theology Olasky says he despises.) Public welfare policies, in these cases, *make more private charitable acts possible.* It would be impossible to exercise civility while driving a car if driving conduct were left entirely to a spontaneous, voluntary social contract. Why might this not be true in other situations involving the basic fabric of our lives?

But we are assured in *The Tragedy of American Compassion* that in the decades since 1930, cold public entitlement has slowly displaced effective voluntary compassion. Olasky acknowledges that the unemployment of the 1930s was different than before, with long-term layoffs that were not due to personal problems. Yet a strong stigma persisted against making use of public relief (which Olasky applauds); aid was generally only given when no relative could support the needy, and federal programs were proposed as short-term solutions primarily aimed at widows, orphans, and the disabled, not as enduring entitlements. The alternative of choice, Franklin Roosevelt's Works Progress Administration, tried to provide income while maintaining a work ethic.

In the process the social work profession organized itself, emphasizing the professionalization of compassion and permanence for their programs. It gained influence in the Roosevelt administration.

Olasky identifies three other subtle changes that directed the nation toward a universalistic welfare system with no work requirements: a decreased sense of personal responsibility and increased emphasis on collective action; a trend toward impersonal urban service over successful personal contact and true suffering-with compassion; and an ideological leftism among social workers that trivialized individuals, viewed income as entitlement, and did not value work or fear pauperization. Olasky dismisses studies undertaken during the following twenty years that claimed stipends do not harm independence and self-respect, or that found that federal involvement reduced administrative abuses, inefficiency and political control.[33] He finds little popular support for universal entitlement throughout the 1940s and 1950s. In the end, he concludes that the New Deal's primary effect was to establish an *organizational basis* for social revolution, not establish the revolution itself.

The 1960s: Revolution in American Compassion

A revolution came in the mid- to late 1960s. At last we come to the meat of the argument: Olasky affirms that, even through the early '60s, "many of the old values were retained both by welfare workers and recipients."[34] Workers in New York were still told that withholding assistance was often as important as giving relief; applicants had to verify eligibility; often unwed mothers had to promise not to have male callers under improper conditions. Shame was still a healthy motivator. "As late as the mid–1960s, only about half of those eligible for welfare payments were receiving them."[35]

This means that Olasky's analysis of the 1960s is crucial to the case he is building that American compassion has taken a tragic turn for the worse. The core of his case is this: the 1960s brought about a sea change in *attitudes.* "The key contribution of the War on Poverty (was) the deliberate attempt to uncouple welfare from shame by changing attitudes of both welfare recipients and the better-off."[36] "Great Society legislation, not so much by extending benefits as by funding advocates to change that consciousness, helped sever welfare from shame in the minds of many dole-holders."[37]

Living on the public dole became not a humiliation, but (in recipients' eyes) a way to preserve dignity. A war on shame was waged, undergirded by "the theologically liberal tendencies within social work (and related fields)."[38] Support for the practice of categorizing individuals as "deserving" or "undeserving" declined,[39] and a growing clamor for state intervention was fueled by a combination of philosophical materialism, economic relativism, and political progressivism. These combined to force the conclusion that eliminating poverty was merely a matter of passing out enough dollars to bring all households' income levels above the poverty line through subsidies.[40] Mainline churches approved of the open-handed attitude toward impersonal support, holding to a social cause and therefore a social solution for poverty. In the process many of the traditional, private social agencies were compromised in their commitment to principles of mutual obligation.[41] The legal profession, for self-serving reasons, fueled the movement away from categorization and discernment.[42] It became difficult or impossible to declare recipients employable and therefore ineligible, or to require that recipients not have a "man in the house."

Thus President Johnson's expansion of Great Society public welfare programs, a sudden replay of the New Deal from a position of economic strength, displayed a rosy disregard for real-life effects, and was based ultimately on a faith, a social gospel walking on earth.[43] It attempted to replace shame with a conviction that the system was the enemy.[44] The result, according to Olasky, was a dramatic increase in the number of welfare recipients from the mid-1960s to the mid–1970s. "The major change was that a much higher percentage of those who were eligible suddenly decided to take advantage of welfare benefits. . . ."[45] "The Great Society's War Against Shame was a success."[46]

I believe that this analysis of the 1960s and its aftermath is simply wrong. It may be that Olasky's background in journalism has led him to his focus on media reports, with their stereotypical portrayal of "welfare mamas" and silence about the majority of urban residents who struggle to lead decent lives. Or it could be that he and I simply have an honest disagreement over the evidence. In any event, we have come to the point where we need to consider some of the current research on the alleged negative work effects and reduction of a sense of stigma due to the modern welfare system.

Consider Robert Moffitt's classic review of the literature by professional economists on the modern history of AFDC and other welfare policies, and those policies' effects on stigma, labor force participation, work effort, intergenerational welfare dependency, marriage and cohabitation, and other behaviors.[47] First, consider the notion of a modern "war on stigma," upon which

Olasky stakes his analysis. I have reproduced Moffitt's figure 1,[48] which tracks the number of AFDC participants and the real (inflation-adjusted) sum of benefits for which families were eligible.[49] The number of participants closely follows the benefit sum. There is no evidence whatsoever of a long-run change in attitudes independent of benefit levels, or change in the stigma associated with welfare receipt. Olasky reports (as an indication of how much things changed during the '60s) that as late as the mid–1960s only about half of those eligible for welfare payments were receiving them.[50] Moffitt's corresponding figure for 1970, at the crest of the sea change in attitudes Olasky asserts, is 38 percent for the food stamp program, 43 percent for the AFDC-U program, and 69 percent for AFDC.[51] This is hardly a successful "war on stigma," especially when we recall that the unemployment and inflation rates in 1970 presented a more economically challenging circumstance than the low-inflation growth of the early to mid–1960s.

As benefits rose from the 1940s through the 1960s, so did participation; when benefit levels fell in the 1970s and 1980s, participation did so as well. There simply was no golden era before the early 1960s, no attitudinal fall from grace caused by Great Society programs.

Now let us review the related work by economists on the effects of the welfare state upon work effort.[52] It is true that only 5–6 percent of AFDC recipients work, though of those who do work, over 50 percent work full-time at low wages.

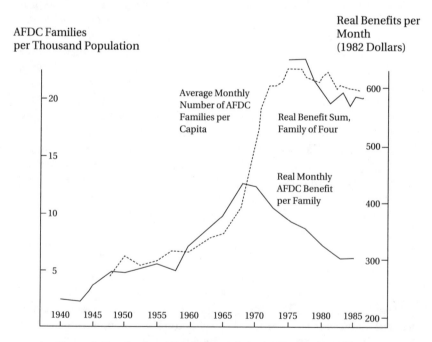

Figure 1. Caseload and Benefit Trends in the U.S. Welfare System

Yet there is not much evidence that these low labor force participation rates are due to the AFDC program. As benefit levels (and the rates at which benefits are reduced as earned income increases, and benefit-earnings ratios, and unemployment rates) have altered dramatically during the last thirty-five years, the labor supply decisions of female heads of households have been extremely inflexible. Employment rates and hours worked by female heads of households were virtually unchanged between 1968 and 1987, despite sea changes in the welfare system. In fact, female heads-of-households (simply "female heads" from now on) as a group have higher employment rates than women as a whole, and work about the same number of hours per year as women as a whole. Their employment rates are about the same as never-married women, and greater than married women, despite lower average wages and levels of "human capital" (such as education). This accounts for the surprising reality that female head earnings are, on average, greater than earnings of other women.

So it is not at all clear that there is a "problem" with low work effort or earnings among female heads that requires a solution. The major difference between female heads and other women is the absence of second incomes to help support children, and the absence of other non-transfer (i.e., non-welfare) sources of income. Sixty percent of the average female-headed-family household income is the female head's earnings, with only 20 percent due to other non-transfer sources and 20 percent from transfers.

There is of course some effect of transfer payments on work effort, but the many studies of this phenomenon converge to the estimate that, for the average welfare family, the loss of earned income amounts to roughly $1000 per year. This is not trivial, but not a large enough effect to be a significant cause of female-headed-household poverty. Put differently, nearly all AFDC recipients would have few enough hours worked and low enough incomes to qualify for AFDC, even if the program had not existed. At most about 5 percent of participants are persons who "switch" from ineligible-employed status to recipient status as a result of the existence of the programs, so that over 95 percent of the caseload would meet the standards for eligibility if no program existed. Thus dependency/participation does not appear to be due to the work disincentives of the AFDC system. If we add in the effect of the Food Stamp program, the additional disincentives appear to reduce earned income by $200 per year; Medicaid appears to have a smaller effect than Food Stamps.

One might fret that, even if welfare benefits have not caused less work effort for the female-headed households that exist, they may have increased the number of such households by restricting benefits to homes where a male is not present, thus reducing work effort via a more indirect means. Perhaps by creating an economic incentive to form female-headed households the welfare system has been a driving force behind the rise of illegitimacy, divorce and cohabitation. But both time-series and econometric studies are unable to find a consistent fit between benefit levels (which have generally been falling since 1975) and illegitimacy, divorce, female-headed-household formation, or fertility rates. If there is a relationship, it appears to be between benefit levels and the form the female-headed household takes (i.e., living with parents or living independently), not (or only very weakly) between benefits and illegitimacy *per se*. Even these potential relationships are empirically much too small to account for the changes in female headship and illegitimacy over the last thirty years.

The cumulative effect of this literature leads me to believe that the 1960s and 1970s do not constitute the social revolution that Olasky reports. But let us rejoin the logic of his book, now approaching its end. Olasky asserts that by 1980 there were several big losers from the entitlement revolution of the 1960s. Social mobility declined, not due to lack of opportunity but presumably due to the change in attitudes Olasky attributes to the 1960s. The remnant of vigorous private empowerment and relief organizations was marginalized. And marriage declined as a viable bond of mutual obligation. Olasky argues that "government entitlements . . . did influence heavily the choice of whether to choose parenting or adoption, whether to marry or not, and whether to live at home or in an apartment." He gives no citation to back this claim, but says that marital obligations decreased as governmental obligations increased, making it viable to raise children alone.

Below, I reproduce figure 4 from Moffitt's paper on the incentive effects of the welfare system.[53] It is clear here that the long-term upward trend in female headship, divorce and illegitimacy are not correlated with the rising-then-falling benefit sum of all transfer payments, and would have an even weaker relationship to AFDC payments if considered separately. "The evidence does not support the hypothesis that the welfare system has been responsible for the time-series growth in female headship and illegitimacy."[54]

I cite these research conclusions that contradict Olasky because I think it is important to pick up the right end of the hammer before you begin striking things. If the changes in welfare policy over the last thirty years have not had a dramatic effect on stigma, attitudes, work effort or marriage patterns, this is news that a conservative should warm to, not try to contradict. It shows that conservatives were right all these years to say that people are not primarily the product of their environment. They are more than that, and less. They have a nature, one that is not that easily corrupted by economic incentives, yet one that often obstinately continues in inappropriate behavior. This also means that conservatives don't need to capture the political process and dramatically reshape welfare policy in order to do good; the policy itself hasn't really ruined people, and public policy changes themselves may not do that much to change people's behavior. People still need to be regenerated, one at a time, and we don't have to wait for the presumed negative effects of the welfare system to be changed before we can dig in and begin to see lives improved.

Olasky ends with a discussion indicating how personal compassion can make a difference in addressing the difficult poverty-related problems of homelessness and the abandonment of women and children. He will find few crit-

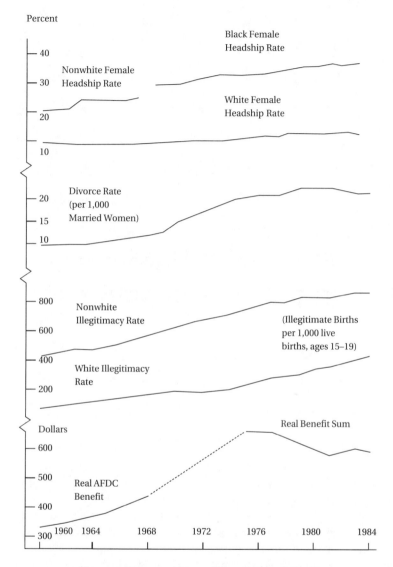

Figure 4. Demographic and Benefit Trends, by Race

ics for the notion that personal, costly compassion, when feasible, is preferable to mass-produced impersonal relief. We may be left wondering if such personal compassion is in fact feasible on a large enough scale, and how churches might begin to point the way toward such compassion now that the political system has essentially accepted Olasky's analysis. These questions will no doubt form a large part of the evaluation of welfare reform in the years to come.

~ 6 ~

Income Distribution
in the United States

George N. Monsma, Jr., Calvin College

Introduction

The slow trend toward a more equal distribution of income among families in the United States from the end of World War II until about 1974 was reversed during the next two decades. The distribution has been roughly stable from 1993 through 1996 (the last year for which statistics were available at the time this was written), but this has left income considerably less equally distributed now than it was in the mid–1970s.

In fact this trend toward inequality was so strong that family income in the United States is less equally distributed now than it has been at any time since World War II. The shares going to the lowest 20 percent, the second 20 percent and the middle 20 percent of families are all lower, and the share going to the top 20 percent higher, than they have been at any other time in the last fifty years.[1] Adjusted for inflation, the average income of families in the lowest 20 percent of the population was about 10 percent less in 1996 than it was in 1974.[2] (Many economists believe the inflation measures used to adjust the data were overestimates of the actual inflation. If so the average income of the lowest 20 percent would not have fallen this much, and may not have fallen at all.) And while the average income of families in the lowest 20 percent was 13 percent above the average poverty-line income for their families in 1974, it was 4 percent below it in 1996.[3]

What has caused these changes? Should Christians be concerned about them? And if so, what policies should we be advocating to deal with them and the problems they cause?

To address these questions this chapter will look briefly at some biblical principles relevant to an evaluation of the distribution of income in a society (section II); present some data regarding income distribution and its changes over the last two decades (section III); discuss the determinants of the distribution of income in a primarily market economy and apply this theory to the United States (section IV); discuss the causes of the changes in the distribution of income during the last two decades (section V); and briefly suggest some policies that might be used to raise the incomes of those at the bottom of the distributions, and thus decrease the inequality (section VI).[4] Throughout, particular emphasis will be given to families in the lower part of the income distribution.

Biblical Principles

Since other chapters have discussed important biblical principles related to an evaluation of a nation's income distribution, particularly the question of justice, only a brief treatment is included here.[5]

God, the Creator of the world, owns everything in it (Ps. 24:1–2). He has entrusted his creation to human beings as his stewards, his trustees (Gen. 2:15; Matt. 25:14–30). Along with this high calling of stewardship, he has given us instructions about how his resources are to be used.

Among his instructions for use of his world are that we are to use it productively to meet human needs (Gen. 1:26–31; 2:15), while also caring for it and preserving it (Gen. 2:15; Deut. 20:19–20; 22:6–7). We are to use it out of love for God and our neighbors (Matt. 22:36–40). An important part of this is using the resources he has entrusted to us to establish economic justice in society (Deut. 27:19; Jer. 7:5–7; Ezek. 18:5–9; Mic. 6:8). All individuals and families have an obligation to act justly in the use of their resources, but those with authority in governments have a special calling to establish justice, and a special responsibility for justice (Prov. 31:8–9; Jer. 22:3, 15–16).

Since we are called to use God's resources to establish economic justice, and since people differ a great deal in their views on what is just, we must ask what the Bible teaches about economic justice.

The laws God gave for the economic life of the people of Israel are a fruitful source of guidance. Enacting these specific laws in the United States is neither required nor wise, given the vast economic, social, and religious differences between the United States and ancient Israel. But if we ask what effects they would have had in Israel if they had been obeyed, this will give us evidence about what is required for economic justice in a society, especially if we find support for these conditions as standards of justice elsewhere in the Bible.

The Mosaic laws granted rights for the use and control of property to families, but limited these property rights in many ways. These limitations, if obeyed, would have assured that all families (and individuals without a family) would always have access to the consumption goods they would need for life in their society. This was done in various ways, including limiting the rights of a farmer to harvest all that his land and labor had produced, and giving the poor and sojourners the right to glean and harvest the corners of the fields (Lev. 19:9–10). In addition, part of the tithe was used to feed the poor (Deut. 14:28–29). Israelites were commanded to give interest-free loans to those in need, and when doing so, necessities could not be kept as collateral and the loans were to be canceled every Sabbatical year if they could not be paid by that time (Deut. 15:1–2, 7–10; 23:19–20; 24:6, 12–13).

But dependence on gleanings, tithes, and loans was not to be the normal condition. The laws also gave each family the opportunity to work to support itself, and, at least in the longer run, the opportunity to control the use of its own labor and a share of the other productive resources of society. Normally each family would have control over the land, labor, and other resources necessary to produce enough for dignified life in its society.

When necessary in extreme circumstances, an Israelite could sell his labor for a period of time, i.e., become an "indentured servant" (this term more accurately conveys the legal status of an Israelite man who sold himself to another Israelite than does the more commonly used term "slave"). Perpetual slavery was forbidden. When the time of service was complete, the master was obligated to free the servant, and give him generous provision from his fields, flocks and vineyards (Deut. 15:12–14).

Families were forbidden to sell the productive land the Lord had entrusted to them. Although they could lease it to another until the next Year of Jubilee, their nearest relatives were to redeem it for them, if possible. They were also allowed to cancel the lease whenever they could return payment for the remaining years (Lev. 25:8–17, 23–28).

Thus the laws the Lord gave to the nation of Israel, if followed, would have provided all families at most times with ownership and control over the resources required to provide for their needs in an agrarian society (i.e., land, labor, and the things needed for growing more food and for sustenance until the next harvest). They also would have provided mechanisms for families to regain these things if they had lost the ability to provide for themselves. And they provided access to necessities during the period when they couldn't provide for themselves.

Are these abiding standards for economic justice, or are they just incidental outcomes of the laws the Lord gave to Israel? Other biblical passages indicate that they indeed are standards for justice. Through his prophets the Lord condemned both individuals and governments when they failed to give all families these opportunities. For example, Isaiah 5:1–7 records the Lord's con-demnation of those who build up such concentrations of homes and land that others do not have enough. Jeremiah 38:8–22 records the Lord's condemna-tion of those who rob others of control over their labor by re-enslaving them after their prescribed terms of service were completed. The prophets also bring the Lord's condemnation on nations and their rulers when they fail to uphold the rights of the poor (Isa. 4:1–10) and on those who live in luxury in the face of poverty (Isa. 3:16–4:1; Amos chapters 4–6).[6] But the Lord promised bless-ings to those who use resources justly and care for the poor (Isa. 58:6–12).

Although the New Testament speaks little about the conditions for eco-nomic justice from the point of view of the society as a whole, nowhere does it contradict or cancel the Old Testament standards for economic justice, and it repeatedly calls us to care for the poor among us.

Christ served the poor (both the materially poor and spiritually poor), and called his followers to follow him in service to those in need (Matt. 11:4–5; Luke 4:18–19; 14:12–14). The epistles call Christians to radical sharing to help the poor (2 Cor. 8:8–15; James 1:27; 1 John 3:16–18), and the early church practiced this (Acts 2:44–45; 4:32–37).

People are called to work to support themselves and others, in the New Tes-tament as well as in the Old (Eph. 4:28; 1 Thess. 4:11–12; 2 Thess. 3:6–13). Thus we can conclude that a just society must provide people with opportunities for such work.

Paul calls rulers God's servants for good and for the restraint of evil (Rom. 13:1–7). Since, in the Old Testament, instructions to rulers about ruling prop-erly included establishing economic justice, and these instructions are not can-celed in the New Testament, we must conclude that rulers' service for good and for the restraint of evil includes establishing justice, in the New Testament era as well as in the Old.

Thus, in summary, the Bible teaches us that:

1. We who have been entrusted with God's resources have only a limited right to the personal use of them and to what we produce with them.
2. All people have a duty to use God's resources productively to meet their families' needs and the needs of others.
3. Societies have a duty to provide just structures (including just systems of property rights).
4. Economic justice requires structures that allow all families access to the basic necessities of life in their society, the opportunity to work to sup-port themselves (including access to the other resources needed to make their work productive), and the opportunity to make responsible deci-sions about the use of their labor and a share of the other resources of the earth.[7] Since these opportunities are influenced by relative levels of income and wealth, as well as absolute levels, economic justice also

requires that wealth, income, and economic power in societies are distributed evenly enough so that all can have these opportunities.[8]

U.S. Income Distribution During the Last Two Decades

No matter how it is measured, the distribution of total family income in the United States is very unequal, and has become more so in the last two decades. Table 1 shows data on family income in 1974 and 1996 for families grouped into fifths of all families, ranked from the lowest-income to the highest-income families. The data are based on the Census Bureau's Current Population Survey, the most extensive and widely used source of data on family income in a given year.[9]

The data in table 1 (see p. 187) show that for each of the four lower fifths, the share of total income received declined. The lowest fifth lost over 20 percent of its meager share, and the second fifth lost over 15 percent of its share; the next two fifths lost lesser proportions of their shares. Only the share of the top fifth increased, and most of its increase went to the top 5 percent of families. The mean income of the top fifth was about seven times that of the lowest fifth in 1974; it was eleven times higher in 1996. The real mean income of the lowest fifth was about 10 percent lower in 1996 than in 1974, that of the second fifth was approximately the same, and those of the three upper fifths rose. Both the absolute and percent increases in real income were greater the higher the fifth.[10]

The data in table 1 do not distinguish among various population groups. But since both the average incomes and the distributions vary between groups, it is important to briefly look at disaggregated data if we wish to have a fuller understanding of the distribution. As table 2 shows, average incomes are lower for blacks and Hispanics than for whites, and the shares of their total incomes going to the lower fifths is smaller. These two factors combine to make the mean incomes of the lowest fifths of black and Hispanic families much lower than they are for whites. Similar patterns were present in 1974.

Although the data in tables 1 and 2 give a picture of the overall distribution, they are not adjusted for any differences that may exist in the sizes of families in the various fifths. It is important to consider this factor, since larger families need more income in order to function at any given level. The Census Bureau also publishes data on the "Average Income-to-Poverty Ratios" for families by fifths. This ratio for a family equals its income divided by the poverty-line income for a family of its size. Table 3 shows these ratios for 1974 and 1996. It shows that large differences remain when the data are adjusted for family size, and that the inequality increased substantially between 1974 and 1994. In 1974 this adjusted-income figure for the top fifth was six times that of the lowest fifth; in 1996 it was ten times higher; both are just slightly less than the proportions in the unadjusted data in table 1. The figures in table 3 also show that the money incomes of the families in the lower fifth did not keep pace with the rising poverty line during these two decades. Family income in the lowest fifth was, on average, 13 percent above the poverty line, although the incomes of many of the families were below it. But in 1996 the average income of the families in the lowest fifth was less than the poverty line. The income-to-poverty ratio remained about the same for the second fifth, and the top three fifths all gained, with the percentage and absolute gains rising as one moves up the income scale.

Another limitation of the statistics presented above is that they include only pre-tax money income. But families' economic welfare is also influenced by taxes and in-kind income. Table 4 contains data for the distribution of "family disposable income" by fifths for 1974 and 1995 (1996 data were not available). This measure deducts net payroll and income taxes from the money income figure used in the data above and adds energy assistance and food stamps to income. The income is also adjusted for the size and composition of the families. Since single individuals are included as families in this data, the figures are not directly comparable to those in the previous tables. These adjustments do not change the basic pattern from that portrayed by the official Census Bureau data reported in table 1; however, the degree of inequality in 1995 and the growth in inequality since 1974 in these data is somewhat smaller.

Table 5 contains income-to-poverty data which include a partial adjustment for taxes and non-cash income. The data are published for households rather than families, and the fifths are based on numbers of persons rather than numbers of families, so they are not directly comparable to the data presented above. The data are only available for a few selected years starting in 1979. Data based on pre-tax money income for households are given for comparison.

As can been seen, the partial adjustments for taxes and non-money transfers reduce the inequality in income (e.g., in 1994 the pre-tax money income of the top quintile was eleven times that of the lowest, but "only" eight times higher by the adjusted measure). And the average income of the lowest fifth comes closer to its average poverty line. But even after this adjustment, much inequality remains, and the lower fifths have still lost ground since 1979 in relation to the poverty-line income.

The highly unequal distribution of income in the United States leaves many people living in poverty, and the number of poor people, and the proportion of the population who are poor, are higher now than they were two decades ago.[11] Table 6 contains data on the proportion of persons and families in various categories who were poor in 1974 and 1996 by the official government definition. (The official definition is based on pre-tax money income, including cash welfare and social insurance payments. The poverty line is adjusted for family size; in 1996 it was $12,516 for a family of three and $16,036 for a family of four.)[12] The proportion of persons living below the poverty level rose from 11.2 percent in 1974 to 13.7 percent in 1996. Likewise, the poverty rates for most groups rose over this period.[13] As can be seen in the table, the poverty rates are higher for blacks and Hispanics than for whites, for children than for adults, and for families where no husband is present than for married-couple families.[14] The figures for black and Hispanic children, and for black and Hispanic families without a husband present, are particularly high, all 40–50 percent in 1996.

The data in table 6 are official poverty statistics, based on pre-tax cash income, including government cash transfers such as welfare and social security payments. The Census Bureau also publishes some statistics based on other income concepts, taking into account some taxes and non-cash forms of income. The most comprehensive of these subtracts Social Security payroll taxes, federal income taxes (net of the Earned Income Tax Credit), and state income taxes from income, and adds to income the values of capital gains received, Medicare, regular-price school lunches, and means-tested government non-cash transfers (such as Medicaid, food stamps, free and reduced-price school lunches, and rent subsidies). It shows somewhat lower poverty rates; for example, 10.3 percent of the population was poor in 1996 by this measure, compared with 13.7 percent by the official measure. Adding the net imputed value of return on home equity reduced the rate to 9.3 percent of the population. But the relative intensities of poverty among persons and children by race and ethnic group reported in table 5 are not changed substantially by these adjustments. Nor is the increase in the percent of the population which was poor over the period since 1979 (the first year for which the adjusted figures are available).[15] And one can question whether the poverty line should not be raised if these non-cash items are included in income; otherwise many families would be removed from the poor category even though they have little available cash income with which to meet their needs not covered by the categorical programs.

The above data are all based on incomes of families (or households) for a particular year. The inequalities and the very low incomes for the lowest fifth in a given year would be less serious if this were just a temporary situation for those with low income. To take an extreme, hypothetical example: if family income were equally distributed over a period of ten years, but for any particular family income varied a lot from year to year, the inequality would not be a serious problem if credit were available at moderate interest rates to those who had to borrow during low-income years. Thus the annual data should be supplemented by data that follow families over a period of time, to see if the distribution is more equal over longer periods of time. Particularly important is the question of whether or not families in the lowest fifth, those whose income in relation to their needs is the greatest, stay at low income levels for long periods of time. This is the issue of family income mobility.

There are fewer data available on income mobility over time than on income in particular years, and the analysis of them presents more problems, but a number of studies have been done with data from the Panel Study of Income Dynamics (PSID). Isabel Sawhill and Daniel McMurrer report on a number of studies using PSID data. Most of the studies found that over various ten-year periods during the last three decades, approximately 40–50 percent of families who started in the lowest fifth had moved to a higher fifth by the end of the ten-year period (these studies excluded families whose chief earner was of school or college age at the beginning of the period, or of retirement age at the end). But many of those who moved up moved only to the second fifth. And many from the second fifth moved down. Even studies that looked at a longer period than ten years do not show much more mobility. Overall, the general pattern shown in a study by Gottschalk for the period 1968–1991 is that over two-thirds of families end in the fifth where they began, or move only to an adjacent fifth.[16]

Looking at the data in another way, Peter Gottschalk reports that averaging incomes over a seventeen-year period (1974–1991) gave an estimate of inequality about one-third lower than using annual income (he used PSID data and measured inequality by the ratio of the income of the family at the ninetieth percentile to that of the family at the tenth percentile in the distribution).[17] Studies that have tried to determine whether the degree of mobility has changed over time have either found that it has not (most of them), or in a few cases have found decreases in mobility.[18] Thus the data indicate that very substantial inequalities in income remain over long periods of time, with many families suffering from low incomes for periods of a decade and more. And there is no evidence that the increase in inequality in annual incomes in the United States has been offset by any increase in mobility over time.

If we compare the distribution of income in the United States to the distribution in other high income countries, we find that the distribution in the United States is less equal than in most. Peter Gottschalk and Timothy Smeeding report that the distribution of disposable income in the United States, as measured by the ratio of the income (adjusted for family size) of the person at the tenth percentile to the income of the person at the ninetieth percentile, was greater in the United States than in any of the eighteen other wealthy OECD (Organization for Economic Cooperation and Development) countries. The average ratio was 3.52; for the United States it was 5.78; the United Kingdom, the next highest country, had a ratio of 4.67. The income of the person at the tenth percentile was only 36 percent of the median income in the United States, compared with an average of 53 percent for all of the countries.[19] In fact, in a comparison of fourteen OECD countries, the people living in households at the tenth percentile had a lower absolute income (adjusted for family size) than people in any of the other countries, even though the median income was higher in the United States than in any of the others. The average income at the tenth percentile in the thirteen other nations was over 20 percent higher than in the United States, although their median income was 16 percent lower, and their average income at the ninetieth percentile was 30 percent lower.[20] Not only is income inequality greater in the United States, it has also been increasing at a faster rate than in most other high-income countries. After examining studies of changes in income inequality during the 1980s in nine-teen wealthy countries, Gottschalk and Smeeding conclude that only two oth-ers, the United Kingdom and Sweden, had increases in inequality close to that of the United States, and Sweden started from such an equal distribution that it still has a much more equal distribution.[21]

Edward Wolff reports on a number of other studies using data from the Lux-embourg Income Study. These studies, using various methods of measuring inequality and data from various years, always found the United States among the most unequal; often it was the most unequal. In a study of seven high-income countries the percent of income going to the lowest fifth was consid-erably lower for the United States than for any of the other countries, both before and after adjustment for taxes and family size. And in a study of eleven high-income countries the inequality, as measured either by the ratio of the income at the tenth percentile to the median income or by the ratio of the income at the tenth percentile to the income at the ninetieth, was consider-ably greater in the United States than in any of the other countries (based on data from the mid–1980s). And the United States was the only country in this study for which the inequality had increased substantially from the late 1970s/early 1980s to the mid–1980s.[22] Regarding the relative degree of mobil-ity in income over time in various OECD countries, Gottschalk reports that the mobility rates in the United States differ little from those of other countries. Thus the higher inequality in annual income is not offset by higher mobility, and the United States remains among the least equal when we look at multi-ple-year earnings.[23]

In summary the data show:

1. The distribution of income in the United States is very unequal.
2. It has become increasingly unequal during the period since the mid–1970s.
3. It is very unequal even when viewed over periods of a decade or more.
4. It is less equal than that of most, if not all, other high-income countries.
5. This inequality leaves the lowest-income people in the United States with lower incomes than those of people in other high-income coun-tries, even though the average income in those countries is less than that of the United States.
6. This inequality leaves many people with meager incomes in relation to what is necessary for them to live and participate in our society.

Determinants of Income Distribution in a Market Economy

In order to understand why we have such a distribution of income in the United States, and why it has changed as it has during the last two decades, we must understand what determines the distribution of income in a basically market economy. In a market economy, the most important determinant of a family's income is the market value of the resources it owns and offers for sale in the market. The income it receives from its resources is reduced by the taxes it pays, and increased by the transfer payments it receives from the government or private sources. The resources of a family include its ability to work productively and the wealth (or property) it owns. The amount and value of each of these, and thus a family's potential income, is influenced by many things. Some of them are, or have been, at least partly within its control. Its choices regarding how much and what kind of education and training its members obtain will have a major influence on the market value of its labor. Decisions about marriage, divorce, and the number of children influence the amount of labor the family has available to offer in the market. Decisions about how many of its members will work for income, how much they will work, and what types of work they will do, strongly influence its labor income. Saving and investment decisions, and the willingness to take financial risk, influence the amount of wealth it has at any given time, which in turn influences the amount of income it can earn from wealth. The health of the members of a family also affects its potential income. All of these things are partly under the control of the members of the family, directly or indirectly. But they are not wholly under the control of the family, and families face different sets of opportunities when making their choices.

Other important influences on a family's income are beyond its control. These include the laws regarding property rights and the initial endowment of wealth it has been given under those laws, which influence the amount of income it can earn from supplying its wealth for use in the economy. The innate abilities of its members will influence the potential labor earnings of the family.

If all markets conformed to the economists' assumptions of the model of perfect competition (which result in a situation in which no one buyer of an input or product can influence its price), the price of every type of resource, whether labor or property, would be determined by the supply of and demand for the particular resource. But this is outside of the control of the family owning some of the resource. It cannot control the quantities of the various types of property and labor that it owns that others bring to the market, but this will strongly influence the market value of the resources our hypothetical family supplies. The demand for resources would be determined by the demand for various products and the productivity of the family's resources in producing those products, which is in turn influenced by the technologies available, none of which they can control.

If all markets were perfectly competitive, the markets for various resources would reach an equilibrium in which anyone willing to supply a given resource at the market price would find a buyer for it. And the market price would equal the value of the increase in output caused by the use of this resource. But actual markets are not perfectly competitive. Often there is excess supply or demand for resources at existing prices for considerable periods of time. When there is an excess supply of labor, some workers cannot find employment. The labor of those who cannot find jobs makes no contribution to family income during the period of unemployment. Discrimination reduces the market value of the labor of some people. In addition, if there are only a few buyers of a resource in a market, this can reduce the resource's market value below the level that would prevail in a more competitive market. (Concentration in output markets also affects the market prices of resources.) Other institutional features (especially those of labor markets) such as the extent and strength of unions, the methods firms use to determine wages and salaries, and the methods they use to select people for the higher-income jobs, are also important influences on the distribution of income. All of these things are largely outside the influence or control of a given family, but all can strongly influence its potential income.

Of course, in the United States, as in all primarily market-economy countries, government policies also strongly influence the levels of market income of various families. Government regulations of many types influence the market values of families' resources. These include labor regulations, antitrust laws, and environmental and safety regulations. Tariffs and other regulations regarding international trade influence the value of various types of labor and other resources. Governments influence the levels of unemployment and inflation through their policies regarding the types and level of taxation and spending, and through their monetary policies; these will also affect the market value of the labor (and other resources) of many families. Of course, the systems of taxation and transfer payments raise the incomes of some families above their market incomes, and reduce the incomes of other below it. Most families have very little influence over any of these government policies.

As we have seen, this method of income determination leads to wide differences in income among families in the United States, with a significant proportion falling below the poverty level. Since families can earn income from their wealth (property) as well as from their labor, the income distribution is influenced by the distribution of wealth. Not as much data are available on the distribution of wealth in the United States as on the distribution of income. The most commonly used data are taken from the Federal Reserve Board's Surveys of Consumer Finances (SCF). The SCF has included both a sample of the general population and a special sample of the richest families, since wealth ownership is so heavily concentrated. Data from the SCF are only available for a few years in the last three decades, but as the data in table 7 show, the distribution of wealth is much less equal than that of income (this is true regardless of the year used).

The estimates depend on the particular definition of wealth used, and the adjustments made to the data. John Weicher of the Hudson Institute, using a broad net-wealth concept (wealth less debts owed) estimated that in 1989 the richest 1 percent of U.S. households owned 35 percent of total wealth, and the top 20 percent of households owned 80 percent of the total wealth, leaving only

20 percent for the other 80 percent of households.[24] Edward Wolff estimated that in 1989 the top 1 percent owned 39 per cent of "Marketable Net Worth" (a very broad wealth concept), and the top 20 percent owned 85 per cent of it. For "Financial Net Worth" (a narrower concept representing wealth more likely to give a potential monetary return), he found the top 1 percent owned 48 percent, and the top 20 percent owned 94 percent. For both definitions the lowest 20 percent had negative wealth; that is, their debts exceeded their assets. For 1983 he calculated an "augmented wealth" figure which included an estimated value of the pensions and Social Security benefits households had accrued. This was less unequally distributed, with the top 1 percent owning 19 percent, the top 20 percent owning 62 percent, and the lowest 20 percent owning 3 percent.[25] But even this measure shows wealth to be much less equally distributed than income. And promises to pay in the future—such as pensions—while valuable, are not available to meet current needs.

Erik Hurst and his colleagues use a different source of data, the Panel Study of Income Dynamics. This has the advantage of allowing an analyst to follow what happens to the wealth of particular families over time, but, as they state, it has the disadvantage that it does not oversample the richest families. Since wealth is so heavily concentrated in the hands of a relatively few families, they cannot accurately estimate the wealth holdings of these families from a general survey. Thus they do not provide data for the top 1 percent of families, and their estimates may well underestimate the concentration of wealth. Indeed their figures based on the PSID show a somewhat lower, but still very high, concentration of wealth, with the top 5 percent holding 44 percent, the top 20 percent holding 75 percent, and the bottom 20 percent having negative net wealth in 1994. If the value of the main home is excluded, the top 5 percent own 54 percent of the wealth and the top 20 percent 84 percent.[26]

Analysts are not agreed regarding the trend, if any, in the distribution of wealth over the last two decades. The limitations of the data, including the limited number of years, the fact that they come at different points in the business cycle, and the lack of full information on the richest families, make it impossible to draw a definite conclusion about a trend. But Weicher concludes that there is no clear trend once the effects of the business cycle are eliminated.[27] Hurst and his colleagues also present some data on the mobility within the wealth distribution of families which retained the same head for the period 1984–1994. Of those families that started in the lowest fifth, 59% were there ten years later, and 24 percent were in the second fifth. Thus only 17 percent had reached the upper 60 percent of the distribution.[28]

Because of this very unequal distribution of wealth, and because of the fact that about 80 percent of market income in the United States is labor income, most families must rely on their labor for the vast majority of their income. Thus low income and poverty are concentrated among families whose members' labor has a low market value. These include families whose main earners are women, members of minority racial or ethnic groups, people with relatively little education, those who are ill or disabled, and young people.

For example, in 1996 the median money income of black, male year-round, full-time workers (YRFT) was $27,136, just 78 percent of the $34,741 of white male YRFT workers. For white, female YRFT workers the figure was $25,358, or 73 percent of that of white males, and for black female YRFT workers it was $21,990, only 63 percent of that of white males.[29] While some of the differences between men and women, and blacks and whites, are caused by differences in education, training, experience, and other characteristics of the individuals or their employment, most studies of relative earnings differences show that these can only account for a part of the differences among these groups. A significant difference remains after making adjustments for such factors. And some of the differences in education, training, and experience are themselves due to discrimination, past or present. Audit studies—in which matched pairs of people apply for jobs, and the experiences of blacks and whites, and men and women, are compared—give additional evidence of discrimination in labor markets.[30] Blacks also suffer from unemployment rates more than twice as high as those for whites, further reducing their relative income.[31] And, as Glenn Loury points out, since conditions in one's neighborhood and social group can strongly influence one's opportunities and behavior, the effects of past discrimination can be passed on to present and future generations.[32] Thus it seems highly probable that discrimination still plays a significant role in the reduction of income for women and minorities. As discussed above, there is some mobility for families in the income distribution over their lifetimes. And there is also considerable inter-generational income mobility, but it is far from true that all children have an equal chance to earn an adequate income when they are adults. Gary Solon, using data from the Panel Study on Income Dynamics, concludes that the correlation of the incomes of fathers and sons is at least 0.4, and most of his estimates are closer to 0.5. This means that a son's income is strongly influenced by his father's.[33] For example, if the correlation is 0.4, the son of a father who was at the fifth percentile of the income distribution[34] had a 42 percent probability of being in the lowest fifth of the income distribution, only a 24 percent probability of being above the median, and only a 5 percent probability of being in the top fifth.[35] Conversely, a son whose father's income was at the ninety-fifth percentile had a 42 percent probability of being in the highest fifth of the income distribution, a 76 percent probability of being above the median, but only a 5 percent probability of being in the bottom fifth. And a son whose father's income was at the twenty-fifth percentile would have a 26 percent probability of being in the lowest fifth, a 39 percent probability of being above the median, and only a 12 percent probability of reaching the top fifth.[36] The association of sons' incomes with fathers' that is implied by a 0.4 correlation is about 4 times greater than that which would be expected due to inherited characteristics.[37]

It is especially difficult for children in poor families to develop their labor resources to the extent that they will earn moderate or high wages when in the labor force, especially if they live in an area which has a high concentration of poor families, if they are in a family which is poor for long periods of time, or if they are members of a racial or ethnic group that suffers from negative stereotypes. Poor children often suffer from poorer nutrition and poorer health care, both of which make it harder for them to develop physically and mentally in ways which make them attractive to employers when they are in the labor force. The schools in poor neighborhoods have poorer outcomes on average, making it more difficult for their students to gain access to the best post-secondary education.[38] There are still substantial financial barriers to higher education for those with low incomes, resulting in fewer students from poor families getting the education which is increasingly required for higher-paying employment. Children growing up in poor neighborhoods have fewer role models of financial success through study and hard work, especially if they are members of groups that have suffered from discrimination. When they are ready to join the job market, they have fewer contacts with people who can help them find out about job openings and recommend them for the jobs. This is very important, because many jobs, especially early jobs, are obtained through informal channels.[39]

Thus it is clear that the income of a particular family, although influenced by the choices of its members, is also strongly influenced by things outside of its control. It is also clear from the preceding discussion that there are many families for whom it is very difficult, if not impossible, to raise their income above the lower end of the income distribution, and that these difficulties can last for long periods of time, and even continue intergenerationally. The fact that the distribution of income has become less equal in the last two decades and that there has been no increase in the mobility, means that it is likely that these problems are greater now than they were two decades ago. In order to gain a better understanding of this it is necessary to examine the causes of the change in the income distribution.

Causes of Increasing Inequality of Income Distribution

The causes of the changes in the distribution of income in the United States in the last two decades are complex and interrelated. There is no clear consensus regarding the degree to which the various factors involved are responsible for the changes. However, two broad areas of causation are changes in the distribution of earnings among workers and changes in family composition and work patterns. Government policies have played a role as well, both directly and via influences on earnings (and perhaps on family composition and work patterns).[40] Since earnings from labor represent the largest proportion of family earnings, any substantial change in the distribution of labor earnings is likely to change the distribution of family income in a similar way. And in fact, the distribution of earnings from labor in the United States clearly has become less equal in the last two decades. This is shown by many studies using a variety of data sources and measuring inequality in various ways.

Table 8 shows the hourly wages for workers at the decile cutoffs for 1974 and 1996. For example, the figure in the first row for all workers in 1974 shows that 10 percent of workers earned less than $5.84 in 1974 (adjusted to 1996 prices) and 90 percent earned above that. The data reveal several noteworthy things. If the correction for inflation is correct, the wages for workers in the bottom 70 percent of the distribution decreased, and those for workers in the highest 30 percent rose. The decreases as a percentage of the 1974 wage were the greatest for the lower-income workers, and particularly for the lower-income males, for whom the decrease for those in the lowest three deciles was 18 percent or more; for the median male worker the decrease was 12 percent. Female workers at all levels of their distribution gained in relation to males, but the lowest deciles still lost in real terms. On the other hand, the highest deciles gained in real income, as well as relative to the lower deciles; this was true for men and women considered separately, and for all workers taken together. The ratio of the wage at the top of the first decile to the median, the ratio of the median to the wage at the top of the ninth decile, and the ratio of the first to the ninth decile—standard measures of the inequality of wages—all rose, whether we look at all workers together or males and females separately.[41]

Table 9 shows that the proportion of employment that pays less than the wage necessary to bring a family of four up to the poverty line, if earned by a full-time worker working year around, has risen from 26 percent to 30.6 percent. The increase is especially high for male workers, although it went down for female workers. On the other side of the wage distribution, the proportion of employment paying more than three times the poverty wage has also increased. Thus the amount of employment paying between the poverty wage and three times it has decreased.

Other data from other sources show a similar pattern. For example, Peter Gottschalk reports that the real, mean, weekly wage for male workers was less in 1994 than in 1973, and the median went down even more, while the real wages of women grew at an annual rate of 2.7 percent during this period.[42] He also reports that real weekly wages fell for males in the lower three-quarters of the distribution, with the percentage decrease larger for lower-wage workers than for those earning more. For the lowest-paid 10 percent of male workers the decrease totaled more than 25 percent over the two decades, while the highest-paid 10 percent of males gained over 8 percent. For female workers, real weekly wages grew across the income distribution, but the increase was less than 10 percent for most in the lowest half of the distribution, while it was over 30 percent for the highest 10 percent.[43] Thus the distribution became less equal for both male and female workers, although the difference between them in average wage declined.

Looking at particular groups of labor, Gottschalk reports that adjusting for education, experience, and region of the country, the earnings gap between men and women decreased from over 55 percent of mean female earnings in 1973 to less than 35 per cent by 1994, but the adjusted black/white gap, which had fallen considerably from 1963 to 1975 remained roughly constant (between 10 and 15 percent) after that.[44]

The data in table 10 show that both the absolute difference, and the ratio of wages of college graduates to those of high school graduates, rose substantially between 1974 and 1996 for both men and women, and by the end of the period the wage for college graduates was about 65 percent higher for both. The real wage, using the standard adjustment for inflation, fell for both men and women with less than a high school education and for men with a high school education, rose for women with a college degree and for both men and women with advanced degrees, and was close to constant for women with a high school education and men with a college degree.[45] Since the wages of the more-highly educated, who started at a higher level, increased relative to those less-highly educated, this contributes to the overall inequality in the distribution of earnings. On the other hand, the reduction in the difference between the wages of men and women at every education level tends to reduce the inequality of the overall distribution. Looking at this in a somewhat different way, Gottschalk estimates that adjusting for other factors, the college premium declined during the 1970s and reached a low point of 31 percent in 1979, but then rose to 53 percent in 1993. He estimates that between 1979 and 1994 the earnings of high school graduates fell by 20 percent, while those of college graduates rose by 5 percent.[46]

Unemployment also became more concentrated during these two decades. In 1974 only 7.4 percent of the unemployed were unemployed twenty-seven weeks or longer, and the average duration of unemployment was 9.8 weeks. In 1996 these figures were 17.4 percent and 16.7 weeks respectively.[47] Long-term unemployment, overall unemployment, and non-participation in the labor force have all increased more for those in groups whose wages are lower and are dropping faster than they are for others. The fact that low and falling wages are correlated with decreases in annual hours worked increases the growth in inequality of earnings.[48]

What has caused these changes in the distribution of earnings? To the extent that wages are set in competitive markets by supply and demand for labor of various types, the answers must be found in shifts in the supply or demand curves. But since institutional factors also influence wage setting, we must also examine their potential influence.

The most common answer given by economists to explain the above changes in earnings is that the demand for labor has shifted away from low-skilled workers and toward higher-skilled workers, and at a faster rate than the supply of labor has shifted toward higher-skilled workers. But this raises the question of why the demand for labor shifted in this way. The common answers are that technological change and an increase in foreign trade, especially in imports from lower-income countries, have reduced the demand for low-skilled workers and increased the demand for high-skilled workers.[49] At the same time, although the proportion of workers with a college education has continued to increase, it has done so less rapidly since 1980 than it did in earlier years.[50]

There is no firm consensus about the degree to which each of these factors has caused the increase in the inequality in earnings. Most economists assign a relatively small role to increases in international trade and a much larger role to technological change, without estimating the exact proportions.[51] This may well be so, but there are some reasons to question how good the evidence for this is. Most estimates of the impact of international trade take one of two approaches: (1) Labor economists tend to assume that it reduces the wage of low-skilled workers by a direct reduction in the demand for low-skilled workers in the United States because of the low-skilled labor "embodied" in imports; since imports are still only a small proportion of total output in the United States, and not all of them are produced with large amounts of low-skilled labor, their estimates of the effects of trade are small. (2) International trade economists try to estimate the effects on wages of low-skilled workers by estimating the relative reduction in prices of goods which use low-skilled workers intensively: These have been small; thus the conclusion is that the effects on input prices have also been small.[52] But since wages are often not set just by a competitive market process that balances supply and demand, there are additional ways that international trade could influence wages of low-skilled workers. Just the threat of moving work to a lower-wage country could be sufficient to lower wages below what they would be otherwise, either during a negotiation with a union, or by a firm setting a wage in a situation of surplus low-skilled labor. If this happens, the wages can be reduced without any increase in imports, and if the firm is not competing with firms which actually do import, the product price may not go down as much as the wages do. In this case, the standard econometric measures will understate the effects of trade.

On the other hand, as many economists have noted, since we cannot directly measure technological change, the estimated effects of changes in technology are usually a residual, that is, what is left after we have explained as much of the change in earnings inequality in other ways as we can. As Peter Gottschalk and Timothy Smeeding say: "Technological change is simply a label for our ignorance."[53]

However, there are good reasons to believe that technological change has played a major role. During a period in which the relative wages of more highly educated workers has been rising, the ratio of highly educated labor to less-educated labor has been rising for a wide variety of industries. This includes both manufacturing and service industries and those not subject to international competition, as well as those that are. This is unlikely to have happened unless the productivities of the more highly educated workers are rising in relation to those of less-educated workers. There is little to explain such a change in relative productivities other than technological change.[54] These intra-industry shifts in employment have been more important in the increase in demand for more-highly educated labor than the inter-industry shifts in employment.[55] However, Robert Feenstra points out that increases in imports of intermediate products and services will lead to such intra-industry shifts in employment. Imports of intermediate goods have increased considerably in recent decades, but these increases are missed by most studies of the effects of trade, which are focused on final products. And they produce changes in intra-industry employment ratios similar to those commonly taken as evidence of technological change.[56] On the other hand, there are a few studies that examine particular technological changes, such as the adoption of computers, that seem to indicate that they do contribute to increasing inequality of earnings.[57] Still, the proportion of the total increase in inequality of earnings caused by technological change cannot be accurately estimated.

We should also note that although the changes in relative wages for workers in different age, race, gender, and education groups can account for much of the increase in inequality, perhaps as much as half of it remains unexplained by these factors. The causes of this are not well-understood by economists.[58] One important factor in this is the increase in volatility of earnings for particular workers (as opposed to longer-lasting changes in relative earnings). But the reasons for this volatility are not well-understood either.[59]

The increasing number of immigrants in the labor force is an additional factor affecting the supply of labor. But most who have studied this have concluded that it is only of minor importance in the increase in inequality of wages in the United States.[60] However, the increase in the proportion of the labor force accounted for by women, minorities, and younger workers, all of whom have relatively low median incomes, has probably also contributed to the increase in the number of low-income earners and to the inequality in the distribution of earnings.

But even if a demand shift brought on in part by changes in technology and increased trade is a major contributing factor to the change in the earnings distribution, this is not a sufficient explanation of it. Although supply and demand are important influences on wages, wages are not merely set in competitive markets where they constantly change just enough to make the quantity of any particular type of labor demanded equal to the quantity supplied. Institutional factors, including governmental policies, the roles of unions and employer organizations, and the views of employers, workers, and the general public regarding fair and proper wages, play a large role in the determination of wages in the United States and in other countries.[61] The fact that institutions are important can be inferred from the fact that even though all industrialized countries have faced similar pressures in the last two decades from the rise in international trade and change in technology, the increase in inequality in earnings has been significantly greater in the United States than in any other industrialized country except the United Kingdom.[62] This is true even though the United States began the period among the industrialized countries with the most unequal distribution of earnings.[63]

Two institutional factors in particular are often cited as playing a role in the increase in inequality of earnings in the United States in the last two decades: the decline in the extent and power of labor unions and the decline in the real value of the minimum wage during the 1980s.

The percentage of workers in the United States covered by unions has been declining for some time, but the decrease became greater during the 1980s. In 1969, 29 percent of non-agricultural workers were unionized; in 1979 this figure was 26 per cent, and in 1989 only 16 percent. Unionization among public employees was growing, so the drop in private sector unionization was even greater, to 12 percent.[64] Since 1989 it has declined further, but at a slower rate. Studies have shown that unions decrease the inequality of earnings among men, for whom they have had the highest rates of membership in the private sector. Several estimates have been made of the relation between the decline in unionization and increase in inequality of earnings in the 1980s, using different methodologies, and they have generally found that it is associated with about 20 percent of the increase in inequality among men, but with little of that among women.[65] However, we cannot be sure that the decline in unionism caused that much of the increase in inequality. As in all cases, statistical association cannot prove causation, and in this case the decline in unionization is closely related to the changing industrial structure and changing composition of the labor force. When potential explanatory variables can influence each other, it is particularly hard to assign estimates to the "causes." But there is little doubt that the drop in union membership in the United States during the last two decades, and unions' reduced power in face of a hostile federal government and the increasing hostility of many employers in the 1980s, played significant roles in the fact that the increase in inequality of earnings was greater in the United States than in most other industrialized countries.

The other major institutional factor that contributed to the increase in inequality in earnings in the 1980s was the decrease in the real value of the minimum wage. The minimum wage did not change in nominal terms from 1981 until 1990, a period of substantial inflation. Thus it lost over 30 percent of its real value during the 1980s.[66] It also declined more than 30 percent in relation to the average hourly wage in manufacturing between 1978 and 1990.[67] Although there have been several increases in the 1990s, bringing it to its current level of $5.15, it is still almost 20 percent below its 1978 level in real terms.[68] In 1968 and 1975, both years of increases in the minimum wage, a person working full-time, year-round at the minimum wage would have earned at or above the poverty line income for a family of three. In 1991, the last year it was increased prior to the 1996–97 increases, such a worker would have earned only 74 percent of the three-person poverty line. And at the 1997 level of $5.15 such a worker would have earned only 84 percent of that poverty line.[69]

However, there is debate concerning how much the decreased real value of the minimum wage in the 1980s affected the increase in inequality in earnings. Different scholars, measuring several different things in different ways, come up with different answers. Nicole Fortin and Thomas Lemieux find that it accounts for 24 percent of the increase in inequality for men, 32 percent for women, and 39 percent for men and women combined (using the variance in the logarithm of wages as their measure of inequality).[70] Others have come up with estimates of 10–50 percent for men, and 30–66 percent for women (the high figures applying to the ratio of wages at the tenth percentile to those at the ninetieth).[71] On the other hand, Michael Horrigan and Ronald Mincy do not ask how the drop in the real value affected the change in inequality, but rather how much higher the earnings share of the lowest fifth would have been if the real value of the minimum wage had not decreased. They come up with modest estimates of 3–4 percent for females and males considered separately.[72]

Some scholars believe the minimum wage has a considerable effect on the wages of poor and low-income families. They point to studies that conclude that over half of those who earn the minimum wage are in families in the lowest-income fifth. And an increase in the minimum wage will usually result in increases for low-income workers whose wages are close to, but above, the new minimum.[73] But Horrigan and Mincy believe that most of the families who will benefit are in higher income classifications.[74] Increases in the minimum wage are often opposed on the grounds that they increase unemployment. While they may do this, most econometric studies show the effect is quite small, even for teenagers, the group that is probably most heavily affected. In the ranges we have experienced in the United States, a 10 percent increase in the minimum wage probably causes only a 1 to 3 percent increase in teenage unemployment, and much less than a 1 percent increase in adult unemployment, if any. And any loss in unemployment is likely to be shared by many workers, since the turnover in most low-wage jobs is quite high. Thus almost all low-wage workers, even teenagers, likely earn higher incomes with modest increases in the minimum wage.[75]

Other government policies have also contributed to the increase in inequality of earnings, but the magnitude of their effect is hard to estimate. In the early 1980s federal government spending on programs to employ and train people who were having trouble earning adequate wages was cut by almost two-thirds,[76] and we have never replaced the programs that provided employment for those who needed such employment and could not obtain it in the private sector. Furthermore, the increases in imports and the effects that they have on earnings have been affected by the government's lowering of tariffs and other trade barriers.

Thus far we have been considering the increase in inequality in the distribution of earnings per worker. But the distribution of family income is also affected by changes in family composition and work patterns, and by changes in government tax and transfer policies.

Demographic changes, especially the rise in the proportion of families without a husband present, have also played an important role in the increase in inequality of family earnings, and of poverty. In 1974, 15.7 percent of families with children under eighteen had no husband present, and 1.7 percent had no wife present; thus 17.4 percent of families with children had only one parent. By 1996 these figures had risen to 24.1, 5.5, and 29.6 percent respectively.[77]

Single-parent families with children have a higher incidence of poverty than married-couple families, so the rise in the proportion of such families contributes to a rise in poverty. In 1996, 41.9 percent of families with children with no husband present were poor; by contrast 20 percent of such families with no wife present were poor, and only 7.5 percent of married-couple families with children were poor. In 1974, 36 percent of poor persons were in families without a husband present, but 41 percent of the total increase in number of poor persons between 1974 and 1996 occurred in such families, so 38 per cent of the poor persons lived in such families in 1996.[78]

These data show that it is not only single-parent status that contributes to poverty. The fact that women receive lower earnings than men contributes to the much higher poverty rates for single-parent families with children with the husband absent, than similar families with wife absent.[79]

It is difficult to determine the relative sizes of these various influences, both economic and demographic, on the increase in poverty rates in the last two decades. This is especially true due to the complex causal interactions of the various factors. For example, the drop in real earnings for men without a college education may affect the rate of marriage, and thus the number of single-parent households. And family structure may influence education and work patterns and thus the distribution of income. Danzinger and Gottschalk estimate that for the period 1973–1991 the change in income inequality and demographic changes contributed about equal amounts to the increase in poverty. The demographic factors contributing to this were changes in the family structure composition of the population, and changes in the racial and ethnic composition of the population, with the former contributing about twice as much to the increase in poverty as the latter.[80]

The increase in the number of working wives in married-couple families is also often suspected of causing an increase in the degree of inequality of family income. But Maria Cancian and her colleagues found that wives' incomes made the distribution of married couples' incomes more equal in 1968, 1978, and 1988, for all such families considered together, and for whites, blacks, and Hispanics considered separately. They also found that over the two decades the equalizing effects grew slightly. Considering married-couple and single-parent families together, incomes of wives in married-couple families generally had a slight, and slightly growing, equalizing effect on the distribution of income. For blacks and Hispanics there were disequalizing effects in the years considered individually; however, these decreased over time.[81]

In addition to the government policies affecting the earnings distribution considered above, other government policies have also played a role in the increase in inequality of income, particularly in the decrease in income for some low-income and poor families.

The value of average Aid to Families with Dependent Children (AFDC) payments, adjusted for inflation, fell considerably during the last two decades. The average monthly benefit per family (in 1996 dollars) fell from $734 in 1970 to $523 in 1980, to $470 in 1990, and to $374 in 1996.[82] This has reduced the level of income of many of our poorest families.

Reductions in the federal income tax in the early 1980s, particularly for high-income families, together with increases in regressive payroll taxes and the shifting of some tax burdens from the federal government to states and localities, whose taxes are, on average, less progressive, contributed somewhat to the increase in inequality of after-tax income in the 1980s. In the early 1990s, this was partially offset by increases in the taxation of high-income families and the increase in the Earned Income Tax Credit for families with low labor earnings.

What was the overall effect of such changes in tax and transfer policies? Edward Gramlich and his colleagues estimated that changes in these policies caused 16 percent of the increase in post-tax, post-transfer inequality during the 1980s.[83] They also estimated that tax and transfer policies would have become less effective during the 1980s even if the laws had not been changed (for example, because the transfers to the poor as a percent of total income would have fallen due to a lack of adjustment for inflation). Including these effects they concluded that "62 percent of the increase in post-tax, post-transfer inequality over the decade can be attributed to changes in pre-tax, pre-transfer incomes and 38 percent to changes in the effectiveness of tax and transfer programs."[84] This is a significant part of the increase in inequality. In contrast, other industrialized nations took actions to help offset the increase in earnings inequality taking place in their countries. As Peter Gottschalk, discussing the period from the mid–1970s to the mid–1990s says: "The United States is the only [high-income, industrialized] country to have experienced a larger increase in the dispersion of family income than in earnings. . . . [other countries] that did experience an increase in earnings inequality then used the tax and transfer system to offset the changes in the labor market outcomes."[85]

Policy Options and Proposals

How should Christians react to this growth in inequality of incomes in the United States, which has caused those with the lowest income to clearly lose ground in relation to those in the middle and to those with higher incomes, and probably has caused a drop in real income for them as well? This situation is unjust by biblical standards, since so many families do not have adequate opportunities to develop and use their resources in such a way that they can become self-supporting, productive members of society and participate with dignity in the various areas of life in society. And children who grow up in chronically poor families, in poor neighborhoods, particularly if they also suffer from discrimination, will have great difficulty in preparing now for such a life in the future.

What policies could the government enact in order to create more opportunities for families to support themselves by their work, and provide other access to income to those who cannot? Other chapters in this volume will discuss a number of these in more detail, but this chapter will conclude with a short discussion of policies that have an important relation to the opportunity for all families to earn an adequate income.

How could we assure that every family of average size which has someone working full-time, year around, at the minimum wage would be able to earn enough for his or her family to escape poverty?

Two policies that have been advocated and used in the United States to raise the net earnings of low-paid workers are the minimum wage and the Earned Income Tax Credit (EITC). Barry Bluestone and Teresa Ghilarducci point out that using a combination of the minimum wage and the EITC to raise the incomes of poor working families has advantages over using either one alone. In 1997 a minimum wage of $7.89 would have been necessary in order for a full-time, year-round worker to earn enough to reach that year's poverty line for a family of four. This is over 50 percent above the level of the minimum wage in late 1997. Such an increase is not politically possible. And if the minimum wage would suddenly be raised by that amount it could well cause much larger increases in unemployment, in relation to the increase, than have been experienced with the smaller increases we have had during most of the history of the minimum wage.[86]

On the other hand, trying to raise the incomes of low-income workers with the EITC alone also has problems. The budgetary cost would be quite high, especially if it is phased out gradually, rather than quickly, as earned incomes rise, in order to decrease disincentives to work and earn more in the phase-out range. And if not combined with a minimum wage, it runs the risk of subsidizing employers who offer only a very low wage, relying on the EITC to induce workers to take the jobs.[87]

However, the two together can complement each other, and in late 1997, together they came close to providing a poverty-line income, when combined with food stamps. At the minimum wage of $5.15 per hour, a worker working forty hours a week, 52 weeks a year, would earn $10,712. Adding an EITC of $3656 (assuming there were two or more children in the family, and no other income), and deducting federal payroll taxes of $819 would leave the family with a net cash income of $13,549 (before state and local taxes). Such a family, if it did not have assets above the eligibility limits, could receive $2808 in food stamps,[88] for a total of $16,357. This is almost as much as the 1997 poverty line for a family of four of $16,400.[89] Does this mean we can declare that a solution to the problem of poverty has been achieved? By no means. Even the family of a worker who could obtain and keep a full-time job, year-round, would have difficulties. Many such jobs do not include medical insurance, and individual medical insurance would probably have been too expensive for a worker earning the minimum wage; but the family would most likely be ineligible for Medicaid unless it had been receiving welfare recently. And, the family would have been ineligible for food stamps if its "liquid assets" exceeded $2000. Counted against this $2000 limit are funds in IRA's and "Keogh" retirement plans, plus the value of its vehicles in excess of $4,650. Thus many families with very low earnings, but with modest assets, are ineligible for food stamps. And food stamps are denied to most legal resident aliens.[90] Furthermore, since the minimum wage is not regularly adjusted for inflation, the potential income of such a worker is already falling further below the poverty line.

As well, many heads of poor families need assistance in obtaining even minimum-wage jobs. They often need child care, assistance with transportation, training in job skills, and/or help in dealing with emergencies that could otherwise result in loss of a job. The experience of states that have actively tried to help their welfare recipients become self-supporting indicate that these things will cost much more than the combination of what the federal government will provide under the Personal Responsibility and Work Opportunity Reconciliation Act of 1996, plus the funds the states had been providing.[91]

In addition, even in periods of low overall unemployment, many low-wage workers are subject to frequent spells of unemployment, which reduce the wages they earn[92] (and their EITC, if their income falls very much). When the unemployment rate rises, low-wage workers often suffer disproportionately from the increases in unemployment, and long-term unemployment rises especially rapidly during recessions. Thus it is important for the government to use fiscal and monetary policies to keep unemployment low, recognizing that it cannot do this perfectly; i.e., there will always be recessions from time to time. Therefore, it will be necessary to provide support for those who become unemployed for significant periods, if families are to have access to necessities at all times.

Thus, unless there is a commitment on the part of federal and state governments to provide affordable access to medical care, child care, transportation, training, and even public sector jobs at minimum wages for those who cannot find jobs in the private sector, we should not expect most of the poor to be able to support themselves with the current level of the minimum wage, EITC, and food stamps.

Furthermore, many of the poor have health problems which will make it difficult for them to work full time, year round. The levels of benefits under AFDC were in most cases inadequate to provide support for families that could not support themselves, and the outlook for adequate support under the new welfare law is not promising.

Simply receiving a poverty-line income does not enable a family to fully participate in the economy and society in the way that is called for by the biblical standards for justice discussed in section II. Further improvement of education and training for low-income people and their children, and for those whose skills have become obsolete, is important to making progress in this area. Vigorous enforcement of anti-discrimination laws and policies is also important in providing just employment and educational opportunities to members of groups that have suffered, and continue to suffer, from discrimination.

Finally, it is important to remember that Christians should also be working personally for justice. We should use our time, talents, income, and wealth at least in part to provide others with the assistance and opportunities they need, just as the Israelites and the early Christians were called to do. And we should work together with others, in our churches and other organizations, to achieve this end. Together, private and governmental actions can do much to make the economy more just and caring for those who are now deprived of opportunities they justly deserve.

Table 1

Income of Families in the United States, by Fifths, 1974 and 1996

	Percent of Total Income		Mean Income (1996 dollars)		
	1974	1996	1974	1996	change
Lowest fifth	5.7%	4.2%	$12,697	$11,388	–10%
Second fifth	12.0%	10.0%	$26,803	$26,847	0%
Third fifth	17.6%	15.8%	$39,191	$42,467	+ 8%
Fourth fifth	24.1%	23.1%	$53,612	$62,052	+16%
Top fifth	40.6%	46.8%	$90,337	$125,627	+39%
Top 5%	14.8%	20.3%	$131,766	$217,355	+65%

Sources: U.S. Census Bureau, "Historical Income Tables—Families, (Table) F–2. Share of Aggregate Income Received by Each Fifth and Top 5 Percent of Families (all Races): 1947 to 1996" (published 29 September 1997); available from http://www.census.gov/ hhes/income/ histinc/f02.html, and U.S. Census Bureau. "Historical Income Tables—Families, (Table) F–3. Mean Income Received by Each Fifth and Top 5 Percent of Families (all Races): 1966 to 1996" (published 29 September 1997); available from http://www .census. gov/hhes/income/histinc/ f03.html.

Notes: A small part of the increased inequality comes from changes in the methods of collecting the statistics between 1974 and 1996. The data in this table include only families, i.e., two or more related people living together. The distribution of income by households (which includes people living alone or with non-related people) is less equal, but the pattern of change has been similar. In 1996 the lowest fifth of households received only 3.7 percent of total household income, and the top fifth received 49.0 percent. In 1974 these figures were 4.4 percent and 43.1 percent respectively. (Source: U.S. Census Bureau. "Historical Income Tables—Households (Table) H–2. Share of Aggregate Income Received by Each Fifth and Top 5 Percent of Households (all Races):1967 to 1996" (published 29 September 1997); available from http:// www.census.gov/hhes/income/ histinc/ h02.html.

Table 2

Money Income of White, Black, and Hispanic Families, 1996

	Whites	Blacks	Hispanics
Mean income	$56,179	$35,592	$34,935
Median income	$44,756	$26,522	$26,179
Share of lowest fifth	4.7%	3.2%	4.0%
Share of the second fifth	10.3%	8.7%	9.3%
Mean income of lowest fifth	$13,097	$ 5,651	$ 7,139
Mean income of the 2nd fifth	$29,059	$15,180	$16,481

Sources: U.S. Census Bureau. "Historical Income Tables—Families, (Tables) F–2 A, B, and C. Share of Aggregate Income Received by Each Fifth and Top 5 Percent of White (A), Black (B), and Hispanic © Families: 1947 to 1996 (A), 1966 to 1996 (B), 1972 to 1996 (C)" (published 29 September 1997); available from http://www.census.gov/hhes/ income/ histinc/f02a. html, /f02b.html, and /f02c; and U.S. Census Bureau. "Historical Income Tables—Families, (Tables) F–3 A, B, and C. Mean Income Received by Each Fifth and Top 5 Percent of White (A), Black (B), and Hispanic © Families:1966 to 1996 (A & B), 1972–1996 (C)" (published 29 September 1997); available from http://www.census.gov/hhes/income/histinc/ f03a.html, /f03b.html, /f03c.html.

Table 3

Average Income-to-Poverty Ratios for Families, 1974 and 1996

	Lowest Fifth	Second Fifth	Middle Fifth	Fourth Fifth	Highest Fifth
1974	1.13	2.24	3.11	4.12	6.69
1996	0.96	2.22	3.37	4.78	9.55

Source: U.S. Census Bureau. "Historical Income Tables—Families, (Table) F–18. Average Income-to-Poverty Ratios for Families, by Income Quintile, Race, and Hispanic Origin: 1967 to 1996" (published 29 September 1997); available from http://www.census.gov/hhes/income/ histinc/f18.html.

Table 4

Family Disposable Income in the United States, Adjusted for Size and Composition of Family, 1974 and 1995

	Percent of Total Income	
	1974	1995
Lowest fifth	5.6%	4.7%
Second fifth	12.2%	10.9%
Third fifth	17.7%	16.5%
Fourth fifth	24.2%	23.7%
Top fifth	40.2%	44.2%

Source: Michael Wolfson and Brian Murphy, "New views on inequality trends in Canada and the United States," *Monthly Labor Review* 121 (April 1998): 14.

Table 5

Mean Adjusted Household Income-to-Poverty Ratios, Pre- and Post-tax, 1973, 1979, and 1994

	Pre-tax Money Income			Adjusted Income*		
	1973	1979	1994	1973	1979	1994
Lowest fifth	0.90	0.90	0.77	NA	0.96	0.89
Second fifth	1.94	2.06	1.93	NA	1.89	1.81
Third fifth	2.82	3.07	3.10	NA	2.67	2.72
Fourth fifth	3.94	4.32	4.61	NA	3.63	3.90
Top fifth	6.87	7.39	8.57	NA	5.85	6.82

*This deducts federal income and payroll taxes (but not other taxes) from money income, and adds the estimated value of food stamps, school lunches, and housing benefits.
**NA = Not Available.

Source: House Committee on Ways and Means, *1998 Green Book*, 105th Cong., 2d sess., 1998, Committee Print 105–7, 1317.

Table 6

Poverty Rates, 1974 and 1996
(Percentage of the persons or families
in the classification which were poor.)

	1974	1996
All persons	11.2	13.7
White	8.6	11.2
Black	30.3	28.4
Hispanic	23.0	29.4
All children	15.4	20.5
White	11.2	16.3
Black	39.8	39.9
Hispanic (1976: 30.2)	NA	40.3
Families		
All	8.8	11.0
White	6.8	8.6
Black	26.9	26.1
Hispanic	21.2	26.4
Married-couple families	5.3	5.6
White	4.6	5.1
Black	13.0	9.1
Hispanic	14.4	18.0
Female householder families, no husband present	32.1	32.6
White	24.8	27.3
Black	52.2	43.7
Hispanic	49.6	50.9

Source: U.S. Department of Commerce, Bureau of the Census, *Poverty in the United States: 1996,* by Leatha Lamison-White, Current Population Reports, Series P60–198 (Washington, D.C.: U.S. Government Printing Office, 1997), pp. C–2 to C–13.

Table 7

Distribution of Wealth in the United States, 1983, 1989, 1994

Wealth Concept, Source, Percent of Wealth Owned and Year

	Top 1%	Top 5%	Top 20%	Bottom 20%
Total Wealth Weicher, SCF, 1989	35%	56%	80%	NA
Marketable Net Worth Wolff, SCF, 1989	39%	61%	85%	–1%
Financial Net Wealth Wolff, SCF, 1989	48%	72%	94%	–2%
Augmented Wealth Wolff, SCF, 1983	19%	36%	62%	3%
Wealth, including main home Hurst, PSID, 1989	NA	47%	77%	–1%
Wealth, including main home Hurst, PSID, 1994	NA	44%	75%	–1%
Wealth, excluding main home Hurst, PSID, 1994	NA	54%	84%	–1%

Sources: John Weicher, *The Distribution of Wealth* (Washington, D.C.: AEI Press, 1996), 13; Edward Wolff, *Economics of Poverty, Inequality, and Discrimination* (Cincinnati: South-Western College Publishing, 1977), 372–373; Erik Hurst, Ming Ching Luoh, and Frank Stafford, *Wealth Dynamics of American Families, 1984–1994* (Ann Arbor, Mich.: Department of Economics and Institute for Social Research, University of Michigan, 1996), 29; also available as PDF file from http://www.isr.umich.edu/src/psid/pdf.html.

Note: SCF is the Survey of Consumer Finances; PSID is the Panel Study of Income Dynamics.

Table 8

Hourly Wage Decile Cutoffs, 1974 and 1996, in 1996 Dollars

	All workers			Males			Females		
Decile	1974	1996	Change	1974	1996	Change	1974	1996	Change
1st	$5.86	$5.17	−0.69	$6.94	$5.68	−1.26	$5.40	$4.96	−0.44
2nd	$7.03	$6.40	−0.63	$8.84	$7.08	−1.76	$6.01	$5.94	−0.07
3rd	$8.35	$7.67	−0.68	$10.41	$8.49	−1.92	$6.73	$6.95	+0.22
4th	$9.67	$8.94	−0.73	$11.94	$10.04	−1.90	$7.59	$8.00	+0.41
5th	$11.08	$10.35	−0.73	$13.62	$11.85	−1.77	$8.49	$9.19	+0.70
6th	$12.75	$12.22	−0.53	$15.16	$13.93	−1.23	$9.53	$10.72	+1.19
7th	$14.78	$14.72	−0.06	$16.90	$16.34	−0.56	$10.77	$12.64	+1.87
8th	$17.04	$17.79	+0.75	$19.16	$19.74	+0.58	$12.47	$15.38	+2.91
9th	$21.49	$23.01	+1.52	$24.30	$25.27	+0.97	$15.32	$19.91	+4.59

Source: Jared Bernstein and Lawrence Mishel, "Has Wage Inequality Stopped Growing?" *Monthly Labor Review* 120, no. 12 (December 1997): 7–9.

Based on data from the Current Population Survey, Outgoing Rotation Group Files. Adjusted to 1996 dollars using the CPI-U-X1.

Table 9

Share of Employment by Relation to the Wage Necessary to Earn the Poverty Line Income Working Full Time for a Full Year, 1974 and 1996

Year	Percent at or below the poverty wage			Percent above three times the poverty wage		
	Total	Males	Females	Total	Males	Females
1974	26.0	14.4	42.8	7.4	11.2	2.0
1996	30.6	24.4	37.4	9.6	12.9	5.9

Source: Economic Policy Institute, DataZone, "Share of Employment for All/Male/Female Workers by Wage Multiple of Poverty Wage, 1973–76," available from http://www.epinet.org/datazone/datapages/povertylevelwages_all.htm and _men.htm and _women.htm; accessed 29 July 1998.

Based on data from the Current Population Survey.

Table 10

Real Hourly Wages by Education, 1974 and 1996, in 1996 Dollars

	Less than High School	High School	College	Advanced Degree	College as a percent of HS
Men					
1974	$12.50	$14.65	$20.47	$24.03	140%
1996	$8.85	$11.95	$19.80	$25.70	166%
Change	-$3.65	-$2.70	-$0.67	+$1.67	
Percentage Change	–29%	–18%	–3%	+7%	
Women					
1974	$7.69	$9.32	$13.55	$17.90	145%
1996	$6.69	$9.12	$15.08	$20.37	165%
Change	-$1.00	-$0.20	+$1.53	+$2.37	
Percentage Change	–13%	–2%	+11%	+13%	

Source: Economic Policy Institute, DataZone, "Men's/Women's Hourly Wages by Education, 1973–96,"; available from http://www.epinet.org/datazone/datapages/wagebyed_men .htm and _women.htm; accessed 29 July 1998.

Based on Data from the Current Population Survey, adjusted for inflation using the CPI-U-X1.

~7~

Redefining Progress: Economic Indicators and the Shalom of God

Timothy Slaper

Introduction

Indicators of social progress suggest a question that typically goes unanswered: Progress towards what? In order to measure progress, one must be able to chart movements toward or away from a particular end. Indicators of poverty, in much the same way, also lack a motivating principle and a social model to which those indicators can be applied to realize a particular end—the end of poverty. While these indicators are conceived with the laudable goal of helping policymakers address social ills, most want for a motivating vision and lack a clear link between policy actions and results.

This paper addresses many of the issues raised by Clifford Cobb, Ted Halstead and Jonathan Rowe in the October 1995 issue of *The Atlantic Monthly* in an article entitled, "If the GDP is up, why is America down?" In the article, Cobb, Halstead and Rowe propose to redefine progress, and propose a new measure of progress, the Genuine Progress Indicator (GPI).[1] The proposal to redefine progress, however, suffers from many of the same flaws as the social indicators movement of the 1960s and early 1970s. The GPI is no better than the indicators of poverty and social progress that were developed at that time. Moreover, the GPI will not accomplish the political and social transformation advocated by the redefining progress initiative.

This does not mean that progress doesn't need to be redefined or even that a new set of indicators is unwarranted. It simply means that in redefining progress and constructing new indicators one must start from first principles. The project represented by this book proposes those first principles and, by doing so, redefines *telos*.

This paper proposes a comprehensive vision, a social *telos*, to serve as the foundation for either using a set of established indicators or developing a new set of indicators to measure justice, poverty and progress. It presents an ethical framework that motivates rectifying social ills and proposes a social *telos* that policy actions are to achieve. The redefining progress proposal is used as a context for discussing the broad range of issues related to indicators of justice, poverty and progress.

This chapter first highlights the inadequacy of using Gross Domestic Product (GDP) as a measure of social well-being or social progress. The first section borrows heavily from the article by Cobb, Halstead and Rowe (C-H-R). The second section presents a critique of the social indicator movement and the redefining progress proposal, and attempts to answer the question: Does it make sense to adopt the GPI? In answering this question, the ways in which the social indicators and GPI consider the poor, and the ways by which those indicators measure the progress of the poor, are highlighted. In the following section, poverty indicators are presented and evaluated according to how well they reflect a Christian moral vision for economic life. The fourth section, using an example, addresses the difficulty of constructing and selecting indicators of poverty and progress. Fifth, a *telos* that serves as a basis for developing indicators of progress and poverty is proposed. In short, this paper makes the ends explicit. The final section suggests a concept and model that, given this vision, may be a useful tool for understanding the dynamics of social production, the dynamics of poverty, and how to monitor progress towards the proposed ends. The paper is written from a Christian worldview.

The Inadequacy of GDP as an Economic Measure

Gross Domestic Product (GDP) has been used for many years as a quick and dirty measure of social well-being. While never intended for such a purpose, the rationale for using GDP per capita (or simply GDP) as a means to gauge whether the citizens of a nation are better or worse off, all other things being equal, has an appeal. GDP measures the value of goods and services a nation is able to produce and thus consume. As an individual's consumption of goods and services increases, so does his or her level of well-being. By extension, if the average consumption of goods and services for the country increases, the country's well-being also increases on average.

There are some important assumptions associated with this line of reasoning, but overall, one can see why an increase in GDP is a handy measure for an increase in social well-being. The more and better food, housing, entertainment, transportation and health services one consumes, the better off one is. Moreover, as a measure of social progress (in contrast to social well-being), GDP per capita is also useful.[2] As GDP increases, other social characteristics improve. For instance, the higher one's income, the more one tends to spend on health care and, as a result, the longer one is likely to live. The more one invests in education, the more productive one is. At an aggregate level, the higher a nation's income, the more educational services a nation can provide to ensure that every citizen is literate and productive. As a nation's income increases, the more it can spend on preserving the environment and natural habitat. Indeed, many studies have found a strong correlation between the level of GDP and other indicators of social progress, e.g., life expectancy, infant mortality and literacy.[3]

But, as anyone who is a critic of the overuse of GDP as a measure of social progress will hasten to say, GDP was never intended to be used as such a measure. Most economists will simply end a conversation about using an adjusted GDP concept, or an alternative economic and social indicator, to measure social progress by simply mentioning this point. GDP is an economic accounting construct that measures recorded market transactions (plus a few estimates of non-market transactions that, if excluded, would create a great asymmetry in the national economic accounts). When there is a record of money changing hands, GDP goes up. That is all GDP measures and all it was intended to measure.

Unfortunately, GDP *is* used as a measure of social well-being and as such misses a lot of beneficial, well-being-enhancing, productive activities. If someone lends a friend her pick-up and helps him move, he is much better off because he does not have to engage a moving company. But, because no money changed hands—except for the requisite purchase of pizza and drinks—GDP doesn't go up. And, if GDP is used as a measure for well-being, neither did social well-being. On the other hand, if he employed a moving company, GDP registers an increase. One can immediately see that GDP does not capture many life-enhancing and life-sustaining activities.

But there is more wrong with GDP as a measure of social well-being. Because GDP is a measure of dollar transactions, it weighs each dollar spent equally. GDP accountants make no distinction between a dollar spent on a wedding and a dollar spent on a divorce. The redefining-progress authors liken this aspect of GDP to the Mad Hatter's accounting system: everything is added. The dollar value of all products and services are summed together as though they were all "good." Everything is added, including products or services on which most would just as well not spend money on, such as prisons, divorce suits and security systems.

There is an additional ethical concern raised by this accounting system that treats every dollar earned or spent equally. There is no attempt to assign greater priority to a dollar earned by someone who is poor and someone who is rich. Arguably, the last dollar earned by the poor person is more important to him than the last dollar earned by the millionaire. In short, GDP and GDP per capita do not disclose who enjoys the increased ability to consume. GDP does not show how many poor there are, how destitute they are, or if their lot improves when GDP increases. As a measure of progress, it ignores a large portion of the population. Even those with no commitment to an ethical system would say that poverty is a social ill. If a measure of social progress ignores a social ill, then that measure is inadequate.

From the perspective of those concerned with the poor, GDP does not even begin to tell the story. In addition to ignoring who gets how big a slice of the economic pie, there are several other issues. Per capita GDP says nothing about the cost of living. A dollar in the United States doesn't buy as much as a dollar in a developing country. A dollar in New York City doesn't buy as much as a dollar in Mississippi. Hence, per capita GDP says nothing about the availability of basic goods and services or a poor person's ability to buy adequate food and shelter. It provides no indication of the availability of free goods and services. It also says nothing about the non-market amenities or unpleasantries a poor person enjoys or endures. Typically, the poor live in areas that are more polluted, more congested, more noisy and more ugly. In short, it says nothing about the quality of life for those who earn less income than the average.

By using increases in GDP as a measure of social progress, one also implicitly assumes that all members of a society enjoy the increases equally. Some cross-national studies suggest that an absolute as well as a relative decline in the average income of the very poor could accompany rapid growth.[4] As a result, the perception of inequitable growth fostered the concern to construct indicators of poverty beyond GDP per capita. This critique of using GDP was bound up in the awareness that growth-oriented strategies failed to account for social structures and the distribution of the benefits of economic growth.

In response to the fact that GDP did not address the issues associated with determining how well one country was faring compared to another, and did not address the persistent problems in the Western countries that many thought would be cured by increases in economic output, social researchers began to look for a new indicator, or set of indicators, that could measure important social developments ignored by GDP. These research efforts in the 1960s and early 1970s attempted to construct measures of economic and social well-being to incorporate the concerns similar to the recent proposal made by C-H-R.

The social indicator movement began in the early 1960s to address the fact that GDP did not tell enough of the development story. Social indicators (SI) were proposed to supply data to help decision making about complex issues, many of which were only tangentially related to economic output.

The SI movement criticized using GDP as a means to monitor progress in three ways. First, GDP omits non-market transactions. Second, money as a measure of value ignores the fact that price signals set by the market are not always accurate and neutral guides for the desirability of products or services. Are attorneys really five times more socially beneficial than teachers? The market says so. Third, it pays no attention to the distribution of benefits among the population at any one time or over time.

A great deal of effort was put into defining a set of indicators that presented a complete picture of social progress. Among them were attempts to modify GDP in order to make an index that is a better approximation of well-being over time and across countries. The most notable efforts were the Net Economic Well-being (NEW) of James Tobin and William Nordhaus[5] and the Net National Welfare (NNW) of the UN Measurement Committee.[6] While interesting exercises, these studies have had little long-term consequence because they have failed to meet the needs of either social researchers or policymakers. Net Economic Well-being (NEW), and measures like the NEW, are neither useful explanatory tools, because they aggregate too many diverse trends, nor a statistic with much policy relevance, because policy makers don't know what lever to pull to improve it.

Physical, non-economic, indices were also proposed. Unfortunately the physical indexes that measured what GDP failed to measure—for example, infant mortality or literacy rates—do not address the issue of distribution. Doctors per capita, for example, does not measure the distribution of health services. The UN Development Programme's Human Development Indicator (HDI) incorporated non-economic data, but was no great advance as an index. The HDI, like GDP, does not take into account the distribution of benefits *and* suffers from an additional problem, that of "normalizing" its components. The HDI is the sum of indices of the normalized components: GDP per capita, infant mortality and literacy. The process of normalizing, or making relative, one country's figures with those of all other countries leads to an unappealing quality: in order for one country's HDI to increase, the HDI of other countries have to decrease. The SI movement lost momentum because the proposed indicators like the HDI couldn't address many of the policy or research issues that motivated it.

Worse yet for the SI advocates, increases in most of the non-economic indicators of development, or social well-being, correlate significantly with increases in GDP. For developing countries, the post-war goal was industrialization and the key indicator of achieving that goal was the growth of per capita GDP. When data across countries are compared, there is a high correlation between GDP and just about every other indicator of progress, e.g., life expectancy and infant mortality. Those examples of countries where the relationship is least likely to hold are South Africa and the OPEC states. In these cases, the high per capita GDP masks the highly unequal income levels that are reflected in the poor health statistics. These results showed that GDP could be used as a reasonable proxy for well-being, social development and, dare one say, progress. After all, concomitant with increases in GDP come increases in material well-being, health, education, and standard of living.

The Genuine Progress Indicator

From the mid-1970s—when the SI movement lost steam—we can fast forward to the Cobb, Halstead and Rowe article "If the GDP is up, why is America down?" In this article, the redefining progress authors tried, in effect, to revive the SI movement.[7] Cobb, Halstead and Rowe critiqued the often-used measure of social progress, gross domestic product, in much the same way as the SI researchers did, and, like the SI researchers, they also proposed using their own measure of social well-being, the genuine progress indicator (GPI).

Their critique of GDP as a measure of progress follows that of the SI movement: GDP presents an inaccurate picture of the economic and social climate. GDP, because it measures only economic transactions, is inadequate for the task for which it is often used, that is, gauging social well-being and providing accurate feedback for policy. Because GDP is a good policy effectiveness indicator for stimulating the economy, and because economic growth has been associated with an increase in social well-being, Cobb, Halstead and Rowe argue that policies to address most social ills have one goal and one indicator in view: increasing GDP. But these economic policies are not scratching people where they itch. Economic growth does not address the many dimensions of social problems.

But there is much more at stake than simply changing the way to measure social progress. Cobb, Halstead and Rowe have a political and social agenda. They want citizens to understand the forces that control their lives. They want the political system to assess and address the anxieties in the land. They hope to strengthen the role of the family. They hope for a more equitable and reasonable tax system. They want a comprehensive social accounting of the costs and benefits of economic and social policies. Few people would argue against this agenda. So why isn't their measure readily embraced? Why did economists, in the main, scoff?[8]

Many economists may well agree that the Cobb, Halstead and Rowe political agenda is desirable, but Cobb, Halstead and Rowe are not going to find too many economists who will champion the adoption of the GPI. There are several reasons. Ironically, the reasons that economists are not likely to join the party are the very reasons why Cobb, Halstead and Rowe think that it is time for the GPI.

The vast majority of economists argue that measures of economic progress must be free of value judgments. Almost to a person, economists are uneasy with imposing subjective judgments about what counts as enhancing social well-being and what doesn't. Let the market decide what is valuable. Then, compile market statistics and report them. The insistence that economics is a value-free discipline, however, is quite ironic; economics is primarily about valuation. The claim that economics is about scarcity is not exactly correct. If scarcity did not exist and everyone could consume as much as she or he wanted, one would still have to rank order what he or she consumed, because humans are bound by time. The process of rank ordering is, quite simply, an exercise in valuation. Even if everyone could consume as much as he or she wanted, one must value one good, service or activity over another in order to determine what to consume first.

Cobb, Halstead and Rowe would also like to see the prevailing economic model reformed, if not replaced. Economics uses many abstractions and assumptions to simplify their analysis. Economists use a model of a person called "Homo economicus" or economic man. Homo economicus is a rational, independent, self-interested, market agent who wishes to maximize his well-being. An important part of the Cobb, Halstead and Rowe agenda is breaking the manacles of economic assumptions about the object of economic investigation. Rather than studying Homo economicus and the measure of his interactions in the market, Cobb, Halstead and Rowe allude to a better model, what one might call "Homo ecologicus." Homo ecologicus is a person who is a rational, interdependent, flesh and blood, civic participant. The genuine progress indicator better describes the world of Homo ecologicus. The GPI captures socially important activities and assets that are invisible to the money economy, and does not add the value of beneficial market activities with malevolent ones. The GPI also embraces cultural, social, institutional and civic values important to Homo ecologicus.

"Fine," the average economist might say. Those are important elements, but those elements are outside the realm of economics. Economists won't play Cobb, Halstead and Rowe's game because their game isn't economics.

But making it the game of economists is high on Cobb, Halstead and Rowe's agenda. They wish to fuse the economic realm with two other critical spheres of human existence currently left out of economic accounting, namely, the functions of family and community and the functions of the environment and natural habitat. Both contribute to well-being and are currently invisible in the national economic accounts. Worse yet, the primary economic indicator often shows increases while social cohesion and environmental sustainability decline. Parents divorce and GDP goes up. A thief breaks into a house, the owner replaces the electronic goods and installs a security system, and GDP goes up. Install a water filter because the local water is foul and GDP goes up. Pave paradise and put up a parking lot and GDP goes up. Cobb, Halstead and Rowe, on the other hand, want to see social and environmental degradation reflected as a negative in the measurement of social well-being.

Cobb, Halstead and Rowe propose an economic statistic that subtracts all costs and adds all benefits of economic activity. Goals for more growth should specify more growth of what product or service, for what purpose, and for whom. An approximation of social and environmental costs, they argue, is less distorting than the zero cost now recorded in the accountant's books. The GPI, they claim, rightly accounts for the costs of crime, self-defense expenditures, resource depletion and habitat degradation, the unequal distribution of income, the household sector, and the loss of leisure. This gets closer to the economy people experience. The GPI measures economic steps forward with social and environmental steps backward.

The early social indicators and the more recent GPI proposal are attempts to measure social and economic phenomena. But what makes for a good measure? The weaknesses of the SI and GPI are explored here in detail with the hope that any other proposed indicator will not fall into the same trap. My own proposal tries to avoid the same pitfalls and, where it cannot, at least admit, its deficiencies.

When recording social phenomena one must keep in mind that there are many things going on everywhere all the time. What one decides to measure and record presupposes that there are certain events worth recording and other events worth ignoring. A social model or theory about how social and economic agents interact usually drives what gets measured and what does not. Measures themselves affect the perceptions of problems and solutions. Models are representations that abstract important elements from the subject of investigation and reassemble those representations for more convenient analysis and manipulation. Policy actions are also based on models because a policymaker must have some presumption about what the result of a policy action will be. In sum, social models and social policy require decisions about which elements are important, hypotheses about how those elements interact, and hypotheses about the results of policy actions.

In management theory, the practice of "managing for results" has gained currency. That is, one must define an objective in terms of an outcome that one can measure and monitor. That may be something quantitative, for example, profits for a year (easy), or qualitative, for example, participatory decision-making (difficult). Social indicators are an attempt to measure desirable outcomes that are not as easy to measure as dollar units of profit. If one is interested in managing for the result of a desirable social process or outcome, then the manager, or in this case the policymaker, should have a model of the social process in keeping with the desired result. "[S]ocial indicators will be most useful to us if they are chosen and designed deliberately and on the basis of the best conceptions and theories we have about the dynamics of the social process."[9]

The aim of the SI movement was to provide guidelines for developing measures to fill the gaps in the socio-economic data. The functions of a social indicator are to simplify observation, ease prognosis, point to policy prescriptions and monitor policy performance. Indicators interpret the advance or retrogression against some norm. They enable policymakers to assess initial conditions, to monitor progress toward a social goal, and to evaluate policies. Indicators organize and present objective information as value-free data, but take on a normative role because they make implicit or explicit assumptions about desirable directions. "In fact, the whole issue is fraught with value judgments and the values involved are of such a fundamental nature that it might not be easily resolved."[10] No wonder economists want to steer clear of such measures as the GPI.

The OECD program for social indicators generated a lot of research into measuring well-being. The program showed that a group of countries could agree on areas of common concern. However, the price of agreement was that "some indicators discussed in the early stages for the administration of justice and social inequality fell by the wayside."[11] The OECD researchers learned that there is no simple and easy way to clearly define the concept of social well-being. They encountered problems of identifying the components of well-being, determining the standard for well-being, and determining who determines the standard.

It is extremely difficult to get a clear definition of the concept of well-being (or the relationship between progress toward some norm and the resulting increase in well-being). Well-being is subjective, involving such characteristics as personality type and psychological make up. Furthermore, because it includes components outside the realm of economic management, it is unsuitable for analytic purposes in econometric models or policy formulation. Trying to make one measure apply to too many concepts or serve too many functions nullifies the usefulness of the measure because there is no unambiguous link between a policy action and changes in the indicator.

The question then becomes: How useful will policy makers find the GPI? The GPI may or may not correspond to social well-being, but what can a policymaker do to improve it? Social and economic relationships are complex. Trying to guide public policy with an all-inclusive measure is like flying a plane with just one dial that registers either a happy face—everything is fine—or a sad face—a crash is imminent. What pedal does one press to make the sad face happy again?

The conceptual and methodological weaknesses of the GPI do not bode well for its future. The SI and GPI suffer the same difficulties and will, no doubt, suffer the same fate. If these were not sufficient reasons for Redefining Progress to go back to the drawing board, the GPI also does not measure up on the philosophical grounds of Cobb, Halstead and Rowe's own critique of GDP as a measure of well-being.

Cobb, Halstead and Rowe argue that the GPI measure will cure economists and the general population of the abstractions and assumptions of the current economic model. With respect to this philosophical attack, how does the GPI measure prevail against the statistical abstractions that serve as a conceptual phalanx against reality? The measure of value of the GPI, like a unit of currency of the current economic model, is also a personal, subjective, "all-in-your-head" assessment of worth. Something has economic value because someone *thinks* it does and is willing to exchange something that someone else *thinks* has value. What *reality,* then, does the GPI measure? By placing money values on everything—including community and nature, for example—are Cobb, Halstead and Rowe not simply increasing the size of the conceptual phalanx? In effect, the economic realm grows to accommodate the sub-realms of community and environment. Worse yet, by applying the yardstick of money to the realms of community and creation, one depreciates their high intangible value. Monetary valuation is useful for measuring the trade-off between benefits and costs among a set of options. The economic trade-off implicit in the GPI scheme suggests that relationships with friends or families can be foregone if the money compensation is great enough.

The basis of valuation that Cobb, Halstead and Rowe use is the same as that of economics. It is human-centered, subjective, and all-in-your-head. Moreover, it presupposes that humans are the measure of all things, not just economic activity. This premise is not acceptable. When the natural habitat is viewed anthropocentrically, the deep ecologists cry "Speciesism!" They question why humans can assume the role of measuring the worth of all life on the planet. In addition, most world religions would also balk at the notion that humans define the meaning and value of themselves, the community, and the environment in which they dwell (but for reasons different than those of the deep ecologists). Finally, a committed humanist as well as a committed Christian may take issue with the instrumentalism embedded in their proposal. Do families and neighbors exist to serve self? That family and community relationships are potentially disposable is implicit in any trade-off scheme that allows a person to place goods and services on the same market scale as family and neighbors.

How will the GPI measure highlight the importance of family, community, and environment? After all, how many policymakers or average citizens understand what is and isn't included in GDP now? Making the elements of community and environment salient is Cobb, Halstead and Rowe's stated goal. Yet, these components of social well-being will go from being invisible in GDP to being scrambled in the GPI. Family and friends, and flora and fauna will not be well articulated in a dollar denominated chop suey that includes everything that has social or personal value. The GPI proposal amounts to nothing more than genuflecting to the altar of economy *uber alles.* Cobb, Halstead and Rowe themselves have succumbed to the imperialism of economics by putting a price tag on everything.

Cobb, Halstead and Rowe assert that the GPI measure will bring about a social and political transformation. But how will this transformation come about? Cobb, Halstead and Rowe, like the SI social researchers that preceded them, have no end to which they gauge progress, or at least an end they make explicit. The type of growth matters, but how and why does it matter? This measure does not go far enough in recalibrating self-perceptions and the understanding of one's civic responsibility. One can argue, as they have, that prosperity has created the attitude that people are independent economic agents in little need of the social and familial ties that nurture and protect. Does using one comprehensive measure have the power to reverse this trend? Will one measure recalibrate citizens' understanding of their civic responsibility? It is not likely.

Cobb, Halstead and Rowe, in determining what is added as good and what is subtracted as bad when calculating their indicator, will find themselves in another quandary. For about two decades there has been a proposal to include "women's work" in GDP so as to acknowledge the value of their labor. Fair enough, but doesn't this mean all labor—market and non-market—should be included? How does a statistician determine whether one type of labor is work and another type of labor is leisure? Monetizing the activities important to some interest group opens the floodgates of monetizing every human activity. Where does one stop? Even sex could be valued at the going rate of prostitution. The logical conclusion of this approach goes beyond counting *some* goods and services as contributing to, and others as detracting from, human well-being. If one were to go through the bother of adding and subtracting— no small task that—one should then value every activity and item according to the degree to which it enhances or reduces well-being.[12]

The most significant critique of the GPI, however, like the critique of the measures developed by the social indicator movement, is theoretical. Any attempt to design a measure of social progress needs a coherent social framework, or social theory, within which this new indicator might occupy the role that money can claim in economic accounting.[13] In the end, the quest to dethrone GDP is misguided. Different accounting purposes need different types of indicators. Only a narrow political strategy can prioritize a single indicator. Compressing many and varied types of data into one indicator obscures rather than illuminates social progress.[14] It will certainly obscure the issue of poverty and income distribution in the economy. While Cobb, Halstead and Rowe have included a component in the GPI to account for changes in the distribution of income, it is inadequate to properly account for the plight of the poor or to provide policy guidance to ameliorate their condition.

An indicator is good insofar as it works to distinguish one policy target group from among others, to monitor and solve problems, or to aid in analysis. Poverty would seem to be a straightforward concept but it is difficult to measure. If poverty is understood to be material want, then the model, concept and measure are simple enough: the lack of money. If the cause of poverty is the subject of interest, then a lack of opportunity may be the appropriate measure and a concept like human capital may be appropriate. But if the cause of poverty is viewed as behavioral, then using a measure of material want or the lack of opportunity will not suffice in measuring the concept or aiding in formulating policy.

Following this line of reasoning, one can choose a concept and model with a view to the kind of public action one favors to alleviate poverty. If one favors income support, then one opts for the concept of absolute deprivation. If one seeks social work solutions, then he can select a behavioral definition. The measure and concept will make it more or less difficult to justify a particular action. "The principal reason that we have no generally accepted measure of poverty, despite considerable interest in the issue, is that proponents of various strategies are revisiting each other's proposal for measures. Insofar as they cannot come to agreement on a policy, it is difficult to come to agreement on a concept and indicator [of poverty]."[15] Only self-delusion allows one to think that one can avoid hypotheses about the cause of poverty and the appropriate policy action when selecting indicators of poverty. Avoiding value decisions when choosing measures is illusory.

The SI movement brought this to light. The SI tried to address the problems associated with using GDP per capita, by developing an alternative set of indicators. Poverty was not seen as simply low GDP per capita. Other elements entered into the consideration of the definition of poverty. But what seemed like better measures—infant mortality and literacy, for example—met problems not unlike those of GDP. The physical indices that attempted to measure what GDP failed to measure also failed to measure the distribution of benefits. Literacy and infant mortality rates, like GDP per capita, are reported as national averages. This suggests the need for local, geographically defined measures. Moreover, like GDP, many indicators implicitly assume the same proportionate scale transformation and linear growth of the concept being measured. That is, if the average number of doctors increases, the indicator implies that everyone enjoys better health care. But that doesn't usually hold true. Using a scale, index or measure that implicitly assumes a linear relationship between changes in high- and low-income groups undermines the usefulness of the statistic.

When developing the social indicators, the SI researchers and other social scientists weighed certain components in the indices more heavily in order to make the indicators more sensitive to movements that were considered more important. As a result, these researchers were criticized for making value judgments about what is most important in development and social progress.

To avoid the value judgments associated with weighing some components of a composite index more heavily than other components, many social researchers use the so-called empirical tradition as a way out of subjective valuations. The empirical tradition in social sciences may be viewed as looking at data without a particular model or theory. One may use this method in the hope of bypassing the problem of defining concepts and models and making value judgments. Unfortunately, in such cases, the concept of interest often becomes whatever the indicators seem to show.

The result of their empirical exercise was the design of very complex measures that overcame the simple or subjective weighting structures in a general index and that quantified the different dimensions of what one might call "the quality of life." These indices applied statistical techniques (factor analysis) to derive a synthetic index, one that evaluates all quality-of-life components according to their statistical significance. The assumption underlying these methods is that variables with high intercorrelations with other indicators (on average) better express the level of development or quality of life than the indicators with low intercorrelations. There is no analytic formula (or motivating model) for such indicators and, in that sense, they are less subjective than weights applied by a room full of social researchers. On the other hand, these indicators may miss what is most important in determining the policy-outcome link.

The foregoing discussion may provide additional insight into how well the GPI and most measures of poverty and progress measure up. The general conclusion: not particularly well. The GPI does not necessarily show social welfare or progress. It does not present social progress in the context of a social dynamic, nor is it helpful in monitoring policy effectiveness. As will be shown below, the plethora of poverty measures falls short for the same reasons. They do not necessarily show the conditions of the poor, nor are they based on a model of the social dynamics of poverty. These measures can be useful in constructing hypotheses about poverty, but they may not be helpful in developing policy options.

The GPI proposal, and the political and social agenda Cobb, Halstead and Rowe advocate, may be a good start in bringing to the table several divergent, and perhaps competing, academic disciplines and political interests to discuss what is meant by progress.[16] Cobb, Halstead and Rowe's stated goals are to change the social and political landscape. What, exactly, is the new political paradigm they advocate? Are justice and equity embodied in their new political paradigm? Is the GPI measure either necessary or sufficient as the first step in reforming the prevailing political paradigm in a way that increases the internal philosophical consistency of American politics? If not, then, according to management theory, theirs is not an appropriate indicator or tool to achieve their goals. The strongest argument for an indicator is if that measure is necessary to achieve one's objectives. People may quibble about the objectives, but unless there is a political discussion about the collective vision for the country, then the discussion about what measure or set of measures to use to measure progress is idle conversation, an academic exercise suitable for those enamored with statistics.

Values, or more precisely, ethics, are at the heart of the discussion. Ethics are the axis of the social and political realignment. Cobb, Halstead and Rowe point out that both major American political camps are quick to speak from the standpoint of values against the moral relativism of the market. That unease with the moral relativism of the market, however, is a far cry from embracing an ethical framework sufficient to realign the market, or any social or political construct, toward a particular goal.

In summary, the GPI proposal, just like the SI movement of yesteryear, has no theoretical mandate to argue in its favor and runs into the same thicket of conceptual and practical problems. While Cobb, Halstead and Rowe would like to see their political and social agenda advanced, and see the adoption of the GPI as an indicator of that advancement, because it is an *ad hoc* hodge-podge of components it lacks a clear link between policy actions and desirable outcomes. Moreover, it still does not adequately address the distribution of social benefits and costs. Their agenda does not sufficiently address the concerns of the poor, nor does their indicator adequately show the conditions of the poor. (Granted, this was not their primary motivation. They are not responsible for failing to accomplish what they did not intend to accomplish.)

My agenda, and the agenda of this book, is economic, political and social justice based on the Judeo-Christian tradition found in the Bible. William Temple argued that the biblical vision is the primary mechanism for the church's influence upon society. It may sound pompous. Many may find it objectionable. But the motivation for proposing indicators and designing policies is nothing less than God's commands. The second mechanism of the church's impact, according to Temple, is to pass to Christians, acting in their civil capacity, the job of realigning the existing order closer to those principles. As Temple points out, technical knowledge and informed judgments are needed at this point. A theologian, for example, is not entitled to make a judgment about how to design an economic policy *as a theologian.* As a result, this book has brought together theologians, political scientists, economists, sociologists and other social scientists to articulate the principles and propose well-researched and practical means to move towards a just and caring economy. If Christianity is true at all, says Temple, it has universal application and all things should be done in accordance with Christian principles.[17]

For the purposes of this agenda, the Cobb, Halstead and Rowe proposal is a good start for discussing the need to redefine progress and develop new indicators, but falls short of ensuring economic justice. In addition, the redefining progress proposal does not go far enough in defining the principles or in developing the policies to realign the social order to correspond to biblical principles. That poverty exists is perhaps a sufficient indication that economic justice is lacking. But how is poverty to be measured? It is to a discussion about measuring poverty and the condition of the poor that attention is now turned.[18]

Measures of Poverty

Social scientists have many tools to measure poverty and to measure changes in how economic output is distributed. After a brief reading of the literature, one may be tempted to say that the poor have been well taken care of, at least based on the sheer volume of indicators and statistics that are available to assess their condition.

The measures of poverty fall within two general categories: relative measures and absolute measures. There are several variations within each of those categories, but the gist of the relative measures is to see how well or how badly the poor are faring compared to the general population. The gist of the absolute measures is to see how the poor are faring with respect to a certain standard of living.

The distribution of income is the most used relative measure. It is usually calculated in two ways: by comparing the observed income distribution against perfect equality, and by comparing different income groups with one another. Income groups are usually broken down in fifths, or quintiles, and then classified within those income quintiles according to other demographic characteristics such as gender, race or educational attainment. The following are ways to break down income distribution and compare income quintiles.

The highest quintile option divides the share of the highest income quintile by the average of all five quintiles. Some social researchers have called this an index of envy because it shows how far away one is from the high life.

From the opposite perspective, there is the lowest quintile option. This calculates the variation in the share of the lowest quintile to the other quintiles. The focus is the poor. When done year to year it shows improvements in the lot of the poorest segment of society. From the perspective of social well-being, the poor, arguably, find that their last dollar received is more beneficial in satisfying human needs than a dollar added to the income of the other groups.[19] The lowest quintile comparison fits well with the Rawlsian notion of justice that gives special weight, or rather the only weight, to improving the condition of the poor. Rawls argues that a society should choose rules (and laws) that protect the interests of society's weakest and poorest members.[20]

One can also use a weighted ratio that assigns arbitrary weights to each quintile, depending how important one wishes to make each income group. By this means one can value a dollar in income in the lowest quintile much more heavily than a dollar earned in the highest quintile. The weights are subjectively applied and often the weighing procedure is not transparent. This method is not favored by many because it is difficult to justify one weighting scheme over another.

The Gini Coefficient is one of the most used measures for comparing income distribution over time and between countries. It compares the difference between the actual income distribution and equal income distribution. It gives equal weight to all income levels. If the Gini coefficient is zero, then income is evenly distributed. If the Gini coefficient is becoming larger over time, then income is becoming more unequal.

The Lorenz Curve is a graphic representation of income distribution relative to equality. Perfect income equality is shown as a forty-five-degree line with the proportion of income on the vertical axis and the proportion of the population on the horizontal axis. If income were equally distributed, 50 percent of the population would be earning 50 percent of the national income. The 50–50 point, plotted on the Lorenz Curve, falls on the forty-five degree line. Unequal income, on the other hand, is plotted as a curve below the forty-five degree line. The greater the inequality, the greater the distance between the curve and the forty-five degree line.

The foregoing statistics measure income distribution. For countries with an economy that is largely formal and recorded, getting income statistics for these distribution indicators is not difficult. The distribution of *wealth*, however, is another matter, even in advanced economies. It is difficult to get both a clean definition of wealth that encompasses all assets, tangible and intangible, and a concept that an economic accountant can measure with a high degree of accuracy and reliability. Wealth can include capital equipment, transportation infrastructure, rights of access to land or sea, education, artwork, natural resources, livestock, and many other things. Wealth can also take forms invisible to the economic accountant. National economic accounts are good at measuring flows over a given time. Stocks of wealth, in contrast, are harder to measure. Wealth can also suffer or enjoy exogenous changes in value— hoola-hoop-making machines may be worth a mint one year and worthless the next, depending on consumer tastes. Yet wealth is critical in assessing longer-term capacity to generate economic output and to earn income.

What is one to make of these relative measures of income distribution? It depends if they are used descriptively or prescriptively. Arguably, indicators should describe the state and direction of income distribution over time. Generally speaking, this approach is fine for descriptive analysis, but it doesn't help select the winning indicator from the list. Whether it is Lorenz Curve and Gini Coefficient analysis; inequality in terms of the lowest quintile or in terms of the average of inequalities; or inequality measured by the variance of logarithms of the different quintiles from perfect equality; all these approaches can be used to describe the state of inequality. There are no criteria for selecting one measure over another other than personal preference. Moreover, many of these approaches have been criticized on the grounds of uncertain relations between money income, social income and social well-being.

Poverty weighting, that is, applying greater weight to low-income gains in income when national income increases, moves from plainly descriptive to opaquely prescriptive. Poverty weighting tries to determine if income increases accrue proportionately or if an increase in income leaves the distribution unchanged. Early studies suggested that indices with poverty weighting yielded lower (adjusted) growth than proportional weighting.[21] In other words, income growth was stronger for the high-income bracket than for the lower-income bracket. One might be tempted to say that, in this case, the policy prescription would be some sort of income redistribution. But would that policy address the root cause of the uneven increase in income between income groups?

In the absence of perfect income equality, the relative distribution analysis so much as says: the poor will be with you always. Why? There will always be a segment of the population that is relatively poor, irrespective of the standard of living of the lowest income quintile. Perhaps the absolutist approach is more promising.

The other general approach is this subsistence, or absolutist, approach. Poverty is measured according to some agreed upon level of subsistence or standard of living that can be purchased by a certain level of income. The poverty line is such a measure. This measure describes the intensity of poverty according to some norm. It measures the number of people, or the percentage of the population, who are below some income threshold. This simple head count method, however, doesn't show the extent of income shortfall from the threshold, or relative movements of income below that threshold. It also fails to count anyone above the poverty line.

The poverty gap is the percentage of shortfall of the average poor person's income relative to the poverty line. This measure is often used in combination with other statistics, for example, with measuring deprivation at various income levels below the poverty line, or with the percentage of national income needed to lift the poor above the poverty line. The general deprivation index shows poverty increasing if the income of the rich rises faster than that of the poor, and, using Lorenz curve analysis or an "ethical prescription," points to necessary changes in income distribution according to some objective. This prescriptive analysis, like the weighted distribution analysis discussed above, presupposes that there are declining marginal gains in social well-being related to increases in income above the threshold.

The social wage is another type of absolute measure. Social wage analysis adds base money income with the social benefits of subsidized education, transportation, health services and the like. Arguably, the social wage is worth more to low income groups who use government-supplied services and subsidies than to high-income groups which do not.

It is also possible to develop an index that combines the averages of thresholds and distributions. For example, the Gini Coefficient can be used to weigh average incomes so that the same unit of income is weighted more heavily if received by a poorer person. But such a weighting system assumes a different utility of money within different groups, which, as stated before, is a value judgment economists are loathe to make, no matter how sophisticated or "objective" the weighting technique. Several researchers have used statistical weighting of index components to remove their personal bias. Unfortunately, these studies cast doubt on the validity of indicators that mix disparate concepts and dimensions.[22]

Are there other precedents for weighing income? GDP places equal weight on each dollar earned or spent. Are other weights theoretically better? The answer is not merely a technical matter. Economists can either create a composite indicator based on some model, a weighting scheme based on value judgments, or use a simple measure that fails to encompass all the necessary dimensions of poverty. What is one to do?

Recently, Amartya Sen developed a measure of poverty that attempts to correct for the deficiencies of the absolute and relative approaches. His goal was to make the measure sensitive to changes in distribution, as well as measure the gap between the poverty line and the income level of the poor. His measure also allows for the statistical decomposition of the poor population. This last feature makes possible the analysis of how much poverty is attributed to various population subgroups, and makes it easier to target various dimensions of poverty. Since Sen's proposal others have advanced distribution-sensitive poverty measures.[23] Unfortunately, despite Sen's specification of the desirable characteristics of an indicator and his care in constructing the indicator, his proposal can also be considered the product of his judgments about what should go into a poverty measure and what shouldn't. In the end, Sen's indicator suffers the same shortcoming of the other poverty indicators: it does not understand the social and economic dynamics of poverty.

Selecting Appropriate Indicators of Justice, Poverty and Progress

There are many ways of measuring poverty. In addition to those described above, there are tracer studies that chart the movements of the poor population from below to above the poverty line. Full-blown profiles of the poor, where they live, their education, their employment rates and their access to health services, are also available. But the issues of interest to this book have yet to be addressed by this plethora of indicators. Do these indicators measure justice? Do they correspond to a model of the social dynamics of the poor? Are they useful in determining the policy-outcome link?

Recall that social indicators will be the most useful and more readily accepted if they are designed on the basis of the best theories and models of the social process. The foundation upon which a compelling social indicator is built is its role in a theoretical model of social relations.

The ideal, the Holy Grail of social indicators, is akin to the central theoretical role of money costs and benefits in the neoclassical economic model, or the role of power relations in the Marxist social model. Both models mandate a certain type of information. The models make certain assumptions about economic and social functions and construct a distinct frame to understand the nature of economic and social dynamics. The models compel the use of a certain type of data and those data, in turn, compel a certain type of analysis. Using just one model, however, can limit a researcher's vision. Someone who uses only one model is more prone to reductionism. Economists are often accused of reductionism, of knowing the cost of everything and the value of nothing. Marxist social theorists, in the same way, seem to see every human activity in terms of a power relationship.

The issue of indicator selection is fraught with either moral-philosophical value judgments about what matters about the human condition, or theoretical value judgments about what matters in one's model. Members of a pluralistic society have different views concerning what matters most about the human condition. Often those who advocate a particular theoretical model do so with religious conviction, as though the model was transcultural, transtemporal, transnational and God-given. Theoretical models, however, even in physics, can come and go.

The solution the present age offers to this dilemma is decision-making by consensus. That is, the first desirable property of an indicator is that all agree on the implicit norms in its construction. My proposal, as shown below, proposes an ethical framework, states the goal and seeks to develop indicators to chart movement toward or away from that goal. That everyone would immediately agree to that framework and goal is doubtful; but, just the same, assume consensus about desirable social outcomes. Given consensus that a just and caring economy is desirable, is the U.S. there yet? How would policy analysts and policymakers know if the country were moving towards or away from the goal? How would model development and measurement proceed?

If agreement is reached regarding ethics, defining goals and developing models become more straightforward. Having defined the goal, it is easier to agree on defining the problem and determining the appropriate model to apply. The choice of the model will dictate the concepts one needs to measure. Then one must ensure that the indicator will measure what it is intended to measure. The measure must have conceptual validity and cohere with the theoretical model that will be used in analysis; if not, the economist must find ways to get those data, and make sure that available data are acceptable and sufficient to carry out the analysis. Finally, when constructing a set of indicators, researchers must ensure that there is a balance between economic and social components.

Those that have traveled this path before may provide some help. Consider the steps in constructing a set of indicators and the desirable properties of indicators listed in table 1 (p. 225). Are GDP, the GPI, or any of the social indicators or measures of poverty presented above adequate for the purposes of ensuring a just and caring economy?

Are there other off-the-shelf indicators or types of indicators that may be of use? Table 2 lists many indicators that are either used now or have been proposed to show social progress. Are these indicators necessary and sufficient for measuring social progress or determining whether a nation is just and caring? Which ones can be excluded? Are there additional measures that need to be included? If so, why? How would the issue of balance between economic and social components be addressed? Do the indicators reflect inputs into a social system, the process of the social system, or outcomes that result from the inputs and social process? Is there a clear link between policy actions and the improvement in the condition of the poor? Are the indicators listed in table 2 a good set of indicators?

While helpful in assessing conditions, these indicators, or measures, are proxies at best. Were policymakers to target these variables, it is very likely that the policy actions would be both expensive and ineffective.

As an example of the issues associated with constructing a set of indicators, consider education. How is progress or success in education measured? The typical and easy answer, test scores, may not be the best.

Education can be viewed as a production process that transforms inputs into outputs (or outcomes). There is a very important distinction between inputs, e.g., money and personnel resources, and outcomes, e.g., test scores and achievement. In addition, the process or system may result in a poor transformation of inputs into outputs.

Measuring education inputs is relatively easy. There are teacher to student ratios, classroom size, average grade point of incoming students, expenditures on teachers' salaries, materials, classroom hours, and the number of volumes in the library, to name a few. Outputs are more difficult because the desired outcome may be difficult to measure. While some graduates may score highly on an exit exam, they may not be intellectually well developed or may not be employable in the local labor market. Just the same, measures of outcomes include the percentage of students gaining admission to the next educational level, grade point average, scores on standardized tests, drop-out rates, average pay of graduates in the labor market and, probably the most important, employability.

Measuring the system and process is more difficult still. Spending a lot of money and using many high quality inputs does not guarantee good results. Often the system does not transform quality inputs into quality output. System characteristics—for example, the type of discipline practiced—are difficult to measure. How are the attitudes of the teachers and the students measured? How does one gauge the relevance of the curriculum apart from the context of the student body and the caliber of the graduates? While the number of volumes in the library may be impressive, what is the quality and relevance of those books? How do the students and teachers use the available resources? How is parent involvement measured? In addition to these questions, one must sort out which data are the most important so that the burden of data collection is not excessive and the analysis is not overwhelmed by the volume of information.

When developing a model to help understand a social process such as education, it is important to create a practical taxonomy of important concepts and variables. Having too few concepts can create as many problems as having too many. Economics uses one category to measure capital and investment. In the real world, the types of capital are many and various, but in the standard economic model, capital is treated as homogenous. Whether one invests in education, heavy presses, inventory, patents or natural resources, capital and its earnings are treated the same way. In this way, capital's productivity can be compared to competing types of investment. But while measuring education by rates of return (either private or social) has theoretical appeal, there are limitations to this approach. In strict money terms, it may not make economic sense to invest in educating handicapped persons, or homemakers, or any other group, if that investment does not provide adequate economic returns. The economic framework is not equipped to model the complex social relationships and social norms, or to evaluate the results, other than in strictly monetary terms. For example, it may cost nothing to impose a different disciplinary regime in a school system, but the returns measured in the productivity of the graduates may be considerable.

Because increases in GDP per capita failed to account for important social outcomes such as rising life expectancy and level of education, and because GDP per capita failed to show who sank in the rising tide that was supposed to raise all boats, the social indicator movement was launched. The GPI is simply a rebirth of the SI movement. The SI movement lost momentum for several reasons. Two of the more important reasons were the lack of an obvious policy-outcome link, and the lack of a social or economic model for which it was an indispensable component. If one were willing to overlook the problems of defining and operationalizing social well-being, there are still the nagging problems of which elements should be measured and what relative importance (or statistical weight) those components should be assigned. The exercise is rife with value judgments. Is GDP per capita more important than the level of literacy? Is the distribution of GDP more important than the distribution of health services? As mentioned above, experience has shown that it is extremely difficult to interpret the meaning of many social measures, especially in the case of composite indices, because they comprise a hodgepodge of subjectively weighed components. The statistically weighed, synthetic indices are not much better. While the statistical techniques removed the subjective bias of a particular researcher or group of researchers, synthetic indicators, more than any other type, obscure the component that is most important in determining the policy-outcome link.

It is important to remember that measures themselves affect the perceptions of problems. Just as a wrong conclusion can result from a single false premise, so can a poor policy prescription result from a poorly designed and applied indicator. Policy actions are based on models of cause and effect. Models abstract important elements from reality and reassemble what are considered the more important elements for analysis and manipulation. For policy actions to serve a purpose, one must have some preconception about what will result from those actions. Typically, that preconception is molded by the outcome as defined by the indicator. In management lingo, the temptation is to manage for changes in the indicator rather than managing for results. Misguided policy actions may simply target the changes in the indicator instead of what the indicator is meant to report.

The proponents of the SI and the GPI do not have a model of social or economic dynamics into which their indicators fit. As descriptive tools, the indicators are interesting, but there is no basis for selecting one particular SI over another. The same can be said of poverty indicators. They are useful tools for describing income distribution or the extent of poverty, but give little insight into the causes of poverty or into the effectiveness of policies which address those causes. Granted, they are helpful in making hypotheses about causes, but testing those hypotheses requires additional data. There is nothing inherently wrong with this approach as long as one is prepared to find root causes. From the spurious use of income distribution indicators, the conclusion of addressing poverty by income redistribution may have arisen. If so, then this is an egregious example of an indicator defining policy options.

In sum, the SI, GPI, and most poverty indicators suffer from three flaws. First, they are not designed according to a model or social theory that explains underlying social and economic dynamics. Second, they do not show the direct policy-outcome link, that is, they do not necessarily show the results of a particular policy action. They do not reflect the input, process and outcome triad. Third, the SI and GPI are not commensurate with the agenda and vision of their proponents. The poverty indicators, on the other hand, are commensurate with the notions of economic justice, albeit on a superficial level.

The Future of Progress: Defining the Ends

The construction of indicators and the motivation of policy actions are driven by ethics, by assessing what is right and what matters most. Instead of merely describing what is, the authors of this book are committed to advancing what ought to be. Typically, critics of measures like the GPI, the net national welfare measure, or similar indicators, focus their attack on the fact that the indicators measure what ought to be instead of what is. These critics point to the value judgments implicit in selecting the social components to include in an index, and in selecting how one component is weighed relative to other components. Having distanced themselves from the messy realm of ethics and from making uncomfortable statements about their values, they consider the case won. As Mishan stated in response to a measure like the GPI, "All efforts to adjust the well-being index to accommodate changes in distribution, intra-generational or intergenerational, must be regarded with misgivings. They are arbitrary or politically biased and are, therefore, invariably a focus of attack."[24] Our project will, no doubt, be attacked in this way. But to reiterate: we are concerned with what ought to be, not simply with what is.

Other critiques of composite indicators question if one weighting scheme is more theoretically sound than another. Typically, the proponents of the new measures are silent on this point because there is no theoretical basis for the weights. The proponents are merely seeking consensus about the inadequacies of the current set of well-being (or poverty) indicators, about the need to construct a new indicator, about what components to include in the indicator, and about what ranking system should be used to weigh the relative importance of those components. The defenders of the old measures are unimpressed with the consensus method of social research. Rather, models and theories should motivate social and economic measures, guide research and inform policy. Without fail, the two groups talk past each other.

Yet another critique of this project questions whether the market—or any institution or social structure like it—can be the subject of moral inquiry. Individuals are moral agents—and, properly, the subject of moral inquiry—but the market, they argue, is not. The market, they suggest, is like the weather, beyond the control of human agents. Some pro-market critics do make normative arguments for the market. For example, they cite the efficiency of market outcomes and the liberty of the market processes. But why are these criteria preferred over others? Why aren't fairness and justice among the evaluative criteria? Whether the debaters admit it or not, there are ethics and values at the core of any discussion about the nature of the market.[25]

I admit that this is an exercise in ethics. It arises from an ethical framework that informs decisions about what is important. Once the proposed understanding of human nature and social dynamics is made plain, the argument should focus on how well the model and indicators correspond to the subject of investigation and the objective of policy actions. Social researchers, whether they be economists, Marxist sociologists or humanists, may disagree with my premises and agenda, but my (and my colleagues') social and political vision will be explicit, the social and economic models coherent, and the policy prescriptions effective.[26] The critics may not agree with the principles, but they will not be able to condemn the project as a product of quack economists or sloppy social scientists.

The goal is a just and caring economy. The ethical framework is the Judeo-Christian tradition of justice, righteousness, shalom, and the kingdom of God. The Bible provides the material to develop these rich concepts, as several other papers have demonstrated.

The importance of starting from concepts and principles and building up to models, indicators and policies cannot be over-emphasized. Working on the margins, that is, taking an off-the-shelf model or measure and making a few minor adjustments, can lead to many philosophical, conceptual and practical difficulties. For example, the GPI, because it attempts to use a money metric for measuring well-being, runs into a philosophical pitfall of placing dollar values on the relationships that form family and community. This is particularly objectionable for Christians.

Human dignity is incommensurate with the all-in-your-head instrumental valuation measured in money. Ultimately, what gives humans, as well as society, plants and animals, worth is that value placed on them by the Creator. Economists call the non-market value of an object its existence value, that is, the intrinsic value placed on something even though it exists outside the realm of human usefulness, whether it is an endangered species or a distant, undiscovered planet. One may take the concept of existence value and extend it to the value the Creator places on something's existence. If, indeed, the world and everything in it is God's, then reason dictates that God could well place value on things which are outside the possibility of human enjoyment or utility. That is, something has value because God is pleased that it exists. Thus the Creator's (absolute) value takes precedence over a creature's (subjective) value.

Humans are created in the image of God. Loving relationships between humans are so important to God that one loves God by loving one's neighbor. Again, the Creator places value on relationships considerably beyond personal, instrumental valuation of "what is in this for me." Humans have value beyond that of objects or plants and animals. To relate to persons as objects denies that they are created in the image of God. Acts of injustice are condemned in the Bible because people are hurt. Hence, to place market prices on relationships with fellow persons who have the *imago Dei* is to arrogantly estimate the value of the invaluable. The Old Testament places such a great importance on human relationships that separation from the religious community of Israel was synonymous with death.

By starting from the principles and concepts of justice and shalom, this book begins with the end in mind. If successful, the fruits of defining the problem, developing the indicators and designing effective policy will be a movement toward greater justice and shalom. The fruit of this project is to redirect the form and structure of institutions to serve human needs. Other authors in this series have unpacked the biblical concept of justice. The concept of shalom, however, may require a little additional attention.

The term shalom is typically translated as "peace." This rendering is accurate but incomplete. Much more than the absence of war, shalom is a peace that speaks to the presence of justice. It means the wholeness, health and harmony of community. It speaks of fruitfulness of farm and family. It connotes rest and the cessation of striving. Shalom is freedom from fear and the presence of joy.

Using shalom as a policy goal brings to the fore the importance of communal and interpersonal relationships and the role of institutions and social structures in fostering fruitfulness, harmony and justice. Using shalom as the fundamental concept tests the process and the outcomes in terms of the good. It explains why social scientists and policy makers need to redefine progress. By embracing shalom as its centerpiece, we explicitly state the social, economic and political goals and begin to flesh out what the proposed political paradigm might look like. It shows why family, community and creation are worth incorporating in one's indicator. It shows why addressing who is progressing is as important as the progress itself. It highlights the importance of the poor. This methodology and ethic helps rank economic and social priorities. In essence, it helps to bring about the just and caring economy this research project is promoting.

Because this process has no hidden agenda and is based on an ethical framework, it can help to accomplish the goal of revitalizing America's public philosophy. It asks and helps to address these questions: What is the common purpose? What is the end of government? What should the relationship of citizens be to the state and each other? Cobb, Halstead and Rowe argue that using a spurious policy indicator—GDP—has resulted in political impoverishment. Using a progress indicator from only one realm of human experience has subtly transformed culture and politics. Like the ancients who began to worship the traits of the gods they themselves created, the United States has experienced a type of economic-totemism.

Cobb, Halstead and Rowe observe, as do other critics of late, that using GDP as a measure of well-being is an outgrowth of a civic and public philosophy that understands the role of government to be that of managing prosperity. Government abandoned the debate over the question of "What is a life that is good?" and embraced the moral imperative of figuring out how everyone can live the good life, i.e., acquire more possessions. Michael Sandel, one such critic, cites the Yale commencement speech of John F. Kennedy as an example of the change. In the speech, Kennedy urged the country to focus on "the sophisticated and technical questions involved in keeping a great economic machinery moving ahead."[27] Politicians have fallen into the same snare as economists. Whether implicitly or explicitly, they operate as though their vocation is the "value-free" pursuit of maximizing GDP. Sandel argues that this has contributed to a bankrupt public philosophy. The agenda of shalom, of charting a course for a just and caring economy, should help bolster a sagging public philosophy.

Measuring Shalom

It is one thing to reconstruct a public philosophy and admit that one's social, economic and political agenda are laden with values, but designing indicators of progress is another matter entirely. These are uncharted waters. Those who devise indicators have often taken the easy way out. They have been content with easily quantifiable concepts that may or may not correspond to the policy goal.

The multitude of income distribution measures and poverty indicators points to redistribution of income rather than to providing each citizen the capacity to earn a decent living or to providing an opportunity to live a healthy life. As other authors have mentioned, redistribution in ancient Israel was a short-term solution to keep someone alive during particularly bad times, or a longer-term solution in the odd case that an individual was incapable of earning an income. Redistribution was not a systemic solution.

The Israelite method of income assurance was to provide each family a means to produce and provide for themselves. The land, the means by which one could provide for oneself, was considered God's. God had resolved that the land—the primary productive asset—would be redistributed regularly so that all families had an equal opportunity to participate in the economic life of the community, and so that economic power would not be concentrated in the hands of any particular group for an extended period of time.

Is there an equivalent set of concepts for today's world? Economics and the other social sciences will be helpful in this search. Education, for example, may be the most important means of production today. Education certainly pays handsomely in the workplace; when researchers link the level of income with education, they find that education explains a great degree of income inequality.

If one is confused as to why society is spending so much on education in poorer areas with little effect, one may have to expand one's understanding of education. Recall that education can be viewed as a process that transforms inputs, for example, teachers and materials, into outputs, for example, graduates with certain abilities. That model may have to be expanded. What Kenneth Boulding has called the "limiting factor" in production may need investigation. Boulding sees production primarily arising out of know-how. Know-how combines capital, labor and materials to produce goods and services. Typically, there is some limiting factor in production. It may be the raw materials, the amount of capital, the type of capital, or some other input. Increasing know-how, or what one might call technology, reduces the limiting factor.[28] Identifying that limiting factor may play a great role in improving education.

It may also play a role in understanding the social dynamics of poverty. Development, according to Boulding, is a process whereby know-how pushes back the limiting factors. It is not a simple process of accumulating capital goods. Identifying the limiting factor in social settings may be difficult and it may be more difficult still to measure, but it may also expand the conception of production from the simple economic model to a more comprehensive understanding of the economic life of individuals and communities.

Of late, social scientists have expanded their understanding of economic production. They have shown that social relationships may also be a necessary input for economic production. These social scientists have adapted a term from economics to describe these relationships. They call them social capital.

In measuring wealth, economists ignore social relationships. This is easy to understand. Social relationships are invisible, not easily quantifiable, and, arguably, outside the domain of economics. Social relationships that are conducive to commerce are simply assumed. Not all economists, however, have made that assumption. Adam Smith spent considerably more time studying the social norms that allowed the invisible hand to increase social production than he did the invisible hand. Unfortunately, the modern, "classically liberal," disciples of Smith have had a bad case of amnesia about what Smith considered more important and have removed the necessary context for the socially beneficial operation of the invisible hand from their analysis.[29]

How do economic agents interact and organize themselves? There is no consensus about how to measure this, or whether it is valid to use the term "social capital" to describe this. But it seems clear that the norms, networks and organizations through which people gain access to resources are critical in producing and trading. Trust, for example, lowers transaction costs and thereby enhances the functioning of the market. Social capital reduces information-gathering costs by helping to spread important market information. Collective decision-making, because it gives a person a measure of accountability to a community, helps the community provide public goods and manage activities that have negative spill-over effects on those who are not direct participants in the transaction, effects that are also known as externalities.

How can the concept of social capital be applied? The concept is still new and, as several social scientists have argued, ambiguous and "under-theorized."[30] Robert Putnam views social capital as horizontal relationships, i.e., social networks and their associated norms.[31] Social capital helps coordination and cooperation to the mutual benefit of members. Civic associations are good proxies for measuring cooperation. But Putnam's concept has been criticized for being functional and, therefore, creating confusion about what it is, how it works, how it comes about and how it is measured.[32]

James Coleman sees social capital as both horizontal and vertical relationships, including corporations and other hierarchies.[33] Coleman's concept and analysis are more precise than Putman's. Coleman views social capital as a resource for individual action and envisages that the social capital framework will bring together social and economic analysis. Currently, both economic and social analysis are deficient. The missing element in sociological models is that there is no engine of action for the social actor, i.e., rational self-interest. The flaw of economic analysis is that a person's actions are shared and constrained by the social context. Norms, interpersonal trust and social organization are important for both social and economic functions.[34]

Coleman views social capital as a resource for helping an actor get things done. However, he does not emphasize the role of legal structures and the government. If anything, argue Brehm and Rahn, Coleman and Putnam present a view of social capital that allows communities to avoid coercive solutions to the problems of public goods and externalities.[35] To put it more bluntly, Coleman and Putnam downplay or ignore the role of government in forming social capital.

The third view places the formation of social capital within the broader framework of government and society-at-large. This understanding incorporates governments, political systems and the system of jurisprudence in forming and maintaining trust. The law of the land, for example, is important because it reduces the uncertainty of enforcing contracts. There appears, however, to be a difference of opinion about what role government has in understanding and forming social capital, and the difference appears to be based on a political divide. For example, Levi sees state institutions performing the functions of intermediation that are Putnam's basis for trust. Putnam, on the other hand, offers little role for government.

The preliminary conceptions of social capital link economic, social and political spheres. All of these conceptions focus on relationships among economic agents and how formal and informal organizations improve the efficiency of economic activities. All these understandings also imply that, because social institutions are public goods, individuals may under-invest in the desirable social relationships which affect those institutions. Hence, there may be a role for public support in building social capital. Associations help coordinate market transactions, reduce the chance of opportunistic behavior by repeated interaction among participants, and enhance trust and reciprocity. Unfortunately, associations are damaged by the mobility made possible by a highly productive economy. Indeed, Edwards and Foley don't see social capital as a particularly useful concept with a profound analytical payoff, but as the latest way to define what has concerned social scientists for years: the rootlessness of individuals who, seeking a better material life, have sacrificed the social integration and networks of a settled society.[36]

Coleman interprets this phenomena using the framework of social capital. "If the first individual can satisfy his need through self-sufficiency, or through aid from some official source without incurring an obligation, he will do so—and thus fail to add to the social capital outstanding in the community."[37] In other words, social capital may depreciate with lack of use. But does the under-investment in social capital mean that there is a role for government to invest in this "public good"? Possibly. Social norms and expectations are embedded in the social capital and in order for those norms to be effective there must be closure. Closure ensures that actions have consequences. Closure assures that an actor that deviates from the established norm is subject to censure. Hence, there may be a role for the state to validate the norms that are needed to provide public goods, to resolve externality issues, and to guarantee closure within and among social organizations.

But closure can also come about by internalizing social norms. Faith, as it turns out, can be a powerful influence in internalizing those norms and creating, in a sense, self-closure. Perhaps that is why Greeley argues that religion is a powerful and enduring source of social capital in the United States, and one with socially and ethically desirable effects. "Only the deliberately blind will continue to ignore religion as a source of social capital or deal only with its negative effects."[38]

Adam Smith would have used the term sympathy as a universal internalized norm,[39] but he might have also gone on to say that one of the two efficient causes for providing adequate goods for the average citizen, and preventing the vulgar accumulation of massive wealth by the very few, was social capital. For Smith, the end, or final cause, of adequate material goods for all people came about by two efficient causes. Efficient cause number one, personal ethics and rules of justice, constrains efficient cause number two, the constant effort of every person to better his or her own condition. Reading Smith and Coleman together makes one wonder if Coleman wasn't a student of Smith. Coleman combines the notion of rational self-interest with the sociological categories of social norms, rules and obligations. Coleman's "engine of action" for a social actor is equivalent to Smith's "self-interest." Personal ethics and rules of justice, Smith's other efficient cause, are equivalent to Coleman's closure and social context that constrain and redirect a person's actions.

Social scientists have only recently begun to refine and measure social capital. This will precipitate, over the next several years, a transformation in the understanding of poverty and how to design policy actions to alleviate poverty. This may follow the transformation in understanding and measuring intelligence. At first, intelligence was measured by the size of people's skulls. Skulls are easy to measure and the units are familiar. As time progressed there were more sophisticated hypotheses about what accounted for high intelligence. New categories to classify intelligence were constructed. Measuring what is easily counted—race, income level, and education level—may give way to measuring the social and institutional arrangements that may be of far greater importance in ascertaining why the poor are poor.

Can social relationships and institutions be assigned a particular value and used as a policy feedback tool? Possibly, but such value assessments should be derived from biblical principles of sin and the law of love. The spiritual cost of sin is infinite. The benefits of the law of love, from the Creator's vantage point, are also infinite. The value of these relationships and institutions is determined by how they contribute to shalom.

In order to define a set of indicators for policy, one needs a well-defined *telos*. The measure of progress must point to an end, a *telos*. In this case, the *telos* is not on a money scale whereby relative costs are totaled with benefits to measure changes in material well-being. Rather, the *telos* is the shalom or peace of God presented in scripture. Perhaps several indices could be developed which chart movement towards or away from that ideal. The indices will probably measure categories and concepts that are now unfamiliar and uncomfortable to us in the way they challenge our values and priorities. Police files record, and newspapers report, social ills, but direct measures of social health are not on the screens of social statisticians. Does anybody know how many people stopped to help motorists change flat tires yesterday? Does anybody know how many people visited the infirm? Does anyone know how many corporate executives have volunteered their time to teach business skills in the community or to help run a homeless shelter?

Conclusion

This paper considers indicators of progress and poverty. It argues that the most important question to ask about progress and poverty is "Progress towards what?" Job number one isn't redefining progress by creating a new indicator. Job number one is redefining *telos*. Only then can a course be charted to realize that *telos*.

This book is attempting to do just that. We propose answers to the most important questions about ends and means. My paper has shown that the standard set of measures of poverty and progress are inadequate. They do not help in understanding the dynamics of poverty and they do not provide an unambiguous link between policy actions and social results. Admittedly, these qualities are difficult to achieve in indicators, but are necessary for the task.

In broad terms, the processes of developing a social model of justice and poverty, and of designing indicators for those models, were also presented according to a biblical vision of shalom.

My recommendations are as follows. One, in constructing a social-economic model and the model's requisite indicators, economists should allow the biblical material to define the concepts, categories and principles. Two, we should apply those concepts, categories and principles to today's social and economic context. In so doing, we must be aware that the understanding and application of the biblical material will be fraught with categories, concepts and principles derived from contemporary social and economic models, current political ideologies and personal biases. As much as humanly possible, we should let the biblical material speak for itself. Three, we can apply off-the-shelf models and concepts that may be useful in conceptualizing the proposed model, in defining the social problem and in making hypotheses about cause and effect relationships. Four, we should construct indicators to manage for results. That is, the indicator itself must focus on the appropriate policy actions and the desired results.

This proposal is only a start. The principles have been set forth and many policies that apply those principles have been presented, but there is still much to do. The development of models of the dynamics of poverty, and development of the data needed for those models, are still in their infancy.

A pluralistic society may balk at using the religious ethic of shalom, but it is the Christian vision. Shalom is part and parcel of the good news of the gospel. Whereas sin is death and destruction, shalom is life and wholeness. The biblical mandates compel us to be concerned for the life of the community and nation. When members of the community are separated from each other, separated from the ability to provide for themselves, separated from life-sustaining health services and separated from the life-enriching natural environment, then the members of the community are separated from the fruit of the kingdom of God. The community is far from shalom and it is our duty to chart a course toward it.

Table 1

Desirable Properties of Indicators

- Developed within a conceptual and operational framework
- Clearly defined and easily understood
- Subject to summing up, that is, they must make sense when added together
- Independent of data collection and, in that sense, objective
- Moderate in the volume of data required
- Limited in number
- Reflect input, process and outcome (pressure, state and response)
- Indicate when a threshold has been exceeded
- Comparable to a benchmark condition or state

(World Bank 1997)

Table 2

How to Measure a Just and Caring Economy?

Are these indicators adequate to show whether
the economy is just and caring?

- Distribution of health resources
- Distribution of income
- Geographic distribution by income level
- Housing statistics
- Cost of living, i.e., purchasing power parity
- Percent of income spent on food
- Persons per square foot of residence space
- Telephones per 100 people
- Access to primary health care, prenatal care and immunizations
- Percent of income for health spending by income bracket
- Infant mortality by income bracket and locale
- Life expectancy by income bracket and locale
- Literacy rate by income bracket and locale
- Access to financial institutions
- Air and water pollution levels
- Ambient noise level
- Average commuting time
- Proximity to recreation areas/libraries
- Spending, both private and public, on education per capita
- Average educational attainment
- Percentage of children in secondary school
- Percentage unemployed
- Labor force participation rate
- Dependent:provider ratio
- Income per capita
- Social wage
- Average wage rate
- Percentage working more than one job
- Average number of hours worked
- Crime rates

~ **Part 2** ~

Empowering the Poor

Components of a Civil Society and Policy Response

～8～

Health Policy
and the Poverty Trap

Finding a Way Out

Clarke E. Cochran, Texas Tech University

Introduction

Poverty and ill health travel together. Persons near or below the poverty line have significantly higher incidences of acute and chronic illness. At the same time, those with such conditions, or those who have suffered serious injury, become more likely to fall into poverty. The conditions co-vary. Poverty puts one's health in jeopardy and ill health, with its attendant high medical bills, impairment of working ability, and days lost from work, makes it difficult to find and hold a decent job.

To a degree this relationship between poverty and poor health is a centuries-old fact of life. However, the particularities of American health and income support programs reinforce the historical connections. Because there is no public guarantee of health insurance, those who need medical care but lack private health insurance can depend upon public programs only if their incomes are low enough to qualify. Additionally, those who qualify for certain income-support programs, such as Supplemental Security Income (SSI) and Temporary Assistance to Needy Families (TANF) automatically qualify for public health insurance in the form of Medicaid. This means that certain poor persons who might be able and willing to work are discouraged from working because it would mean loss of health coverage for them and their children. Indeed, if health insurance were available to all persons, one barrier to work would be removed and public assistance expenditures would immediately decline substantially.[1] Empowering the poor requires creative public and private approaches to breaking the destructive connections between poverty, ill health, and impaired access to health care.

The medical system reflects the power relationships of society at large. It also has unique institutions of power that block access for the poor. The poor lack not only money; they lack the social, and often the intellectual and linguistic, resources to negotiate a medical system with centers of authority and hierarchy and with peculiar languages and rules.

The Primary Barrier: Lack of Health Insurance

The poor and near-poor do not get the health care they need to become productive members of the economy because they often lack health insurance.[2] Having a low income and being uninsured are positively correlated. The problem is particularly acute for the "working poor" and their children. These are persons who work full- or part-time in low-wage jobs that do not provide health insurance benefits. Health insurance and employment go together in America, yet the percentage of workers covered by private, employment-based insurance has declined in the last 15 years. Moreover, the costs of health care take a higher proportion of income the lower one's income.[3] This means that low income workers with family health problems have less money available for decent food, shelter, additional education, job training, or other requisites of social advance. It means also that the poor go through life sicker than the non-poor and die earlier. There is some evidence that these gaps are widening.[4]

The poorest of the poor often are eligible for publicly financed Medicaid and for a variety of other national and state programs that pay for health care. Moreover, it is often claimed, any person without insurance has access to care when needed through public hospital emergency rooms and other public clinics for the uninsured. Though there is some truth to this claim, there is as much untruth. First, these alternatives do not cover all medical needs, nor are they always available when needed. The uninsured are four times more likely than the insured to report an episode of needing and not getting medical care. They are three times more likely to report problems in paying medical bills. Persons at risk for, and persons having, a ruptured appendix are more likely to be uninsured.[5] Second, as David Hilfiker points out, in his poverty medicine practice there was frequently a large "gap between what was theoretically available to the poor and what was actually accessible."[6] Third, even after getting access to care, insurance makes a great deal of difference in how one is treated within the health care system itself. Though the uninsured enter hospitals sicker than the insured, they receive fewer diagnostic procedures and leave the hospital sooner. They are less likely to receive coronary bypasses and are one to three times more likely to die in the hospital. "Dumping" uninsured patients from private to public emergency rooms remains a stubborn problem.[7] These findings hold even for children, the group (next to the elderly) best covered by public insurance. Their access to the kinds of medical care needed to allow them to grow up to be fully participating members of American society very much depends upon whether or not they have health insurance.[8]

Lacking insurance is not an isolated phenomenon. Rather, both the number and percentage of uninsured are increasing dramatically. An estimated 42 million people (15.6 percent of the population) were without health insurance for significant periods of time in 1996. This figure included 31 percent of persons below the poverty line. Though only about 13 percent of the total population, poor people make up 27 percent of the uninsured. The number of uninsured children grew to 10.6 million in 1996 (about 15 percent of all children). Young adults (18–24), Hispanics, African-Americans, persons with less education, part-time workers, and foreign-born persons had the highest rates of uninsurance. More than half of poor, full-time workers (52 percent) were uninsured in 1996.[9]

Effects of Race, Ethnicity, and Residence

Income and employment alone do not determine the links between poverty and ill health. Certain racial and ethnic groups, as might be expected, are more affected by the connection than others. African-Americans, Hispanics, and Native Americans in particular are likely to be poor and to have limited access to health care resources. To some extent, race and ethnicity are proxies for low income. Because these groups are disproportionately below the poverty line, they disproportionately suffer the combined effects of life below that line. But there is more.

Many studies document the effects of racial discrimination in health care. African-Americans suffer disproportionately from certain health conditions; yet they do not receive the treatment needed to cure or alleviate these conditions. They are discharged "quicker and sicker" from hospitals, do not receive the same treatments as white persons for similar conditions, even when insured, and are discriminated against in admission to nursing homes and other facilities.[10] These effects exist even in Medicare, where African-Americans and whites have exactly the same insurance coverage.[11]

Hispanics also have particular problems in accessing medical care. Language barriers, discrimination because of doubts about legal status, and differences in cultural practices interfere with access to health care.[12] Native Americans suffer the twin effects of poverty and geographical isolation. Most reservations are far from state-of-the-art medical facilities.

Place of residence affects many others. Changes in the health care system have produced hospital closures in rural areas and central cities. Physician-to-population ratios are twice as high in suburban areas as in rural counties and the central cities of major metropolitan regions.[13]

The System of Private Insurance

Because state and federal laws require hospitals, especially public hospitals and private hospitals that operate emergency rooms, to accept all persons in medical need, everyone in America has some access to health care. If you are sick enough or hurt enough, some medical facility somewhere has the obligation to treat you. This kind of access, however, is very often too late, too costly, or inappropriate in terms of treatment and location. Moreover, it can also be of significantly lesser quality than regular, insured access to medical care, as noted above.

In short, access to the health care system at the appropriate time and place, for the right treatment, and without overwhelming financial burden depends upon possession of health insurance. And health insurance is tied to employment, at least for the working population. The majority of working-age Americans and their dependents obtain health insurance in connection with employment. Employer-sponsored insurance for workers and (frequently) for their dependents evolved in the mid-twentieth century as the preferred means of covering the health needs of Americans.

This system, however, is breaking down. The retired elderly (for the most part), the disabled, and the unemployed, of course, never had access to this system. Hence, the Medicare and Medicaid programs, described below. Recently, however, private, employment-based insurance coverage itself is declining. Job growth today is in the service sector, part-time employment, self-employment, and in contractual employment. These sectors traditionally do not offer health insurance benefits to the same degree as the manufacturing and blue-collar sector. Moreover, even those employers offering insurance have increased employee cost-sharing, making it more expensive for the worker, especially for dependent coverage. Changes in dependent coverage have left many children with diminished access to health care. Thus, there has been a steady decline in private, employment-based insurance over the last decade.[14] About two-thirds of uninsured workers work for firms that do not offer insurance. Another 20 percent work for firms that offer insurance, but these workers cannot afford the premiums. Individual policies not connected to employment are too expensive for the poor or lower middle class. Very few workers are uninsured by choice. The vast majority have no employment-based access to it or cannot afford it at their low wages.

Public Insurance and Other Public Programs

A system of public health care was developed in this nation to meet the needs of those without access to private insurance. Medicare and Medicaid, inaugurated in 1965, represented the largest public response. Medicare covers Social Security-eligible retired and disabled persons, as well as those with terminal kidney disease. Medicare covers virtually all the elderly; fewer than 1 percent lack insurance. Because of coverage limitations, however, many of the poor elderly have exorbitantly high out-of-pocket medical expenses.

Medicaid is a jointly operated federal-state health care program for those who receive public assistance, particularly SSI, the former AFDC, and the new TANF, as well as other persons who meet the various states' definitions of medical indigence. In addition, some poor Medicare recipients can receive Medicaid to help with medical needs. This Medicare-Medicaid link is especially important in connection with nursing home care. Medicaid covered thirty-five million persons in 1995 at a cost of $151 billion. Children were nearly half of those covered. Adults of working age were another 23 percent. However, expenditures for children and adults were only about 30 percent of the cost of the program. The elderly, blind, and disabled (about 28 percent of the Medicaid population) accounted for nearly 60 percent of spending. Long-term care accounts for over one-third of Medicaid spending. Medicaid pays for 47 percent of total nursing home care in the United States and 14 percent of home health care.[15]

Eligibility expansions in Medicaid in the late 1980s and early 1990s partially offset declines in private insurance coverage, especially coverage of children.[16] Nevertheless, many adults and children are not eligible, and parents fail to enroll many eligible children in Medicaid. Private insurance, Medicare, and Medicaid together furnish health insurance coverage to approximately 84 percent of the population. This leaves 16 percent, approximately forty-two million persons, without public or private insurance.

Other public programs do give episodic health care to many of the uninsured. They are often collectively referred to as the health care "safety net." These are the Veterans Administration health care system, the Indian Health Service, state and local departments of public health, public hospital emergency rooms and satellite clinics, and the network of Community Health Centers (CHC) and rural health clinics. Currently, nearly seven hundred CHCs serve about eight million persons, nearly half of them children. The number of uninsured seen at CHCs rose dramatically in the 1990s, placing them under severe financial pressure. The present safety net is not adequate to overcome the effects on health or income of the lack of good, regular access to mainstream health care.

Foundational Biblical Principles Related to Health Care[17]

Healing is a manifestation of Jesus' own action. "Health care is holy ground," in the words of Sr. Julianna Casey.[18] God cares about creation, providing the gift of healing skills for its restoration and as a sign of creation's ultimate wholeness. Any particular act of healing stands neither on its own nor as its own justification. All point toward the final healing of a broken creation (2 Cor. 5:18–20). Jesus frequently healed particular individuals of a variety of physical and (some might say today) emotional maladies. These included leprosy (Matt. 8:1–4; Mark 1:40–42); blindness (Matt. 20:29–34; Mark 10:46–52); muteness (Luke 11:14); hemorrhage (Matt. 9:20–22; Mark 5:25–34); and possession (Luke 9:37–43). He restored the dead to life (e.g., Mark 5:35–42). Jesus' cures were never simply for the personal, physical benefit of the one healed. They were signs of a deeper healing of soul in response to faith. The cures were also signs of the reign of God breaking into history. In the words of Pope John Paul II, "These cures, however, involved more than just healing sickness. They were also prophetic signs of his own identity and of the coming of the kingdom of God, and they often caused a new spiritual awakening in the one who had been healed."[19]

Health care touches the heart of the gospel. Those committed to imitating Christ's healing can never allow their work to be commodified and packaged for the exclusive good of the well-insured. Christian commitment to health care is intimately bound up with the coming of the kingdom.

Even more profoundly, Jesus does not simply *heal* the sick; he *identifies himself* with the sick. "I was sick and you visited me" (Matt. 25:36). "He took our infirmities and bore our diseases" (Matt. 8:17; Isa. 53:4).[20] On the cross Jesus takes on the whole weight of physical and moral evil, especially suffering and death. Therefore, Christians have always imitated Jesus' healing action; from Peter in Acts to the healing ministry of monasteries, to modern hospitals and clinics. Remembrance of his words and deeds becomes the ground of Christian healthcare ministry and public advocacy.[21]

Christian Principles for Public Policy

There are seven "fundamental commitments" that orient Christian approaches to government and to public policy generally. They are: (1) the social nature of humanity; (2) the reality of sin; (3) the limits of government; (4) commitment to the common good; (5) commitment to justice and fairness; (6) protection of human dignity; and (7) stewardship. The commitments that ground Christian approaches to policy are neither ideological nor partisan. They transcend the political categories that frame the policy debates of particular eras.

General principles, however, are inadequate for sustained analysis of the complex policy questions characteristic of health care. Such analysis requires that principles be more carefully specified and applied to real, public policy challenges. It is easy, but unprofitable, to move directly from the cry for "justice" to condemnation of a Republican or Democratic proposal for Medicare. The Christian analyst or citizen must unpack the specific meanings of justice for health care and carefully explore the likely consequences of policy changes. Policy inquiry takes time, energy, and willingness to confront intricacy and doubt.[22]

Specific Implications for Contemporary Health Care Policy

These seven general commitments need connection to the specific characteristics of health and healing before policy implications can be drawn. Given the profound connection of these concepts to all facets of life, it is not possible to explicate them fully.[23] Health is first of all a gift, part of God's promise of "life in abundance" (John 10:10). Health is the whole and proper functioning of mind, body, spirit, and emotion. Such wholeness enables fully human social relationships, contributing to the human flourishing that God intends. But humans are not always fully alive; mind, body, spirit, and emotion do not always function properly. The fall makes healing an essential part of human life and of church mission. Healing (and medicine, one of its instruments) is also a divine gift, the presence of God to human brokenness. Healing is, therefore, a fundamental part of Christian community life. Witness the large number of Christian health care institutions. Healing is a restoration of the gift of health, a faithful response to God the redeemer.

But the kingdom is both now and not yet. Neither health nor healing may be treated as final, nor can their ambiguity be denied.[24] There are two reasons for this. First, "Those who are well have no need of a physician, but those who are sick" (Luke 5:31). Flourishing health is often a temptation to pride, to independence from the giver of life. The power to heal also tempts pride when healers see themselves as gods instead of servants of God. Second, suffering is part of the human condition in a broken world. Not every injury or sickness can be mended. Suffering and death are also part of the fallen world that health care confronts. Though healing is sometimes possible, medicine ultimately cannot defeat death. The deepest mystery of faith is that God in Christ shared human suffering and death. Therefore, simple presence with the suffering and dying is as basic to Christian life as curing—thus the ministry of Mother Teresa's nuns in the slums of Calcutta. "Care" is one name given to this presence with the sufferer. Both care and cure are part of ministry, parts that can come into tension with each other in the tangled world of modern medicine.

These reflections bear upon the principles of human community, sin, and the limits of government. God's intention is for healthy persons to live in community, an intention marred by sin. Suffering and affliction insult the integrity of person and community. The temptation is to insulate the healthy from the sick, who are kept on the edges of the community, especially if their conditions are incurable. Keep them outside the camp and force them to cry "leper" should they encounter one of the whole! The example of Jesus, however, forces the community to struggle to include the sick, injured, suffering, and dying as fully as possible in social life. Because government has responsibility for the common good it can assist in this struggle. Yet government itself is limited and cannot take the place of health care personnel, families, or churches in the effort to care and cure. The paragraphs below outline specific implications for health care policy.

Health Care and the Common Good

The perceived relationship between health, health care, and the common good has varied through history. When the healing and caring arts were largely the possession of families, their relation to the common good was more indirect. As the meaning and production of medicine became more social, particularly in the twentieth century, their relation to the common good become more direct, with a corresponding increase in the responsibility of public authority.[25]

What does it mean to say that medicine becomes more social? Today the knowledge of medicine, both in its healing and its caring aspects, cannot be contained by families or even by well-trained medical professionals. Medicine in the late twentieth century is a social art; that is, its divisions (nursing, obstetrics, psychiatry, surgery, and so forth) are distributed among specialists who (in the best of circumstances) work together for the good of particular patients. Moreover, the advancement of medicine in the form of research and development is also a collective enterprise, often heavily financed by government. Finally, the specialists who hold and advance medical art receive their education in institutions founded and supported by the public through philanthropy, public financing, and (often) public governance.

Therefore, the health care system is both a common good, in the sense that it is a good produced by the common action of society and its representatives, and at the same time a *means* to the common good, in the sense that it assists individuals to remain members of the community in the face of illness and injury. Because government has a primary responsibility to promote the common good, it has an obligation to develop policies that assist the health care system to be both a common good and a means to the common good. But government does not have the sole or final responsibility. The health care system itself has responsibilities, as do families, churches, and other associations. Individuals, civil society, and government form a web of responsibility.

Justice and Health Care

If institutions of health care have a social character and if Christians hold to the view that the common good is the focus of public action, then justice in the distribution of health care means distribution primarily according to the need for health care. Society uses various principles fairly to assign benefits and burdens to citizens. Different spheres of society appropriately employ different bases of distribution. College professors aim to assign grades on the basis of merit or achievement; the same principle is used for prizes in an athletic competition. Parents distribute slices of cake at a children's party according to strict equality lest fights break out. Numerical equality also governs votes in a democratic society. Love and affection are distributed according to mutual attraction and the bonds of marriage, family, and friendship. Cameras, blue jeans, automobiles, pencils, and diamond rings are distributed according to the logic of the market, which is free choice according to one's financial resources. No single principle of justice covers all spheres of life, and principles of fair distribution in one sphere do not translate directly to other spheres.

Need is one of the principles of distribution recognized in some spheres, but not others. Need is a poor principle for distributing grades, but the proper principle for distributing emergency food supplies. Need is also the proper principle for distributing health care when that care is recognized as a common good. Health is necessary for a community's proper functioning. Good health facilitates social interaction and economic enterprise. Medical care is not equivalent to health, but health care is one of the principal means of preserving and restoring physical, mental, and emotional functioning. Therefore, societies that value health, and that have the financial and technical means to develop modern systems of medical care, recognize that health care is a need of all citizens.

Need's prime competitor as a distributive principle in American society is the market. Commitment to laissez-faire capitalism promotes a vision of the market as the single metaphor for life. Yet the market, however appropriate for the distribution of commodities, depends upon an individualistic perspective foreign to commitment to the common good. It treats health care as a commodity like cameras, cars, pencils, and blue jeans. Those with the money (or in this case, the health insurance) may purchase the care they need (or perhaps only want). Those without financial resources receive inferior care or no care at all in meeting basic health needs. The American tendency to make health care a market commodity produces very high quality technical care, but at the highest cost and with the worst access in the industrialized world.

Basing health care justice on need, instead of other distributive principles, also recognizes the fundamental dignity of all human persons and their equality as citizens. To refuse to cover all citizens with health insurance and to make those without means wait in endless lines, jump through demeaning qualification procedures, and accept second-rate facilities while their fellow citizens have ready access to the best care, very clearly divides citizens into first and second class. It is as though some required special approval in order to vote, while others walked right into the polling place.

This argument that health care is most properly distributed according to need rather than by market mechanisms lies open to a number of objections and requires considerable clarification, which cannot be given here.[26]

To define a product as a need is not to say that its production and distribution *must* be social. Market mechanisms allocate essential resources such as food. Rather, this definition implies that government has a fundamental duty to assure that, whatever the distributive mechanisms employed, justice is done and needs are met. For example, government food stamps supplement the market resources of low-income families. Social responsibility for health care does not exclude indispensable personal responsibility or a role for civil society. Individuals and their closest family members are certainly obligated for their own health care, especially when many of its means are largely under their control (good eating habits, avoidance of smoking and excessive alcohol consumption, sufficient rest, and the like). Individuals and families also bear responsibility for treating and/or paying for minor health needs (such as Band-Aids and inexpensive analgesics to care for childhood scrapes and bruises). They may even assume responsibility for part of the sophisticated and expensive care given by the medical system (insurance deductions and co-payments). Responsibility for the health and safety of workers falls notably to employers. The health care system itself also has a duty to meet health care needs from its own resources (charity care). Churches and other associations provide care that is not a public, private, or health system responsibility (for example, the health needs of illegal immigrants).

The language of individual responsibility can be used far too glibly. Many persons (with mental or physical handicaps, with addictions, or with damaged social skills) are only marginally capable of personal responsibility. Moreover, the language of individual responsibility is often an excuse for denying public responsibility to provide adequate medical treatment, counseling, addiction treatment, and housing for the poor.[27] The obligation for meeting needs is a shared responsibility, which especially includes the obligation to manage the financial risks that accompany medical care. Insurance, public and private, is the principal mechanism of sharing risk.

Government and Shared Responsibility for Risk

The preceding does not require that society exercise its responsibility solely through government programs. No nation with a system of universal health care does so, and it is neither necessary nor desirable for the United States. Various public and private insurance mechanisms help to share risks.

Speaking of access to care is often short-hand for access to insurance against the financial risk associated with falling sick or becoming injured. Insurance does not prevent sickness or cure it; insurance makes it financially less burdensome to take relatively costly preventative measures (an annual physical) and assures both provider and patient that the cost of treatment (or a substantial portion of it) will be paid. Removing this financial uncertainty provides peace of mind to provider and patient, thus facilitating treatment decisions. It also ensures that the high cost of paying for accident or illness will not be financially devastating in the long-run, but will be apportioned within the community.

Insurance is fundamental to a modern system of health care. Yet risks for accident or illness are not spread evenly over the population, and some risks are partially controllable by individual or family choices (for example, types of hobbies, smoking, alcohol consumption, type of occupation, place of residence). Moreover, placing persons or families at some financial risk encourages sensible use of health care resources (for example, co-payments and deductibles discourage unnecessary physician visits). Placing physicians or hospitals at financial risk (as in HMOs or other forms of managed care with capitation) discourages over-treatment.

It is not a matter of either government or personal or civic responsibility alone. The three go together. The challenge of health care in the 1990s is to distribute risks fairly among individuals, families, employers, providers, and insurers. The greatest danger to the need principle is that the insurance market will segment risks in such a way that those who need health care the most (those with pre-existing conditions, for example) will bear an exorbitant share of the risk or be unable to obtain insurance at all.[28] In general, these considerations direct Christians to favor insurance market reforms that remove unreasonable barriers (e.g., pre-existing condition exclusions) and that guarantee access to insurance and to health care to all who need it. They steer Christians to oppose policy proposals that segment the insurance market into high- and low-risk categories, giving favorable treatment to the latter, who are most often those with higher incomes.

Dignity, Freedom, and the Vulnerable

Threats to health make persons especially vulnerable to the loss of human dignity. The special solicitude that Christ enjoins his disciples to take for vulnerable and marginal persons ("the least of these my brothers and sisters") reinforces the principle of need. Poor persons and racial minorities have worse health conditions than the average American does. Yet they have the most difficulty gaining access to care. Children and the frail elderly also require special protection, because they cannot provide care from their own resources and are unable effectively to advocate for themselves within the complex health care system. It is difficult to see how Christians can be "pro-family" without supporting guaranteed access to the kinds of health care that can heal family members. Sick and injured persons are vulnerable to misplaced attention (or lack of attention) from others. Without medical care and appropriate supporting environments, their physical and mental health deteriorate further. They become unable to participate in the normal activities of living and in customary social interactions.

These vulnerabilities hold even more for persons with congenital or acquired mental impairments, severe physical disabilities, and stigmatized diseases such as AIDS. Addicts too, despite the often self-imposed quality of their health needs, become extraordinarily vulnerable to neglect and exploitation. Just as Jesus restored lepers to his society, Christians have an obligation to work to integrate medical outcasts into society.

Jesus came to liberate captives (Luke 4:16–21). Health care is one way to liberate human beings and restore their human dignity. Those captive to disease, frailty, and injury depend upon health care for restoration into the freedom of citizens and the liberty of sons and daughters of God.[29] These special vulnerabilities dictate that those who possess special health care resources (doctors, nurses, dentists, for example) have a *duty* to provide care to those most vulnerable, those with the greatest need. Moreover, society has a duty to allocate resources and to regulate the health care field to assure the proper treatment of the vulnerable; for example, by funding and regulating care through programs such as Medicare and Medicaid.

Stewardship and Recognition of Limits

Though the previous principles bestow resources of time, attention, and wealth on the sick and injured, it is incumbent upon Christians to acknowledge limits. "There is no perfect correlation between health and happiness, between length of life and satisfaction with life, or between the health of individuals and their common good as a community."[30] This is not to say that there are *no* correlations. Rather, it is to assert that the body insists on death and that pain and suffering infect a fallen world, whose redemption is both now and not yet. The natural span of life limits the legitimacy of cures attempted on seriously ill and dying persons.

The issue is not that the United States spends too much on health care in some abstract sense, but that health care dollars spent on futile attempts to extend life (for example) entail neglect of the health needs of children (for example). Moreover, the debate must not be one of more treatment versus less treatment. The problem is not quantitative, but rather a question of appropriate treatment. Curative, medical interventions are not the exclusive model; rather, the full range of professional health care, including palliative care, comfort care, and reassuring presence fall within the scope of health care. Christians insist on never abandoning the old or the vulnerable. They press, therefore, for more appropriate kinds of care for those at the end of life. Concern for costs never permits the tragic tradeoff between sanctity of life and scarcity of resources.[31] Therefore, Christians must become witnesses for different ways of doing health care that respect both stewardship of finite resources and the infinite value of each person.

Christian Community as Witness

Christians not only react to, or advocate for, public policy; they are also deeply embedded in the health care system itself. This location is institutional, not simply personal or professional. Recall the thousands of Christian hospitals, clinics, nursing homes, hospices, home health care services, and other institutions large and small. Christian concern extends simultaneously to public advocacy for policies that reflect their faith and to rendering direct service according to that same faith.

Policies that do not discriminate against religious providers are as essential in health care as in education and other social services. These services, enacted in love and according to the fundamental principles above, are sacramental witnesses to Christ's presence in the world, especially his presence to the vulnerable. The Christian community testifies that another way of life, different from the life of the world, including a different way of health care, is indeed possible and salvific.[32] Faith witnesses to the reality of hope in the face of pain and loss, to life in the midst of suffering and death. This testimony at the end of the twentieth century must generate ways of doing medicine in tension with the dominant paradigm, which has produced great scientific and technological advances but has left many without care and subjected others to excessive treatment.

Assured Health Care

For those able to work, assurance of health care coverage for themselves and their children removes an important obstacle to seeking and taking employment. This is particularly true for part-time, temporary, or contracted employment. The 1996 welfare reform legislation recognized the centrality of health insurance for former public assistance recipients by providing one year of transitional Medicaid coverage once employment has been found. This provision, though needed, is not sufficient. The kinds of jobs available to former public assistance recipients most often do not carry private health insurance or health insurance with affordable premiums. After a year, unavailability of insurance provides a stimulus to move back to public assistance for those who have eligibility remaining. One challenge of a truly effective strategy of creating the kind of just and caring economy that empowers the poor is to assure health insurance coverage for all persons. This means longer transitional Med-

icaid, and provisions for health insurance for part-time and temporary workers. Ultimately, it means universal health insurance coverage.

Health insurance is a vital part of the comprehensive approach to a "just
and caring economy." It complements the measures described in this volume's
other chapters: sound wages, access to capital, food stamps, the Earned Income
Tax Credit, and employment conditions. Together these describe a basic, minimum set of resources that a modern, prosperous, democratic society owes to
all citizens through a combination of market forces, civil society, and government programs.

It is vital to remember that there is no possibility for many of the poor to
find employment that will support themselves and their families. Many of the
poor cannot work: the frail elderly, persons with severe disabilities, the
addicted, and those with marginal intelligence. Assuring health insurance for
all, even if that could be accomplished for all the employed, will require more
adequate Medicare and Medicaid programs for those who cannot work, or
more effective programs as their replacements.

Moreover, lack of insurance does not generate all of the barriers to the health
care system. Even if all persons were guaranteed public or private health insurance coverage, millions of persons would find it difficult to get the care they
need. Many Medicaid-eligible persons today, for example, do not take advantage of the insurance offered. Millions of children lack their complete vacci-
nation program, despite the availability of free shots. Assured insurance is part
of the picture; effective work by churches and other non-profit organizations
is the other part needed to empower the poor with respect to health care. Civil
society, as described in the chapter by Stephen Monsma, will always remain
an indispensable part of the web of institutions, practices, and attitudes that
form a just and caring health care system. The following section discusses various means of assuring health insurance to all Americans. The section after
that considers the barriers that would remain even under a system of assured
coverage. The final sections discuss the essential role of churches, community
organizations, and other non-profits in overcoming the barriers.

Health Insurance for All?

The latest opportunity for federally guaranteed health insurance coverage
for all Americans was lost in 1994 with the defeat of the Clinton health-care
plan and all other Democratic and Republican plans for major, health-care
reform. This is not the place to discuss why it failed, its place in the history of
failed attempts at national health insurance, or the details of possible major
health reforms.[33] Suffice it to say that there are only three general ways to guarantee a minimum package of health insurance benefits to all Americans.

First, abolish Medicare, Medicaid, and the system of private employment-
based insurance and replace them with some form of "single-payer" plan oper-

ated at the state or national level. The radical disruption of the health-care system and the major tax revisions needed to finance such a plan make it impossible to enact in the foreseeable future.

Second, retain Medicare for the elderly and disabled; mandate that all employers provide health insurance for their employees and employee-dependents, and share the cost of premiums, and develop a Medicaid-like program to cover all the unemployed (and possibly part-time employees). This would build on the current system but require significant coercion of employers, and would require the public to subsidize premiums of employers with relatively low-paid workers. This is the most likely direction of major reform, but the 1994 failure postpones it for at least ten years.

Third, retain Medicare for the elderly and disabled, mandate that all working persons purchase individual private insurance policies for themselves and their dependents, and develop a Medicaid-like program to cover all the unemployed (and possibly part-time employees). The subsidies, accounting, and difficulty of administering an individual mandate make this option both politically and administratively unfeasible in anything like the near-run.

This is not the place to debate the advantages and disadvantages of each of these approaches. Choosing among them (and their many variations) requires complex calculations of effectiveness, and uncertain predictions about the future. These are subjects of legitimate debate. However, it is vital to state once again the importance of working toward a version of universal coverage. Given how essential health care is to maintaining the ability to function effectively within contemporary economy and society, citizens cannot preserve human dignity or contribute productively without effective access to the health-care system. Considering the very high cost of health care itself, and the insurance that is the chief means of access to it, without guaranteed access many citizens will be temporarily or permanently relegated to the economic second-class. Moreover, it violates the duty of care that human beings owe to each other to allow some to suffer pain, disability, and indignity because they lack the financial resources to purchase the medical procedures for restoration to normal and healthy functioning. Here is one striking way to frame the issue: "As a matter of national policy, and to the extent a nation's health care system makes it possible, should the child of a poor American family have the same chance of avoiding preventable illness or of being cured of a given illness as does a child of a rich American family?"[34] The correct answer, of course, is "Yes." With regard to preventing illness and curing conditions affecting children, there should be no room for wealth to determine the outcome. All developed nations, except the United States, design their health-care systems in such a way as to make possible universal access to basic services for all children (and adults) without regard to income or wealth.

This principle does not entail, however, that all persons must have equal access to all of the benefits available within the American health-care system. It entails, instead, that all must have access (through universal insurance coverage) to all of the basic or essential services. Beyond these services, there is another level of benefit which individuals may freely purchase, either through their own means entirely or in conjunction with employer-provided insurance. Food is analogous. Justice requires that all must have a diet sufficient to sustain healthy life. Beyond that, individuals may use whatever discretionary income they have to purchase gourmet meals, expensive steaks, or junk food. A two- or three-level health care system does not violate justice if the first level includes access to comprehensive health care services without financial burden or dignity-sapping measures like long waits in dingy offices.

This principle is relatively easy to state but difficult to put into practice. There is no universal agreement, in general or specific terms, about what counts as basic or essential services. Developing a definition of essential health care services is complex and contentious.[35] Here is Daniel Callahan's general description of a "minimal level of adequate care," which consists

> first, of full support for caring (that assistance, and those institutions, that sick, dying, and disabled individuals need to tolerably bear the burdens of their condition); second, of full support of those public health measures that promote general societal health as well as access to primary and emergency care; and third, of access to more individualized forms of cure compatible with a sensible allocation of resources to the health sector in relationship to other societal requirements.[36]

This kind of general approach usefully reminds us of the importance of caring and of public health, as well as of the curative measures of the medical system. It reminds us as well that health care is only one component of a just and caring economy and that it has limits in relation to other components. Callahan's definition, however, does not describe what specific treatments would be part of a list of basic services, partly because there is no universal agreement and partly because the list must change over time with changes in medical technology and in the delivery system. Probably the most useful approximation to thinking about such a list would be to take one that already exists, Medicare or Medicaid, for example, though each has important gaps. They provide a useful starting place in that arguably every citizen deserves access to the procedures covered by these programs.[37]

Any health care reform, lacking either a government-run system or a coercive mandate on employers and/or individuals to purchase insurance, would not assure coverage to all, even for basic services. Anything less than these measures falls short of justice's requirement of access to health care for all. There are many means to accomplish universal access and Christians should continue to debate their merits, while politically advocating universal coverage. The political impossibility of these measures in the next ten years, however, is clear. Therefore, the challenge is to work in the near run for more modest and achievable reforms in existing programs and for incremental expansions of insurance coverage. Such incremental reforms pertain to Medicare, Medicaid, children's health, and health insurance market reform.

Medicare

Although Medicare is an essential component of health care for the elderly poor, it contains significant gaps that imperil their health and well-being.[38] Medicare does not cover ordinary long-term nursing home or home health care. Those who need these services and cannot pay for them directly must depend upon Medicaid, which requires making sure that one becomes truly poor in order to achieve eligibility. Medicare does not cover most prescriptions, yet these take a large bite out of the incomes of the chronically-ill elderly. Medicare does not have a cap on out-of-pocket health care expenditures, placing the incomes of the elderly in jeopardy. Finally, there is no public or private coordination of the many health-care and daily-living needs of the frail elderly. As part of the safety net for the poor, Medicare requires reform to close these gaps, in conjunction with the private and religious initiatives described below.

There are three other significant policy developments affecting health insurance for the non-elderly poor: reform of Medicaid in the direction of managed care; the state Children's Health Insurance Program (CHIP); and reform of insurance markets.

Medicaid Reform

The Medicaid program dodged fundamental restructuring in 1995. Proposals to change it from an entitlement to a block grant were supported by most congressional Republicans and by many state governors. The 1996 welfare reform legislation left most features of Medicaid intact, even maintaining the old AFDC qualifying rules. Indeed, transitional eligibility for Medicaid was enhanced for those moving from welfare to work. However, because families usually find out about their Medicaid eligibility in connection with receipt of cash assistance, reforms in cash assistance have the potential to *decrease* Medicaid rolls.

The action now lies with state experiments aiming to bring Medicaid under the aegis of "managed care." The promise of these experiments, carried out under waivers granted by the Clinton administration, is to move Medicaid enrollees from a fee-for-service system into managed-care networks. In theory, this move should reduce costs (managed care is believed to be cheaper than fee-for-service), expand the pool of physicians accepting Medicaid patients, and free up dollars to expand Medicaid eligibility to more of the near-poor. This section will evaluate these proposals and the potential for managed care Medicaid to increase health insurance coverage among the poor.

Until the early 1990s enrollment of Medicaid beneficiaries was chiefly in traditional fee-for-service medicine. Although Arizona had created its Medicaid program under managed care from the beginning, it was only gradually that other states began to experiment with this form of health-care delivery for some adults and children. These experiments had to be approved by the Department of Health and Human Services, usually through what are known as section 1115 waivers. By 1993 however, states like Oregon, Florida, and Tennessee had begun to enroll all or most of their Medicaid populations in managed care plans.[39] What is the impetus to change Medicaid in this fashion? First, most private health insurance plans have moved toward managed care in an effort to reduce costs. It seems anomalous to leave the poor in fee-for-service medicine. Second, low Medicaid fees discouraged physicians from accepting Medicaid patients. The assured monthly income per enrollee that is part of managed care may attract more providers. Third, any money saved by the use of managed care mechanisms can be used to make more persons eligible for Medicaid. If it could be well implemented, Medicaid-managed care seems like a win-win-win proposition for state governments, providers, and patients.

The 1997 federal Balanced Budget Act contained a number of provisions designed to encourage managed care in Medicaid and to enroll more persons.[40] First, it repealed the "75/25" rule that required at least 25 percent of enrollees in a Medicaid-managed care plan to be privately insured. The new law made it easier to start "Medicaid-only" plans. Second, the law required that recipients must have a choice of managed care plans and freedom to change plans. Third, and very important, "presumptive eligibility" became an option for states, which may enroll persons in Medicaid and begin benefits before completion of the lengthy forms and qualification procedures. Fourth, the law gave states the option of ensuring a continuous twelve months of eligibility if changes in family income would have removed a child from continuing to qualify for Medicaid. Another innovation related to Medicaid is the CHIP program described below.

Medicaid-Managed Care's Potential

Managed care does have the potential, if properly implemented, to enhance access and continuity of care for the poor. Medicaid enrollees should have more continuous contact with a managed care organization (MCO) than with individual doctors. Moreover, good MCOs have financial incentives to do the kinds of preventative care and follow-ups that enhance health and well-being. If cost savings are realized, it may be possible for states to cover more persons. Managed care could be particularly important in delivering coordinated chronic and acute care to the poorest of the elderly, those dually eligible for both Medicare and Medicaid.[41] The actual record of the states with regard to cost savings has been mixed, and it is too early to evaluate quality of care; anecdotal evidence is also mixed in this regard.

Moreover, there are worrisome aspects.[42] First, there is potential for deceptive marketing practices by MCOs looking to make a fast buck by enrolling recipients without providing a standard of care comparable to private insurance. This is particularly a problem if the states allow "Medicaid-only" MCOs. Quality assurance efforts in the states have lagged behind managed-care implementation.[43] Second, because the premium is on getting managed-care contracts with the lowest bid, high-cost providers may be left out. This is particularly important for academic medical centers and physicians practicing in low-income areas that heretofore have provided a large percentage of care to the Medicaid population.[44] Third, and analogously, traditional "safety net" providers such as public hospitals and community health centers could be outbid for Medicaid contracts by MCOs organized around private hospitals. Since Medicaid is now an important source of income for these institutions, they could be left to treat the uninsured without the resources to do so.[45] Finally, a managed-care organization may bid for and obtain a Medicaid managed-care contract and provide good care, but then abandon the contract or Medicaid patients if it finds their care too costly. There is some evidence of such occurrences.[46]

Part of an effective strategy for empowering the poor is to ensure that Medicaid eligibility is expanded to cover a larger proportion of the poor and that implementation of managed care does not come at the expense of quality health care for the poor, or at the expense of the health care organizations that constitute the safety net for the uninsured. These goals call for following specific measures: substantial (one- to two-year) transitional Medicaid eligibility for former public assistance recipients; requirements for Medicaid MCOs to include a substantial percentage of non-Medicaid beneficiaries or substantial quality-assurance and compliance measures for Medicaid-only MCOs; requirements that managed care contracts include traditional safety net providers if their costs are substantially similar to other providers in the contract; and managed care contracts of sufficient length to ensure continuity of care for the Medicaid population.

Children's Health

Incremental expansion of health insurance coverage in the short-term will come through new federal and state programs to provide health insurance coverage for children. Despite the fact that, in terms of empowering the poor, the most pressing health care needs involve working, low income adults, political sympathies lie with children. Virtually all initiatives to expand insurance coverage for the poor are directed at children.

Extending insurance coverage to more children became politically popular in 1996–1997. Proposals for doing so involved creation and enforcement of court orders that non-custodial parents cover their children under employment-based health insurance; block grants to the states for children's insurance; and additional federal Medicaid funding to expand Medicaid to more children. This section will focus on the potential of the Children's Health Insurance Program (CHIP), the most important health insurance provision of the 1997 Balanced Budget Act. It is incumbent upon advocates for the poor to monitor and lobby for effective state implementation of this legislation.

CHIP creates a five-year, $20.3 billion federal block grant to the states to provide child health assistance to uninsured, low-income children.[47] States may use these funds to expand coverage under Medicaid or to create or expand separate, child health insurance programs. States doing the latter have wide discretion on how to determine eligibility, but must comply with federal guidelines on benefits and cost-sharing. States must also spend some of their own funds under either option. The Department of Health and Human Services must approve state plans under CHIP.

The advantage of taking the Medicaid expansion option is that the administrative apparatus is already in place in all states. Moreover, Medicaid regulations define a fairly broad package of health care coverage. The Medicaid option also permits a slightly more generous federal match of state dollars. This option permits states to increase eligibility standards to cover children who did not qualify for Medicaid under state rules in effect on April 15, 1997.

The second option—expanding or creating new, child health programs—gives the states great flexibility but forbids them from transferring children from Medicaid to the new program. Administrative issues become important, since states have to decide whether existing or new state agencies should administer programs created under CHIP, or whether to privatize program administration. Separate programs have four options for meeting minimum federal benefit standards: (1) coverage equivalent to the Federal Employees Health Benefit Plan; (2) coverage equivalent to the state employee benefit plan; (3) coverage equivalent to the benefits offered by the commercial HMO with the largest enrollment in the state (excluding Medicaid enrollment); and (4) "benchmark equivalent coverage," which is a plan based on one of the first three options, but with certain allowable alternatives.

The possibilities here are complex and states have varied in their approaches to implementation. In general, Medicaid expansion does more for children in most states. Therefore, unless a separate state plan offers substantial improvements over Medicaid, advocates for the poor should favor Medicaid expansion. Moreover, they should push for the most generous definitions of eligibility possible.

It is possible for states to take creative steps to expand coverage and to assist poor people toward the health necessary to support work and family. Many states have taken steps to include health insurance in child support settlements. Others have expanded Medicaid coverage substantially. Maine recently implemented a program to train former public assistance recipients for jobs handling HMO enrollment under Medicaid. Minnesota has reduced child uninsurance to about 3 percent through a combination of Medicaid and MinnesotaCare, a voluntary subsidized insurance program for low income persons.[48]

Outreach under Medicaid and CHIP

For a wide variety of reasons, the availability of health insurance does not ensure that eligible persons will take advantage of it. Outreach efforts to enroll those eligible are vital to program success in both Medicaid and CHIP. During the mid–1990s approximately 20 percent of all children under age eleven who were eligible for Medicaid (about 2.7 million children) were not enrolled. Causes include parent ignorance or irresponsibility, complex bureaucratic qualification procedures, lack of publicity, unavailability of providers for those enrolled, cultural barriers, and other factors. Whatever the explanations, major outreach efforts are necessary to get the coverage to those who need it.[49] Here the churches can make important contributions. For example, child care programs operated by churches and other non-profits are natural locations for information and enrollment. In February 1998 President Clinton announced new federal budget proposals and public-private partnership initiatives designed to enroll children.

Other Expansion Possibilities

Although the focus of recent attempts to expand insurance clearly rests on children, efforts should continue to expand coverage to other groups. Natural candidates are the parents of Medicaid-eligible children, workers between jobs and therefore without insurance, and the near-elderly who lose employment-based insurance.[50] President Clinton and some congressional Democrats floated ideas about the second of these alternatives in late 1997. President Clinton proposed a variation of the third through expansion of Medicare in his 1998 legislative agenda. However, the form in which he proposed it would make such additional insurance affordable only for the upper-middle class and upper class. For reasons described above, a just and caring economy includes access to basic health insurance for low-wage and part-time workers and for those workers of any age who have lost employer-based insurance temporarily. Despite the dim prospects at this writing (June 1998) for the incremental proposals floated in 1997 and 1998, no incremental reforms go far enough unless they include these groups of workers.

Insurance Market Reform

Some of the barriers to health insurance coverage are created by the private health insurance market. "Experience rating" and "risk selection" methods mean that insurers have both the tools and the incentive to avoid insuring or to increase premiums to very high levels for persons with pre-existing conditions or otherwise at risk for needing health care. Older persons, sick persons, persons in high-risk occupations, and persons who work for small businesses find it either impossible to obtain group or individual coverage, or the coverage they can find comes at too high a price. Federal ERISA law (Employee Retirement Income Security Act) places severe restrictions on the ability of state governments to enact insurance requirements on self-funded insurance plans, the dominant force in the employer insurance market.

The 1996 Health Insurance Portability and Accountability Act (HIPAA) aimed to reduce some of these barriers. The legislation does enable formerly uninsurable individuals to purchase insurance, but it will not make substantial impact on the number of uninsured persons. This legislation, and similar efforts at the state level to broaden coverage in certain sectors of the market, are laudable and should be supported by Christians. For example, HIPAA contains a provision through which health professionals who donate time to free health clinics may receive special protection from medical malpractice suits.

Managed-care regulation is currently a major item on state and federal legislative agendas. The aim of such legislation is to protect managed-care enrollees from some of the perceived abuses in the economic and organizational incentives of managed care. Although none of these regulations, laudable as they might be, will do much to extend care to the poor, it is important to ensure that the protections available to the privately insured are also mandated for Medicaid-managed care.

Barriers to Health Care Unrelated to Insurance Coverage

There are three significant barriers to health care access among the poor that are relatively unrelated to income or insurance. First, certain groups have unique obstacles to health care, particularly immigrants, both legal and illegal. Second, many of the poor engage in irresponsible behaviors that interfere with obtaining needed health care. Third, the structure of the health care system itself makes it difficult for persons without educational resources and social skills to find the care they need.

Immigration

Persons residing in the United States illegally have a difficult time meeting their health care needs. Usually working for very low wages and existing on the margins of society, they cannot afford to pay for health care and they are not entitled to coverage under federal or state programs, except emergency medical care for life-threatening conditions. Even when some family members are legal residents, or even citizens, they may decide not to apply for the benefits the law gives them for fear of exposing those in the family who are not legal residents.

Legal residents who are not citizens do qualify for some federal and state health care programs, and they may receive coverage through employment. However, recent changes in the law have tightened and restricted the kinds of benefits for which such persons qualify. Although 1997 legislation removed some of the most harsh exclusions on legal immigrants, important ones remain, particularly for those legally entering the country after August 1996.

Though nations and their governments must recognize the difference between citizens and strangers, Christians may not. Therefore, it is incumbent upon the Christian community to find or invent ways to meet the health care needs of the "strangers" among us.

Responsibility Issues

Even when poor persons have Medicare, Medicaid, or some form of private insurance, they may not always use their access in appropriate ways.[51] This statement, of course, is not true of all the poor, and numerous middle-class families have similar responsibility issues. However, the circumstances of hardscrabble daily life often make it difficult for poor persons to exercise responsible decision-making for themselves and their children. Addictions interfere with responsibility; shifting addresses make it difficult to track patients, and for patients to keep appointments with health care providers; compliance with directions about self-care or medications can be spotty. Appointments are not kept, even at free clinics. Promises to stop smoking or to stop drinking are broken. Tens of thousands of children eligible for free vaccinations do not receive them. Similar numbers of children eligible for Medicaid are not enrolled because of parental fear (among immigrants) or simple inaction. Again, the call for Christians to be healers in Jesus' footsteps means finding or inventing new ways of enabling the poor to overcome these barriers, or to bring care directly to the poor.

Health Care Structures

Responsibility issues interact with barriers in health-care structures themselves. What looks like irresponsible behavior is sometimes simple lack of the intellectual, emotional, or social resources to negotiate one's way through large, bureaucratic institutions. Linguistic and cultural barriers on both sides—health professionals and clients—exacerbate non-compliance. Health care for the poor is often delivered in public hospitals largely staffed by foreign medical graduates, thus creating a double cultural barrier, or by young residents passing through toward more rewarding placements. Waiting rooms are crowded, appointments difficult to obtain, and transportation to health-care facilities expensive or erratic. Public hospitals are often underfunded and understaffed. Functional illiteracy leads to imperfect compliance with medical directives. One way to change these structures is to develop and improve policies that aim to increase the number of minority health-care providers, since members of minority groups are more likely to return to poor communities after medical training than white professional are to locate there.[52]

Civil Society and Health Care Problems Among the Poor

The barriers to health improvement among the poor (thus, also, the health barriers to moving out of poverty) cannot be addressed solely by expanded government health care, the dominant theme of the previous pages. Both "top down" (expanded insurance coverage financed and/or mandated by government) and "bottom up" (civil society) approaches are simultaneous requirements. The values of citizenship, equality, and justice demand that every American have guaranteed insurance that will be the ticket into the health-care system when its services are needed. We must work toward health insurance for all, while taking advantage of short-term opportunities (CHIP, for example) to expand coverage of particular groups of persons in need.

Simply guaranteeing insurance to all will not remove all barriers to health and well-being. The kinds of personal and structural barriers to health just described cannot be overcome by government spending or promises of guaranteed coverage. Urban and rural communities, and the Christian congregations embedded in them, can find ways to provide care for immigrants, encourage responsible behavior from parents and adults, and help the poor to negotiate the labyrinthine pathways of the health-care system.

Civil Society and Health Care

We should not think of health-care provision in either/or terms: either government insurance or church-financed clinics; either community-focused continuity of care or centralized, professional, acute medical care. The Christian community must do both: bear witness to the need for personal, caring interaction with the ill and injured, and prophetically challenge public institutions to do justice. Focus has been on the political system and public policies for so long that it is time to re-assert the importance of the local community—the neighborhood, town, or congregation—in the health of citizens and, especially in the present context, of the poor. Outreach efforts, community health centers, parish nurses, hospices, and congregations are locations for deeply personal restorative care that includes everyone in the circle of God's love. There is now, both within the church and within government and secular society generally, renewed concern for community and congregation.[53]

The following discussion represents a civil society strategy for assuring access to health care. It is not simply a matter of recognizing the importance of the local community vis-a-vis large government institutions. In addition, the local community often can provide a more appropriate setting for aspects of health care that are not managed well by large, tertiary care medical complexes. This may be true especially of the basic health needs of homeless persons, single mothers, the elderly living at home, drug addicts, street people, and the unemployed. Often their health care needs are basic and chronic—eye examinations, dental checks, blood pressure screening, and the like. In the local community these services can be given on the spot when the person is ready and the need is evident. Complex, expensive surgeries are best handled in medical centers and paid for by social insurance. Basic needs may best be met for the poor in a close-to-home setting and paid for through a variety of mechanisms.

Earlier sections have described the kinds of government programs needed. The following sections discuss the private and, especially, church-based structures required to empower the poor with regard to their health.

The problems in health care parallel those in society at large. Often there is no buffer between the lone and vulnerable individual and large public or private institutions. Religious institutions can play a vital role because they are already deeply embedded in communities and neighborhoods and in the health-care system. They provide a natural link between public funds and entitlements, and the individual, one-on-one work necessary to bring people into a healing relationship with the medical system.[54]

There are many examples of creative civil-society approaches to meeting the health needs of the poor and near-poor. Here we can briefly describe only a few: community health centers; traditional, hospital-based community outreach; Christian ministries dedicated to the most wretched of the urban poor; comprehensive poverty medicine programs; and parish-based ministries focusing on health and well-being in addition to traditional curative health care.

Community Health Centers

Federal, state, and local governments already cooperate with religious institutions in establishing and maintaining the hundreds of community health centers in rural and inner-city neighborhoods. These centers, and officially established "look-alikes," receive federal funding as part of block grants to states and local communities. Their special role is whole-person health care for a local community. Situated in the community, they may receive both Medicare and Medicaid reimbursements, but they also have the obligation to serve uninsured persons on a sliding-scale fee basis.

Because community health centers often incorporate attention to outreach and follow-up, social services, and transportation, they can work on and encourage the kinds of compliance and personal responsibility that are impossible for public hospitals and large Medicaid MCOs to encourage. But Medicaid-managed care and other health system changes place substantial pressure on community health centers. In some states, community health centers have been frozen out of Medicaid-managed care contracts. This loss of Medicaid funding impairs the ability of the community health centers to offer reduced-cost services to persons without insurance. Some have closed their doors or substantially reduced services.[55] In other places, however, community health centers have banded together to form their own Medicaid MCOs in order to retain the business and to take advantage of their unique positioning in the Medicaid market.

Finding ways for local churches and other religious organizations to work with community health centers is an important challenge of the next decade. One way might be to use parish centers or child care facilities as community health center satellite centers, especially for enrollment, outreach, and basic health education.

Church-Affiliated Health Care Institutions

Churches and religious organizations operate numerous health care facilities—hospitals, clinics, and nursing homes being the most prominent. These have a legal and moral responsibility, as well as a responsibility to the faith that created them, to benefit the communities in which they are located. This benefit is not only in the form of medical care for the particular individuals that enter them. Responsibility extends to community education and outreach programs, special services made available to the community as a whole.

As many of these institutions merge with, or sell out to, larger not-for-profit and for-profit health care systems, large sums of money are obtained by the religious groups and boards that founded and govern them. These sums need to be reinvested in the communities themselves to establish programs to meet the needs that government programs cannot meet: anti-violence and youth activities; special clinics for immigrant communities; health screening and other forms of preventative care offered regularly, for free or at low cost, in poor neighborhoods.

Whether non-profit (including religious) health-care institutions provide sufficient "community benefit" to justify their tax-exempt status is now a hot topic in the literature.[56] Religious hospitals, nursing homes, and other care centers were traditionally ways that religious communities responded to newly emerging needs. Religious institutions now face the challenge of inventing new institutions to respond to new needs. Perhaps such institutions could take the lead in establishing creative forms of community care for the elderly in the twenty-first century, such as new kinds of addiction treatment or basic care for the homeless.

Many religious hospitals have taken the lead in such community service for many years. St. Mary of the Plains Hospital in Lubbock, Texas offers one example of these kinds of community outreach.[57] Operated by the Catholic Sisters of St. Joseph of Orange as part of their national network of hospitals, St. Mary commits 10 percent of its bottom line to community outreach. Although some of these funds support poor hospitals in the St. Joseph system, most of the money remains in the local community. That community has the city of Lubbock (200,000 population) as the urban hub of a ten-county, rural Texas area. In the mid–1990s St. Mary funded a community health assessment and a media campaign to publicize its results. From this assessment, it developed four strategic priorities for its outreach work: (1) increase community-wide efforts to reduce risks of premature cardiovascular disease and cerebrovascular disease deaths; (2) expand community-wide efforts to reduce the risk and promote the early detection of cancers; (3) expand awareness of and access to mental health and substance abuse services; and (4) expand access to primary medical and dental care, especially for the working poor and indigent population.

More tangibly, the hospital funds, fully or partially, a variety of services in the ten-county area. Services are free or on a sliding scale according to income, and include the following:

- The Community Health Center of Lubbock.
- A mobile mammography van, a mobile dentistry van, and a mobile clinic which travel a regular schedule to the rural communities within a one hundred-mile radius of the city. These vans also provide special services to migrant workers during the summers.
- Co-sponsorship of a prenatal nurturing program with a Baptist-supported children's home.
- St. Mary Counseling Center, adjacent to the Community Health Center.
- Health-education programs at various sites in the region.
- A school-based neighborhood center in a poor area of the City of Lubbock, offering health education, literary training, parent-school cooperation, and other activities.

Even if universal health insurance were to become established in the United States, these kinds of outreach efforts by religious, health-care institutions would continue to be needed. Absent such insurance, their presence is vital to helping the poor to be fully functioning members of society.

Urban Health Care Ministries

There are a wide variety of health-care ministries specifically directed to the urban poor, the homeless and the addicted. Some are run by congregations;

others are freestanding. They share a commitment to offering medical care in the gaps of the established health-care institutions. They provide free or minimal cost physician services, nursing, and immunizations, and they do it at the doorsteps of those who need it. The most powerful account of the spiritual, emotional, and medical resources needed for this kind of ministry is David Hilfiker's *Not All of Us Are Saints: A Doctor's Journey with the Poor.* Hilfiker describes two ministries in Washington, D.C., with which he has been affiliated: Christ House and a network of clinics (Columbia Road Health Services, Community of Hope Health Services, and a clinic at the So Others May Eat soup kitchen).

Christ House is a medical recovery shelter for homeless, addicted men. It takes men too sick to be on the streets who commit to remaining clean and sober. The men live in the house, together with a community of physicians, staff persons, and their families. This Christian community fills the gap that exists between conventional homeless shelters, which provide little or no health care, and the very limited in-patient recovery programs in the inner cities. In addition to providing treatment for addiction, Christ House becomes a Christian community for the men who live there.

Columbia Road Health Services and its affiliated clinics were founded by Washington's Church of the Saviour, and are now supported by, and affiliated with, other congregations in the Washington area. As of the early 1990s, Columbia Road was a complete family-practice clinic with over fifteen thousand patient visits a year, predominantly from the refugee Hispanic community. Such refugees were and are largely ineligible for government-funded programs, except emergency treatment. Without clinics like Columbia Road, they would have nowhere to turn for ordinary treatments for accidents and illnesses that are less than life- or limb-threatening. Of equal significance, these poorest of the poor have access to a community that loves them.

The commitment of these ministries and many others like them is not simply to serve the poor or to be present *for* the poor, but also to be *with* the poor. Poverty medicine, which they exemplify, is a spiritual journey as much as, or more than, the delivery of health care.

Poverty Medicine

Poverty medicine is quite different from other forms of health care. To serve the poor effectively means surrendering the power of the health professional. It requires willingness to live with chaos, tolerance of racial and cultural differences, acceptance of lack of trust in health professionals, and attitudes of attention, care, hope, and listening often neglected in conventional medical training and practice.[58]

The Christian Community Health Fellowship (CCHF) is approximately two decades old. It is a "national network of Christian health professionals committed to living out the Gospel through health care among the poor."[59] The network is national but the commitment is international. Members work in health ministries in Latin America, Africa, and Asia. The majority work in urban and rural poverty areas of the United States.

The CCHF quarterly, *Health and Development,* is published with another quarterly, *The Apprentice,* for medical, nursing, and allied health students. CCHF also has an annual conference and serves as a clearing house for news and information about poverty medicine. Professionals looking for internships or full-time employment in poverty medicine can find opportunities in health-care facilities needing their assistance. CCHF helps to make the match. Primarily however, CCHF publications and conferences serve as a forum where health-care professionals can share the stories of their spiritual journeys with the poor: struggles, failures, mistakes, successes, and growth. Poverty medicine is not simply conventional medicine practiced in a particular setting; it is a way of being and of living the spiritual journey.

Parishes and Christian Health Professionals

New structures do not always need to be built outside of the local congregation and apart from the personal responsibilities of Christian health professionals. Many of the elderly and the poor are connected to congregations. Congregations also are home to dentists, nurses, physicians, and other health professionals. There are three different yet complementary features of a creative congregational approach: care for individual health-impaired members of the congregation; a holistic concept of health; and, especially for congregations located in poverty settings, outreach and advocacy for the uninsured in their localities.[60]

Individual Ministry

Congregations can set up home visitations to the elderly and the chronically ill using parish volunteers. Such efforts can provide continuity and coordination of care and also encourage wellness at a personal level. Persons who already visit shut-ins for prayer and fellowship can be trained to make basic health assessments and to watch for warning signs of impending health crises. The parish nurse program is one model for congregational outreach. Such programs generally involve a congregation employing a registered nurse to serve as a resource for health and wellness in the parish. Often the employment is in conjunction with a local religious hospital. The parish nurse does not so much see individual patients when they are ill as serve as a resource for medical information, coordinating health fairs and setting up various health screening opportunities using parish facilities.

Congregations can also assemble the health professionals who are already members of the congregation to plan health and wellness opportunities, to staff health education programs, and to meet the needs of individual members of the congregation who find it difficult or impossible to access the medical system in the conventional ways. Mentally ill persons, for example, may be enabled to function within the community by having a network of friends and support from the congregation to call upon when life seems to be spiraling out of control. Congregations can be places that connect and coordinate multiple community resources for those members (and neighbors) who lack the resources to do their own coordination.

Focus on Health

The institutional health system in the United States is really a *sickness* system. Its focus is on treating illness and injury and returning the individual to as fully functional a life in society as possible. That is its great virtue and its weakness. Healthful living, which includes spiritual and emotional health as well as physical wholeness, is marginal to the enterprise of health care. Yet the poor often have special difficulties maintaining health in its fullest sense, and these difficulties translate into barriers to their full participation in a just and caring economy.

The key is to think of those aspects of health and wellness that take place outside the walls of traditional health-care institutions. This way of thinking is really a public-health, rather than an illness, approach. It looks at whole populations, particularly in the neighborhoods served by individual congregations, and gives highest priority to illness prevention. "What if every house of worship was committed to ensuring that at least between their steps and the church or mosque or synagogue down the street, no child would be hungry or unimmunized, no pregnant mother would lack prenatal care, none seeking freedom from drugs was denied help, no elder was isolated, nobody suffering from mental illness was stigmatized?"[61] Other health-related needs that can be addressed (at least in part) at the local congregational level include nutrition, violence prevention, family communication, and the development of parks for exercise, social interaction, and healthful air, water, and vegetation.

One example of a religious foundation encouraging such local initiatives is Wheat Ridge Ministries, which makes grants focusing on holistic medicine, parish nurse programs, and seed money for local "health and hope" ministries. Another is the Lutheran Charities Foundation in St. Louis, which supports such ministries as Our Little Haven, a nonprofit that facilitates foster-care placements for HIV-positive children, and a Community Summer Sports Program at Ebenezer Lutheran Church. In San Francisco the Vesper Society makes grants that forge collaboration between health institutions and faith communities. Many of these foundations derive their funding from the sale of religious hospitals to for-profit or other not-for-profit hospital systems as part of the reduction of the hospital sector.[62]

Outreach to the Uninsured

Millions of persons, especially children, are eligible for Medicaid or other publicly funded, health-care programs, but are not enrolled in them. Expanded Medicaid eligibility in recent years, combined with the decline in welfare rolls (a traditional form of qualifying for Medicaid) means that the gap between eligibility and enrollment may grow. Barriers to enrollment include complexities of qualification, parental dysfunctions, lack of transportation, limited education or language skills, and lack of information.

Churches cannot remedy all of these, but many are located in urban neighborhoods or rural towns where the poor live. Some of the eligible, but unenrolled, are church members. Congregations can take responsibility for outreach to such persons, informing them of their eligibility for Medicaid, CHIP, or other public programs, going with them to enroll, translating, and so forth. Suburban partner churches of inner-city churches can help with the costs of printing informational materials, funding transportation, and other logistical support. The federal government has invited such civil society approaches to help fill the uninsurance gaps. The 1997 Balanced Budget Act simplified qualification procedures for Medicaid, and in February 1998 President Clinton announced a government-wide effort to enroll uninsured children, provide financial incentives to state enrollment efforts, and invite the private sector to help get the word out to eligible persons.

Conclusion

A genuine community-health focus, the incorporation of civil society perspectives with traditional health-care policy concerns, demands a set of relationships different from the state- or market- or profession-centered health-care system currently dominant in the medical field.[63] Without a change of focus the health-care system will not operate effectively for those at the margins of the economy. A just and caring economy includes a just and caring health care system that prevents cost and access obstacles from becoming barriers to a dignified life for low-income persons. More than that, an effective health-care system is an essential condition for fulfilling the gospel mandate to follow Christ the healer, and for fulfilling the duty of government to ensure that all citizens receive the essentials of life.

More specifically, a just and caring society features a health-care system that provides universal access to curative medicine, preventative health care, and compassionate care for those with chronic conditions. Universal access may be achieved through any one of a variety of schemes, but its enactment is a vital goal for Christian political action. Because its achievement is some years away, short-range, incremental measures are also important. The following steps should be pursed:

- First, expansion of Medicaid and the Children's Health Insurance Program to cover the maximum number of the unemployed or uninsured, the poor, and the near-poor, especially young children and young adult workers.
- Second, aggressive cooperative efforts by local governments and civic organizations (especially churches) to inform people of the eligibility for Medicaid and CHIP.
- Third, protection of essential "safety net" institutions such as neighborhood clinics, public hospitals, departments of health, and community health centers.
- Fourth, resistance to legislative proposals such as medical savings accounts that would further fragment the health care financing and delivery system.
- Finally, effective mobilization of community health and well-being ministries by local congregations, religious hospitals, nursing homes, and parachurch institutions.

Such ministries not only close the gaps left by traditional health care institutions, but must also model new ways of thinking about and practicing health and healing.

Neither government alone, nor health-care providers alone, nor churches and civil society alone, but rather all together can create the health-care segment of a just and caring society.

～ 9 ～

Taxation
and Economic Justice

John E. Anderson, University of Nebraska

Introduction

The biblical account of the Israelite boy who had the audacity to face the Philistine giant Goliath reveals the real source of David's courage and strength. What power is capable of enabling a young shepherd boy with just a sling and five smooth stones to overcome a battle-tested behemoth with sword and shield? It is a little known fact of the Old Testament, yet the scriptures clearly reveal the source of David's empowerment: tax incentives. Yes, that is right, tax incentives motivated David to accomplish his remarkable feat. King Saul had promised tax breaks to the man who would kill Goliath. Read for yourself: "The king will give great wealth to the man who kills him. He will also give him his daughter in marriage and will *exempt his father's family from taxes* in Israel" (1 Sam. 17:25b, emphasis added). You see, it was the promise of tax breaks that motivated David. Of course, King Saul did offer his daughter in marriage as well, but I am sure it was the tax breaks that motivated his actions. What else could account for such valiant behavior?

While we in political-economic culture do not rely on promises of the president's daughter and tax breaks to assure national security in our day, we certainly do believe strongly that taxes are responsible for motivating all kinds of behavior. Witness the constant public policy debate over tax incentives for education, health care, retirement savings, home ownership, and a host of other behaviors we believe to be in the public interest. We enact tax policy as if it were the only factor that motivates behavior. To the Christian observer of public policy that is an inadequate view, of course. Just as the Christian understands that David was motivated by factors other than tax breaks and the offer of the king's daughter, so the contemporary Christian policy observer understands that modern behavior is not driven entirely by tax incentives.

Yet the tax system is a powerful tool for implementing incentives for individuals and firms to alter their behavior. The tax system affects labor-supply decisions, savings decisions, investment decisions, and a host of other decisions. The tax system is also used to alter the distribution of income. The extent to which the tax system may be used as a tool for achieving economic justice is the focus of this paper. In the process, we will have to consider both efficiency and equity issues.

I have elsewhere examined biblical principles that are appropriate to consider in the design of a tax system.[1] Rather than repeat that material here, I will summarize those biblical principles in section two of this paper and then proceed, in section three, to consider applications of those principles to specific tax policy issues that affect the usefulness of taxation as a tool of economic justice in section three. Section four describes income inequality measures and the effects of taxation. Section five focuses on equity and efficiency issues in optimal taxation. Section six contains a review of major proposals for fundamental tax reform and includes evaluation of each proposal with respect to its effects on economic justice. The final section of the paper contains a summary and conclusions.

Biblical Principles and Taxation

Render to Caesar

It is often asked whether a Christian is obligated to pay taxes to a secular government. The answer is provided in scripture and is unambiguous. Paul teaches in Romans 13:1–7 that Christians are to submit to authorities, and that submission includes the payment of taxes. He says:

> This is also why you pay taxes, for the authorities are God's servants, who give their full time to governing. Give everyone what you owe him: If you owe taxes, pay taxes; if revenue, then revenue; if respect, then respect; if honor, then honor (Rom. 13:7).

Notice that Paul not only gives the command to pay taxes, he also explains *why* the Christian is to do so. The command is given in the context of submission to authority, including civil authority. That authority has its origin in God's sovereignty. Civil governments are ordained by God and Christians should pay their taxes to them.

Indeed, Jesus Christ was asked this very question. The Pharisees inquired of him: "Is it right to pay taxes to Caesar or not?" (Mark 12:14). Of course, the Pharisees knew that answering this question would be fraught with difficulty, since to say yes would be to appear to violate Yahweh's authority as King of Israel, while to say no would be seditious, directly challenging Rome's authority.

The Romans divided the kingdom of Herod the Great, king of the Jews, in 4 B.C. Herod's three sons ruled the divided kingdom and levied taxes on Jewish citizens. There was no religious objection to paying the taxes since Herod's sons were Jews. The region where Jesus primarily lived, in Galilee, was ruled by Herod Antipas until A.D. 39. The southern region, called Judea, including its capital, Jerusalem, was ruled oppressively by Archelaus.[2] In fact, after nine years of rule, the Roman Emperor removed Archelaus in order to prevent a revolt, and made Judea a Roman province, setting a political appointee as governor over the region. As a result, the Judeans had to pay taxes to Caesar. In A.D. 6 a census was taken to determine the tax yield of the newly formed province. While Jewish teaching had always maintained that it was proper to pay taxes to secular governments (see Ezra 7:21–23), a new view of taxation began to circulate about the time of this census. According to the new view, Yahweh alone was King of Israel, hence payment of taxes to Caesar could be considered high treason.[3] While payment of taxes to pagan rulers was not an issue for Jews of the Dispersion, for those in Judea it could be considered inappropriate. This made the Pharisees' question difficult. To answer that payment of the tax to Caesar was appropriate risked offense to Judas the Galilean and his followers who argued that Yahweh alone was worthy of tribute. On the other hand, to answer that payment of the tax to Caesar was not appropriate risked charges of sedition against Rome. The Pharisees thought they had Jesus trapped.

Jesus' response was simple yet profound. He asked for a coin and was given a Roman denarius. He asked whose name and face appeared on the coin. Since the coin had Caesar's name and face stamped on it, he concluded that the coin must be Caesar's. Therefore, the coin should be given to Caesar. Jesus said "Render to Caesar the things that are Caesar's, and to God the things that are God's" (Mark 12:17 NASB). The verb "render" which Jesus used in this encounter meant to return something that belonged to another. He instructed his hearers to pay Caesar's tax with Caesar's coin. With this instruction, however, he also revealed that what is important in life is to discover God's claims on us and make sure that those claims are met. His focus was on God's kingdom, not Caesar's kingdom.

We also have a biblical account of Jesus teaching that it is proper to pay an ecclesiastical tax. Matthew 17:24–27 describes temple tax collectors asking Peter whether Jesus paid the temple tax. Peter's response was that Jesus did pay the tax. Later Jesus asked Peter "From whom do the kings of the earth collect duty and taxes—from their own sons or from others?" (v. 25). Peter responded that they collect taxes from others. Jesus drew the conclusion that "the sons are exempt" (v. 26). After establishing his tax exemption, he went on to say, "But so that we may not offend them, go to the lake and throw out your line. Take the first fish you catch; open its mouth and you will find a four-drachma coin. Take it and give it to them for my tax and yours" (v. 27). Four drachmas was exactly the required tax for two people. Jesus' teaching here is about citizenship in God's kingdom, not about tax payment. Yet the event illustrates that Jesus was willing to pay a tax, even one from which he knew he should be exempt. There were, however, observers who drew the incorrect conclusion that he was encouraging them to avoid paying taxes (Luke 23:2).

The biblical witness reveals that our Lord paid both civil and ecclesiastical taxes and that Paul taught that Christians are required to pay taxes to whom they are due. As a result, we have clear normative instruction to do the same. Scripture also teaches that God's laws are supreme, however, and if the Christian is asked to violate God's law the Christian has no choice but to violate a human law that is in direct opposition to God's law (Acts 4:19). As a result, there may be circumstances in which the Christian may support tax resistance. As a general rule, though, Jesus taught that payment of taxes is right and proper. He even went out of his way to pay taxes that he considered inappropriate.

Justice

The preeminent biblical principle that must characterize society, including its tax system, is justice. Isaiah the prophet was told that the Lord "looked for justice, but saw bloodshed; for righteousness, but heard cries of distress" (Isa. 5:7). This passage makes it clear that God looks for justice in human social systems. When he finds justice lacking his judgment follows. God instructed the Israelites to "Follow justice, and justice alone so that you may live and possess the land the Lord your God is giving you" (Deut. 16:20). Thus, we know that God's direct intention is that justice be served in human society.

God himself is perfectly just and by his justice he is exalted (Isa. 5:16). When Solomon, in his prayer, described the characteristics of an ideal human ruler, he asked that God would "endow the king with your justice" (Ps. 72:1). As a result, we know that justice is required of human government. In the specific context of this paper, we know by extension that tax systems must be just in order to meet God's standard.

Justice in a tax system and its administration has many aspects. We will consider several aspects of justice in the following sections. Justice in enabling people to earn a living wage will be emphasized as we consider ways in which the tax system can enhance the after-tax incomes of low-income, working families. We will also consider aspects of justice in the tax-rate structure and in the administration of the tax system.

What Structure of Tax Rates Should Be Used?

The first tax recorded in scripture is that imposed by Moses, associated with the taking of the census of Israel as described in Exodus 30:12–16. This tax was a half shekel in amount and was collected from all men twenty years of age or more. The Lord's instructions are recorded as follows:

> When you take a census of the Israelites to count them, each one must pay the LORD a ransom for his life at the time he is counted. Then no plague will come on them when you number them. Each one who crosses over to those already counted is to give a half shekel, according to the sanctuary shekel, which weighs twenty gerahs. This half shekel is an offering to the LORD. All who cross over, those twenty years old or more, are to give an offering to the LORD. The rich are not to give more than a half shekel and the poor are not to give less when you make the offering to the LORD to atone for your lives. Receive the atonement money from the Israelites and use it for the service of the Tent of Meeting. It will be a memorial for the Israelites before the LORD, making atonement for your lives.

Notice that the required atonement money was a head tax. The rich were to give no more than half a shekel while the poor were to give no less. It would appear that all paid the same half-shekel tax.

The second tax recorded in scripture is that imposed under the reign of King Joash, implemented in order to repair the temple. The biblical account is as follows:

> At the king's command, a chest was made and placed outside, at the gate of the temple of the LORD. A proclamation was then issued in Judah and Jerusalem that they should bring to the LORD the tax that Moses the servant of God had required of Israel in the desert. All the officials and all the people brought their contributions gladly, dropping them into the chest until it was full. Whenever the chest was brought in by the Levites to the king's officials and they saw that there was a large amount of money, the royal secretary and the officer of the chief priest would come and empty the chest and carry it back to its place. They did this regularly and collected a great amount of money. The king and Jehoiada gave it to the men who carried out the work required for the temple of the LORD. They hired masons and carpenters to restore the LORD's temple, and also workers in iron and bronze to repair the temple.

> 2 Chronicles 24:8–12

Joash instructed the priests to collect the temple tax in three parts: (1) the tax associated with the census, (2) the money received from personal vows to the Lord,[4] and (3) voluntary contributions (2 Kings 12:4–5). We have seen that the tax associated with the census was a head tax of half a shekel. The money received from personal vows to the Lord, however, was not uniform in amount. In general, the tax was *ad valorem*, based on the value of the asset. The account in Leviticus 27:1–88 provides further, detailed information on the amount specified. The required amounts were specified for persons dedicated to the Lord, animals offered for sacrifices, houses, land and other assets. Provisions were also specified for the redemption of these assets, generally requiring a 20 percent redemption fee. One provision of the law makes it clear that the rate of taxation was modified for the poor. In particular, the law specified that: "If anyone making the vow is too poor to pay the specified amount, he is to present the person to the priest, who will set the value for him according to what the man making the vow can afford" (Lev. 27:8 NIV). Hence, the tax which was otherwise an *ad valorem* tax was modified and made an ability-to-pay tax for the poor. The priest used his judgment to assign an amount based on the person's ability to pay.

We see from the early accounts of taxation in scripture that taxes were levied in three fundamental ways: head taxes, *ad valorem* taxes, and ability-to-pay taxes. As a result, it is clear that there is no unique biblical method of taxation that can be claimed to the exclusion of all others. Nevertheless, there are Christians who make the claim that the perfect, biblically faithful tax is a flat 10 percent tax, modeled after the tithe. For example, James Gwartney has made the case this way:

> If God were supportive of schemes which take disproportionately from the rich in order to assist the poor, surely he would have used this techniques (sic) to finance his work. But he did not. The tithe treats the rich and poor alike. Both are required to contribute the same proportion of their income to the Lord's work. Thus, God's method of raising funds fails to provide support for progressive taxes and other re-distributive policies.[5]

The biblical admonition to tithe (Deut. 14:28) comes in the context of the community supporting the weak and those without access to the means of production. The tribe of Levi did not have land, as did the other tribes in Israel. Land was the primary factor of production in that economy. The motivation for the tithe was that they might "eat and be filled" (Deut. 14:29 RSV). Further, God's blessings were promised to obedient tithers. Stephen Mott suggests that the message of this passage is "a principle that an adequate portion of private production be gathered for the needy rather than to focus upon the particular proportion appropriate for the Hebrew village."[6]

We see that both head taxes and ability-based taxes were levied in ancient Israel. Why a combination of taxes rather than one single tax? It would appear that the combination of taxes reflects the reality that individuals live in community. The head tax applies to everyone in the community, thus supporting community life. Ability-based taxes take into account the special circumstances of the individuals within the community, however. Thus, we see a tax system in Israel that reflected both community and individual realities.

Compassion

God requires Christians to have an extraordinary regard for the poor; that is abundantly clear from scripture. The biblical witness teaches that an economic system that disregards the powerless, widow, sojourner, and alien brings God's judgment (see Lev. 25:35 and Deut. 26:12). God's concern for the marginalized is everywhere in scripture. Does that mean that the poor should therefore be relieved of all tax liability? Should our tax system have such generous exemptions that the poor pay nothing? Probably not, since scripture also teaches that personal responsibility is important. We see in scripture that each individual is accountable. John Mason has examined the system of assistance for the poor in ancient Israel and found that those programs required reciprocity. Wealthy members of the community were required to provide assistance and the poor were required to work.[7]

Christopher Wright sees the biblical prophets' concern for the poor as a warning against the view that wealth is simply reflective of God's blessing. He says:

> In championing the cause of the oppressed in this way, [the prophets] exonerate God from the suspicion of being actually on the side of the wealthy and powerful, who could point to their wealth and power as apparent evidence of God's blessing on them and their activities.[8]

Careful interpretation of scripture is required when considering passages having to do with the rich and poor. Biblical writers often write in a stylized fashion, employing stereotypical characterizations of rich and poor. When James writes of the poor in the first chapter of his epistle, for example, he is referring to the *pious* poor while his references to the rich typically imply the *impious* rich.[9] His terms "rich" and "poor" are not morally neutral. The poor to whom James refers are poor precisely because they lead pious lives, refusing to engage in impious activity that bears an unjust economic return. On the other hand, the rich to whom James refers are rich precisely because they have unjustly gained wealth from the poor. James's strong warning against wealth-based partiality in the church strikes at the heart of the Christian's faith-claim. James confronts *sola fide* Christians with the examples of Abraham and Rahab, who demonstrated their faith by their actions. In the same way, he calls Christians to demonstrate their faith through their deeds, specifically emphasizing their treatment of the poor. In chapter 5 of his epistle, James condemns rich Christians for sins that are directly related to their use of wealth, and calls those Christians to be compassionate and just in their economic dealings.

But what is the relationship between compassion for the poor and justice? In the context of a tax system, for example, how do we combine compassion for the poor with justice? Does compassion require a very highly progressive tax-rate structure? If so, doesn't that violate the requirement of justice—requiring of each his due? I will suggest that a tax system should incorporate a degree of compassion in its design, including exemptions, credits, and the shape of the rate structure itself. That system, once established, should then be administered with perfect justice—giving each his due. In this way, compassion and justice may be fulfilled without confusing the two.

Carl Henry has warned that Christians should not confuse compassion and justice. He has advised that in contemplating policy issues from a Christian perspective, we should not

> ... elevate compassion as the essence of divinity and subordinate to it all other divine perfections, including righteousness or justice. One consequence [of doing so] is that God is depicted as not seriously offended by sin and iniquity; another is that the concept of justice itself is weakened, while that of compassion is distorted.[10]

In the work that follows, I will attempt to emphasize both God's requirement that public policy be just and that it reflect his compassion for the poor. Indeed, a Christian view of tax policy that is grounded in the requirement of justice must include compassion for the poor as well. In this sense, there is no confusion of the two. These two biblical concepts are not antithetical. Rather, the two concepts are integral parts of God's mandate.

Stewardship of Resources

When God created the heavens and the earth and filled the earth with his creatures, he commanded humanity to be stewards of his earth and its resources (see Gen. 1:26–30 and Ps. 24:1). A primary role fulfilled by the discipline of economics is to articulate specific means by which we can accomplish that command. Economics, understood in a Christian way, is all about how we can be good stewards. That includes the economics of tax systems and the insights provided by modern economic theory regarding the ways in which various tax policies have the effect of wasting resources. Indeed, the concept of efficiency in economics captures the primary concern of economists to not waste resources. We will investigate the many implications of this stewardship concern, or the efficiency aspects of taxation, in later sections of the paper. It must be laid alongside the more commonly articulated equity/justice concerns when one is attempting a fully Christian treatment of tax policy issues.

Application of Biblical Principles in Tax Policy

Justice, Compassion, and the Role of Redistribution

We will consider the biblical requirement of compassion for the poor and the mandate for justice as we contemplate the role of the tax system in redistribution of income. To do so, we will begin with a consideration of the efficiency-equity trade-off and then proceed to consideration of justice in the administration of the tax system. Issues in redistribution will then be considered.

The Efficiency-Equity Tradeoff

Economists use two standards by which to judge a tax system: efficiency and equity. By efficiency, we mean the effect of the tax on distorting economic decisions, resulting in wasted resources. We measure such inefficiency in terms of the *excess burden* of the tax; the welfare loss over and above the tax paid. Equity is measured along two dimensions: vertical and horizontal. Vertical equity requires that two families on different rungs of the income distribution ladder be treated differently. We expect that the high-income family should pay more tax than the low-income family. Of course, the degree of difference in relation to income is debatable. By horizontal equity, we mean that two families with equal income should be treated equally. We expect that similar incomes should result in similar taxes.

In the world of tax policy, we recognize that there is a fundamental relationship between efficiency and equity. Pursuit of efficiency, in terms of implementing taxes that distort economic decision-making the least, can have unfavorable equity consequences. For example, the classic Ramsey Rule, which suggests that excise taxes be levied in inverse proportion to the elasticity of demand for commodities, would have us apply high rates of taxation to gasoline and low rates of taxation to fine china. In doing so, however, we may violate the most basic concept of equity. Consider a wealthy family living in Manhattan, without a car but with a strong demand for fine china with which to entertain; such a family would pay a small proportion of its income in tax if taxed according to the Ramsey Rule. At the same time, a poor family in rural Mississippi, which depends on an old, gas-guzzler car to transport three family members long distance to minimum-wage jobs, would pay a high proportion of its income in tax. Efficiency is served by following the Ramsey Rule, but equity, in terms of vertical equity, may well be violated.

Modern tax theory has combined the dual concerns for efficiency and equity in the so-called optimal tax literature. Models have been developed in that literature which explicitly combine the concern for minimizing the welfare cost of taxation with a concern for income distribution as well. We will consider the combined concern for efficiency and equity in section five of this paper.

Justice in Administration of a Tax System

Justice requires that each person receive his due. In taxation, justice requires that similar taxpayers receive similar treatment. If you and I both own similar houses in a neighborhood, the property tax system should value those homes similarly and our tax bills should be similar. If not, our sense of justice is violated and we have reason to question the assessor. If Mr. Erickson and Ms. Ramirez have similar incomes, we expect the income-tax system to tax them similarly. If not, our sense of justice is violated. In every tax context you can imagine, justice requires equal treatment of equals. In public finance this concept is called *horizontal equity*. Two people of equal income should be taxed equally. Further, we should expect the tax collection agency to treat these two individuals similarly.

Recent criticism of the Internal Revenue Service (IRS) has focused on horror stories of the unequal treatment of taxpayers. Reform of the IRS, such as that suggested in the report of the National Commission on Restructuring the Internal Revenue Commission, is necessary in order to assure justice.[11] We expect that taxpayers should be treated equally, not singled out for harassment. In the process of reform however, we must think broadly about the demands of justice. For example, one criticism voiced loudly in the press regarding IRS audit practice relates to the Service's practice of auditing large numbers of low-income taxpayer returns. On its face, that seems unfair. When one realizes that low-income returns often include fraudulent claims for the Earned Income Tax Credit (EITC), however, one realizes that justice demands high audit frequencies in this case. One should not tolerate fraud in the name of compassion.

Another proposal—to transfer the burden of proof from the taxpayer to the IRS–has recently been signed into law by President Clinton. This reform also appears, on the surface, to improve the justice of tax administration. Yet we must realize that it is a fundamental principle of law that the party controlling the evidence has the burden of proof. The taxpayer controls the evidence in our system of taxation, keeping records and receipts. In switching the burden of proof to the IRS, which lacks the evidence, we may only encourage additional fraud in the tax system. Once again, we should not sacrifice justice in our pursuit of compassion (or votes!). Of course, we must also uphold the fundamental legal presumption of innocence until guilt is established.

In the administration of a tax system we must hold to the highest standard of justice. We must assure that each taxpayer receives his due. Audits must be objective and impartial. Tax evasion must be pursued and evaders punished. Without justice in administration the tax system crumbles into a capricious mess. The following section of this paper describes how we measure income inequality, and then presents evidence on how the tax system affects income distribution.

Income Inequality and the Effects of Taxation

In order to understand the potential for taxation as a tool of economic justice, we must first determine the determinants of income inequality. Once we have identified the sources of income inequality, we can evaluate the potential effectiveness of the tax system in relieving that inequality. We begin by describing properties of the income distribution and then, using those properties, we move to a consideration of recent research on the sources of income inequality. We leave to George Monsma a more general description of income inequality measures and causes. Here we focus on the specific role of the tax system in affecting income inequality.

Decomposition of Inequality by Source of Income

Nonspecialists will need to bear with me as I walk through some technical but extremely important material related to the sources of income inequality in the United States. The traditional method of measuring income inequality is to compute the Gini coefficient, which ranges from zero, indicating perfect equality of income (each person earns the same amount of income), to one, indicating perfect inequality of income (one person earns all of the income). A useful feature of the Gini coefficient is that it is additively decomposable, following the method of Lerman and Yitzhaki, and can be used to decompose overall inequality into its various sources.[12] If income is derived from K sources, we can decompose the Gini coefficient G as follows:

$$G = \sum_{k=1}^{K} S_k G_k R_k$$

where S_k is the kth component's share of income, G_k is the kth component's Gini coefficient, and R_k is the so-called Gini correlation—the kth income component's correlation with total income (the covariance between the kth income component and the cumulative distribution of total family income divided by the covariance between the kth income component and the cumulative distribution of the kth income component).

Table 1 (p. 292) reports the decomposition of the Gini coefficient by income source, using adjusted family income among persons for the years 1970, 1980, and 1990. The first data column of the table reports the share of adjusted family income attributed to each of eight sources. The family head's wage and salary income is, of course, the largest source of income, accounting for 51.5 percent of family income in 1990. The share of family income derived from the head's wage and salary has declined in marked fashion from 1970, when this income source accounted for 60.6 percent of family income, to 55.6 percent in 1980, to 51.5 percent in 1990. Spousal earnings have increased in importance as the share of family earnings due to the spouse has risen from 11.8 percent in 1970 to 16.5 percent in 1990. The share of income derived from capital income has risen from 3.9 percent in 1970 to 6.8 percent in 1990. Finally, other income sources account for 5.8 percent of family income, up from 1.5 percent in 1970.

These are simply the changes in income shares, however. It is important to also consider the associated Gini coefficients for each of these income sources, reported in the second data column of table 1. At the same time that the share of income derived from family-head wage and salary income was declining, the Gini coefficient for that income source was rising substantially. The increased Gini coefficient indicates a more inequitable distribution of family-head wage and salary income. The share of overall inequality due to family-head wage and salary income fell from 59.5 percent in 1970, to 57.9 percent in 1980, to 51.7 percent in 1990, as reported in the far right-hand column of table 1. On the other hand, the share of overall inequality due to spousal earnings rose from 16.2 percent in 1970, to 17.3 percent in 1980, and 20.4 percent in 1990. Capital income accounts for a growing share of inequality, as reflected in the rising share reported in the table, from 6.3 percent in 1970, to 9.5 percent in 1980, to 10.8 percent in 1990. Other income also accounts for a growing share of inequality, rising from 0.8 percent in 1970, to 3.7 percent in 1980, to 5.3 percent in 1990.

What does this decomposition of income inequality tell us about the potential role for tax policy to affect income inequality? Karoly concludes that changes in tax policy would actually have little impact. She states that, if her estimates are correct,

> there may be little opportunity to use the tax system to redress the rise in pre-tax income inequality that has occurred since the 1970's. Although changes in the degree of progressivity of the tax system may be justified on other grounds, it is not clear that they can be used to significantly counteract other factors—such as family composition changes and the changing wage structure—that have contributed to increased disparities in the distribution of income.[13]

Of course, the reason for her conclusion rests in the sources of inequality that her study reveals. Much of the growth in income inequality in recent history is due to fundamental shifts in the earnings of family members, with less reliance on the family head's wage and salary income, which has a relatively low Gini coefficient (i.e., is less unequal), and more reliance on the spouse's earnings which have a relatively high Gini coefficient (i.e., is more unequal). Add to that an increasing reliance on capital income with a very high Gini coefficient, and you have an increasingly unequal distribution of income, an inequality that has nothing to do with tax policy.

Taxation and Poverty

How do government transfer programs and the tax system affect income inequality? Table 2 provides alternate measures of income inequality for the current measure of income used by the census, as well as for five alternative measures. The first row of the table reports that, using the current measure of income, the first population quintile earns 3.7 percent of the income in the economy while the top quintile earns 48.6 percent. These income shares reveal a substantial inequality of income. One of the frequent criticisms of such data however, is that government transfers and taxes are not taken into account in computing these shares. The third row of the table presents income shares that reflect after-tax income and the fifth row of the table reflects correction for transfers. Income shares reported in the fifth row indicate slightly less income inequality, but still reveal substantial inequality. The Gini coefficient has been reduced from 0.444, using the current measure of income, to 0.394, reflecting a somewhat more equal distribution of income. The transfer and tax systems in the U.S. do have some impact on reducing measured income inequality, but that impact is very modest.

How does the U.S. tax system affect poverty? In order to answer this question we must consider both the federal income and payroll taxes. Table 3a reports poverty thresholds for the year 1995 for families of various sizes with specified numbers of children. This table is based on a special technical report of the U.S. Census Bureau. A family of four with two children, for example, would be considered to be in poverty if their income was below $15,455. A single mother with one child was considered to be in poverty with an income below $10,504. Table 3b reports corresponding income tax thresholds for families of various sizes for the same year in order to facilitate comparison. That table indicates that a family of four faced an income tax threshold of $16,550 if we consider only personal exemptions and the standard deduction. If we add in credits provided on the income tax for such a family, the taxable income threshold was higher: $22,362. With the income tax threshold above the poverty line, it is clear that a family with income at the poverty line will not face a federal income tax liability. Indeed, they may receive a check from the IRS due to refundable credits.

This is not the full story, however, as the family is still subject to payroll taxation. The last column of table 3b provides an estimate of the combined income and payroll taxes for families with income at the poverty threshold. These figures range from $685 for a single person, to $1,054 for a family of four, to $400 for a family of six. Notice that the EITC and other credits on the income tax are clearly offsetting substantial payroll taxes required of low-income families. While the payroll tax is a flat-rate tax applied to all payroll earnings, with no exemption at the low end, credits on the income tax help to reduce the combined impact of the two federal taxes.

How effective is the U.S. income tax system in reducing poverty? Table 4 provides information on antipoverty effectiveness of tax and transfer programs in 1996, the most recent year for which data are available. The table lists poverty reduction, due to a number of sources, for all persons in poverty, the elderly and children. The table reveals very clearly that the EITC is most effective in reducing poverty for children. Overall, the EITC is responsible for a 3 percent reduction in poverty, a modest contribution at best. Among the elderly poor, the EITC does not help at all. But for children, the EITC is a very powerful antipoverty program. Social insurance, means-tested cash transfers, food and housing benefits, and the EITC all combined to remove 5.3 million children from the poverty rolls. Notice that the EITC removes approximately the same number of children from poverty as does social insurance, and more than means-tested transfer programs. Only food and housing benefits combine to remove more children from poverty.

Because of its beneficial effects in removing work disincentives for AFDC recipients, and its impact in reducing poverty among children, we will return to a fuller discussion of the EITC in section 6.

Policy Conflict

It is often the case that policy objectives are in conflict. Pursuit of improvement in the tax system according to policy objective *A* may actually cause the tax system to become worse when judged by policy objective *B*. The reality of tax policy is that we have many policy standards, and even an apparently simple issue can involve multiple policy conflicts. As an example of this difficulty, we will consider marriage bonuses and penalties in the following section. This policy issue is currently receiving a good deal of attention in Congress and from Christian commentators who believe that there should be no "marriage penalty." By itself, that is certainly an admirable policy objective. There is a problem, however, in that resolution of this policy issue may only be accomplished by violating other policy objectives that Christians also hold to be important.

The Case of Marriage Bonuses and Penalties

There are inherent policy conflicts involved with the income tax and marital status. Table 5 illustrates those conflicts. Consider the first row of the table where we have two couples with equal family income of $60,000. Couple *A* is a married couple where each spouse earns $30,000 while couple *B* is a married couple where one spouse earns $60,000 and the other spouse has no income. A reasonable policy objective across this first row of the table is horizontal equity, so that these two couples with equal income pay the same tax. Justice requires this outcome.

Another policy objective to consider, however, is marriage neutrality within the tax system, so that a couple pays the same tax regardless of their marital status. This objective is illustrated in the first and last columns of Table 5. In the first column, we would like the tax system to treat couple *A* in the same manner, whether the couple is married (row one) or not (row three). Similarly, we would like the tax system to treat couple *B* in column three the same whether they are married (row one) or not (row three).

Finally, we may have the policy objective of applying a progressive rate of taxation to income, so that as income rises, the marginal tax rate rises. This objective is illustrated in the third row of table 5. Under progressive income taxation, couple *B*, with a combined income of $60,000 per year, pays a higher marginal tax rate than the individuals in couple *A*, who earn $30,000 per year.

The fundamental difficulty in tax policy as it relates to marriage is that these three policy objectives cannot be met without creating marriage bonuses and penalties. If we are willing to give up any one of the three policy objectives, we can eliminate marriage bonuses and penalties. As long as we wish to retain all three of these policy objectives, however, we will necessarily have marriage bonuses and penalties in our income-tax system.

Table 6 illustrates the distribution of marriage bonuses and penalties by adjusted gross income in 1996. The upper panel of the table reports the percentage of tax returns that have marriage penalties, are unaffected by marriage, or have marriage bonuses. For couples with AGI less than $20,000, the majority benefit from marriage bonuses (63 percent) or are unaffected (25 percent). Just 12 percent of the returns in this income class are affected by a marriage penalty. As income rises, however, the number of returns with penalties rises to 44 percent and 54 percent in the table. For incomes between $20,000 and $50,000, 44 percent of the returns have penalties while 55 percent have bonuses. For incomes above $50,000 those figures are reversed, with 54 percent of the returns with penalties and 44 percent with bonuses.

How big are these bonuses or penalties? The middle panel of table 6 reports that, on average, the penalties are 2.0 percent of AGI while the bonuses are 2.3 percent of AGI. Of course, the size of the bonuses and penalties, as a percentage of AGI, varies inversely with AGI.

The bottom panel of table 6 reports the total dollar value of all bonuses and penalties. The income tax confers bonuses amounting to $32.9 billion while inflicting penalties amounting to $28.8 billion. The effect is a $4.1 billion net marriage bonus. Notice that most of the bonuses and penalties are in the higher AGI classes.

This brief discussion should at least make it clear that the so-called "marriage penalty" is quite a bit more complicated than it sounds, and that the elimination of *any* circumstance in which marriage might cost taxpayers money would both compromise other tax policy objectives and cost the Treasury some $30 billion a year.

Equity and Efficiency Issues in Optimal Taxation[14]

Modern public finance has been dominated by a combined concern for both efficiency and equity in taxation. The innovation of the optimal tax literature was to explicitly combine these concerns. Efficiency aspects of taxation are included in optimal tax models as labor supply is endogenous, incorporating an efficiency cost of the tax. Specifically, we assume that labor (measured in hours of work) depends upon the gross wage per hour w, the elasticity of labor supply with respect to the net wage, the time endowment L_0, and the marginal income tax rate t. Revenue generated by the tax is given by the product of the tax rate and the labor earnings: $R=twL$. Clearly, for a value of $t=0$ there is no tax revenue generated. As the tax rate is increased there may be revenue generated, but the general relationship between the tax rate and tax revenue is ambiguous in sign; it may be either positive or negative. It is possible that an increase in the tax rate will reduce revenue if the labor supply response is strong enough.

As the rate of taxation initially rises above zero, revenue is generated for a small tax rate t. But for larger values of t, an increase in the tax rate may reduce revenue. There is some tax rate that generates a maximal amount of revenue. Beyond that tax rate, increases in the tax rate have the effect of reducing revenue. In a simple and well-known model described by A.B. Atkinson, that tax rate has been computed to be $t=1/(1+\varepsilon)$. At tax rates above this level, revenue falls with increased tax rate. At rates below this level, revenue rises with increased tax rate. If the elasticity of labor supply with respect to the net wage is 0.3, for example, the revenue maximizing tax rate is $t=0.77$.

The optimal tax rate can be expressed in a form that reveals the efficiency and equity aspects of the problem. The tax rate can be shown to depend upon the tax rate t, the elasticity of labor supply with respect to the net wage, the coefficient of variation of the gross hourly wage distribution, and a parameter capturing our taste for income redistribution.[15] A zero value of Υ indicates distributional indifference (equal social marginal value of income for all) while a value of Υ approaching infinity captures the Rawlsian objective of maximizing the welfare of the least well off person in the income distribution.

In this formulation of the problem, there is a convenient decomposition of the optimal tax rate into the product of two components. The first term captures the efficiency aspect of the problem while the second term captures the equity aspect of the problem. The efficiency aspect of the problem is determined entirely by the labor supply elasticity. The larger the elasticity of labor supply, the larger the efficiency cost of redistribution through a linear tax mechanism. That is, the more responsive are workers to after-tax wages in their labor supply, the greater the efficiency cost of income redistribution, because as the tax rate is increased to facilitate redistribution, less labor is supplied by workers. As a result, there is a high efficiency cost of redistribution. This result is expected if we recall the simple Ramsey Rule from the policy world of indirect taxation. According to that rule, tax rates should be set inversely proportional to elasticities in order to minimize the excess burden of taxation for a given amount of revenue generated.

The equity part of the decomposition is more complex. It depends upon all three parameters: ε, η, and γ. First, the wage dispersion measured by η is involved—as the degree of inequality in wages rises, the optimal tax rate required rises as well, other things being equal. Second, the elasticity of labor supply with respect to the net wage ε is involved since the gross wage w depends on this parameter. The larger the elasticity of labor supply with respect to the net wage, the more gross wage earnings rise with w, causing the income tax rate to be more effective in redistribution. Third, the value of γ which indicates distributional preference also affects the equity term in the above equation. If we attach no weight to redistribution, only caring about total income, $\gamma=0$ and the optimal tax rate is subsequently zero. For positive values of γ, the greater our preference for redistribution the larger the optimal tax rate, other things being equal. For example, if we assume that $\gamma=0.5$ and $\varepsilon=0.3$, then the optimal tax rate can be computed to be $t=0.23$. As γ approaches infinity the equity term approaches one and the optimal tax rate approaches $(1+\varepsilon)^{-1}$. For a value of $E=0.3$, for example, the optimal tax rate is $t=0.77$.

Table 7 illustrates the optimal tax rate for various values of the parameters. Retaining the same values for ε and η, we can examine the effect of increasing γ. As γ rises from zero to 0.25, the optimal tax rate rises from 0 to 14 percent. Additional one-quarter increases in γ raise the optimal tax rate to 25 percent, 32 percent, and 38 percent. Further increases in γ cause the optimal tax rate to asymptotically approach the rate of 77 percent. These examples illustrate the sensitivity of the optimal tax rate to the distributional parameter. The more income inequality we are willing to tolerate, the lower the optimal tax rate. The more income equality we desire, the higher the tax rate required.

We now must specify an objective function that will enable us to select the best tax rate from among the many possibilities that exist. A simple objective function that is often used in the optimal tax literature is to specify that the social, marginal value of income to a person is proportional to her wage rate: $w^{-\gamma}$. By specifying the value of the parameter γ we can characterize a number of alternative views regarding redistribution of income. For example, a person who is completely indifferent to alternative distributions of income would have a value of $\gamma=0$. That would result in a constant, unitary, social, marginal value of income. On the other hand, a person who considers it most important to make the least well off person as well off as possible would have a value of γ approaching plus infinity. In this case, the social marginal value of income for a person with a high wage approaches zero while that for a person with a low wage is very large. As an intermediate case, consider the person who has a value of $Y=0.5$. This person would compare a high income person (whose wage is nine times larger than a low income person) and attach a weight of one-third as much to a dollar increase in the affluent person's income.

Redistribution Pessimism

Atkinson has well summarized the pessimism that has come to surround contemporary discussions of redistribution through the tax system. This pessimism is grounded in the belief that marginal reductions in income inequality through the use of a more progressive income tax are very costly in terms of efficiency effects. Most notable in this regard is the work of Browning and Johnson.[16] Using the case they describe as most plausible, which embodies a compensated elasticity of 0.312, they derive estimates of the gains or losses of net equivalent income from a one percentage point increase in the linear income tax rate. Table 8 provides a summary of the dollar gains and losses, measured in terms of net equivalent income, that would be experienced by the five quintile groups as a result of a 1 percent increase in the marginal tax rate used to finance an increase in basic income. Taxpayers in the bottom two quintiles gain the equivalent of $47 and $33 dollars each, for a total gain of $80. But taxpayers in the upper three quintiles lose the equivalent of $279 in income. The source of those losses, of course, is the distortion the higher, marginal tax rate causes in labor markets, resulting in lower income. This loss of income must be considered as well as the benefit of redistribution for low-income households. Browning and Johnson conclude that "the marginal cost of less income inequality is surprisingly high even when labour supply elasticities are relatively low."[17] Evidence such as this has led to substantial resistance to income redistribution through more progressive taxation.

Is Redistribution Pessimism Justified?[18]

We should consider whether such pessimism regarding income redistribution through more progressive taxation is justified. There are, in fact, a number of reasons to question the prevailing pessimism in this regard. The analysis above is based on just one form of tax effect on economic decision-making: labor supply. Changes in the tax system affect a wide range of other activities in addition to labor supply. For example, a change in the marginal tax rate will potentially affect savings, investment, and risk-taking as well. Suppose for a moment that the tax-rate increase has the effect of increasing taxpayers' willingness to hold risky assets (since the higher marginal tax rate provides a greater subsidy to potential losses), which fuels increased entrepreneurial activity, which stimulates growth. It may be that the subsequent growth in the economy provides a type of dynamic efficiency that is not considered in the static view of efficiency employed in the literature cited above. The criticism here is that existing models that have led to redistribution pessimism have been extremely narrow in their focus. The sole supply-side effect is typically a labor-supply response. All other forms of response to changes in the tax system are typically ignored. Some of those potential effects move in the opposite direction.

While labor supply has been incorporated in the models used in the optimal, linear income tax literature, the particular form of labor-supply response included is limited. The models generally incorporate labor-supply response in terms of hours of work. There are, of course, effects on labor force participation rates. Suppose for the moment that we have a linear income tax system, with a basic income guarantee and a single marginal tax rate. Such a tax system may reduce the disincentive to work that exists under the current U.S. tax and transfer system. If so, labor supply response—measured in terms of labor force participation—may be greater than we would otherwise have expected. But a person who returns to work then moves out of a position of receiving the income guarantee and moves into a position of paying a positive income tax. We cannot simply assume that other dimensions of response to changes in the marginal tax rate will operate in the same direction.

The empirical evidence we have on labor-supply response is voluminous but limited. The literature is voluminous, with a plethora of studies each providing a view of labor-supply response which takes into account a myriad of econometric issues that provide more accurate estimates. Most of the studies in the labor-supply literature are cross-section studies based on subgroups of the population. For example, the work of Jerry Hausman excludes workers that are self-employed, under twenty-five or over fifty-five years of age, farmers, single women without children, and the disabled.[19] Each group excluded makes the remaining sample more homogeneous, which has the effect of making the estimated labor-supply responses less representative of the entire population.

There are also potential problems due to the often wide confidence intervals on the estimates of labor-supply elasticities, which reduce our confidence in the results. Finally, our estimates of labor-supply elasticity suffer from the inevitable problem that cross-section estimates are not properly derived from a controlled experiment in which a control group has no change in tax treatment while an experimental group experiences a change in tax law. Time-series studies suffer from the problem of confounding events that distort our picture of the partial effect of the tax law change. In all, there are a number of reasons to be cautious regarding the efficiency effects of redistribution. These concerns do not suggest that studies which indicate the efficiency cost of redistribution is large are systematically biased or otherwise unreliable. Rather, these concerns are intended to provide a cautionary note so that the estimates can be understood within a specific context. There may indeed be reason to believe that the efficiency cost of redistribution through the tax code is large, but our models are not yet sufficiently comprehensive and robust to allow us to draw that conclusion with certainty.

Charles Ballard has estimated the efficiency cost of increased progressivity as well. In his most preferred estimation he finds that transferring one dollar from upper income groups to lower income groups has an efficiency cost of $0.50 to $1.30. While this estimate is for the same type of demogrant simulated by Browning and Johnson, Ballard also estimates the effect of an alternative redistributional mechanism which he calls a notch grant. Using this mechanism, a grant for low-income groups is financed through an increase in the marginal tax rate for higher-income groups, combined with a wage subsidy for low-income workers. Both high-income and low-income taxpayers are assigned exogenously and both face linear budget constraints. The efficiency cost of both of these redistributional methods is found to be far lower than that for the demogrant. The demogrant is a funding mechanism whereby the marginal tax rate is increased by one percentage point for all households, and the resulting revenue is distributed in equal, per capita, cash grants.

Another policy alternative is to provide increased progressivity through an expansion of the earned income tax credit (EITC). Robert Triest estimates that the efficiency cost of improving progressivity this way is less than $0.20 per dollar of income redistributed, if the redistribution is financed through tax-rate increases for middle-income taxpayers. His assessment is that the efficiency cost of redistribution "varies considerably with the type of tax reform considered." He also makes note of the fact that he is only modeling one distortion due to taxation: individuals' hours-of-work decision. He cautions that "I may be missing the most important distortionary effects of taxation affecting very high-income households." Despite these caveats, he concludes that:

> The simulations do suggest that the efficiency cost of increasing progressivity by rasing the marginal tax rates faced only by very high-income households is likely to be much greater than if the progressivity-increasing reform were instead financed by raising the marginal tax rates faced by moderate income groups.[20]

The conventional wisdom on labor-supply elasticities for the past two decades has been that prime-age men are quite unresponsive to wage changes, while women are quite responsive. That view has been based on the research of Hausman, Burtless, Hausman, and others. That literature is briefly summarized in Burtless and Bosworth.[21]

On the High Income Laffer Curve[22]

Joel Slemrod argues that before we can consider the question of whether we *should* tax the rich more, we must answer the logically prior question of whether we *can* tax the rich more. Perhaps it is the case that a higher rate of taxation applied to the rich yields no revenue. If that is so, then only pure envy motivates calls for higher tax rates on the rich. There is no revenue derived from such increases. As an alternative, perhaps it is the case that a higher rate of taxation applied to the rich yields some revenue, but also induces strong behavior responses that bring with them large excess burdens. In that case the added revenue may not be economically justified. For both reasons, it is important to understand how the rich react to changes in tax rates, in order to know whether they *can* be taxed more and to inform our view of whether they *should* be taxed more. Slemrod summarizes his findings with this concluding statement:

> In sum, with respect to two aspects that differentiate the rich from the non-rich—the importance of capital income, and the flexibility of the form of compensation—I have uncovered no evidence of a significant behavioral response to

the marginal tax rate. There is, however, evidence of a significant response of capital gains realizations to the tax on capital gains; exactly how substantial is the long-run elasticity of this response remains a controversial issue. Thus, in assessing the behavioral response of the affluent, it is important to consider separately the marginal tax rate on ordinary income and the effective tax rate on capital gains.[23]

In summary, we have been considering whether attempts to use the tax code in a progressive manner to reduce income inequality violate the goal of efficiency (and thus stewardship), or actually are successful in yielding the results that are being sought. We can say that though redistribution does have efficiency costs, and though those who are taxed do respond to the nature and form of that taxation, we cannot conclude from the available evidence that the use of tax policy for modest redistribution efforts in the interests of justice is either hopelessly inefficient or ineffective in accomplishing this goal. Yet those seeking greater economic equity through the use of the tax code must be aware of the limits of this strategy.

Fundamental Tax Reform and Economic Justice

Fundamental Tax Reform Plans

A number of plans for fundamental tax reform have been proposed in recent years. Table 9 summarizes the features of five alternatives to the current income taxes (personal and corporate): a federal, retail sales tax, a value-added tax (VAT), the Armey-Shelby flat tax proposal, the USA tax, and the Gephardt tax plan. A brief description of each tax plan follows. Distributional properties of each plan, compared with the current tax system, are then considered.

National Sales Tax (NST)

The federal government could adopt a retail sales tax in much the same way that forty-five states currently apply retail sales taxes. The *ad valorem* tax would apply to the value of final goods, and possibly services as well. Only final sales are taxed by a sales tax, exempting intermediate goods from taxation. The reason for this exemption is to avoid the problem of the cascading of the tax, with very high rates of taxation resulting in production processes with many steps, where intermediate goods are passed on to other firms for additional finishing. A uniform tax rate would be applied to sales anywhere in the country. This is the quintessential consumption tax.

Since consumption expenditures rise at a decreasing rate with income, however, the sales tax is quite regressive. The effective rate of taxation (tax paid divided by income) falls as income rises. States generally relieve that regressivity by exempting essential commodities such as food (for home consumption), prescription drugs, and in some cases, clothing.

Value-Added Tax (VAT)

A value-added tax taxes the value added at each stage of production. Value added is measured by gross receipts less expenses for raw materials or intermediate goods purchased by firms. There are three variants of the VAT, distinguished by their treatment of depreciation and investment. The gross-income type of VAT allows no deductions for depreciation or investment. The net-income type of VAT allows a deduction for depreciation of capital equipment and plants. The consumption type of VAT allows a deduction for investment expenditure, which is equivalent to expensing. VATs are very broad-based taxes. As a result, they can generate large amounts of revenue at very low rates. In order to relieve the regressivity of VATs, countries often zero rate certain commodities considered essential. Zero rating simply means that the tax rate applied to those essential commodities is zero. VATs are very common taxes in the rest of the world, but in the U.S. the only VAT is Michigan's Single Business Tax.

Armey-Shelby Flat Tax

The Armey-Shelby flat tax plan is an adaptation of the flat tax proposal of Hall and Rabuska.[24] The tax is best thought of as a consumption-type, value-added tax that would be applied in two pieces. A consumption-type VAT taxes gross receipts, less the cost of raw materials, intermediate goods and investment. The deduction of investment expenses for new machinery, equipment, and facilities is what makes this version of a VAT a consumption-type VAT. In terms of simple national income accounting, national income or product Y is comprised of the components C, consumption expenditures, and I, investment expenditures, according to the formula $Y=C+I$. If investment expenditure is deducted, we are left with consumption expenditures. This consumption-type VAT is then applied in two parts. First, a tax is applied at the household level on wages, salaries, and pension benefits. Second, a tax is applied to all businesses on their gross receipts less wages, pension contributions, raw materials costs, and investment. Table 10 provides details on the major aspects of the plan.

USA Tax

The USA tax plan is a hybrid of two forms of taxation. First, households are subject to a personal consumption tax applied to income, less deductions and exemptions, and an unlimited savings allowance (hence the name of the tax—USA). Households are also given a refundable credit for the employee's portion of the payroll tax. Second, businesses would be subject to a VAT, less a credit for the employer's portion of the payroll tax. As a result, the USA tax is a progressive consumption tax. It differs from our current income tax system in that it taxes consumption rather than income.

Income Tax Reform

Various proposals have been suggested for reforming the existing income tax system. One such plan is the Gephardt plan, named for its sponsor, Representative Richard Gephardt. This plan is a modification of the current income tax system, building on the concept of base-broadening embodied in the Tax Reform Act of 1986 (TRA86). This plan eliminates deductions for state and local taxes paid, charitable contributions, and pension contributions. Employer-provided health insurance benefits and municipal bond interest are added to the tax base. Both the Earned Income Tax Credit (EITC) and the mortgage interest deduction would be retained. As a result of the base broadening, the rate structure of the income tax would be lowered, with the bottom rate at 10 percent and a progressive rate structure rising to 34 percent at the top. On the corporate side, the plan would retain the corporate income tax but eliminate exemptions and deductions often called *corporate welfare.*

Another income tax reform plan is that of the late economist Joseph Pechman, who suggested that the current system be modified further in the direction of TRA86, with generous family and child exemptions and an EITC to hold down the tax burden on low-income families and the working poor, with deduction elimination for the purpose of base-broadening; and with a two-bracket rate structure of 15 percent and 30 percent.[25]

Distributional Effects of Tax Reform Plans

Table 10 provides Aaron and Gale's estimates of the distributional effects of the major alternative tax systems, compared to current law.[26] These estimates are based on the results of a complex microsimulation model that the Brookings Institution has developed for evaluating tax and transfer programs. The upper panel of the table provides estimates of the average tax paid by income, while the lower panel provides average effective tax rates. Figure 1 plots the average, effective tax rates by income to provide a picture of each tax system.

Under current law, the average, effective tax rate begins at 2.7 percent for households with taxable income in the range of $5,000 to $10,000, and rises monotonically to 41.6 percent for households with taxable income between $99,000 and $100,000. The average, effective tax rate is 25.8 percent. While the average, effective tax rate is virtually identical for all four alternative tax systems in the table, the distribution of effective rates by income is very different across the alternatives. The flat tax and VAT are both less progressive than current law. Both would increase the effective rate of taxation for low-income households. The VAT increases the effective tax rate for households up to $90,000 of taxable income. Thereafter, the VAT reduces the effective tax rate. Clearly, the VAT would reduce the progressivity of the current tax system substantially. In terms of consequences for the poor, the VAT is the most threatening proposal on the horizon. The only way to relieve the tax burden on the poor under a VAT is to zero rate necessities and provide large exemptions. After all, the flat tax is a VAT and its effective tax rates are more progressive due to the liberal exemptions it incorporates. While a VAT could be configured to be less demanding of low-income households, most proposals for a federal VAT would be quite threatening to the poor.

The flat tax is the next most progressivity-reducing proposal. Compared to current law, the flat tax would increase effective tax rates for households with taxable incomes up to $99,000. For households above that income level, the flat tax would reduce the effective tax rate substantially. Notice, however, that the flat tax raises the effective tax rate substantially at low- and moderate-income levels, but raises effective rates only slightly for middle-income households.

The USA tax would generally lower the effective tax rate for households with income of less than $90,000. Above that level, it would apply higher effective tax rates. As a result, the USA tax would be more progressive than the current tax system. The Pechman plan would also be more progressive than the current tax system. While it mimics the effective rate structure of the USA tax up through income of $60,000, thereafter it applies higher effective rates, making it more progressive than the USA tax up through the $99,000 income level. At the top end, the USA tax applies a higher effective tax rate.

The distributional properties of each of the tax reform plans described above represent the direct effects expected. The Aaron and Gale microsimulation model is a static model, hence dynamic effects are not included. The issue of static vs. dynamic simulation is controversial, not so much because of genuine differences of opinion regarding the effects involved, but because of the potential to bias the results of dynamic simulations with appropriately selected elasticities. There are, of course, indirect effects to consider as well.

Fundamental tax reform may have indirect effects on macroeconomic variables as well. For example, proponents of the flat tax, such as Hall and Rabuska, believe that pre-tax interest rates are likely to fall by 2 percent. Alan Auerbach estimates that the flat tax would lower pre-tax interest rates by about 1 percent.[27] Others, such as Gentry and Hubbard, believe that the adoption of a flat tax would raise pre-tax interest rates.[28] Of course, the effect of a flat-rate tax on pre-tax interest rates will depend crucially on household saving behavior in response to the tax. Research provides mixed evidence on the sensitivity of savings response (that is, how much money households choose to save) to tax changes. As a result, we cannot know with any degree of certainty the direction of such indirect effects, much less their magnitude. While indirect effects will occur, it is not wise or prudent to build one's case for tax reform on those effects.

The prospect of fundamental tax reform brings with it concern for a number of other effects that should be considered. For example, transition issues and effects are very important. If we were to adopt a tax plan that eliminates the mortgage interest deduction, for example, we would expect that the demand for owner-occupied housing would shift downward, reducing prices and quantities cleared in housing markets, other things being equal. Since owner-occupied homes are the primary source of wealth for most families, this tax policy change would result in a reduction in wealth for many families. Those effects could be substantial. As a result, the transition from the current system to the flat tax system would be fraught with difficulties, each with distributional effects worthy of consideration.

Evaluation of Fundamental Reform Proposals

A concern for biblical justice in enabling people to earn a living wage requires a tax system that complements wages in such a way as to result in adequate after-tax earnings. Given the key features of each fundamental reform proposal discussed above, which tax system would most clearly facilitate biblical justice? Each reform proposal has its merits. From the policy viewpoint of biblical justice, however, there are clear differences among the proposals based on their distributional impacts. The Pechman Plan for modifying the income tax, and the USA tax, which would move us in the direction of a savings-based tax, are clearly preferable. Both the VAT and flat tax (in any of its variants) are inferior. Grounded in a biblical concern for the poor, and desiring to see working households earn a living wage, we suggest that reform in the spirit of the Pechman Plan or the USA tax be pursued.

What about all the other advantages embodied in VAT and flat tax proposals? Isn't the simplicity of a flat tax "postcard-sized tax return" reason enough to favor that proposal? Not really. Under the current income tax system most taxpayers do not itemize. As a result, many file Form 1040EZ, which could easily be reduced to the size of a postcard. In fact, many taxpayers now file their tax return on the telephone in a matter of minutes, without ever sending anything to the IRS. Indeed, there are numerous proposals for moving toward a return-free system, even with the current income tax.

What about simplicity? Isn't the current tax system hopelessly complex and in need of complete overhaul to make it simpler? That is a matter of perspective as well. Taxpayers balance competing policy objectives all the time. One policy objective is simplicity, another is minimizing tax liability. Consider a simple example. Suppose that you are a homeowner with a mortgage. Under current law you have the choice of filing a simple Form 1040EZ, taking the standard deduction, or filing Form 1040 with Schedule A, on which you itemize your deductions, including mortgage interest and local property taxes paid on your house. For most homeowners, the sum of their mortgage interest and local property taxes exceeds the standard deduction, so it makes sense to itemize. As a result, their tax liability is reduced. But, of course, they have a choice. If they prefer simplicity they can take the standard deduction. Most of us will forego simplicity in exchange for a lower tax liability. Simplicity is an overrated virtue. In fact, the transition from an income tax system to a consumption-type value added tax in the form of a flat tax, would be the most complex change in the history of U.S. tax policy. Lovers of simplicity beware. The current income tax system can certainly be greatly simplified. Congress has the opportunity to do so regularly. Other policy objectives usually win out over simplicity, however, and the tax code becomes increasingly complex.

Would a single tax rate not be far better than the current graduated rate structure? Actually, this is one of the most trivial aspects of a flat tax plan. If the argument is that the computation of a tax liability is simpler when there is one rate, it must be noted that tax tables make computations very simple. A taxpayer in the 32 percent tax bracket does not first compute the tax owed in the first 15 percent bracket on income in that bracket, and then compute the tax owed on income in the 28 percent bracket, and finally compute the tax owed on income in the 32 percent bracket, summing all of the amounts to get total tax liability. Rather, the taxpayer simply looks up taxable income in the tax table and finds the total. By no means is it simpler to ask taxpayers to compute the tax owed as 17 percent of their taxable income.

Of course, the more important aspect of moving to a single tax rate relates to removing the difference between the tax rate applied to personal income and the tax rate applied to corporate income. Any difference between the two rates leads to arbitrage. Taxpayers have an incentive to misreport one form of income as the other to take advantage of a lower rate. It does not take a major reform, moving away from income taxation to a consumption-type value added tax, to reduce the difference in rates on the personal and corporate income taxes. Indeed, this is just one aspect of integration of the two income taxes that could be accomplished without major reform.

Transition costs are also worthy of mention. Marginal changes in the current income tax system have relatively small marginal costs associated with them. Reform proposals to switch to a completely different tax base will bring with them very large transition costs. Not only would accounting systems have to be changed with different information requirements, but there would also be large costs associated with hold-harmless provisions of a major reform. Any major reform creates groups of winners and losers. The losers will lobby for provisions to hold them harmless from the negative effects of the reform (in comparison to the *status quo*). Those provisions will be very expensive for the rest of the taxpayers.

We have stressed the Christian concern for biblical justice and emphasized the corresponding concern that a tax system enable the working poor to earn a living wage. Distributional consequences matter. As a result, we have suggested that reforms similar to the Pechman Plan or the USA Tax are likely to be more rewarding efforts than implementation of a VAT or a flat tax. If we were to pursue a reform of the income tax system with an eye toward implementing biblical justice, expansion of the EITC or similar mechanisms would be required. In order to advance our thinking along that line, we will now consider the EITC in greater detail, looking for ways to expand or adapt such a mechanism to facilitate our policy objectives.

Income Tax Reform: A Critical Role for the Earned Income Tax Credit (EITC)

The earned income tax credit (EITC) provides income tax reduction for low-income working households. The taxpayer must have positive earned income in order to be eligible for the credit. Hence, no credit is provided to taxpayers unless they are working and have earned income. For example, a taxpayer with two children and earned income of $8,000 in 1997 would qualify for a credit of $3,200, reflecting a credit rate of 40 percent. The maximum credit that the taxpayer with two children could earn is $3,656. There are three separate schedules for the EITC; which one applies depends on the number of dependents. Once the maximum credit is reached, increases in income have no effect on the credit amount. The credit is constant over a range of income. For higher income levels however, the credit is phased out and eventually the household may have income too high to qualify for the credit.

An important feature of the EITC is that the credit is refundable. This means that the taxpayer can receive the full amount of credit for which the taxpayer qualifies, even if the taxpayer has an income tax liability that is smaller than the credit. For example, if the taxpayer owes $1,200 in tax and qualifies for a credit of $3,200, the taxpayer receives a check for $2,000 from the IRS. The credit is fully refundable. In fact, the credit is also front-loaded through an advance payment option so that the taxpayer can receive the credit in her paychecks during the year, rather than wait until after filing her tax form at the end of the year.

The EITC provides substantial assistance to low-income families. In 1997, for example, a total of 18,652,000 households received the credit. Each household received an average credit of $1,443, for a total credit amount of $26.9 billion.

Figure 2 illustrates the EITC mechanism, plotting the tax credit as a function of earnings. A household with zero earnings receives no tax credit, so the graph of the credit begins at the origin in the figure. As earnings rise above zero, the tax credit rises as well. This is the phase-in range where the taxpayer receives a credit equal to a portion of earnings. The credit reaches a maximum amount when earnings are equal to E_1. After the phase-in range, there is a range of earnings from E_1 to E_2 over which the credit remains at the maximum amount. This range of earnings is called the stationary range since the amount of the credit does not change with earnings. Once earnings reach E_2, however, the credit is phased out as earnings increase. At earnings level E_3, the household receives no credit at all.

For a family with two children in 1997, for example, the EITC provided a credit rate of 40 percent of earnings up to a maximum credit of $3,656. Families were eligible for the maximum credit with earnings of E_1 = $9,140. The phase-out range began at an earnings level of E_2 = $11,930 and continued up through earnings of E_3 = $29,290, applying a phase-out rate of 21.06 percent. Table 11 reports these parameters of the EITC for 1997. While the parameter values differ for families of different sizes, the basic structure of the credit remains the same. The earnings levels E_1, E_2, and E_3 are indexed to the inflation rate and are adjusted annually.

Taxpayers are not eligible to receive the tax credit if their disqualified income exceeds $2,200. Disqualified income is income from interest (both taxable and non-taxable), dividends, net rent and royalty income (positive), capital gains (net, positive), and net passive income (positive) that is not self-employment income.

For purposes of qualifying for other means-tested assistance programs such as AFDC, Medicaid, SSI, food stamps, and low-income housing programs, the tax credit received is *not* counted as income. Furthermore, the credit is not counted in the computation of benefit levels in these programs. This has been the case since 1990. Prior to that time, the credit was counted as part of the eligibility standard.

Table 12 reports the distribution of tax returns with EITC in 1997. Only 29 percent of the returns with an EITC were joint returns. Nearly 71 percent of the returns with an EITC were either head-of-household or single-filer returns. Virtually all of the returns with an EITC report income of less than $30,000. In fact, most of the returns report less than $20,000 income.

Interaction with the Income Tax Structure

Once a family is in the phase-out range there is also an interaction with the positive income tax to consider. Figure 3 illustrates the interaction of the EITC with the income tax structure. As income rises from zero to E_1 the household pays no tax but receives the credit. Once income reaches E_1 the credit is at its maximum and further increases in income result in no tax and no additional credit. After income level E_2 however, the credit is phased out. The household still pays no tax, but their EITC is being reduced as their income rises. Once the household income reaches E_t however, the income tax threshold has been reached and the household must begin to pay income tax. Of course, its EITC is larger than its income tax liability, so the household still receives a check from the IRS. There comes a point, however, where household income tax liability begins to exceed its EITC. That income level is labeled E_v in Figure 3, and represents a break-even point where tax liability first exceeds the credit amount. As income increases further, the credit is phased out and income tax liability rises. Once income reaches the level E_3, the household no longer qualifies for the EITC and the credit amount is zero. At this point the household is out of the credit program and in the income tax system.

Notice that the household is confronted with four different tax rates as its income rises from zero to E_3. For income levels between zero and E_1, there is no tax but an EITC credit rate that results in a combined effective marginal tax rate of minus the credit rate. For income levels from E_1 to E_2, there is no tax and a constant credit, yielding a combined effective marginal tax rate of zero. For income levels from E_2 to E_t, there is no tax, but an EITC credit phase-out rate is applied, resulting in a combined effective tax rate equal to the credit phase-out rate. For income levels from E_t to E_3, both a marginal income tax rate and an EITC phase-out rate are applied. The effective combined marginal tax rate is the sum of these two rates.

A family of four in 1997, for example, began to pay income tax once their income exceeded $17,500 (the sum of four personal exemptions of $2,650 and a standard deduction of $6,900). The marginal tax rate applied to income was 15 percent. Since a family with income in this range is also eligible for the EITC, albeit at a phase-out rate, there is an important interaction to consider. On the margin, income is taxed at the 15 percent rate above the income threshold of $17,500. But at that level, the EITC phase-out rate was also 21.06 percent. Thus, each additional dollar of income above $17,500 was taxed at a 15 percent rate and subjected to EITC phase out at a 21.06 percent rate—a combined rate of 40.06 percent. Thus, households with income in this range were subject to very high marginal tax rates. Indeed, the rate applied exceeded the maximum income rate of 39.6 percent that was applied to high-income taxpayers with incomes of at least $271,050.

Interaction with other Means-Tested Assistance Programs

Steuerle traces the origins of the EITC and reveals that it was originally designed as a mechanism to encourage Aid to Families with Dependent Children (AFDC) recipients to work.[29] Since one of the fundamental policy dilemmas involved in providing AFDC recipients with assistance for their children is that the financial assistance can be a disincentive to work, it is important to reduce or eliminate that disincentive. The EITC was designed to accomplish that policy objective.

For purposes of qualifying for other means-tested assistance programs such as AFDC, Medicaid, SSI, food stamps, and low-income housing programs, the amount of EITC received is *not* counted as income. Furthermore, the credit is not counted in the computation of benefit levels in these programs. This has been the case since 1990. Prior to that time, the credit was counted as part of the eligibility standard.

Effects on Poverty

The EITC plays a role in reducing poverty as well. Table 4 reports the combined impact of the EITC and federal payroll and income taxes in removing 1.7 million persons from poverty, or a 3 percent reduction in the number of persons in poverty. Of course, payroll and income taxes paid would have the effect of increasing the number of people in poverty, so the reduction reported in table 4 is due to the powerful impact of the EITC not only overcoming the negative effects of federal taxes in causing poverty among low income families, but providing a net reduction in poverty overall.[30]

An expansion of the EITC with a greater credit percentage over the phase-in range (earnings from zero to E_1), a higher maximum credit, and an expanded phase-out range (E_2 to E_3) holds the prospect of providing substantial assistance to the poor, assistance consistent with biblical justice in enabling them to earn a living wage. This policy is also consistent with the biblical stewardship mandate because it recognizes that work is part of the creation order and encourages work effort.

Summary and Conclusions

We have established that Christians must be concerned about issues of economic justice, and that the tax system is an important part of that concern. It is right and appropriate for Christians to pay taxes to secular governments. Tax systems employed by those governments must administer the taxes in just ways, giving each taxpayer his due. There is no single method of taxation prescribed in scripture, however. We find examples of head taxes, *ad valorem* taxes, and ability-to-pay taxes in scripture. Christians are also compelled to be compassionate and provide assistance to those in need. Yet we should not confuse compassion with justice in administration of a tax system.

The biblical mandate to be stewards of God's creation means that in tax policy we should be concerned with designing tax systems that waste as few resources as possible. Efficiency in taxation is our rightful concern. We must also be concerned with equity in taxation, both from a horizontal point of view and a vertical point of view. The effects of our tax system on income distribution deserve careful consideration. Further, the trade-off between efficiency and equity in taxation must be carefully considered. Both policy objectives are relevant to the Christian concern for justice in taxation.

Research on the sources of income inequality indicates that there may be a very limited potential for using the tax system to redress the growing inequality we presently experience in the U.S. economy. Fundamental changes in family composition and wage structure cannot be undone through tax policy. Research on optimal taxation that combines efficiency and equity policy objectives has generally been pessimistic regarding the potential for redistribution of income through use of taxation. There may be large efficiency costs associated with small improvements in income distribution. But there are a number of reasons to believe that the optimal-tax literature has been overly pessimistic regarding the scope for redistribution. Newer research indicates that the efficiency costs of redistribution may not be as large as earlier evidence indicated.

Finally, we considered a number of proposals for fundamental tax reform and evaluated each with regard to its impact on the income distribution. A value added tax in pure form would be much less progressive than the current income tax system. The so-called flat tax, a variant of the value-added tax, would also be substantially less progressive than the current system. Other variants of the income tax, such as the USA tax or proposals suggested by Gephardt or Pechman, would make the present income tax more progressive. With small efficiency costs associated, these plans are clearly preferable from the perspective of biblical justice. While none of these proposals should be considered inherently any more Christian than another, the thoughtful Christian policy analyst should evaluate each with a focus on both efficiency and equity implications. Unless there are clear efficiency gains involved, the Christian concern for economic justice means we should be vitally interested in the distributional aspects of each reform proposal. Those proposals that move our tax system in the direction of a less progressive incidence of tax burden should be carefully considered for other redeeming value. In the absence of clear evidence that efficiency gains would be large, it may be more appropriate to focus our attention on reforming the existing income tax system and gaining additional progressivity, greater horizontal equity, and increased efficiency through base-broadening and rate reductions.

To the extent that we wish to build greater progressivity into the tax system, we should consider expansion of the Earned Income Tax Credit or other similar mechanisms. This method of building progressivity into the system has many advantages. First, it rewards work. Taxpayers do not receive the credit unless they have earned income to report. As their earned income increases their credit also increases, but only up to a clear limit, after which the credit is phased-out with further increases in income. Second, evidence indicates that this mechanism is especially effective in reducing poverty for children. While other transfer programs play a role in reducing poverty for single persons or the elderly, this mechanism is most effective in targeting poverty relief for children. Further, expansion of the EITC can be an integral component of a policy plan to enable the working poor to earn a living wage. This is the essence of biblical justice.

Table 1

Decomposition of Gini Coefficients by Income Sources
(Adjusted Family Income Among Persons)

Income Source	Year	Share of income (S_k)	Gini (G_k)	Gini correlation (R_k)	Share of inequality (I_k)
Head's wage and salary	1970	0.606	0.492	0.721	0.595
	1980	0.556	0.527	0.717	0.579
	1990	0.515	0.563	0.713	0.517
Head's self employment	1970	0.080	0.947	0.521	0.109
	1980	0.055	0.954	0.445	0.064
	1990	0.054	0.957	0.506	0.065
Spouse's earnings	1970	0.118	0.812	0.610	0.162
	1980	0.134	0.781	0.600	0.173
	1990	0.165	0.764	0.648	0.204
Others' earnings	1970	0.077	0.877	0.458	0.086
	1980	0.075	0.877	0.456	0.082
	1990	0.068	0.886	0.419	0.063
Means-tested transfers	1970	0.010	0.958	−0.672	−0.017
	1980	0.010	0.946	−0.706	−0.019
	1990	0.008	0.947	−0.708	−0.014
Other transfers	1970	0.057	0.851	−0.038	−0.005
	1980	0.071	0.820	−0.073	−0.012
	1990	0.064	0.837	0.018	0.002
Capital income	1970	0.039	0.924	0.638	0.063
	1980	0.057	0.891	0.676	0.095
	1990	0.068	0.886	0.720	0.108
Other income	1970	0.015	0.962	0.203	0.008
	1980	0.041	0.917	0.351	0.037
	1990	0.058	0.892	0.409	0.053
Total income	1970	1.000	0.361	1.000	1.000
	1980	1.000	0.363	1.000	1.000
	1990	1.000	0.399	1.000	1.000

Source: Karoly (1996).

Table 2

Percentage of Aggregate Income Received by Income Quintiles and Gini Coefficient by Definition of Income, 1995

Definition of Income	First Quintile	Second Quintile	Third Quintile	Fourth Quintile	Fifth Quintile	Gini Coefficient
Current measure	3.7	9.1	15.2	23.4	48.6	0.444
Current measure less government cash transfers plus capital gains and employee health benefits	0.9	7.2	14.7	24.2	52.9	0.509
Prior measure less taxes	1.1	8.4	15.9	24.9	49.7	0.481
Prior measure plus non-means tested government cash transfers	3.9	10.6	16.3	23.6	45.5	0.412
Prior measure plus means-tested government cash transfers	5.0	10.8	16.3	23.3	44.5	0.394
Prior measure plus return on home equity	5.2	11.0	16.3	23.4	44.1	0.388

Source: U.S. Census Bureau.

Table 3a

Poverty Thresholds, 1995

Size of Family	Poverty Threshold ($, for all households)	Number of Related Children under 18 years of age (for householders under 65 years of age)				
		0	1	2	3	4
1	7,763					
2	10,259	10,205	10,504			
3	12,158	11,921	12,267	12,278		
4	15,569	15,719	15,976	15,455	15,509	17,909
5	18,408	18,956	19,232	18,643	18,187	20,364
6	20,804	21,803	21,890	21,439	21,006	23,627

Source: U.S. Bureau of the Census, March 1996 Current Population Survey.

Table 3b

Income Tax Thresholds, 1995

Size of Family	Personal Exemptions ($)	Standard Deduction —Joint ($)	Income Tax Threshold ($)	Income Tax Threshold ($) including EITC and other credits	Combined Income and Payroll Taxes at Poverty Level ($)
1	2,500	3,900	6,400	7,356	685
2	5,000	6,550	11,550	11,550	759
3	7,500	6,550	14,050	19,387	1,027
4	10,000	6,550	16,550	22,362	1,054
5	12,500	6,550	19,050	23,426	371
6	15,000	6,550	21,550	24,491	400

Source: Congressional Budget Office.

Table 4

Effectiveness of Antipoverty Programs, 1996

Category	Group		
	All persons	Elderly	Children
Total population (thousands)	266,218	31,877	70,650
Number of poor persons (thousands):			
Cash income before transfers	57,228	15,977	16,642
Plus social insurance	39,459	3,905	15,426
Plus means-tested cash transfers	36,529	3,428	14,463
Plus food and housing benefits	32,251	2,936	12,576
Plus EITC and less federal			
payroll and income taxes	30,538	2,943	11,341
Number of persons (thousands) removed from poverty due to:			
Social insurance	17,769	12,072	1,216
Means-tested cash	2,930	477	963
Food and housing benefits	4,278	492	1,887
EITC and federal payroll			
and income taxes	1,713	(7)	1,235
Total	26,690	13,034	5,301
Percent of persons removed from poverty due to:			
Social insurance	31.0	75.6	7.3
Means-tested cash	5.1	3.0	5.8
Food and housing benefits	7.5	3.1	11.3
EITC and federal payroll			
and income taxes	3.0	–0.0	7.4
Total	46.6	50.1	31.9

Source: 1998 Green Book, Tables H–23, H–24, and H–25.

Table 5

Policy Conflicts and Marriage Bonuses/Penalties

Couple A: married with both spouses earning $30,000 each	Policy objective: Same tax (equal treatment of married couples)	Couple B: married with one worker earning $60,000
Policy objective: Marriage neutrality		Policy objective: Marriage neutrality
Couple A: not married, each person earning $30,000	Policy objective: Progressive tax	Couple B: not married, one worker earning $60,000

Source: For Better or for Worse: Marriage and the Federal Income Tax, Congressional Budget Office, 1997.

Table 6

Distribution of Marriage Bonuses and Penalties by Adjusted Gross Income, 1996

	Less Than $20,000	$20,000 to $50,000	More Than $50,000	All Incomes
Returns in Income Category (Percent)				
With Penalties	12	44	54	42
Unaffected	25	1	3	6
With Bonuses	63	55	44	51
	100	100	100	100
Penalty or Bonus as a Percentage of Adjusted Gross Income				
Penalties	7.6	3.2	1.6	2.0
Bonuses	5.0	2.6	2.0	2.3
Total Penalties and Bonuses (Billions of Dollars)				
Penalties	0.9	9.6	18.3	28.8
Bonuses	3.9	8.7	20.3	32.9
Net Effect on Tax Liability (positive indicates net penalty, negative indicates net bonus)	−3.0	0.9	−2.0	−4.1

Source: For Better or for Worse: Marriage and the Federal Income Tax, CBO, 1997.

Table 7

Optimal Tax Rates for Various Parameter Values

Labor Supply Elasticity E	Wage Dispersion Measure η	Distribution Preference Parameter γ	Optimal Tax Rate t
0.3	0.4	0.00	0.00
0.3	0.4	0.25	0.14
0.3	0.4	0.50	0.25
0.3	0.4	0.75	0.32
0.3	0.4	1.00	0.38
0.3	0.4	5.00	0.68
0.3	0.4	10.00	0.74
0.3	0.4	100.00	0.77

Source: Atkinson (1995).

Table 8

Gains and Losses from Increasing the Income Tax Rate

Quintile	Gain/Loss ($) Resulting from a 1 Percent Increase in a Linear Income Tax Rate
First	+47
Second	+33
Third	−11
Fourth	−72
Fifth	−196
Total	Gains: +80 Losses: −279

Source: Browning and Johnson (1984).

Table 9

A Comparison of Major Tax Reform Plans

Tax Provision	Current Law	Retail Sales Tax	Value-Added Tax	Armey-Shelby Flat Tax	USA Tax	Gephardt Plan
Change in the system	none	Replaces individual and corporate income taxes and estate tax	Replaces individual and corporate income taxes	Replaces individual and corporate income taxes and estate taxes	Replaces individual and corporate income taxes; offsets payroll tax	Modifies current tax system
Individual-level tax summary	Imposes graduated rate tax on wage and capital income with exemptions and deductions	Eliminates individual-level income tax	Eliminates individual-level income tax	Imposes single-rate tax on wages and pension distributions with large exemptions and no deductions	Imposes graduated-rate tax on wage and capital income less savings and other deductions, with a credit for employee payroll taxes	Broadens base and reduces rates relative to current system
Tax base						
Wages and salaries	yes	. . .	. . .	yes	yes	yes
State and local bond interest	no	. . .	. . .	no	no	yes
Other interest, dividends, rent, royalties	yes	. . .	. . .	no	yes	yes
Realized capital gains	yes, at preferred rates	. . .	. . .	no	yes	yes
Health insurance	no	. . .	. . .	no	no	yes
Employer pension contribution	no	. . .	. . .	no	no	yes

(continued)

A Comparison of Major Tax Reform Plans (*continued*)

Tax Provision	Current Law	Retail Sales Tax	Value-Added Tax	Armey-Shelby Flat Tax	USA Tax	Gephardt Plan
Employee pension contribution	no	...	...	no	no	yes
Accumulation in pensions	no	...	...	no	no	yes
Pension receipts	yes	...	...	yes	yes	yes
Social security	yes	...	...	no	yes	yes
Deductions						
Non-pension savings	no	...	...	no	yes	no
Mortgage interest	yes	...	...	no	yes	yes
Charitable contributions	yes	...	...	no	yes	no
Property taxes	yes	...	...	no	no	no
State and local taxes	yes	...	...	no	no	no
Tax rates (%)	15,28,31,36 and 39.6	...	...	20 in transition year, 17 thereafter	8,19,40	10,20,26,32, and 34
Exempt range ($)						
Single person	6,400	...	...	10,700	6,950	7,750
Married couple	11,550	...	...	21,400	12,500	13,850
Family of four	16,550	...	...	31,400	17,600	19,350
EITC	yes	...	...	No	yes	no
Payroll tax credit	no	...	...	no	yes	no
Child care credit	yes	...	...	no	no	no

(*continued*)

A Comparison of Major Tax Reform Plans (*continued*)

Tax Provision	Current Law	Retail Sales Tax	Value-Added Tax	Armey-Shelby Flat Tax	USA Tax	Gephardt Plan
Business-level tax summary	Corporations pay essentially a flat rate tax on net income; other businesses pay taxes under individual income tax	Imposes a flat-rate tax on sales to consumer by all businesses	Imposes a flat-rate tax on all business sales to consumers and other businesses less costs of inputs and capital goods	Imposes a flat-rate tax on value-added base less wages and employer pension contributions	Imposes a flat-rate tax on value-added base with export exemptions plus refundable credit for payroll taxes paid by employer	Retains the current tax and cuts "corporate welfare" by $50 billion (no details specified)
Tax base						
Sales of goods and services	yes	yes	yes	yes	yes	yes
Financial income	yes	no	no	no	no	yes
Foreign-source income	yes	no	no	no	no	yes
Deductions						
Wages and salaries	yes	no	no	yes	no	yes
Employer pension contribution	yes	no	no	yes	no	yes
Investment	depreciated	no	expensed	expensed	expensed	depreciated
Payroll taxes	yes	no	no	no	credit	yes
Other taxes	yes	no	no	no	no	yes
Interest paid	yes	no	no	no	no	yes
Health insurance	yes	no	no	no	no	yes
Tax rates (%)	35	17	17	17	11	35
Foreign trade	in general, taxes export sales	taxes imports; exempts exports	taxes imports; exempts exports	taxes exports; exempts imports	taxes imports; exempts exports	in general, taxes export sales

Source: Aaron and Gale (1996).

Table 10

Distributional Effects of Alternative Tax Systems

Family expanded income in thousands of dollars	Current law	Flat tax	VAT	USA tax	Pechman plan
		Average taxes ($)			
5–10	175	318	448	182	171
10–20	627	872	1,300	518	517
20–30	1,686	2,175	2,905	1,470	1,422
30–40	3,159	3,633	4,644	2,691	2,716
40–50	5,023	5,299	6,496	4,336	4,324
50–60	7,145	7,204	8,709	6,187	6,214
60–70	9,785	9,914	11,292	8,580	8,898
70–80	13,284	13,718	14,733	12,110	12,956
80–90	18,562	19,460	19,578	17,808	19,605
90–95	26,714	27,531	25,951	27,705	29,099
95–99	43,375	43,896	38,521	47,994	48,894
99–100	223,953	186,045	141,535	256,108	219,109
Total	11,834	11,825	11,831	11,832	11,865
		Average effective tax rate (%)			
5–10	2.7	4.9	6.8	2.8	2.6
10–20	6.1	8.5	12.7	5.1	5.1
20–30	10.8	14.0	18.6	9.4	9.1
30–40	14.8	17.0	21.7	12.6	12.7
40–50	18.2	19.2	23.5	15.7	15.7
50–60	20.5	20.7	25.0	17.8	17.9
60–70	22.5	22.8	25.9	19.7	20.4
70–80	24.4	25.2	27.0	22.2	23.8
80–90	26.4	27.7	27.8	25.3	27.9
90–95	29.0	29.8	28.1	30.0	31.5
95–99	31.3	31.7	27.8	34.7	35.3
99–100	41.6	34.5	26.3	47.5	40.7
Total	25.8	25.7	25.8	25.8	25.8

Source: Aaron and Gale (1996).

Table 11

Earned Income Tax Credit Parameters, 1997

Number of children	Credit rate (percent)	Minimum earnings for maximum credit, E_1 ($)	Maximum credit ($)	Phaseout rate (percent)	Phaseout range	
					Beginning earnings, E_2 ($)	Ending earnings, E_3 ($)
0	7.65	4,340	332	7.65	5,430	9,770
1	34.00	6,500	2,210	15.98	11,930	25,750
2 or more	40.00	9,140	3,656	21.06	11,930	29,290

Source: Committee on Ways and Means, Green Book, 1998, p. 867.

Table 12

Distribution of Tax Returns with Earned Income Tax Credit, 1997

Income Class ($)	Joint Returns		Head of Household and Single Returns		All Returns	
	Number (1,000s)	Amount ($millions)	Number (1,000s)	Amount ($millions)	Number (1,000s)	Amount ($millions)
0 to 10,000	681	924	4,495	4,816	5,175	5,740
10,000 to 20,000	1,615	3,592	4,824	9,270	6,439	12,862
20,000 to 30,000	2,038	2,873	3,067	3,900	5,106	6,773
30,000 to 40,000	920	711	730	602	1,650	1,313
40,000 to 50,000	112	93	18	18	130	111
50,000 to 75,000	29	35	5	12	33	47
75,000 and over	0	0	0	0	0	0
Total	5,394	8,229	13,139	18,618	18,534	26,847
Percent distribution by type of return	29.1	30.7	70.9	69.3	100.0	100.0

Source: Green Book, 1998.

Figure 1. Distributional Properties of Major Tax Plans

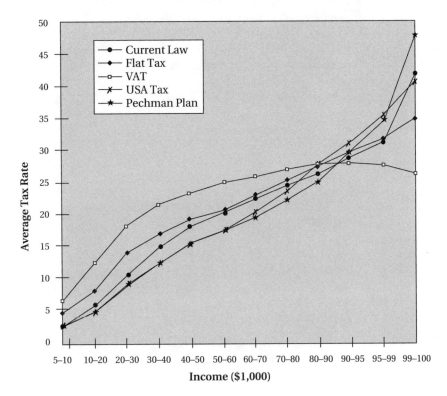

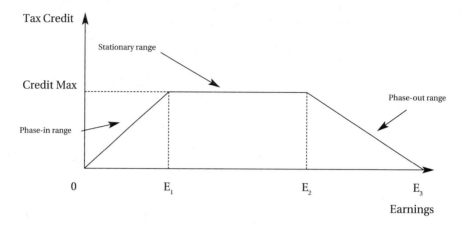

Figure 2: Earned Income Tax Credit Design

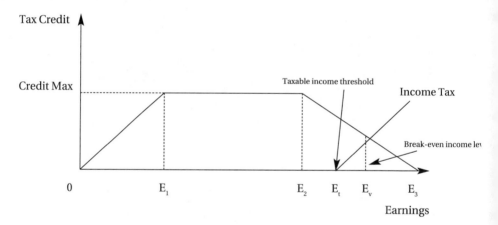

Figure 3: Earned Income Tax Credit and the Income Tax Structure

~ 10 ~

Just Schools

Doing Right by Poor Kids

Charles L. Glenn, Boston University

Introduction

To put it plainly, good education is usually experienced in good schools. Whatever makes it more likely that poor children and youth will be profoundly and positively influenced by good schools should be encouraged by public policy. Whatever reduces the availability of such good schools to poor children and youth, or limits their influence, should be identified and opposed as a source and an expression of injustice.

Good education is usually experienced in good schools. Before getting to policy specifics that sentence must be unpacked. What is "education," what is "experience," what are "schools"? The answers are not as obvious as they may seem.

"Education" is not the same as "instruction," though education usually includes instruction. Instruction involves teaching skills or imparting information, whether face to face or (increasingly) through computer programs and other means. Of course it is of immense importance in an information-based economy which demands so much in the way of competence in order for one to participate successfully. As we will see, competent and well-planned instruction is especially important for poor children and youth, who are the least likely to receive it.

But education rightly understood is something broader; it involves the shaping of a whole person. This includes intellectual competence, certainly, but also desires, loyalties and virtues, the settled disposition to exercise good judgment, self-control, courage and commitment to justice. Good schools educate along that whole range, as do good families, good churches, and good summer camps. Bad schools and mediocre schools shape students too, but the lessons they teach do not deserve to be called education in the sense used here. Parents correctly fear that they get their children back from such schools as worse persons than when they sent them.

And education needs to be *experienced.* It is quite possible to attend school for years without really experiencing education. We experience only what we make our own through active engagement and reflection. There is a fundamental difference between idly watching a sitcom on television and experiencing a film or play which moves us deeply to sorrow, delight, or both. Good schools provide an experience of education that makes a lasting impression on mind and character. Bad schools often provide another sort of experience; at best they are endured like a bad dream that fades away when we awake with no lasting impression.

Even in a good school, however, some children may fail to experience a good education. A boy or girl who does not understand English may sit all day in most American classrooms without being educated. Other pupils are prevented by some physical or psychological condition from making their own what the school is seeking to teach them. Factors related to social class and to race—including expectations attached to each by teachers and social analysts and often internalized by children and their parents—have an impact which is easier to measure than to explain or remedy. And we are increasingly aware that family breakdown, and other traumas of private life, can make it much more difficult for a child to learn what schools teach.

Finally, good education is experienced in good *schools,* though of course not only in schools. A school is more than the sum of its classrooms and its teachers; the school as a whole makes an impact, whether for good or ill. Research suggests, for example, that effective bilingual education programs are almost always located in schools whose overall program is effective.[1] That sounds obvious, but in fact most educational reform efforts have been designed and implemented with little eye to their effect on schools, and in not a few cases they have undermined the capacity of schools to provide a coherent and purposeful experience of education. To stay with the example of bilingual education, the whole tendency of regulation and professional specialization has been to weaken the links between bilingual pupils and the teachers and schools that deal with them.

Compensatory and special education teachers too often pull children out of their classrooms in ways that disrupt the ordinary course of instruction, while it is an unusual urban public school today that does not have a variety of outside specialists and funded projects scarcely related to the core mission of the school. Some have suggested that one reason why inner-city Catholic schools seem to produce better results for at-risk pupils is that Catholic schools have neither the specialized funding nor the detailed regulations with which policymakers, in their well-meaning way, have plagued the public schools.[2]

This suggests that educational policymakers need to devote more attention to whether particular measures strengthen or weaken schools as institutions. This is not to minimize the significance of improving classroom instruction, or of setting higher standards for student learning, or of producing a more coherent curriculum. Nor should my failure to discuss early childhood education (including home-based interventions), or vocational and school-to-work programs, or the ramifying field of special education, or teaching methodologies, be taken to mean that any of these is unimportant. Education reform is a puzzle with many pieces; to change the metaphor, there is no magic bullet to win this battle.

Good Education

Good education, then, is something whose value goes far beyond marketable skills. Even from the perspective of employers, we have been told again and again, qualities of character and the ability to learn are more important than vocational training. Emphasis on character is necessary for schools which serve poor children. What, for children of the middle class, is a desirable and important aspect of education, for many poor children is absolutely make-or-break; poor children will need an extra measure of focus, discipline, courage, and practical wisdom to make a success of their schooling . . . and their lives. "Sacred and secular moral orientations are well developed in high-achieving [low-income, black] students," anthropologist Reginald Clark found. Some will be fortunate enough to learn such virtues at home;[3] few will learn them in typical urban public schools.

The solution is not to impose, through mandatory schooling, a government-adopted orthodoxy on beliefs and values. Those who have studied the controversies surrounding American public schools cannot fail to be struck by how often they involve a conviction on the part of parents that their children are being taught to despise values held by the parents themselves. Important as it is that schooling promote the development of good character, this is not something that government (or the education establishment) should seek to dictate in a way which casts parents and families as the problem. Some parents are abusive, of course; some families are not healthy places for children; and society has a duty to intervene in such cases; but educational policy should not be made on the basis of the aberrant cases.

There is a better way. Schools, if they are an expression of the civil society rather than of the state, can be one of the settings within which adults and children cooperate to make decisions about, and to sustain, a common enterprise, and thus can be important character-forming institutions. It seems likely that public schools in small towns often have something of this nature as well, though the combined effects of state regulation and of the professional socialization of teachers place it under threat.

Public schools that are enmeshed in large and bureaucratized systems, by contrast, provide little scope for parents, or indeed teachers, to act as responsible adults, and thus to model behavior for children. Despite much talk in recent years about "school-based management" and "shared decision-making," reports from the field indicate that actual results have been disappointing. Not only is the scope for decision by teachers and for participation by parents generally limited, but the reality of these limits can encourage factionalism and irresponsibility. After all, if little is really at stake in decisions, those making them can indulge themselves in behaviors that are the opposite of the principled responsibility and mutual accommodation which they should be modeling.

Most non-public schools, by contrast, have no assurance of survival if those who are directly involved fail to act responsibly, not just from time to time but consistently over the course of years. Parents will not make the sacrifice to keep their children in these schools—nor teachers the financial sacrifice to teach in them—unless they are convinced that the education and the environment are distinctive in a positive way. Typically, parents are required to volunteer at inner-city private schools, and thus become more engaged in the school's life.[4] Students who attend schools marked by clarity of focus, involvement, and a sense of responsibility for the school's survival are more likely to learn by example a disposition to act virtuously.

In a recent national study, 71.4 percent of the teachers in small (less than 150 students) private schools agreed that "colleagues share beliefs and values about the central mission of the school," compared with 40.8 percent of those in small public schools. In large schools, with more than 750 students, both numbers dropped, to 49.4 percent in the private, and only 26.2 percent in the public, schools.[5] This helps to explain why many studies have found a "Catholic school advantage" in the education of at-risk urban pupils. Data from the massive *High School and Beyond* longitudinal study have been used by Chubb and Moe (1990); by Coleman, Hoffer and Kilgore (1982); Coleman & Hoffer (1987); and most recently, by Bryk, Lee and Holland. All have noted that

> the achievement growth benefits of Catholic school attendance are especially strong for students who are in one way or another disadvantaged: lower socioeconomic status, black, or Hispanic. . . . The dropout rates from Catholic schools are strikingly lower than those from public schools or other private schools. This reduced dropout rate holds both for those who show no signs of problems as sophomores and for those who as sophomores are academically or disciplinarily at risk of dropping out.[6]

Each of these studies dismisses the common assumption that Catholic schools do better because they are selective. Contrary to the conventional wisdom that Catholic schools simply do not admit or quickly expel potential trou-blemakers, they rely much more heavily than do public schools upon social-ization to maintain order and motivation. In their sample of inner-city, pri-vate, K–8 schools, Cibulka and his colleagues found that a child's behavior was the primary criterion for admission in only 6 percent of the cases, rising to 15 percent when the child was transferring from a public school. More than half (56 percent) of the principals said that they frequently or sometimes admitted pupils who had had discipline problems in public schools. Often, in fact, par-ents turn to a private school only when their child has had trouble in public school, counting on the reputation of private schools for strict discipline to bring about a change in behavior. While the *threat* of expulsion may exist as a powerful sanction, the rate at which it actually occurs is quite low. In an aver-age year, 71 percent of the schools in the sample had no expulsions at all.[7]

Bryk and his colleagues found that "the achievement of students in Catholic high schools was less dependent on family background and personal circum-stances than was true in the public sector" and "the achievement advantage of white over minority students increases in public high schools during the last two years of schooling, whereas the minority gap actually decreases in Catholic schools."[8] Such outcomes lend powerful support to the contention that social justice requires that we make it possible for poor parents to choose non-pub-lic schools.

Of course, the explicit curriculum of schools, and the way it is taught, can and should contribute powerfully to the formation of character through guided reflection on stories (both fictional and historical) and through the daily class-room and schoolyard habits which, for children, are a primary opportunity to acquire the settled disposition to do what is right.[9] In this respect, as well as in their organizational context, public schools are often at a disadvantage. Con-troversy almost invariably surrounds efforts to introduce questions of "values" in schools operated by government and backed by mandatory attendance laws. The almost invariable result is a kind of "defensive teaching," which seeks by all means to avoid controversy and thus fails to engage the ultimate—or even the antepenultimate—questions of life. Schools that are morally incoherent, as too many American schools are, cannot help their pupils to acquire the inner consistency of sentiment and outer consistency of behavior worthy of free women and men.[10]

Curriculum Content and Emphasis

Many poor children—in cities and in rural areas—are not exposed to the same learning opportunities as are middle-class children. While there has been considerable progress in strengthening the curriculum since the flurry of crit-ical reports in the 1980s,[11] minority students continue to lag behind. Review of high school transcripts in 1992 found that Hispanic graduates were less likely than non-Hispanic, white graduates to have taken algebra II (46.9 percent versus 59.2 percent), calculus (4.7 percent versus 10.7 percent, despite the inspiration of Jaime Escalante!), or physics (15.7 percent versus 25.9 percent).[12] Black students were even less likely than Hispanic students to have taken algebra II, but somewhat more likely to have taken calculus or physics.[13] The one curriculum area in which Hispanic graduates—not surprisingly—had a slight advantage over white, and a large advantage over black, graduates was in having taken two years of a language other than English.

Despite the fact that the aspiration levels of black students for higher education are similar to those of white students, they are less likely to go on to college (30 percent versus 38 percent), and they are much less likely to complete four or more years of higher education by the time they are twenty-nine (13.6 percent versus 29.7 percent).[14] There can be no question that some of this disparity reflects the cost of higher education, but some also reflects the fact that they have been less exposed to a college-preparatory curriculum, and that their skills may be less adequate for college study despite earning a high school diploma.

Hirsch cites recent research showing that the disparity (at least 16 percent lower wages for blacks of the same grade level completed) is because blacks have been, on average, less well educated by the schools. Most of the existing wage disparity, that is, some 12 out of 16 percent, can be explained by *a disparity in actual educational attainment.* After matching black and white earners by their actual educational level rather than by nominal grade level, the black-white wage disparity drops to less than 5 percent.[15]

On the National Adult Literacy Survey (1992), "Hispanics with a 4-year college degree had prose literacy scores resembling those of whites with a high school diploma." Thus "the differences in the labor market opportunities of Hispanics and whites . . . may be related to the differences in the literacy levels of both groups at similar levels of educational attainment."[16] Similarly, the literacy of black high school graduates was similar to that of white non-graduates.[17]

In other words, participation in formal schooling—even when they complete school successfully—is doing less for black and Hispanic youth than it is for white, non-Hispanic youth. They are being shortchanged, and part of the problem—it has become increasingly clear—involves "making allowances" in a well-meaning way for their presumed inability to handle a demanding curriculum. West Indian sociologist Maureen Stone, a critic of sentimental approaches to the schooling of poor and minority children, has studied the resistance of minority parents to "multi-racial" programs in English schools serving Afro-Caribbean pupils. Concern on the part of educators for underachievement led, through a fundamental misunderstanding of the causes of underachievement, to an emphasis upon "social, as opposed to educational goals" and thus to an emphasis on activities designed to raise the self-esteem of black pupils rather than to develop their academic skills. "In spite of contradictory research evidence," Stone points out, "the belief in black low self-esteem persists, and along with it goes the parallel belief that schools can and should compensate black children for the negative social stereotypes which exist in the wider society."[18]

West Indian parents created "Saturday schools" to teach academic skills that the schools were neglecting in favor of multicultural programs designed to enhance self-esteem. "[S]chools have concentrated on 'relationships' and on the 'soft-option' approach," writes Stone. "Without exception, people working in the West Indian community groups stress the importance of hard work, high aspirations, willingness to sacrifice and belief in one's ability to succeed as the only possible way forward. . . ." She described the resentment of many West Indian parents at multicultural programs that she characterizes as "a misguided liberal strategy to compensate black children for not being white," and as "aimed at 'watering down' the curriculum and 'cooling out' black city children while at the same time creating for teachers, both radical and liberal, the illusion that they are doing something special for a particularly disadvantaged group."[19]

Rather than seeking to promote minority cultures, Stone argues, schools should concentrate on providing minority children with access to successful participation in the mainstream of society. She insists that "the community, parents and children are sufficient guardians of the black cultural inheritance. Schools have to be about something else." After all, "if you really want to reduce educational and racial inequality, the best way is by providing your pupils with the skills and knowledge they need to make their own way in the society in which they live."[20]

In support of this emphasis, Stone quotes the Communist theoretician Antonio Gramsci. So does E.D. Hirsch in a recent, devastating critique of the educational status quo. Gramsci insisted that political progressivism demanded educational conservatism. The oppressed class should be taught to master the tools of power and authority—the ability to read, write, and communicate—and to gain enough traditional knowledge to understand the worlds of nature and culture surrounding them. Children, particularly the children of the poor, should not be encouraged to flourish "naturally," which would keep them ignorant and make them slaves of emotion. They should learn the value of hard work, gain the knowledge that leads to understanding, and master the traditional culture in order to command its rhetoric, as Gramsci himself had learned to do.[21]

Too often, in programs for minority children, questions of identity and culture have been stressed more than improving the content and methods of instruction.[22] Lisa Delpit, an African-American reading specialist, describes the "negative outcry in the black community when well-intentioned white liberals introduced 'dialect readers.' These were seen as a plot to prevent the schools from teaching the linguistic aspects of the culture of power."[23] As Gramsci pointed out seventy years ago, "without the mastery of the common standard version of a national language, one is inevitably destined to function only at the periphery of national life, and, especially, outside its national and political mainstream."[24]

Hirsch makes a powerful case that a fundamental inequity grows out of the well-meaning willingness to adapt the curriculum to the supposed interests of different groups of pupils. Without a content-rich curriculum, the learning of luckier students snowballs to their initial advantage, while that of the less fortunate ones, dependent on what the incoherent American school offers, never even begins to gather momentum. The lack of shared knowledge among American students not only holds back their average progress, creating a national excellence gap, but more drastically, holds back disadvantaged students, thus creating a fairness gap as well.[25]

Hirsch concludes that "a systemic failure to teach all children the knowledge they need in order to understand what the next grade has to offer is the major source of avoidable injustice in our schools." Other countries have managed to reduce the gap between the high-achieving schools and the low-achieving schools by achieving more clarity about what every child should be enabled to learn:

> Among Finnish schools, only 2 percent of schools showed below-standard average achievement; in Japan, it was 1 percent; in Korea, 5 percent; in Sweden, 1 percent; and in Hungary, 0 percent. Among the noncore countries, the percentages of schools below par were: Australia, 8 percent; the Netherlands, 16 percent; England, 19 percent; and the United States, 30 percent. . . . Remarkably, in France the initial gap between advantaged and disadvantaged students, instead of widening steadily as in the United States, decreases with each school grade. By the end of seventh grade, the child of a North African immigrant who has attended two years of French preschool (école maternelle) will on average have narrowed the socially induced learning gap. Such success in achieving fairness is explained at least in part by the fact that national systems which have core curricula are able to provide a school-based education which relies relatively less on the undependable home curriculum to supply the prior knowledge needed for learning in each grade.[26]

By contrast, "In the United States, the all-too-consistent correlation between low academic performance and low economic status shows that something more than innate talent is determining the results." The current pedagogical fashion of "Developmentalism," Hirsch charges, "withholds academic knowledge on principle. But in the current social context it withholds it differentially, according to social class."[27]

Maintenance of Minority Languages

Bilingualism is a good thing, and education which promotes real proficiency in two or more languages, while stressing academic content as well, is very desirable. Five of my own children have received their elementary education in a bilingual (Spanish/English) inner-city school, and my most recent book argues strongly for such integrated, "two-way" bilingual education.[28] A well-run bilingual program can also be a very good way to educate immigrant and other language-minority children, as we will see below.

Under some circumstances, however, maintenance of an ethnic group language, whether that is promoted by social conditions or by public policy, tends to support the continued separateness—even the segregation—of the group that speaks it, in a way that is harmful to the general interest as well as to that of individuals in the ethnic group. It is undoubtedly for this reason, as Edwards pointed out prophetically, that "despite much propaganda, we do not have unequivocal evidence of widespread support for active policies of bilingual education (in its maintenance form) and cultural pluralism. Nor do we have such evidence from ethnic groups themselves."[29] This is increasingly apparent even in the United States, where bilingual education has been, for several decades, the touchstone issue for Hispanic activists.

> Elected Hispanic officials surveyed in 1983 supported bilingual programs in general but with some questions about the programs' effectiveness. . . . Half said that all regular school classes should be taught in English with Spanish used only for "supplementary courses. . . ." Ninety-seven percent of the leaders were opposed to teaching all courses in Spanish, and few saw language as the basic cause of either dropouts or youth unemployment. The leaders tended to favor some kind of an effort to retain Spanish in other ways but not as an educational panacea or a substitute for learning English.[30]

Immigrant parents, as we have seen recently in the controversies over bilingual education in California, are especially likely to question language-maintenance efforts in schools if they believe there is any chance this will limit the acquisition, by their children, of the majority language. "Significantly, much of the pressure for learning English comes from Hispanic parents."[31] Mexican-American parents surveyed by the Educational Testing Service in 1987 supported bilingual education and said it was important that their children speak Spanish well, but rejected instruction in Spanish nearly four to one if it would take time away from learning English. Cuban-Americans were even more adamantly opposed to cutting into the time available for teaching English.[32] The leading authority on bilingual education among the Indians of the Southwest mentions a pueblo where bilingual education was opposed "because it might bring the school into areas best left to the home and the community," and other cases in which language minority groups saw it as threatening the access of their children to the economic rewards associated with proficiency in the majority language.[33]

Maintenance of their home language is, as noted above, not always a primary concern in the demands made by immigrant parents upon official education systems, despite the painful language gap that may exist between the immigrant generations. Asian parents in the United States are much more likely than Hispanic parents to favor teaching their children "only in English," and to believe that instruction through the home language would interfere with learning English.[34] Parents recognize that their children need to acquire proficiency in the language of the society, and when instruction through the home language becomes the primary focus, it is usually because of the involvement of progressive intellectuals and educators in formulating the agenda of the parents.

The irony of this debate is that even multi-year, separate, bilingual education programs of the sort common in the United States do not, in most cases, preserve the active use of the minority language unless that use is strongly reinforced by the social environment in which the pupil and her family live. The danger associated with bilingual programs of inadequate quality is not that they will reinforce pupils in a minority language which they are almost invariably in the process of abandoning, but that they will prepare them inadequately to function with a high degree of proficiency in the majority language. In other words, the danger is that the pupils will come out badly educated, not that they will be well-educated in a minority language. Would that they were!

Louis Porcher noted, decades ago, that the ideological commitments of the French Left to "Third-Worldism" led to efforts to address the needs of the children of immigrants as though they had nothing in common with French children from poor families. These efforts stressed institutional and structural remedies, linguistic over conceptual considerations, at the expense of attention to pedagogical strategies in the classroom.

All of a sudden, on the basis of the educator's generous intention of preserving the cultural identity of the foreign child, he is thrown involuntarily into a world different from that of his French peer; thus objectively, though without anyone noticing it, he is cut off from the world in which he lives here and now.[35]

It should be noted that proficiency in a language other than that of the school, is of itself by no means a barrier to success in school and may indeed be associated (whether as cause or effect) with academic achievement, provided that the pupil is also proficient in the language of the school. A study conducted by the Educational Testing Service in conjunction with the National Assessment of Educational Progress concluded that "whether or not one comes from a home where a second language [that is, other than English] is frequently spoken is not the critical issue, but rather the central question is whether or not one is competent in English."[36] Among Indochinese refugee youth, "English proficiency was the key sociocultural variable which was predictive of psycho-social adjustment."[37] In other words, maintaining the heritage language is an option, and often a highly valued one, but becoming proficient in the language of the school is essential.

Such findings have nothing surprising about them, of course; speaking the language of the host society well is fundamental to success and positive adjustment. The hesitation that many immigrant parents feel about school policies that promote retention of their home languages has to do, not with a rejection of those languages, but with concern about diversion of energy and time from the majority language and from academic subject-matter, and with isolation of their children in a separate instructional track.

Standards and Expectations

Economist John Bishop has pointed out how crucial are the "signals" which the educational system gives about whether effort on the part of students and of their teachers has a significant pay-off. "Most American secondary school teachers," he writes, "do not feel individually accountable for the learning of their students. . . . Only coaches, band conductors, and teachers of advanced placement classes are exceptions. They teach in environments where student achievement is visible to parents and colleagues and, as a result, feel accountable for outcomes." The incentives for student effort are much weaker here than they are in countries with high-stakes examinations. After all (despite our national commitment to an ideology of equal educational opportunity for all), "in the United States access to quality teaching and supportive peers depends on parental ability to buy or rent a home in a suburb with excellent schools. In France and the Netherlands access to the top upper secondary schools depends primarily on achievement in lower secondary school."[38]

The American educational system is both enormous and highly complex, with over 15,000 public school districts ranging in size from a handful of pupils to over a million, and many thousands of non-public schools. There is no bureaucratic mechanism for central control of what goes on in all these schools, or for control of what teachers expect of their pupils; nor would creating such a mechanism be likely to improve matters. It is for this reason that Bishop and other economists are interested in the signals which are communicated to teachers and pupils by society and the economy as well as by government at its various levels. Some have proposed "an overall approach, strengthening performance incentives, and a set of decision rules, comparing benefits with costs, that have proved extremely useful in enhancing business performance, even if they have been largely ignored by schools."[39] Simply increasing expenditures on education, they argue, will not achieve the necessary reforms. "Our panel of economists sees no reason to believe that increases in spending would on average be any more effective than past spending, particularly when they rely on the same people operating with the same basic incentives." The favored remedies of the educational establishment, such as reduced class size, teacher salary increases, and more computers, have not produced notable improvement in outcomes. For example, student performance in most classes is unaffected by variations in class size of, say, fifteen to forty students. Nevertheless, even in the face of high costs that yield no apparent performance benefits, the overall policy of states and local districts has been to reduce class sizes in order to try to increase quality.[40]

One powerful form of signals for school people is provided by the decisions which parents make to enroll their children in one school rather than another. A report by the National Center for Education Statistics found that in 1993, 20 percent of all schoolchildren in grades three through twelve attended schools that their families had chosen for them: 11 percent in public and 9 percent in private schools. Of the remainder, however, the parents of 39 percent reported that their choice of residence had been "influenced by where their children would go to school." Thus "higher family income facilitates both public and private school choice." Of families with incomes over $50,000, 72 percent had their children in private schools, public schools of choice (such as magnet schools), or schools which had been selected through residence decisions.[41] Poor parents are much less likely to be able to exercise school choice through either residential or private school decisions, but more likely to benefit from publicly sponsored choice opportunities like magnet schools and charter schools. In one way or another, then, many American parents make decisions about schools, and this represents a form of accountability to which school administrators are more sensitive than they usually admit.

But parent choice without adequate information about school quality cannot have a powerful effect on the improvement of instruction, since parents are constrained to choose on the basis of generalized reputation, "climate," and the social class of the students enrolled. Good information about student outcomes is essential both for choice-based accountability and also for government oversight of the adequacy of all schools. And that means some form of testing.

It is ironic that many of those most concerned with educational equity tend to be opposed to standardized tests, which they see as discriminating against poor and minority children. To take one among numberless examples, a lawsuit was filed in October 1997 in U.S. District Court in San Antonio, seeking to block the use of a test that Texas requires for earning a high school diploma. The suit was brought on behalf of seven minority students who had failed the test. The plaintiffs charged that the test was discriminatory because the rate at which black and Hispanic students passed the test was significantly below that of whites.

Now it is true that tests literally "discriminate" between those who can demonstrate certain competencies and those who cannot—that is their primary purpose—and it is also true that poor and minority children on the average perform less well on standardized tests than do middle-class white and Asian children. The reasons for this disproportionality, which affects black students even when social class is held constant, are poorly understood. There is good reason to be cautious in using standardized tests in ways which have serious consequences for the children who take them. On the other hand, tests are the most powerful means which we possess to determine whether schools are succeeding or failing, and in what respects, and they also give unmistakable signals to the students themselves about the importance of their academic work. Thus the Texas Commissioner of Education insisted that the graduation test did not discriminate against minority students, and that "We cannot lower our expectations and our standards because of the ethnicity of a child."[42]

Hirsch points out that

> fairness in schooling cannot be isolated from excellence in schooling. Fairness and excellence invariably go together in national systems of education because the educational principles and arrangements that elicit the best performances and highest competencies from advantaged students also elicit the best from disadvantaged students . . . .
>
> The final irony of the antitesting movement is that in the name of social fairness it opposes using high-stakes tests as gatekeepers, monitors, and incentives—functions that are essential to social fairness.[43]

The primary author of one of the classic studies on educational inequality, Hirsch points out,

> parried the implicitly condescending view that tests are biased because the middle class places more value on cognitive skills than the lower class does. And finally, he repudiated the [National Education Association] objection that standardized tests contain "complex language and obscure vocabulary," saying, "If the NEA no longer thinks it is worthwhile to teach students how to read [complex] prose, this may explain why students are less capable of doing so."[44]

There is indeed a serious danger lurking in the temptation to shield poor children from evaluations in which their performance is likely to show at a disadvantage. While this is often justified in the name of protecting their self-esteem and motivation to learn, it may in fact have the opposite effect. Americans share an unwillingness to impose unpleasant demands upon our children, leading in turn to drastically low expectations of what competencies they should be expected to master and to widespread complacency about the feeble performance of American students.[45] Setting high expectations, of course, would make it inevitable that many students could not achieve them, at least initially; thus, these expectations would be contrary to the "zero failure" principle expressed by self-esteem advocates. As Chester Finn observes, "most American teachers and principals strive to give students and parents only positive feedback, encouragement, and reinforcement."[46] On a policy level, much of the opposition to national standards and standardized assessment is expressed in terms of their allegedly devastating effect upon the happiness of America's youth. "Happy but dumb" isn't much of an ambition for our children!

The other fundamental flaw in American education is even more damaging: low expectations for minority and poor children, what Finn calls "a poisonous brew of humanitarianism and condescension."[47]

Well-meaning white liberals seem to assume that black and Hispanic children must have low self-esteem by the very fact of living in this "racist" society; the unspoken assumption seems to be, "I wouldn't feel good about myself if I were black or Hispanic"! Schools should therefore devote considerable attention to reassuring these children that it is acceptable to be what they are; this should be done by making the curriculum "relevant" and taking care not to impose the majority culture.

Thus bilingual education programs are increasingly justified not so much for linguistic reasons as on the psycho-political basis that some years (five-to-seven are commonly suggested) of instruction primarily through the ancestral language is essential to the self-esteem and subsequent educational success of language minority children. Some advocates go so far as to urge that it be provided even to those who come to school speaking only English, since "the language spoken by the child in the home is, in itself, essentially irrelevant."[48]

Research support for this policy prescription is notably weak. For example, a study of 270 Puerto Rican children in grades four through six in Chicago found that "bilingual students who read only English adequately had significantly more positive self-esteem scores than those who read only Spanish adequately. ... Students who had participated in a bilingual program reported significantly less positive self-esteem scores than those who had never had this type of experience. .... The language of the dominant culture appears to be a key factor in the self-concept development of these students."[49] A study of Mexican-American students in California found that those in bilingual programs had lower self-concept (and reading scores) than those in the regular program.[50] Another found that limited-English-speaking children matched English-speaking children in self-concept, and concluded that "[w]hile instruction through the native language may provide linguistic and conceptual advantages, these findings called into question one of the most frequently cited rationales for bilingual education, its positive effects on self-concept."[51]

Nor, in general, is there good evidence that minority children suffer from low self-esteem. Dutch research on the self-concept of adolescents from ethnic minorities found that their lower social status, relative disadvantage, and frequent confrontation with prejudices and discrimination did not lead to lower self-esteem.[52] A review of ten years of American research on the subject found no clear evidence of low self-esteem among black youth.[53] In fact, as a lead editorial in *The Economist* put it, prescriptions for poor children that focus upon making them feel good about themselves are "Bunk. The characteristic that in the past drove generations of immigrants from the underclass to prosperity was not self-esteem, it was self-discipline. The reason that Japanese schoolchildren—and the children of Asian immigrants in America—learn so much more than their American counterparts is discipline, not self-esteem."[54]

To the extent that educators come to see the development of self-esteem in children as a primary goal in itself, they risk neglecting their primary mission of "helping children achieve competence, perseverance, and optimism—the real contents of self-worth" through the achievement of the academic goals of schooling.[55]

Education should be organized around high expectations, and schools should make clear how students will know when they have reached each stage toward realizing them; American families, employers and colleges should stress consistently that nothing less than a determined effort is acceptable. Within the context of such clarity about the academic purposes of schooling, it will be appropriate also to ensure that our classrooms are humane and supportive, places where children experience merited feelings of satisfaction from their real achievements, without being discouraged by the difficulties associated with learning.

Unfortunately, American educational fashion has grown rather apologetic about standardized tests, preferring what is called "authentic assessment" such as portfolios of student work or the observing of group projects. "Teaching to the test" has become almost a definition of limited and inadequate instruction. As with most clichés, this one is based upon partial truths; no test can assess all that it is worthwhile to teach, and preparing students to do well on a mindless test is a waste of their time and teachability. But a well-designed assessment can organize instruction in a purposeful way and concentrate the minds of teacher and students alike.

"It has been shown convincingly," Hirsch points out, "that tests and grades strongly contribute to effective teaching. . . . Quite unambiguous analysis showed that students who took courses for a grade studied harder and learned more than students who took the courses for intrinsic interest alone."[56]

Standardized tests have their limits, but they have the advantage of permitting comparison between education outcomes in different schools and classrooms—especially if evaluated in a way which takes into account the "value added" in relation to the starting point of the children at, say, the beginning of the year—and in reducing the "inexpungible arbitrariness . . . at the heart of grading performance-based assessments."[57] Objections that standardized tests are "biased" because they draw upon information and assumptions which minority children do not share equally with the white, middle-class majority have been met in part by extensive efforts, over the past quarter-century, to eliminate test items on which systematic differences in response can be identified. Such efforts to make the tests bias-free can only go so far however; as Hirsch observes,

> the principal unfairness connected with testing consists in a failure to prepare students adequately for the competencies for which they are to be tested. These competencies usually require a great deal of intellectual capital. . . . [T]he public elementary schools of the United States provide neither equality of opportunity nor equality of result. Comparative studies show that our system affords far less equality of educational opportunity than exists in most developed nations. . . . In a mediocre school system, the competence gap between social classes widens

during the school years, In a good, coherent school system with definite year-by-year goals for all students, early, systematic compensation becomes possible, and the competence gap is narrowed.[58]

In other words, schools fail to teach minority children much that is common knowledge to most majority children, and then tests that assume such knowledge are accused of bias. Surely the charge should rather be directed against the schools!

There are dangers associated with using tests as a means of holding school staff accountable for results. When outcomes have consequences for teachers, schools sometimes create an environment that is relatively inhospitable to academically disadvantaged students, provide course offerings that predominantly address the needs of academically advantaged students, fail to work aggressively to prevent students from dropping out of high school, err on the side of referring "problem" students to alternative schools, err on the side of classifying students as special education students where the latter are exempt from statewide testing, or make it difficult for low-scoring students to participate in statewide exams. These practices are designed to improve average test scores in a school, not by improving school quality but by catering to high-scoring students while ignoring or alienating low-scoring ones.[59]

What's more, middle-class parents may avoid schools with low average test scores, even if these are the result of the social class background of the pupils and not of inadequate instruction; this makes it more difficult to integrate such schools or, in mixed neighborhoods, to keep them integrated. It is for these reasons that there has been considerable interest in finding some way to measure the "value added" by a school. Do its pupils do better or worse than would be expected, given social class and other background factors?

Ideally, we would know not only how much each school has added to the performance of its pupils, but also how much each teacher has added each year. After all, "the average test score reflects information about school performance that tends to be grossly out of date. For example, the average test scores for a group of tenth-grade students reflect learning that occurred from kindergarten, roughly ten-years earlier, through the tenth grade. . . . A performance indicator that fails to localize school performance to a specific grade level or classroom is likely to be a relatively weak instrument of public accountability."[60]

While there are powerful arguments for taking a "value added" approach to accountability—despite very considerable technical difficulties in doing so—there are also policy arguments against such an approach. Could it not lead to having lower expectations for groups of children because of their background, to settling for lower achievement from them, or even to not trying to teach them the whole curriculum? Only with great care should an accountability structure be implemented which makes allowances on the basis of the social class—much less the race—of pupils.

Experienced

Exposure to a rich and demanding curriculum is not sufficient unless students are able to come to grips with it successfully. For example, the ability to understand and to draw inferences from fairly complex written material is essential to success in high school, but many students cannot do so. Despite significant progress between 1975 and 1992, in the latter year "17-year-old Hispanics were now reading at about the same level as that of 13-year-old whites," and the results had improved little since 1984.[61] Reading proficiency of black pupils at seventeen in 1992 was similarly "about the same as that of 13-year-old whites."[62]

High expectations are a cruel joke, critics from the Left insist, if society is not prepared to invest the resources necessary to enable poor children to meet them, and prepared to create schools that are supportive as well as demanding. Simply raising standards for high school graduation, for example, will not help those pupils who cannot meet them; just schools must have effective strategies to intervene in support of poorly performing students.[63]

It would be nice if we could say with some confidence that if America would simply spend more money on its public schools, the achievement gap between poor and middle-class children, and between black and Hispanic children on the one hand, and white and Asian-American children on the other, would be eliminated. Jonathan Kozol (of whom more below) seems to assume that. Unfortunately, we do not have anything approaching agreement about what specifically we should be spending more money on. Economist Eric Hanushek points out the stunning fact that "after allowing for inflation, expenditures per pupil [in the United States] have increased at almost 3.5 percent per year for 100 years."[64] The results of schooling have remained disappointingly flat, at best, in recent decades. The response of public schools is simply to pile on more and more supplemental programs and other nostrums, without facing up to the need for fundamental change. This has led Hanushek to conclude that there is "a case for holding down funding increases to force schools to adopt a more disciplined approach to decision making," based upon practices of proven effectiveness.[65]

The situation is especially important, as we have seen, with respect to Hispanic students, and the National Research Council recently undertook a massive review of the research carried out over the past 30 years—costing some $100 million—on how language minority children can be educated effectively. The review written by Diane August and Kenji Hakuta produced a few glimmers of what we can with confidence say works; for example, we apparently know that direct instruction in phonics and other "processing" skills is more important for these children than it is for middle-class, English, monolingual children. While "whole language" methods have their place in stimulating language use, "many believe that [language-minority] children are at considerable risk in classrooms that provide only a whole-language environment with no direct reading instruction."[66] That is important to know. But it is depressing to learn that, though researchers have found out quite a lot about how children in general learn, we do not know much about how any of this applies to language-minority children. "With regard to reading instruction in a second language, there is remarkably little directly relevant research." How should instruction in content areas be sequenced? "At this point, we know next to nothing about these questions."[67]

August and Hakuta take a refreshingly agnostic position on one of the central articles of faith of bilingual-education advocates: that children must be taught to read first in the language which they speak at home.

> It is clear that many children first learn to read in a second language without serious negative consequences. These include children in early-immersion, two-way, and English-as-a-second-language based programs (ESL programs) in North America, as well as those in formerly colonial countries that have maintained the official language [of the colonizer] as the medium of instruction, immigrant children in Israel, children whose parents opt for elite international schools, and many others . . . The high literacy achievement of Spanish-speaking children in English-medium Success for All schools . . that feature carefully-designed direct literacy instruction suggests that even children from low-literacy homes can learn to read in a second language *if the risk associated with poor instruction is eliminated.*[68]

The authors conclude candidly that "We do not yet know whether there will be long-term advantages or disadvantages to initial literacy instruction in the primary language versus English, given a very high-quality program of known effectiveness in both cases."[69] Only those familiar with the field can appreciate how heretical this concession is, and how unwelcome it will be to those who urge that it is essential to postpone exposure to reading in English until reading is solidly mastered in the home language. It is disheartening, however, to learn that an insufficient attempt has been made to understand the cognitive processes underlying successful transfer of first-language literacy skill to the second language, the limitations on that transfer, the conditions that optimize positive and minimize negative transfer, or the differences between children who manage learning to read in a second language well and those who do not.[70]

We have been told so often that "research proves" that literacy must first be developed in the home language if language-minority children are not to be permanently damaged in their cognitive development.[71] August and Hakuta's review of the whole field suggests that this assertion has been accepted too uncritically without further investigation of whether it is true, how it might actually occur, and what can promote it.

The National Research Council study also undercuts a primary justification for much of what is done in the name of "multicultural education." Contrary to the common practice of encouraging children to celebrate their ethnic distinctiveness, the study found that "to increase positive intergroup contact, the salience of group characteristics should be minimized, and a superordinate group with which students from different cultural and language groups can become identified should be constructed."[72] In other words, well-meaning efforts to persuade the children in a class to identify how they differ "culturally" because of their differing ancestry are likely to be counterproductive.

This is not the place to enter into a discussion of the debates on teaching methods which fill the pages of the professional journals, but it may be worthwhile mentioning the positive endorsement, by the National Research Council study, of the Success for All program developed by Robert Slavin and his associates. This appears to have "significant and important effects on the achievement of English-language learners, regardless of whether they are in a primary language [i.e., 'bilingual'] or sheltered English program." Contrary to the present educational orthodoxy, there is nothing in the Success for All literature indicating that cultural validation or cultural accommodation per se is an important element of the program or, indeed, that culture plays any direct role at all (aside from language). Success for All is an intensive, prescriptive, well-conceptualized program designed to help as many children as possible leave third grade reading at grade level.

In effect, Success for All operates on the premise that children are children and deserve to be taught in a challenging and effective way that enables them to succeed. As a result, culturally and organizationally, "the program is no different for African American students in Baltimore than for Latinos in bilingual education or sheltered English programs in California or for Cambodians in an ESL program in Philadelphia."[73]

This approach, they note, "runs counter not only to much of the accepted wisdom in the school reform literature, but also to previous efforts to disseminate and replicate effective programs" in its assumption that a model can, in effect, be plugged in successfully with different teachers and different types of students.[74] If it turns out that Success for All does in fact offer such a replicable and effective package, we may find the question of when to use home language and when to use English becoming a distinctly secondary consideration rather than the all-important symbolic issue it is today. That is, we may conclude that it is a very good thing to teach children bilingually because they are quite capable of learning, and learning through, two languages, and because proficiency in two languages is better than in one, but not—as we have long been told—because that is the only educationally responsible way to teach language-minority children.

What we can learn from models that seem to work, like Success for All, is that children are best served by well-planned and consistent instruction by well-trained teachers, and by being provided with "a balance between instruction in basic and higher-order skills at all grade levels."[75] There is nothing astonishing about that, but it should be a warning against the fads that sweep through

American public education. It should also dispel the despairing conclusion that nothing schools can do makes any difference against the effects of class, race, and family breakdown. Hanushek points out that "in inner-city schools, the progress of students with a good teacher can exceed that of students with a poor teacher by more than a year of achievement during a single school year."[76] When all is said and done, as research in England has shown, "school matters."[77]

Cultural Diversity

There is an unfortunate tendency toward stereotyping in attempts to adapt school programs to the supposed demands of cultural diversity. It is conventional wisdom, for example, that Latino pupils recoil from the competitive atmosphere that allegedly rules in American classrooms, and would do better if instruction were organized on a cooperative basis. Actual research on preferred styles, however, found in one case that Anglo pupils were more cooperative and less competitive than Latino pupils![78] Research has also failed to confirm the belief that Mexican-American teachers, parents, and children differ from their Anglo counterparts in how they perceive classroom interactions.[79] Common sense and the research on styles of cognition suggest that there is *far more difference within ethnic groups* in how individuals learn or relate to school than there is between groups.

Even when there are culturally based differences in learning style, it is not clear what implications for instruction are appropriate. A study of American Indian children in school found that their participation styles were very different from those of non-Indian American children; the researcher concluded that placing the Indian children in a separate class, while it would reduce that conflict, would prepare them poorly for participation in the wider society. "The point is not that one set of values or behaviors replaces the other, but that the children have access to both sets so that they can form from both their unique bicultural identity."[80] "Culturally relativistic" teachers, influenced by anthropological literature on culture and teaching for altruistic reasons, may reinforce the ways in which Indian children differ from academically successful, majority children.[81] Too much "sensitivity" can mislead children about the real costs of succeeding in the dominant culture, costs that cannot be wished away.

We should thus be on our guard against an overemphasis of the ways in which groups of pupils differ, while remaining keenly sensitive to how individual pupils differ in their strengths, their needs, and in how they learn. If our laws primarily protect the right to be different—as they should—our policies, by contrast, should be concerned above all to make it possible for pupils to participate fully in all the opportunities that our educational systems make available. This may well mean some loss of distinctiveness, some (dare I say it?) assimilation or adaptation to the majority. So long as schools simply facilitate this possibility, without requiring conformity, they should not be accused of violating the right to be different.

Integration

One more aspect of school experience should be mentioned: the effect of the environment created by other pupils. One of the most firmly established facts about achievement is that it is affected by "the educational background and aspirations of other students in the school. 'Children from a given family background, when put in schools of different social composition, will achieve at different levels.' This composition effect . . . is . . . particularly strong for low-income students."[82] This finding has been confirmed by the massive amount of data available from the National Education Longitudinal Study of 1988. One analysis "found that low income students in schools with low concentrations of such students score higher than their counterparts in schools with high concentrations of low income students." A review of research found that "school-level SES [socio-economic status of pupils enrolled] affects students' chances of graduating as well as how much they learn, after controlling for family background."[83]

It is thus not surprising that the achievement of pupils in schools with a high concentration of poor children—whether these schools are located in a city, in a suburb, or in a rural area—lags far behind and has serious consequences for their futures.[84] There are more such schools in cities, of course, and an urban location does have an additional negative effect on whether former high school students go on to further education or to full-time work.[85]

Racial and social class integration, and the integration of LEP children with children for whom English is the first language, are important for *educational* reasons. Real integration is more than a matter of putting children in the same building; it requires attention to the details of grouping for instruction, to the nature of the instruction itself, and to the overall *ambience* of the school.[86] Real and effective integration is an educational strategy, not a form of social manipulation as its opponents charge.

Given the high degree of residential segregation in many American cities, such integration cannot be provided without active efforts to achieve desegregation of schools. Desegregation by itself does not guarantee integration which is educationally meaningful, but segregation guarantees that integration cannot occur!

Several years ago I had occasion to rethink the desegregation strategy which I promoted in Massachusetts in the early 1970s as the state's civil rights enforcer and the principal author of the desegregation plan implemented in Boston in 1974.[87] The underlying premise of that plan, I now understand, was a profound mistrust of ordinary parents and a determination to require them to overcome their prejudices and fears and send their children to the schools that we selected for them, in order to serve the common good. We were arrogant, and we were wrong. Racial integration, like any legitimate end, should be sought by legitimate means, and simply substituting our "expert" judgment for that of parents was wrong.

How would I do it if I could do it over? I would seek to base school assignments, so far as possible, upon well-informed parental choice. This would in turn have the effect—if done right—of encouraging diversity and school-based decision making, and of weakening the stifling effect of a hierarchically organized school system. Treating everyone in similar formal circumstances the same way is one of the virtues of bureaucracy, but it is antithetical to the suppleness and responsiveness of good education. A system that must promote parental choice in order to achieve race desegregation will not find its efforts successful unless it can learn to allow decisions about the character and organization of each school to be made by those directly involved, both staff and parents.

Including a few magnet schools, as was done in the second-stage Boston desegregation plan implemented in 1975, does not have the same effect; it accommodates the most engaged teachers and parents but at the expense of depressing the energy level and the prospect for improvement of other schools even further. The reports I prepared for the Federal District Court "revealed many problems with the way the process of providing information and encouraging choices was handled. In particular, there seemed little expectation that individual schools (apart from the magnet schools) would develop distinctive themes and encourage parents to take advantage of the possibilities for choice."[88]

In 1989 the Court permitted the school system to implement a new approach to desegregation, based upon a model developed originally in Cambridge and subsequently employed with good results in other Massachusetts cities. Known as "universal controlled choice," this assignment strategy abolishes school attendance districts and requires all parents with children entering either the system or a new level of schooling to indicate preferences that are then accommodated to an extent consistent with school capacities and racial guidelines. Automatic assignment of pupils to schools on the basis of where they live is abolished, and parents receive information and (if they wish) counseling about all options before indicating ranked preferences. In the event of oversubscription to a school, the available spaces are assigned randomly.

The goal of universal controlled choice has been to extend the benefits of choice—amply demonstrated for some schools and some pupils by magnet schools—to all schools and all pupils, and specifically, (1) to give all pupils in a community (or in a geographical section of a larger city) equal access to every public school, not limited by where their families can afford to live; (2) to involve all parents (not just the most sophisticated) in making informed decisions about where their children will go to school; (3) to create pressure for the improvement, over time, of every school through eliminating guaranteed enrollment on the basis of residence; and (4) where necessary, to achieve racial desegregation of every school with as few mandatory assignments as possible.[89] Four well-staffed parent information centers were established in Boston, at state expense, and the staff of each school were helped to develop materials explaining their programs to prospective parents.

While desegregation remained an objective and a requirement, the role of compulsion was greatly reduced; only about 5 percent of children each year are assigned to schools that their parents have not expressed a willingness to accept. Of course, having offered parents a choice, the pang of disappointment is all the keener for those who do not receive their preferred assignment, and this is particularly true for middle-class parents who, in the past, almost had a monopoly on applications to the magnet schools. In Boston, black and "other minority" parents are actually more likely than white parents to be given the school assignment they sought for their children.[90]

Magnet schools and controlled choice are not painless ways—there are no such things—to achieve racial desegregation, but they have the positive side-effects of increasing parental awareness about and demands upon schools, and of forcing urban public schools to begin to behave more like private schools, which must satisfy their "customers."[91]

In Good Schools

To start at the most basic level, a good school must be a safe school, and it must feel safe to all of its students and teachers. The 1993 Household Education Survey found that "about half of 6th-through 12th-grade students personally witnessed bullying, robbery, or physical assault at school, and about 1 out of 8 students reported being directly victimized at school." Students at private schools were much less likely to report such incidents than were students at public schools.[92] Nor, despite inclusion of school safety among the National Education Goals, is the situation getting better: "the percentages of public secondary school teachers reporting weapons possession as a moderate or serious problem . . . almost doubled from 1990–91 to 1993–94—from almost 11 percent to about 20 percent." This was an especially acute problem in large public secondary schools, where, in 1993–94, 26.5 percent of teachers reported that weapons possession among students was a problem, and 47.4 percent reported that physical conflicts among students was a problem.[93]

A disorderly school environment has an especially severe impact on minority students. "Hispanic seniors were more likely than white seniors to report that disruptions by other students interfered with their learning, that fights often occurred between different racial/ethnic groups, and that they did not feel safe at their school. Furthermore, Hispanics were almost three times as likely as whites to report that there were many gangs in their school."[94] Similarly, "Black sophomores were more likely than their white peers" to report disruptive behaviors in their schools.[95]

There is a growing recognition that the push in the 1970s to expand the due process rights of high school students in discipline cases, while it corrected some abuses, undermined the ability of administrators and teachers to maintain a focused environment. A standard reference on school law reminds officials that "liability never results from too much due process, but damages can be assessed if violations of procedural rights result in unjustified suspensions, expulsions, or other disciplinary actions. . . . Courts will carefully study the record to ensure that any procedural deficiencies do not impede the student's efforts to present a full defense."[96] Robert Hampel points out that there were more suits on behalf of public school students challenging teacher, principal, and school board practices between 1969 and 1978 than in the previous sixty years, and that "the percentage of cases decided in favor of students rose dramatically, from 19 percent (before 1969) to 48 percent (1969 to 1978)."[97] Gerald Grant brilliantly described the downward spiral of an urban high school caught in the disruptions of the 1970s—as well as the way to reverse that spiral. Describing several Catholic schools that serve poor and minority children, he writes of an

> orientation . . . emphasized not only in catalog rhetoric but at every important juncture in the life of the school. Much effort is spent in communicating the ideals for which the school stands, and in encouraging a dialogue with a public about those ideals. There is a deeply embedded belief that education is inseparable from the concept of what constitutes a good life and a good community.

In good schools, "intellectual and moral virtue are seen as inseparable. . . . Teachers must have equal concern for mind and for character, schools should be neither morally neutral factories for increasing cognitive output nor witless producers of obedient 'well-adjusted' youngsters." Teachers in such schools "expressed a belief in the saving power of the community and expressed great reluctance to expel or give up on a difficult student."[98]

Organizational Context

It has frequently been noted that "the larger size and often burdensome centralized bureaucracy of urban schools can restrict the independence and collegial support among school staff and create a more impersonal environment for students."[99] An especially powerful case for the negative effects of such an organizational environment (quite apart from the social environment of poverty and family breakdown) was made by Chubb and Moe. In a deservedly influential book they argued that "schools are largely explained by the types of environments that surround them" and that "the freer schools are from external control—the more autonomous, the less subject to bureaucratic constraints—the more likely they are to have effective organizations."[100] Decentralization may lead to efficiencies by shortening the hierarchical lines of control, but it leaves in place the subordinate situation of the school as a unit within a large organization constrained by bureaucratic rules, rewards and sanctions, and culture.

Urban teachers and those in urban, high-poverty schools reported less influence over their curriculum than most teachers had in other locations. Teachers' perceptions of the level of teacher absenteeism were higher among urban teachers than among teachers in other locations, even after taking poverty into account.[101]

If there are some advantages possessed by non-public schools which have a religious identity, and especially in how they serve students who are in some way at risk, the advantage does not consist in superior financial resources or more highly educated staff; quite the contrary. The National Center for Education Statistics report cited above found that in 1993–94, 42 percent of the public school teachers, but only 30 percent of the private school teachers, had earned master's degrees. This is at least partially explained by the fact that the average salary range from the least to the most experienced teachers was $34,200 to $54,900 in public schools, and $22,000 to $32,000 in private schools. On the other hand, 36 percent of the private school teachers, but only 11 percent of the public school teachers, pronounced themselves "highly satisfied" with their jobs. An important element of this satisfaction seems to be that they feel more sense of control over significant aspects of their work. For example, 59.2 percent of private school teachers (versus 34.9 percent of public school teachers) reported they had a great deal of influence over discipline policies, and 55.7 percent (versus 34.3 percent) over curriculum.[102]

This sense of satisfaction is shared by the parents who send their children to schools on the basis of the parents' own choice. Parents whose children had been assigned to a public school were significantly less satisfied with the school (48.7 percent) than were parents who had chosen a public school (61.2 percent), but those who had chosen a private school were the most satisfied (82.5 percent). The smaller size of the private schools—those in central cities averaged 191 pupils, contrasted with 516 in the public schools—undoubtedly helps to create a calmer and more purposeful climate. Students in grades six through twelve reported feeling more secure in private schools, though these are by no means inviolate havens: 32 percent reported they had witnessed incidents of robbery, bullying, or physical attack, contrasted with 58 percent of those attending assigned public schools.[103] Perhaps the most significant difference, however, is one of *attitude,* which no doubt reflects a large element of self-selection among those families who make the sacrifices to send their children to private schools. While 46.4 percent of central-city, public secondary teachers reported serious apathy among their students, this was true of only 10.7 percent of the central-city, private secondary teachers; 32.5 percent of the former but only 5.4 percent of the latter complained of "disrespect for teachers."[104]

It seems obvious that motivated students, a relatively safe and focused environment, and a size that allows the students and adults to know one another well, would more than offset the public school advantage in resources such as computers and master's degrees. A further advantage enjoyed by the faith-based private schools has already been mentioned: clarity about goals and shared values. The NCES study found that 71.4 percent of the teachers in the small (less than 150 students) private schools agreed that "colleagues share beliefs and values about central mission of school," compared with 40.8 percent of those in small public schools. In large schools, with more than 750 students, both numbers dropped, to 49.4 percent in the private and only 26.2 percent in the public schools.[105]

This is, of course, one of the reasons why urban parents are disproportionately likely to enroll their children in private schools, even though many can ill afford to do so. While 13 percent of suburban students are in private schools, this is true of 17 percent of urban students.[106]

Voice and Choice

Much lip-service is paid to the importance of involving parents—especially poor parents—in the schooling of their children, but in fact most schools do very little to make that possible. Despite the labors over several decades of those who have a vision for this dimension of public schooling (like my former colleague Don Davies and my colleague Vivian Johnson), the results have been exemplary but not widely emulated.

Periodically, attempts have been made to require that schools provide parents with a voice in decision-making; few of these attempts have enjoyed much success. For example, the federal compensatory education program mandates a parent voice in decisions and sustains an expensive apparatus of consultation, but most observers note that few rank-and-file parents participate in any meaningful way.[107] State laws frequently mandate parental advisory councils for bilingual and special education, for school-based management, and for other reform initiatives. Most such councils are notably ineffective. Similar efforts in other countries have the reputation of either being simply dominated by the professionals or as engaged in endless wrangling with them.[108]

A very different situation is created when parents actually control a school, as may be the case with a charter school or with a "grant-maintained" school in England which has exercised its right to "opt out" of the local education authority and operate as an independent public school. In such cases, there may still be tension with the professional staff or a supine inclination to defer to their expertise, but there is at least the potential of a meaningful voice in fundamental decisions about what happens in the school. The most notable American example of what could be called serious parental voice has been in

Chicago, where state legislation gave significant power over individual schools to elected councils.[109]

The difficulty of making parental "voice" work effectively—at least where poor parents are concerned—has led to increased interest in parental choice as a means of ensuring that school staff are accountable and responsive to those most affected by their work.[110] The haphazard parental choice of schools, which already exists on a very large scale in the United States, has tended to increase social and racial segregation, but almost all of the planned and publicly sponsored school choice has been intended to achieve racial (and thus to some extent social class) integration. In short, everything depends upon how it is done. Briefly stated, there must be (1) an outreach process for ensuring that all parents have equal access to good information about the options available, which requires extra effort to reach and to counsel those who are usually left out of the loop; (2) an assignment or admission process which is transparently honest and fair, which cannot be manipulated, and which makes the schools which are more in demand accessible to families who would be excluded by relying on residential criteria; and (3) an educational improvement process which seeks to increase the number of schools or programs which well-informed parents would want for their children, and which intervenes helpfully with those schools unable to attract enough applicants.

Adequate Support

There is no need to belabor what no one denies: poor children as a group do not do well in school.[111] The only relevant policy questions are: do we as a society care? and, is there any form of governmental intervention which would make a significant difference? Jonathan Kozol, in a very influential book, argued that in fact we do not care, and are therefore directly responsible for the school failure of poor children; this should indeed be considered the failure of our society rather than of the children. Contrasting the expenditure levels in urban schools and in the most affluent suburban districts, he suggests that the disparities are directly responsible for the dismal school careers of many inner-city children.

Kozol rejects excuses for unequal schooling that point to the dysfunctional families of many inner-city children, since "government is not responsible, or at least not directly, for the inequalities of family background. It is responsible for inequalities in public education. The school is the creature of the state; the family is not."[112] That begs the question, of course, whether equal expenditures by government would overcome the effects of the social forces which provide so much of the miseducation of poor children, including the bad decisions of the parents of many of them. Of course it would not.

The weakness of Kozol's case is that the linkage between expenditure and achievement which he assumes is simply not there. The social class and other family characteristics are far more predictive of pupil achievement than the amount spent on the school. Indeed, average per pupil expenditures in many cities are well above those in middle-class suburbs (not included in his statistical charts) where pupil achievement is substantially higher. An important study carried out for the National Research Council by a distinguished panel of economists found "no reason to believe that increases in spending would on average be any more effective than past spending, particularly when they rely on the same people operating with the same basic incentives."[113]

The same objection can be raised to proposals by some in Congress that schools and districts be required to meet "opportunity to learn" standards before children are held accountable for their performance on assessments. All of the conditions—primarily, though not exclusively, resources—that are necessary for language-minority or other at-risk students to achieve to their maximum potential should be in place in every school before a system of national or state testing is required. Unfortunately, as another National Research Council study (already cited above) points out, "the research base for defining the most important and effective resources and conditions for English-language learners is very weak."[114] That is a stunning conclusion. After all these years and all these studies, we apparently still don't know what resources and what conditions make a difference for these students. What did those tens of millions of dollars go for, we want to ask. Are we still just flying by the seat of our pants in educating millions of children?

This is not to dismiss the central message of Kozol's book: hundreds of thousands of poor and minority pupils attend public schools that do not have the resources or the flexibility to meet their needs. The needs of many (by no means all) of these children are enormous, and meeting them would go far beyond what has been the traditional role of day schools. As the Coleman Report concluded a quarter-century ago, "equality of educational opportunity through the schools must imply a strong effect of schools that is independent of the child's immediate social environment, and that strong independent effect is not present in American schools."[115]

Greatly increased expenditures through the schools attended by poor children would be justified only if the funds were used in very different ways than at present; simply increasing the amount and intensity of what schools do now would not provide poor children with what they need to experience and sustain academic success. Even a notably optimistic account of what can be done to break the cycle of poverty concluded that there is "a fundamental contradiction between the needs of vulnerable children and families and the traditional requirements of professionalism and bureaucracy . . . [which] helps to explain why programs that work for populations at risk are so rare. . . ."[116]

Schools That Have an Impact

James Coleman, the source over the years of so many important insights about the education of poor and minority children, suggested that there was a growing need to replace the neighborhood-based "common school" with a new institution, capable of having a far more intensive effect upon children than is possible for public schools as presently constituted.

> It is a demand not for further classroom indoctrination, nor for any particular content, but a demand for child care: all day, from birth to school age; after school, every day, till parents return home from work; and all summer. . . . As the social capital in home and neighborhood shrinks, school achievement and other growth will not be increased by replacing these resources with more school-like resources—that is, those that produce opportunities, demands, and rewards— but by replacing them with resources which produce attitudes, efforts, and conception of self—that is, those qualities that interact with the ones provided by the school [to produce achievement] . . . some indication of what these resources must be like can be seen in the character of the currently eroding institutions that have provided the social capital in the past. Their essential qualities have been, I believe, attention, personal interest and intensity of involvement, some persistence and continuity over time, and a certain degree of intimacy.[117]

It should be noted that Coleman's concern, in this article, is not with poor families exclusively, but with what he sees as a general decline in the ability and willingness of parents to provide a consistent structure of expectations and attitudes that will lead to success in school. Even parents whose "human capital"—educational level and income—has grown may have a diminished "social capital" of legitimacy in the exercise of authority in relation to their children and a diminished willingness simply to pay attention to their children. The decline of residential communities and of the institutions of face-to-face socialization have placed a burden upon schools that they cannot adequately bear. It is poor children who are most vulnerable to the effects of this loss, and who most urgently need new institutions, beyond the nuclear family, within which they can find both emotional safety and encouragement.

In 1994, 25 percent of children lived in single-parent families. The figures for minority children are even higher. In 1994, 59 percent of black children lived in single-parent homes compared with 19 percent of white children and 29 percent of Hispanic children. These data on children in single-parent families represent children's living status during a single year. Many more children are affected over their lifetimes by the impact of divorce. As social science examines the emotional and psychological consequences of single-parent households, the economic consequences are already clear. Single-parent families tend to suffer severe economic disadvantages.[118]

But the economic disadvantages, it has increasingly become clear, are less crippling than some of the other effects of a disrupted family life upon behavior, motivation, and application to schoolwork. Schools find themselves faced with serving many children—the majority of their students, in some cases—for whom they should be providing a powerfully socializing experience to make up for lack of structure, direction and support in the home. The challenge is comparable to that faced by schools serving large numbers of refugee children whose lives have been disrupted by war or famine; but in some respects the former is even more difficult because the deprivation experienced by many of the children growing up among us may be more hidden and may go back to birth and before.

Bureaucratically structured institutions, like government, human service agencies and public schools as now constituted, are not well equipped to meet such needs. Osborne and Gaebler classify functions according to which of three "sectors" is best able to carry them out. Government is best at "policy management, regulation, ensuring equity, preventing discrimination or exploitation, ensuring continuity and stability of services, and ensuring social cohesion. ..." Business is best at innovating and adapting to rapid change. It is what they call the "third sector" of voluntary, non-profit organizations that is "best at performing tasks that generate little or no profit, demand compassion and commitment to individuals, require extensive trust on the part of customers or clients, needs hands-on, personal attention . . . and involves the enforcement of moral codes and individual responsibility for behavior."[119]

The strengths of "third sector" organizations are very much those called for by Coleman. He argued that schools outside the public sector that are freely chosen for their religious or pedagogical character are better able to set and enforce expectations that lead to achievement, especially for poor and vulnerable children, than are public schools enrolling pupils on the basis of residence.

Family background makes much less difference for achievement in Catholic schools than in public schools. This greater homogeneity of achievement in the Catholic sector (as well as the lesser racial and ethnic segregation of the Catholic sector) suggests that the ideal of the common school is more nearly met in the Catholic schools than in the public schools.[120]

This leads to his conclusion, which I share, that "the strict separation of church and state, as practiced in America, has been harmful to the least advantaged and particularly harmful to children in the black community."[121] It is important that it become more feasible for new kinds of schools to be established, schools that are based upon shared beliefs about education and the formation of character, whether these schools have a religious basis or not and whether they are operated by government or by "third sector" organizations. Such schools should, as Coleman suggests, provide a far more intensive and extensive environment for children than is possible for public schools as now constituted and staffed.

This will require an increased commitment of funding so that caring—not custodial—adults will be available to provide a range of learning experiences and support for children and youth twelve hours a day or more. It will require summer programs of equal intensity, the option of residential programs for some, and outreach to families in their homes (routine in Europe but almost unheard-of in American education). In short, it will require "comprehensive and intensive services" provided by staff "with the time and skill to establish relationships based on mutual respect and trust."[122]

When the idea of "urban boarding schools" was raised by Coleman and others thirty years ago, it seemed an insult to the adequacy of inner-city parents. Now many of those parents are themselves crying out for help, for anything to give their children a safe environment wherein they can grow. Public policy should no longer ignore what parents tell us by putting their children in non-public schools which parents cannot well afford.

Final Thoughts

With all the warranted concern for the effectiveness of American schools in producing measurable achievement, it is important to keep in mind that education is more than the acquisition of academic skills and knowledge. Three other functions of formal schooling deserve our attention, not because they are important to the effective functioning of schools (sometimes they may in fact reduce efficiency), but because they are morally important.

The first of these is the relationship of schools with families who are the primary educators of their children and—however imperfectly—the protectors of their interests. The second is the importance of racial and class integration in schools for the health of a pluralistic society, and the third (in some tension with the second) is the potential significance of schools as contexts for the rebuilding of civil society where it has become almost non-functional.

A school is an extension of and in some ways an agent of, the family, extending its educational mission. The legal catch-phrase *in loco parentis* has too often been understood to mean that schools should act in place of, rather than on behalf of, parents. When, under a compulsory system of schooling, teachers set themselves against parents, or see parents as a problem to be evaded or overcome, a fundamental principle of a free society is violated. Of course, there are some family situations so terrible that outside intervention is appropriate in the interest of the hapless children, but universally applicable policy should not be based upon the hard cases.

Alignment between schools and families is also important as an element of effective education. The sense of continuity between family and school sends a powerful message to children that they will learn because the adults in their lives share a commitment, and that learning what schools teach is not an abandonment but rather a confirmation of what their families stand for. This respect for parents as educators and guardians of the interests of their children, and not a blind faith in educational markets, is the really compelling reason to dismantle command-driven educational bureaucracies and create systems of parental and teacher choice among schools that are free to be distinctively excellent.

The second priority that we should pursue "because it is right" is the integration, in schools, of those children who, because of race, home language, or poverty are at risk of living their lives as adults apart from the society and the productive economy.

> There is substantial agreement about the nature of the social problem. A class of Americans, heavily poor and nonwhite, exists apart from the social mainstream. That is, it has very little contact with other Americans in the public aspects of American life, especially in schools, the workplace, and politics. . . . There is also substantial agreement that the solution for the disadvantaged must mean integration, that is, an end to the separation so that the disadvantaged can publicly interact with others and be accepted by them as equals.[123]

Though the importance of such integration into the society is clear to conservative social analysts like Lawrence Mead, and helps to explain the anxiety about separate bilingual programs and about the multicultural emphasis now fashionable, the goal of school integration seems to have dropped off the public policy agenda. Kozol observes that the "dual society, at least in public education, seems in general to be unquestioned. . . . The fact of ghetto education as a permanent American reality appears to be accepted."[124] While this reflects in part the stormy history of urban school desegregation in the 1970s, it surely also betrays a lack of confidence in the capacity of American society to provide spaces where racial and class differences can be put aside in the interest of a common purpose.

The fact is that the race desegregation of schools, while it has been overtaken by massive demographic change in the largest cities, has not been a failure in its results for millions of minority and white pupils. The remarkable growth of a black middle class and the generally positive attitudes of white adults toward residential and social integration, compared with the situation forty years ago, have been furthered by integration in schools, working together with other societal changes.[125]

Important as these considerations are, it has become clear that integration by itself, like the other external interventions described above, does not have a powerful enough effect on what actually occurs in the learning process to overcome the barriers facing poor and minority children. As Coleman wisely pointed out decades ago, "integration is important to both white and black children principally for other reasons. We are committed to becoming a truly multiracial society."[126]

Too often, top-down efforts to achieve racial desegregation of schools have resulted in polarization rather than mutual understanding. This is why some of us have become convinced that integration strategies based upon parental choice are far more likely to achieve success. Moving beyond magnet schools (urged by Coleman in his 1967 article), a number of cities in Massachusetts have adopted policies that make school choice universal and seek school improvement along with stable integration. While the present policies do not go far enough to encourage the development of new schools within and outside the local public systems, they have demonstrated that urban parents can be given the information to make responsible school choices within a framework that ensures fairness and desegregated enrollments.[127]

Educational policy should have as a fundamental premise that it is desirable that those groups of pupils who are commonly marginalized, and for whom there may be no assured place in adult society, should experience the school as a place where they truly belong. To accept this premise would require designing policies of public funding so that they reward successful efforts to achieve integration, and designing systems of accountability for academic outcomes so that they do not penalize schools for having become integrated.

A third priority for educational policy, whose justification goes beyond the efficiency of schools, is that they should become an occasion to rebuild the civil society. We can see something like this happening in Poland and other nations emerging from the Communist effort to subordinate all aspects of society to the State and the Party. In the face of pervasive cynicism and mistrust of government initiatives, groups of parents and teachers have come together to create hundreds of schools that reflect shared convictions about education. Most of these schools are small and struggling—they have no powerful sponsors or endowments—but they are serving to create the "communities of memory and mutual aid, of character and moral discipline, of transcendent truth and higher loyalty" that are essential to a healthy civil society. Within such schools, shaped by the free collaboration of adults, children can experience the "'embedded relationships' that produce moral integrity" and make a free society possible.[128]

It has become increasingly clear that American inner-city areas (it will not do to use the mocking euphemism "communities") have been experiencing, over the past three decades, a collapse of the civil society that had earlier provided structure and dignity even in the face of poverty. William Julius Wilson attributes this collapse to the exodus of middle-class and stable working-class black families from areas to which they had previously been confined by housing discrimination and other barriers. Their loss

> made it more difficult to sustain the basic institutions in these neighborhoods (including churches, stores, schools, recreational facilities, etc.). . . . As the basic institutions declined, the social organization of inner city neighborhoods (sense of community, positive neighborhood identification, and explicit norms and sanctions against aberrant behavior) likewise declined.[129]

Is it too much to hope that schools which truly belonged to parents, schools freely created or chosen by them, could serve as a focal point for the growth of new community, indeed for the revival of civil society where it has been profoundly damaged? Certainly there is reason to believe that something like this has occurred around hundreds of "community schools" and inner-city parochial schools that struggle to survive, like the hundreds of parent-run schools that have sprung up in Poland, Russia and other nations on the arduous road to freedom.

In brief, the leading educational policy challenge facing American government at all levels is to increase school autonomy and appropriate educational diversity while at the same time achieving clarity about the expectations of what every pupil will learn. To meet this challenge, we will need careful legislative drafting, experimentation with charter schools and other forms of choice-related diversity, and a willingness on the part of administrators and teachers to abandon the mental habits of bureaucratic functionaries and to think and act as real educators.

If there is any single message in the analysis and discussion above, it is surely that there is no single solution to the failure of the American educational system to serve poor children effectively. To some extent, indeed, the various measures which our society and government should take could cancel each other out unless they are designed and implemented with great care. For example, I have called for greater autonomy of individual schools and also for more explicit common standards with real consequences for failing to help students to meet them. Balancing standards and autonomy can be done, but only with close attention to how each affects the other.[130]

Here, briefly, are the primary recommendations which emerge from the discussion above. They are offered with the caution that they are not intended to stand in isolation from each other or in isolation from the discussion from which they emerge. Not everything which is important can be reduced to a policy recommendation!

- Poor children deserve a rich curriculum, one which introduces them to the heritage of a culture which they need to be able to share with the children of middle-class families in order to participate fully in all that this society makes available.
- Schools which serve poor children should be held to high standards for the skills and the knowledge which they will be helped to acquire, and students and their teachers should be keenly aware of the personal importance of meeting these expectations.
- Although accountability requires a societal consensus on the essential knowledge and skills which students should acquire, and for which educators will be held accountable, it is also important that schools have the "elbow-room" to develop and express a distinctive character based upon a shared understanding of the untestable goals of education.

- Since poor children, even more than those from middle-class families, require well-planned and consistent instruction by well-trained teachers, it is essential that the incentive structure for teachers encourage the best to make a long-term commitment to working with poor children, and that teacher training prepare them for such assignments.
- Since, in general, small schools have proven to be more effective than larger schools, especially with poor children, the present trend toward teacher-initiated charter schools, magnet schools, and schools-within-schools should be encouraged and facilitated by flexibility about staffing ratios and other requirements.
- Schools should be seen, and should function, as civil-society institutions in close partnership with families, not as branch offices of government, and their governance structure should resemble that of non-profit associations more than that of bureaucratic hierarchies.

~11~

The Good City

Inner-City Poverty and Metropolitan Responsibility

John D. Mason, Gordon College

Introduction

An uncomfortable question drives this inquiry into our society's moral sympathies and reigning systems of moral obligation. If the realities of our inner cities are as damaging as authoritative observers have chronicled, why has our response as a society to these damaging realities been so restrained? In the summer of 1993 we found ourselves mobilizing without difficulty both private and public responses to severe flooding along prominent midwestern rivers in which there was virtually no loss of life, albeit great damage to property. What has prevented us then, from mobilizing in a similar way to attack the harmful conditions of our inner cities[1] where great loss of life and life-sustaining hope have been occurring for years?

The answer to this question turns in part on the perceived causes of inner-city poverty, an issue that finds learned analysts generally dividing into two camps: one emphasizing the behavior of those within the inner city, the other appealing to socioeconomic processes within the broader metropolitan region and beyond. Indeed, the realities surrounding our inner cities—both life within them and the larger society's response to them—are among the most complex social realities facing us today: so much so that New York's Senator Moynihan counseled us some years ago to pursue a policy of "benign neglect." Since we understand so little about the socioeconomic dynamics surrounding our inner cities, more harm than help may come from rushed efforts to "do something." If so, then we should respond slowly.

This essay reflects the spirit of Moynihan's suggestion, though my focus is less on the socioeconomic measures he had in mind than on how we as a society should conceive of moral responsibility for the pockets of concentrated poverty within too many of our inner cities. Martin Marty has written recently that on the moral/political front "the United States is paralyzed and . . . its moral, spiritual, and intellectual capital are in need of restoring."[2] Thinking of the problem at issue in this essay, I concur. Swept up in the unsettling social forces of industrialization, urbanization and secularization, as our nation has been for over a century, and amidst attempts to fit our unique system of federalism to these forces, we have been confused as to the urgings of moral obligation. Any agnosticism about what to do on the socioeconomic front, then, is far more than uncertainty about the consequences of proposed initiatives and extends to confusion over who should bear the cost of these initiatives. We need, therefore, to shore up our understandings of moral obligation—and, when it comes to the conditions of our inner cities, this implies special attention to rehearsing our traditions of moral obligation surrounding the meaning of metropolitan responsibility.

A central concern of this essay is, therefore, the "moral philosophy" surrounding space—using this older notion which links social science with ethics. On the one hand, how in fact do we (as households, firms, government agencies, and other institutions) respond to spatial constructions of concentrated poverty—and, given these responses, what ameliorative measures seem most feasible and effective? On the other hand, how should we address the existence of concentrated poverty, and should we refine and extend our existing moral sympathies? As part of our exploration we wonder particularly whether some level of "physical proximity" between poor and non-poor becomes a necessary condition both to elicit a greater sense of personal and corporate responsibility among members of society and to establish more effective remediation efforts as a result. If so, this reality speaks to measures—such as the disruption of neighborhoods by major highways, or the use of land-use controls to establish and maintain more economically homogeneous communities within metropolitan regions—that affect physical proximity between poor and non-poor.

The physical and moral dimensions of space have long dogged us as a society. In an earlier century we first encountered the difficult and continuing question of whether to allow or disallow the political annexation by central cities of surrounding communities. We have lived through an era in which we allowed, legally, the preferences of the majority group of citizens to dictate housing and seating space for citizens of distinct ethnic and racial backgrounds.

In one sense, therefore, the difficult realities of our inner cities today are but continuations of these earlier struggles. The 1960s, however, gave the spatial realities surrounding our inner cities a particularly deadly face amidst the riots and fires that broke out in a number of cities: so much so that the oft-quoted aphorism of the 1968 Kerner Commission ("Our nation is moving toward two societies, one black, one white—separate and unequal . . .")[3] has come to haunt the last third of the twentieth century.

It is not obvious, almost thirty years after Kerner, whether the national government realistically can or even should attempt to mount and sustain an aggressive response to the situations within our inner cities. There has been a clear shift in political power at the state level of government away from central cities to suburban communities,[4] combined with a restructured federalism vesting more responsibility with the states than has been true for much of the twentieth century.[5] Given these patterns, it is unclear what sympathies for addressing the harmful realities of our inner cities can be found for national efforts. If greater and more effective efforts to redress these difficulties flow from physical proximity between poor and non-poor, ought then the normative response reside within metropolitan regions?

So it is that the moral focus increasingly has come to center on local responsibility. But what can and should this mean? Formal metropolitan government, practiced in many parts of the world but rarely in the U.S.,[6] is considered by most as a "nonstarter" on the American scene. This being the case, the quest for local responsibility moves in the direction of (a) regional cooperative arrangements, (b) strategic steps that central cities can take to bring economic well-being to their people, and (c) private—often faith-initiated—measures. Thirty years from the riots of the 1960s, with poverty increasingly found in concentrated pockets in or near our central cities, we have waning confidence that existing forms of local responsibility offer clear relief—at least any time soon, with too much damage done while we wait. But, given our present sympathies, hope seems only to reside with local efforts.

Thus this essay is framed. How ought we to think morally about our metropolitan regions and particularly the meaning of local responsibility?[7] Asked differently: Given the distinct character of our moral sympathies, who should become primarily responsible for addressing the difficult realities of our inner cities? What blend of private and public efforts is appropriate, and how should public responsibility be assigned within our federal system of government? If there is a thesis to be tested here, it is that a workable system of moral obligation for the difficult realities of our inner cities, which fits our sympathies as a society, must embrace a greater commitment to local (or metropolitan) responsibility. Concentrating upon the poorer and weaker members of our inner cities will give our inquiry clarifying focus.

Section I of this chapter lays the necessary foundations in social science for the primary appeal to our moral sympathies as a society, an appeal made in section II. In section I we consider an emerging picture of concentrated poverty within the metropolitan regions of the United States, along with the socio-economic dynamics which both give rise to and maintain these pockets of concentrated poverty. The impact of concentrated poverty upon those who must dwell within these pockets is assessed, along with developments which could promise some relief from these conditions.

The distinctive thrust of this essay comes in section II, where we revisit biblical teaching and commentary (the "biblical tradition")[8] in a quest to clarify our moral sympathies surrounding metropolitan responsibility. In an otherwise secular and pluralistic era and setting, why make an appeal to the biblical tradition? First and foremost is the conviction, shared by faithful Jews and Christians over the millennia, that moral insight to guide our daily walk amidst the practical problems of the day is found through struggling to apply God's law to those problems. As these problems change over the centuries we need continually to rehearse the biblical materials in order to refine our moral discernment. A basic hermeneutical assumption resides herein: that the Creator of this world knows best how it does and should function, and that the Bible offers instruction (generally in the form of ethical emphases) which, when combined with careful study of the world, helps us sort our way through the problems we face.

The position being advanced here is developed systematically by C.J.H. Wright. He writes: "What God did with Israel in their land functions for us as a model or paradigm from which we draw principles and objectives for our socioethical endeavor in secular society." And again:

> The purpose of redemption is ultimately to restore the perfection of God's purpose in creation, that perfection which sin and the fall have corrupted. Israel, as God's redeemed community, was to have been a "light to the nations"—not just the vehicle of God's redemption, but an illustration of it in actual historical life. Israel's socioeconomic life and institutions, therefore, have a paradigmatic or exemplary function in principle. It is not that they are to be simply and slavishly imitated, but rather that they are models within a particular cultural context of principles of justice, humaneness, equality, responsibility, and so forth which are applicable, *mutatis mutandis,* to all people in subsequent cultural contexts.[9]

Those who share this conviction today obviously are not the first to do such work, and thus we expect to learn from those who have struggled with this same project over the millennia. In short, it is our conviction that God has a mind on spatially related moral realities and thus what responsibility for the more vulnerable members of our metropolitan regions should mean in the late twentieth century, and desires us to rigorously consult the Bible and broader biblical tradition to help achieve a greater *shalom* within society.

An appeal to the biblical tradition carries a second motivation—the unique cultural setting of the U.S. From the earliest presence of European settlers on this continent the biblical tradition has had a determinative influence in the systems of moral obligation that have informed and constrained us as a society.[10]

Several centuries later, and amidst the pressures of secularization and a thicker state-church wall than exists in many nations, belief in biblically based dogmas remains a distinctive trait of our society. Moral obligation in America, in other words, remains closely tied to biblical instruction; gaining greater clarity into the moral implications of that instruction should help us resolve our problems.[11] This is the case within society at large; it is even more obvious when our focus becomes the inner city, where a growing number of learned voices contend that the institutions holding the greatest hope for relief of poverty and despair are religious institutions (particularly Christian faith and Christian churches).[12]

As we observe in section II, the "city" of the Bible occupies the central part of the larger "economic region" surrounding it, including its outlying villages. The city represented protection and security for the citizens of its economic region, security seen especially in the walls, watchtowers, and gates surrounding the city. The principal gate of the city, through which people passed in and out to do their daily business, became the physical setting for effecting justice within that society, and an important defining component of justice in the legal documents that have been passed down to us was special concern for the most vulnerable members of society.

If the central city in the biblical tradition promised greater security, the exact reverse too often exists today, when the central city represents fear of physical harm, and movement to the surrounding region offers greater hope for safety and opportunity. Though forms of metropolitan governance to address the difficult realities confronting us probably are politically unlikely to develop, Christian families and organizations can help lead society by acknowledging and acting upon legitimate forms of metropolitan responsibility, reaching out to assist our most vulnerable "extended" neighbors, and therein serving as catalysts for broader initiatives to this same end.

Though the Bible and traditional commentary speak of both poverty and city life, the settings involved are far removed from those of America's inner cities in the late twentieth century. The same could be said of the earlier traditions of moral obligation within the U.S. Though one might think that by the late nineteenth century urban conditions began to approach the reality of life in the inner city today, we argue in section I that considerable social distance separates the earlier conditions of our inner cities from the realities of the present. Hence this inquiry into moral obligation must begin with the socioeconomic dynamics that both give rise to and surround our inner cities today, for it is only through careful interaction with these dynamics that we discern questions to ask both of the biblical tradition and of the earlier moral sympathies of our society.

The Inner City Today

A good city will not allow conditions harmful to its citizens to persist for prolonged periods—a moral commitment applying particularly to the most vulnerable citizens of the city, since they are least able to defend themselves. The figurative—if not literal—walls of the city are intended to protect its residents from such conditions. Whether through private or public measures (more likely, some combination of both) the citizens of the good city will assume responsibility for attacking the harmful conditions, seeking to assure its members that their efforts to better themselves are worthy efforts—that they can hope for the future. The geographic reach of this good city extends far beyond the "walls" of the central city to the broader economic region within which the city lies—such that the responsibility we observe properly can be called a metropolitan responsibility. So it is that the prophet Jeremiah instructs the Jewish exiles in Babylon to "seek the peace and prosperity of the city . . ." (Jer. 29:7), and so it is, when God sees harmful conditions persisting in Jerusalem (if not the entire land), he longs "for a man among them who would build up the wall and stand before me in the gap on behalf of the land . . ." (Ezek. 22:30).

Our quest for the good city begins, therefore, with inquiry into whether (and how) harmful conditions confront members of the city—a quest quickly leading to the pockets of concentrated poverty we call here the "inner city," where virtually all observers grant that unusually difficult realities face those who dwell there. Our attempt, in this section of the essay, is to assess the extent and nature of these realities as a necessary first step for understanding what a proper response should involve. We recognize this task to be peculiarly subject to exaggeration, with attendant consequences—and that this danger confronts those on *all* sides of the issue. We argue that due to the lives both lost and stunted, and the hopes dashed, redressing the difficult realities of our inner cities ranks among the most important tasks facing society and deserves far greater attention than it has received.

The risk attending our assessment is that of encouraging excessive pessimism, which (a) fails to appreciate the often heroic efforts being taken by many within and without the inner city, and (b) potentially reinforces a selfish desire among many outside the inner city to avoid at all costs the seemingly contaminating conditions of life there. Danger attends those with more optimistic views as well; as much as we want to acknowledge the natural processes of urban revival and to praise innovative initiatives, an overly positive assessment can reinforce an all-too-convenient desire by those outside our inner cities to put this problem out of sight and out of mind.

In this section of the essay we observe both a growing concentration of poverty within neighborhoods where most of the other residents are poor or near-poor, and what may well be a growing economic stratification within society generally. We then wonder over the consequences of the emerging concentration, noting various so-called "neighborhood effects," especially the development of a condition of "social isolation" within the inner cities which limits the ability of residents within these neighborhoods to perceive and grasp economic opportunity within the larger metropolitan region. The historic formation of our metropolitan regions within which this concentration is occurring is then reviewed; we note how this process was not solely a spontaneous one and that state intervention was used in a number of strategic ways to bring us to where we are today. In this context we also consider how families use the existing structure of metropolitan regions, and the implications of this for poorer households. Finally, we ponder the potential for steps which could overcome these difficult conditions, from the natural forces of economic revival to strategic governmental measures.

Geographic Concentration of Poverty

Reading social reality is never easy. This warning noted, our best grasp of social reality tells us that since the 1960s the poor and near-poor within the U.S. increasingly reside in neighborhoods where a goodly share of their neighbors are also poor and near-poor. As economic opportunities have allowed most households to move comfortably above poverty levels, using a part of their income to obtain housing in non-poor neighborhoods, poorer households find themselves surrounded more and more by other poor and near-poor households. By extension, therefore, this same process finds non-poor households positioning themselves in neighborhoods occupied primarily by other non-poor residents. Table 1 presents the percentage of overall U.S. poverty located within three conventional geographic areas, along with the "poverty rate" for each area (the percentage of an area's residents that are poor).

Table 1

Geographic Composition of Poverty in the U.S. for Selected Years[13]

	1969	1979	1989	1996
Area poor population as % of total *U.S.* poor population				
Metropolitan Regions				
Central City	34.1	39.6	42.7	42.8
Outside Central City	22.1	29.1	28.6	34.4
Outside Metropolitan Regions	43.8	31.3	28.7	22.8
Area poor population as % of total *area* population (poverty rate)				
Metropolitan Regions				
Central City	14.9	16.5	18.0	19.6
Outside Central City	8.1	8.0	8.1	9.4
Outside Metropolitan Regions	19.2	15.4	16.9	15.9

For the years noted the largest portion of the poor (top half of the table) increasingly is found in our central cities, growing from 34 percent in 1970 (an amount less than that residing in areas outside metropolitan regions) to 43 percent in 1996 (approaching double that found outside metropolitan regions). Casual observation would suggest that these poor are not scattered uniformly about all neighborhoods of our central cities, but live generally in concentrated locations, a few of which gather labels like "ghetto" and "slum."[14] The table shows a growing portion of the poor (at an even faster rate of increase) within suburban areas as well. Once again, casual observation finds much of this poverty concentrated within inner-ring suburbs and older industrial communities within metropolitan regions, and not spread uniformly throughout the communities and neighborhoods of our metropolitan regions.

The second set of percentages in table 1 shows the "poverty rate" for each area—the percentage of each region's population comprised of poor residents. Whereas poverty rates in suburban areas and areas outside metropolitan regions seem to have stabilized in recent decades, the poverty rate within our central cities has continued to increase—testimony, we suspect, to continued movement out of the central cities by non-poor residents. Were we to observe the *racial composition* of the poor living in the central cities of our metropolitan regions, and using the two years 1969 and 1989, we get the results noted in table 2. The percentage of central city poverty comprised of whites falls substantially, from 47.5 percent in 1969 to 34.9 percent in 1989; the percentage of central city poverty comprised of blacks falls mildly, from 40.3 percent in 1969 to 38.2 percent in 1989 (rising above the number of white, poor residents in the process); and the percentage of central city poverty comprised of Hispanics rises substantially, from 12.1 percent in 1969 to 23.3 percent in 1989.[15] Not only is poverty increasingly found in the central cities of our land, but it is becoming increasingly black and Hispanic in that setting as well.

Table 2

Racial Composition of Central City Poverty for 1969 and 1989[16]

	1969	1989
Percentage (%) of Poor Central City Residents who are:		
White (non-Hispanic)	47.5	34.9
Black	40.3	38.2
Hispanaic	12.1	23.3

But is this picture still too blurred? To observe a growing concentration of U.S. poverty within our central cities may mask even greater levels of concentration within distinct pockets of our central cities. Paul Jargowsky provides the most careful evidence to date of a greater level of concentrated poverty via his detailed examination of metropolitan statistical areas (the Census Bureau's conception of metropolitan regions) for what he calls "high-poverty neighborhoods"—census tracts in which at least 40 percent of the residents are poor. He finds that from 1970 to 1990:

1) the number of high-poverty neighborhoods more than doubled;
2) the total number of persons living in these neighborhoods increased from 4.1 million to 8 million;
3) the percentage of all poor people in the U.S. residing in these areas rose from 12 percent (1.9 million) to 18 percent (3.7 million)—from 3 to 6 percent among the white poor and 26 to 34 percent among the black poor.[17]

Jargowsky offers the following characterization of the process at work over these years.

> The rapid expansion of ghettos and barrios documented in this chapter is not only a human tragedy but also an intensification of the divide between the "haves" and the "have-nots" within metropolitan areas. Almost all of the growth of high-poverty neighborhoods takes place within the confines of political jurisdictions of central cities or, in some cases, inner-ring suburbs, caused in part by middle-class flight and commercial abandonment. In contrast, wealthier suburbs and other outlying areas are growing rapidly and trying to shield themselves from the problems associated with the inner city. Whether intentional or not, the process represents a retreat from the concept of community and has very serious long-run implications for American society.[18]

Table 3

Number of Census Tracts by Poverty & Distress Status for the 100 Largest Central Cities, 1970–1990[19]

Census Tracts	1970	1980	1990
Total number of tracts	12,584	13,777	14,214
Percent of city total	100.0	100.0	100.0
Poverty tracts	3,430	4,713	5,596
Percent of city total	27.3	34.2	39.4
Extreme poverty tracts	751	1,330	1,954
Percent of city total	6.0	9.7	13.7

(continued)

Number of Census Tracts by Poverty & Distress Status
for the 100 Largest Central Cities, 1970–1990[19] (*continued*)

Census Tracts	1970	1980	1990
Distressed tracts	296	1,513	1,850
Percent of city total	2.41	11.0	3.0
Severely distressed tracts	166	562	566
Percent of city total	1.3	4.1	4.0

In a similar study Kasarda chose census tracts from the one hundred largest central cities and examined them over the 1970 to 1990 period in four categories: (1) *poverty tracts* (in which at least 20 percent of the residents were poor), (2) *extreme poverty tracts* (in which at least 40 percent of the residents were poor—Jargowsky's "high-poverty neighborhoods"), (3) *distressed neighborhoods* (census tracts in which the portions of poverty, joblessness, female-headed families, and welfare receipts were one standard deviation above the 1980 national-tract mean for each of these attributes), and (4) *severely distressed neighborhoods* (in which he adds teenage school dropout rates to the four attributes used for *distressed neighborhoods*). As table 3, above (reproduced from Kasarda's article), shows, with the exception of the change in *severely distressed tracts* from 1980 to 1990, there is a dramatic increase in the number of census tracts represented by each of the four dimensions that he isolates over the entire period.[20] We draw particular notice to the 160 percent increase in *extreme poverty tracts* from 1970 to 1990.

The U.S. Census Bureau reports for each year the portion of overall income received by families, arrayed in quintiles (20 percent groupings) from poorest to richest; that is, we are given the portion of overall income received by the poorest quintile of families within our society, the second poorest, the middle quintile, the second richest, and the richest quintile. Mayer collects these data for families within metropolitan statistical areas (MSAs) to trace the "central city" location of each quintile from 1964 through 1994, finding what turns out to be a consistent rank order for all years, from the poorest to the richest quintile (top to bottom in figure 1), in terms of the likelihood of central city location (with members of the poorest quintile always the most likely to live in the central city). Figure 1 is reproduced from his paper. The left axis of the figure shows the greater or lesser likelihood that a family within a given quintile will live in the central city compared to the average family overall. In 1994, for example, a family from the poorest quintile was almost 1.4 times as likely to live in the central city as the average family, and a family from the richest quintile was about .7 times as likely as the average family overall to live in the central city. Over the entire period observed, only the poorest quintile increased its likelihood to live in the central city. "While urban families at the bottom of the

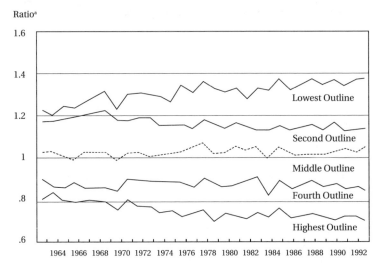

Figure 1. Central City Concentrations of Family
Income Quintiles (MSA Residents)[21]

income distribution have always disproportionately resided in central cities, this pattern has become more pronounced in the last three decades."[22]

Two qualifications are in order with regard to a growing concentration of poverty within U.S. society. First, not all residents of "high-poverty neighborhoods" (*extreme poverty tracts* for Kasarda) are poor; according to Jargowsky, 46.9 percent were poor in 1990, up from 45.6 percent in 1970. That is, on average, just over half of the residents of "high-poverty neighborhoods" were non-poor. The non-poor residents of these neighborhoods would, however, be affected by the adverse realities (higher crime rates, poorer quality public schools, etc.). Therefore, the adverse social impact of these neighborhoods is greater than the poverty numbers themselves might indicate.

We will review the work of Cutler and Glaeser in our discussion of neighborhood effects (and social isolation) below.[23] They test those metropolitan statistical areas with at least 100,000 people (a total of 209 MSAs) for the effects of greater and lesser segregation of black residents, and find that in more segregated communities blacks are significantly worse off than they are in non-segregated communities (measuring success by high school graduation rates, employment, earnings, and not becoming a single mother). Their notion of "ghetto" is tied to segregation and not high-poverty neighborhoods as such, and they examine the effects on entire communities, not census tracts. We suppose it could be that all of the adverse social consequences they discern are crowded into certain neighborhoods of these broader communities, but their data cannot tell us this. But there is a presumption in their work that adverse consequences may affect larger areas than only high-poverty neighborhoods.

Secondly, the vast majority of the U.S. poor do not reside within "high-poverty neighborhoods" (12 percent of all the poor in 1990, up from 7 percent in 1970; 25 percent of all black poor in 1990, up from 16 percent in 1970).[24] Kasarda's work (see table 3 above) found significant growth in the number of *poverty tracts* (in which the poverty rate was at least 20 percent rather than the 40 percent figure used for *extreme poverty tracts*) within the one hundred largest central cities—evidence that a concentration among poor residents is occurring at a more general level than only among *extreme poverty tracts*.[25] Acknowledging an arbitrariness in using a 40 percent census tract poverty rate as the definition of a "high-poverty neighborhood," Jargowsky observes that neighborhoods with 20 to 40 percent of their residents in poverty "generally had a quite different look and feel than high-poverty neighborhoods do." His observation offers a helpful reminder that most central city neighborhoods are not "ghettos" or "slums" (to use his terms), but simply home for families struggling with the normal vicissitudes of life. Even so, it seems more likely that neighborhoods surrounding his "high-poverty neighborhoods" will experience more of the undesirable adversities connected with those neighborhoods than will other residential settings of our metropolitan regions—such that our notion of "inner city" is not identical with Jargowsky's "high-poverty neighborhoods" (or Kasarda's *extreme poverty tracts*).

As the previous paragraph makes clear, discerning neighborhoods that are basically normal and healthy, and neighborhoods that are unhealthy, is not an easy task. To make the cut at a 40 percent poverty rate seems too arbitrary to us. Our casual judgment is that most households within society would find more neighborhoods than those identified by the 40 percent poverty rate to be unhealthy. But what other definition does one use? The point we want to make here is that some degree of casualness surrounds this question, which then prompts us to suggest a formal (albeit operationally casual) definition of "inner-city" neighborhoods. Inner-city neighborhoods are those neighborhoods experiencing such problems that most residents, when they are able to do so, will try to relocate away from them. Such a definition—realizing that operationalizing it for empirical purposes could raise serious problems—probably reflects how most within society distinguish the "inner city" from other neighborhoods.

We lack careful evidence of the extent to which poor residents within all geographic regions of society are congregating primarily among other poor residents, and if they are—at levels below the 40 percent tipping point, at least—whether this is cause for worry. Figure 2 shows the poverty rate within society as a whole from 1959 through 1996, suggesting that a "concentration" of poverty in the 10 to 15 percent range may create no more difficulty than families face in otherwise normal circumstances. What we do not know, however, is whether our average neighborhoods are experiencing a 10 to 15 percent poverty rate, or whether—which seems the more likely reality—poverty slowly is becoming more concentrated in select neighborhoods within society.

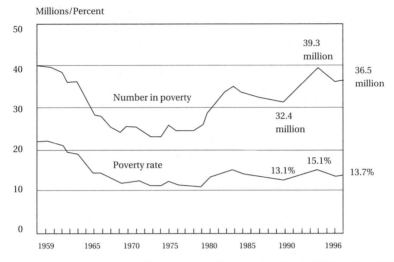

Figure 2. Overall Poverty Rate for the U.S., 1959 to 1996[26]

This brief rehearsal of the available evidence suggests to us a growing concentration of the poor in neighborhoods comprised increasingly of other poor residents—one piece of what may be growing economic stratification within society generally. The leading voice sounding the larger warning is Douglas Massey. In his 1996 presidential address to the Population Association of America he worries about a worldwide spatial concentration along economic/class lines. "The industrial revolution of the nineteenth century . . . allowed the affluent to distance themselves spatially as well as socially from the poor, causing a rise in the levels of class segregation and a new concentration of affluence and poverty."

> The juxtaposition of geographically concentrated wealth and poverty will cause an acute sense of relative deprivation among the poor and heightened fears among the rich, resulting in a rising social tension and a growing conflict between the haves and the have-nots . . . we have entered a new age of inequality in which class lines will grow more rigid as they are amplified and reinforced by a powerful process of geographic concentration.[27]

Massey ties these developments primarily to economic realities: the computerization of production, the globalization of capital and labor markets, and the fragmentation of consumer markets.[28] These forces are aided by political choices. "Insofar as the boundaries of local governmental units can be arranged to approximate the geographic contours of concentrated affluence and poverty . . . the potential for reinforcing class advantages and disadvantages will be maximized." Dire consequences of all this fall upon those living in poor neighborhoods. "The spatial concentration of affluence and poverty thus raises the odds that affluent children will receive a superior education while poor children will get inferior schooling." Massey goes on to state: "[A]s the density of poverty increases in cities throughout the world, so will the density of joblessness, crime, family dissolution, drug abuse, alcoholism, disease, and violence. . . . The concentration of affluence will create a social environment for the rich that is opposite in every respect from that of the poor." Stirring up memories of the contentious debate set off by Oscar Lewis in the 1960s over the existence of a *culture of poverty*, Massey claims "[o]nce such a subculture [of concentrated poverty] becomes established, it acquires a life of its own that contributes independently to the perpetuation of educational failure."[29]

We suspect Massey may intentionally exaggerate a bit to draw attention to potentially dangerous trends. Exaggeration contains a danger, however: that others will find evidence seemingly contrary to the warnings being sounded and then dismiss the potential dangers which may in fact be slowly accumulating. Nonetheless, along with Massey, we are worried. We suspect, for example, that the public schools in the U.S. generally may be more economically stratified today than at any time in our history.

The evidence finding a growing concentration of poverty within U.S. society seems substantial. Let us, therefore, read these signs carefully. Due to the work of Kuznets, particularly, we have come to expect a period of growing economic inequality as a (seemingly) necessary part of economic development.[30] But the U.S. in the late twentieth century already has developed economically. A sustained growth in economic inequality and poverty at this stage of economic growth poses troubling ethical questions. The degree to which we should become troubled, however, turns on the social consequences of the growing concentration—the issue we now pursue.

Consequences of a Growing Concentration of Poverty

How troubled should we be by a growing concentration of poverty within society? Our reading of the emerging evidence suggests that we should be very troubled. Those growing up within "high-poverty neighborhoods" suffer higher levels of harmful social outcomes than otherwise, which show up anecdotally in media accounts and systematically in a growing literature going generally under the rubric of "neighborhood effects." The most cited of the adverse consequences include poorer quality job information networks (and thus higher levels of unemployment and job-related idleness), high levels of welfare involvement, high levels of female-headed families and non-marital births, excessive criminal activity, and too many public schools limited in their efforts by the conditions of the homes and streets.

Urban researchers' files and shelves are filled with both heroic and tragic stories of life in the inner city. But in arranging these, how do we avoid the biases of anecdotal evidence to make a carefully balanced assessment? Fortunately, others have been at work on this issue to help us out, with Jargowsky's work proving especially insightful. The first paragraph of his book notes: "In these 'deadly neighborhoods' families have to cope not only with their own poverty, but also with the social isolation and economic deprivation of the hundreds, if not thousands, of other families who live near them. This spatial concentration of poor people acts to magnify poverty and exacerbate its effects."[31]

Using the 1990 census, Jargowsky constructs a "sociodemographic portrait" of high-poverty neighborhoods and finds considerable heterogeneity. "The most visible sign of neighborhood poverty and abandonment is dilapidated housing." Men are nearly twice as likely to be out of the labor force than is true in other neighborhoods, though the majority of residents do have jobs (which are more likely to be low-skill and service-sector jobs than in other neighborhoods). Working from data for one point in time, however, he is reluctant to observe obvious neighborhood effects. He does observe that the sharpest division between high-poverty neighborhoods and the rest of society is the prevalence of single-parent families.

Seemingly contrary to the dire picture painted on his first page, Jargowsky stresses that his larger message is that these neighborhoods are not as difficult as many think them to be. "[R]esidents of high-poverty neighborhoods are not nearly so cut off from the mainstream economy and mainstream values as popular stereotypes suggest."[32]

> The extreme poverty of ghettos and barrios notwithstanding, the popular and politically exploitable image of ghettos and barrios as places where everyone drops out of school, no one works, and everyone receives welfare, is a gross distortion of reality. Many of their residents work, albeit at lower-skill occupations, for fewer hours and lower wages. Earnings account for about the same proportion of total income in ghettos and barrios as elsewhere. Although households on public assistance are more common in these high-poverty neighborhoods, most residents receive no government assistance. Most of the teenagers are in school. People who work tend to be employed in the same industries as residents of other neighborhoods and spend about the same time commuting to their jobs. Although census data do not allow for analysis of such aspects of ghetto life as the levels of crime or drug use, the picture that emerges is not the popular image of ghetto neighborhoods as otherworldly, a class apart.

The dominant characterization of the inner city to this point has been William Julius Wilson's notion of "social isolation"[33]—an observation which has occasioned a rich and growing literature. As non-poor residents of lower-income, central city neighborhoods move away from these neighborhoods, those remaining behind slowly become isolated from the world of regularized work.[34] They no longer have good information about which firms are hiring and the types of jobs that are available. There are fewer regularly employed workers who can vouch for a young man or woman to an employer in the informal process used to select new workers. Those growing up in these neighborhoods no longer have numerous examples and role models surrounding them of men and women who regularly go off to work, making the necessary sacrifices required of stable employment.

> Thus, in a neighborhood with a paucity of regularly employed families and with the overwhelming majority of families having spells of long-term joblessness, people experience a social isolation that excludes them from the job network system that permeates other neighborhoods and that is so important for learning about or being recommended for jobs that become available in various parts of the city. And as the prospects for employment diminish, other alternatives such as welfare and the underground economy are not only increasingly relied on, they come to be seen as a way of life.[35]

In their provocatively entitled "Are Ghettos Good or Bad?" Cutler and Glaeser note how ethnic ghettos through history, especially when all income classes have lived together, have not always been damaging. Yet today, where African-Americans reside in racially segregated communities, they experience substantially worse outcomes, both absolutely and relative to whites: lower high school graduation rates, greater idleness (not in school or working), less earned income, and a higher incidence of single motherhood.[36] Clearly building on this work, Glaeser writes: "Cities throughout history have contained distinct ethnic districts. But rarely have they been so isolated and impoverished as the African-American districts found in U.S. cities today." Glaeser continues: "Economic conditions in African-American ghettos have deteriorated quite sharply over the past three and a half decades." He concludes, "The empirical evidence clearly indicates that ghettos hurt blacks a great deal."[37]

In a review article on inner cities, Mills and Lubele use a large number of general social indicators (not tied to the inner cities as such) to compare the U.S. with other societies, noting how "[i]nspection of the [evidence] makes clear that the U.S. performance is among the worst of the countries included for most of the social indicators." The link to the inner cities in this comparison is their claim that "the poor U.S. performance relates strongly to the racial composition of the population." In drawing inner city and suburban comparisons within the U.S., they note "[t]he easy conclusion is that inner city, especially minority, residents have lower incomes and more social problems than suburban residents by almost every available measure." And, "most measures of the gaps between inner cities and suburbs have widened" in recent decades.[38]

A more complete review of the inner city today than this essay can offer would weigh the evidence for each of a number of potentially adverse neighborhood effects.[39] The one piece we choose to engage is the structure of labor market opportunity facing inner-city residents, because of the strategic importance of steady employment and adequate earnings in helping people overcome other adverse conditions.[40] As with most alleged neighborhood effects, considerable debate surrounds the question of how inner-city residents view and respond to labor market opportunities—a debate that has been raging at least since John Kain's seminal article in 1968.[41] The essential questions are as follows:

- Has the demand for entry-level jobs for high-school graduates, jobs that hold a potential for either decent pay or promotion potential, changed from an earlier era, such that it is more difficult for low-skilled workers today to find good entry-level jobs?
- Has the spatial structure of jobs (specifically, the movement of decent-paying, entry-level jobs from the central cities to outlying communities of our metropolitan regions) changed in such a way that hearing of, obtaining, and regularly getting to jobs is more difficult today for the normal inner-city resident?
- Have the social changes cited above made job-related efforts more difficult today than in an earlier era?
- Do inner-city residents, and particularly young black men, encounter various forms of job-related discrimination in a way that was not true in an earlier era?

Each of these questions has become fertile ground for considerable scholarly activity.

One position, generally aligned with conservative voices, argues that anyone who really wants to work will make sure they hear of decent entry-level jobs, get hired, and find transportation to and from the jobs. As Mills and Lubele (hardly conservative voices) put it in their review article on the inner city, if blacks migrated all the way from the rural South to northern and eastern cities in an earlier day in a successful search for work, they can get from the inner city to surrounding suburban communities today.[42] A standard refrain of those sympathetic to this view is to point to the experience of recent immigrants who locate in our inner cities and are able to find work.

Wilson and his associates, observing especially the inner city of Chicago, help us understand the importance of job information networks and how, because of the relatively fewer number of employed people within these neighborhoods, young workers both fail to hear of job opportunities as effectively as in an earlier day, and do not have as many helpful role models of employed people from whom they can learn what measures must be taken to become a successful worker today. We find considerable sympathy with this view, in good part because of the substantially changed institutions of civil society today (important elements of which are the structure of the family, the existence of voluntary associations such as the local church,[43] and the informal system of moral restraint and encouragement that characterizes neighborhoods). Teens particularly need to be in reasonably close proximity to their part-time jobs. If "teen-type" jobs increasingly are found in the regions outside the central cities, then inner-city teens face greater difficulties than earlier in developing work-related experiences, along with whatever consequences attend relatively greater levels of labor-market-related idleness. This reality during one's teen years would then condition the prospects for labor market success later in life.[44]

To sort through these contending voices we must consider briefly several issues relating to the condition of labor-market opportunity confronting the inner city, an important one of which is the much-researched question of the number of good entry-level jobs within the broader economy (jobs tradition-ally found in the manufacturing sector). The emerging consensus argues that far fewer of these jobs are available today to otherwise unskilled workers; good entry-level jobs now require greater levels of education than earlier.[45] The impli-cation of this for residents of the inner city becomes obvious: the need for good educational outcomes—and thus for both good schools and an environment conducive to taking advantage of the proffered schooling. Unfortunately, nei-ther of these conditions are in place in far too many inner-city neighborhoods.[46]

Another crucial piece of the labor-market condition facing the inner city is the long debate over a "spatial mismatch" of jobs and workers—whether it is substantively harder for workers today to know about and get to jobs that are not close to one's dwelling. There are at least two parts to this question: whether good entry-level jobs within the metropolitan regions of our country are mov-ing away from the central city to the outer rings of suburban communities, and (if so) how difficult is it for inner-city residents to know about and get to these jobs? The answer to the first part of the question is clear. Over the past thirty years there has been a steady movement of good entry-level jobs away from the central cities to the shopping centers, warehouses, and manufacturing facilities now located nearer the beltways surrounding the cities. There clearly is a spatial separation between job location and inner-city dwelling. But should this spatial dimension really make much difference? Most suburban residents routinely live with lengthy commutes. Why should space matter all that much for those who truly desire to work?

The crucial part of the question then becomes the second one, whether it is substantively harder today for inner-city residents to hear about and get to jobs spatially separated from their homes. On the one side are those who argue that space itself is not a serious barrier (after all, behold the recent immigrants who manage the difficulties).[47] The opposing side points to longer and more difficult out-commutes for central city residents, made far more difficult for those who do not have cars.[48] A phenomenon like commuting time can be measured. Much more difficult to measure precisely are the consequences of the "social isolation" that has emerged—of a neighborhood environment with far fewer employed men and women than most of us have observed growing up, isolation such that the normal job information network is seriously dimin-ished and youngsters are not socialized to the world of work in the same way as those living in other parts of the nation are. Add to this the anecdotally attested reality that educational achievement often is discouraged by street life, and the existence of public schools struggling valiantly, but too often inadequately, against broader social realities not faced by schools outside these areas, and we find here a world far removed from that of the typical household outside these pockets of concentrated poverty—a world that *has* to seriously complicate the effort to find and hold a good job.[49]

One final labor market reality must be considered, the question of discrimination faced by inner-city residents. A growing number of careful observers offer us insight into the existence of likely discrimination faced by those who indicate (or even subtly signal) their residence as the inner city, a condition especially true for young black males.[50] It appears that employers may engage too often in a form of behavior economists dub "statistical discrimination." Working from a presumption (probably true) that inner-city males are more likely to have some history of criminal involvement, an employer then presumes that any young male from the inner city who applies for a job brings with him a criminal record, and consequently, the employer is reluctant to hire the young man. One might "understand" the employer's dilemma; we should struggle far more to sympathize with the frustration which a wrongfully affected young man must experience.

Working through the arguments over the precise nature of adverse social consequences facing the inner city today, and struggling to draw reasonable conclusions, we are led to the view that in a number of very specific ways times have indeed changed: that for young men and women escaping the influence and lure of a street that is less healthy in a number of ways than earlier, and gaining a good education in the process, is considerably harder today; and that because of the confluence of changed conditions discussed above, grasping labor-market opportunity is a more difficult task today than it was several decades ago. Not that overcoming the combination of these difficult circumstances cannot be done by unusually motivated and situated individuals, but the general realities of the inner city militate against such motivation and favorable settings. The institutions of civil society which provide a rich social fabric to assist the processes of growing up, getting a good education, and finding a good job, have been allowed to disintegrate over the past several decades, and this social reality, combined with a changing employment picture, explains a significantly changed opportunity structure.

With regard to the social consequences of life in the inner city, and thus the implications of a growing level of concentrated poverty, our general conclusion is a very gloomy one. The neighborhoods of our inner cities are settings in which few of us would want to bring up our children. These are not healthy neighborhoods and those who can do so typically seek to move away from them. We cannot help but conclude that life is a lot harder in these neighborhoods. Unusually strong labor-market opportunities, mixed with unusually strong families, should help young men and women growing up there to weather the adverse conditions of these neighborhoods, but they will get little help from a failing civil society. The benefit of hindsight helps us understand how crucial spatial proximity between the more and less vulnerable members of society has been throughout history for generating a healthy society. The implicit moral demands flowing from this spatial proximity have provided an important seedbed for constructing and interweaving a number of the institutions of civil society. Care for the more vulnerable by the less vulnerable has been *the*way of holding society together throughout history. What new things do we know today, and what new institutions do we propose, that would let us move away from this provision?

Construction and Use of Metropolitan Regions

Our attempt in section I of the essay is to read the signs of the times and to render a faithful account of social reality in the inner city today. Our ultimate purpose, however, is to determine moral responsibility for these social realities. In some sense the ligatures of moral responsibility must relate to the historical formation of our metropolitan regions. In what sense, if any, can an emerging structure of concentrated poverty be considered purposefully constructed, and, to the extent this could be shown, what moral implications flow from this? An alternative story could find individuals and families going about the routine business of the day, seeking to improve their situation in life, and in the process finding themselves amidst an emerging concentration of poverty that was not intended. What moral implications then arise from this historical account? We suspect truth is some mixture of these two scenarios, that the continued existence of concentrated poverty within society represents a complicated tapestry of sins of commission and of omission.

We can offer here but a thumbnail sketch of the process by which our metropolitan regions came into being.[51] With the substantial growth in economic activity and immigration throughout the nineteenth century, the central cities of the nation routinely sought and received from state legislatures the right to annex surrounding areas. After all, the central cities offered better school and water systems and there was little resistance from the annexed areas. As the nineteenth century flowed into the twentieth, more and more of the annexation efforts were contested by the surrounding suburban communities and were defeated, and soon the era of routine annexation largely ended. Starting in the 1920s, and expanding considerably in the post–World War II era, the politically autonomous suburban communities began embracing zoning regulations, an outcome of which has been to lessen the otherwise spontaneous growth of scattered-site, lower-income housing that developers were all too ready to construct. The use of government power—both that of acting on annexation requests earlier, and particularly the strategic use of various land-use controls more recently—clearly has contributed to a greater concentration of lower-income housing and peoples in the central cities of the country than otherwise would have resulted.

The mid-decades of the twentieth century also found the federal government assisting access to housing. As a generalized result, the non-poor received substantial benefits from two opportunities: (1) increased mortgage availability through the Federal Housing Administration—which, by program design, assisted housing purchases primarily in non-poor areas (thereby encouraging metropolitan sprawl); and (2) the deductibility of mortgage interest payments from one's income tax liability, the benefits of which became more substantial with the rise of tax rates during and following World War II. Housing assistance to the poor, on the other hand, primarily took the form of public housing projects, typically concentrated in central city neighborhoods. Government measures, in other words, served to enhance a spatial separation between poor and non-poor.[52]

A similar picture emerges when we consider government-supported public transportation systems. The most subsidized forms, rail lines and subways, served largely to allow suburbanites to travel more quickly to and from the central city, leaving the less subsidized bus lines to serve central city residents. The construction of interstate highways and beltways obviously favored citizens using cars, typically those residing in outlying regions.[53] Our point in this brief historical account is to suggest that the government hardly has been a neutral player in the development of the spatial structure of metropolitan regions, and that the increasing concentration of the poor is an outcome in part of legislatures responding to the wishes of the non-poor electorate. This is not necessarily to conclude that those pressuring the government to act intended to create harmful concentrations of poor citizens. A more likely scenario, to our mind, is one in which normal folk, seeking what all normal folk want (some degree of control over their environment and safety and a good education for their families), unfortunately contributed to a spatial outcome that contained harmful consequences for poorer families. And because this outcome was not intended, we should now own up to the situation and redress these harmful spatial realities.

As an outcome of the measures noted here, and fed by the understandable desires of families who could afford it to find more spacious housing and grounds in suburban areas than those allowed in the central cities, most metropolitan regions in the U.S. today are comprised of checkerboards of politically autonomous municipalities, almost uniformly with an older central city surrounded by inner- and outer-ring suburban communities. The question then becomes how households use these regions, and whether such use contributes to the emerging pockets of concentrated poverty that we now observe. We should not begin with a dark assessment, however, but note first how the political structure of our metropolitan regions contains beneficial properties. Such a structure provides households with the opportunity to move among differing municipalities, to seek the distinctive combination of local public goods and amenities which best suit the preferences of any given household. Moreover, the fact of households choosing among municipalities sends signals to municipal governors to offer more "household-relevant," local public goods at more efficient costs than otherwise would be the case. Finally, numerous municipalities means smaller communities than otherwise, thereby allowing any one household greater potential for involvement in and control over its political well-being. Most of us would agree that unless there are significant social costs created in the process, these outcomes clearly are preferred to more constrained choice, less inter-municipal competition, and larger political units. And so it is that a normative presumption often follows from observing families exercising these mobility options: that the choice presented allows greater levels of family satisfaction than in metropolitan regions comprised of fewer or even a single municipality.

These beneficial potentials embedded within politically complex metropolitan regions were anticipated in a famous 1956 paper by Charles Tiebout— and economists have come to describe our metropolitan regions as "Tiebout worlds." Tiebout's argument for the beneficial properties of complex metropolitan regions was built on clearly specified assumptions, the most important of which is that "consumer-voters are fully mobile and will move to that community where their preference patterns . . . are best satisfied."[54] That is, a family unhappy with where it presently is living has the potential to move to a number of other municipalities within its metropolitan region—a process which should force the community being left behind to consider improving its offerings of public goods.

Before we are willing to accept the contemporary structure of our metropolitan regions as obviously better than the feasible alternatives, we need to ask what the implications of a Tiebout world are for the poorer households of our metropolitan regions. In particular, how realistic is the assumption of "fully mobile consumer-voters" for lower-income households? For these families a relocation would be difficult under any circumstances. Compounding this, the presence of zoning limitations within many suburban communities (by requiring larger lot sizes and restricting the availability of rental housing) reduces the supply of available housing units and thereby raises the cost of housing from what otherwise would be the case. The presence of class- and/or race-based real-estate practices makes the picture even bleaker.[55] In other words, a presumption of "fully mobile" households (whatever this might mean) seems terribly unrealistic when the frame of reference is poor families.

The more plausible reality within our metropolitan regions, therefore, is a truncated Tiebout process, whereby non-poor households are fully mobile and the poor are not. What likely outcome would this process generate? Unfortunately, the following scenario seems all too likely. Consider a responsible municipality (call it "our community") within which are found several neighborhoods of poor residents. Anxious to care properly for its more vulnerable citizens, our community raises revenues from its non-poor residents to offer the services needed to help these vulnerable citizens overcome their difficulties. This commendable action creates two undesirable incentives, however. First, the non-poor citizens of our community will now consider moving to another municipality with fewer poor citizens in order to escape these types of tax obligations.[56]

Second, the poorer citizens from surrounding municipalities are induced to migrate to our community. In part this occurs because rental rates for housing in our community will be dampened by the process of non-poor households leaving, making our community relatively more attractive. This will occur as well because of the very competition embedded within the Tiebout process. In their quest to make themselves attractive to new households, municipalities face a competitive incentive to lessen services for their more vulnerable members and "free-ride" off of our community's efforts in this regard. To the extent they do this, they signal to their poorer citizens to relocate to those communities like "ours" which do offer such services.[57]

The spatial structure of our metropolitan regions presents more than an opportunity for families to choose among an array of housing/community options. It also places severe restraints upon the efforts of communities in which there are inner-city neighborhoods to address the adverse conditions considered above. The net result of all this is that not many "our communities" will exist within metropolitan regions, and those that do will face loss of non-poor residents and a growing concentration of poverty, and will ultimately be forced to cut back on their services to their more vulnerable citizens. This scenario seems very much like what we are observing today—and the situation appears to be deteriorating. "Flight-from-blight is thought by many writers to be self-reinforcing. The more higher income people leave inner cities for suburbs, the worse the concentration of poverty and social pathology in inner cities becomes. And the worse inner cities become, the more higher income residents move to suburbs."[58]

We draw two morals from this story. The first is the message that most economists working in this area have trumpeted for years: the redistributive function of government must be handled by the national level of government to avoid the type of competition noted here.[59] Redistributive efforts need not be handled solely by the government, however. The second moral we draw is that greater family-to-family assistance will be forthcoming when there is spatial proximity within a community between the poor and non-poor residents. This is a reality the Tiebout process seems designed to thwart, presuming (as it does) that the likely outcome of household mobility will be homogeneous municipalities along a number of different dimensions, including income levels.

In our assessment, the freedom allowed in a Tiebout world encourages an irresponsible form of both community and metropolitan governance. In its place we need to nurture an ethos of mutual assistance for those within our metropolitan regions who are most vulnerable. To work towards such an ethos we need to reconceive the moral meaning of metropolitan responsibility.

Municipal autonomy, like individual freedom, must be joined by proper forms of municipal and individual responsibility. But we anticipate the arguments to be made in section II and the conclusion of the essay. Before undertaking that discussion we should consider one final issue surrounding the state of the inner city today: the extent to which forces are at work which will undermine the growing concentration of poverty found there.

Likelihood of Correction

Our assessment of the inner city to this point has not been an encouraging one. Things are getting worse with time rather than better. The political structure of our metropolitan regions presents a difficult-to-refuse opportunity for the non-poor to avoid contact with, and responsibility for, the poor of their community by relocating to municipalities with fewer or no poor neighbors. Though each of us routinely treats metropolitan regions as social and economic wholes—living, working, shopping, worshipping, and relaxing in different communities throughout the entire region—we then retreat behind the political jurisdiction of our community of residence and bear little direct political or economic responsibility for the larger region we so freely use.

In the midst of this otherwise gloomy assessment, however, are there forces at work to provide some relief and ultimate reversal to what has been occurring in our inner cities? In this subsection we examine four categories of possible improvement: a) place-based initiatives designed to bring economic revival to the inner city; b) mobility strategies, assisting those who live within the inner city to find jobs and/or housing outside the central city; c) income redistribution measures, providing both stick and carrot for escaping the consequences of inner city life; and d) restructured government oversight to create workable forms of metropolitan responsibility for inner-city poverty. If there is any hope for improvement it most likely will come as a result of steps in each of these four categories.

Place-based Initiatives

Virtually everyone in the broader society supports economic revival within the inner city. Those who live there want to see their neighborhoods improved and job opportunities found closer to home. Those living outside these neighborhoods want these good things as well, and often find that this approach makes fewer demands upon them in the process. As much as we might hope for spontaneous economic growth, the likelihood of this happening without some form of government support, however limited, would be as unlikely in the inner city today as it has been in the broader economy throughout our history (thinking, for example, of government assistance in the funding of canals and railroads in an earlier day, and general oversight of the money supply and the investment sector at all points of our history).

Michael Porter has taken the lead in emphasizing the economic potential for private investment within the inner city today. Sharing our judgment that "[t]he economic distress of America's inner cities may be the most pressing issue facing the nation," and concerned that the existing approaches are inadequate for the task, he sees the relevant question as "how inner-city-based businesses and nearby employment opportunities for inner city residents can proliferate and grow."[60] The key is to discern and promote the "competitive advantage" of the inner city, which for most metropolitan regions includes particularly the strategic factor of location related to the downtown area and the opportunity to complement existing business "clusters" unique to a given city. Another key advantage is the flip-side of the seeming disadvantage of inner-city location noted above: a concentration of low-wage laborers. A successful strategy for attracting private investment will require efforts from business, government, and the nonprofit sector, with each being asked to break existing stereotypes about the inner city and take what appear initially to be sacrificial steps (such as hiring local laborers). With regard to government's role, the needed changes call as much for terminating measures which hinder economic development as they do for positive steps which can fuel the potential for economic revival.[61]

Porter's voice is not the only one calling for business and the broader society to pay greater attention to the inner city. The prestigious Committee for Economic Development issued a special statement in 1995, with a stronger call for governmental measures than Porter allows.[62] In April of 1997 the ninety-first American Assembly, prompted by Porter's challenge, convened to consider the theme "Improving the Economic Health of America's Distressed Communities" and issued a brief statement gathering general agreement of the conferees. Their statement assigns a greater role to inner-city community organizations and emphasizes necessary steps to improve the quality of the inner-city workforce.[63]

A broader set of initiatives can be lumped under the category of "community development,"[64] running from formal community development corporations (CDCs)—generally non-profit organizations seeking to improve life in inner city neighborhoods—through housing and producer cooperatives, to efforts to convince lending agencies to target loans for inner-city development ("greenlining"),[65] to government investments in infrastructure and subsidies (both direct and tax-based) designed to encourage private investment. This last measure, the creation of tax-based inducements (called by some "enterprise zones" and others "empowerment zones"—thus EZs) tied to specified geographic areas, has been popular across the political spectrum and seems to provide benefits to the firms using the tax breaks, but their track record in actually creating jobs and improved lives for inner-city residents has not been all that clear.[66]

In our analysis of the likely consequences of increasing levels of concentrated poverty, we argued that where the institutions of civil society are healthier the harmful impact of concentrated poverty will diminish. That insight applies with equal vigor to the hope for successful community development. We are becoming increasingly aware of the crucial role played by inner-city churches in leavening neighborhoods in a number of healthy ways.[67] This realization should not be as surprising as it seems to be for some, since members of this particular institution are encouraged by their faith commitments to sacrifice for the good of others. We read of voluntary outpourings of money and especially time by Christian neighbors (especially women) of inner-city poor families through much of the nineteenth century,[68] and we hope that a similar response might be forthcoming among Christians scattered about metropolitan regions today. Our hope is tempered, however, by the dual realizations that these non-poor neighbors today most likely have relocated to the suburbs and that a far higher percentage of women in the late twentieth century are working outside the home than were doing so in the nineteenth century.

As encouraged as we are by the enthusiasm which many bring to place-based initiatives and the desire to create economic opportunity within the inner city, our pessimistic assessment is that the deteriorating social conditions in most of these settings makes the likelihood of these efforts yielding substantial and sustainable economic improvement anytime soon terribly problematic. In his treatment of this general approach, Nicholas Lemann notes how a bottom-up, neighborhood revitalization strategy has characterized the federal commitment since the 1960s, regardless of the political party in power, and with negligible results.

> The problem is that on the whole, urban slums have never been home to many businesses except for sweatshops and minor neighborhood provisioners. . . . [T]o try to create a lot of new economic activity in poor neighborhoods is to swim against the great sweeping tide of urban life in America. Inside the ghetto, it usually does no harm—but it doesn't help much either. Outside the ghetto, though, it does a great deal of harm. Attempts at economic revitalization often take the place of other efforts that would do much more good (especially improving schools, housing and police protection), and they establish a public mission that can't be accomplished.[69]

Given decades of private and public actions which have laid the foundations for the current conditions of our inner cities, any lasting success in correcting these conditions will require sacrificial efforts by far more of us than those living in these neighborhoods. Sadly, the support for place-based initiatives too often seeks to avoid this truth, and for that reason will prove inadequate.

Mobility Strategies

With the movement of good entry-level jobs away from the central cities and the damaging impacts attending living amidst concentrated poverty, the appeal of mobility strategies becomes obvious. On the one hand, one expects little social resistance to the movement of workers to jobs, especially if the entrepreneurial efforts are privately arranged. The main question then becomes whether, given the considerable subsidies expended over the past century to provide transportation into and around the central city, subsidies which have largely benefited those living in suburban areas, the government now should undertake similar efforts to assist those living in the inner city to get to and from jobs outside the central city. We find ourselves in sympathy with a public initiative, even as we see few efforts toward this end within metropolitan regions around the nation.

On the other hand, when the mobility question involves efforts to relocate poor households away from pockets of concentrated poverty to suburban communities, great resistance has been encountered. Indeed, several state government mandates upon suburban communities to allow the construction of scattered-site, lower-income housing have prompted well-known and long-lasting legal battles.[70] The reasons for resistance need little rehashing, involving as they do some mixture of an understandable concern over deterioration in one's property values and the appearance and spread of adverse social conditions accompanying the relocation, along with a distressing desire among too many to avoid contact with and responsibility for the poorer members of our metropolitan regions. That such moves would prove beneficial for the poor of the inner city, as well as involve fewer adverse social consequences than suburban residents typically fear, finds empirical support from a court-ordered relocation effort in the greater Chicago metropolitan region (generally known as the Gautreaux program). Using controlled studies comparing inner-city families who relocated, either to other inner-city settings or to suburban communities, those who moved to the suburbs experienced improved schooling and employment outcomes.[71]

There seems little reason to believe that suburban resistance to such efforts has lifted, and we do not expect to see much movement on this front in the foreseeable future. To the contrary, the rise of private, gated communities around the country, which generally are protected from the legal mandates upon suburban communities to allow the construction of low-income housing, makes us wonder if the degree of social resistance actually is growing with time. What deserves mention, as we end this discussion, is how the private sector stands ready to provide the desired housing; the primary roadblock lies in the use of local government power to prevent this—one more reminder that government can be as much of a hindrance to redressing the difficulties of our inner cities as it can be a lever for improvement.

Income Redistribution Measures

Some observers have differentiated between place- and people-based initiatives. It seems to us that all measures ultimately are people-based. We have in mind in this category steps to assist poor families (as families) where they live without affecting directly the neighborhood around them or moving them to a job or new house. Two specific programs will concern us: welfare reform and choice-related educational initiatives (both of which are treated at more length elsewhere in this book). It has become conventional wisdom for many today to view poverty within our inner cities as an outgrowth of the welfare programs inaugurated initially in the 1930s and then modified and expanded in the 1960s. This is not the place to discuss the highly contentious issue of welfare and welfare reform.[72] Our specific concern is over the likely effects of the welfare reforms of 1996 (Personal Responsibility and Work Opportunity Act— PRWOA) upon life among the poor in the inner city. Will the strong work-mandates enacted have the desired effect of moving welfare-involved adults from heavy welfare reliance to greater independence and provide hope to their children for a better future in the process?

The relevant portions of PRWOA for our purposes are two: (a) the general requirement that virtually all welfare recipients find paid employment within specified time periods (differing by state), and (b) the use of federal block grants to states as the direct national commitment to assisting poor families. By mid–1998 the states and recipients were still working through the early phases of the time restrictions of PRWOA, and authoritative evidence of both how the states are administering the law and how families are responding to the changes remains some months away. The success of "workfare" requires changes at several levels: recipients need to prepare for, seek, and then find and hold jobs; welfare bureaucrats need to apply the proper mixture of carrot and stick; employers need to hire and then retain welfare recipients; and the now-working parents need to find adequate daycare for their children.

In general, we see no reason to doubt that inner-city welfare recipients will be any less willing to enter into the new process as recipients elsewhere in society, and we presume that welfare bureaucrats will be as determined within offices serving the inner-city as anywhere else. Moreover, we presume the difficulties of finding suitable daycare arrangements to be little different in the inner city than in other parts of our metropolitan regions—even as we worry greatly about the adequacy of this provision for lower-income parents anywhere in society. The linkage we worry most about, and which makes us question the ultimate success of workfare for the inner city, is the willingness of employers to hire welfare recipients "from those neighborhoods."[73] The unique difficulties discussed above surrounding labor market opportunities for those living within the inner city apply with particular force to the likely success of workfare in this setting.

Finding employment will be difficult enough. Tending the store at home while the parent now is away more regularly, and more weary while at home, becomes an entirely different worry which has received too little attention.[74] We are concerned about far more here than the adequacy of daycare arrangements. There is reason to worry that the children of workfare parents will receive less supervision as one outworking of welfare reform, and this potential takes on far greater significance within the environment of the inner city.

The second important piece of PRWOA for our purposes is the block grant arrangement for funding workfare. Most of the debate over this new system has turned on the implications of interstate competition for state supplements to the federal block grant, with the critics arguing that once a downturn in the economy arrives the states will cut their spending levels at the expense of their poorer citizens—the so-called "race to the bottom." This likely scenario worries us as well. When our focus becomes the inner city an added worry emerges. Given the shift in political power away from the central cities to the suburban communities, it seems likely that the poor of the inner city will be at a distinct disadvantage in the grab for the remaining federal funds.

If welfare reform holds limited obvious potential benefit to inner city residents, the second income redistribution measure we emphasize—choice-related educational initiatives—holds perhaps the greatest practical hope. It is no exaggeration to argue that publicly assisted education has been one of the most important forces over the past two centuries in positioning members of society for seizing economic opportunity.[75]

Educational choice in one form or another has been the growing edge with primary and secondary schooling for some years. Earlier steps created magnet schools, generally built around distinct educational emphases. This approach tended practically to confine choices to large school systems, which had the numbers to make the specialization possible. The most recent experiments with choice come in two versions: (a) the charter school movement, which extends the potential for greater choice within the public arena; (b) a voucher system, which allows publicly funded choice to enter the private arena as well. Both of the current versions have received considerable criticism from the existing educational establishment, which expresses an important fear that public charters or private schools receiving public funds will draw off the more motivated students and families, leaving the public schools to handle the more difficult students and students with parents who show limited concern for their education.

Our reaction to the choice-related developments is full-speed ahead on all fronts. The unpleasant but harsh reality in our inner cities is that the existing public schools are already handling primarily the more troubled and troubling students, an outcome compelling those families who can to remove their children from these schools to private or suburban public alternatives. If greater choice were made both better known and more financially available, the existing condition could only improve. We must believe that most parents want their children to succeed in their schooling and would use the possibilities afforded by greater choice to find educational options better suited to the needs of their children. We would also expect the existing public schools, initially left with fewer students on which to concentrate, to improve their performance; the new presence of greater competition should work in this direction as well. We are encouraged in our conviction by the accumulating evidence from several inner cities around the country in which greater choice has been afforded. In these cases students seem to be aided by these reforms and not harmed.[76]

Restructured Government Oversight

We examined above the incentive properties implicit in the current structure of metropolitan government, whereby non-poor citizens in communities containing inner-city neighborhoods can find, through relocation, a way not only to avoid contact with any adverse conditions attending concentrated poverty, but also to avoid being taxed locally to assist their poorer neighbors. For some observers the logical solution to this seeming dilemma has been the formation of metropolitan governments to replace the existing checkerboards of politically autonomous municipalities. Brookings Institution economist Anthony Downs long has been trumpeting this theme.[77] However rational this alternative political arrangement may appear, it long has been viewed as "un-American." This society's distinctive commitment to individual freedom has a political counterpart in its equally strong moral commitment to municipal autonomy and local control.

The politically relevant form of metropolitan governance in most parts of the country, therefore, will have to be some variation on regional governmental cooperation among otherwise autonomous municipalities. Such arrangements have long been in place in limited arenas like transportation and waste disposal, where each municipality receives obvious and direct benefits. The types of cooperation needed to address the difficult realities of our inner cities however, are likely to confront suburban communities initially with costs rather than benefits, posing major problems to their willingness to participate.[78] Achieving workable metropolitan alliances of the types needed, therefore, will require creative political entrepreneurialism. A recent example of this can be found in the Minneapolis-St. Paul metropolitan region, where strategic coalitions were built between the central city and older, inner-ring suburbs experiencing similar neighborhood difficulties, coalitions which created sufficient political muscle at the state level to force promising forms of regional cooperation.[79]

It is one thing to hold up forms of metropolitan cooperation which could bring some relief to inner-city neighborhoods. It is quite another thing to find sufficient political will to effect the needed cooperation. We observed above the likely impact of interstate competition working to limit the willingness of states to supplement federal welfare block-grants. A similar competition exists between municipalities when it comes to taxing their citizens to share the burdens of the inner cities within their metropolitan region. We see implicit evidence of this in the dogged reluctance of suburban communities over the decades to allow the construction of scattered-site, lower-income housing within their borders.

Given these political realities it is unlikely that corrective measures will be forthcoming any time soon through municipal cooperation at the local level.

Any real hope for corrective relief on the public front, therefore, will have to flow from the state or federal levels. But this only returns us to the discouraging picture we painted in the introduction to this essay, where we noted how political power at the state and national levels increasingly has shifted from the central cities to the suburban communities.[80] Our society confronts an unpleasant conundrum when it comes to conventional politics and the difficult conditions of our inner cities. Our traditional systems of moral obligation locate both private and public responsibility for the most vulnerable members of our inner cities at the local level, but the raw politics of the local setting keep thrusting the ball upward to the state and federal levels of government.

One solution to this conundrum would find citizens of metropolitan regions who are willing to sacrifice for the good of their region offering leadership, in both private and public ways, in working toward the needed corrections. Because Christian commitment is ideally built on a foundation of sacrifice we might expect the needed leadership to emanate from this faith community. For this to happen, however, greater insight into the moral meanings of local responsibility within a metropolitan context is needed—the task that becomes the main pursuit in section II of the essay.

We have struggled in this section to paint a realistic portrait of life today in the inner cities of our metropolitan regions. Despite glimmers of light, conditions in these neighborhoods are both unacceptably difficult and becoming worse. Moreover, too few forces are at work to offer a realistic hope for correction—certainly any time soon, with far too much damage done while we wait. An unfortunate realization, when we examine the historical and contemporary structure of the inner city within its larger geographic context, is that the office of government has as often been the source of the problem as it has been the means for relief and improvement. Non-poor members of society generally are more politically active and adroit, and have used their leverage through the institution of government too often at the expense of the poor.

This otherwise gloomy assessment is not ours alone; indeed, we understand it to represent the consensus view. Mills and Lubele conclude their review article on the inner city by noting how the U.S. ". . . has among the worst measures of most social indicators in the industrialized world," and that "[i]nner city-suburban gaps in social indicators are large and have increased by most measures during the last 30 years."

> A dramatic and deeply disturbing phenomenon to people who were socially and intellectually concerned in the mid–1960s, is the paucity of progress that has been made in solving socioeconomic problems and in reducing racial tensions during the subsequent thirty years. One can argue that governments have done too much or too little, but one cannot argue that the effort has been negligible. . . . The tendency of scholars has been to accept the proposition that programs have been well-intentioned, but have been badly designed or administered and to suggest changes that will improve performance. A rising tide of skeptics . . . claims

that government programs are part of the problem, not part of the solution, and that many programs should be swept away, not reformed.[81]

We end section I, therefore, by noting a reigning agnosticism among prominent experts about what socioeconomic steps we can take that will yield clear improvements. For example, Glaeser concludes a recent piece with the following observation: "While the evidence justifies action, policymakers have little idea about what should be done. In the past, many well-intentioned interventions caused more harm than good."[82] Downs adds the following to this litany of woe:

> Although the serious negative impacts of this process [of the non-poor relocating away from inner city neighborhoods to suburban communities] on society can be perceived when the process is viewed as a whole, no important actors in either the public or private sector are motivated to react to these overall consequences. Each is faced with incentives that are based on its serving the welfare of only a small, parochial part of the entire area. Therefore, it remains in the interest of all groups that enjoy mobility to continue withdrawing from the core area, further weakening its viability.[83]

We must not end our analysis of the inner city today on a negative note. To achieve the needed correction this nation must do at least two things: (a) revisit the meaning of local responsibility for the conditions of the late twentieth century, and (b) give fresh attention to what moral force will motivate citizens to sacrifice for the good of the larger society. Given who we have been as a people, an important element of both these tasks is to refine our understanding of the norms of the biblical tradition. It is our hope that Christians will be willing and able to offer crucial leadership when others within society either are unwilling or unable to do so.

The Biblical Tradition and the Good City

In this section we seek to ground our search for the appropriate meaning of moral responsibility for our inner cities in the "biblical tradition," that tradition which starts with the documents of the Bible and extends through the many efforts over the centuries by those who find this teaching authoritative to apply the biblical materials to the realities of their day. We approach the biblical tradition in the way faithful Jews and Christians have over the centuries: convinced that the God of the Bible—the Master of the universe—created this world in such a way that if we use the freedom granted us in a responsible manner we can know personally within ourselves and interpersonally within all structures of society a level of peace (what the Bible calls *shalom*) otherwise not attainable.[84] What we expect to find in our interaction with the biblical tradition are ethical emphases concerning the possible meaning of metropolitan responsibility, rather than precise institutional instructions.

An appeal to a traditional religious source for moral guidance today hardly is as capricious as some would have it. A society of more than a few related people must rely upon some moral authority that will indeed limit freedom and will coerce in various ways. The hard reality of scarcity compels this, even were all of those within society totally unselfish saints anxious to respect the desires and rights of others. Some system of moral obligation, some set of values, will be imposed upon us—ideally with our participation through a properly designed democratic process. To argue that because the U.S. is a "secular" society we should not allow public appeals to religiously based morality to constrain us strikes me as a bit silly. *Some* moral tradition and some set of values will dominate; it cannot be otherwise. We have one tax system, one welfare system, one system of property-rights assignments, and the list goes on. These systems necessarily reflect values drawn from some moral tradition. We struggle to understand why, in the public arena, moral traditions lacking direct rootage in traditional religious conviction should be granted privileged status. To the contrary, the relevant and helpful discussion would ask which of the various moral traditions, and which set of values, offer greater scope for adjudicating among what clearly is a growing cultural/moral diversity within society. In this dynamic process values drawn from traditional religions should hardly be ruled out of bounds. If only because they have stood the test of time, it may well be that many of the values commended in traditional religions offer less capricious and more respectful social mores and structures than many competing alternatives.

The arguments of this section can be summarized as follows. The consistent testimony of the biblical tradition charges the less vulnerable members of society with a special concern for the more vulnerable members (what some have called a "preferential option for the poor"), a responsibility carrying particular significance for those less vulnerable members who live in reasonable proximity to the more vulnerable in our midst. Working from the form in which this responsibility was construed in the living context of early Israel, we conclude that reasonable proximity extends throughout the "economic region" within which one dwells and normally functions: a geographic space which for most of us would comprise the metropolitan regions of which we are a part— and thus the commended norm today of "metropolitan responsibility." God issues a call today, as he did in Ezekiel's time, for "anyone among them who would repair the wall and stand in the breach before me on behalf of the land" (Ezek. 22:30, NRSV). This plea must be heard today as more than a good metaphor. We need to discern how a breach in the (city) wall, which exposes the most vulnerable within the city to grave harm, does indeed affect adversely the broader land (and certainly the metropolitan regions of our land). The moral weight of the plea falls heaviest upon those who live by the authority of the biblical tradition, and thus Christian men and women should be taking the lead in treating metropolitan regions morally as in fact we all do economically.

In our quest for moral insight we draw on biblical materials that are in some cases at least three millennia old. An understandable and appropriate question to ask, therefore, is how these materials can offer useful guidance for the late twentieth century and a vastly more complex socioeconomic setting. A systematic answer to this question cannot be constructed within the confines of this project. Our understanding of what the biblical writers and compilers intended is that the Pentateuch provides an ethical foundation: that within the numerous legal and extralegal provisions designed to inform life in early Israel, God encoded ethical emphases or guidelines that form a normative foundation which then finds further expression and refinement in the remainder of the Bible. These ethical guidelines, informed by helpful commentary from the Jewish and Christian faith communities over the centuries which have sought application to their contemporary settings, are to be held up before all nations as a measuring rod for discerning what are just and righteous institutions and behaviors. Indeed, I wonder if the proffered moral insight may well have been delivered in "primitive" socioeconomic settings *precisely* because we could grasp ethical nuances therein that would be masked in more complex settings.[85]

We conclude this subsection of the essay with the two main arguments we proffer herein. First, in our inquiry into the biblical tradition to bring fresh moral insight to the meaning of local responsibility today, we should pay particular attention to the pentateuchal materials. Second, a basic intention of God's relationship with faithful Jews and Christians is greater *shalom* for all peoples and nations. In this regard, those of us committed to the biblical tradition must at least consider how our deportment will be perceived by and bring blessings to others. We submit that our responsibility extends beyond this, however, and includes entering the various "public squares" of society to work towards behaviors and structures that help achieve God's desired *shalom* for this world. We do not in any sense undertake these tasks in a triumphalist way, knowing as we do how easily sin can tarnish even our most well-meaning efforts. But undertake them we must, contending respectfully with others for means and ends that—after due diligence in searching the counsel of the biblical tradition—we deem will please the God who created and loves this world.

The Significance of Spatial Proximity

Without embracing, necessarily, particular (exploitation) theories about how poverty arises within society or distinct (generally socialistic) measures for responding to poverty—arguments which occasionally attend the theological affirmation dubbed a "preferential option for the poor," we do affirm the basic ethical thrust of this affirmation: that the presence of a demeaning poverty within society should exert a prominent claim upon our moral sympathies and should demand that we act to remove this scourge. We find this ethical emphasis to echo the systematic teaching of the Bible. The (covenantal) foundations of this instruction are laid in a number of pentateuchal passages specifying precise measures for assisting households facing difficulty: the use of compassionate loans (Exod. 22:25–27; Lev. 25:35–38; Deut. 15:1–11), ultimate release from an indebtedness that entraps one (Exod. 21:1–11; Lev. 25:8–55; Deut. 15:12–18), access to fallow-year fields and gleanings (Exod. 23:10–13; Lev. 19:9–10, 23:22, 25:1–7; Deut. 24:19–22), and the right to receive a part of the third-year tithe (Deut. 14:28–29, 26:12).

The pentateuchal instruction finds both affirmation and illustrative application to a number of social settings in prophetic commentary (consider Ps. 113:5–8; Isa. 10:1–4; Ezek. 16:49–52; and Amos 3:6–10, as representative of numerous other texts). Consistent with the claim of Jesus in Matthew 5:18, the "Law and the Prophets" provided the moral foundations for Christian teaching as well (Luke 16:19–31; 2 Cor. 8:1–15; 1 John 3:16–20), and we read in the Acts and elsewhere of the struggle by members of the early Christian community to live out these teachings in practical ways (Acts 2:42–47; 6:1–4, 1 Tim. 5).

The relevant questions surrounding this instruction concern not its central ethical thrust but how the counsel should be applied in practice. Who in fact were the most vulnerable members of society, how and how much should they be assisted, and what expectations should be placed upon them in the process of assisting them? Which less vulnerable members should bear this responsibility: only extended family members of the adversely affected persons, all households within the economic region surrounding those in need, or all less vulnerable members within the greater society generally? Should the assistance be effected solely or primarily through private charity, or are there grounds for government-mediated redistribution?

In our effort to grasp the unique nature of moral responsibility in early Israel, and what God intended for his people and for us today, it will prove helpful to recreate as best we can how the specified provisions were lived out in practice. To do so, we trace out initially the socioeconomic setting within which hardship would arise.[87] The pentateuchal narratives and legislation picture a primitive, agricultural, subsistence economy.[88] Productive property (primarily land) was held privately by extended-family units, but these property rights were attenuated by obligations to the broader community. For example, normal productive activity on a piece of land was to cease one year out of seven with the natural growth made available to the more vulnerable members of the community. Furthermore, any one piece of land was not to be alienated more than fifty years from the extended family of original ownership (Lev. 25).

The basic social unit was the extended family (*beth'ab* or "house of the father") consisting of a father/elder, mother, unmarried children, married sons with their wives and children, any servants, and possibly a few aliens (or sojourners)—all of which could amount to as many as fifty members or more, but could also be quite small (e.g. Naomi and Ruth). Of almost comparable social importance was a larger unit, the *mishpahah,* or what Gottwald calls a "protective association of extended families."[89] The most likely occasion for the development of a *mishpahah* would be the aging of an extended family, as each of the sons becomes the head of his own *beth'ab,* with grandchildren and (less frequently) great-grandchildren, all typically situated within the same local geographic region. The members of different *beth'avoth* would be brothers at the patriarch level and cousins of different degrees at the lower levels.[90]

Israelites generally married within the *mishpahah;* members of a *mishpahah* could exact retribution or redeem a member sold into slavery, and local justice was performed by the elders of the *beth'avoth* within a *mishpahah* (elders at the gate). DeGeus writes: "The *mishpahah* was the principal form of organization and social grouping in ancient Israel, and . . . for landowning Israelites it practically coincided with the town."[91] A *mishpahah* could consist of twenty to fifty *beth'avoth*[92] and thus would possibly comprise a small village or extended neighborhood of a larger city.

We find, then, a land-based subsistence economy with a fringe of market-based earnings and primitive but growing commercial and capital markets.[93] In this agrarian setting substantial variation in income would occur due to varying weather and other natural events (insect, disease, and predator damage), with sickness and injury frequently enough hindering productive activity. In addition to the economic provisions for the land and emerging markets, there would have been inheritance practices and transfer obligations.

To the extent that there was a governing authority in the modern sense, it was comprised, for most citizens, of the heads of the *beth'avoth* (the elders) of one's village or city, who typically convened at the main gate of the city and interpreted and enforced God's law (the so-called law of Moses).[94] A telling passage from the Book of Job offers rich insight into the normative nature of the Israelite governing authority in early Israel:

> When I went to the gate of the city and took my seat in the public square, the young men saw me and stepped aside and the old men rose to their feet; the chief men refrained from speaking and covered their mouths with their hands; the voices of the nobles were hushed, and their tongues stuck to the roof of their mouths. Whoever heard me spoke well of me, and those who saw me commended me, because I rescued the poor who cried for help, and the fatherless who had none to assist him. The man who was dying blessed me; I made the widow's heart sing. I put on righteousness as my clothing; justice was my robe and my turban. I was eyes to the blind and feet to the needy; I took up the case of the stranger. I broke the fangs of the wicked and snatched the victims from their teeth.

> Job 29:7–17

Job joins the other elders before the people in the "public square." In such capacity righteousness and justice are the legal norms, clearly requiring special concern for more vulnerable members of the community. These "judges" hardly were passive officials. Job saw himself as eyes to the blind, feet to the lame, and father to the needy. The picture is one in which the local governing authority not only issued decisions on contested claims, but actively intervened to make sure that righteousness and justice characterized the community. The normative standard for all this—the standard that decreed righteousness and justice and that specified detailed applications in a vast number of cases—was God's law.

In its earliest history the documents tell us that Israel was to have no permanent central government, neither king nor standing army, making her unique among the nations of that time (and ours).[95] Equally unique was the instruction that those responsible for Israel's cult (the sons of Levi) were to be granted no allotment of land and were to depend upon voluntary offerings (Num. 18:8), accompanied by numerous admonitions to other Israelites not to forsake them (Deut. 12:19). It seems likely these provisions were intended to avoid the twin dangers (seen frequently in the surrounding nations of the time) of concentrated economic and political power: the use of power for selfish ends to the detriment of common Israelites (2 Sam. 11; 1 Kings 21; Amos 2:6–10; 5:12), and the merging of political-economic power with the cult, thereby wrongfully appropriating the true King's name for unrighteous ends.[96]

Despite the warning of God through Samuel (1 Sam. 8), Israel succumbed to the temptation to be like the surrounding nations and embraced the monarchy. Israel's king, however, was to be different from those other kings. Just as with the city and village elders, Israel's king should be a steward of the covenant conditions of the law (Deut. 17:14–20) working to establish justice and righteousness (1 Kings 10:9), with special concern for the most vulnerable members of society (Ps. 72:1–4, 12–14; Jer. 22:15–17). He was to protect property rights so that each family could sit under its own vine and fig tree (Mic. 4:4).

Within this socioeconomic setting of early Israel, how were households facing hardship to be assisted? Were an otherwise able-bodied Israelite household to fall on hard times, the most likely form of assistance would have been a compassionate loan from another member of one's *beth'ab*—the implicit presumption of a loan being that the family could generate sufficient surplus beyond their own needs to repay the principal of the loan (an unlikely outcome for households weakened through some circumstance). If other family members were unable to manage this, the next appeal would be to an economically viable *beth'ab* of the same *mishpahah,* perhaps an uncle on the father's side (Num. 27:9–11). Access to gleanings may well have been reserved for less economically viable households suffering hardship, with the presumption once again that this would start with the fields, vines, or trees of one's *beth'ab* and then extend out to those of uncles and cousins.[97] Beyond the specific provisions noted above, economically less vulnerable members of society were admonished generally to care for the poor and needy in ways such as sharing feast days with widows, orphans, and aliens (Deut. 16:11–14). This is taught clearly in pentateuchal passages like Exodus 22:21–24, Deuteronomy 15:11, and 24:10–15; it is affirmed throughout the Old Testament in passages referring to the "poor and needy," and it stands implicit in God's whole treatment of Israel (Deut. 6:10–13, 8:7–9:6).

Only when appeals for assistance within one's *mishpahah* were exhausted would a household facing hardship approach others within their immediate region, more than likely making some demand upon local government officials in the process. Within the confined social reality of most villages and cities those households experiencing severe hardship would have been known, with someone calling the situation to the attention of the elders gathered at the gate. Facing such an appeal, how should they then respond? The stipulations of the law (and general covenant obligation) in this regard were clear—the community should not allow a family to be devastated by economic adversity. Whether one or several of the elders would become "eyes to the blind and feet to the needy" (Job 29:7ff) directly, or admonish other members of the community to do so, it seems hard to imagine how cases like these could have avoided some form of local governmental oversight.

We should not be surprised, therefore, to observe Nehemiah's response to the returned exiles when (amidst rebuilding the ruins of Jerusalem) he was confronted with practices which violated the pentateuchal instructions at issue before us:

> When I heard their outcry and these charges, I was very angry. I pondered them in my mind and then accused the nobles and officials. . . . What you are doing is not right. Shouldn't you walk in the fear of our God to avoid the reproach of our Gentile enemies? I and my brothers and my men are also lending the people money and grain. But let the exacting of usury stop! Give back to them immediately their fields, vineyards, olive groves and houses, and also the usury you are charging them. . . . Then I summoned the priests and made the nobles and officials take an oath to do what they had promised. . . . At this the whole assembly said, "Amen," and praised the Lord. And the people did as they had promised."
>
> Nehemiah 5:6–13

Nehemiah both accuses and gives a mandate to the "nobles and officials"—to carry out their responsibilities, personally and publicly, toward the most vulnerable members of society. Similarly, we are told that a proper king and ruler does not pursue women, drink wine or crave beer, lest he forget what the law decrees and deprive the oppressed of their rights; in an active sense, he should speak up for those who cannot speak for themselves and defend the rights of the poor and needy (Prov. 31:1–9).

In most cases the level of governmental oversight would have been local.[98] Even with the descriptions of a king pleasing to God through his active concern for the poor and needy (Ps. 72:1–4; Jer. 22:15–17; Prov. 31:1–9), the likely extent of his oversight probably was the capital city in which he served as chief among the elders rather than over the entire land—testimony, once again, to a local expression of government engagement. Though the authority of this text for our purposes may be questionable, there is at least one case in which the central government acted to prevent grave social harm to an entire nation of vulnerable families. We refer to parts of the Joseph narrative in the latter chapters of Genesis. Having ascended to great authority under the Pharoah, this son of Jacob acted to preserve the developing people of Israel (along with other peoples) from the ravages of severe famine. The narrative is not without its troubling elements, particularly the *quid pro quo* for assistance to the Egyptians: the concentration of all landed property into the hands of the Pharaoh.[99]

We summarize our brief attempt to reconstruct the likely "system" for assisting households facing hardship in early Israel with the following attributes. Those poor who were "really in need" (the *'ani* and *'ebyön*—Hebrew terms for the "poor and needy" persons mentioned so frequently in biblical passages— as apart from those the Bible calls idlers or sluggards) were deserving of assistance; indeed, the reference in a number of texts to the "rights" or "cause" of the poor (Exod. 23:6; Deut. 24:17, 27:19; Job 36:6; Ps. 140:12; Prov. 29:7, 31:9; Isa. 10:2; Jer. 5:28, 22:16) would seem to create binding legal significance for a number of the provisions. A compassionately administered work expectation placed before those receiving assistance was fully consistent with the biblical provisions. The standard to be used in providing assistance was sufficiency for need, with a liberal rather than niggardly interpretation of that standard.[100] The ultimate objective of this network of law-like provisions for assisting the most vulnerable members of early Israelite society was maintaining and (where necessary) restoring the economic viability of the basic family unit.

The question needing greater clarification, if we are to lift moral insight from the biblical tradition to address the troubling realities of our inner cities, asks whether those who live within a "prudent social and economic reach" of the most vulnerable bear a greater responsibility for offering assistance than do those who live beyond this prudent reach. Were a vulnerable person's (extended) family unable to provide adequate assistance, should the next appeal be to those less vulnerable persons living within a prudent social and economic reach of the vulnerable person, rather than to the broader society as a whole?

It should be obvious from what we have presented concerning early Israel, that the primary location of moral responsibility for the most vulnerable members of society lay at the local level, both through private and public responses. To the extent we intend to gain broader moral insight from these materials, an obvious question becomes whether what we find here reflects anything more than the given state of economic development of that time and the then- existing social arrangements. Extended and related families living in close spatial proximity are the exception today rather than the norm, certainly in economically developed societies and increasingly in all. Early Israel had far poorer means of movement and communication than we do today. Can we really presume that forms of moral accountability suitable for early Israel offer useful insight for us today?

Granting the legitimacy of this question, our hermeneutical commitment compels us to ask whether greater ethical insight for our contemporary struggles may be found in Scripture than we might normally presume. Our first response, therefore, is to observe how the law code and surrounding narratives instructing early Israel, which both enjoined a systematic redressing of demeaning poverty and called upon *all* members of society to take an active part in this, was in fact *not* the normal and expected social reality for that time and place. Far more typical was a social setting in which the least vulnerable sought a safe distance, socially and economically, from the more vulnerable members of society, and used their influence to structure society in ways to maintain and further this. Our insight in this regard is not only a matter of comparing known law codes. The archaeology of early Israelite cities bore marked differences in precisely this regard, with fewer obviously privileged neighborhoods. Our point here is that to affirm in law and practice a high degree of local responsibility among all citizens for the more vulnerable households was not at all typical of the era and context.

Secondly, the lived experience of early Israel demonstrates the fundamental importance of family responsibility. Though clearly manifest most typically in a local context, the responsibility for family members was crucial enough to transcend local space—at least if we consider the examples of both Abraham (Genesis 24) and Rebecca (Genesis 27:46ff), who sent their sons to related *mishpahah*-members in distant lands to find spouses. Similarly, were we to situate the moral responsibilities embedded within the pentateuchal provisions within the world of the New Testament, the obligations falling to members of a *mishpahah* would seem to shift to members of the church (the world-wide body of those committed to the Lordship of Jesus Christ). We can deduce this (among other possible appeals) from Paul's admonition to the Christians in Corinth to give sacrificially for their more vulnerable fellow church members in Jerusalem (1 Corinthians 8). Most of us would affirm a fundamental commitment to family responsibility today, even as we observe how often it seems to be lacking in practice.

Third, given the virtually universal commitment to local responsibility in the provisions designed for early Israel, we are compelled to wonder whether there exist distinct social dynamics for any society at any point in history that can be found only at this spatial level of moral responsibility. Does, for example, personal assistance carry with it interpersonal attributes which serve to lessen the potential for demeaning dependency among more vulnerable households? When the less vulnerable invest their time are they then more likely to invest their money, such that greater levels of assistance will be forthcoming through a more heightened level of local responsibility than has been evident in the late twentieth century? Could it be that when individuals become active personally in offering assistance to the most vulnerable households within their prudent social and economic reach, that character is formed (on both sides of the relationship) in ways otherwise not possible, that, in other words, a commitment to exercising individual responsibility in this way represents the necessary counterpart of a commitment to individual freedom, and that individual freedom wanes when this responsibility is relaxed?

In our pondering of the prudent benefits of local forms of moral responsibility for our most vulnerable households, and observing therein an ideal of voluntarism, we emphasize as well how the controlling moral instruction lifted from the biblical materials does not foreclose the strategic mediation of government in standing ready to assure that an adequate level and appropriate forms of assistance are forthcoming. To be sure, government mediation can become problematic as well and contribute to the problem rather than lessening it, but it must be seen as a potential part of our normative response.

We have argued on biblical grounds the fundamental importance of a local responsibility for the most vulnerable households in our midst. We make this argument within a contemporary world of economically developed societies in which local responsibility increasingly has been allowed, if not encouraged, to lapse. Does our modern approach represent a wise shift, given the obviously changed socioeconomic conditions brought on through industrialization and urbanization? Or could it be we have lost something in the shifting spatial location of moral accountability, struggling as we have in our attempts to both understand and respond institutionally to these revolutionary social forces? At the least, the biblical tradition would have us raise these questions.

The Moral Reach of Spatial Proximity

We have used the phrase "prudent social and economic reach" to describe the spatial limits of moral accountability. But what sweep of geography does this notion cover? In our search to locate the proper meanings of moral responsibility for the difficult realities found in the inner cities of our metropolitan regions today, we need more refined insight. Local responsibility for the most vulnerable households in society is commended to us, but what spatial limits should this responsibility know? What, in practice, is the prudent social and economic reach for which we should bear relatively greater moral accountability? My attempt to address these questions begins with the socioeconomic setting of early Israel and the likely relationship of the central (walled) city to the region surrounding it.

Two works provide the most detailed understanding of the city in early Israel, both entitled *The City in Ancient Israel:* one by Frank Frick and the other by Volkmar Fritz.[101] We use the arguments of these two works as a foundation to organize our presentation. Frick writes self-consciously in the context of nineteenth- and twentieth-century anthropological conceptions of the city and wonders, accordingly, how much we impose modern analytical categories and the urban consequences of industrialization back upon pre-modern societies. Removed as we are in the late twentieth century from an earlier fascination with the modern city, we typically associate urban areas with the undesirable social side-effects of industrialization. Consequently there has developed a tendency to associate many of life's problems generally with urbanism and, in reaction, to romanticize village life, in the biblical world as well as today.

For example, Gottwald understands early Israel to be primarily a rural/village people organized administratively along tribal (sh*e*vātîm) lines, as "... a territory within which the [tribe] lived, the settlements and fields which it occupied and cultivated and grazed, and the natural resources of the region which it exploited."[102] With the advent of the monarchies, Gottwald argues, David ruled initially through the established tribal units, but Solomon then abolished these for more hierarchic structures, with the ultimate outcome being a tension between two "antagonistic morphemes": urban statism and rural tribalism. Urban statism, essentially borrowed from the pre-existing Canaanite society, represents social and economic stratification with power centered in the city, which then exploits the surrounding villages and region to supply the desires of the urban elite. As helpful as we generally find his work we sense Gottwald envisions an antagonism between city and village/region which fails to offer a plausible rendering of the lived experience of early Israel even into the era of the monarchies.

Undertaking a search for the historic meaning (etymology) of "city" ('*îr*) Frick searches the probable languages of origin and concludes that "the word for 'city' includes within its general frame of meaning the connotation of protection for its inhabitants and those of the immediate environs." Observing that the predominant way of understanding the city in the Old Testament was "as a walled place of refuge," he summarizes:

> [I]t can be said that the word '*îr* covers the following range of meaning in the Old Testament: (1) a fortified structure for defensive purposes; (2) a walled, permanent settlement; (3) a quarter within such a settlement, especially the citadel containing the temple of temples and the administrative quarters; and (4) in a more comprehensive political and economic sense, the city includes the citadel, the fixed settlement, and is the center of and marketplace for the surrounding secondary settlements of a less permanent nature.[103]

The city represented, therefore, protection or security for those who lived and worked both within its walls and in its surrounding environs. The biblical writers typically use the word "city" for walled settlements, in contrast to secondary settlements or villages (häsër), which are not so much smaller but of less permanent nature, and dependent upon the city within whose protective region they lay, such that we find a number of references to a particular "city and its villages" or a "city and its daughters" (Num. 21:25, 32:42; Josh. 15:32–62, 18:24,28, 19:6–23; Judg. 1:27; 1 Chron. 4:33; Isa. 42:11; Jer. 49:2; Ezek. 26:6). "The mother, while having the primary function of producing children, also had considerable authority over her daughters, hence the analogical control of a mother-city over the dependent daughter-villages. The mother had major responsibilities in caring for the children, and similarly, the city provided protection for its dependent daughter-villages."[104]

Frick observes an Israelite society remaining predominantly pastoral throughout the period of history seen in the literature of the Old Testament, and displaying an interdependence between rural and urban rather than a conflictual or exploitative relationship. "[T]he city proper and its hinterland, including the city's fields and villages was a self-contained, self-sufficient independent unit of human society where sovereignty was vested in the city dwellers and their representatives."

> [C]onsiderable evidence [exists] in the Old Testament for a "commuting" pattern on the part of urban dwellers. This pattern involved the city as a "bedroom community," to use contemporary parlance. A not inconsiderable proportion of the city's lower class would leave the city in the morning to spend the daylight hours as agricultural laborers [and] then return to the city for the night. Thus, a rigid rural-urban pattern cannot be imposed upon the Old Testament.[105]
>
> We have already asserted, on philological grounds, that the city and its hinterland formed a unit. Here, this unity is seen from an economic perspective. The inhabitants of the city are basically dependent on the produce from the fields immediately surrounding the city, with some goods being brought in from a greater distance . . . As the population of a city grew, the acreage of the fields on which the city depended had to increase. . . . As this expansion continued, the fields soon became so distant from the city that they could not be protected. The result in this instance was a movement from the city to the villages, or alternatively, the establishment of "cities" (i.e., fortified settlements) which were still subservient to and allied with the "mother city.[106]

In seeking a possible distinction between "fields" and "pasture lands" Frick speculates on the possible size of the economic region surrounding a city. Working from the presumed speed of oxen and donkeys, he discerns a feasible limit of four hours a day "commuting" time. Hence, the ". . . periphery of the city's cultivated fields should not be much more than four miles distant. This limit could be extended in peaceful times when the security provided by the city was not necessary and more of the population could move out of the city and establish temporary residence in villages."[107]

In his description of the city in early Israel, Volkmar Fritz relies more than Frick upon archeological evidence. Tracing the evidence for the rise and fall of city life in Palestine, he observes radical changes in the nature of the city around 1200 B.C. (roughly the time an Israelite presence appears in Palestine): a breakdown in the system of independent, Canaanite city-states and a notable rise in the number of non-urban settlements lying mostly outside the vicinity of the former urban centers, particularly in the mountainous eastern part of Palestine. "Instead of the few urban centres which held sway over the respective surrounding area through deployment of their power, the country is now covered by small villages, which subsist through the cultivation of fields and meadowland in the immediate vicinity."[108] These agricultural settlements ("an extraordinary phenomenon" for the time, Fritz notes) were constructed less with defense in mind than access to fields and herds outside the settlements. Most of the houses within these settlements were of roughly equal size, and their architecture no longer bore a Canaanite character.

If Frick stresses continuity between rural and urban, and between village and city, Fritz observes a sharper break between village and city and—similar to the arguments of Gottwald noted above—associates the latter with the rise of the monarchies in early Israel.[109] Whether in village or city, however, Israel's settlements were unique for the time in their lack of careful planning and relative absence of prominent "public" buildings (temples, palaces, and civic and defense-related buildings). Of two excavated villages Fritz writes: "The completely irregular pattern of streets does not allow recognition of any planning; the only concern here was with access to the houses." He also writes: "The extremely irregular method of building is conspicuous. . . . Public buildings are absent, and what was once the temple is subdivided by means of partition walls and used as a place of dwelling."[110]

With few exceptions the monarchic-era cities of early Israel displayed these same attributes, creating at least questions about the presumed differences that arrive with the monarchy. Kinneret was built during David's reign, with a palace at the center, extraordinarily strong fortifications, and with what seemed to be "a special planning concept for the city"—but this was the exception. More typical was Megiddo, which grew out of a Canaanite city. "In contrast to the ordered layout of the palace precinct, the rest of the city only shows minimal signs of planning. The pattern of streets cannot be discerned, and a particular set of planning precepts does not seem to have been followed." Even after further building of the city under Solomon (1 Kings 9:15), with buildings for administration, ". . . when compared with the royal building measures in the [Canaanite] city of the ninth century, the number of buildings with an official function was minimal."[111]

In early Israelite cities in general, beyond such basic signs of planning as putting a single gate at the lowest point of the city (to allow proper drainage) and assuring an adequate water supply, "[t]here was no further planning behind the system of streets, which can rather be described as twisted alleys between the rows of houses" (140). Cities with military or administrative functions showed more signs of both planning and public buildings, but (once again) far less than in other cities of that era. Cities other than these "were self-governing in all legal and economic matters. This self-government is a legacy of the tribal constitutions of the pre-state period, according to which both the tribe as well as the smaller units of clan [*mishpahah*] and family [*beth'ab*] had a right to independent decision-making in all matters which affected them."[112]

Fritz joins Frick in understanding the economic structure of the early Israelite city. Most city inhabitants were farmers who cultivated fields and gardens in the vicinity of the city, with fields found in the valleys and plains, vineyards and olive groves on terraced slopes, and animals grazed farther up the slopes. "Since no craftsmen's workshops have been discovered in cities to date, it has to be assumed that the workshops of both the potters and smiths must have been situated outside the city. Both of these crafts rely on large quantities of combustible material, and thus the production sites may have been situated near an area of forest."[113]

The general portrait offered us in these works is reflected well in the book of Ruth. Boaz, whom we presume to be a town elder (Ruth 4:1) and hardly a peasant-farmer being exploited by city aristocrats, lives in the city and goes out to his fields to oversee his work crews (2:4, 9). Ruth and Naomi also live in Bethlehem and Ruth goes out to glean (2:2) and then brings the gleanings into the city to her mother-in-law (2:18). When they are cleared to marry, the community's affirmation may well suggest that Ephrathah was one of the village "daughters" of Bethlehem (4:11). When contested issues arose, such as the status of Boaz as the kinsman next in line to marry Ruth—and thereby to assume whatever responsibilities this entailed—these were to be handled at the city gate, that place where people went in and out to conduct the normal affairs of life (4:2).

The conception of early Israel that emerges, therefore, is of a series of largely independent economic regions containing a relatively large walled city near the center and a number of villages spreading out from the city which existed in a symbiotic relationship with the city. Many of those who worked the lands surrounding the city lived within the city and moved in and out of the city gate(s) to conduct the normal affairs of life. At least a number of shepherds would have slept in makeshift settlements beyond the clustered housing of larger villages and cities. The need for water, in an area of the Middle East experiencing a few days annually of heavy rainfall, meant the functioning economic region needed to be broad in order to gather as much rainfall as possible—and that residents would not want to dwell too far from the limestone-lined cisterns that held the water. One strategy to prevent wasteful water run-off during the few rainy days was terracing, a labor-intensive process most likely requiring cooperative efforts—certainly within the economic region of a given city and its villages, and possibly among contiguous "mothers and their daughters." It seems probable that this reality would have called for larger rather than smaller regions so as to assure a sufficient number of laborers for terracing.

In an era without modern fertilizer it seems likely that extensive use was made of fallowing, a practice requiring more lands than otherwise (because some fields lay idle in any one year). Moreover, some land would have been committed to olives, figs, and grapevines, and could not be used throughout the year for other crops. In other words, the whole lifestyle and mindset of a people who "cut their teeth" in the hill country of eastern Palestine would include relatively large and economically coherent regions, with densely packed villages and cities and surrounding lands necessary for growing, grazing, and water recovery.[114]

That the city lay at the center of a number of villages (suburbs?) which then shared responsibility for the welfare of the city, finds expression in an interesting case study within the biblical record, the rebuilding of the walls around Jerusalem as overseen and recorded by Nehemiah (see especially Nehemiah 3). From the detailed biblical account of who was involved in this project we read that those who lived in the city labored on this project, and with what appears to be special concern for sections of the wall nearest their houses— testimony, it would seem, for bearing greater responsibility for the economic and social space closest to one's residence. The task, however, was not only for those living within the protective custody of Jerusalem's walls. Laborers from a substantial region surrounding Jerusalem are mentioned as well: the Tekoities (Neh. 35:5, 27) from south of the city; men from Gibeon and Mizpah (Neh. 35:7, 15, 19) to the northeast; inhabitants from Zanoah (v. 13) to the east, residents from Beth-zur and Keilah (vv. 16–17) to the southeast, along with priests "from the surrounding region" (v. 22). Williamson observes that workers from throughout the five administrative districts comprising the province in which Jerusalem lay (the metropolitan region of greater Jerusalem?) were involved in the project, suggesting an area "no more than 40–50 kilometers wide [and possibly 30 kilometers high]."[115]

We have attempted to portray the likely structure of the city in early Israel and its relationship to the region surrounding it, in a quest for the limits of spatial proximity and the meanings of moral responsibility for households facing hardship. The main question driving us in this pursuit is how this people construed the "prudent social and economic reach" within which greater moral accountability adhered. As a practical matter, less vulnerable families would have been most likely to make compassionate loans to those within their immediate neighborhood, and those needing to glean would have sought out fields not too distant from their dwelling. These practical realities accepted, the spatial reach of moral responsibility more than likely encompassed the entire economic region within which a family *(beth'ab)* lived.

From all we can tell the coherent economic unit was also the dominant political unit as well. As Frick observes, ". . . the Old Testament nowhere delineates laws regarding city-village relationships, nor is the village an entity for which there is a precise definition."[116] Certainly in the pre-monarchic era of Israel's history the most likely political unit would have been the same informal economic units just reviewed, with any broader affiliation being with the tribe with which the peoples of the region were aligned. The biblical documents suggest that under Solomon's reign particularly, the land of Israel was organized along more structured political lines (1 Kings 4:7–19), albeit these most likely reflected the extant regions of a "city and its villages" without necessarily honoring the tribal affiliations. An economic whole becomes a moral whole, a reality reflected nicely in the following text from Deuteronomy: "All these blessings will come upon you and accompany you if you obey the Lord your God: You will be blessed in the city and blessed in the country" (Deut. 28:2–3).

We conclude, therefore, that moral responsibility for households facing hardship extended beyond one's immediate neighborhood to the broader economic region within which a family was situated: a moral relationship of interdependence between central (walled) city and surrounding villages and fields, in which the central city/mother bore protective custody over the surrounding villages/daughters. The objective of this symbiotic relationship was the security and protection of all those who lived within the economic region, a general obligation upon *all* Israelites within the region complementary to the more particular responsibility carried by less vulnerable households.

In our quest for added insight into the moral meanings of spatial proximity, let us go beyond socioeconomic structure and explore the meaning and significance of otherwise mundane phenomena like bricks and mortar. We consider here three related elements of the Israelite city: its walls, main gate, and seemingly unplanned layout. Relatively little need be said about the nature and function of city walls, given their obvious defensive function. Indeed, as noted above, it appears the name "city" derives from the protective function of the walls for those within them. The point we want to make here is that the walls served this function for the entire surrounding region.

From what we know about other prominent peoples of that era, power typically was vested in the hands of an elite that controlled a standing army and served as patrons to the dominant cult. In this context, it is far less obvious how the main city gate became the center for political and social life in the cities and villages of early Israel. There was obviously the necessity to pass through the gate regularly to conduct the normal affairs of life, and the likely tendency for people to gather there (generally at the end of the day as they came through it to their homes from fields and workshops). But this presumes political control resided far more with the common people than a select few, a revolutionary reality for that day.[117] But let us observe what we find herein: *the going in and out.* The entire region was in fact an economic, political, and social whole and the gate then symbolized this wholeness. The significant center of their economic and political life was not some palace or citadel at a high point within the city where the social elite lived, nor on some hill or mountain outside the city, but a lowly gate strategically placed between city and surrounding region where the common person regularly trafficked.

Third, we are compelled by the archaeological evidence to wonder over the seemingly unplanned layout of Israelite cities during the entire pre-exilic era of her life in Palestine (and especially in the pre-monarchic era), and over the fewer and smaller public buildings within the cities, in comparison to non-Israelite cities of that era. It seems extremely unlikely that economic factors alone would compel such differences. Our best guess as to the origin of this unique pattern is that a more aggressive level of city planning would have required too great a centralization of political power, with the attendant dangers therein—especially, we presume, unacceptable levels of economic inequality. In other words, what we see in these distinctives at the local level may reflect what we noted above at the national level, that Israel was to have neither king nor standing army: an apparent preference of Israel's God for more decentralized political and economic arrangements, with as much of the business of government handled either through non-public, voluntaristic means or at the local governmental level.

As we have observed throughout this section of the essay, we find in the lived experience of early Israel a number of unique elements for that time and place—and now again we observe an unusual degree of socioeconomic *shalom* between central (walled) city and surrounding region. What are we to make of these unique elements? Gottwald attributes them to the unique social composition of early Israel, made up primarily of the politically and economically disenfranchised lower classes of the Canaanite city-states on the western plains of Palestine, classes of people who slowly infiltrated the eastern hill country and established far more egalitarian socioeconomic arrangements than they had previously endured. Granting a plausibility to Gottwald's thesis for some of the observed differences, as an alternative explanation to the biblical account it calls for too large an epistemological stretch. That otherwise dispossessed peasants who only had known Canaanite gods and had no extant models of egalitarian, democratic structures would contrive all of what we observe in early Israel, seems implausible to us—unless a distinctive moral/religious Presence (the God of the Bible) is introduced. We are forced to the conclusion, therefore, that Israel was unique because her God was unique, and that because of this the socioeconomic structures and meanings embedded therein hold normative ethical content for all peoples and all nations to the present.

Thus, according to the best attempts we have today to recreate for us how life was lived in early Israel, we do not see in early Israel the level of antagonism between city and surrounding region that we find in the previous and co-existent Canaanite city-states. The situation in the Canaanite city-states was similar to what we discern in virtually all societies of that era: a concentration of political and economic power in the hands of a few, concentration which led generally to an oppressive organization of the regions and peoples surrounding the cities to the benefit of the city-elites. To the contrary, we find mutually supportive relationships that portray the entire region as a complete socioeconomic unit. This assessment, along with our first wonder over the unplanned nature of Israelite cities, should be seen in the context of other significant differences characterizing early Israel: their devotion, for example, to one God who was not embodied in the various structures of creation (including sovereigns) but who stood above and beyond the created world; their commitment to structures more economically egalitarian and politically democratic than those of surrounding societies. The extension of this uniqueness is a working model of the entire (metropolitan) region as a socioeconomic whole rather than a model of conflict between those who live and work within the central city and those who live and/or work in the regions surrounding the central city.

Theological Commentary on Spatial Proximity

We argued in the preceding two sections that families in early Israel were expected to exercise protective responsibility for the most vulnerable households residing within a prudent social and economic reach surrounding them. Though the ideal response would have been a voluntary one, the instrument of government was an expected part of the normative response for accomplishing the important task of assuring each household adequate protection and hope for the future. Moreover, the moral reach of spatial proximity more than likely extended throughout the economic region of which the Israelite family was a part—a reach which would practically invite government participation in most cases. We now investigate whether further moral insight is afforded us by pursuing uses made within biblical commentary of the spatial images embedded in the basic social and economic framework developed above. For example, consider the image used by the prophet Ezekiel expressing God's lament when he "looked for a man among [the residents of Jerusalem] who would build up the wall and stand before me in the gap on behalf of the land so I would not have to destroy it, but I found none" (Ezek. 22:30). How are we to understand here the role of a city wall with reference to the land of Israel? Jerusalem was not a fortress city on Israel's border which would represent actual protection for the land. Is this reference therefore simply a compelling metaphor or could it represent a more functional relationship, that the fate of the land turns in part upon the condition of the cities?

We begin by recalling a number of references, such as Ezekiel 22:30, to walls and gates, references which seem clearly to refer to spatial realities broader than the particular city to which the gate and walls belong. Prior to this verse there is no reference in the chapter to any destruction of the city wall as such. What we find is a long recitation of sins on the part of the people, and particularly of sins committed by the religious and political leaders of the people, who are presented as actively oppressing, rather than passively failing to act, when others oppress. Among the offenses, mention is made at several points (vss. 7, 12, 29) to injustices inflicted upon those we have considered above as the most vulnerable members of society—the orphans, widows, and aliens. "The people of the land practice extortion and commit robbery; they oppress the poor and needy and mistreat the alien, denying them justice" (Ezek. 22:29).

In other words, this well-worn passage (Ezek. 22:30) that we have lifted out for emphasis uses what would seem to be a broken city wall to reflect a general condition of sinfulness among the people in all parts of the land, with an accompanying call for faithful action both to redress the existing condition and prevent further injustice. A very similar picture emerges in Isaiah's call for one to correct injustice by becoming a "Repairer of Broken Walls" and "Restorer of Streets with Dwellings" (Isa. 58:12). Jeremiah's reference to the "city gates of the land" (Jer. 15:7) and the description in Proverbs of the commendable wife's husband, who "takes his seat [at the city gate] among the elders of the land" (Prov. 31:23) also use city-related references for spatially broader moral realities.

To the extent that the metaphorical use of a city wall and gates in passages like those cited here provide additional moral insight, they help to broaden the spatial reach of responsibility beyond the city and its environs to the entire land. Solid and intact walls are designed to offer protection and security for those within; the gates in early Israel were settings for the determination and adjudication of justice. Israel's religious and political leaders especially are admonished in these passages to actively set right what injustice had broken and to assure protection for those who were vulnerable.

The meaning of the metaphors, then, seems obvious: disobedience and injustice throughout the land are pictured through broken walls and references to the gate, and actions to correct what is broken and to set right the injustices are expected—given the nature of the complaints—of the political or religious leaders. We move in these images from the broader reach of the land to the bricks and mortar and physical space surrounding a city wall and gate. But could something more be at work here? Is there any sense in which attention to city walls, and efforts to bring justice to all those for whom the elders gathered at the city gate bore responsibility, will help the broader land realize a greater *shalom?* That is, can we move the direction of causation from the city outwards to the land?

We find no direct instruction to this effect and advance the question only as a possibility. What teases our thinking, however, are those verses scattered throughout the Bible, generally deemed to be eschatological, which suggest a movement in history toward the city: such that we are tempted to speculate whether in the mystical linkage between what we know now and what will be known when God's Kingdom is fully revealed, faithful efforts to work towards the desired state of earthly *shalom* place upon us special demands to attend far more carefully than we have to this point in history to the conditions and structures of our metropolitan regions. Could it be, in other words, that the health of the city today carries a special relationship to the health of the entire land? The evidence here is inferential, at best, but nonetheless suggestive, and contributes to the general argument we are advancing in this essay that we need in the U.S. to find new and renewed forms of responsibility for the most vulnerable households of our metropolitan regions.

We cannot develop the biblical material in this regard in any sort of systematic framework. Most Christian readers will be familiar with the last two chapters of Revelation, which present God's future reign in our midst as set in a most unusual city. Careful examination of this text should thrust us back to the latter chapters of Ezekiel and the careful specifications of the temple, along with concern for proper spatial arrangements of the land in and around the city which houses the temple. We read in Hebrews 11 how Abraham was "looking forward to the city with foundations, whose architect and builder is God" (Heb. 11:10).[118] Our more speculative musings could be extended to texts not generally understood in a spatial sense. For example, should anything be made of Christ's "use" of the metropolitan region of Jerusalem in the days leading to his crucifixion: staying with friends in a suburb of the city, dramatically entering the city (through a gate) upon a blanket of palms, walking to and from the city each day, eating the Passover meal within the city and then retiring out of the city for prayer, and then a trial within and crucifixion without the city walls? Might we rethink the parable of the good Samaritan (Luke 10:25–37) in terms of space as well as cultural and religious distinctions? If the proper neighbor in this passage came from Samaria (some distance from the Jericho road), then the commended neighborliness knows a much broader spatial reach than we typically imagine.

In other words, how are we to think of the city? How is it that the Bible locates our future hope in a city rather than (say) a garden or an exurban estate with attractive grounds to walk in, visages and smells to please us, and fruit trees and vegetables to nourish us? If the city is indeed our future, should we then be far more concerned for the proper structures and moral meanings of city and metropolitan life? I suspect so.

To conclude this section of the essay we explore a spatial setting often used to represent a social ideal, the condition in which each family can live, eat, sit, and socialize "under its own vine and fig tree" (1 Kings 4:25; 2 Kings 18:31; Mic. 4:4; Zech. 3:10). Like the images of walls and gates, this one also contains real significance for that time and location, which then serves a more abstract significance. The vine and vineyard, providing a major part of the food supply, find numerous uses throughout the Bible, from Joseph's dream that ultimately brought him to the attention of the Pharaoh (Gen. 40:9–15) to the illustration of Jesus as the vine and his faithful followers as branches (John 15:1–8).

I have long treated these texts and this image as affirming the importance of local control, of the family that owns its own house and lands and exercises a healthy degree of control over them within the social context of the surrounding community. The contemporary embodiment of this objective, I have presumed, would be found in smaller communities and greater municipal autonomy, in contrast to a more inclusive notion of metropolitan responsibility. Given this working presumption I expected this image to offer a good test case for my thesis calling for greater metropolitan responsibility. As it turns out, however, this image actually supports that thesis.

Of the many references to vine(s) and fig tree(s) in combination, the four noted just above ("under one's own vine and fig tree") present an ideal state of family security and contentment. The first two speak to the present day of the text, as a description of life in the land under the administration of Solomon (1 Kings 4:4, to "live under . . .") and as an enticement by an invading king to throw their allegiance to him (2 Kings 18:31, to "eat from one's . . ."). The second two use this earthy ideal to describe how things will be "in the last days" (Mic. 4:1ff, to "sit under . . .") or "in that day" (Zech. 3:10, to "invite one's neighbor to sit under . . ."). In all cases the objective of the image seems clear, to paint a condition of family security and contentment, an image of the freedom to go about one's work without fear of invasion from without or losing one's patrimony from within, or otherwise being troubled by forces beyond the family's reasonable control—one piece of a larger socioeconomic *shalom* within society.

What I had not anticipated when I began working with this image more carefully was the spatial sweep of the ideal condition. In my naiveté I had conceived of the vine and fig tree lying just outside the family's house, and hence as being an affirmation of very local control. The far more likely reality would have found the house within the city/village and the vines and fig trees in the surrounding region. In several of the other texts linking these two fruits (Deut. 8:6–9 and Joel 1:12, among others) we find a rich variety of crops and livestock which clearly would have been found in the regions surrounding the city/village, with grains in the flatter valley areas outside the city or village, trees on the abutting slopes, and livestock farther up the hillsides and farther removed from the city/village. The picture we are offered, then, is one in which the family feels secure and content both within the city where it resides, and in the economic region surrounding the city where the family's crops and livestock were to be found. It would appear, therefore, that this image serves an ethical commitment to metropolitan responsibility more than it does a narrower and exclusive commitment to local responsibility.

The Scripture's moral counsel seems clear. As metropolitan regions are coherent economic and social wholes, so they should be coherent moral wholes. We should be working toward models of metropolitan responsibility, being led particularly by concern for how existing structures and behaviors impact the most vulnerable members of these regions. Granting the practical reality by which the less vulnerable families of early Israel most likely would have assisted the more vulnerable ones within a fairly narrow spatial proximity, the thrust of the moral instruction handed to us extends the limits of moral obligation from one's immediate neighbors to at least the broader economic region in which a typical family conducted its normal affairs of life.

Conclusion

For reasons too poorly understood and too complex to untangle fully in this essay, U.S. society has been struggling in the second half of the twentieth century to grasp the morally appropriate assignment of responsibilities for redressing the damaging realities of our inner cities. We have inherited an otherwise commendable commitment to personal (and, by extension, municipal) liberty, but we struggle today to both conceive of, and practice proper forms of, responsibility as the necessary moral counterpart. This reality presents both an opportunity and responsibility for those who seek to live by the moral counsel of the biblical tradition to step forward and stand in the gap, to (with Nehemiah) weep over the broken walls and burned gates of the city, and then to walk the walls and examine the gates,[119] all in preparation for offering practical leadership to help our society work toward a greater portion of God's desired *shalom* to our metropolitan regions.

My counsel to "walk the walls" is tendered both literally and figuratively. I have found it a helpful practice to actually walk the streets and tour the neighborhoods of cities, stopping occasionally to pray over what I observe, and then subsequently to think through what has been learned—a discipline offering crucial input for both knowing the texture of the city and discerning what steps might bring improvement. This walk should also take us through the difficult intellectual terrain that is required to discern measures which seem likely to yield *shalom* in our cities. The ultimate outcome of our walk, however, must be what Nehemiah and all his co-laborers from throughout the greater metropolitan region of early Jerusalem achieved—the practical rebuilding of the walls and restoration of the gates.

As we pray over and walk among our metropolitan regions in a search for measures which will allow all families to live securely and contentedly under their own vines and fig trees, our moral counsel is sharpened by two ethical touchstones lifted from the biblical tradition: 1) we must extend special concern to the most vulnerable members of society; 2) we must treat metropolitan regions morally as the social and economic wholes they in fact are. Accordingly, those scattered about our metropolitan regions who submit themselves to the moral counsel of the biblical tradition might strategically begin more intimate communication and cooperation than generally has been the case. In doing so it would seem prudent to grant greater voice and leadership to those ministering within our central cities in order to understand the damaging social realities being experienced there, and for those who minister in the communities surrounding the central cities to exert greater voice and leadership in addressing the harmful side effects of our otherwise desirable commitments to personal and family freedom and municipal autonomy. The limitations on this essay do not allow review of the many commendable steps that already are underway in this regard, nor do they allow exploration of additional measures which might be taken. We can only remind ourselves of, and thereby challenge ourselves with, the biblical instruction that a few righteous men and women can save a city (Gen. 18:23ff.; Jer. 5:1).

If I have done my job well in this essay, and if my interpretive understanding of the biblical tradition is correct, then my conclusions should help the U.S. resolve the dilemma it confronts in properly assigning moral responsibility for the troubling realities affecting the inner cities of our metropolitan regions. Our work here should edge us toward a more effective resolution of the dilemma in two ways: 1) by helping the U.S. understand better the nature of its moral sympathies, a tradition of local responsibility for the problem areas of society; 2) by providing a theory of motivation lacking in our dominant systems for specifying moral obligation, which will compel citizens to work towards those behaviors and structures which promise greater *shalom.*

Our deepest roots of moral obligation as a society reveal a strong commitment to personal liberty along with its necessary companion, commitment to personal responsibility. This commitment to personal liberty and responsibility finds its public counterpart in a commitment to municipal liberty and responsibility. We see little relaxation today in our commitment to personal and municipal liberty. It is far from clear, however, what the tug of personal and local responsibility should mean today and to what extent our nation remains committed to it.

I affirm in this essay two ethical touchstones to guide us: a special commitment to the most vulnerable households in our midst and an admonition to treat municipal regions as moral wholes. Robert Goodin observes that western societies in a number of ways affirm a special commitment to the most vulnerable persons and households in their midst, offering as evidence such practices as care provided voluntarily to vulnerable members of one's family and certain others, as well as court decisions which hold employers legally accountable for work conditions that could harm unwitting workers. Perceiving what he calls an "orthodox" model of moral obligation, in which we bind ourselves morally and legally only to those responsibilities for which we formally and voluntarily contract, Goodin argues that in point of fact we bind ourselves in far more ways than this. He then argues that the best explanation of our behavior is that we actually incur responsibilities for those around us who are especially vulnerable to us.

> It is their vulnerability far more fundamentally than any voluntary act of will on your part, which explains the moral force of the promissory obligation. When, as occasionally happens, no one is relying upon you to keep your promise, then virtually no moral force attaches. Conversely, whenever there are people relying upon you to do something (and you know, or should know, of their vulnerability to your actions and choices), you have the same sort of special obligation. Those obligations are, then, independent of any promises or other voluntary acts of will on your part.[120]

Building from such observations Goodin proposes an alternative model of moral obligation which fits better who we in practice reveal ourselves to be—a reading of social and moral reality in which we allow ourselves to bear special responsibility for those who are vulnerable to us, and then calls us to spend efforts teasing out what both vulnerability and an appropriate response to vulnerability should mean in practice. I find his argument persuasive, in good part because it comports so well with the norms of the biblical tradition as I have understood them in this essay. Were we to embrace this framework for construing moral obligation, those of us who live in and use metropolitan regions regularly would ask in what ways those within those same regions who are constrained by circumstances to live within the pockets of concentrated poverty are especially vulnerable to us, and how we should take steps to assist them.

In other words, because responsibility has a spatial dimension, the supposedly private realm of personal responsibility and the public realm of municipal/metropolitan responsibility begin to merge. This moral reality would seem to be one obvious teaching of the Luke 16:19–31, wherein the rich man should have known the nature of his obligation to poor Lazarus. It would appear consistent as well with the historical roots of our moral sympathies as a nation: the republican sympathies obligating the proper gentleman to bear a special responsibility for those in his area vulnerable to him; the liberal commitment to limited government, with its implied presumption that responsible citizens will handle as many of society's problems as possible privately so as not to create an undue demand for government action; the religious sympathies of a goodly share of the households committed to the same biblical tradition I have been exploring in this essay.

Hence, a properly construed "metropolitan responsibility" represents who we have been as a people morally and, until an alternative conception of these moral sentiments can find broad acceptance, a properly construed notion of metropolitan responsibility would seem to offer our best contemporary working model of moral obligation. Embracing this self-understanding, and then undertaking the hard work of finding workable means of putting it into practice, should help us to sort our way more effectively through our current flounderings to locate the appropriate level of government for handling various civic responsibilities.

The second way in which the ethical framework of this essay can nudge society toward a more effective response to the harmful realities besetting the inner cities of our metropolitan regions is by offering a workable theory of motivation. The leading systems of moral obligation in the modern era, and particularly the dominant tradition of liberalism, remain incomplete at a crucial point: offering us a theory of motivation to compel the ordinary citizen to sacrifice towards the accomplishment of properly chosen public objectives. Indeed, it would appear there is little in these systems of moral obligation to even encourage us to live contentedly within our private domains without in smaller and larger ways continually seeking access to the public purse to enhance our well-being, efforts which then make the accomplishment of truly legitimate social objectives far more difficult to achieve. If the primary agenda of liberalism is the defining and protecting of individual liberties,[121] what compelling reasons will induce citizens to limit their own desires and demands and place the proper needs of far more vulnerable members of society ahead of the needs of their families?

If we consider the biblical tradition as one system of moral obligation, then we have, for those committed to this tradition, the most compelling of all theories of motivation. The very God worshipped within this tradition draws us to himself through the sacrifice of his Son, and asks those who would serve him to sacrifice for others that they too would come to know and worship this God, and that the world within which all humans exist in common would be marked by growing manifestations of socioeconomic *shalom*. This hope for both a personal and social *shalom,* with particular concern for those living within the inner cities and metropolitan regions of the nation, motivates this essay.

~ 12 ~

Organizing the Poor

Helene Slessarev, Wheaton College

Introduction

There can be no genuine solution to the growing crisis of poverty in America unless those most hurt by its impact on their lives get more power. The growth of economic inequality and the political disenfranchisement of poor working people demand that Christians engage in an incarnational ministry among the poor, working together as they organize to transform their communities and workplaces. For many evangelicals, who have shied away from involvement in either community or labor organizing, this will require some rethinking about how they view themselves, the poor and the church's calling to social-justice ministry. I hope what follows will initially be thought-provoking, but ultimately serve as a call to action.[1]

Organizing is the process by which a community of people come together to deal corporately with those forces that are exploiting them and causing their powerlessness. It allows people to recapture their humanness by rebuilding the relational bonds of civil society that have been broken in the process of economic disinvestment. Ordinary people gain the capacity to rebuild the mediating institutions in their communities—families, congregations, local unions, local political parties, block clubs, neighborhood schools, and other civic institutions that allow them to enter the public discourse from a position of greater power. Organizing the least powerful in our society strengthens the democratic traditions that we uphold as a nation but often find difficult to practice. Empowering those without money and influence has become more important at a time when the influence of big money has so clearly overwhelmed the political process. Rather than the poor being dependent on government largesse or private charity, organizing emphasizes self-help and self-reliance, enabling the poor to figure out their own solutions to the problems they face. Although Christians should not stand on the sidelines of the fight for justice, they cannot simply act on behalf of the powerless. Poor and working people have to be able to decide the priorities and goals for which they intend to fight. The task of the church is to join with them to take responsible action to identify and deal with the forces that are destroying their communities.[2] In doing so, the church itself is revitalized and strengthened.

While there has been little visible large-scale protest, ordinary Americans are increasingly engaged in local organizing aimed at winning immediate, tangible results. As these efforts gain in power, they have the potential to transform communities and workplaces. While community organizing can take a wide variety of forms, the focus of this paper will be on the work of people of faith in community organizing, and in support for labor organizing.

For many Christians, the influences of America's free market ideology has led to the embrace of a theology that blames poverty on personal sin rather than structural inequities. This results in an emphasis on ministries that seek the moral uplift of the poor, rather than ones that seek to change the structural causes of poverty. While there are certainly people who are poor because of their own moral shortcomings, that is not the primary cause of poverty. Over the last two decades, the benefits of America's economic prosperity have become increasingly uneven, as the salaries of employees at the top of the economic ladder have risen, while families in the middle have seen their incomes stagnate or slip, and those at the bottom have suffered "the equivalent of a Great Depression." Beginning in the 1980s, real wages for the least skilled workers actually fell, even though the economy was booming, leaving increasing numbers of working people with incomes below the poverty line. This stands in sharp contrast to the 1960s when expanding work opportunities led to rising wages. The situation became worse in the early 1990s when, for the first time in modern economic history, U.S. poverty rates did not fall with economic growth.[3] With the decline of unions and the globalization of the economy, the power of employers in the labor market has become so dominant that corporations have been able to reap record profits while holding wage increases for white and blue collar workers to a minimum, despite low unemployment rates.[4] Poverty rates have continued to rise, especially among children and young adults. According to the United Nations' *Human Development Report, 1997,* one in four American children now lives in poverty, the worst record among the leading industrialized nations.[5]

These trends are the outgrowth of an enormous economic transformation in which America's traditional manufacturing jobs have moved to export platforms in developing nations, while thousands of new jobs have been created in high technology and service occupations. In a June 1997 meeting of the world's leading industrialized nations President Clinton referred to this process of economic change as "creative destruction" and called on other world leaders to follow this country's lead.[6] Yet this form of economic creativity has left many workers downsized out of their jobs. Others who lack an adequate education find themselves at a severe disadvantage in the labor market, while this trend also robs those communities that once served as sites of industrial production of their economic vitality. The loss of manufacturing jobs has had a particularly severe impact on the job prospects of minority men who live in poor urban communities. It has been estimated that between 30 and 50 percent of the employment gap between white and black youth can be explained by differences in job accessibility.[7] The impact of vanishing manufacturing jobs has also led to a deterioration of older working-class suburbs whose whole way of life revolved around the presence of one or two large factories.

The disappearance of jobs from older urban communities left a vacuum that has been filled by a flourishing street corner drug trade that leaves in its wake the destruction of already fragile families and the proliferation of gangs, violence, and ultimately death. Basic city services such as garbage removal, street repairs, and police protection are neglected, while the quality of public education has declined precipitously. Many families who have the financial resources have chosen to leave, while young professionals who have grown up in those communities are not returning, transforming what were once economically mixed communities into neighborhoods that house primarily poor people. In the nation's one hundred largest central cities, nearly one in seven census tracts is now at least 40 percent poor.[8] The areas of greatest job growth are now located in distant suburbs which often have virtually no public transportation systems and limited low-income housing opportunities.

Despite recent rhetoric against the evils of welfare, for many years it was the favored policy choice of Democrats and Republicans alike. While long-term dependency on public aid is clearly detrimental to its recipients, from a political standpoint providing a minimal income to the poor was regarded as more palatable than the alternatives of opening up the suburban housing market, creating access to the areas of job growth, and constructing functional educational systems. By simply removing a large segment of unemployed adults from the labor force, the need to tackle such thorny issues as the dislocations caused by deindustrialization and poor-quality public schools was avoided.

Beginning in the early 1980s, the federal government steadily dismantled programs designed to provide training and entry-level jobs for the long-term unemployed. In August of 1996, Congress transformed the long-standing Aid to Families with Dependent Children (AFDC) benefits into a block grant program, ending its 60-year-old status as a federal entitlement program. The measure is harsher than any that currently exists in other Western industrialized nations and harsher than any previous welfare reform legislation enacted by Congress. Peter Edelman, who served as the Assistant Secretary of the U.S. Department of Health and Human Services until he resigned in protest in 1996, has termed the legislation, "a war on poor people."[9] The new law places a heavy emphasis on work, requiring states to place recipients in jobs after twenty-four months and cutting off all financial support to poor families after sixty months. Many states have implemented stiff sanctions that can lead to a sudden loss of benefits to the whole family. The new law is predicated on the belief that years on public aid engenders dependency and therefore recipients must be forced to go to work. However, it ignores the fact that most of the women will remain poor even once they are working because the jobs open to them pay wages that will leave them well below the poverty line.

A Lack of Large Scale Protest

Neither the worsening income inequality nor the disappearance of federal income entitlements for single parents has resulted in vocal protest from the people most severely affected. In contrast to the widespread unrest over similar trends in Europe, Americans have thus far been willing to accept a high degree of income inequality. The European reaction to cuts in social welfare has been "vastly bigger, more emotional, and more dangerously volatile."[10] In France, Germany, Italy, Spain, and Belgium public sector unions have repeatedly protested government austerity programs by staging walkouts at airports, bus terminals, railroads and post offices. The large numbers of unemployed have strengthened these countries' commitment to a politics of economic solidarity. The trade unions have mobilized against threatened cuts in health and pension benefits in both France and Germany. In 1997 French voters threw out the conservative Chirac government and elected a coalition government led by the French Socialist Party, which promised to lessen the negative effects of government budget cuts needed to bring that country into compliance with the Maastricht monetary accord. Yet, the new government has also been besieged by protesters. On June 12, 1997, thousands of demonstrators from throughout western Europe converged on Amsterdam for a day of protest against the lack of a social contract in the proposed European monetary union.

In the United States, poor and working people are not nearly as well organized on a national level. While there are numerous examples of successful community organizing efforts, along with a reinvigorated union movement, neither has achieved the breadth needed to reverse these negative economic trends or restore the lost social safety net. The Association of Community Organizations for Reform Now (ACORN), which has won some remarkable victories in fighting for living wage ordinances and mortgage equity in a number of cities, has found itself rejecting almost every plan to address the issues facing its constituency at the national level because they are simply not winnable right now. Madeleine Talbott, the director of ACORN in Chicago, describes the dilemma: "At a day to day level it's exciting because we are winning on our issues in some very low income communities. But still, we cannot keep up with everything that is being taken away with the attacks on immigrants, welfare reform, etc."[11]

In a society where political power is increasingly determined by money and connections, as evidenced by the revelations concerning the 1996 Presidential campaign, poor working people who have access to neither of these resources are increasingly marginalized. Within the political arena, power is manifested through the ability to control the policy agenda and set the parameters of the public debate. The dominant political institutions are structured so as to control the scope of conflict by keeping certain issues out of the political arena, while allowing others to come to the forefront. Thus, those individuals and groups who possess the ingredients of political power can control the content of the political agenda. The reverse of this is also true, namely, that those people or groups who are powerless lack control over the content of the political agenda. One of the remarkable aspects of the 1996 debate on welfare reform was the lack of discussion of certain critical issues, such as the availability of low-wage jobs in areas of highly concentrated poverty, the necessity of job training to achieve long-term improvements in wages, or whether it is really in the best interests of young children for their poor mothers to be working.

In order to understand the lack of political protest at the national level one must come to terms with the shifts in political power that have occurred over the last several decades. First, poor working people have been rendered ever more powerless and stigmatized as the resources needed to move out of poverty have declined. As a result, they have become ever more reluctant to believe in the possibility of change, or that they possess the creative capacity to affect their surroundings. One of the most striking manifestations of this has been the declining rates of voter participation among low-income and less-educated voters.

Table 1

Distribution of American Voters by Income in the November 1994 Elections

Income	Percent Voting
Under $5,000	20.0%
$5,000–$9,999	23.5%
$10,000–$14,999	33.0%
$15,000–$24,999	40.4%
$25,000–$34,999	44.9%
$35,000–$49,999	50.1%
$50,000–$74,999	58.3%
$75,000 and Over	63.7%

Source: U.S. Bureau of the Census, Table 13: Voting and Registration of Family Members, by Race, Hispanic Origin, and Income, Release date 4 June 1996.

Table 1 shows a clear correlation between voter participation and income, with the percentage of voters among the poorest Americans only one-third as high as among the wealthiest.

Finding themselves caught between the American myth of equal opportunity and their own inability to achieve their personal dreams, poor people often "internalize their powerlessness as their own fault, rather than as a response to system-wide discrimination."[12] Indeed, powerlessness leads to a sense of victimization that can become immobilizing. It is a testimony to Martin Luther King and the other organizers of the civil rights movement that they understood that their battle for freedom would be won only if large numbers of ordinary Southern blacks underwent a personal transformation and became conscious of themselves as purposeful actors infused with a sense of dignity and self-worth. Long years of oppression had beaten them down so badly that they doubted their own capacity to improve their conditions. In the South the strategy of non-violent, direct action became the means by which thousands of blacks divested themselves of their traditional passivity, breaking forever the image of the "shuffling Negro."[13] Only then could institutional change occur.

Second, population shifts away from the nation's urban centers have decreased their numerical representation in state legislatures and the U.S. House of Representatives, thereby altering the balance of power between cities and suburbs. The suburbanization of American politics was quite evident by 1990, when 170 Congressional Districts had majority suburban populations, while only ninety-eight were majority urban. Since the suburbs are more heavily middle class and Republican, it has given the Republicans a decided edge in Congressional elections and has pushed the Democrats to become more responsive to the political interests of middle-class taxpayers.[14] As suburban rings expand outward, there is a growing economic gulf between the well-to-do suburbs with little available affordable housing, and the older suburbs that are also experiencing heavy job losses and rising poverty. The proliferation of these small governmental units allows wealthier homeowners to pay only for those basic governmental services for which they have a need, such as schools, parks, fire, and police protection. These residents are less accountable for the well-being of others with lower incomes who cannot afford to buy into their municipality's discrete set of services. Thus, declining schools and poor services in big urban centers are of little direct consequence to a growing number of American voters who do not come in contact with people living in economic hardship.

The Democrats, who were the architects of much of the civil rights and anti-poverty legislation of the 1960s and 1970s, are now afraid to propose anything that smacks of redistributing resources from wealthier suburbs to the inner urban core. The Clinton administration has been marked by a high degree of economic conservatism, including its early emphasis on deficit reduction, the signing of NAFTA, and the enactment of a welfare reform package that contained no resources for job creation, as had earlier been recommended by the President's own welfare task force. Clinton's only anti-poverty measure has been the enactment of empowerment-zones legislation in 1993, which is the Democratic version of enterprise zones—first championed by conservative politicians in the early 1980s as the favored policy remedy for urban disinvestment.

Finally, the loss of power on the part of intermediary organizations that historically played crucial roles in the expansion of national policies aimed at alleviating poverty has contributed to the absence of protest at the national level. While poor people have seldom had direct input into the political decisions that affect their lives, there have long been certain intermediary organizations that advocated on their behalf.[15] Intermediaries are organizations "devoted to service in the public welfare," or groups whose potential constituents are drawn from the same class as those who have been politically disenfranchised, or whose potential constituents are attracted to policies which appear to serve the interest of lower-class or minority groups.[16] These groups supply important resources, particularly policy expertise, money and access, that are usually lacking on the part of the poor. Several of the most important of these organizations, such as the AFL-CIO (the umbrella organization for the nation's labor unions) and the national civil rights organizations (NAACP, the Urban League, and Operation PUSH) have experienced a loss of energy and direction.

Most not-for-profit organizations that work in poor communities are restricted by their tax-exempt status from engaging in lobbying activities. This has left a handful of public-interest groups to advocate on behalf of poor people's interests before state and national bodies. As a result, the interests of the poor often come to be represented indirectly. For example, public service employee unions such as AFSCME and SEIU, concerned about their own members' jobs, lobby against cuts in state and federal social services. AFSCME has emerged as a vocal opponent of the welfare reform legislation because the expansion of workfare programs poses a direct threat to their own members' jobs. Big city mayors and black congresspeople lobby for more aid to cities, which will indirectly provide benefits to the poor who are concentrated there. The American Hospital Association is one of the leading supporters of Medicaid because those dollars are crucial for many of its member institutions. Even the Children's Defense Fund, one of the strongest anti-poverty lobbying organizations in the country, has, for political reasons, chosen to focus on kids, thereby helping their poor parents only indirectly.

The Biblical Call for Justice and Empowering the Poor

Since God created each of us in his image to be free, loving, and joyful people, those who treat others as objects rather than creatures of God by mistreating or abusing them provoke his wrath. As children of a loving God, all humans have an intrinsic claim to be given their due, simply because they are human. Just as we are given God's grace without our meriting it, and are invited into a relationship with him, so are we bound in turn to treat others with the same grace, simply because of our common bond as God's children. This concept of justice lies at the heart of the Christian tradition.

As Ron Sider and Steve Mott point out in chapter 1, while God does not object to the accumulation of wealth per se, he is displeased by the amassing of wealth through economic exploitation and impoverishment. There are hundreds of biblical texts that show God's special attentiveness to the poor and the needy who are the perennial victims of injustice by the powerful and greedy. Recognizing that human sinfulness will always lead the powerful to take unfair advantage of those with less power, God has created government to be an instrument of justice. Only in government do we find the power necessary to create a just social order that will enable people to live together in at least a measure of harmony, so that each of us has the opportunity to become the reasoning, choosing, loving human beings that God intends us to be. Contrary to many modern economists, if each person is simply allowed to pursue his or her private interest it will divide the community, since private good and common good are not the same. Therefore, there must be something that moves everyone toward the common good, and that something is government.[17] Christians often shy away from involvement with government because they fear that power is inherently evil. Yet, it is not power that violates justice but a misuse of power that "disregards the intrinsic claim of a being to be acknowledged as who they are in the context of all beings."[18]

Organizing the poor empowers the people who are most directly suffering economic and social injustice to act collectively on their own behalf, thereby taking control over their destinies and more fully becoming equal members of the community. It does not suffice to have others speak on behalf of the disenfranchised. This is made abundantly clear by the prophet Isaiah in the following familiar passage,

> The Spirit of the Sovereign Lord is upon me, because the Lord appointed me to bring good news to the poor. He has sent me to comfort the brokenhearted and to announce that captives will be released and prisoners will be freed. He sent me to tell those who mourn that the time of the Lord's favor has come and with it, the day of God's anger against their enemies. . . . They will rebuild the ancient ruins, repairing cities long ago destroyed. They will revive them, though they have been empty for many generations.

> Isaiah 61:1–4[19]

In this passage, the people who will rebuild the city are not the powerful, but the poor, the brokenhearted, the prisoners and captives referred to in the first sentences. The prophet has been sent to give them the news of God's special favor so that they can take action to recreate their community. Jesus does the same in his ministry which at its core has the same message of empowerment. At the very beginning of his public ministry Jesus announces his purpose on earth by reading those same words from Isaiah:

> The Spirit of the Lord is upon me,
> for he has appointed me to preach Good News to the poor.
> He has sent me to proclaim that captives will be released,
> that the blind will see,
> that the downtrodden will be freed from their oppressors,
> and that the time of the Lord's favor has come.
>
> Luke 4:18–19

Each of the groups of people referred to in this passage—the poor, the captives, the blind and the downtrodden—are suffering from common forms of human distress from which Jesus intends to free them. The linking of these two passages ties Jesus to Israel's long prophetic tradition in which God sends a prophet to warn the nation of its wrongdoing and to call upon it to fulfill its God-given responsibilities.

The incarnation itself, which lies at the heart of our faith as Christians, epitomizes God's passion for the disinherited as well as his desire to speak directly to them. The very fact that our Savior was born into a poor carpenter's family, among a people oppressed by one of history's mightiest military powers, speaks as a witness to God's love of the poor. The circumstances of Jesus' birth placed him with the great mass of people on the earth who are poor. To quote Howard Thurman, "If we dare take the position that in Jesus there was at work some radical destiny, it would be safe to say that in his poverty he was more truly the Son of man than he would have been if the incident of family or birth had made him a rich son of Israel."[20] It is a life in Christ that gives the poor an ability to heal the wounds of fear, hypocrisy, and hatred, and to resist the crippling calls for vengeance. In Jesus' time the poor were not only the economically deprived but included the lame, the sick, the widows and orphans. Each of these groups of people had no income and therefore were forced to resort to begging, a humiliating act of dependence on charity. Through their faith in Christ, the poor are empowered and regain the dignity that has been stolen from them, enabling them to meet their oppressors as equals before God.

The sick, who were counted among the social outcasts in Jesus' time, had become resigned to their lot until Jesus awakened in them a belief that they could and would be cured. Jesus awakened this faith in them. In John 5, Jesus comes to the pool at Bethesda which is surrounded by crowds of sick people—blind, lame, or paralyzed. One of the men lying there has been sick for 38 years. Jesus asks him if he would like to get well and the man replies that he cannot because he has no one to help him into the pool. Jesus then tells him, "Stand up, pick up your sleeping mat and walk!" The man is instantly healed. Jesus was the initiator of faith, yet once it was awakened it could be spread from one person to another. Before Jesus approached him, the man at Bethesda believed he could not be cured without someone else's help. Jesus tells the man he has to do it himself and he is healed. Wherever the general atmosphere of fatalism was replaced by an atmosphere of faith, the impossible began to happen.[21]

Once the sick were empowered through faith, their illnesses were healed and they were reunited with society. Jesus, by his acts of healing, did not simply restore physical health but also carried out a profound act of justice. Jesus empowered those considered to be sinners, and others who had been marginalized in Jewish society, through his friendships and his acts of healing.

The Evangelical Response to Poverty and Oppression

Given the high value placed upon adherence to biblical truths by evangelical Christians, it is rather remarkable that the Bible's many references to the sin of oppression against the poor and weak are so frequently overlooked. For the most part, middle-class evangelicals view poverty as the result of some moral failing rather than due to the sins of the larger economic or social system. Having soundly criticized the social gospel movement of the early twentieth century for its emphasis on the attainment of the Kingdom of God on earth and its inattention to evangelism, evangelicals have failed to construct their own theoretical explanations of the causes of poverty. Instead, they fit poverty into their understanding of personal sin, viewing it primarily as the result of individual immorality. This has made it easy to embrace the various "blame the victim" theories generated by neo-conservative social theorists and politicians who have stigmatized poor people by arguing that they somehow have "a hidden investment in victimization and poverty."[22] While correctly identifying common attitudes among the poor, this approach never connects deviant social behavior to the alienation of the poor from the broader society. Thus, most middle-class evangelicals fail to comprehend the link between poverty and powerlessness that leaves poor people constantly in a reactive mode, having to respond to the actions of others.

Modern Christians have largely accommodated their theology to the demands of a market-driven capitalist economy that elevates the rights of individual property owners above the pursuit of the common good. In looking back over the history of American Christianity it is almost startling to discover the extent to which the early Puritans who settled New England held what to us would seem to be an almost radical notion of a society that protected the common good. The Puritans created state governments that were committed to placing the interests of community ahead of the aspirations of individual businessmen. "Especially in the first several decades of settlement, before the merchant class had become strong enough to sway public policy, the courts did not hesitate to put these traditional views into practice by regulating trade that they saw as posing a threat to the Puritan community."[23] In 1639, a Boston merchant was tried and convicted for "oppression," defined as the making of excessive profits in trade. He was fined by the court and censured by the church. The Boston minister, John Cotton, took the opportunity to outline certain business practices that he condemned, including:

- that a man might sell dear as he can, and buy as cheap as he can;
- if a man lose by casualty of sea etc., in some of his commodities, he may raise the price on the rest;
- that, as a man may take advantage of his own skill or ability, so he may of another's ignorance or necessity.[24]

This notion of the common good vanished with the growing commercialization of the economy, which increasingly stressed individual ability and financial success over promotion of the community's general welfare. Given that Protestants had been the first settlers in most of the American colonies, their descendants now occupied the key positions of power in the economy and political life. Gradually, their religious views accommodated themselves to the unfettered pursuit of profit. The old religious ideology was replaced by a secular, patriotic one, according to which the United States was the best and freest society possible in that each individual was economically independent and able to rise in wealth and status. The existence of rich and poor was accepted by explaining it as the result of individual merit and exertion. Poverty was seen as the result of idleness and vice.[25]

The rise of urban poverty precipitated a crisis in the Protestant conscience. During the latter half of the nineteenth century, prevailing convictions about self-help and laissez-faire economics, together with a disdain for the new immigrant working class and their unions, led to great class antagonisms on the part of many Protestants. Those Protestant leaders who knew most about the real conditions of the poor during this period were often the evangelists who sought to convert the urban poor. Such work gradually led them to embrace the importance of supplementing preaching the gospel with simple acts of Christian charity. The social gospel movement went still further to call for the need for comprehensive reforms of the social and economic order. Their reform proposals were essentially identical to those of the Progressive reformers who called on government to alleviate the harsher consequences of industrialization. In the process, they subordinated the importance of traditional evangelism, thereby permanently linking progressive politics with non-evangelistic Christianity.[26] According to George Marsden,

> The result of this conjunction of theological and social crisis was that twentieth century American Protestantism began to split into two major parties, not only between conservatives and liberals in theology, but correspondingly between conservatives and progressives politically.... This development, which was gradual, has sometimes been called the "great reversal" in American evangelicalism. Until this time in American history considerable numbers of revivalist evangelicals had always been in the forefront of social and political reforms (anti-slavery-for instance) even though many other evangelicals had been socially conservative. In the twentieth century however, evangelical participation in progressive

reforms, except for some of the older crusades such as for prohibition, dwindled sharply.[27]

The evangelical retreat from involvement in social and political reform was so complete that they were never drawn into the most significant church-based social movement of the twentieth century: the civil rights movement of the 1950s and early 1960s. White evangelicals remained on the sidelines even as mainstream Protestant denominations were actively engaged in the struggle for civil rights, mobilizing their members for the Southern protests and successfully lobbying to secure the votes of many midwestern Republican congressmen on behalf of the historic 1964 Civil Rights Act. Their lack of presence during the most momentous social movement of the disenfranchised to occur in their lifetime has left modern evangelicals particularly ill-equipped to embrace a theology of empowering the poor, given that the most visible poor in the United States are now people of color. Their absence has also isolated present-day white evangelicals from the mainstream of the black church and its leadership, whose understanding of the struggle for social justice was forged in the crucible of slavery and Jim Crow. The black church was founded on a radically different vision of the United States—not as the new Israel, but as the new Egypt—giving it a radically different theological framework for understanding the call to social justice. Believing that America had a responsibility to compensate African-Americans for the injustice of slavery and Jim Crow, civil rights leaders of the 1960s, most of whom came out of the black church, had demanded that government provide assistance to the black poor. This view of the government's responsibility stands in sharp contrast to that held by many evangelicals, who are suspicious of government control and prefer that churches were more at the center of a system of caring for the poor. Yet it is doubtful that churches, especially African-American and Hispanic congregations who generally have numerous members who are themselves in dire need, would have the capacity to play such a role without continued government financing. In fact, long before Congress passed the Ashcroft amendment, loosening restrictions on churches receiving social-service contracts, black churches were actively lobbying for money to construct senior citizen centers, day care centers, and Head Start programs.

In recent years, suburbanized evangelicals have been rediscovering urban ministry, recognizing that there is a crying need for the gospel among the dispossessed. The growth of these ministries is somewhat ironic in that it comes at a time when many evangelical churches are actively backing political candidates who support cuts in social programs that in turn contribute to a worsening of poverty. So, while evangelicals supported cuts in government-funded social services targeting the poor, they have supported the creation of Christian organizations that minister to the growing population of poor people. Many of the people who have answered a call to urban ministry have sacrificed their personal comfort and well-being, choosing to relocate into poor communities. This has become a distinctive feature of Christian community development ministries whose leadership and staff are strongly encouraged to move into the communities in which they are working so that "their lives, their children, their resources, their connections . . . become sturdy strands that are rewoven into the fabric of the community."[28] Increasingly, their work has focused on rebuilding poor communities through church planting, housing rehabilitation, job training, after-school tutoring, and youth mentoring programs. Nonetheless, all too frequently, these ministries operate out of the assumption that since they are led by Christians trained in ministry they know what is best for the community. While residents may serve in advisory capacities, they are often not present on boards of directors that tend to be geared primarily towards securing funding from outside of the community, not towards promoting decision-making leadership from within the community. This approach ultimately robs poor people of responsibility for dealing with their own problems in much the same way that many government sponsored programs have done. The inappropriateness of this approach lies in its perception of "the community and its people as an object to be ministered to and the church as the subject—the only viable change agent in that community. Such an attitude is actually colonialist in nature, and reveals a paternalistic attitude towards people."[29]

Few of these ministries, including those that seek to transform communities through economic development efforts, are engaged in community organizing. According to Mike Miller, director of the ORGANIZE Training Center in San Francisco, evangelicals are leery of joining community organizing efforts that are broadly interfaith in nature, bringing together Catholics, liberal Protestants, Jews and Muslims into affiliated networks. Miller also believes that they are uncomfortable with using conflict tactics to bring pressure to bear against cases of systemic evil.[30]

Faith-based, community organizing efforts are growing nationwide. There are now numerous examples of successful citywide organizing networks built upon a foundation of individual church participation. Many of these local efforts are tied to one of several larger national networks of community organizers that provide training and other resources to local organizing efforts. All community organizing begins with the premises that 1) the problems facing distressed communities do not result from a lack of effective solutions, but from a lack of power to implement these solutions; 2) that the only way for communities to build long-term power is by organizing people and money around a common vision; and 3) that a viable organization can only be achieved if a broadly based indigenous leadership—not one or two charismatic leaders—can knit together the diverse interests of their local institutions.[31]

Saul Alinsky, the pioneer of community organizing, created the first community-based efforts by organizing the already organized, which meant bringing together already existing groups into collective action around particular issues. Today, poor communities are much less cohesive than in Alinsky's time, so that it is necessary to bring individuals into relationship with each other first and then take on issues that grow out of the stronger bonds that are created through relationship building. As communities of faith, churches are ideally suited for the task of rebuilding a relational community. Yet, in poorer communities, many churches are themselves experiencing the same loss of cohesiveness as they struggle to survive in an increasingly barren environment. Thus, organizing becomes a means by which such congregations are able to reconnect with their own members and with the broader community around them.

Congregation-based community organizing seeks to build a church with the dispossessed. When a church seeks to empower the poor, it incarnates itself in that community. The church becomes flesh of the people's flesh and bone of the people's bone. It enters into the life of the community and becomes a partner with the community in addressing that community's need. That means the church asks the people of the community to instruct it as it identifies with the people. It respects those people and perceives them as being people with great wisdom and potential. Such a church joins with the people in dealing with the issues that the people have identified as their own. This is the approach in which the most authentically Christ-like ministry is actually done.[32] In undertaking community organizing, the church is coming alongside the members of its community and working with them as they empower themselves. Empowerment cannot be another "service" carried out by the church.

The book of Nehemiah provides us with some powerful insights into the steps necessary to engage in successful community organizing. Nehemiah was a Jew serving as cup bearer to Artaxerxes, the king of Persia. When one of his brothers came to tell him that Jerusalem lay in ruins, Nehemiah was struck with a deep grief for the suffering of his people. In his heart, he empathized with the plight of the Jewish people even though he was not living in Jerusalem. The decision to engage in community organizing must come out of a sense of pain for the suffering of a powerless people. Nehemiah then prayed, asking God's forgiveness for the sins of his people and his own; he beseeched the Lord to grant him success in his undertaking.

In carrying out his plan of action, Nehemiah first went to the King of Persia and enlisted his support, as well as that of the Queen and the governors of the provinces west of the Euphrates. Nehemiah was systematically building a base of support for his efforts, which included people were are not themselves Jewish. Of course, as the king's cup bearer, Nehemiah had an unusual degree of access to key political rulers and officials. Modern organizers would generally not start by getting support from corporate executives, mayors, and government bureaucrats before starting an organizing project. Nehemiah then went to Jerusalem and investigated the state of the city's walls. Only after gathering support for his project and gaining a first hand assessment of the situation, did he speak to the local city officials, telling them "how the gracious hand of the Lord has been on me and about my conversation with the king" (Neh. 2:18).

He assured the city officials that they would not be alone in their work of rebuilding the walls. Upon hearing this, the officials agreed and they took up the task of reconstruction. Nehemiah was the catalyst in mobilizing the people of Jerusalem to solve their most pressing problem: the rebuilding of the city's walls. Nehemiah does not take on the task himself, nor does it happen through the intervention of outsiders. As in Nehemiah's case, most organizing campaigns start out with a small number of people who come together around a shared vision and set of values. They then go out and draw others in by giving them a sense that change is possible. The Book of Nehemiah provides a lengthy account of exactly who rebuilt each portion of the wall, giving the reader a deep sense that it was a community-wide effort, with large numbers of people involved in the work. The entire wall was reconstructed in only fifty-two days.

The community's effort to rebuild the city's walls did not go unchallenged by its enemies, since clearly there were those who had benefited from the destruction of the wall. Nehemiah tells us that Sanballat the Horonite flew into a rage when he saw the wall going up, while Tobiah the Ammonite mocked the effort. These men were responsible for maintaining order throughout Canaan and were nominally accountable to the King of Persia. The Ammonites and Arabs were benefiting from the trade and industry in the region by exploiting the Jews' cheap labor. In other words, those who resisted the rebuilding of the wall were the political and economic leaders of the region who had benefited from the weaknesses of the Jewish people and therefore had no desire to see them become empowered.[33] As the wall rises, so does the intensity of the opposition, forcing Nehemiah to place half of the people on guard against their enemies, while the other half continued the work. The work on the wall also brought to the forefront conflicts among the people of Jerusalem because the city's officials and nobles had been enriching themselves by lending money to the poor at high rates of interest. An economic stratum among the oppressed Jews were practicing business in such a way that poorer Jews were falling into impoverishment. This too is generally the case in poor communities today. Greatly angered, Nehemiah called a public meeting to demand an end to these exploitative practices.

Nehemiah exemplifies several very important leadership qualities that must be present among community organizers. During the twelve years that he was the governor of Judah, he did not personally profit from the work. He made himself one with the people rebuilding the wall. "I devoted myself to working on the wall and refused to acquire any land. And I required all my assistants to spend time working on the wall" (5:16). Nehemiah did not exempt himself from the arduous task of rebuilding the wall. Upon seeing the wall completed, Jerusalem's enemies escalated their attacks, threatening Nehemiah and spreading false rumors about him. Nehemiah was not the initiator of this antagonistic relationship, yet by continuing his efforts to reestablish the security of Jerusalem, he elicited a powerful response that became very personal in nature.

Only by relying on his faith in God was Nehemiah able not only to withstand these attacks but also to discern the intentions of false supporters. Nehemiah tells us that he prayed for strength to continue the work in the face of these threats.

Rebuilding the walls was not Jerusalem's only problem, simply its most pressing one. If the city was once again to flourish as the center of Jewish life, people had to return to live there. Nehemiah tells us that after the wall was completed, "the city was large and spacious, but the population was small. And only a few houses were scattered throughout the city" (7:1). After rededicating themselves to the Lord, the leaders of Israel agreed to return to live in Jerusalem. The decision to commit to rebuilding Jerusalem as the center of the Jewish people's religious and economic life took place only after the people were brought into a much deeper relationship with God. By reaffirming that they were a people of God, the Jewish people were able to reestablish a sense of themselves as a nation. The same is true in poor communities today, where marginalized people can recapture a sense of their own creative possibilities through an embrace of the gospel because it is indeed "good news to the poor."

The continued validity of Nehemiah's strategy for organizing the poor and politically disenfranchised can be seen in the work of young civil-rights workers in the deep South during the 1960s. Like Nehemiah they were convicted by their faith and love of their people, who were suffering unmentionable hardships in the hidden corners of the deep South. Civil-rights workers went into small towns where most blacks were too frightened to even attempt to register; they lived with local families, often earned their own keep, and slowly gained people's trust, until a few courageous people were willing to take the risk of trying to register.[34] The spirit of Nehemiah remains vibrant in communities across America, wherever people of faith are engaging in organizing efforts aimed at restoring the powerless into community.

Community Organizing in Action

For people who have been marginalized by mainstream society, the church is often the one institution that offers them the space to freely develop their leadership abilities by serving in various leadership roles, as deacons, trustees, musicians, and teachers. This makes the church an excellent starting point for building a powerful community organization. Those members of a congregation interested in initiating an organizing effort begin by reaching out to other members of their church, listening to their concerns and hopes, and engaging them more deeply in the life of their congregation. Then members reach out to neighbors of the congregation, knocking on doors, meeting one-on-one to ask them what they see as pressures affecting the quality of family and neighborhood life. Greg Galluzo, head of the Gamaliel Foundation, one of the national organizing networks, emphasizes the importance of these one-on-

one meetings as the foundation for any organizing project. "If you understand the depth of our lack of community, you understand our lack of relationship building. We need one-on-ones because people don't know each other."[35]

Quite often this process of initial networking will enable the church to reconnect to its immediate neighbors, reestablishing itself as an institution relevant to their lives. As the church becomes active in the broader issues of the community, new leaders emerge from within the congregation who become engaged not only in the broader organizing efforts but in the life of the church itself. Pastors whose churches have become involved in community organizing note "how much better organized their own parish committees are, how much more eager lay people are to become involved and participate in church activities."[36] Father Michael Jacques, whose church spearheaded the formation of All Congregations Together (ACT) in New Orleans, has seen new leadership emerge in his church "from people I never imagined" it would.[37] Bishop George McKinney, pastor of St. Stephen's Church of God in Christ in San Diego, explains his commitment to community organizing by saying, "Because of the church's involvement in addressing certain social and justice issues, we have been able to present God to many who would never have come to church. Thus, community based organizing has been used by God as a tool of evangelism."[38] Father Michael has seen how participation in community organizing has increased a sense of ownership in the church and pride in the community. "It restored those old time concepts of building relationships and looking out for each other."[39]

Modern organizing at its core is concerned with building relationships, out of which common issues will eventually emerge. The foundation of these relationships is an agreement on a set of values, enabling people from very diverse backgrounds to find common ground.

In Chicago, during the formation of a metropolitan-wide network of churches and local unions called United Power for Action and Justice, initial participants spent months discussing the values on which the broad-based effort would be based. In a region which remains seriously divided by race, class, and geography, that discussion has led to the formation of an organization that, remarkably, encompasses people from the city and suburbs; from various religious denominations including Catholics, Protestants, Jews, and Muslims; and from various ethnic, racial, and economic backgrounds. After two years of organizing, including a founding meeting attended by over 9,000 people, the organization has yet to define its issues agenda.[40] Centering the organization around a common set of values has been the first step in organization building. Extensive conversations have taken place between leaders from different faith and other institutions in which they have shared their stories and learned each other's hopes and concerns. Only after this base of relationships has been firmly established will the organization move into issues. It is the common values, the relationships established, and the desire to have the power to hold large institutions of business and government accountable that are the organization's glue. Issues come and go; values, relationships, and the need for community power continue.

There are several principles that shape community organizing in every city in which it is taking place. The first is that people are organized based on their self-interest. Self-interest is not seen as a person's narrow individualistic desires, but rather one's long-term interests. Theologically, the concept of legitimate self-interest rests on Christ's commandment to love others as ourselves, which contains an assumption of self-love. "Self-interest is more a discovery of who someone is, which is gained in the course of doing work."[41] The process of conducting hundreds of one-on-one conversations about people's most heartfelt concerns regarding the quality of life in their community is used to shape the organization's action agenda. It is a non-ideological agenda, resting on the common sense of the ordinary people involved in the organizing. Ed Chambers, director of the Industrial Areas Foundation, maintains that the principle of self-interest appeals to moderates, who see themselves as neither politically liberal nor conservative.[42]

Another core principle holds that one should fight for winnable goals which can appear to be relatively insignificant in the early stages of an organizing campaign. Yet, every victory expands the pool of leadership, seasons people in victory, and thereby increases the organization's power to take on still larger issues. Finally, community organizers believe in what the IAF calls "the iron rule": never do for others what they can do for themselves. It is this principle that distinguishes community organizations from social service organizations. As the IAF explains in its literature,

> This cuts against the grain of some social workers and program peddlers who try to reduce people and families to clients, who probe for needs and lacks and weaknesses, not strength and drive, not vision and values, not democratic and entrepreneurial initiative. The iron rule implies that the most valuable and enduring form of development—intellectual, social, and political—is the development people freely choose and fully own.[43]

The iron rule has meant that the IAF never agrees to initiate an organizing campaign until the local denominations have committed the financial resources to sustain the first several years of the effort. When asked why the new, IAF-sponsored organization in Chicago has yet to engage in any actions since its founding meeting in October 1997, Chambers replied, "We're still busy building a network of 175 dues-paying organizations."[44]

After identifying a set of issues, every organizing campaign has a research phase which focuses on two elements: who makes the decisions, and who gets the money. Out of this research comes an institutional analysis of the power relationships and the points of possible intervention that could result in change. As is the case with every other aspect of the work, the research work is carried out through a team effort by the organization's collective leadership.

Once the research has identified a set of winnable goals and the targets, the organization engages in a series of actions aimed at bringing about the desired change. An action focuses the organization's energies on achieving certain results: bringing police attention to neglected drug traffic, winning favorable insurance rates in a neighborhood previously redlined, or building a branch bank in a neighborhood that has none. The action fuels the organizing process—it is the womb of discovery—discovery of self, of values, of power. New leaders come to the fore. As was the case in the Book of Nehemiah, actions create reactions from opponents which require flexible and factual decision-making by the collective leadership. Action enables the organization to grow, to deal with more complex issues, to win more substantial victories, and thereby again increase its growth.[45] Each action is followed by a time of reflection and evaluation when the leadership team assesses both the action's accomplishments and weaknesses.

Most of the early community organizations started by Alinsky were restricted to a single neighborhood, which limited the range of issues they could address. Critics charged that they tended to pick safe issues that were winnable but did not bring significant improvements to the life of the community. Until recently, the types of issues taken on by community organizing campaigns tended to focus on the quality of life of the immediate neighborhood, including improved neighborhood schools, community policing, money for affordable housing, and an end to the redlining of poor and minority communities. In San Francisco, organizers working in the city's Tenderloin district organized tenant unions among residents of individual low-income apartment buildings. In other cities, organizing efforts have led to an involvement in community development projects that create new job, training, and housing opportunities for residents. However, according to a report prepared by the Woods Charitable Fund of Chicago, some of the more fundamental problems created by urban restructuring—"including poverty policies, racism, the eroding job and wage base, drugs, and crime policy—have largely eluded the organizing agenda. Moreover, local community groups have too often been excessively focused on short-term, winnable fights and too little on the need to do ongoing organizing among their grassroots base."[46]

Over time, the organizations have come to recognize that without a broader base of support it is difficult to achieve the level of power needed to change the behavior of the larger institutions located outside the community, such as banks and government bureaucracies, that were negatively affecting the neighborhood. Increasingly, community organizing strategies are aimed at building citywide, and even regional, networks of congregations. Reverend Dennis Jacobson, the pastor of Incarnation Lutheran Church in Milwaukee and a leader in Milwaukee Inner City Allied for Hope (MICAH), a network of thirty-six inner-city churches, admits that at present Wisconsin's governor writes MICAH off, just as he writes off the inner city of Milwaukee. "We have to build a larger power base because a lot of issues that affect our communities are statewide issues."[47] Recognizing the need to build more broadly, MICAH established a regional planning council to work on recruitment strategies for suburban churches. These regional networks will of course represent a wide variety of interests, but it is hoped that they will be held together by a common set of values so that they will be able to support each other as the network attempts to address broader issues such as regional transportation, drug addiction, and low-paying jobs. Reverend Ellwanger, another pastor involved in MICAH, foresees that a metropolitan strategy will demand a more sophisticated approach to organizing. "It is a challenge to organize suburban congregations who generally don't see the injustices themselves. In the city you don't have to convince people there is injustice, you have to convince them we can work together."[48]

Community organizing has become increasingly professionalized. In contrast to the organizers who were hired by Saul Alinsky thirty years ago, most of whom were young and without family responsibilities, enabling them to work for virtually no income, today's organizers tend to be older, better-trained people who are making long-term commitments to this type of work. They are long-term employed by an organizing network that sustains itself by requiring its member organizations to pay dues. There are now several national and regional organizing networks that provide training to new grassroots activists, ongoing consultation, and staff to local organizing campaigns. Perhaps the most prominent is the Industrial Areas Foundation (IAF), founded by Saul Alinsky and now run by his successor, Ed Chambers. Headquartered in Chicago, the IAF links together nearly 50 local organizations nationally, involving more than 1.5 million people, with its strongest presence in the cities of the northeast and southwest. The Gamaliel Foundation, also headquartered in Chicago, has built a strong presence in a number of other midwestern cities, including Milwaukee and St. Louis. The Pacific Institute for Community Organizations (PICO) originated in 1972 through the work of two Jesuit seminarians in Oakland, California, and is now active in seventy cities in the United States. The organization's core beliefs reflect its deep religious roots. PICO believes "that people are precious, and because they are precious, they deserve to live in a world that is just. Justice is a product of the interaction of the spiritual and social dimensions of our lives. Organizing is a tool to integrate those two pieces: the spiritual and social, and create a world of dignity and justice for all families of our community."[49] Finally, DART is a network that primarily works in the southeastern part of the United States.

Evangelical churches have largely remained disconnected from these organizing efforts for reasons that have already been discussed. There has, however, been a small scale effort to make community organizing "thinkable" among evangelicals and other theologically conservative Christians. Founded in 1997, Christians Supporting Community Organizing is encouraging churches in the Anabaptist, Baptist, Evangelical, Holiness, Pentecostal, Reformed, and Wesleyan traditions to "explore congregation based community organizing as a means to bring forth powerful action in the world that remains faithful to the mandate of the Scriptures."[50] The organization was initiated by Marilyn Stranske who has personally visited with several hundred Christian leaders throughout the country in an effort to build support for the creation of this organization. CSCO has sought to provide congregations from this part of the church with opportunities for training, reflection, and education that supports them in their exploration of congregation-based organizing. The organization has prepared some excellent educational and training materials that enable evangelical Christians to examine the biblical grounding for community organizing, something that remains underdeveloped in much of the existing congregation-based work. Its goal is not to form a new network but to encourage churches that become interested to join one of the existing local networks in their cities.

A Look at Organizing in Four Cities

Perhaps the best way to illustrate how community organizing actually works and what it is able to accomplish is to take a closer look at the work being done in four different cities. Each of these cities has congregation-based community organizing networks that are at least eight years old and have won some significant victories in that time. Each of them rests on a core of inner-city pastors, representing a broad range of both Catholic and Protestant denominations. Each has received strong support from the black church, including Baptist, AME, and Church of God in Christ congregations. The pastors who helped found the network, and continue to play leadership roles in each of these cities, all come to community organizing through a personal background in either the civil-rights movement or peace and justice issues combined with a sensitivity to the groans of people in their congregations and the communities they serve.

East Brooklyn, New York

East Brooklyn Congregations (EBC) is an IAF-affiliated organization comprised of fifty local congregations in the East Brooklyn and Oceanhill-Brownsville neighborhoods of New York City. EBC's chairperson is Reverend Johnnie Ray Youngblood, who pastors St. Paul Community Church, a five thousand member church in East Brooklyn. Reverend Youngblood's commitment to community organizing came through an increasing sense of the gap between the present and eternity that exists in too many churches.

> From reading Martin Luther King I recognized that we have to demand justice. Dietrich Bonhoeffer's *The Cost of Discipleship* taught me that when Jesus calls a man, he calls him to come and die, in order that he may be reborn. I tried

to move from defensive to offensive, seeing that the church has to move from defensive to offensive. That is the meaning of the Word becoming flesh. Suddenly the incarnation became very large and possible to me. I had to teach it, preach it and then do it.[51]

Youngblood's work of community transformation began within the walls of his own church. In taking over the pulpit at St. Paul's, Youngblood did not want the church to exist in a telephone booth as the work world passed him by. He began to preach using passages from the Bible such as John 5 to show the congregation how some people have been down so long that they have become comfortable in their despair. He began to push the congregation to do things for itself. Tithing increased and the money was used to help children with their tuition. The church started to do missions, bring in outside speakers, and expand its staff. With $100,000 in the bank, it picked up a few pieces of property. Although the church had been activated from within, it still could not get anything done in the larger community, encountering the ineptness of their local politicians at every turn. It was at that point that Youngblood was approached by IAF, which requested that he send two of the church's best lay people to IAF's ten-day organizer training. His members returned enthused and convinced him that he should become involved. "I then went to the ten-day training myself. It made me a better pastor, preacher, and man. It knocked the walls out of my ministry by making me see that I am not just the pastor of a church, but of a community."[52]

Following the strategy of initially going after small, winnable victories, EBC's first campaign forced the borough president to put up 32,000 street signs throughout the eastern section of Brooklyn. Without the signs it was virtually impossible for anyone new to the community to find his way, including relatives coming to visit residents. During its research phase, EBC documented every single street lacking a street sign. Sixteen years later the organization founded by Youngblood and a group of other ministers has truly recreated community by building 2,300 single-family homes in a devastated section of Oceanhill-Brownsville and forcing the Board of Education to create two new high schools. They secured an agreement from five local banks that they would hire students who were from those schools and had a 95 percent attendance rate and "A" and "B" averages. After documenting that the largest owner of property where illegal activity was taking place was the City of New York, they have gotten increased police patrols in neighborhoods plagued by crime.

The construction of the new homes drew its inspiration from a sermon delivered by Reverend Youngblood out of Nehemiah. He had preached on the verse where Nehemiah tells the city officials in Jerusalem, "you know full well the tragedy of our city. It lies in ruins and its gates are burned. Let us rebuild the wall of Jerusalem and rid ourselves of this disgrace!" (Neh. 2:17). The resultant housing development is aptly named Nehemiah Homes. Prior to their construction, the price of a private home, even in the worst slum of New York City, exceeded what a letter carrier or bus driver could afford, forcing many families to flee the old neighborhoods. The EBC began with a vision of constructing an enormous number of new homes in the midst of the decimated, predominantly black neighborhoods of East Brooklyn where drug dealers ruled the streets, even in daylight. Repeated break-ins and theft had driven out legitimate store owners. Block after block had been bulldozed into rubble, giving the neighborhoods the appearance of a war zone.

In conjunction with the IAF staff and a builder, the EBC leadership team developed a set of rules that would shape the character of the undertaking. They would build only single-family homes to create a clear sense of accountability. The houses would be owned rather than rented so that each resident would have an emotional and financial stake in the experiment's success. The homes would be attached to each other to hold construction costs below $50,000 per unit. They would be built in the thousands, rather than in the small numbers of most pilot programs, to foster a renewed sense of neighborhood. Finally, the organization would not rely on any gifts or grants from the public sector.[53] The houses were paid for through the creation of a revolving loan fund that received its seed money from the Missouri Synod Lutherans and the Catholic archdiocese. The costs were made affordable by securing state-subsidized mortgages at 9.9 percent interest and by a hard-won agreement from Mayor Koch that the city would condemn the land, provide tax deferrals, and offer interest-free loans totaling another $10 million. The result was the rebirth of a community. The price of the homes was set at an affordable $48,000 and nearly half of the new homeowners, with an average income of only $25,000, moved directly out of housing projects.[54] EBC now also owns a pre-fab factory that builds the walls of the homes before they are transported to the construction site, providing permanent jobs and further lowering construction costs. The organization is in the midst of raising the money for Nehemiah II. This time, Youngblood's church is putting up $4 million towards the revolving loan fund. Concerning the housing construction, Youngblood says, "My image of a Christian is with a sword in one hand and a trowel in the other."[55]

Baltimore, Maryland

Baltimoreans United in Leadership Development (BUILD) has been a national leader in developing creative responses to the changing structure of work. BUILD, also an IAF affiliate, was founded in 1977 from among primarily black congregations, including Episcopalians, Presbyterians, United Church of Christ, Baptists, Lutherans, and AME Methodists. It is the next incarnation of the local civil-rights movement, having been organized by many of the same people.[56] Again, local ministers involved in BUILD testify to the impact that IAF's ten-day training had on the pastor's relationship to their own congregations. Reverend Doug Miles, pastor of Brown Memorial Church, describes how the training altered his view of ministry: "The church had been functioning so that if the pastor was not involved, the program did not go. I began to see the fallacy of that. The ministry was not something I was responsible for; it was something the church was responsible for. I began to see the need to share responsibility, not to be afraid of training people to become leaders."[57] Miles took that lesson and instituted a leadership development program in his church, tying the ten-day principles to scriptural and theological reflection. As a result, his church grew several fold.[58]

Today BUILD is the largest, mainly black, local organization in the country.[59] The organization's first decade was spent focused on education issues, with its efforts culminating in the creation of Baltimore's Commonwealth of Schools, which combined incentives from business groups for high school graduates along with training in the essentials of democracy for the system's students.[60]

In the late 1980s, BUILD shifted its focus to Baltimore's changing labor market. Baltimore is a city undergoing radical economic transformation. Stable lifetime jobs in heavy manufacturing are gone, having been replaced by highly mobile, often temporary, service employment. The public sector is contracting out many of its jobs to private sources that pay far less. In Baltimore, a city custodian once earned $13.00 per hour; as of June 1998 that same job, done through a private contractor, pays only $4.25 per hour with no benefits.[61] Since the 1960s the city has lost 350,000 residents.

BUILD won the first living-wage ordinance in the country, covering all employees of companies that have contracts with the city. BUILD had first sought an agreement that any company receiving a city subsidy be required to pay $7.70 an hour. This would have included not only firms receiving contracts to do work directly for the city, but also those receiving the many types of subsidies offered to firms as a means of stimulating the local economy. However, after a number of large actions in which they turned out several thousand supporters, they realized that they did not have sufficient power to win that broader demand. The city council finally passed an ordinance that set the living wage at $7.70 an hour plus benefits, which is based on calculating 110 percent of what it takes a family of four to live if the main breadwinner is working 2,000 hours a year.[62] BUILD had pursued the ordinance after their research revealed the highly fluid nature of service employment, which they recognized would make it difficult to successfully demand wage increases from individual private contractors, since it would only give a competitive advantage to those firms that kept their wages at a minimum. However, they saw that the point of leverage over these firms was to force the city, which is a huge purchaser of their services, to require the payment of an adequate wage.

While living-wage campaigns in a number of other cities have consulted with BUILD since their victory, none of the other campaigns have taken the next step beyond securing the ordinance. While participation from organized labor is not unusual in various citywide organizing networks, BUILD has actually organized a new local specifically for the workers of the firms doing business with the city. They have organized a union local around the people benefiting from the living wage, treating the new American Federation of State, County and Municipal Workers Union (AFSCME) local as another unit within BUILD, with the same status a member church would have. At its core, the vision behind the creation of the Solidarity Sponsoring Committee (SSC), as the organization is called, is the recreation of civic engagement for low-wage workers. According to BUILD's organizer, Jonathan Lange, "For many members, SSC is probably the only organization they belong to. They may claim to be members of a particular church, but they are not known there. The union has also not been in relationship with them." SSC is rebuilding these lost relational bonds by creating something of a hybrid between a church and a union. Lange explains, "SSC meets every other Saturday, we have a chaplain, and we meet in a church."[63]

For six months prior to beginning the union organizing drive, BUILD clergy and organizers visited with workers to hear their stories. BUILD's leaders had promised to dedicate one day a month to these visits. Often they would meet the workers at bus stops while they were commuting from one part-time job to another. BUILD served hot tea on winter nights at the bus stops, which proved to be one of the most effective ways of building relationships with the workers.[64] The creation of this new union has only been possible because BUILD's strong base of support has been able to protect the workers as they have organized. "The churches have been able to loan these workers their political clout."[65] At one point during the organizing drive, 60 BUILD clergy and lay leaders prayed in the lobby of a hotel in a visible show of support for the effort, forcing one employer from his anti-union stance to one of neutrality.[66]

Borrowing the Nehemiah Homes concept from East Brooklyn, BUILD has already erected four hundred new homes. It has been able to lower the income necessary to move into one of the homes so that workers in SSC can afford to buy them. Through opening up the possibility of home ownership to low-wage workers, BUILD is enabling them to build up equity, further adding to their long term income stability. According to Lange, "Conservatives love our campaign because it is wage-based. They can see that the tyranny of government contracts is driving wages in these firms to a minimum. The living wage is in effect stipulating a minimum wage."[67]

New Orleans, Louisiana

The statement of purpose of All Congregations Together (ACT) reads: "ACT's mission is to develop and train local leadership, to improve the quality of life for all families, uphold the democratic traditions of our country, and provide opportunities for people of faith to demonstrate faith in action."[68]

ACT is the result of seventeen pastors of different denominations coming together in 1989 to form a sponsoring committee for the purposes of exploring the creation of a faith-based community organizing network. As a group, they decided to affiliate with the Pacific Institute for Community Organizing (PICO). After a year of conducting research through one-on-one meetings, the congregations agreed that drugs were the issue that cuts across all areas.[69] Just one of the founding churches alone held 1,800 one-on-ones within the congregation and another five hundred to six hundred within the surrounding neighborhood to determine the main issues and build support for ACT.[70] Over the next several years ACT discussed and held a series of actions on the drug issue, calling on the mayor to join them in developing a comprehensive drug policy but getting little positive response. During the 1993 mayoral campaign, ACT approached both of the mayoral candidates with its issues and platform. The ACT platform was based on having surveyed 500,000 people.[71] One of the candidates, Mark Morial, embraced the platform, going so far as to hang a copy of it on the wall of his private office. Upon his election, Morial began to address ACT's agenda, which by then had shifted to the more general issue of public safety. ACT holds monthly meetings with the mayor and he continues to respond to their issues. The organization's success in securing a positive response from government officials is due to its size and the respect it brings to the table as representing a moral community. ACT resists the danger of co-optation by its political partnerships by adhering to the principle of having no permanent allies and no permanent enemies, only permanent interests.[72]

In confronting the crime issue, ACT congregations held a series of public meetings with local beat police, detectives, and the police superintendent; out of these meetings a new working relationship between the community and police has emerged. One of ACT's parishes, St. Peter Claver's, was able to reduce its crime rate to one of the lowest in the city by organizing its members to keep weekly records of crimes they witnessed and then reporting them at church on Sunday. Each Monday the church's leadership takes the list of hot spots to the police captain who has agreed to make the identified sites a priority.[73]

ACT's alliance with the mayor has given it the clout to take on larger issues. ACT has developed a critical role in local policy making. Many of the elected officials who did not take ACT seriously are now out of office and most of the current ones work in partnership with the organization.[74] After deciding that the New Orleans schools were in serious trouble, ACT held an action with members of the Orleans Parish School Board in May of 1998. Each of the seven board members was asked to make a public commitment to the reform platform developed by ACT's education committee. The platform included: a commitment to openness and accountability by a board with a flagrant history of closed-door meetings and deals; ACT's involvement in the search for a new superintendent; the creation of after-school learning centers; and textbooks for every student. When two of the board members failed to endorse the platform, ACT called for their resignations. Even the New Orleans press called ACT's demands for reform reasonable and constructive. Eventually, one of the two board members who initially resisted ACT's demands reached out and signaled that he wanted a new relationship with the organization. Still, when asked what he sees as the biggest obstacles to ACT's continued success, Father Michael's first response is, "City government and local politicians who don't want the community to become empowered."[75]

Milwaukee, Wisconsin

As is the case in other older American cities that were once manufacturing centers, Milwaukee has seen the number of family-supporting jobs decline. The replacement jobs are often at minimum wage, leaving many families without the resources needed for absolute necessities. Eighty-seven percent of the children enrolled in the Milwaukee Public Schools are from families whose incomes are below poverty. The schools are beset with a 60 percent dropout rate between eighth and twelfth grade.[76] Many of the city's black neighborhoods are undergoing a second transition, this one based on class, rather than race. It is in this context that MICAH was formed eight years ago. Affiliated with the Gamaliel Foundation, MICAH is now composed of thirty-six churches from eight different denominations. The organization seeks to respond to the issue raised in Micah 6:2, which reads, "And now, O mountains, listen to the Lord's complaint! He has a case against his people Israel! He will prosecute them to the full extent of the law." For pastor Dennis Jacobson, "a church-based organization has been a great way to live out what I preach on Sunday." When asked what he saw as the theological significance of his church's involvement in community organizing, Reverend Jacobson replied that "If the Sermon on the Mount is separated from the Great Commission, it is heresy. It is wrong to emphasize either one without the other."[77]

MICAH's greatest successes have been securing increased mortgage lending from area banks, winning a city ordinance requiring that 25 percent of all Department of Public Works jobs go to the inner-city unemployed, and reducing crime. The organization has spun off a community development corporation. Reverend Ellwanger, whose church is also a member of MICAH, tells of an effort by his church to address crime in the neighborhood:

> There had been a couple of gang related shootings and a couple of church members' homes had been shot into. The church's core team called the police and contacted other neighbors. We discovered that one particular tavern was the focal point for one of the gangs in the neighborhood. The taverns have a strong lobby, but because we are part of MICAH we were able to get copies of several police reports on arrests at the tavern. On one occasion, the police had found guns, drugs, and underage patrons. With that information we went before the licensing commission which decided to suspend the tavern's license for thirty days. The tavern owner threatened to go to City Council. But, through MICAH we

were able to buttonhole a couple of aldermen we knew. When we showed up with placards and MICAH members from various churches, the aldermen knew they couldn't ignore MICAH. The vote to shut the tavern was fourteen to three.[78]

MICAH is currently working on education issues. After extensive searching for a winnable strategy to tackle education issues, the leadership team decided that the single most important change in the schools, a change that could improve student performance, would be to lower the teacher/pupil ratio to 1:15. The organization estimates that it would require an additional $80 million in annual spending. "We cut through a lot of possible ways of solving this educational dilemma. The clergy are at the point of realizing this is something we can do in this generation."[79] Despite its victories, Dennis Jacobson believes that MICAH has not yet found an adequate way of addressing job loss. "MICAH's strength—its church base also tends to be parochial."[80]

Faith-Based Organizing Outside the Church

Faith-based community organizing does not take place only within the context of congregations. All too often the very poor have become so disconnected from any form of associational life that not even churches can reach them. Pursuing a solely congregation-based strategy risks leaving out these people. John Donahue, the Executive Director of the Chicago Coalition for the Homeless and a former Catholic priest, explains his work with the homeless as being primarily an effort to recreate relationships. "The gospel message is that Jesus came to be homeless, he identified with the struggle of the poor. We go down there (to Lower Wacker Drive) and say to the homeless men, 'Come along on a journey. We're not going to give you anything.' We're trying to build a sense of belonging, a sense of community. You have to build off of love."[81]

In Chicago there is currently an effort to create a collaborative network among those grassroots organizations doing organizing primarily with the very poor because they are concerned that as the big networks like IAF and Gamaliel pursue larger metropolitan strategies, the voices of this constituency will be lost. "We see it as a strong unified block to deal with poor people organizing around justice and inequality. The voice of the poor has to be made known."[82]

ACORN, whose campaigns on behalf of the living wage and for home mortgage equity are recognized nationwide, bases its work on a community organizing strategy of building small, local, neighborhood groups. The groups are formed by knocking on every door in the community, then calling for a general meeting with the hope that 10 percent of the households will show up. Any one neighborhood may have as many as ten to twelve small ACORN groups which form the basic building blocks of all of the organization's work. The chair of each group sits on a citywide ACORN board. Madeleine Talbott, the head of Chicago's ACORN chapter, explains that for her members, their personal faith and ACORN are often the two most important things in their lives. Her twenty-three years of organizing among the poor have taught her that faith-based organizing is not just about institution-based organizing.[83]

Religious Support for a Revitalized Labor Movement

American unions reached their peak in the mid–1950s, during the heyday of American mass production manufacturing. Despite the Congress of Industrial Organizations' (CIO) efforts during the 1930s to organize all-inclusive unions that would bring all production workers in a given industry into one union, the Achilles heel of American labor has been its inability to address issues of racism within the economy and among its own membership. As the industrial workforce became increasingly composed of non-white workers, organized labor made little effort to expand its ranks to these employees. The only unions that invested in significant organizing efforts were public sector unions such as the American Federation of State, County and Municipal Employees (AFSCME) and the Service Employees International Union (SEIU). Instead, an aging leadership, ensconced in the AFL-CIO's headquarters a few blocks from the White House, grew increasingly disconnected from the growing insecurities confronting American workers. While living off of a $4 billion annual budget drawn from the dues paid into the aggregate of all unions, the old guard spent no more than 5 percent of that income on organizing new members.[84] Since unions are the key mediating institution designed to buffer ordinary workers from the negative effects of a dynamic capitalist economy, their weakened state has had a severe impact on the living standards of the bottom rungs of the labor market. According to Thomas Kochan, an economist at MIT, there is a clear connection between stagnating or sinking incomes on the one hand and the limited influence of the labor movement on the other.[85]

The election of John Sweeney, the former head of the service employees union, as the new President of the AFL-CIO in late 1995 has led to a long-awaited reinvigoration of the labor federation. The federation is launching bold new organizing campaigns, flexing its muscle in national politics, and asserting its views on key policy issues of direct interest to its members. Indicative of the change in attitude, the AFL-CIO has pledged to put one-third of every dollar it receives in dues into new organizing.[86] It has established a new organizing department that is aggressively seeking to bring in new members. For the first time in a generation organized labor has focused on lower-wage workers, including immigrants and part-time employees. Unions have finally directed their attention to lifting up those at the bottom of the economic ladder, like janitors, sales clerks, hotel maids, farmworkers, and even workfare participants.[87] The focus is on organizing service sector workers because their jobs cannot so easily be shipped overseas. According to John Sweeney, Las Vegas—with its thousands of service jobs—is "the hottest union city in America."[88]

Another example was the week-long strike against United Parcel Service in August of 1997. This was one of the first strikes in decades that involved labor's lower castes to capture the national spotlight. In this case, the walkout by 165,000 teamsters was on behalf of part-time parcel sorters and truck drivers who earn roughly $10,000 per year. Unlike strikes by the upper crust of organized labor, such as airline pilots and baseball players, this one resonated with a large segment of American society that is concerned that corporations no longer have a commitment to their employees, that they are engaged in too much downsizing and are using too much contingent labor.[89]

The AFL-CIO's new commitment to organizing is leading it to seek out new relationships with the religious community. The result has been the formation of thirty-six religion and labor groups in cities throughout the U.S that are bound together in the National Interfaith Committee for Worker Justice. The interfaith network is led by Kim Bobo, who spent ten years working for Bread for the World before coming to Chicago to work for the Midwest Academy, another organizing training center. While there, she volunteered to build religious support for the Pittston Miners. She discovered that it was not hard to find support among churches, because whether a church supports labor organizing is "more about class than about theology," with those churches whose members are suffering the ill effects of economic restructuring more prepared to lend support to the new organizing drives.[90] Since 1995, Bobo has built an extensive network of religious supporters who work hand-in-hand with local unions. The National Interfaith Committee has produced a wealth of teaching material for the church, is working with religious schools, and is bringing the religious community into direct support for organizing among low-wage workers. One of the Interfaith Committee's most important projects is its support for poultry workers, who now number 200,000 and are mostly black and Hispanic women.[91]

In some cities the ties between churches and unions began because the churches wanted to support labor issues and in other cases the union people came out looking for religious support. The religious community sees many of the new labor issues as being family issues because the low wages and long hours that many workers are being forced to work are hurting families. Peter Laarmann, the pastor of Judson Memorial Church in New York City, is a leader in the local Interfaith Committee in that city. He explains the origins of their local committee: "The impetus for the current effort came from the younger leaders within the labor movement who felt that their backs are up against the wall. They can see that the themes of a living income, health care, and honoring women's work are also issues that religious leaders are articulating."[92]

Conclusion

The current resurgence of both community and union organizing represents an effort on the part of poor and low-income people to take greater control of their own futures. Faith-based community organizing as a strategy can clearly work hand-in-hand with churches' existing commitments to evangelism and community development. None of the churches involved in community organizing is simply building a large service organization which interacts with the residents of their community as clients. Instead, they have led their congregations into a search for creative solutions to the systemic problems that plague their communities. The relational foundation of all of the work assures that it represents the heartfelt interests of broad numbers of people. The work of community organizing is clearly laying the foundation for a radically different relationship between those in power and the poor. By organizing large numbers of people around a common set of values and issues these organizations are developing a new paradigm of political accountability. Rather than aligning themselves with either political party, they are forcing politicians and government officials to align themselves with the poor. The pastors who have committed their churches to engage in organizing have found that it transforms their own understanding of their calling as well as the life of their congregations. Their churches become revitalized and the meaning of worship is deepened.

At present, neither community nor union organizing has the power to successfully place the interests of the poor onto the national policy agenda. Many of the most critical economic issues can best be addressed at the national level. On the other hand, if the devolution of social programs to the states continues, there will in fact be new opportunities for statewide organizing efforts to influence those legislative outcomes. In response to the increasingly complex needs of communities, organizing networks are developing new levels of sophistication, adopting more metropolitan and statewide strategies, and building alliances with sympathetic politicians as necessary steps to increase their power. In doing so, they must take care to preserve a focus on the interests of those people who are suffering the greatest hardships. Only by doing so, will this work continue to be a reflection of Christ's incarnational presence in our midst. In Matthew 25:40 the Lord reminds us that "when you did it to the least of these my brothers and sisters, you were doing it to me."

∼ 13 ∼

Business and Empowerment

Management Systems with a Heart for the Poor

Joseph A. Maciariello, Claremont Graduate University/
Claremont McKenna College

Introduction

I have written this chapter for Christians and others who are interested in exploring the relationships between biblical assumptions concerning human nature and the management of work. I have done so because I believe that the moral and cultural systems derived from these assumptions are beneficial to the management of economic organizations in general, and are particularly beneficial to the management of organizations which function within systems of democratic capitalism.[1]

Accordingly, I believe it is proper for executives who are also Christians to seek to infuse the management systems of their organizations with values that are derived from the Christian faith. While this chapter is primarily Christian in its orientation, the human values endorsed within it are compatible to a significant extent with those of Judaism. In fact, many of the attributes of human nature and many of the examples which are examined in the chapter are drawn from the Hebrew Scriptures.

One reason for my focus on Scripture is because of the continuing centrality of biblical values in national life. Richard John Neuhaus writes that "give or take two or three percentage points, all the relevant research tells us that 90 percent of the American people claim to be Christian or Jewish, and 95 percent say that they believe in God." Neuhaus goes on to argue that "the Judeo-Christian tradition provides 'the meaning system' or the 'plausibility structure' of American moral discourse, personal and public."[2] Therefore, an examination of biblical assumptions about human nature, work and management is highly relevant for American executives, since the management systems of all organizations are deeply influenced by the assumptions made about human nature and work.

Insights from biblical teachings and compatible secular and religious literature provide much wisdom as to how organizations may be managed to achieve both morally just and economically sound results. But the management systems that result from the application of biblical values are very different than systems whose design reflects purely secular values. The differences are especially profound in terms of their impact upon human beings, especially upon the least privileged members of society.

It should not be surprising that significant differences do exist in the design of management systems when constructed under the influence of biblical versus secular values. God's ways are not our ways. And we should expect God's ways to be more effective and more just in dealing with the problems of management, given the nature of humankind. Knowledge of and relationship with God ought to result in profound insights into the design of management and economic systems. Moreover, we learn from Scripture that God is very interested in the topic. As the Creator, he delegated the management of his creation to humankind:

> What are human beings that you are mindful of them, mortals that you care for them? Yet you have made them a little lower than God, and crowned them with glory and honor. You have given them dominion over the works of your hands; you have put all things under their feet.[3]

God has given humanity responsibility for the management of his creation. Should he not also provide insight as to how it should be managed so as to produce just and effective outcomes? And should he not also hold humanity accountable for the management of his creation? I believe so, and these premises serve as the foundation for this chapter.

The church as an institution does have a responsibility to contribute to the solutions to the problems of business and society. But it is also the responsibility of Christians who are in positions of authority in business and government to put the Golden Rule into practice in the various decisions made in these institutions. It is the responsibility of Christians to integrate their Christianity into their actions in whatever organizations they find themselves engaged. C.S. Lewis has stated this general proposition clearly:

People say, "The Church ought to give us a lead." That is true if they mean it in the right way, but false if they mean it in the wrong way. By the Church they ought to mean the whole body of practicing Christians. And when they say that the Church should give us the lead, they ought to mean that some Christians—those who happen to have the right talent—should be economists and statesmen . . . and that their whole efforts in politics and economics should be directed to putting "Do as you would be done by" into action. If that happened, and if we others were really ready to take it, then we should find the Christian solution for our own social problems pretty quickly. . . . The job is really on us, the laymen.[4]

This chapter involves an examination of the major themes in the Bible as they affect the management of work. The general approach taken is to consider all truth, sacred and secular, to be God's truth and to seek consistency between biblical principles and related management principles derived from secular sources. The chapter then demonstrates how these themes have been applied effectively in certain American companies. The examples are analyzed in terms of systems of management in order to facilitate their description and analysis. A systematic analysis of these examples should help executives to transfer relevant practices to their organizations.

Work and Human Nature: Implications for the Design of Management Systems

Work and Human Nature

Work is instrumental to personal, family and community economic well-being. It is also important as a contributor to the dignity, self-worth and self-respect of the human person. It is a major point of connection between the individual and the welfare of the community at large. It provides for a "sense of belonging." As a result, unemployment is devastating not only because of its economic impact, but because it means exclusion from participation in the larger society with significant loss in dignity and also with loss of the social benefits that are derived from affiliation with society at large.

The biblical view of work assumes that the process of growth and development of the person at work is as important as achieving the goals and objectives of the work itself. Work is effectively linked to the nature of humankind when the firm is managed so as to develop God's image in the worker. This was stated skillfully by C. W. Pollard, Chairman of ServiceMaster:

When the purpose of the firm is linked to the growth and development of a person in God's image, it unleashes powerful forces in the mind and the spirit of the worker.[5]

In much of the secular management literature, "management" is defined as the process of getting work done through people. The biblical view is different. Here management is viewed as a process of developing people through work. This represents quite a different perspective on work, and quite a different beginning point for the design of management systems!

People are developed in the process of work as godly attributes are promoted, modeled, and encouraged.[6] The image of God in humankind is enhanced as people are managed so as to promote the qualities of:

- *moral discernment:* the ability to discern "right" from "wrong";
- *dignity:* the sense of self-worth and self-respect;
- *rationality:* the ability to reason, to choose, and to change;
- *creativity:* the ability to learn, to adapt, and to innovate;
- *community:* the ability to relate to others; and
- *mastery:* the capacity to develop self-mastery and to manage God's creation effectively.

Major changes have taken place over the last fifty years in the nature and composition of work which make the issues addressed in this chapter especially relevant and timely. Rapid advancements in technology, communications, and transportation have made global enterprise a reality. Global competition has placed increased competitive pressure on various work groups while providing unprecedented opportunities for other groups.

Corporations are acquiring their resources and marketing their products and services globally. Underdeveloped economies, with low wage rates, are increasingly being used for routine manufacturing, thus displacing the traditional production worker in advanced economies. As late as the 1960s, the production worker could command good wages in the United States. With the rapid advances in technology and the advent of globalization, however, many of the lower-end production jobs have disappeared from advanced economies. Unskilled work in manufacturing in the United States has been largely displaced by mechanization and automation, leaving service jobs and knowledge jobs for those workers previously engaged in manual production jobs.

These trends have resulted in sharp shifts in absolute and relative wages in the United States. Lester Thurow, Professor of Economics and former Dean of the Sloan School of Management at MIT, has addressed the potential for these trends to produce social unrest in the United States:

> No country without a revolution or a military defeat and subsequent occupation has ever experienced such a sharp shift in the distribution of earnings as America has in the last generation. At no other time have median wages of American men fallen for more than two decades. Never before have a majority of American workers suffered real wage reductions while the per capita domestic prod-

uct was advancing. So on Labor Day this year, as with a lot of Labor Days, most laborers don't have a lot to celebrate. The median real wage for full-time male workers has fallen from $34,048 in 1973 to $30,407 in 1993 [in 1992 dollars].[7]

The impact of these trends upon the poor has been especially devastating, both in terms of unemployment and in terms of the level of real wages.

Production and service workers in the United States are losing their bargaining and political power: production workers because jobs are moving overseas and being automated, service workers because many of these workers are employed in small establishments, thus making it difficult to organize them into effective bargaining units. The result is that there are large pools of production and service workers who are becoming increasingly marginalized. The growing alienation among these segments of the workforce represents a major social problem.

The solution to these problems lies in equipping the workforce with the tools and attitudes necessary to shift its orientation from the requirements of production and service jobs to the requirements of knowledge jobs. Knowledge jobs involve "knowledge work." Knowledge work consists of the application of knowledge to work. In order to successfully adapt to rapidly changing products, markets, and opportunities, organizations must seek to design management systems that facilitate learning processes which improve the ability of all the people within these organizations to acquire new knowledge, to learn, and to adapt to the new requirements of work.

Management Systems

Executives design general management systems to assist in the twin tasks of bringing unity out of the diverse efforts of dissimilar organizational units, and of steering the organization as a whole toward its goals and objectives.

Management systems are used both to assist the organization in managing ongoing operations and in managing change, change which may be reactive in response to a threat or proactive in response to an opportunity in the environment.

Management systems are essential in modern organizations because they are needed to keep these often large, complex, far-flung organizations in excellent order, or at least as close as possible to a state of good order—often referred to as a state of "control." The designer of management systems seeks to identify principles or levers that may be applied by executives to organizations so that those executives may attain positive results and avoid negative results. An executive seeks to raise the performance of his or her organization according to the goals, objectives, and purposes established for it, while simultaneously resisting the negative entropic tendency of all organizations to go out of control.

If management systems are to be "designed with a heart"—designed according to compassionate biblical principles—each aspect of these systems must embody godly values. Otherwise executives who espouse these values verbally will not be able to implement them. If values espoused are to be congruent with values in action, each subsystem and component of the management systems of an organization must be designed to reflect these values. Otherwise, the values espoused become mere platitudes; they do not affect the design of management systems and they do not affect the actions of the organization.

The primary characteristic of those management systems which embody godly values is that they focus upon people and their growth and development in godliness. In the management of work, God's emphasis is first upon people, not upon programs or systems. Therefore, management systems, and the programs that are implemented through them, should be designed to serve people and assist in their growth and development as these people work towards fulfilling the purposes of an organization.

Change—creative destruction—is at the heart of our system of democratic capitalism. The distinguished economist Joseph A. Schumpeter made this point in a compelling way many years ago:

> Capitalism, then, is a form or a method of economic change and not only never is but never can be stationary. The opening up of new markets, foreign or domestic, and the organizational development from craft shop and factory to such concerns as U.S. Steel illustrate the same process of industrial mutation—if I may use a biological term—that increasingly revolutionizes the economic structure from within, incessantly destroying the old one, incessantly creating a new one. This process of Creative Destruction is the essential fact about capitalism. It is what capitalism consists in and what every capitalist concern has to live in.[8]

"Creative Destruction" has become even more the norm in advanced capitalistic economies. As a result of the accelerated rate of change in the application of new knowledge to work, stable environments and stable command and control management systems appear to be a thing of the past. Organizations and people must, in this environment, learn to accept and thrive on change, especially change in the nature of work and in the management of that work.

Management systems are designed by executives to carry out the functions inside the firm that markets carry out outside of the firm. These functions include: allocating the human, financial, and physical resources of the organization; coordinating the activities of various parts of the organization in an attempt to achieve unity of purpose among the various parts; assessing the performance of individuals who have responsibilities for these resources; and distributing rewards to personnel based upon their performance in accomplishing predetermined goals and objectives.

These functions are in turn carried out in a number of planning, resource allocation, and control processes such as: strategic planning, operational planning, capital budgeting, reporting, and monitoring of performance.

These systems, to function effectively, must be integrated into the structure and processes of an organization. Integration of systems requires us first to consider the leadership philosophy, values, and style of management of the executives whose actions are to be guided by these systems. Leadership philosophy has a dominant influence upon each of the subsystems of the organization's overall management system. Because of the dominance of leadership philosophy, values, and management style upon the design of management systems and upon the growth and development of people, the examples in this chapter will focus primarily upon these aspects of an organization's management system.

Philosophy and style affect the levels of autonomy accorded people and the methods of accountability imposed upon people in an organization. They therefore have a direct impact on the way the planning, reporting, and control processes are carried out and on the degree of oversight top management chooses to have over subordinates. Philosophy and style also influence the human resource management systems of an organization. All of these issues, in turn, have an influence upon an organization's strategic planning, resource allocation, and reporting processes.

The degree of oversight of executives over operations affects the nature and timing of the reviews of plans that must take place in order to coordinate and integrate the decisions of the organization. Finally, levels of autonomy and accountability measures in turn affect the design of the reward system used to further encourage people to accomplish desired results. Each of the other subsystems of management follows from leadership philosophy and style.

In order for management systems to be effective, the various subsystems should be internally consistent with one another, and the formal and informal dimensions of these systems should be consistent across formal and informal boundaries. But internal consistency is not enough! The systems should also be designed to be consistent with the requirements imposed upon them by the various environments faced by the organization and by the various strategies being pursued.

These are tall orders for the work of management systems. These systems, to be effective, must be designed with wisdom and knowledge. The direction for the design of management systems is embodied in the values that are used to guide their design. The management systems of many, if not most, public companies are guided predominately by shareholder values. They are designed to continually support the formulation and implementation of strategy and to link resource allocation decisions and performance measurement activity to approved strategies—all directed toward increasing shareholder wealth. These systems link compensation to individual and unit performance so as to encourage the desired results for shareholders. While these systems are not and cannot be designed to disregard customer and employee interests, they are usually designed to give top priority to shareholder interests.

Management systems guided predominately by shareholder values are to be contrasted to management systems guided by biblical values. The latter are designed to develop people and to balance the responsibilities of the organization to customers, employees, shareholders, and communities. They are designed with a heart! And the key to their design lies in the philosophy and values of top management. Executives who are interested in promoting these values in their management systems must pay particular attention to the matter of executive succession. The management systems themselves should be designed to insure that the values of the organization are perpetuated.[9]

Management systems do matter! Their designs differ, sometimes in dramatic ways, and these differences do affect people and performance. Each design embodies implicit (if not explicit) assumptions about how best to motivate the people of an organization to perform efficiently and effectively. Designs do and must differ because of differences in markets, products, technology, and competition, but they also differ significantly because of differences in the leadership philosophies and styles of executives who employ them. And these philosophies and styles embody different assumptions about human nature and motivation.

This is not a new problem in management. Some of the great writers, and their classic works on management theory, have dealt with this problem, including Douglas McGregor in his *Human Side of Enterprise.*[10] A key question for McGregor is: What assumptions about human nature are more in tune with humankind's actual nature, and how can these assumptions be appealed to in order to bring forth more effective managerial control? This is precisely the question addressed in this chapter. While many secular management writers have assumed a view of human nature that is consistent with the biblical view,[11] none of these previous writers has taken a management systems view of the problem. Nor have previous writers looked at the impact upon motivation and performance of values derived from the biblical tradition as they are imbedded within the design of management systems.

Figure 1 is a diagram providing a highest-level summary view of the task involved in the design of management systems. As the diagram shows, executives design management systems, including formal and informal management systems. These design variables influence a set of motivational variables which, as they interact with the people, environment, technology, and work of an organization, lead to performance.

Figure 1. The Impact of Management Systems upon Performance Through the Intervening Variables of Human Motivation

Certain moral and cultural values are required in the design of management systems because they affect the motivational variables found in figure 1. Organizations consist of cooperative systems of relationships, which depend for their effectiveness upon a certain amount of goodwill among their constituents. On this issue, the following insights of Michael Novak are as applicable to individual companies as they are to the free enterprise economies of which they are a part.

> Without certain moral and cultural presuppositions about the nature of individuals and their communities, about liberty and sin, about changeability and history, about work and savings, about self restraint and mutual cooperation, neither democracy nor capitalism can be made to work. Democratic capitalism is more likely to perish through its loss of indispensable ideals and morals than through weaknesses in its political system or its economic system. In its moral-cultural system lies its weakest link.[12]

Within the set of companies examined in this chapter, I am especially interested in how these systems are designed so as to induce high levels of dignity, morality, rationality, creativity, mastery, and community, attributes identified previously in part II. We will not find, nor should we expect, utopian solutions to the design of management systems, because companies must design systems which deal realistically with the realities of human weakness and sin. Moreover, we should not be shocked to find a number of companies which do induce high levels of godliness by their system designs but which do not explicitly espouse biblical values.

General Model for the Design of Management Systems

We need an "engine of analysis" to describe and analyze the effects of executive leadership, values, and beliefs upon the management systems of an organization. The success of the companies described in part III of this chapter is difficult to understand apart from the impact of the values of their key executives upon the design of their system of management. It is the entire system of management as affected by the organizations' values that makes it possible for these companies to operate as economically successful and morally just organizations. If other companies are seeking to duplicate the results achieved by these firms, they must understand the interrelated "systemic effects" of values upon the design of the management systems of these organizations. We turn to this subject next.

Adaptive management systems consist of a set of formal and informal systems which are designed to assist management in steering an organization toward the achievement of its purpose by bringing unity out of the diverse efforts of subunits and of individuals.[13] These two sets of systems are distinct but highly interrelated, and sometimes indistinguishable, subdivisions of management systems. They are considered adaptive if the two systems are internally consistent—consistent with one another and designed to permit learning so as to continually meet the competitive challenges in the environment.

Formal systems make possible the delegation of authority in that they make explicit the structure, policies, and procedures to be followed by members of the organization. Formal documentation of these structures, policies, and procedures assists members of the organization in performing their duties. Figure 3 contains an overview of a generic set of five mutually supportive management subsystems and is useful for describing the formal aspects of management systems. This system of structures, procedures, and patterned responses assists management in planning and maintaining strategies to meet organizational goals in rather predictable environments.

The formal subsystems are designed to focus upon the needs of customers and markets, to be consistent with the informal systems of the organization, and to be mutually supportive. Moreover, each subsystem should be designed to include explicit provision for managing both short-term concerns and the innovations necessary to remain competitive in the long run.

The subsystems of the formal management systems, shown in figure 2, are: management style and culture of the organization; infrastructure; rewards; coordination and integration; and control process.

All organizations also have informal dimensions. These informal dimensions consist of interpersonal relationships, which are not shown on the formal organization chart. Barnard defines the informal organization as "the aggregate of personal contacts and interactions and the associated groupings of people."[14] Informal systems form a companion set of systems to the formal, and complement the formal systems in a manner similar to the way the informal organization complements the formal organization.

Informal systems require of management a mindset that differs from that required to operate formal structures, policies, and procedures. "Formality" in these systems leads to a pattern of defined behaviors and expectations that are made explicit. "Informality" refers to a pattern of interacting roles.

Figure 3 contains a summary of the structure of a set of mutually supportive management subsystems that comprise the informal systems. This set is symmetrical to the formal set presented in figure 2. Therefore, for the formal infrastructure, the informal counterpart is emergent roles. Emergent roles are the informal relationships and responsibilities that emerge based upon expertise, experience, and trust. Emergent roles are those roles which build cooperative norms and facilitate problem solving and learning through the development of informal working relationships. These informal contacts promote compatibility among personnel, build community, and encourage the willingness to serve organizational purposes.

The remaining three outer boxes are recognition and rewards, informal coordinating mechanisms, and style and culture. Recognition and rewards consist of personal feedback based upon performance. Informal coordinating

Figure 2. Formal Management Systems

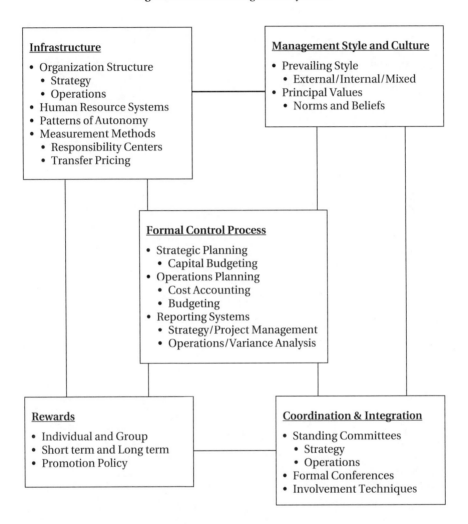

mechanisms are cooperative networks of relationships that emerge as a result of socialization and mutual adjustment. Style and culture consist of the prevailing style of management and the principal values of the organization.

The informal management process consists of activities engaged in by members of the organization outside of the formal management process when those members encounter non-routine decision making, such as realignment of goals, or when they seek new information to increase understanding of problem areas and of potential solutions.

These informal management systems supplement the formal systems by increasing the organizations' ability to learn and to make adaptive responses.

Figure 3. Informal Management Systems

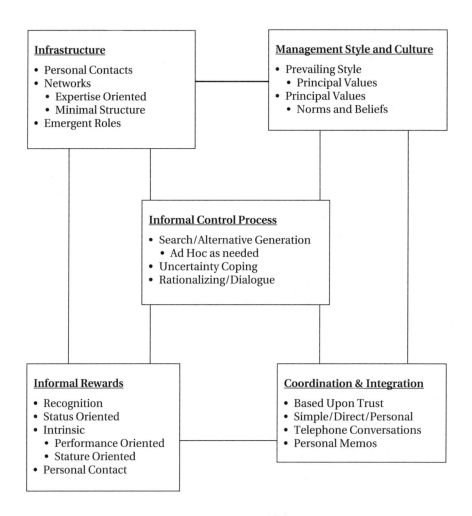

Informal systems usually develop as either complex patterns of interpersonal activities, or as temporary structures controlled by the prevailing culture, both of which support management in adapting and maintaining the organization in the face of environmental changes. As with the five formal subsystems, each of the informal subsystems should be designed to be mutually supportive.

It is beyond the scope of this chapter to examine the details of each of the subsystems of formal and informal management systems. But it is critical to recognize that if the biblical values described in this chapter are to be congruent with those values actually implemented by organizations, these values must affect the detailed design and operation of both the formal and informal management systems represented in figures 2 and 3.[15]

As we have seen, leadership style and values are crucial determinants of the design of management systems. The leadership style supported in the Bible is one that recognizes and attempts to capitalize upon the dignity of human beings, not only as a means to other goals but as an end in itself. The key concept is one of nurture for the good of those served. This leadership style is significantly different than what we find in most organizations. Christ taught and illustrated this style, which may be called *servant leadership.* Numerous passages in the New Testament contrast the approach to leadership to be employed by the followers of Christ with the leadership style often employed by others in positions of authority.[16] The following passage illustrates these contrasting leadership styles.

> Jesus called them and said to them, "You know that among the Gentiles those whom they recognize as their rulers lord it over them, and their great ones are tyrants over them. But it is not so among you; but whoever wishes to become great among you must be your servant, and whoever wishes to be first among you must be slave of all. For the Son of man came not to be served but to serve, and to give his life a ransom for many.[17]

A study of the leadership characteristics of Christ and his disciples reveals certain critical characteristics of the servant leader. Here is a summary of these characteristics:[18]

- A natural servant spends considerable time with his or her people, listening, building relationships, making himself or herself transparent to followers—sharing joys, fears, and tears.
- The leader separates the important from the urgent, always keeping his or her focus on the mission of the organization. This requires the leader to neglect much of what is clamoring for attention.
- The servant leader is accepting of people and empathetic towards their needs but not always satisfied with their performance; again, the leader is easy to please but hard to satisfy.
- The servant leader demonstrates acceptance, which requires tolerance of imperfection. For example, Christ showed amazing tolerance of imperfection with the apostle Peter despite a series of acts on Peter's part which were contrary to Christ's mission. Christ illustrated that an ordinary person with character flaws is capable of great devotion if wisely led.
- The servant leader has true affection for followers even when followers do not deserve such affection.
- The servant leader employs motivational schemes to build people up, not to manipulate or use them to achieve the leader's objectives.

- The servant leader relies primarily upon the power of persuasion and not upon the power of coercion. Nevertheless, the power of coercion is sometimes needed in service to the mission of an organization in light of the sinful nature of humankind. Persuasion, however, is always to be preferred.

The causes of the increased pace of change in the world of commerce include an explosion in new knowledge and technology, in industrialization, in world population and in the interdependence of the world business system. This rapid rate of change places a premium on the ability of people and organizations to learn and to adapt proactively to competitive threats and to new opportunities. An organization's ability to develop and sustain competitive advantage is dependent upon its ability to continually learn and to create knowledge. Increasingly, this competitive advantage resides in its people, more specifically in its highly trained knowledge workers.

The challenges facing organizations can be met by redesigning management systems so as to facilitate learning, that is, by creating the learning or adaptive organization. Drawing from studies by Senge[19] et al.,[20] a learning organization requires the development of five personal and organizational disciplines:

- systemic thinking about business processes and problems;
- personal mastery, requiring the creation of conditions for personal vision, learning, and growth;
- shared visions, growing out of the dreams of individuals, of what a group, multi-disciplinary team, policy committee, concurrent engineering group, planning group, executive staff, or the organization as a whole would like to create;
- the development of new and improved mental models of the cause and effect relationships which affect business problems; and
- the development of processes for team learning, in which individual members of a unit may learn to work together in harmony, using their peculiar skills to reinforce the talents of others on the team so as to create solutions that are superior to the solutions which could have been produced by team members working independently on business problems.

The development of each of these disciplines may be encouraged or discouraged by executives in the way they design their formal management systems and influence their informal management systems. It becomes largely a matter of executive leadership. And the results have a dramatic effect upon the ability of the organization to develop God's image in people. The examples in the next section of this chapter illustrate the management systems of four public companies in the United States. These companies do a particularly good job of developing these learning disciplines in their people.

Examples of Morally Just and Economically Sound Management Systems[21]

The ServiceMaster Company

ServiceMaster is a public corporation whose shares are traded on the New York Stock Exchange. Its nearly 50,000 employees operate in thirty-nine countries on five continents and serve over 9.6 million customers. ServiceMaster offers an array of services through its three operating units: Consumer Services; Management Services; and a developing unit, ServiceMaster Employer Services.

Services offered by ServiceMaster include residential and commercial building cleaning; lawn care and pest control; home appliance warranty and inspection; maid, plumbing, and furniture repair services; facility maintenance and management services for health care, education, and business customers; management services for long-term health care facilities; and special disaster/restoration services such as cleanup efforts for the 1995 Oklahoma bombing disaster.

For the year ending December 31, 1997, ServiceMaster had operating revenues of $4 billion. The company achieved a 24 percent annual compounded rate of growth in earnings per share for the past twenty years and has increased dividends for twenty-eight consecutive years. ServiceMaster was incorporated in 1947, thus completing 50 years of operations as a corporation in 1997. On December 30, 1986 ServiceMaster was reorganized as a publicly traded limited partnership. As a result of the requirements of current tax law, the company has reincorporated as a Delaware Corporation—The ServiceMaster Company—effective December 26, 1997.

The values at ServiceMaster are very much concerned with developing God's image in people. They are values I would call theocentric. The management systems at ServiceMaster are designed to manage work in a way that attempts to implement the biblical view of work and management.

The four objectives of ServiceMaster, which express these values are:[22]

1. To Honor God in All We Do
2. To Help People Develop
3. To Pursue Excellence
4. To Grow Profitably

To see the logic of these objectives and values consider that:

- Objective one follows from the biblical counsel to honor and glorify God in all that is done. This is accomplished at ServiceMaster by applying moral standards to activities of the organization and seeking to enhance

God's image in all the stakeholders of the firm, especially the service provider.

- Objective two follows from number one. Developing God's image in people honors God.
- Objective three, pursuing excellence, is derived from numbers one and two. Using resources, material and human, in an increasingly productive manner honors God.
- Finally, if the first three objectives and values are adhered to diligently, profitability (objective four), while not guaranteed or a logical result of the first three objectives, becomes an excellent measure of how well a firm is doing in meeting the wants of society.

The first two objectives are considered "end" goals whereas the second two objectives are considered "means" goals. In other words, ServiceMaster starts with the premise that people are created in God's image. This premise provides the energy for carrying out the second objective with real integrity. At ServiceMaster management is viewed as the process of developing people through work. Objective three reflects stewardship activities and is consistent with the biblical view of the appropriate use of resources. Objective four is a means of providing the resources for carrying out objectives one and two.

While management and Service Partners (employees) may espouse a diverse range of personal faiths or have no professed faith, the philosophy of management at ServiceMaster is based upon biblical principles and upon the example of Jesus Christ. As a result, servant leadership is the dominant style of management at ServiceMaster. Servant leaders are those who are leading in such a way as to put others ahead of themselves. And this follows directly from objective one (to honor God in all that is done).

This section of the chapter examines the selection, training, and evaluation process in the two largest divisions of the company: the Management Services Division and the Consumer Services Division. Taken together, the selection, training and evaluation processes of these two divisions illustrate a dynamic process for training and developing people, a process which over the years has led to the transformation of thousands of entry-level employees into people with high levels of responsibility and self-esteem.

The Management Services Division of ServiceMaster provides outsourcing services to three large business segments: health care, education, and business and industry. At the end of 1997, ServiceMaster provided management services to approximately 2,500 customers, producing operating revenues of over $2.1 billion. Services provided to these institutions included general maintenance, housekeeping, equipment maintenance, laundry and grounds, materials and energy management, and food services. ServiceMaster provides these services by hiring its own employees and by managing the employees of customer organizations.

ServiceMaster's Management Services Division uses the S.T.A.R. system. S.T.A.R. is an acronym for the Selection, Training, Assessment, and Recognition process within the division. Personnel selection and Training are issues that are part of the infrastructure in the formal and informal management systems of figures 3 and 4. The assessment process is a part of the management control process in these diagrams. Finally, the rewards and recognition process is part of the formal reward subsystem in figure 3 and the informal recognition system in figure 4.

From the four key objectives at ServiceMaster follows the company's theory of the business. The theory of the business provides major focus for the control processes of organizations. Put succinctly, ServiceMaster is in the business of training and developing people, and their people service systems reflect this emphasis. As a result, the S.T.A.R. system is at the heart of the management systems at ServiceMaster.

In the selection of Service Partners, ServiceMaster looks for attitudinal variables, especially the attitude of prospective employees towards work and service. The company believes that if people bring the right attitudes to work, the appropriate aptitudes can be taught through formal and on-the-job training.

The formal ServiceMaster Service Partner selection tool that is used in the Management Services Division is an instrument whose design is based upon the attributes of their most successful Service Partners. This tool is the product of a management process in which division managers simply ask: What are the personal characteristics that our most successful Service Partners have brought to the job? With these attributes in mind, they then look for new Service Partners who possess characteristics which closely mirror those possessed by their most successful Service Partners. These characteristics include: a good work ethic, a sense of responsibility, trustworthiness, and a desire to provide service. Managers are looking for people who desire to become professionals and who seek to grow as individuals.

ServiceMaster does take risks with people during the selection process and management does make mistakes. ServiceMaster managers will take a person with a rough demeanor if they believe the person will show responsibility toward the work to be done and if they believe the person desires to grow. They are seeking people who are likely to be responsive to managers and to organizational training processes whose purpose is to develop people. Managers seek to take a Service Partner and, through a process of listening, caring, and showing compassion to the worker, tap the deep motivational variables which will transform the employee into a productive Service Partner. ServiceMaster hopes that the caring attitude of management, coupled with the development resources of formal training, will tap into the inner nature of Service Partners and transform them into people who eventually will be willing to take on increased responsibilities.

The company has seen persons from very disadvantaged backgrounds respond to this form of recruitment, caring, and personal development. Many of these people later move on to supervisory positions in the company. In fact, ServiceMaster's Management Service Division seeks to fill 20 percent of its supervisory positions from the pool of Service Partners. But it should be said that not all of the managers at ServiceMaster are equally good at developing this class of service provider. Managers are selected for various competencies and some may not be as strong as others at developing people. Nevertheless, this is the ideal for managers at ServiceMaster.

The company does make mistakes in recruiting, but it tends to "hang in there" with employees and "go the extra mile" until it is clear that employees have given up on themselves. This pattern reflects the corporate philosophy. Because the organization has committed itself to honoring God in all it does and to developing people, managers tend to keep marginal Service Partners until it is absolutely clear that they are not going to make it. The cost of this approach is that they can wait too long to "cut the cord." Waiting too long becomes the cost associated with the values of the company. The potential benefits, however, are substantial.

Once a Service Partner is recruited, the company turns to training. Training in the Management Services Division begins on the first day of employment with a basic orientation, through the use of a checklist of activities, to the company and to the specific work assigned to the Service Partner.

The second step involves one-on-one training with the partner's immediate supervisor and with the manager of the unit. After the service worker has been performing the job for a time, refresher training is carried out according to a schedule, set in advance. Managers are held accountable for this training, which consists of skill development for the relatively new partner and recognition activities for the partner who has been performing the job for a number of years. Skill training is devoted to improving the processes which partners are already using.

Beyond refresher training there are monthly team meetings in which the team reviews a checklist of potential problems which may occur on a job. Included is an analysis of potential opportunities which may exist to perform the job more efficiently and effectively. Also included in these monthly meetings are scheduled issues such as safety training. More importantly, monthly meetings are used by ServiceMaster to provide training in "life skills." Life-skill training deals with issues that are intended to assist employees in their growth and development. Included in this category of training could be classes in the preparation of income tax forms and in English as a second language (ESL), or even instruction in getting a library card.

Many of the managers at ServiceMaster do have strong operating values for training and believe that every opportunity at the work place should be used to train. But they also believe that before Service Partners are made aware of "how much managers know" they first must be made aware of "how much you care." Reiteration of values during training is one of the biggest differences between ServiceMaster and other companies. Many companies espouse values very similar to those of ServiceMaster but not as many work to carry out these values in day-to-day activities. This is what separates ServiceMaster from most other companies.

In summary, the overall purpose of training at ServiceMaster is to foster dignity, maturity, growth, and development in its Service Partners.

A Service Partner's performance is evaluated based upon the quality of his or her work. Supervisors assess the quality of work utilizing standardized inspection forms. These inspections are carried out at regularly scheduled intervals, but the Service Partner being evaluated does not know the precise dates of inspections. The results of the inspection are shared with the Service Partner.

Absenteeism, a major problem for this category of worker, varies account-by-account, depending on the quality of the management servicing the account. If managers demonstrate that they care for Service Partners and seek their growth and development, and in the process help the Partners to become professionals, both absenteeism and turnover rates drop precipitously.

Turnover rates among Service Partners average about 25 percent in the Management Services Division. These turnover rates are only a fraction of what is experienced in the industry in general. But turnover rates are very much a function of the manager in charge of a facility. At John F. Kennedy airport in New York City, for example, where ServiceMaster provides cabin-cleaning service for Delta Airlines and for a number of international carriers, turnover rates dropped from 100 percent to 5 percent as a result of management-initiated programs. These programs included ESL training and provision of transportation vans to transport Service Partners to and from work.

Evaluation leads to recognition and rewards. Growth in salary and responsibilities for Service Partners comes as a result of being promoted to supervisory positions. While Service Partners are paid by the hour, supervisors are generally salaried.

Promotion opportunities exist in the form of moving up in rank at a customer facility or moving geographically within the company. In some cases, the customer of the company subsequently employs people hired by ServiceMaster.

Whether ServiceMaster is able to move Service Partners beyond the minimum wage in a given position within the Management Services Division depends upon the nature of the contract negotiated with the customer. Nevertheless, the idea behind Service Partner employment is to honor God and develop people. So if ServiceMaster is able to affect the lives of those who are willing to grow into larger roles at ServiceMaster, or to grow with other companies, the company believes it has fulfilled its objectives. This kind of behavior on the part of employers is uncommon.

If the manager genuinely cares about Service Partners and is seeking to develop their talents and to help them grow in responsibility, then the manager hears fewer complaints about the $5.15-an-hour minimum wage being paid. Service Partners get the idea that although they may only be earning the minimum wage, somebody in the company cares about them. Employees who have trouble in this environment are ones who are not treated with dignity and respect. Upper level managers often find that service employees are eager to share their employment experiences with them and they are especially sensitive to supervisors or managers who do not treat them with respect. If a manager snubs the Service Partner, it provokes attitudes of defiance. Treating Service Partners with respect leads them to behave in kind.

The work processes at ServiceMaster are devoted to adding dignity to the Service Partner and to building self-esteem. The processes and equipment used by ServiceMaster add to the development of people, and this is a substantial reward for employees. While rewards are for what a person does at ServiceMaster, recognition comes for who a person *is*. And adding dignity to work reflects the belief at ServiceMaster that all people are made in the image of God and deserve dignity and respect.

Standardized, technical work processes at ServiceMaster are designed to make jobs simpler and more productive. In housekeeping, service employees are provided with lightweight tools that are easy to use. Providing such tools says volumes to people who are providing basic services, a kind of work which few people wish to do. As a result, Service Partners feel better about themselves, and have greater self-respect and dignity.

As an example, assume the company employs a middle-aged woman who is arthritic but must work because she is divorced and has a child or two in college. Assume further that ServiceMaster provides a light-weight vacuum cleaner that fits on her back so as to facilitate vacuuming executive staircases somewhere in a hospital, a business, or an airport concourse. She might be grateful for the modern tool. Assume the manager explains to her that the reason for the lightweight equipment is to make the job easier for her to accomplish and to help fulfill the company's third objective, to pursue excellence. At that point, she may make the connection between the values of the company and her own dignity and become a more productive, loyal, and motivated employee. The incident, in effect, becomes an opportunity for teaching whereby the company may infuse the employee with the values of the company around a case illustration that makes the point in a concrete way. Values espoused and values in action become one for the employee.

In the management academies of the company, the training for managers emphasizes that there are certain opportunities for teaching in which to transmit the values of the company. Managers want Service Partners to see that the company is serious about honoring God and developing people. Moreover, if the Service Partner is convinced that the company does believe in pursuing excellence, and cooperates, then the company will keep the account and will succeed in growing profitably. If the company keeps the account, the money will continue to flow and job security will exist for the employee. When the manager is in the loop, the good equipment and job simplification programs bring the four values to the level of the service employee, and the values become a source of informal rewards.

Numerous other examples exist of the relationship between people, tools, and the work. A short person may be provided a short mop. Lawn technicians (in the Consumer Services Division) may be provided a twin hose so they don't have to walk as far to accomplish the lawn-feeding job. The result is that a technician is capable of doing more lawns. But it also makes his or her life much easier. It can be explained either way or both ways; it is up to the manager. The idea is to link technology and the work back to the four objectives to which ServiceMaster is committed.

ServiceMaster is not an unusual company in the rewards it provides, except that it places normal recognition activities—birthday celebrations, pride days, recognition of the work of Service Partners by the customers served, etc.—into the category of rewards. But what is different is that the company actively looks for ways to say to employees, "You are worth something. You are created in the image of God and have inherent dignity. You can better yourself." These activities are all directed towards building self-esteem in the service employee. ServiceMaster thinks of these latter, dignity-enhancing activities as *recognition activities.*

For some services, managers are required to regularly schedule a "pride day" at the customer facility. On pride days employees wear flowers, and as they go about their regular duties, customer personnel ask them about the flowers. Normally, customer representatives participate in the pride day activities and thank the workers for the work they are doing on behalf of the customer organization. These activities are intended to impart the values of ServiceMaster and to be sources of self-esteem for the Service Partner.

ServiceMaster's Consumer Services Division is a group of companies that provide services to over 9 million consumers, mostly households, through a network of more than 7,500 service centers.[23] Of these companies, three have become household names in the United States: Terminix, the market-share leader in termite and pest control; TruGreen-ChemLawn, the dominant commercial lawn care provider in the United States; and ServiceMaster Residential/Commercial Services (Res/Com), which provides carpet and upholstery cleaning for homes and businesses, small scale janitorial services in commercial buildings, and heavy cleaning services including disaster cleanup services. Res/Com includes over 4,500 distributors and franchisees. Many of the franchisees are part of distributors that are not company-owned. These three companies within Consumer Services provided customer-level revenues in 1997 of over $2.5 billion.

In addition, the Consumer Services Division includes Merry Maids, primarily a franchised service, providing housekeeping services for approximately 225,000 homes in the United States and representing approximately 40 percent of the organized market for housecleaning services in the United States; American Home Shield, which sells warranties for the repair and replacement of home appliances, heating and plumbing systems; Furniture Medic, which provides furniture repair services through its 550 franchise locations; and Rescue Rooter, the nation's second leading provider of plumbing and drain cleaning services. AmeriSpec, which was acquired in 1996, has been integrated into American Home Shield (AHS). AmeriSpec is a leading inspector of homes for buyers, sellers and agents, inspecting for over four hundred items in a home, including, structure, plumbing, electrical, heating and air conditioning, and the condition of roofs. It operates through 257 franchise locations in the United States. AHS markets its services through real estate offices, buyers and sellers of homes, and through independent repair contractors.

The practices regarding Service Technician recruiting, training, and evaluation in Consumer Services are similar to those in the Management Services Division, but some differences exist. First, entry-level standards are often different in the consumer segment than in Management Services. There are many more points of entry in the Consumer Services Division, and considerable potential exists for upward mobility for people at the service provider level.

Terminix and TruGreen-ChemLawn are mostly company owned. Because of the nature of the work, which at Terminix involves the use of pesticides for killing household pests, and at TruGreen-ChemLawn involves the use of chemicals for lawn care, technicians in these companies must pass an aptitude test in addition to meeting certain standards regarding minimum age, education, and character.[24] These two companies require people who are more technically proficient since they have to assess chemicals, and measures and rates of application of chemicals. As a result these positions are much more highly paid than those in Management Services, although there are multiple points in both companies where entry-level service employees may assist the technical specialist and then move into specialist and technician roles. Moreover, TruGreen-ChemLawn utilizes telemarketers, which are entry-level positions requiring the applicant to possess certain skills in reading, writing, and oral communication. On the whole, there is considerably more mobility at the lower levels in these two companies than at the Service Partner level in the Management Services Segment.

American Home Shield requires various levels of expertise at the service-employee level. It too has telemarketers to market their warranty services through real estate agents. In addition it utilizes highly trained professional account representatives to call on real estate offices. It also maintains telephone operators in Iowa who take service calls and dispatch repair employees to customers' homes. To go into the home to repair an appliance, or make the decision to replace it, requires considerable expertise.

Turning to the franchise operations, ServiceMaster Residential/Commercial Services, Merry Maids, AmeriSpec, and Furniture Medic, we observe a more indirect but pervasive influence of ServiceMaster on recruiting service personnel. Consumer Services offers franchisees the same kinds of tools Management Services uses in the selection, training, and rewarding of service employees.

Training within Consumer Services varies somewhat from Management Services but there are strong similarities. At Terminix, training for each technician begins with books, workbooks, and videos, and then proceeds to mentoring programs where trainees are placed with experienced employees. In this phase, they do both classroom training and on-the-job training in a "show-and-tell" manner. They do this for a set period of time depending on the minimum standards of Terminix and on specific state regulations. Certain goals are set for each period during this initial training phase. Higher-level training involves special state certification training programs. Beyond that level, they may seek higher certification levels in Urban Pest Control offered at universities. Individual performance determines the levels of certification which technicians are encouraged to seek.

At TruGreen-ChemLawn, training is very similar to that at Terminix. It involves classroom work plus on-the-job training. Entry-level training consists of training on the legal aspects of performing services on someone else's property; on how to provide customer service; and on how to troubleshoot for problems. State certification proceeds from the initial training effort. Beyond that, the technical staff of TruGreen-ChemLawn conducts short, topical training sessions.

At the management levels of the Consumer Services Division, a whole series of courses are offered which deal with basic and advanced issues of management. These courses are offered all over the United States. There are currently 119 courses taught by the combined training staff of the Consumer Services Segment. Managers of the division are constantly refining and updating their skills.

The provision of training is part of the agreement new franchisees sign with Consumer Services. Franchise owners are offered courses on how to set up their organization, including how to account for operations. They are taught how to recruit appropriate service personnel and how to deal with legal liability issues that arise in the course of providing services. Liabilities always exist when a service is provided on someone else's property.

As in the Management Services Division, managers within Consumer Services deal with various personal issues in the training process. For example, a large franchise owner in Yakima, Washington, said, "In many ways I have to parent my employees because of the deficiencies in the parenting process." This reflects the owner's concern not only for productivity but also for the development of people to correct problems emanating from the lack of family nurture within society.

Another executive reports that "Many of the people we get in these entry level positions do not have the experience, education or 'street sense' that you would like and you end up doing a lot of things," such as providing employees with basic education, helping them start savings accounts, and teaching them about the importance of getting involved in company sponsored retirement programs. For example, many of the branch managers help employees make decisions about whether they should purchase a new or a used car.

Experience in Consumer Services indicates that managers who get involved from the outset in these kind of training issues will end up being the successful ones, because these employees will become very loyal and motivated to perform for the company. Employees respond positively because they know that somebody cares for them—it is not just doing a job. They respond by showing up for work and by getting proper rest so that they can do their jobs effectively. This is an example of managers developing a work ethic in people who do not already possess it.

Will this training process work for all potential workers? Yes, in theory it can work; but there are real, practical limitations to the process. All potential workers cannot meet initial recruiting requirements. Each of the companies has a set of screens through which employees must pass. If a service provider has to go into homes, he or she must be bonded, and some potential workers are not bondable given their backgrounds. These impediments will show up in routine drug, motor vehicle, and general background checks.

Many of the service providers in the Consumer Services segment are not supervised closely throughout the day since they are out working in customer homes. To solve many of the potential training problems that service workers have, supervisors must provide one-on-one contact. Here is where the practical limitations of the training methods lie; service providers must possess at least a modicum of self-motivation and drive because once they leave the presence of the manager they are on their own.

Can the company create this self-motivation and drive in employees during training? One executive states, "I think you can draw it out. You can create the environment wherein the employee can develop." But, he adds, "all you can do is to provide the environment, including encouragement, nurture, resources and training to do the job, and then it is up to them." If the employee does not respond, the company cannot continue to provide employment.

At TruGreen-ChemLawn, all specialists are reviewed annually. Informal reviews provide continual feedback. In addition, pay-for-performance programs are set up to provide quick feedback. Reward systems are very similar at Terminix. Terminix sets pay for performance if specialists achieve quality levels. In addition, sales personnel are all on commission. Hourly workers receive annual reviews and raises. The largest group of employees at Terminix, the pest control technicians, are paid based on a quality index. The quality index is an index of the number of customers they had at the end of the month divided by the number of customers they started with at the beginning of the month. Technicians receive incentive awards and are eligible for various kinds of recognition awards.

American Home Shield has a formal evaluation process for determining the promotability of employees. The sales force is paid on commission, so feedback is built into performance. Some members of the sales force exceed $100,000 in annual compensation. As in all companies within ServiceMaster, employees are recognized for length of service.

ServiceMaster Residential/Commercial Services terminated more franchisees in 1997 than ever before. This was done to ensure that a uniform level of quality of service is being provided to customers. Strong industry quality standards exist in this division. These quality standards are geared toward different segments of the Res/Com market. For example, there are QRV standards, signifying a franchise as a Quality Restoration Vendor for disaster restoration. There are QSC standards, established for Quality Service Contractors, which apply to commercial cleaning operations. Res/Com seeks to promote these standards for their franchise owners as a basis for renewing the franchise agreement. Of course, it is in the interest of the franchisee to attain these standards. Doing so is good for business and franchisees are naturally entrepreneurs.

Significant opportunities for promotion and upward mobility exist with Consumer Services, both in company-owned and franchise operations. At Terminix, TruGreen-ChemLawn, and American Home Shield (mostly company owned and operated), people move every day from minimum-wage jobs to jobs that pay well above the poverty level for a family of three. This reinforces the tremendous upward mobility within the Consumer Services Division of ServiceMaster.

Every one of the TruGreen-ChemLawn branch managers begins at the entry level. Jay Jeffries, the current Director of People Services for TruGreen-ChemLawn, started at the technician level there. Nearly all of the crew chiefs, supervisors, and forepersons at Terminix have come from the ground up. In addition, there is considerable mobility—from the mail clerk to executive levels—at the headquarters of the Consumer Services Division in Memphis.

Franchisees are very motivated by profitability in the franchise operations of Consumer Services. Ample opportunities exist for entrepreneurs within the division, since a franchise normally involves relatively low capital outlays. For example, the franchise license fee in Res/Com is between $10,000 and $15,000. The necessary tools and products add an additional $25,000. If conditions are right, Res/Com will proceed to add a new franchise with as little as $9,000 down and finance the remainder. Payback of investment is normally between three to five years.

Having reviewed the selection, training, and evaluation processes within ServiceMaster's two largest divisions, we now return to issues concerning the implementation of the values of the company.

In light of the above training, rewards, and recognition processes, how might we evaluate the effectiveness of the servant leadership style at ServiceMaster? Robert Greenleaf suggests that the best test of servant leadership is: "Do those served grow as persons? Do those being served grow healthier, wiser, freer, more autonomous, more likely to become servants? And what is the effect on the least privileged in society?"[25]

The servant style of leadership practiced at ServiceMaster does have a very positive influence on the multitude of service providers employed by the company and its franchisees. Clearly the pool of service employees from which they draw contains a large number of people caught in a vicious cycle of failure and low self-esteem. The implementation of ServiceMaster's commitment to developing people through training and motivational programs assists these "least privileged" ones to break this cycle of failure and low self-esteem. This is a very significant social accomplishment.

ServiceMaster is a particularly important example of what a company may do for "empowering the poor," because the type of employment that the company offers is particularly suitable for first jobs for people who are presently poor and on welfare. The company operates in, and is representative of, the largest sector of the economy, the service sector, which accounts for in excess of 60 percent of the total employment in the United States. Furthermore, ServiceMaster works very hard to transmit to Service Partners the culture of responsibility and self-respect that is needed to succeed and improve one's well-being in this economy.

Finally, I believe (as does ServiceMaster) that "biblical ways in management will bring biblical results," meaning that economic justice and profitability are consistent objectives, at least in the long run. Economic justice and profitability are not in conflict in organizations which are devoted to providing "ethical goods and services" for society. This concept is probably not generally accepted by those public companies that place strong primary emphasis upon the maximization of shareholder wealth. They should consider that ServiceMaster has achieved an average compounded rate of return on equity of 24 percent over the last twenty-year period![26]

ServiceMaster has achieved an 18.7 percent annual compounded growth rate in earnings per share for the past twenty-seven years and has increased dividends for twenty-eight consecutive years. It has nearly 50,000 employees and operates in twenty-four countries on five continents. Its customer level revenues in 1997 were over $5.6 billion. It seems logical to ask whether a company that is so big and so global in its operations can maintain the integrity of its values, especially as its primary growth is being derived from acquisitions in the Consumer Services Division.

The answer is in the acquisition process. Acquisitions are driven by compatibility with the values and mission of ServiceMaster. While there are very few companies just like ServiceMaster, there are enough that share ServiceMaster's basic beliefs (at least as they affect business practice) to make "value compatibility" a realistic prospect. Following are some examples.

ServiceMaster purchased Terminix just over ten years ago. What was very evident to executives at ServiceMaster were the core values of Terminix, especially how they perceived and treated their people. This was compatible with ServiceMaster's business practices, even though Terminix had no acknowledgment of God in its corporate objectives. But Terminix understood the connection between the success of the business and the process of developing people. Thus it was an easy company for ServiceMaster to assimilate without changing its core values. Terminix essentially came to the same core values as ServiceMaster, though they started from a different (but compatible) position.

Ned Cook sold Terminix to ServiceMaster at a lower price than another company had offered him. He did so because of the compatibility of the values of the two organizations and his concern for which company was more likely to treat his people well. He thought that the people within Terminix would be better cared for by ServiceMaster than by the other company. This speaks volumes about the values of Terminix and those of ServiceMaster.

What about the acquisition of TruGreen-ChemLawn? Again, the compatibility started at the business level, not at the religious level. Many of the ideals expressed in the four objectives of ServiceMaster were found at TruGreen-ChemLawn. They believed that the only interaction that counts in the service business is the interaction between the service employee and the customer. TruGreen-ChemLawn has always believed that people were the most important part of their organization. Now they have been a part of ServiceMaster for eight years and are able to fully accept the four objectives of the company. It is most evident upon entering an office of TruGreen-ChemLawn.

The story in the franchise businesses is similar. Most of the franchisees will have either a strong faith or they will believe that the four objectives are really a good way to conduct business. Many of them select ServiceMaster for that very reason. ServiceMaster does not force the four objectives or their values upon its acquisitions or upon its franchisees, but there is a strong and real corporate culture that permeates the entire company.

Thus the basis for ServiceMaster's success in maintaining its core values while growing very rapidly is to acquire companies and franchisees whose beliefs and practices are compatible with ServiceMaster's and to work to assimilate these beliefs and practices into the culture of each new organization. One can sense a difference between the depth of the four values in the company-grown Management Services segment and the acquisition-built Consumer Service Division, but the differences are only of degree, not so great that they affect business practice. But the experiences of ServiceMaster illustrate that it involves time and effort to blend the key values of two different organizations, no matter how close they are when they begin the process.

ServiceMaster is an exemplary company in many ways. It develops a culture of work that is deeply in accord with biblical values. It focuses enormous attention on developing people and providing those at various service levels of society with dignity and self-respect. It also provides a way out of the economic difficulties faced by the poor. Nevertheless, many entry-level service jobs in the United States and at ServiceMaster pay only the minimum wage, currently $5.15 per hour. This is considerably below the poverty level for a sole provider with a family of three. The United States poverty level for a family of three is $15,300, which means that many service personnel at ServiceMaster must find ways to supplement their income or reduce expenses. This may be done in a number of ways that resemble the manner in which European immigrants dealt with life upon immigration to the United States in the nineteenth and twentieth centuries. Often the service employee will work a second job or will live in an extended family in order to meet economic obligations.

Moreover, unless the contract calls for it, the Service Partner will not have health-care benefits. As Christians we must recognize that this is far from ideal, and that the lack of such benefits can be a profound obstacle to the health and job performance of the worker. We should continue to seek a society in which all persons' health-care needs are fully met. Nevertheless, current realities are what they are. There are growth opportunities at ServiceMaster for those who wish to grow in responsibility and income, but it does take time. In addition, other remedies are available in the United States to assist lower income people. These are discussed at length in the last part of this chapter.

Growth in responsibility and income at ServiceMaster requires the service employees to develop a strong ethic of work and responsibility. It requires training and education and it may also require that they leave ServiceMaster for higher paying jobs. Nevertheless, ServiceMaster does have a culture of work that is successful in transforming people, imparting dignity to people, and providing hope. So while ServiceMaster may not move all of the Service Partners considerably beyond the minimum wage, the company does affect the lives of these workers in a way that is positive and potentially life transforming. Moreover, ServiceMaster does provide the pathway for people who are willing to grow in responsibility and salary within ServiceMaster or with other companies. This pathway would not be provided if ServiceMaster and companies like it did not make the effort. It is truly a God-honoring and people-developing approach.

The model of training and development at ServiceMaster provides one very powerful approach toward solving the economic problems of the poor in the United States through employment in the service sector of the economy. But to go further, we have to move on to examples of companies in the manufacturing sector of the economy that are able, through their recruiting, training, and evaluation processes, to move their entry-level workers into higher levels of economic remuneration. Lincoln Electric provides an example of an American company that has done this for over a century. We turn now to examine the way they do it by examining the relevant parts of their management systems.

Lincoln Electric Company

Lincoln Electric was founded by John C. Lincoln, an engineer, in 1895 and was initially involved in the manufacture and repair of electric motors. The company was incorporated in Cleveland, Ohio, in 1906. James Finney Lincoln, John Lincoln's brother, joined the company in 1907, at which time John, the

President, began to devote his efforts to the development and use of welding machines and welding products. James, the vice-president of the company, became the general manager and operating head of the company in 1911. In 1914, at the beginning of World War I, Lincoln began to demonstrate the advantages of arc welding for attaching and repairing two metals, and the war provided the opportunity to develop this technology fully.

Lincoln Electric is now the world's leading manufacturer of welding products and equipment. Lincoln's welding products and welding consumables are marketed throughout the world. Welding products include arc welding machines, electrodes, power sources, wire and feeding systems, and environmental systems for handling the fumes from industrial welding processes. Lincoln's products are used for cutting, manufacturing, and repairing metal products. Lincoln is also a producer of a variety of electric motors, for various niche markets, ranging in size from one-third to 1,250 horsepower. Lincoln Electric became a public company in 1995. Its shares are traded on the NASDAQ Stock Exchange. At the end of 1996 Lincoln had a direct, worldwide employment level of 5,971.

Sales in 1995 exceeded $1 billion for the first time in the company's history. Significantly, Lincoln Electric reached the $1 billion milestone in sales in its hundredth year of operation. Sales in 1996 were $1.1 billion. Net income in 1996 increased 20.8 percent to $74.3 million over 1995. For the quarter ending March 31, 1997, net sales were $280.7 million and net income for the quarter increased to $21 million, a 27 percent increase from the first quarter of 1996.

Lincoln operates three manufacturing facilities in the United States: in Cleveland, Ohio ("The Ohio Company"), Gainesville, Georgia, and Monterey Park, California; and fourteen facilities in ten foreign countries. Foreign manufacturing operations currently exist in Sydney, Australia; Toronto, Canada; Sheffield, England (two); Grand-Quevilly, France; Rathnew, Ireland; Pianoro, Milano, and Celle Ligure, Italy; Mexico City, Mexico; Nijmegen, the Netherlands; Andebu and Stavern, Norway; and Barcelona, Spain. In addition Lincoln is adding manufacturing capacity in Cikarang, Indonesia, in order to serve the Asian region more effectively.

The values of the company, as developed by James F. Lincoln, have been stated completely in the three books he has written.[27] In particular, his book *A New Approach to Industrial Economics*[28] describes the key values he developed to run the company. These values have had a powerful influence on the design of the management systems at Lincoln and have contributed significantly to employee welfare and to the company's long-term agility, competitiveness, and success.

At the highest level of company values is Christ's Sermon on the Mount. In particular, James F. Lincoln attempted to guide the development of the business operations of Lincoln Electric by the Golden Rule:[29] "In everything do to others as you would have them do to you."

James Lincoln sought to apply the Golden Rule first to the customers of Lincoln Electric and then to Lincoln's employees. Stockholders had third priority but James Lincoln believed that if the Golden Rule were applied to customers and employees, shareholders would end up in better shape than if the firm attempted to serve stockholder interests primarily. Moreover, James Lincoln sought through employee stock ownership programs to make employees owners. He did not see any final conflict among the three stakeholders but saw that their interests were congruent with one another—at least in the long run.

Lincoln believed that the application of the Sermon on the Mount should proceed as follows:[30]

1. Recognize that the greatest economic need the worker has is for income and security in that income, and that both labor and management have the same interests. Yet the need for security in income can only come from satisfying needs of customers on a continuous basis. Therefore the customer is the key stakeholder whose needs are to be satisfied, and this should be done by applying the Golden Rule in the relations of the company to customers. *(Formal and Informal Rewards and Formal Control Process, and Values)*

2. Achieving the needs of the customer on a continuous basis is a function of staying in touch with the needs of the customer. This happens, in turn, by both management and the worker applying continuous efforts to increase *quality, customer service,* and *productivity,* which in turn will provide the customer new and improved products, higher quality products and reduced prices. *(Formal and Informal Control Process, and Values)*

3. The worker is to be provided with the most modern tools of production (methods and machines), as well as continuous training and skill development. Moreover, the worker is encouraged to participate in solutions to all kinds of work related problems. Not only do these efforts raise the productivity of the worker and the quality of work, but they also develop talents and raise the dignity, creativity, and self-respect of the worker. *(Formal Control Process, Formal and Informal Coordination and Integration, Informal Rewards, and Values)*

4. Continuous cost reduction is to be passed on to the customer in the form of lower prices, which along with continuous increases in quality, and the development of new and improved products, will result in fulfilling the Golden Rule to the customer. *(Formal Control Process and Values)*

5. Increased productivity, quality, and innovation is to be directly rewarded by a merit system that puts no upper limit on what a worker can earn but one that simultaneously penalizes workers for lack of productivity and for poor quality and absenteeism. The result is an incentive system which provides strong formal rewards according to variables which mat-

ter a great deal to the customer and which increase the economic and social status of the worker. *(Formal Control Process and Formal and Informal Rewards)*

Average total wages at Lincoln have always been above average for the Cleveland area. This has occurred because the piece-rate system is set up to allow an employee of normal productivity to earn a competitive base wage, but the bonus system allows those who work with extreme diligence and ingenuity to earn bonuses equal to or in excess of base pay. So strong is the bonus plan that factory workers have been known to earn over $100,000 per year! In 1996, the earnings of the average production worker at Lincoln were $62,000.

What is so striking about the results of the Lincoln piece-rate and bonus system is that they are so much at odds with the norm in the United States (as described in part II above). One becomes convinced that we as a nation can do much better.

6. Employees, by contributing to continuous progress and by maintaining a cooperative and trusting attitude towards management, can meet customer needs and thus achieve full employment. Therefore, in conjunction with principles 1–5 above, the Golden Rule is implemented with respect to the customer, to labor, and to management. *(Values, Formal Process, and Formal and Informal Rewards)*
7. James Lincoln recognized that the shareholder deserves a fair return on investment, but to the extent the company is already launched and successful (that is, it is not a new venture sponsored by venture capitalists), the stockholder really does not do much to contribute to the success of the company and is not terribly committed to the company, its customers and workers. Nevertheless, although Lincoln went through a tough economic period during the late 1980's and early 1990's, stockholder returns have now returned to levels that are considered excellent by the United States investment community. *(Values and Rewards)*

In summary, the forces that have put pressure on median wages in the United States, globalization and automation, have also been faced by Lincoln Electric. Yet its management systems, while being severely tested, have clearly produced more equitable results for its workers than those results experienced in the remainder of the Cleveland area and in the United States.

Lincoln Electric's recruiting process is very selective. The company is looking for the kind of people ServiceMaster is so good at developing: those who have a sense of responsibility, understand the work relationship and are eager to learn, grow, and develop. This makes Lincoln considerably more selective in initial employment recruiting than ServiceMaster is but the results are very impressive. Their first-line recruits include a portion of people from the lower socio-economic class, and the company has been without equal in the United

States in providing opportunities to bring these people to very high levels of skill, judgment, productivity and economic status.

Herman Miller, Inc.

Herman Miller is a leading designer and manufacturer of furniture and furniture systems. Herman Miller is today a global company employing approximately seven thousand people. Sales in the fiscal year ending May 31, 1997 were approximately $1.5 billion, of which $1.24 billion was from facilities in the United States. By comparison, sales in fiscal year 1996 were approximately $1.28 billion, of which $1 billion was from facilities in the United States. This represented a 16.5 percent increase in sales over fiscal year 1996. Net income increased 60 percent, from $17.1 million to $27.4 million. Sales and income have now increased for eleven consecutive quarters. Approximately one-third of the company's sales in Europe consists of exports from the United States.

The primary segment of the furniture market served by Herman Miller is the office furniture segment. In 1997 approximately 90 percent of the company's sales were in the design, manufacturing, and sales of office furniture, office furniture systems, and related products. Office furniture systems are interrelated pieces of furniture that may or may not be used together. Herman Miller in its design of open space has exhibited product leadership. This leadership is displayed in its innovative modular office equipment, including moveable, partial and full-height office walls, as well as in its office-seating furniture.

To a lesser extent, the company also designs and manufactures furniture for various other customer markets, such as health-care and residential markets. Innovative products for the health-care market include furniture for storing and retrieving materials and supplies in health-care facilities and laboratories. Herman Miller is a publicly owned company whose shares are traded on the NASDAQ Stock Exchange.

D.J. DePree formed the company in 1923 while working for Star Furniture Company in Zeeland, Michigan. Star Furniture was a small furniture manufacturer, incorporated in Michigan in 1905. DePree had an opportunity to purchase the company as a very young man, and with a loan from Herman Miller, DePree's father-in-law, he purchased Star and renamed the company after his father-in-law. The company remains headquartered in Zeeland, Michigan, a small town of approximately 5,500 residents, adjacent to Holland, Michigan.

In the early days of the company, DePree stuck to the manufacturing of "knockoff" furniture, furniture from various periods of history. This furniture served the residential marketplace. In the late 1930s DePree developed a number of associations with furniture designers and as a result developed an interest in the design of modern residential furniture. Slowly the company got involved in the office furniture market and by the early 1960s began to see itself as primarily in the office furniture business—which is true to this day, although they still serve multiple markets, including the residential market.

The company has been a design leader in office furniture. Its patented "Action Office" furniture is believed to be the first approach to the "open office system" which, as a concept, seeks to employ furniture to maximize efficient utilization of office space. The company holds trademarks and patents on a number of innovative office furniture designs and systems.

D.J. DePree was a devout Christian, and his influence, and the influence of Christianity, have always been pervasive in the company. DePree instilled strong Christian values into the company—values that took hold because he acted according to those values in his behavior with employees, customers, and all other constituents of the business. He believed strongly in equity, fairness, and participation, values and practices which he derived from his Christian faith. D.J. DePree led the company until 1962 when his eldest son, Hugh DePree, became CEO.

In 1949, DePree was listening to a lecture at Michigan State University by a young professor who had just moved to Michigan State from MIT. His name was Carl F. Frost, a former student of Joseph Scanlon at MIT. DePree was convinced by Frost's talk about the so-called "Scanlon Plan." It provided a statement of the way DePree had been managing and about the way he thought management should be done. It reflected the approach to management that DePree had already adopted.

The Scanlon Plan emphasizes the importance of participation, fairness, equity, merit, and trust, all virtues that were consistent with DePree's beliefs

Figure 4. The Principles of the Frost-Scanlon Process

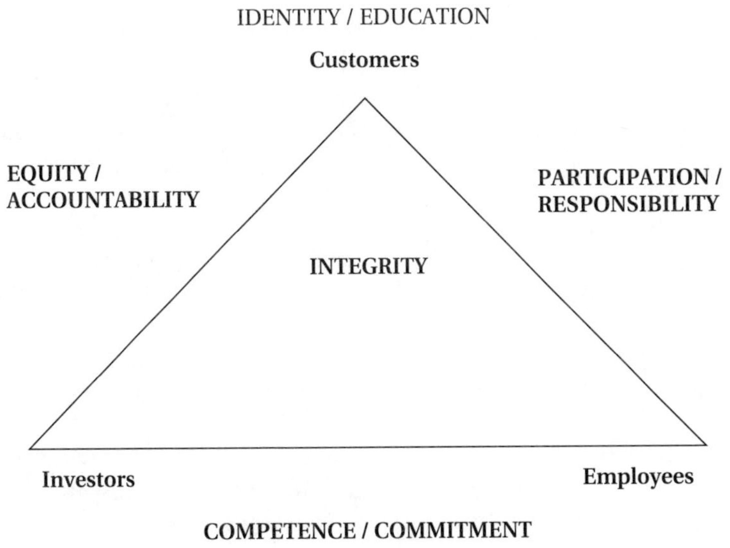

IDENTITY / EDUCATION

Customers

EQUITY /
ACCOUNTABILITY

PARTICIPATION /
RESPONSIBILITY

INTEGRITY

Investors   **Employees**

COMPETENCE / COMMITMENT

(values in Figures 3 and 4). As a result, DePree invited Frost to come to Herman Miller as a consultant, and Herman Miller became the first company in western Michigan to adopt the Scanlon Plan as a participatory form of management. Frost continues his association with the company to this day.

The principles behind the participatory management approach Frost developed, which he calls the Frost-Scanlon Plan, are portrayed in figure 4.[31] Many of the ingredients of the Frost-Scanlon Plan have been put into practice at Herman Miller over the years and still characterize the company's attitude towards employees.

Customers are at the pinnacle of the Frost-Scanlon Plan; without their satisfaction, investors will not receive an adequate return nor will employees receive bonus compensation. In fact, if customers are disaffected, investors will lose capital and employees will lose their jobs.

Investors and customers are seen as having very little loyalty. Investors and customers are egocentric: if they get a better deal elsewhere they will abandon the company and go elsewhere with their capital and with their purchases. Therefore, the survival and prosperity of the firm rests upon the way employees meet customer and investor needs. This represents an accurate portrayal of the way capital and product markets work in a competitive society.

How are executives and employees expected to meet the demanding and ever-changing needs of these two powerful sets of stakeholders? By adopting a set of four principles along with related management processes for carrying them out. A brief explanation of these principles and processes follows.[32]

Identity/Education. Executives and employees must come to the realization that the survival of their company and the survival of their jobs are at risk. Reality is harsh and demands continuous change, and this is the only context in which to view the task of managing our personal, professional, and organizational lives. Executives and employees come to understand these realities through a process of education into the realities of the business. The goal of the education process is for all to comprehend the nature of the competitive reality and to accept this reality. This process of education creates identity of executives and employees with the needs of the organization. The process of education is to be carried out continuously by management. *(Formal and Informal Control Process, and Formal and Informal Coordination and Integration)*

Participation/Responsibility. Once employees understand the realities of the business and accept them, they are encouraged to take responsibility for their domain of work. Once they take personal responsibility for their domain, they are expected to participate in management decisions affecting that domain, including making suggestions for improving processes and products.

The principle of participation and the process of taking responsibility means that relationships between management and employees should be cordial and constructive and not adversarial in nature. *(Values, Formal and Informal Control Processes, Infrastructure, and Coordination and Integration Systems)*

Competence/Commitment. Responsible participation and identity require that employees commit to a process of continuous growth in competence. The realities of the market place demand a competent work force, one that is continuously learning. The company has a responsibility to help here; one of the ways in which Herman Miller does help is through the widespread use of cross-functional teams whereby each member contributes and learns from the others. *(Formal and Informal Infrastructure, and Coordination and Integration Systems)*

Equity/Accountability. Employees are accountable for the results of their operations. Processes of accountability are established for each employee to ensure customer satisfaction and good investor returns. In return, the company commits to sharing the results equitably with employees through a bonus and associated profit sharing programs. *(Formal Control Processes, Infrastructure, and Rewards)*

In the middle of the triangle drawn to describe this system is the word INTEGRITY (in leadership style). If integrity is present in the leadership of the organization, all other principles and processes have an opportunity to flourish. If it is not present, the other principles and processes will not be able to function effectively. Under Frost's definition, integrity is closely related to the practice of management that constantly seeks to pursue social justice in its dealings with employees, customers, and investors.

This brief description of the Frost-Scanlon Plan makes evident its compatibility with the values of the founder of Herman Miller, D.J. DePree, and why he might have been attracted to the Scanlon Plan as he heard Carl Frost present it in 1949. To arrive at a concise statement of the key operating values of Herman Miller, consider the following quote from D.J. DePree: "A business is rightly judged by its products and services, but it must also face scrutiny and judgment as to its humanity."[33] This credo is etched permanently into the wall at the company's headquarters in Zeeland, Michigan.

Herman Miller has recently published a *Blueprint for Corporate Community* ("The Herman Miller Way").[34] The blueprint represents a formal restatement and clarification of the corporate philosophy of management; it attempts to define what Herman Miller is, what Herman Miller aspires to become, and how it intends to operate. The company is now engaged in a dialogue with all of its executives concerning the blueprint. The ultimate objective is to attain buy-in at all levels of the company, with the major effort to do so taking place in fiscal year 1998. *(Formal and Informal Coordination and Integration)*

The Blueprint emphasizes seven points:

1. The company seeks to provide "extraordinary value" to customers in the form of products and services that improve their businesses and their lives.

2. The company is a values-driven community of over seven thousand employee-owners who are performance oriented in terms of the customers they serve.
3. Herman Miller draws strength from diversity because diversity enhances its ability to be creative in the solutions it provides customers. In the process, the people of Herman Miller grow in relationships, creativity, skills, and problem-solving ability.
4. As employees create value for shareholders they create value for themselves, since the company believes in encouraging employees to become owners. This provides incentives for employees to be good stewards of the resources entrusted to them.
5. The company emphasizes innovations in product design which result in improvements in customer operations.
6. The company seeks in its decisions to be a good steward of the environment, not only because it may be good for business but because it is the right thing to do.
7. The company is committed to the truth and to integrity in all of its dealings. This is done by keeping promises—to customers, to shareholders, and within the company. The company seeks to "walk the talk" contained in the blueprint.

Management at Herman Miller seeks to capitalize on the distinctive talents of each individual. In that sense, the philosophy of management might be characterized as participatory, enabling, and empowering. Top management is concerned with unleashing and developing the gifts and talents of its people. Success has always come to Herman Miller by seeking good designs for its products and by pursuing a respect for the dignity and talents of its people.

Herman Miller is similar in many respects to both ServiceMaster and Lincoln Electric, and different in some very important ways—which adds other dimensions to the biblical view of management systems. The company's emphasis on the Frost-Scanlon Principles and the influence of the DePree family on the company operations for over 70 years have resulted in instilling values into the company which are deeply biblical.

The company's values and management systems seek to bring unity out of the diversity of the work force and to build a strong sense of community and loyalty among employees. The company has pursued policies that have been guided by integrity and have resulted in deeply moral behavior with regard to the treatment of all of its employees, customers, stockholders, and suppliers. In addition, the company has pursued strong environmental and social responsibility within the communities in which it has operated.

The Scanlon Process seeks to develop God's image in personnel by tapping the rational and creative attributes of all of their employees. Historically, the company has placed a strong value on its relationships with its people, and has attempted to be equitable in sharing the fruits of the company's effort with the entire work force in the form of egalitarian wage and salary structures, profit sharing, and stock ownership programs which affect practically all of Herman Miller's employees. The Frost-Scanlon Processes lead to a strong sense of dignity among the employees at Herman Miller. The commitment of the company to the development of the talents of its entire work force creates the opportunity for all to develop a sense of mastery in their work.

Nevertheless, the nature of the work force and the culture is different at Herman Miller than at ServiceMaster and Lincoln Electric. Unlike service partners at ServiceMaster, Herman Miller's employee-owners do not start off at the minimum wage, but at a wage and bonus level that is fully sufficient for the support of family life. Unlike those at Lincoln Electric, the incentives at the production level are not strong enough to yield the extraordinary levels of productivity and wages realized by the production worker at Lincoln. But as at ServiceMaster and Lincoln, the employees have a sense of dignity and equity and a chance to grow and develop, to reach their God-given potential, and they are encouraged to do so.

The former chairman and chief executive officer of Herman Miller, Kermit Campbell, who was the immediate successor of Max DePree in both roles, attempted to capture the essence of how he saw the culture at Herman Miller. He did this by describing his view of the "wise" corporation.

> I think corporations in the future will have a difficult choice: Will they have it as their goal to be successful? Or will they choose to pursue wisdom as a corporation? If they choose to pursue worldly success, they will probably achieve it. Many companies are finding this success, though I believe it may be short-lived. Success has always come to Herman Miller as the result of pursuing something else—good design, for example, or respect for people. It is not a matter of either/or, it's a matter of which one comes first. I think corporations will choose more and more to pursue wisdom first. There are some characteristics of corporations that survive long enough to be eligible for wisdom—just as there are some requirements for people who live long enough to earn the right to become wise. We have to be alive; we have to survive financially. We have to have skilled people who know their jobs and how to do them. We have to have products that truly solve our customers' problems.[36]

I believe Herman Miller has shown much corporate wisdom, and has shown that this wisdom is not at odds with strong profitability and employee welfare.

Donnelly Corporation[37]

Donnelly Corporation is a leading global manufacturer of mirrors and glass products for automobiles. The company is the world's leading supplier of rearview mirrors to the global automotive industry. The company serves customers throughout the world, from manufacturing locations in the United States and Europe through joint ventures in Asia. Net sales for fiscal year 1997 were a record $671 million, and net income after taxes was approximately $10 million. Since 1995 the company has almost doubled sales while profits have been approximately flat. Their corporate headquarters are located in Holland, Michigan. The company is a public corporation, incorporated under the laws of the State of Michigan; its shares are listed and traded on the New York Stock Exchange.

John Fenlon Donnelly ran the Donnelly Corporation for approximately fifty years until his death in 1986. The management systems at Donnelly resemble those at Herman Miller. They too are based on the Frost-Scanlon plan.

Paul Doyle, Director of Organizational Development, and Carol Kaplan, Director of Compensation and Benefits, have recently stated what makes Donnelly Corporation different, and these differences are why I see Donnelly fitting precisely into the class of public corporations I have used as examples in this chapter. Doyle and Kaplan state:

> What makes Donnelly's experience unique is that for 65 years our leaders have worked hard to learn how to tap the full potential of every person associated with our company. John F. Donnelly for many years taught us that the greatest reward for a person's work is not what they get from it, but what they become by it.[38]

The following selected passages from an address of Robert Doyle, former Director of Personnel of Donnelly Corporation, provide insights into the strong Christian legacy left by John Donnelly for Christian executives and for the practice of management.

> This is the major point I wish to make today: what made John Donnelly unique among business leaders, and the reason for his success as a CEO, was his religion. For John, religion was not something saved for Sundays, it was the driving force in his life and in everything he did. . . . You cannot possibly understand John's actions and his successes without understanding his very strong religious motivations. Like all businessmen, John studied and practiced management, marketing, finance and technology, but as he did, he sought to use the knowledge and skills of the businessman in a Christlike manner. This was the dimension that gave John his edge. Under John's leadership we never hesitated to act on a matter of social justice. We attempted a variety of affirmative action plans and participated in programs to employ the unemployable. John viewed the company as an institution of society and the community and, therefore, an institution with a responsibility to and for the community. . . . John was not unique among CEO's in his extensive knowledge, or in his practice of the cardinal virtues I have described, rare but not unique. Still he was considerably more successful than most in creating an organization whose hallmarks were participation, equity and trust.[39]

The major difference between Donnelly Corporation and the other three companies whose management practices were described previously is its profound understanding of the nature of work and the design of management systems that are explicitly designed to tap the full potential of people. Moreover, Donnelly defines "the people who matter to the organization" very broadly. These consist of a partnership among five constituents, each of whom make contributions to the organization and each of whom are owed inducements by the company.

The five constituents form a five-part model. The partners' and Donnelly's intended contributions to their welfare are described below.

- *Customers:* Donnelly seeks to exceed customer expectations in the provision of its products and services and realizes that, as an original-equipment manufacturer selling to the global automotive industry, it must do so in a world of intense competition.
- *Stockholders:* Donnelly is committed to providing outstanding investment returns to its long-term shareholders.
- *Employees:* The company seeks to be an employer that satisfies its employees. Donnelly has been named one of the ten best companies to work for in America (see footnote 37), eloquent testimony that the company does satisfy its employees.
- *Suppliers:* The company seeks to establish long-term relationships with its suppliers in a partnership mode of operations. This means few, but very loyal, supplier relationships, involving true partnership activity in fulfilling mutual interests.
- *Communities:* In the communities in which Donnelly operates throughout the world, the company seeks to become an exemplary citizen, valued by the communities and respected for what it does and how it carries out its operations.

Conclusion: Implications for Government, Business, and Non-Profits

Training and education policies on the part of both government and business are necessary to address the growing social problems created by the rapidly changing demands on the worker which have been caused by the changing composition of work.

Productivity and innovation, although requiring and using labor and capital as contributions, rely upon the application of knowledge as a key ingredient. Therefore, knowledge, and the application of knowledge, are becoming the most consequential economic factors for generating economic improvement in an advanced economy such as ours.[40] This must be emphasized in programs for the training and education of the disadvantaged.

The biblical conception of humankind leads to a significantly different view of human behavior and human dignity than do some influential views from science and behavioral science. In the latter, man is oftentimes viewed as a machine with certain chemical and physical properties, whose behavior is controlled by heredity and by environmental or "operant" conditioning. There is no free will and no human dignity possible under this view.[41]

While the biblical view does not deny the role of conditioning as a powerful influence on behavior, it does recognize that humans have a mind and free will, and as a result are able to think and act autonomously. Humankind has inherent value, self-worth, and dignity. Moreover, by recognizing and cultivating these inherent characteristics within the context of work, the manager unleashes very powerful, positive qualities in the worker and in the organization.

R.C. Sproul has developed these themes in detail:

> Where human dignity is cultivated in a work environment, increased production and higher quality are its inevitable byproducts. . . . The worker has a heart, and it breaks within him when he is treated without dignity. When his dignity is honored and the void is filled, then the sanctity of labor—his labor—is affirmed.[42]

Thus the effective executive will think of his or her responsibilities in terms of "the development of people in the process of managing work."

To exalt the worth and dignity of persons in management does not require executives to denigrate the need for profit. Profit is essential for economic exchange and investment. Without profit, investment will not take place. Without increased investment, productivity will be adversely affected. The result will be a decline in the standard of living, thus working to the detriment of the welfare of workers. Not only is profit consistent with human dignity, but pride in workmanship and human dignity are both bolstered when workers become owners and thereby participate in the economic success of their companies and of the economic system as a whole.

By developing and encouraging worker participation in employee stock-option programs and other company incentive plans, and by encouraging participation in the equity investments of pension funds operated on behalf of employees, executives may encourage significant employee involvement in ownership of their own company. Thus, there need not be a conflict between the needs of the employee and the needs of stockholders.

Yet in the relationship between labor and capital, biblical teaching advises us to give priority to the needs of labor. The right to ownership and management of private property and to profit is strongly affirmed in the biblical tradition, but the use of private property is to be governed by the social good.[43] Human beings are created in the image of God; capital is an aggregation of material objects, produced as a result of combining natural resources and labor. As a result, it is not proper or moral to consider labor as merely an economic resource to be used by executives to generate profits. And it is not proper to view management as the process of getting work done through people.

The laws of a nation should promote economic efficiency and simultaneously emphasize social justice. They should emphasize personal responsibility, personal incentives, full employment, a living wage, and appropriate social provision for health care, unemployment, disability, and retirement. The experiences of the companies in this chapter demonstrate that the trade-off between economic efficiency and social justice, when the motivational effects of treating people with dignity and respect are considered fully, is not nearly as extreme as that assumed by economic theory.

If democratic capitalism has as its purpose to serve the common good, then one has to look at the question of income distribution. And here the evidence of growing inequality over the past twenty-five years in the United States is not encouraging. Under either the traditions of civic republicanism or biblical ethics, economic growth must support the common good for it to be socially desirable. Here I find compelling the notions expressed not only by Pope John Paul in *Centesimus Annus* but also those expressed by Jonathan Boswell:

> If balanced, sustained economic performance is sought, it seems that to desire it primarily for its own sake is unwise, even self defeating, not to mention ethically unsound. If we seriously want it, it appears that we should want something far more, namely a social change extending particularly, though not exclusively to the economic system itself. We would accept that enterprise makes full practical and ethical sense only in and with as well as for community. We would acknowledge that economic health and a community renaissance are inseparable, and that of the two it is a community renaissance that would come first.[44]

Given the crucial nature of work and its importance to the spiritual, psychological, creative, and economic dimensions of life, unemployment and underemployment are devastating to the human condition, resulting in poverty and humiliation. There is something seriously wrong with any social and economic system that fails to provide the necessary incentives and opportunities for good work to those willing to seek it.

Democratic capitalism is the system that is potentially most effective in developing the higher nature of humankind while diverting many of the weaknesses and sins of human beings to outcomes that are socially desirable. Yet, unless the policies of business and government are sound and moral, unacceptable levels of unemployment, great income inequality, and much hardship will continue to be the result. These results are not inevitable in an advanced economy such as ours, as the case examples in this chapter illustrate.

The process of moving people from welfare to work, and then from work at the minimum wage to work for the wages required to sustain a family, cannot be accomplished by the independent efforts of business or government alone. Moving people from welfare into productive work is most effectively achieved through cooperation among the various groups representing society: government, business, and non-profit organizations. The chapter concludes by reviewing examples of cooperative efforts among government, business, and non-profit institutions in the cities and states in which the companies described in this chapter are located.

Good Samaritan Ministries, Holland, Michigan

Good Samaritan Ministries (GSM) is a faith and church-based institution that is part of a broad coalition of government, business, and non-profit institutions in Ottawa County, Michigan. The purpose of the coalition is to move people from the welfare population into productive work. The mission of Good Samaritan is to work with a network of local churches and equip them to attend to the physical, social, emotional and spiritual needs of welfare families in the county. The work of Good Samaritan also includes training clients to prepare applications for Medicaid and for property tax relief. Clients are also assisted in preparing their income taxes and, if eligible, obtaining the Earned Income Tax Credit.

Good Samaritan is under contract with the Family Independence Agency of the State of Michigan and with Michigan Works, an agency of Ottawa County. The charge to GSM under these contracts is to work with a coalition of other non-profit institutions and business organizations on one hand, and with local churches on the other. Once Michigan Works refers a client, Good Samaritan's professional staff attempts to assess the needs of the client and then with the client's participation and permission seeks to make a referral to an appropriate local church. Participating churches in turn provide mentors to each person referred to them. Mentors commit to "come alongside" each person and help meet his needs—physical, social, emotional, and spiritual—during the period in which he is making the transition from welfare to work. In the process, churches may also impart spiritual values that are intended to assist these people in the business of life. The spiritual dimension, of course, requires the desire and consent of the participant.

To make the mentoring project effective, Good Samaritan asks a participating church to identify five to seven people who are willing to serve on a relational ministry team. Ministry team members are asked to commit to remaining in an accountable relationship with the participant for up to one year. Good Samaritan then trains team members to minister to the clients who are referred to them. GSM provides training in structured relational ministry techniques. The training includes techniques of listening, problem solving, goal setting, financial planning, and spiritual support. In addition, team members are provided information on how to access help for their clients from various state and county agencies. They are also taught how to provide clients with child care and transportation services and how to meet other miscellaneous needs of their clients. Good Samaritan then follows up with the ministry team and provides additional training as needed.

Good Samaritan is one of four non-profit institutions in the county which contract with the state and county to coordinate the services necessary to place, train, and care for all the needs of people moving from welfare to work. The other three non-profits which contract with state and county agencies are:

- Kando Industries, which provides job training and placement;
- Life Services Systems, which provides transportation services; and
- The Children's Resource Network, which provides child- and day-care services for children of people moving from welfare to work.

These four non-profit institutions are supported both by private contributions and by public funds. In addition, each of them utilizes volunteer labor.

The entire work-to-welfare coalition is coordinated by the Project Zero Initiative of Ottawa County, a state-supported initiative. The coalition has been very successful in removing people from welfare and placing them in gainful employment. The welfare population of Ottawa County as of April 1998 was only fifteen families, leading the *Washington Post* to cite Ottawa County as the first to solve the welfare problem during this new era of workfare. The Director of Good Samaritan, William Raymond, recognizes that this effort is at present being assisted by very positive economic conditions, which have moved the starting wage to between $6.00 and $7.00 per hour for entry-level jobs in the Holland area. This is significantly above the minimum wage of $5.15 per hour, although it is not enough to move a family of three or four above the poverty line.

Ottawa County is one of twelve pilot sites in Michigan in which non-profit institutions are being supported by public funds to assist in the welfare-to-work program. Ottawa County/Good Samaritan was the first Project Zero site to work with faith-based mentoring and a network of churches, but other counties in Michigan are now developing the mentoring component. Kent County (Grand Rapids) and Berrian County (Benton Harbor and St. Joseph) have established coalitions and church networks. These coalitions are also working to connect mentors with families. Good Samaritan has provided consultation and technical assistance to both counties in order to facilitate these mentoring programs.

Good Samaritan has been in existence for nearly thirty years. The relational ministry and mentoring portions of the work of GSM have been in existence for ten years. Good Samaritan receives 25 percent of its funding from public sources and 75 percent from private sources. These private sources include donations from individuals, churches, businesses, and the United Way. Approximately half of the funds necessary to support the relational ministries and Project Zero program within Good Samaritan come from public sources.

The program appears to be effective in preventing large-scale recidivism among the portion of the welfare population that has been placed into productive work. Good Samaritan serves approximately fifty welfare clients at a time. GSM does not report a heavy overlap with previously trained, placed, and mentored welfare clients.

The demonstrated effectiveness of Good Samaritan and the Ottawa County coalition has stimulated significant interest from other cities. Good Samaritan has had representatives of twenty-eight states and over one hundred cities throughout the United States contact them and ask for various kinds of assistance in exploring and adopting the coalition concept to assist at-risk families. They now have commitments from two states to provide assistance in developing similar coalitions in those states. Clearly, the coalition concept put into place in Ottawa County can be extended to many additional states and counties throughout the United States.

ServiceMaster's Partnership with Goodwill Industries and the North Carolina State Government

ServiceMaster is in partnership with the state government of North Carolina to facilitate the state's welfare-to-work program, which is designed to train, employ, and empower the poor. Under this arrangement, Goodwill Industries is funded by the state to work with welfare recipients. Goodwill provides personal counseling and initial skill training in order to place welfare recipients with ServiceMaster. Goodwill then follows up on these employees to evaluate their progress as service partners, assessing how the people are doing at what they are supposed to be doing. In order for Goodwill to provide the necessary initial training required by ServiceMaster, the company has been involved with Goodwill in identifying the skills, values, and sense of responsibility which the company requires of its service partners.

Neither Goodwill nor the state of North Carolina subsidizes ServiceMaster. But if Goodwill identifies deficiencies in the performance of service partners, the organization does provide the training necessary to bring these people up to the performance level required by ServiceMaster.

To summarize, this example of moving people from welfare to work involves the interaction among all three sectors of society: government provides funding to a non-profit organization, which in turn works with a corporation in order to develop the skills of welfare recipients so that they become employable.

An Alternative to the Three-Sector Programs

One possible model of a public-private partnership is for state and national government agencies to partner directly with ServiceMaster, and with other companies that have effective programs for developing people. The companies selected could take over the process of training and placing employees in various service and manufacturing occupations. Treating people with dignity and respect during training would contribute to their success and development during their working lives. These people would be treated well and trained well and thus prepared and motivated to enter the work force. It would be especially helpful in developing these employees if they could be placed in organizations which have deep values concerning the dignity and development of their people.

The disadvantage of this model relative to the North Carolina-Goodwill-ServiceMaster model is that members of the welfare population often require remedial services (e.g., transportation, child care, and health care). Industry is not in a good position to provide these services given the nature of their economic responsibilities. As we have seen in the Good Samaritan example and as we will see in the next example, these remedial services may be provided more effectively and at lower expense by a coalition of non-profit institutions with financial assistance from business. Financial assistance from business may come in the form of direct contributions to relevant and effective non-profit institutions. It is not unusual for businesses to contribute to local charities, especially those that are effective in serving the disadvantaged.

The Case of St. Clair Avenue in Cleveland

Will coalitions of government, business, and non-profits like those in Holland, Michigan, and in North Carolina work in all situations to move people from welfare to work? I think not. To explain, I will draw on a situation from the very street on which Lincoln Electric is headquartered: St. Clair Avenue in Cleveland, Ohio.

The downtown area of Cleveland has enjoyed a remarkable renewal during the last twenty years. Rosabeth Moss Kanter, noted professor at the Harvard Business School, reports that this turnaround "was orchestrated by a few dozen chief executive officers of big companies" with headquarters in Cleveland.[45] This renewal is nowhere more evident than on the lakefront end of St. Clair Avenue, near Jacobs Field and the Rock 'n' Roll museum. This urban renewal effort is a remarkable testimony to what can be done through corporate involvement in the civic affairs of a community.

But separating Lake Erie and the headquarters of Lincoln Electric are eight miles of some of the worst poverty in the United States, an area more representative of conditions in a third-world country. Clearly the people who live on St. Clair Avenue are not employable by Lincoln Electric. The only thing Lincoln and its employees can do for these people is to be a good corporate citizen and to support non-profit and relief agencies that are attempting to deal with the human problems on St. Clair.

One obvious fact about the people on St. Clair: like so many of the urban disadvantaged in the United States, they have suffered from a breakdown in family structure. Because the culture of work and good work habits are first taught in the family, the breakdown of the family on St. Clair means that little of this culture is being developed in the home. A large number of the people living on St. Clair are African-American. According to national statistics, approximately 70 percent of African-American children are born out of wedlock, and in many of these cases their fathers escape responsibility for the care of their own children. The legal system in the United States has not been effective in holding these parents responsible.

The evidence of slums, idleness, drugs, crime, and violence on St. Clair creates what appears to be an almost hopeless situation for the kinds of coalitions of government, business, and non-profit institutions described above. For this portion of our society more drastic steps seem necessary to move the poor from streets like St. Clair into productive work.

The people on St. Clair are not homogeneous. Some simply lack basic education and skills to enter the work force. Programs may be developed by government to separate these people from this hopeless environment and move them into a more controlled environment in which they can obtain the basic skills and attitudes needed to enter the workforce. Once these problems are remedied, coalitions like those that exist in Holland, Michigan, and in North Carolina could be effective in moving these people into productive work. With the assistance of government and non-profit institutions, Lincoln could then help develop these people and place them into productive work.

The issue related to those on St. Clair who suffer from more serious social, legal, physical, and mental problems is not how to move these people from welfare to work, but rather how to restore their dignity as human beings. This requires a massive relational ministry on the order of the Sisters of Charity of Calcutta. This would be a one-on-one relational ministry that must be owned by all of us: government, non-profits—including churches—and businesses, like Lincoln, that have a stake in the conditions of their neighborhood.

This section on proposals for adopting welfare-to-work programs ends on a hopeful but sober note. Many coalition efforts like those in Michigan and North Carolina may be effective in moving the welfare population into productive work. But in extremely depressed urban areas there are no simple answers. In some of these areas a focused effort by government, business, non-profits, churches, and neighborhood groups can make some improvement. Many such coalitions throughout the United States are reporting some progress in blighted areas in spite of formidable odds.[46] As the model urban renewal effort of downtown Cleveland illustrates, nothing is impossible, especially when God, his people, and all people of goodwill own the problem and begin to act to solve it.

~ 14 ~

Transforming American Welfare

An Evangelical Perspective on Welfare Reform

Stanley W. Carlson-Thies, Center for Public Justice

Evangelicals contemplating welfare policy cannot avoid one thing: God does not give anyone or any society the option of closing their ears to the cries of the poor and oppressed. Whether we think government welfare programs have been a waste or are a necessity, whatever role we believe the church should play in assisting the needy, all who claim to follow God's ways must have a heart for the poor. Yet it is obvious that not all help is equally helpful; indeed it has become apparent that programs of assistance can even have unintended negative effects. So beyond the intent to help, we require wisdom about effective assistance.

Clarity about compassion is especially needed these days as debate continues over charity and justice and about the roles of church and government in helping the needy, and as our nation continues to reconstruct its welfare programs. Committed to biblical wisdom and zealous that congregations and Christian ministries should fulfill their tasks, how should evangelicals evaluate the dramatic changes in the public welfare effort? In this essay I suggest biblical standards for effective assistance, evaluate recent welfare reforms, propose principles for improving welfare, and conclude with a challenge for evangelical action on behalf of the poor.

The "Welfare" Imperative

It is a strict duty of justice and truth not to allow fundamental human needs to remain unsatisfied. It is also necessary to help needy people acquire expertise, to enter the circle of exchange, and to develop their skills to make the best use of their capacities and resources.[1]

That those who have enough are accountable to come to the assistance of those who have not is the unmistakable message of the Bible, from start to end. Some four hundred verses attest to God's concern for the poor and to our obligation to meet their needs if we are able.[2] Demonstrating love for others is an obligation second only to our duty to love God totally, Jesus reminded us (Matt. 22:34–40). The prophets continually warned the people of God that worship unaccompanied by justice and mercy is abhorrent to God, and in the New Testament James confirms their word by including care for the needy in his definition of true religion (James 1:27). Nor is the call to love our neighbors addressed only to those who claim to love God; the pagan king Nebuchadnezzar was warned by Daniel that if he was to be restored to humanity he must, among other changes, renounce wickedness "by being kind to the oppressed" (Dan. 4:24–27, NIV).

Such care for others is to be manifest in the structures and patterns of our interactions; the Scriptures require, for instance, that laborers be given a fair wage, weights and measures be accurate, justice in the courts be administered without favoritism to the wealthy, and flat roofs be fenced lest the unwary plunge over the edge. The Bible anticipates as well that there will be crises due to accident, injustice, or brokenness—emergencies that can be overcome only by special help—and when such crises occur, we who are able to help are obligated to be Good Samaritans and not to walk by on the other side of the road. The Bible does not, however, simply demand a compassionate response to such need. It also guides us to understand what kind of assistance should be given. Three principles stand out.

First, the aim of help is to enable the family or person to take care of themselves. In the guidelines for assistance detailed in the Pentateuch, those who had suffered an economic setback but remained able to work were to be offered a no-interest loan; the loan could be forgiven, but the intent was to make it possible for the family to work itself out of its crisis. Families unable to take care of themselves in the marketplace, even with the help of a free loan, were to be given the opportunity to glean in the fields, using their own labor to harvest grain and fruit left behind. Those unable to act on their own behalf at all were to be supported from income raised through the third-year tithe.[3] Similarly, in the New Testament the apostle Paul gathered support from the far-flung churches for the relief of their poor brothers and sisters in Jerusalem (1 Cor. 16:1–4), and yet declared that the able-bodied must pursue honest work, not only to support themselves but to be able to contribute to others (Eph. 4:28; 2 Thess. 3:10).

Thus help should not be unconditional and undemanding. Rather, true assistance is designed to draw on and to build up the capabilities of those in need. Assistance to overcome a crisis—"welfare" help—should aim to restore persons and families to their diverse responsibilities or callings and not become a substitute way of life.[4] But though conditional, biblical help is not pinched. The second principle of assistance, thus, is that help should be generous, sufficient to restore and ensure a reasonable and decent place in society. The well-off are not to cling to their riches but to share with others. The general standard, as John Mason points out, is "liberal sufficiency for need."[5]

The third principle is that multiple agents are responsible to assist the poor.[6] Both the Old and New Testaments emphasize that families, nuclear and extended, are to care for their own needy members. Economic institutions have a role; the poor were able to glean because farmers were required not to strip fields and orchards of all the harvest. The church is to care for its own and also others. Government, too, as the institution charged to promote public justice, must play a part. The godly king, as described in Psalms, "will defend the afflicted among the people/and save the children of the needy; he will crush the oppressor" (Ps. 72:4, NIV). Job, who had been a village elder clothed with public authority, recalls being honored "because I rescued the poor who cried for help, and the fatherless who had none to assist him" (Job 29:12, NIV). The apostle Paul emphasized the high dignity and indispensability of political authorities, who are instituted by God to punish wrongdoers and uphold those who do good (Rom. 13:1–7).

Involvement by the government is important because the needy require assistance even when those who can help are not moved to generosity, because poverty can have systemic causes necessitating a large-scale response and legal changes, and because resources are not necessarily located in the areas of greatest need.[7] As Jonathan Edwards remarked, impoverished families should not "be left to so precarious a source of supply as voluntary charity," for they should have "something sure . . . to depend upon."[8] Government may rightly step in to ensure that help is forthcoming as needed.

Such a formulation rightly emphasizes that the government's role is not exclusive but rather supplementary. Its task is to ensure that justice is done, and not necessarily to step in itself, for it must take care not to displace others who have their own responsibilities to help the needy. And when government must act, its own help should, as much as possible, aim to uphold those other institutions. The ways government provides direct help—programs and checks—are impersonal and abstract, whereas a renewal of responsible action and a recovery of direction and drive require personal, direct, and morally authoritative assistance. When poverty is entrenched, the help likely to be most effective "comes from people with deep moral and religious commitments, and very often from those who work for explicitly religious organizations."[9] Thus government should, when possible, work with, rather than substitute for, the assistance efforts of the institutions that are closest to those in need. It is these organizations that can and should bear *direct* responsibility for people in special need. Government policies should not sidestep or displace families, churches, schools, and independent service agencies. To the contrary, the law and public funds should go, first of all, to support the institutions and organizations that can minister directly and personally to people, helping them recover their own accountability.[10]

In evaluating welfare policies and welfare reform, then, we should consider whether and how government cooperates with nongovernmental assistance efforts, whether programs and policies are designed to assist people to become independent of help, and how generous and reliable is the assistance offered. And throughout, we must be careful to see that people are actually helped, and not merely judge how well policies, programs, and reforms are designed.

The Trajectory of American Welfare

Compared to other wealthy democracies, America has never had a full "welfare state." The western European and Scandinavian countries, along with others, such as Canada, have adopted a more systematic governmental approach to alleviating needs and protecting against vulnerability; they cover more policy areas, and they spend more on their public programs.[11]

Yet while conservatives thus vastly exaggerate when they damn the American "nanny state," they are right to see that our own welfare programs have a pattern and a logic, and that our own design has been deeply flawed. Such flaws in the architecture and aims of our own system mean that criticism may not be confined to how far short of the European model our system has fallen. Our own approach may have been smaller-scale, but it has suffered from being overgovernmentalized and by focusing too much on income maintenance. It is both ironic and significant that the better-developed welfare states themselves are also in the throes of reconstruction in order to come to grips with the same problems.[12]

A determined government welfare effort in the United States began in the 1930s with the New Deal. Before that time, assistance for the needy was mainly local and typically supplied by charities, many of them faith-based, often working with, and supported by, local governments. Such assistance, as Marvin Olasky and others have shown, had many positive features. It acknowledged the poor as accountable persons with a spiritual and moral dimension who should be strengthened to overcome the challenges facing them and who needed, as much or more than material resources, true neighbors on whom they could rely.[13]

This charitable response to poverty became increasingly strained as the nation developed, however. Families were increasingly dependent on a cash income and on the health of the formal economy as the nation industrialized and became urbanized. Yet at the same time the ability of charities to respond was diminishing as ideas about poverty and charity changed, as those with resources had less time to volunteer, and as the rich and poor lived farther and farther apart.[14] The catalyst for radical change was the Great Depression. It produced wide-scale poverty which clearly had systemic, and not only personal, causes. And it overwhelmed not only the charities but also local and state government resources.

The New Deal was American society's response, an evolving and rather unsystematic attack on the crises of unemployment and poverty. It inaugurated a wide range of federal government employment, welfare, and social insurance programs, often carried out in conjunction with state governments. Some programs were temporary, such as the public-employment programs; others, such as Social Security, were the planned beginnings of a major change in responding to vulnerability; yet others, notably the Aid to Dependent Children (later Aid to Families with Dependent Children) program, were minor efforts that mushroomed into key elements of the American welfare system.[15]

To this legacy was added a new dimension after the Second World War, when the federal government took on a commitment to promote full employment and to supervise the economy for the good of all. In the 1950s a federal responsibility to increase the access of low-income families to housing and to promote urban development were added. In the 1960s, sparked by the exposé of continued poverty, expanded and new federal programs, notably government health insurance for the aged and poor, were added as part of President Lyndon Johnson's Great Society and War on Poverty. And through the 1970s and into the 1980s this collection of initiatives was further developed.

This six-decade trend of social activism in America was in many ways a positive one. It acknowledged that poverty can be due to systemic or external causes and is not always the result of personal or moral deficits. It presumed that the needy should receive help, so that lack of will or insufficiency of resources on the part of charities or lower governments may not be the final word if the federal government is able to respond. The New Deal/Great Society tradition presumed as well that persistent and prevalent poverty calls for a deliberate and significant commitment by the nation.

However, this tradition of social assistance also included several profoundly negative features. The rhetoric, from the beginning, termed assistance a hand up, not a handout, and yet the main emphasis in fact became income maintenance, that is, supplying to the poor the resources they lack. Few questions were asked about why families needed assistance or about what they should do, or stop doing, in order to advance.[16] Government turned extensively to nongovernmental organizations to deliver services to the needy, and yet because it treated those organizations like extensions of itself, their ability to offer personal and moral assistance was compromised, and poor families, even when their help was delivered by nonprofit organizations, often became isolated from their own communities.[17] Focused on the relations between the poor person or family and the public programs intended to rescue them, government officials and society in general paid insufficient attention to the declining health of civil society, such as the collapse of families and the atrophy of social networks in the poorest communities.

Welfare became, in short, not only government-supported but governmentalized, separate from and often in tension with the assistance offered by real neighbors and by the institutions of civil society. Rather than being devoted to empowering families for independence, the aim and effect of welfare became, to a great extent, the maintenance of poor families and communities in their poverty and dependence on others. The symbol of welfare became the public assistance office whose employees seek not to help families regain their footing but rather to determine what size government check they are eligible to receive.[18] Such a system rightly satisfied virtually no one.

Welfare Reformed

American welfare has always been a work in progress, constantly criticized and redesigned. Many of the changes and criticisms have been about extent: the range of benefits and the numbers of beneficiaries, the total cost and size of programs and agencies. However, equally persistent and important have been criticisms and changes relating to dependency. President Franklin Roosevelt at the very outset warned against the "dole" as a soul-chilling force that should be avoided as much as possible by giving people work opportunities instead.[19] His concern was revived in the later 1960s, resulting in modest work requirements for some AFDC recipients (the WIN program). Continued concern resulted, in 1988, in adoption of the Family Support Act, a compromise reform of the AFDC program that united conservative demands for work requirements with liberals' insistence on providing government services to prepare people for work.[20] However, these and other attempts to ensure that welfare became a pathway to independence resulted in few significant changes in either the actual workings of the programs or in their outcomes.

Radical change in both policy and practice is now underway. The 1996 federal welfare reform law (the Personal Responsibility and Work Opportunity Reconciliation Act) made a long list of changes: totally replacing AFDC with a new program called Temporary Assistance for Needy Families; cutting federal social spending, particularly by changing the food stamp program and making immigrants ineligible for many federal social benefits (both of these changes have largely been reversed by later action); increasing subsidies for child care for poor families; strengthening the enforcement of child support obligations; and more.[21] Beyond the details, the 1996 federal law, along with the experimental modifications already made by many states to their AFDC programs under waivers from the federal government, have changed the entire course of American welfare. We can best summarize the redirection under three heads.

From Increasing Federal Dominance to Increased State and Local Design and Control

After six decades, the trend of growing federal control over social welfare has been reversed. The federal government no longer operates a national welfare program in conjunction with the states; it now sends its funds to the states as block grants, leaving it to the states to operate their own welfare programs, within certain federal guidelines. Each state now has its own welfare system, and many of them have, in turn, authorized the counties beneath them to design their own systems. The federal role now is limited mainly to sending out the fixed sums to which each state is entitled, ensuring that states report the main features of their redesigned programs, monitoring state compliance with certain performance goals, and facilitating the sharing of information and design ideas between states.

States and localities are using their new freedom to craft distinctive programs that take account of the specific characteristics of the welfare populations in their respective jurisdictions, the particular balance of economic opportunities and barriers, and the distinctive array of nongovernmental resources.[22] Programs can become more effective as a result, although at the same time great variations in benefits are developing.

From Income Maintenance to Empowerment to Independence

As signaled in the change from Aid to Families with Dependent Children to Temporary Assistance to Needy Families, welfare assistance is now intended to prepare families to provide for themselves through employment, rather than to be an alternative source of income. The typical employee in a welfare office is now someone mandated to help a welfare client prepare for work, and no longer a specialist in the rules governing eligibility for cash grants.

The push into employment has elements of both "help" and "hassle," to use the terms of Lawrence Mead.[23] "Hassles" include the five-year lifetime limit on federal welfare aid, the requirement that able-bodied adults, in order to receive cash assistance, either be working or engaged in activities to make them employable, and the rule in many states that applicants must search for work even while their eligibility for benefits is being assessed. "Help" includes services ranging from conventional job training to volunteer mentors that help families improve their life-skills; employment supports such as child-care subsidies and transportation assistance; and income supplements such as federal and state EITC programs and the continuation of Medicaid benefits during the first year of work.[24]

Other rules and programs encourage additional positive life-choices by individuals and families that have requested assistance, such as avoiding pregnancy outside of marriage, completing high school, enforcing payment of child support, and ensuring that children receive vaccinations.

From Government-centered Welfare to Partnerships With Community and Faith-based Groups

Welfare has also been changed into a government effort that works in partnership with various organizations in civil society. Everywhere welfare agencies are creating formal and informal networks with employers to discover how to prepare clients for employment and to secure jobs for those clients. To provide the mentoring that is the key to a successful transition to independence for many families, welfare agencies are linking with social groups and congregations, connecting with preexisting networks of congregations that offer assistance, or constructing their own networks of congregational mentors. Welfare officials are working with other public officials and with community groups to figure out how prospective employees can move between home, work, and child-care provider despite the inadequacies of most public transportation systems.

The change of the welfare program to empowerment has forced state and local officials to seek out and partner with these and other community resources. The federal law, in addition, includes a specific measure, the "Charitable Choice" provision, designed to expand the involvement of the faith community in the public-welfare effort.[25] Charitable Choice requires government not to discriminate against religious organizations when contracting for services or determining which groups are eligible to receive vouchers to provide services to welfare families. In addition, it protects the religious character of organizations that accept public funds to provide services while also ensuring that recipients are not coerced into religious practices. These features are intended to encourage more faith-based organizations to offer services to welfare families while ensuring that such organizations can retain their nongovernmental character, thus remaining able to provide a different kind of service than government agencies themselves can offer.

These are radical changes, going to the very heart of the public-welfare effort in America. They are more than paper changes. States, and in many cases, counties, have actual control of welfare in their jurisdictions and have created new programs and new partnerships. Time limits have imparted a sense of urgency to welfare families, to case workers, and to community groups. The federal welfare block grants to the states carry with them both incentives for good performance and fines for violating the rules or failing to move sufficient numbers of recipients into employment. This time the actual practice, and not only the formal rules, of government welfare in America is being dramatically changed. What happens to families that turn to government welfare is very different now than even a year ago.[26]

These dramatic changes in the course of American welfare are highly positive, in principle. Welfare ought to help people move to independence rather than maintaining them in their poverty and dependence. Employment is positive, not only because of the income it gives to families but because it imparts a fruitful structure to the lives of the employees and also to their families and neighborhoods.[27] Work is one of the main ways people use the gifts God has given them and by which they contribute to others. The devolution of authority to state and local governments has energized them to become problem solvers rather than simple implementers of rules dreamed up in far-away Washington, D.C. The development of partnerships acknowledges that the well-being of the needy is a responsibility of everyone and not just government,[28] while not simply dumping the poor on the steps of churches and charities.

Yet in both details and in several main features, the new trajectory of American welfare is troubling and even in some respects mistaken. A series of problem areas indicates the need to reform welfare reform itself.

An Unreliable Safety Net

The most basic cause for concern is just the uncertainty that exists about the situation of many of the thousands of families that have left the welfare rolls since the federal and state programs have been radically changed. It is not that a larger population on assistance or a growing welfare budget is a positive thing; these are, rather, signs that many of a society's families for some reason are unable to provide for themselves. But the point of welfare is to offer assistance when families have no other recourse. When the welfare rolls shrink it should be because fewer families need assistance.

But that is just what is unclear in the current era of welfare reform. Without a doubt the new policies and programs have assisted or persuaded many families to make a successful transition to independence. However, from the start there has also been evidence, fragmentary but persistent, that other families are not receiving help they need because they have been cast off support before they are ready, are required to work without access to daycare or other essential supports, were sanctioned for unintended or petty offenses, have been misled by rumors or misinformation that they are not eligible for help, or were thrust insufficiently prepared into work that will not sustain their families.

No one knows what proportion of the families off welfare are now truly self-supporting, and no one is sure just how many families are no longer receiving aid they need. The numbers do not appear to be very large; certainly the critics who predicted that thousands of families and children would be left destitute, sleeping on the streets, misjudged both the nature of the changes and the capabilities of most welfare families.[29] Nevertheless, there are at least five serious problem areas.

Time Limits

Time limits affirm that welfare is intended to assist a family in achieving independence, not to be a substitute for the family's own activity. But not all families will be able to achieve independence fast enough. A portion of the case load can be exempted from the five-year federal lifetime limit on aid, but it is uncertain that the exemption is large enough to cover all families that will require it; indeed, no one can be sure if the exemption is too large or too small.[30]

Moreover, while time limits provide just the catalyst some families require in order to successfully strive for independence, in other cases the limits are counterproductive. Mothers have been forced by the time limits to drop out of education or training programs that would have prepared them for well-paying jobs. Because receipt of even minimal, federally funded cash benefits keeps the five-year clock running, states are unable to use partial benefits as a supplement to wages, forcing some families to choose between independence without sufficient income or continued dependence on welfare. Time limits have also damaged an innovative and effective Maryland program that enlisted churches as caseworkers to get families off welfare within six months. Before the federal law was passed, the program gave the churches an entire year's worth of a family's welfare checks, producing a lump sum that could be used to pay off debts, buy a reliable car, or purchase specialized training. But using up the extra six months of a family's life-time benefits is very risky, so the program now can only provide a smaller nest egg.[31]

The basic problem is that time limits are a crude way to implement the "tough love" approach that should characterize welfare. Some get a chance to loaf when they need a firm push; worse, others are cut off from help even though they cannot make it on their own. Time limits are too crude an implementation of the dual biblical principles that assistance should stimulate the poor to do everything they can themselves and yet provide generous help.

"Work First"

To help welfare families move to independence, most states have adopted a "work first" or "rapid attachment" strategy of minimal training and maximum pressure to get able-bodied adults to take the first job available, with little regard for the nature of the job, the adequacy of the pay, or the career interests of the employees.[32] Training and education programs in the past too often became substitutes for employment. By contrast, employment of any kind puts a person on the path to other job opportunities and helps him or her to sort out interests and skills. Any job allows the person to build a record of reliability and requires her to develop the organizational and coping skills needed to succeed as an employee. Most important, being thrust into employment is the only way some welfare recipients are able to overcome their fear of failure and to discover their capabilities.[33]

But Work First is inadequate as an empowerment strategy. While almost anyone can get hired when unemployment levels have been very low for so long, many find retaining employment to be a challenge that is beyond them when they are confronted with conflicts on the job, the difficulty of moving between work, day care, and home, or the complexities of reorganizing family and personal patterns to support employment. It may take several tries before a new employee is able to settle into a job; for others, a mentor or caseworker readily available to give advice and encouragement is needed. In all these cases, independence requires supportive services along with the strong push into the workforce.[34]

But getting a footing on the bottom rung of the job ladder is not enough, either. Increasingly, jobs that pay enough to allow a family to advance require specialized skills and education, and not just a good attitude, experience, and energy. Without additional assistance, even the most willing employee can remain stuck in a job that pays so little that the family can hardly sustain itself once transitional benefits like salary supplements and Medicaid eligibility run out after a year. As a legislative audit in late 1998 of Virginia's welfare program noted, many of the welfare recipients who had successfully found and retained employment were earning so little that they required supplemental welfare benefits in order to make ends meet—supplemental help that counts against the five-year lifetime limit.[35] And jobs at this lower end, even if they pay enough, are likely to be seasonal or short-term, or to go offshore or disappear entirely in a recession. So training and education opportunities need to be offered. However, the federal welfare law's time limits and its heavy stress on getting recipients into work make it difficult for states to offer such career building tools.[36]

Furthermore, the Work First approach is particularly inadequate for the harder cases on the welfare rolls. As one researcher notes, these families typically need, in addition to intensive job-preparation and job-retention assistance, help "in battling domestic violence, drug and alcohol abuse, and mental illness." Participation in programs to address such challenges, however, cannot be counted by the families involved as a required work activity, and although a state may provide such services using its own funds if it chooses, it cannot count families participating in them as part of its work participation quota.[37]

Employment is the right goal for welfare families, and requiring work is appropriate. However, the Work First approach is not adequate for the real task, which is empowerment to independence.

Child Support or Dads?

In recognition of the reality that family breakdown and nonformation are key causes of contemporary poverty, the goals of the new TANF program include promoting marriage and strengthening two-parent families. Yet the new rules in fact perpetuate the traditional American welfare focus on mothers and children, giving inadequate attention to the noncustodial fathers. These fathers come into view mainly through the requirement that mothers establish the paternity of their children, and the states' obligation to aggressively pursue child support payments from noncustodial parents. In other words, the fathers appear essentially only as sources of income, as wallets.

Indeed, noncustodial fathers (and mothers) ought to fulfill their financial responsibilities to their children. And enforcing that obligation may have the additional benefit of discouraging family abandonment and promiscuous sexual activity. However, by paying insufficient attention to the circumstances of the fathers and by ignoring the emotional dimension of family life, the policies may do little good and actual harm.

Usually only $50 per month of the collected support is passed through to the mother and children, with the rest reimbursing the government for the welfare payments it has been making to the family. Getting the father to pay the child support thus does little to actually bind him and the mother together for the sake of their children. And the fathers often are neither in regular employment nor very good prospects for well-paying jobs. Unless they—just like the mothers of their children—are not only expected to be employed but also assisted into the workplace, they may be unable to provide the required child support. The consequence is likely to be this: by identifying the father of her children as required, the mother may actually gain almost nothing in child support payments while alienating the father, who had been providing informal support and at least periodically visiting the children.[38] This is not a very promising way to increase the volume of child support payments, ensure that abandoned families receive the funds they need to become independent of government support, and encourage fathers and mothers to cooperate for the good of their children.

The Crisis of Big Cities

However well the various states are doing in slimming their welfare rolls and assisting families to move into employment, almost all of them are finding the least success in their large urban areas. Between 1994 and 1997, for example, the welfare rolls in Milwaukee declined 40.1 percent, a huge change, but much less than the 55.6 percent decline in the state of Wisconsin; Los Angeles County declined 4.6 percent while California as a whole was down 6.2 percent; and the Philadelphia area dropped only 8.5 percent compared to 17.7 percent for the state of Pennsylvania.[39]

The greater difficulty in helping people move from welfare to work in large urban areas is hardly surprising. Our big cities are home to concentrations of the most needy and dependent families. Their public schools typically do a poor job preparing students for life. Jobs have been moving elsewhere, and public transportation systems are usually not well designed to move inner-city residents out to the places of greatest job growth. Crime and taxes are high, and city services, including welfare bureaucracies, are often dysfunctional. Residents who succeed move out, leaving behind those most in need of the departing role models. Civil society is often minimal; most neighborhoods host more liquor dealers and social-service institutions than citizen associations, thriving churches, libraries, or sports clubs. Disproportionately of minority race or ethnicity, residents looking for work may face discrimination on the basis of both race and zip code.[40]

In short, our big cities house concentrations of families needing special help, while their economies offer fewer opportunities and both their governments and their civil institutions are less capable of providing assistance. And yet there is little, if anything, in the new welfare policies that takes special note of the characteristics and challenges of the welfare problems of large urban areas.[41] The presumption is that urban poverty is just more of the same, just larger numbers of essentially separate instances of poor families. But poverty is more entrenched in center cities and government's efforts to help have less to build on. An adequate response to the multiple problems of cities will require both much time and systemic approaches that promote economic development and the revitalization of civil society. If, instead, time limits are blindly applied and the needs of the poor in cities are addressed only through individualized services, it is likely that many families will end up off welfare and yet without employment, despite their own best efforts, or else, to avoid that injustice, will have to be maintained in dependence on public support. Neither outcome fulfills the goals of welfare reform.[42]

Dysfunctional Government

Welfare reform is a positive change for the poor to the extent that it combines "help" with "hassle"—services and other supports with the requirement to become self-supporting. Combining the two is a form of social contract; indeed, in many states, in order to receive support the head of the household must enter into a formal agreement with the welfare agency in which the obligations of the two parties are specified, and the requirements laid upon the families are conditional so that the unavailability of employment or day care is a valid reason not to be working.

All of this is an acknowledgment by the lawmakers that to succeed, welfare reform needs not only willing families and an economy of opportunity but also adequate government services. And yet, although the current radical redesign of welfare policy has produced a profound transformation in the actual operations of the welfare programs in the various states, those welfare systems are plagued by greater and lesser problems. Even Wisconsin, long noted as a state that stresses good governance, and one of the states that has worked the longest and most determinedly to restructure its programs, has experienced serious failures. One account in late 1998 noted that

> [o]n paper, no state has done more to replace welfare checks with workers' supports. But a year after moving from the shelves to the streets, Wisconsin's celebrated effort bears only an intermittent likeness to the program of customized employment services outlined in planning documents. . . . In practice, even supporters of the program complain that uneven casework and unresponsive bureaucracies can make services cumbersome, if not impossible, to use.[43]

Other problems in state programs are caused by policies brought into conflict by welfare reform itself. Many states, for example, operate diversion programs, which fulfill a TANF purpose by giving families a lump-sum payment that allows them to overcome an emergency without enrolling in welfare. However, under the rules of the food stamp program, such payments must be counted as regular income, even though their purpose is to allow the family to cope with a temporary and extraordinary need. Unless this conflict in rules is cleared up, families living close to the edge can find it necessary to reject the diversion payment and go on welfare, in order to preserve the food stamp benefit that keeps them above water.[44]

Such problems, along with others such as mistaken information dispensed by overburdened caseworkers, and ineffective assistance rendered by staffers required to transform themselves, in short order, from keepers of bureaucratic rules to energetic employment specialists, have caused at least some families to lose benefits or services which they are supposed to be able to receive. Welfare officials may well be willing to redress such injustices by relaxing penalties or allowing the families to re-enroll in programs. But regaining welfare benefits is not the same as gaining independence. Especially in large cities and in the case of clients with multiple problems, these governmental and administrative dysfunctions are likely to create significant barriers for families doing their best to fulfill their own responsibilities.

Such problems do not prove that welfare reform is fated to fail or destined to generate multiple injustices. The 1996 federal law in fact is very flexible, emphasizing goals as much as specific rules, so that states have considerable latitude in how they design their services; moreover states have the option of offering additional services if they are willing to use their own funds. Several major features of the original law have already been changed (e.g., those concerning immigrants), significant additions have been made (the Welfare-to-Work program adopted in 1997), and congressional backers of the reform have indicated a willingness to consider further changes if necessary.[45] Moreover, states have plenty of money to use for expanded services, because their block-grant allocations are based on welfare rolls much larger than the current ones. Furthermore, states have been willing to set aside penalties and to bend the rules when welfare families have failed to meet goals but have tried their best.[46]

Yet the fact that justice requires that rules be bent or set aside, unexpected surpluses be available, or significant innovations be made to basic features of the federal law, points to flaws in the basic design of welfare reform itself. Fair treatment—in this case, access to needed help—should be, as far as possible, the routine outcome of programs and policies, and not dependent on exceptional circumstances.

Transforming Welfare

It would be presumptuous and fruitless to propose specific remedies for the various areas of concern noted above. However, the existence of these problems suggests underlying flaws in the design of the current round of welfare reform that require attention to ensure that the changed programs in fact provide more effective compassion for the needy.

A Guarantee of Assistance

The single most important change that should be made is to restore a federal commitment to help destitute families.[47] This would clarify what welfare reform is actually doing and confirm what welfare should be.

The basic concept is just this: people in need deserve assistance, and others able to assist them should come to their aid; conversely, people and institutions with resources should be prepared to respond to neighbors who might fall into crisis, and if any neighbors do fall into crisis they should be able to count on help. A guarantee of assistance means that people who come to the end of their own resources should find there a Good Samaritan.

However, such a commitment does not mean that assistance should be unconditional. The point is to help the person or family toward health and not to enable continued mistaken choices or destructive activities. Assistance not only may be, but should be, conditional upon those in need bending every effort to help themselves. Further, a federal guarantee in this sense does not mean that the federal government, or any government, must be the provider of assistance. The responsibility to assist is a differentiated one in which government is only one participant. However, charged with promoting public justice, government, and ultimately the federal government, should oversee the common good, including monitoring how persons and other institutions fulfill their responsibilities and, when necessary, acting as the provider of assistance at last resort.

But a commitment to assistance should not be understood as a legal "right" to welfare benefits. The "rights" concept is counterproductive in the case of welfare, as Paul Marshall has pointed out. It presumes that the key relationship is between government and the needy person, when in fact the institutions of civil society have indispensable roles. It suggests that the person in need should only receive, when instead the exercise of personal responsibility should be present. And it implies that assistance should be standardized when flexibility and diversity are, in fact, the hallmarks of effective help.[48]

There can be no legal guarantee that people will be given exactly the assistance they deserve as creatures made in the image of God. Systems fail; sufficient resources are not always available or appropriately deployed; needs are complex and those attempting to help are not omniscient; and people in need sometimes reject precisely the best assistance. The idea of a commitment to assist only affirms that a society and its government must do what it can when its members need the assistance of others.

Americans, indeed, believe this. If not, welfare would have been abolished, not reformed. Yet, paradoxically, welfare reform was driven, in part, by the desire to end an entitlement to welfare. There were two main motives for this. One goal was to rein in welfare spending perceived to be out of control. In fact, spending on programs for the poor is not very large in the United States. And surely it is shameful that the most powerful and wealthy country in the history of the world would entertain the idea that adequate care for its poorest members is beyond its capabilities. The real problem with welfare spending has always been not its magnitude but the ineffectiveness of the programs it paid for.

The other objection to welfare entitlement was that it fostered in both the needy and in programs of assistance the idea that help is a one-way street requiring the needy to be mere "recipients" and not actors, and that no questions could legitimately be asked about choices and behavior.[49] However, these pernicious notions are not inherent to the idea of assistance, to the assistance relationship, or to the idea of an entitlement or guarantee of help. A guarantee of help means surely, but only, that the poor should be able to count on those who can aid them, to do so. But such aid must be calculated to actually assist them to be restored to the ability to fulfill their varied responsibilities or callings in life. That means that it must be conditional.

Yet, though conditional, assistance should be available. This requires serious rethinking about at least four issues. The first is the "family cap"—the federal authorization that states may refuse to provide a welfare family additional benefits upon the birth of a child conceived while the mother was on welfare. The intention to discourage parents from having additional children when they are unable themselves to support them is right. But the whole purpose of welfare is to provide assistance in a crisis, and that crisis may well be the result of a mistake, to which welfare mothers are no less prone than are others. Simply expanding benefits to the family encourages bad choices as well as genuine mistakes, but capping the benefits can harm innocent children, leading even to abortion. The best solution, allowed by the federal law but not accepted by all states, is to provide support for the child in the form of vouchers or direct payments to suppliers which can be used only for items needed by the new member of the family.

The second problem is the insufficient assistance offered to noncustodial fathers, to couples without children, and to single adults. Since the New Deal, the focus of American welfare has been on families with dependent children, which generally has meant mothers and their children. However, as noted above in the discussion of child-support enforcement, these are not the only ones who may require special assistance in order to become able to take care of themselves. Some forms of help are available: various programs operated by charities, food stamps, emergency medical care, state or local general assistance programs in some places,[50] and so on. Are these sufficient? Surely one concern of genuine welfare reform would be to examine how such persons fare when they meet a crisis that is beyond their own capabilities.

A third important issue is the situation of the working poor, whose ability to earn a sufficient income is being eroded by changes in the American economy.[51] The working poor, of course, are not welfare families dependent entirely on government benefits. But according to biblical principles, it is not only the wholly dependent who should be helped; indeed, as we have seen, a basic principle of help is that it should activate and supplement the efforts of the poor themselves. Our tendency to shy away from assisting all but the worst off, lest we help make people dependent, needs to be resisted. The federal (and in some places also, a state) Earned Income Tax Credit is a good way to help those who are helping themselves. Now that welfare itself is being reoriented to emphasize empowerment, perhaps it will be possible to consider whether the working poor should receive additional assistance, such as help to gain further training or education.

The fourth issue is put in stark terms by Glenn Loury, who notes that "the personal resources, job skills, and child-rearing capacities of a sizable minority of welfare recipients are severely limited." If such families are simply cut loose because they have exhausted their five years of benefits, then "the perfectly foreseeable consequence," Loury emphasizes, is "a humanitarian disaster."[52] Such a disaster cannot be justified by showing that the families received abundant services during those five years; that the 20 percent exemption from the five-year benefit limit has already been filled; that the families have consumed many thousands of dollars of taxpayer and private funds; that only a few families are involved; that making exceptions to the rules may lead others to demand the same; or that the public is just tired of welfare programs and welfare excuses. A different response will be needed, a response grounded in the reality that each member of these families is made in the image of God.

Renewed Federalism

The radical devolution of welfare design to the states and, in some states, further down to counties, has been a key reason welfare changes legislated in Washington have actually been implemented. And devolution has simultaneously allowed and required officials to come up with more effective programs that involve partnerships with community organizations.[53] The result has been real welfare change that, albeit imperfectly, combines both services and requirements and actually promotes independence.

But devolution has had the additional and negative consequence that poor Americans have in effect become citizens, respectively, of the fifty separate states or even of smaller sub-state jurisdictions. What benefits they can receive, what requirements they must meet, and what services they are offered by government all vary widely depending simply on where they happen to be located. Cash benefits are twice as large in some states as in others; some states enforce a family cap and others not; some states have accepted the federal time limits while others have imposed shorter ones; some states have developed effective job-preparation programs and others have not; some have mobilized a sufficient array of child-care providers while others cannot assure mothers required to work that their children will be safely cared for; some local welfare agencies have developed partnerships with the faith communities while others appear to have little consciousness of the importance of such networks. In short, how a welfare family is treated—with regard to both the help it receives and the requirements it must meet—is increasingly a function not only of what the family needs in order to reestablish itself but of where the family resides.[54] This consequence of devolution neither fits the intentions of welfare reform nor the biblical standards for effective help.

The growing divergence in treatment also works against the aims of welfare reform in another way. The early fears that giving states so much control would spark a "race to the bottom," with every state competitively cutting its benefits to avoid becoming a "welfare magnet" have proven mistaken.[55] However, various states have tried to keep out "outsiders," for example, by limiting the benefits of newcomers to the level in their state of origin for some period.[56] But moving to another state may be precisely what some welfare families should do. Moving could reunite a mother with her extended family, giving her a vital source of help and guidance. Moving could be the best way for her to find an appropriate job, or any job at all. Ironically, moving could be the only way the family will get the opportunity to experience a welfare system that has become truly effective.

Moreover, radical devolution confines states to their own resources, pushing them back toward the vulnerable positions they were in before the New Deal. Of course states are now receiving large sums from the federal government in the form of their welfare block grants, and the 1996 federal law also made some provision for states that need extra federal help due to demographic changes or economic difficulties. But the logic of devolution goes against redistributing funds from wealthy states to those with greater needs. And radical devolution diminishes the ability of the federal government to rescue the states by sending them extra funds when a severe national economic downturn reduces their revenue but requires them to spend more to counteract expanded need. In an emergency, no doubt expanded federal contributions to the states would be authorized. But if such extraordinary action is foreseeable and legitimate, then devolution should even now be tempered with a greater acknowledgment of the positive aspects of the national framework within which the states exist.

Poor Americans, whatever else they are, are citizens of the United States and not only residents of particular states or localities. They should be able to count on the help the whole nation can mobilize if their particular locality experiences a crisis. Moreover, as citizens of the United States, poor Americans, no matter in which state they live, should be able to count on a common standard, some uniform level of help, and, equally, some uniform set of expectations about what families and persons themselves must achieve.[57] Federalism is supposed to entail precisely an arrangement of commonalities along with differences. Devolution, for all its benefits, needs to be counterbalanced by a stronger idea of what Americans owe to each other and can expect of each other.

Empowerment to Independence

One of the commonest criticisms of welfare reform is that pushing families off welfare is not the same as enabling them to become self-sufficient. In fact the federal and state reforms acknowledge this truth by coupling time limits and other disincentives with services and other supports for families required to move into the workplace. However, as we have seen, the Work First strategy can thrust families into work insufficiently prepared to move beyond low-level employment, and time limits and other rules make it difficult for states to offer families with extensive handicaps all of the help they need. Welfare reformers were right to search for ways to keep welfare from becoming a substitute for work, but in the process they overcompensated, neglecting too much the reality that many families require extensive assistance if they are to be capable of taking care of themselves.

If the goal of welfare is to empower families to take care of their own responsibilities, then the focus should be equipping those families for success in the marketplace and life, and not how to most effectively move them off the welfare rolls. Incentives (e.g., greater income from employment) and disincentives (various requirements to keep making progress) need to be maintained, but in many states a greater stress is needed on how to get the family moving up the job ladder. Families that make it past the bottom rung are less likely to

fall back onto welfare the first time the economy slows or some personal crisis arises. Parents for whom work is more than a way to escape welfare are better role models for their children and their neighbors. Moreover, work should
be an expression of calling, a way for a person to contribute his or her gifts and
talents to others.

Taking empowerment seriously is a philosophical reorientation that
requires policy and program changes. Time limits and overly narrow definitions of acceptable activities that prevent welfare recipients from adequately
equipping themselves for careers should be changed.[58] Unemployment insurance rules need to be modified so that welfare recipients newly in the workplace who get laid off are able to count on this normal employment support
rather than having to go back onto welfare.[59] Welfare officials and congregations in more places need to join together in mentoring programs, like Mississippi's Faith and Families effort and the VESTIBULE program in Charlotte-
Mecklenburg County, North Carolina to maximize support for families trying
to make the transition from welfare to work or to retain their jobs once they
obtain them.[60]

Welfare reform has increased the number of the working poor-families that,
while not dependent on welfare, do not on their own earn enough for a decent
life. To say that these families' transition into work represents no progress
would demean the many American families that over the years have willingly
accepted low-wage jobs rather than go on welfare. We should acknowledge
instead that the plight of all of the working poor has been brought into relief
by the families newly moving from welfare to bottom-rung jobs. Taking welfare reform seriously entails going beyond the narrow focus of traditional welfare programs: "Part of the challenge of welfare reform will be providing a new
kind of assistance—one that helps low-income working families make ends
meet and also helps them keep jobs and move up the earnings ladder."[61]

Expanding Partnerships

As noted before, the logic of welfare reform has driven state and local officials to search for a wide range of partners: mentors for welfare families, businesses that will agree to hire trained welfare recipients, synagogues willing to
expand the capacity and hours of their day-care facilities, community colleges
that can offer job-focused training, churches able to host after-school programs for students whose mothers are at work, and more. Notwithstanding
this creative flurry, states and localities have been slow to implement the one
specific partnership directive of the 1996 federal law—the Charitable Choice
requirement intended to make government contracting and voucher programs
more hospitable to faith-based organizations.

The delays are due in part to the sheer volume of the policies and programs
that state and local officials have had to design and implement. More than two

years after adoption of the federal welfare reform law, states were still struggling with such basic requirements as developing the capability to track lifetime welfare use and to collect all of the child-support payments that are due families on welfare. Compared to these obligations, Charitable Choice must seem not very pressing. Moreover, since Charitable Choice directly conflicts with the "no aid to religion" misinterpretation of the First Amendment that was predominant for many years, some state and local officials suspect that it may be unconstitutional.[62] Certain religious-liberty groups not only encourage that view but have threatened to take officials to court if they contract with religious organizations that do not put their faith on the shelf.[63] And whatever they think of the larger constitutional issues, many officials are very reluctant to accept the right of faith-based organizations under Charitable Choice to use religious criteria in their hiring decisions, regarding it as a return to the old days of illegal discrimination rather than as the only way mission-oriented groups can maintain themselves.

Reluctant officials have not been pushed very hard by the faith communities in most places. Mainline Protestants, many Catholics, and most Jewish groups accepted the pre-Charitable Choice rules as establishing a reasonable balance between church and state; in any case, their chief preoccupation in welfare reform has been to ensure that government does not relinquish the primary role in assisting the poor. Evangelicals and other theologically conservative groups, on the other hand, continue to suspect that cooperation with government will eventually lead to secularization. Many, claiming that serving the poor is the task of the church, would rather see government go away than partner with it.[64]

Public officials should not wait for pressure from the faith communities before taking Charitable Choice seriously, of course. It is the law of the land, a nonoptional requirement that accompanies the federal welfare block grants that states receive. Yet for the requirement to make a difference in practice requires cooperation from both public officials and the faith communities. Public officials have to be willing to look beyond the large, religiously affiliated nonprofits they are used to working with and reach out to the many smaller and dispersed churches and parachurch ministries that have in the past declined to cooperate with government. For their part, faith-based groups that have long taken care to avoid contact with government will have to learn how contracting works and who does what in the public sector if they really desire a chance to work with the welfare department.

Extensive cooperation also requires creative new structures and policies because most faith-based organizations are too small to deliver the volume of services required by typical government contracts. Charitable Choice itself acknowledges vouchers as an alternative to contracts: welfare authorities can authorize many different organizations to provide the needed services, giving recipients a certificate redeemable at any of the providers. Recipients can then exercise choice, government can work with many small organizations, and the organizations can avoid being tightly controlled by government. Contracting itself can also be modified, for example, by requiring large agencies to sub-contract with faith-based and other community groups, or by utilizing non-profit intermediary organizations that network together many congregations and other small organizations.[65]

Reconstituting America's Assistance Network

Charitable Choice is a key tool for the reconstruction of America's welfare system because it requires government to be more hospitable to faith-based organizations in its procurement policies—when it purchases services for the poor from outside organizations. Charitable Choice creates the opportunity for faith-based programs and organizations to be at the heart of our society's official assistance system. During the debates leading up to the 1996 federal welfare bill, there was much talk about transferring welfare from government to churches and charities. Instead, by adopting Charitable Choice, Congress and the president chose to require government to include religious organizations when it spends funds to buy services.

But, of course, partnerships when government contracts or uses vouchers are only a part of the changing landscape of social services. Welfare officials have entered into a wide range of new partnerships with churches, synagogues, and other faith-based organizations in which the religious organizations agree to provide mentoring and other services without payment. Both Faith and Families and the VESTIBULE program are examples. Many other new partnerships have also being constructed, often without any direct connection with government. The Jobs Partnership of Raleigh, North Carolina, and an increasing number of other places, knit together employers ready to hire welfare recipients and other unemployed people with congregations that cooperate to prepare the prospective employees to be reliable workers. STEP Richmond (Virginia) is one of a number of nongovernmental efforts that connects suburban congregations with inner-city ministries that have many opportunities to serve but few resources. Project QUEST in San Antonio, Texas, an initiative of the Industrial Areas Foundation, brings together businesses, congregations, city government, educational institutions, and others in a program that trains welfare recipients for specific jobs and works intensively with them to enable them to overcome their other problems.

Yet another approach is being tried in Maryland. Applicants for welfare assistance there are required to cooperate with caseworkers "in seeking and using programs and community and family resources that may be available to the recipient."[66] In this way government encourages families in need to turn first to those closest, who bear the first responsibility to help, and shows respect for, rather than usurping, the helping agencies of civil society. Of course, such a policy would be mere cynical loadshedding if caseworkers were not ready to step in when family and community cannot or will not. And a government that is serious about civil society will go beyond a measure like this to a serious effort to revitalize institutions that have atrophied and been shoved aside in the drive to create a government-centered assistance network.[67]

Renewing nongovernmental assistance is a complex task and a controversial one as well. Restoring to families, churches, neighborhood groups, charities, companies, and other social institutions a significant responsibility and capability to respond to poverty and social distress seems to many to be an effort to let government off the hook and to consign the powerless to arbitrary treatment. Indeed, opponents of the American welfare state too often have played the same game, proposing to dismantle welfare in the mere hope that churches and charities will arise to take over, or suggesting that government welfare spending is not needed if citizens are required to help the poor by donating to the charity of their choice, receiving in return a credit against the taxes they owe.[68]

Such schemes rightly seek to energize communal and personal acts of service to neighbors in need, to reverse the governmentalization of social care that became the hallmark of the New Deal-Great Society project. However, the way forward will not be found by going back. Government must continue to play a key role. Care for the poor must not be dependent on whether their neighbors at the moment feel generous, how much empathy is aroused by a particular person's need, or the happenstance that resources and needs are found close together. An adequate response to significant poverty requires a way to identify and prioritize needs and to marshal dispersed resources. That public justice task belongs to government. The challenge is not to cycle back from government to civil society, but to devise effective ways for the two sectors to work together. And because the actual construction of a new assistance network comprised of both governmental and nongovernmental institutions is a complex task that will take many years to accomplish, it is imperative that the poor are not prematurely cast out of the current welfare system with the rationale that a better system exists in policymakers' minds.

Welfare Reform's Challenge to the Evangelical Church

This essay has sought to develop an evangelical Christian perspective on welfare reform and poverty. However, an evangelical response to welfare reform and poverty must go beyond analysis. As the Bible makes abundantly clear, knowing what to do is worth nothing without action. Evangelicals may not stop at evaluations and recommendations. The question is what we should do in this era of opportunity and danger. So I conclude with three challenges to action.

The Full Gospel Includes Serving the Needy

Evangelicals treasure it as a wonderful assurance that, though our sins be "like scarlet," they can be washed "white as snow" (Isa. 1:18, NIV). But what are the misdeeds that necessitate this application of God's mercy? The accusation Isaiah had just pronounced against God's people was that they had blood on their hands because of their neglect of the poor and the weak. Thus, the Lord commanded, "Stop doing wrong; learn to do right! Seek justice, encourage the oppressed. Defend the cause of the fatherless, plead the case of the widow" (1:16b–17, NIV). Think of it: issues of social justice at the heart of the message of redemption! But it should be no surprise to find this in the book of Isaiah, for it is the consistent message throughout the Bible.

So it is not farfetched to read the cry for welfare reform of our day, and the plea from officials to the churches to engage in love of neighbor, as calls from the Lord. We must not merely sit through this era during which our nation's assistance network is being reconstructed as if this was a matter irrelevant to people of faith, a marginal issue or a concern that distracts us from what is really important. Indeed, we must love the Lord our God with all our heart, but we must also love our neighbors as ourselves.

In the nineteenth century, evangelicals were known as people who were engaged with society as well as with souls.[69] Tragically, at the start of this century evangelicals underwent a "Great Reversal," persuading ourselves that the Good News addresses the heart and not life in the world, sinfulness and not poverty.[70] The tragedy of persistent and entrenched poverty, and the challenge of welfare reform, have led increasing numbers of evangelicals to repent and to work to recover the full gospel, inspired in many cases by the leadership of the Christian Community Development Association, headed by John Perkins and Wayne Gordon.[71] Are we seeing a recovery of social compassion in the evangelical church? We must pray that it is so, for it is a nonoptional part of orthodox belief and life.

Accepting the Challenge of Partnership with Government

Evangelicals are rightly wary of government rules and government money that threaten the spiritual mission of congregations and parachurch ministries. So even if government officials are seeking to partner with evangelical and other faith-based anti-poverty programs, why should evangelicals cooperate with them if the price is losing the defining characteristics of their organizations?

The danger of secularization must be taken utterly seriously. But we should not let our fears paralyze us. Government policy and practice have not been as anti-religious as we might guess based on some well-publicized instances.[72] Moreover, the key problem has always been not government rules but the loss of conviction and nerve by Christian ministries themselves.[73] But now Congress and the president, by means of the Charitable Choice provision, have specifically addressed the major legal problems. It is now the law of the land that state and local governments may not discriminate against faith-based organizations that want to compete to provide welfare services using public funds. And it is now the law of the land that if such organizations receive contracts or become eligible to accept vouchers to provide services, all levels of government are bound to protect their religious character and practices.

What a tragedy it would be if, just at the moment when public officials are coming to evangelicals and to other faith communities for help, and just when government has adopted new rules designed precisely to be fair to faith-based organizations, evangelical nonprofits and churches were to refuse to move boldly ahead by taking advantage of the new opportunities to serve our neediest neighbors as part of a reconstituted public/private effort.

Vocation and Not Only Volunteerism

At this time when America is laboring to build a better welfare system and the door is open for evangelicals to propose new directions, we must be careful not to limit our witness and actions by focusing on volunteerism to the neglect of renewing our vocations. Volunteering to help the poor is essential, without a doubt. It is a salutary impulse when Christians discard the notion that love for neighbor is best expressed by paying taxes for government social-service programs or sending donations to private or Christian charities. The Good Samaritan, of course, was the person who actually stopped and got directly involved.

And yet the commandment to come to the aid of the poor is not intended to guide only our use of our volunteer energy. It must determine as well the way we carry out our vocation, our primary calling in life. We must not zealously serve soup to the homeless each Saturday afternoon while neglecting the cause of the poor during our weekday occupations as mayor, banker, zoning official, housing developer, employer, lawyer, or day-care provider. How hypocritical it would be for a businesswoman to volunteer an evening each week to help prepare welfare mothers for employment and yet to refuse to consider whether her own company should hire a person who has never before had a real chance at a job. How tragic it would be if a public official serves energetically as a church deacon but neglects to consider the plight of the poor when the government makes decisions about schooling, the police, or welfare services.[74]

The temptation to think of serving the poor mainly as a voluntary activity and not as a responsibility of our vocation may be especially strong for American evangelical Christians. For we have a well-developed sense that we must serve God in ministry but we have an equally strong but mistaken tendency to think of ministry as limited to spiritual or church service. So when we hear God's call to the evangelical church to recover a neglected part of its witness and activity, we think of asking our congregation to take on a new task in its neighborhood or we respond to the plea for help that comes from parachurch ministries that serve the needy. And, indeed, these are things we must do.

And yet we must not forget that God's call to the church is a call to believers in every walk of life. The constructive contribution the evangelical church should make to welfare reform will go beyond new congregational programs and beyond innovative evangelical nonprofits. It will be expressed as well in creative legislative proposals, strong advocacy in the corridors of power for the weak, and practical wisdom about how to better knit together government assistance for the poor with the work of the churches.

~ 15 ~

Rebuilding Marriage and the Family

David P. Gushee, Union University

Introduction

This essay considers an aspect of the problem of poverty that is increasingly recognized: the connection between poverty and the changing structure of the American family.* If the reader has managed to get this far in our volume, she will have had ample opportunity to consider numerous matters of debate and controversy. But it is fair to say that few if any of the issues discussed heretofore match this one in terms of the intensity of the passions they evoke.

In late 1997 I attended a lecture in which William Galston, former Clinton administration official and one of the leading analysts of the issues we will discuss here, made the claim that the single best predictor of economic well-being for children is membership in a two-parent family. That claim is by now exceedingly well documented, as I will show. But the largely liberal crowd that day was, to put it mildly, not receptive. As seems to happen every time this particular piece of data is reported, the crowd attempted to overcome hard facts with angry rhetoric. They interpreted Galston's reporting as an attack on legitimate lifestyle choices—or worse, as a subtle racial smear. Galston stood his ground, and surely he had experienced the same kind of response dozens of times before. But he still seemed a bit surprised at the intensity of the emotion his comments engendered.

I stand with Galston. While I am sensitive to the emotions at stake here, and have no interest in attacking any individual or group, the data speak for themselves. The central thesis of this chapter is that the restructuring of the family—in particular, the decline in the two-parent family and the rise in the number of single-parent, especially female-headed, households—is one of the most negative developments occurring in contemporary American life. The data related to the link between family structure and poverty reported in this study will give ample empirical support to this assertion.

However, from a Christian ethical perspective this claim has independent normative status. That is, on the basis of biblically grounded moral convictions, I would be opposed to the decline of the two-parent family regardless of whether or not an empirical link to poverty could be demonstrated. It seems appropriate to outline here some of the key theological/moral norms that shape my understanding of the nature of the family, parenting, and the well-being of children.

- God created human beings male and female for the purpose of relational partnership, procreation, and childrearing, and the undertaking of stewardly responsibilities on the earth (Gen. 1:27–28).
- God intended joyful, lifetime, monogamous, heterosexual marriage as the moral, legal, and social framework within which human beings are to experience this male/female union, which at its best reaches the heights of human experience on this earth (Gen. 2:18–25).
- God intended that children should be conceived and reared within the bounds of the marriage relationship rather than in other relational contexts, though of course God's love extends without partiality to all children (Luke 18:15–17).
- Divorce is never God's intention for marriage. While divorce is on occasion morally permissible in a sinful world (Matt. 5:31–32, 19:1–9; 1 Cor. 7:10–16), it falls well short of God's plan for family life, and as such carries with it a variety of destructive built-in consequences.
- Children are the living embodiment of the "one flesh" union that is marriage (Gen. 2:24), and as such normally experience divorce as a near-literal sundering of their very personhood. That divorce (and other forms of partial or total orphaning) is harmful to children is not only established, empirical fact but also a corollary of biblical teaching on marriage and family life.
- All participants in family life—men, women, and children—are more likely to find love, security, stability, serenity, and wholeness within the context of a just, loving, and intact family structure than in any alternative living arrangement.

- The God revealed in Jesus Christ is characterized by love, compassion, and mercy. He is a God who hears the cries of the oppressed, the broken, and the wounded and seeks avenues of liberation and healing (Luke 4:18–20). Both poverty and family breakdown, and the two together, are contexts of oppression, sorrow, and misery. God sides with the victims, and seeks human partners in the work of the reconstruction of family life.

- Both in terms of God's design of family life and the simple logic of everyday life, the economic well-being of family members is most likely to be advanced within the intact, two-parent family structure. The scripture witnesses relentlessly to the economic vulnerability and need of the widow and the orphan—of whom there are, in modern form, all too many these days—and calls on the people of God to do the work of God by acting on their behalf (Exod. 22:22–24; Deut. 10:17–18; Job 24:9–10, 21; Job 31:16–18; Ps. 146:9; Isa. 1:17; 1 Tim. 5; James 1:27).

- Involuntary poverty violates God's intentions for human beings, and God is especially concerned with the well-being of those who are at risk of such poverty (Deut. 15:1–11, and hundreds of other passages).

Finally it is important to add the following normative statements with regard to the *who* and the *how* of response to the problems emerging at the intersection of family breakdown and poverty.

- Because family life is both irreducibly personal and profoundly social, a variety of moral actors bear different measures of responsibility for addressing problems emerging in families.

- Men and women who conceive children and/or marry, bear the primary responsibility for performing their moral obligations with reference to each other in marriage and to the children they bring into the world.

- Agencies of civil society, such as the media, civic organizations, activist bodies, and other cultural entities, have a share in the responsibility of helping to create a societal moral climate conducive to marital and familial well-being.

- The church, understood as a body of disciples of Jesus Christ, committed to be his agent and committed to the advance of the kingdom which he inaugurated (Matt. 6:10, 33), is to serve as a means of personal and social transformation in this and other areas of moral concern.

- Agencies of government, in their function of securing public justice and protecting the innocent (Rom. 13:1–7), bear the obligation, within appropriate limits, to establish mechanisms to ensure precisely such justice in law and public policy related to marriage and family life.

Grounded in these moral convictions, this monograph will proceed in the following way. First, we will sketch the available empirical data concerning the reconfiguration of family life in the United States over the past thirty-five years, focusing on out-of-wedlock births and divorce. Next we will consider available evidence related to the economic impact of these changes in family structure.

Part II combines analysis of the causes of the problems discussed in part I with exploration of both current and prospective responses on the part of governmental and non-governmental bodies. The hope animating this chapter is that as a nation we can begin to rebuild the family through the aggressive implementation of some of the responses discussed herein.

Family Reconfiguration and Its Economic Impact

There can be no doubt that we find ourselves in the midst of a radical and ongoing restructuring of American family life. The family in which resident children are the biological children of the man and woman with whom they live is increasingly the exception rather than the rule.

The increasing institutionalization and "normalization" of out-of-wedlock childbearing is one major source of this reconfiguration, as we shall see. Cohabitation, which we shall not consider here, is a second. Divorce is the third. These trends in combination have formed a kind of pincers movement, to borrow a military metaphor, that attacks the marriage-based nuclear family from all sides and threatens to encircle it, bringing not only a steady decline in the number and stability of such families but also a variety of negative economic consequences as well. Let us look briefly at the data concerning the restructuring of the family.

Family Reconfiguration

Rise in Out-of-Wedlock Births

The total number of children born out-of-wedlock reached 1.29 million by 1994. These 1.29 million births represented 32.6 percent of the total number of births. The percentage of out-of-wedlock births increased from 5 percent in 1960 to 11 percent in 1970, then up to 18 percent in 1980, on to 28 percent in 1990, and now to the current figure of just under 33 percent.[1] The most recent figures indicate that this increase in the rate may be slowing or even dropping, especially among teenagers. But no one anticipates approaching a return to the illegitimacy rates of even fifteen years ago.

It is illuminating to segment these statistics by race and age. First, race. In 1994, 25.4 percent of white births, 43.1 percent of Hispanic births, and 70.4 percent of black births were to unmarried mothers. While Hispanic and black illegitimacy rates are higher, the unmarried birth rates are rising somewhat faster among whites than among other groups. And, of course, these rates are considerably higher for all three groups today than they were even ten years ago. The 1985 out-of-wedlock birth rates were the following: white, 14.5 percent, black, 60.1 percent, Hispanic, 29.5 percent.[2] Across American society we are witnessing the deinstitutionalization of marriage as the normative context for the birth of children. That process is proceeding more quickly in some groups than others, but everywhere it proceeds apace.

In terms of the age of unmarried mothers at the time of birth, the statistics offer an important corrective to the tendency to lump together the out-of-wedlock birth issue with concerns related to "teen pregnancy." The fact is that both in terms of absolute numbers and percentages it is women in their twenties (especially their early 20s) who have the most out-of-wedlock births. In 1994, 53.2 percent of all out-of-wedlock births were to women in their twenties, as compared to 30.5 percent to teens.[3] Yet we must still remember that the United States teen pregnancy numbers and percentages are the worst of any major industrialized country, and our overall out-of-wedlock birth rates places us fourth among industrialized nations as of 1995.[4]

In summary, the following can be said about out-of-wedlock births in the United States.

- Nearly one in three American children are born out of wedlock at this time.
- Out-of-wedlock birth is the predominant experience in African-American life and the trend is moving in that direction for Hispanics and white Americans.
- The rate of increase in out-of-wedlock births has been precipitous over the past thirty-five years, though at this time there are some signs of a slowdown.
- Nearly two-thirds of all out-of-wedlock births are to women ages fifteen to twenty-four. Given the nature of our career and vocational preparation system, it is easy to predict the difficulty that many of these women will have in providing for themselves and their children.
- The problem of large numbers of births to unmarried women is not confined to the United States. However, the U.S. faces the issue at a particularly acute level at this time in comparison with other similar nations.

Rise in the Divorce Rate

In recent years the nation has begun to awaken, as if from a fog, to the fact that the divorce rate has skyrocketed over the past thirty to thirty-five years. It is not that the age of mass divorce, as it has been aptly called, has not been well-documented. Both hard data and mountains of anecdotal evidence as to our "divorce epidemic" are readily available. But only in recent years have the consequences of divorce as a mass phenomenon become a matter of growing public concern. Still, there is much public education needed as to the facts of the matter even as we begin to discuss what can be done to counter this trend. Let us consider some of the key statistics.

In 1996 there were 2.34 million marriages and 1.15 million divorces in the United States.[5] Sixty-five percent of these divorces involved children, over one million of whom experience divorce each year.[6] The number of divorced Americans went from 4.3 million in 1970 to 17.4 million in 1994.[7] Projecting current statistics, over 40 percent of first marriages initiated today will end in divorce, and more than 60 percent of remarriages will fail.[8] Our divorce rate remains the highest in the industrialized world.[9]

Overall trends related to divorce are, if anything, more staggering than those we examined concerning illegitimacy. They can be summarized as follows: the divorce rate, and the number of divorces, doubled between the late 1960s and the late 1970s. Throughout the 1980s, and thus far in the 1990s, the divorce rate has remained fairly steady, with some evidence of decline in the most recent numbers, which are the best (in terms of rate) since before 1975.

The numbers are sufficiently high that it is fair to say that divorce has become deeply woven into the fabric of American life. The average American will either be divorced, be the child of divorce, or have family members who have endured one or both of these experiences. While divorce has always existed in this nation, and a longer-term study would indicate a steady rise since the turn of the twentieth century, current divorce rates and absolute numbers are much higher than at any time in our history. Divorce has become a fundamental part of the life experience of millions of American children. A first divorce tends to introduce a pattern of even greater fragility and instability into family life, as evidenced by the especially high breakup and divorce rates of cohabiting and remarried couples. Whereas rising rates of divorce, like rising illegitimacy rates, are international phenomena, the relative place of the U.S. vis-a-vis like countries is quite different—we easily "lead the pack" with regard to divorce, but can be found among other nations with regard to births to unmarried women.

The Result: The Reconfiguration of the American Family

The illegitimacy and divorce (and cohabitation) pincers movement, as I have called it, has demonstrably reconfigured the American family. Let us consider numbers, percentages, and trends related to one primary indicator of this reconfiguration: the shape of the American "family household."

In 1996, there were just under 100 million American households. The U.S. government defines a household as comprising all persons who occupy a housing unit, such as a house or apartment. Approximately 70 million of these households were defined as "families." The federal government defines a family as "a group of two or more persons related by birth, marriage, or adoption and residing together in a household" (*U.S. Statistical Abstract 1997*, p. 6). Some 54 million of these families consisted of married couples (without children).

That leaves approximately 16 million families of some other shape. Twelve and a half million of these are female-headed; the rest are male-headed.

Perhaps most germane to our topic is the configuration of households in which there are children present. This reduces our number of families to consider from 70 million to 37.1 million. Of these 37.1 million, in 1996 only 25.3 million included "two-parent family groups," while 9.9 million were single-parent, female-headed, families. Here we are not considering whether these two parents are the biological mother and father of the children or whether they are married.

Expressed in the most important percentages, in 1996 numbers we find that barely 68 percent of families with children under the age of 18 include two parents; the rest (32 percent) are headed by single parents. Of these single-parent families, 85 percent are headed by women. Fully 27 percent of all families are now headed by single mothers.[10]

We can summarize the overall trends related to the reconfiguring of the American family in the following way:

- Since 1960 the percentage of families headed by a single parent has tripled. The great majority of these families (85–90 percent) are female-headed. The rate of increase may be slowing slightly at this time, but the cumulative effects are still staggering. Single parenting has definitely become the norm rather than the exception in black family life, but the trend exists across the board.

- It is the *combination* of non-marital childbearing, cohabitation, and divorce that together are creating the reconfiguration of the American family. Since at least 1990, the annual number of out-of-wedlock births (1.165 million in 1990 and rising) has exceeded the number of children for whom divorce creates a single-parent home (1.075 million in 1990 and holding steady). Thus it is illegitimacy rather than divorce that today claims the dubious distinction as the leading cause of the reconfiguring of the American family.

- A childhood spent entirely with both of one's married biological parents has by now become the minority childhood experience in American life. Children increasingly live in households consisting of their never-married, and/or cohabiting, and/or previously married and/or remarried mother (and/or other household residents), all in various stages and configurations. One study places the proportion of those children living with both biological parents at a mere 36 percent.[11]

Economic Impact of Family Disintegration and Reconfiguration

In this section we will consider what connection exists, if any, between the reconfiguration of the American family, which we have just outlined, and the economic well-being of those families. We will focus our attention on the situation facing never-married mothers and their children on the one hand, and divorced mothers and their children on the other. The news is distressing.

Impact upon Unmarried Mothers and Their Children

The research evidence is in and it is indisputable: "children born outside of marriage are 30 times more likely to live in persistent poverty than children whose parents got and stayed married."[12] There are other ways of making the claim of a direct connection between out-of-wedlock births and poverty:

> The rise in nonmarital births is cause for serious concern because most children born outside of marriage live in households that are very poor: 54 percent of the families of children with never-married mothers had incomes below the poverty line in 1989, compared to 27 percent of divorced families and 7 percent of married-couple families with children.[13]

Suzanne Bianchi and Daphne Spain have put it this way: "The . . . median income of a family with a never-married mother is only about half that available in a family with a divorced mother. Two-thirds of children with a never-married mother live in poverty."[14] Princeton sociologist Sara McLanahan sums it up: "the bottom line is: The more single parents and the more out-of-wedlock single parents, the more poverty."[15]

It is not all that difficult to anticipate the reasons why unmarried mothers and their children would have such profound economic difficulties, more profound even than the problems facing the divorced mother.

- *Education.* Never-married mothers, as we saw above, tend to be younger, on average, either than married or divorced mothers, with the majority between the ages of fifteen and twenty-four. For this reason, as Bianchi and Spain have argued, they are quite unlikely to be college graduates, and, in fact, less likely to be high school graduates than are divorced or married mothers.[16]

- *Employment.* Thus, as might be predicted and as the data bear out, unmarried mothers are less likely to be employed than are divorced mothers. Lacking adequate education, they tend to lack the educational prerequisites for obtaining employment, especially for obtaining employment in well-paying jobs and jobs with fringe benefits such as health insurance. Further, they tend to lack the qualifications and skills for advancing in the jobs they do get. Thus, according to Bianchi and Spain, "only 39 percent of children with a never-married mother live with a parent who is employed, compared with 69 percent of those with a divorced mother."[17]

- *Childcare.* All working parents face the issue of child care when they have preschool-age children. However, both the never-married and the divorced mother face this issue with particular acuteness. Child care expenses are beyond the reach of both the unemployed and many employed unmarried mothers. Lacking family members, friends, or any other source of child care, as is so frequently the case, the unmarried mother is frequently shut out of the workplace—or hindered in the workplace—due to child-care problems.

- *Paternal Support.* According to Bianchi and Spain, "never-married mothers find it harder to get income from the fathers of their children than divorced or separated mothers."[18] Married women expect and receive financial support from their husbands in the raising of their children. Divorced women also expect (though only some of the time receive) some child-support payments from their ex-husbands. However, the never-married mother is far less likely to receive any income support whatsoever from the father of her child. In some cases, this is because paternity has never been claimed or established. It also appears to be the case that fathers feel less sense of responsibility to the children of women they have never married than in other scenarios. As well, legal enforcement of child support for unmarried mothers lags behind that for the divorced, though the latter is itself a major issue.

The net result for children of unmarried mothers of this lack of resources for financial well-being can be summarized in the following way:

> Eight to 12 years after birth, a child born to an unmarried, teenage, high school dropout is 10 times as likely to be living in poverty as a child born to a mother with none of these three characteristics.[19]

Indeed, if one projects the lives of these boys and girls ahead several years, it is clear that many find themselves repeating the experience of their own childhood:

> Research shows that children born to single teenage mothers are more likely to drop out of school, to give birth out of wedlock, to divorce or separate, and to be dependent on welfare.[20]

As they repeat the life trajectories of their mothers, these now-grown men and women begin to visit their problems and disadvantages on their own children. According to Maggie Gallagher, children raised by single parents have twice the risk of becoming unmarried teen parents themselves.[21] Thus the vicious cycle of poverty rolls on, a cycle which so many have noticed and which seems so very difficult to arrest.

Impact upon Single Mothers, Divorced Fathers, and Their Children after Divorce

The 1985 publication of Lenore Weitzman's *The Divorce Revolution: The Unexpected Social and Economic Consequences for Women and Children* (Free Press) can arguably be seen as the first volley of a significant mainstream scholarly counterattack on the divorce culture in which we find ourselves.

Weitzman appears to have been the first researcher to raise the economic justice question vis-a-vis the issue of divorce. By 1985 rumblings concerning the psychic pain of divorce for adults and children had begun to be heard. But to that point no one had documented the disastrous economic consequences of divorce for divorced women and their children.

Weitzman's key figure was shocking. She claimed that women with minor children experienced a 73 percent decline in standard of living during the first year after divorce, whereas their husbands enjoyed a 42 percent increase in their own standard of living. She envisioned an increasing economic cleavage between the married and the unmarried, and between men and women, and in particular feared the development of a permanent underclass of divorced women and their children.

Weitzman's figures have been quoted widely. However, more recent research has cast doubts on her original calculations, though not their general import. In a 1996 *American Sociological Review* article, Richard Peterson examined the same numbers that Weitzman worked with and found that the corrected figures should be a 27 percent drop in standard of living for women and children, and a 10 percent increase for men after divorce.[22]

William Galston, analyzing the data produced by the Panel Study of Income Dynamics, offers numbers similar to the revised figures: a 30 percent drop in standard of living for women and children after divorce and a 10–15 percent increase for divorced men.[23]

It made a certain intuitive sense that single mothers and their children would face economic stress and that their male counterparts would prosper. After all, as Bianchi and Spain point out, mothers who gain custody of their children (the great majority) face several impediments to economic well-being: "their reduced income has to stretch further than their former husbands', their responsibilities for child care impede their ability to work full-time, and the child support they receive seldom compensates for the loss of a husband's income."[24] These impediments threaten the well-being of all who live in such households. Meanwhile, men get to keep most of their income, usually are not hit with large child support obligations or alimony payments, and most no longer invest in the support of their families as they would if they were still living with them.

However much sense this may make intuitively, at least two recent studies have found an actual loss in standard of living for noncustodial divorced *men,* and not just for divorced women and their children. Bianchi and Spain find that the drop for men is 6 percent,[25] while Stroup and Pollock claim that the income drop for men is actually 10 percent.[26]

This particular research question must be seen as open at this point. Nor is it clear, if it is the case that men's incomes are dropping after divorce (though not as much as women's), why this should be the case. A 1993 study by Biblarz and Raftery found that divorce increases a father's odds of winding up in a "low occupational stratum."[27] Perhaps this effect is due to the "tremendous emotional and economic stress [divorce causes] for individuals and families," including men.[28] Wallerstein and Blakeslee have written eloquently of the way in which marriage structures adult personhood; perhaps divorce diminishes the overall life competence of a certain percentage of men who experience it, and thus diminishes their economic performance as well, at least for a time.[29] Men who cohabit or remarry after divorce are also stressed financially if they seek to provide for both households.

But let us return to the main issue, the economic impact of divorce on those who unquestionably bear the greatest share of its cost: divorced women and their (custodial) children. Whether articulated in sensational or understated tones, the overall reality is clear, as Theresa Mauldin has said: "Numerous studies have found that marital disruption has detrimental economic effects on women and their children."[30]

In particular, divorced (and never-married) women and their children constitute a disproportionate share of the poor and of recipients of welfare payments. According to 1993 Census Bureau statistics, only 13 percent of women who received AFDC benefits were married with their husbands present; the other 87 percent were either separated (17 percent), divorced/widowed (23 percent), or never married (48 percent).[31] Eggebeen and Lichter have calculated that "increasing family breakdown accounted for almost half the increase in child poverty in the eighties."[32] Children who experience divorce "are almost twice as likely to be living in poverty than they were before the split."[33] McLanahan and Sandefur have claimed that "the average child from a nonpoor family will suffer a 50% drop in income after divorce."[34]

The effects of divorce on the economic prospects of its children extend well beyond the early childhood years. Divorce, as Biblarz and Raftery have claimed, "decreases the family's ability to pass [economic] advantages on to their children."[35] There are many reasons for this. Divorce, as has been repeatedly shown, has devastating emotional and behavioral consequences for children. Children from single-parent and disrupted families are two or three times more likely than children in two-parent families to have emotional and behavioral problems. They are more likely to have academic problems and/or drop out of high school, become pregnant as teens, abuse drugs, attempt or commit suicide, engage in violence, become mentally ill, and get in trouble with the law.[36]

The disadvantages that divorce brings into the lives of children have definite economic implications. Wallerstein and Blakeslee found that fully 40 percent of the young men in their longitudinal study of children of divorce are drifting. Fewer are going to college—in large part because they cannot afford to pay their own tuition and are not receiving any parental financial support— and fewer are finishing college even if they do start.[37] In a time in which the demands of the global economy make education and vocational competence all the more important, children of divorce—like their mothers—compete on an uneven playing field.

Barbara Dafoe Whitehead's summary is apt:

> Widespread divorce has generated new forms of inequality for women and children. It has contributed to greater economic insecurity and poverty among women and children, and it has been a principal generator of unequal opportunities and outcomes for woman and children. . . . It is hard to think of any recent economic force that has been as brutally efficient as divorce in transforming middle-class haves into have-nots.[38]

Divorce, it is now abundantly clear, has become one of the most important economic justice issues of our time.

In Summary: Family Reconfiguration and Its Connection with Poverty

David Popenoe has written:

> I know of few other bodies of data in which the weight of evidence is so decisively on one side of the issue: on the whole, for children, two-parent families are preferable. . . . If our prevailing views on family structure hinged solely on scholarly evidence, the current debate would never have arisen in the first place.[39]

Popenoe's comments were intended to address the entire issue of family structure and its impact on children's well-being. But they make a fine summary of the particular issue of the relationship between family structure and poverty which is our focus in this chapter. They also allude to the political/cultural debate in American public life that has raged for several years over the rise in single-parent families.

The raw fact of the matter is this: *the best predictor of financial well-being for children and women is marriage, while the best predictor of poverty is single motherhood.* Marital status has come to exceed education, race, neighborhood, family background, or any other predictor of financial and economic well-being.[40]

David Ellwood, in reflecting on the life-chances of children, summarizes the evidence this way: "the vast majority of children who are raised entirely in a two-parent home will never be poor during childhood. By contrast, the vast majority of children who spend time in a single-parent home will experience poverty."[41] In any given year, half of the children in one-parent families will experience poverty, versus 15 percent for those in two-parent families. Over the course of an entire childhood, 73 percent of children from one-parent families will experience poverty at some point, versus 20 percent for children from two-parent families. Only 2 percent of children in two-parent families will experience persistent poverty, as opposed to 22 percent of children from one-parent families.[42]

It is possible, of course, to frame the matter more positively. As Frank Furstenburg has written: "Marriage gives all parties involved an economic boost. In fact, stable marriages could be perpetuating the growing division between the haves and the have-nots. Marriage, quite simply, is a form of having. Children growing up with both of their biological parents are likely to be more educated, and to have better job skills and a more secure sense of themselves."[43]

In his 1992 article, David Popenoe, quoted above, made glancing reference to "the current debate." What debate, exactly, was that? It had to do with whether society should accept as a matter of course and without objection the reconfiguration of the American family. The issue was perhaps engaged most effectively in Barbara Dafoe Whitehead's landmark 1993 *Atlantic* piece entitled, "Dan Quayle Was Right." Quayle had attacked the TV sitcom "Murphy Brown" for what he called its glorification of single motherhood and its apparent message that marriage is no longer relevant or preferable to other family forms. For this attack Quayle was roundly scorned as a cultural philistine. Yet Whitehead's article marshaled the kinds of data we have looked at here and concluded that, in fact, on every front, Quayle's basic claim was simply empirically correct.

Since that time the cultural landscape has begun to change, and those who make the argument for the preferability of marriage over single parenthood are less frequently laughed out of court. Yet at times they still are, despite the mountains of data, only a small portion of which I have presented here. I suspect that is because facts prove at times to be inconvenient obstacles to the conclusions that we feel compelled to draw for reasons of our own ideology or self-interest. The fact that women, their children, and possibly even men benefit economically from being situated in intact marriages, and suffer when the reverse is the case, is one such inconvenient fact. That is, it is inconvenient for those whose worldviews require the legitimation of easy entry into and exit from marriage, and perhaps for those whose own life choices are implicitly called into question by the evidence at hand.

Rebuilding the Family: Guideposts for the Way Ahead

In part II of this monograph, we proceed on the basis of the evidence available to us to consider what can be done to address the heartbreaking, often unjust, and frequently economically disastrous breakdown of the family.

To do so will require us to discuss both the causes of the problems we have been naming and the various responses that have been or could be offered, on the assumption that responses to problems tend to reflect either explicit or implicit analyses of the causes of those problems. It will also require us to distinguish between and among solutions that are best located at the governmental, civil society, church, and individual/family levels.

Analysis of why human beings behave as they do is the perennial task of many disciplines of study. We are a mystery to ourselves, despite the increasingly sophisticated analytical tools now available to us in a variety of fields. We can and must use these tools, as long as their use is grounded in a biblical framework of interpretation concerning the nature and responsibility of human persons. So we enter into a discussion of the causes of family breakdown, and of the possibilities for altering these behaviors, with appropriate humility and caution and from within the framework of a biblical worldview.

Addressing the Problem of Out-of-Wedlock Births

Sexual Character and Personal Responsibility

There is an irreducibly personal dimension to the problem of out-of-wedlock births, and thus an irreducible personal responsibility. Children are conceived as the result of sexual intercourse between a man and a woman. Where that sexual act is voluntary on the part of both persons, both share fundamental responsibility for its consequences. Whatever else may be said about the causes of illegitimacy, this is where we must begin.

Sexual desire is one of the most compelling features of human existence. Scripture indicates that sex is one of the good gifts of God's creation (Prov. 5:18–19). We seek sexual contact for many reasons; among these are the desire for partnership, intimacy, and love, for physical pleasure, and for children. Within the context of marriage, sexual activity undertaken for these purposes is not only morally responsible but also rich with meaning, pleasure, and fulfillment.

Yet the need to discipline one's sexual drives is a fundamental dimension of character and moral responsibility. The introduction of sin into God's good creation has distorted every aspect of human personhood and relationships. Sin in the area of sexuality carries with it the potential for considerable harm of all types: exploitation, degradation, oppression, violence, disease, unwanted pregnancy, and the disfiguring of human personality.

The need for sexual self-control is a recurrent theme in Scripture (Matt. 5:27–30; 1 Corinthians 7). It is understood that such self-discipline will be a mark of the people of God, while at the same time constituting a highly desirable character quality for any human being. Training the young in self-discipline in the area of sexuality has long been understood to be a fundamental task of a range of agencies of human socialization: the family, the religious community, the schools, and the broader culture in its other expressions. The goal of these efforts is the production of grown men and women who will handle their sexuality responsibly. We will speak of these other agents below. Yet we must begin with the recognition that ultimately the responsibility rests with the individual.

Thus the first response we must make to the problem of out-of-wedlock births is simply to call men and women to a reclaiming of personal moral responsibility in the area of sexuality. That the current trend toward sexual irresponsibility is profoundly harmful to all concerned is an outcome that could easily have been predicted within the framework of biblical thought. Now it is likewise reaffirmed by an avalanche of data from the social sciences.

There are a host of practical aids to such moral responsibility that are available through a variety of publications and other outlets. The person who would seriously seek to avoid sexual intercourse outside of marriage can find many suggestions for how to do so, such as hints on how to avoid situations in which unplanned, impulsive sex is likely to occur. Abstinence from intercourse is the only foolproof birth prevention method. Given the pressures of our sexual drive, abstinence is extremely unlikely to be maintained unless it is a conscious decision, buttressed by the support of a key reference group, and strategically and prudently considered.

A second-best form of moral responsibility in the area of sexual conduct is the faithful use of effective birth-control methods. Here we confront an issue of considerable sensitivity for individuals, faith communities, school districts, and even for federal government policy.

Confining our discussion to personal responsibility at this point, we must say the following: first, because no birth-control technology is 100 percent effective, we are in every case dealing with a second-best option. Some pregnancies will occur. Second, birth control cannot be counted on to prevent sexually transmitted diseases, such as AIDS. Third, from a biblical perspective sexual intercourse outside of marriage falls outside of God's will. The use of birth control may lessen the likelihood of creating further moral problems, but it is at best a concession to sin. Fourth, it is difficult to simultaneously be fully committed to sexual abstinence outside of marriage and at the same time make preparations for sexual activity.

For these and other reasons, many Christians have tended to oppose the availability of birth control devices and sex education involving birth control, at least to the young. We will return to this issue later, but must say this: at the level of personal moral responsibility, while sexual intercourse outside of marriage violates God's will, such intercourse apart from birth control risks further violation of that will. It also threatens to bring into the world a child at risk of all manner of social ills, including poverty, from the very beginning of its life. Personal moral responsibility involves a hard-eyed realism about one's own likely behavior, and a willingness to deal responsibly with its implications.

Sexual Character and Civil Society

Even as we speak of the irreducibly personal dimension of this issue, we must also attend to the social context in which sexual character is formed or deformed. Sin is personal and social. So is character. The personal and the social continually interact with one another in an endless feedback loop.

The current trend toward personal sexual irresponsibility is incomprehensible apart from awareness of broader social and cultural changes. Perhaps the best way to summarize the issue is as follows: the traditional agents of sexual socialization—which largely fall within the realm of civil society—are no longer performing this task adequately. The family, religious communities, schools, civic agencies, neighborhood leaders, media personalities, entertainment providers, and so on, no longer transmit a coherent message of sexual responsibility. Thus it is unsurprising that the kind of sexual character we seek and need is increasingly scarce. It is also unsurprising that a reclamation of sexual responsibility must involve the efforts of all of these agents of civil society.

It is not always easy to identify the source of broad shifts in cultural attitudes. Yet it is possible to spot the existence and the consequences of such shifts. One such shift was the so-called sexual revolution which hit western society in the 1960s. The sexual revolution is aptly named, for it did amount to an overturning of the longstanding cultural moral norm—itself rooted in the Judeo-Christian moral heritage—that sex should be inextricably related to the marriage relationship.

Instead, as articulated with vigor in both popular and scholarly venues, the sexual revolution proposed an ethic not of sex-within-marriage but of sex-with-mutual-consent. Sex, it was argued, could and should be delinked from the marriage relationship. Sexual activity was instead appropriate wherever two consenting adults chose to engage in it. It was assumed that "the Pill," which was just then coming into wide availability, would take care of any risk of pregnancy, and at this stage there was little concern related to sexually transmitted diseases. Thus the only barrier standing between persons and full sexual fulfillment was believed to be the outmoded, conventional, Judeo-Christian sexual ethic.

Today it is possible to see a third competitor for the prize of reigning sexual ethic in American life: the sex-within-loving-relationships ethic. This ethic argues that sexual activity is morally permissible within any loving relationship—married or unmarried, homosexual or heterosexual, whatever permutation one might name. I tend to see the loving relationship ethic as a kind of post–1960s compromise between the older traditional/Christian ethic, on the one hand, and the Playboy/James Bond mutual consent ethic on the other. By now it has become, in my view, the prevailing popular sexual ethic in North America. Even a large number of traditional church bodies have either considered subscribing to it or already do so in one form or another.

A final wrinkle in cultural attitudes should here be noted: the removal of social stigma vis-a-vis what used to be called "illegitimacy" but now tends to be called "births to unmarried mothers"—the terminology I have tended to employ here. The promise of the birth-control revolution proved illusory. Today, thirty-five years after the Pill became widely available, fully half of all pregnancies are unintended, while some 65 percent of births to unmarried women are unplanned.[44]

Perhaps due to the brute fact that unintended pregnancies have become an everyday occurrence, or perhaps because of broader attitudinal changes toward marriage, the previous social stigma associated with out-of-wedlock pregnancy and birth has declined precipitously.[45] Note again the statistic just cited related to unintended pregnancies to unmarried women. It is significant both that so many unmarried women unintentionally end up pregnant, but also that so many of these pregnancies are in fact intentional. One recent article cited poll date in which 55 percent of teenage girls say they would consider having a child out of wedlock.[46]

What all of this amounts to is a thorough, though not total, cultural delinking of sex, reproduction, and marriage. What for the whole of human history had been inextricably joined has now been sundered. This delinking is then communicated to successive generations through both the lives and the explicit moral norms of a range of agents of civil society—beginning within the family, which is more and more likely to reflect in its very history the kind of delinking we are discussing.

How shall Christians and other concerned people respond to such a wide-ranging shift in cultural moral standards? It seems to me that the best response is to initiate a social countermovement with three dimensions: first, the embodiment of Christian sexual character within disciplined families and communities of faith; second, direct cultural engagement with prevailing moral norms; third, strategic targeting of particular areas of civil society for transformative effort.

As Christian theologian Stanley Hauerwas and many others have argued, the focus of Christian moral effort should be the identity and integrity of the churches themselves. It can be argued that this should always and everywhere be the focal point of Christian moral concern; but it is an especially acute issue in our own post-Constantinian, post-Christian society.

It is now essentially impossible for Christians to use what remains of our social and political power to coerce our secular society to conform to our moral vision. However, what we can at least do is live out our convictions in full view of a skeptical society. We can make of Christian family life something approximating our vision of God's intention for family life. We can demonstrate disciplined sexual character and its joyful outcomes in life.

We can also create congregations of highly committed, mutually accountable Christian brothers and sisters who can together become mini-communities of sexual character. Such congregations will have an impact on their communities through their individual members and families, through the public proclamation of Christian sexual morality, and through the creative ministries and programs for developing sexual character (such as the True Love Waits campaign) that they initiate in their congregations and localities.

At both local and national levels Christian scholars, activists, and church leaders can and must engage the new cultural sexual paradigm with vigor and skill. Its failures are obvious, yet it still commands powerful support among those who generally hold the levers of access to public opinion. Yet such access can likewise be gained by articulate Christian thinkers and leaders who can then offer a clear alternative vision. Here I am thinking about universities, their presses and journals, major newspapers and magazines, research and advocacy organizations, and so on.

One particular arena of civil society in need of engagement is the entertainment industry. As of 1992 the average daily television viewing per American household had reached seven hours. "In the prime afternoon and evening hours the three largest TV networks broadcast a total of more than 65,000 sexual references each year."[47] The great majority of sexual acts and references did not involve married couples. Many organizations are attending these days to the entertainment industry and its simultaneous reflection and reinforcement of damaging cultural trends. That industry should remain a focal point of concern for Christian engagement, not only via outside critiques but also through the infiltration of the industry by committed Christians.

Our nation needs moral and spiritual renewal. This summary may be a commonplace or be perceived as a cliche. Yet no one, to my knowledge, has offered a compelling alternative. Given that reality, we need to think more concretely and clearly than we have so far about strategies for making that renewal happen.

Sexual Character and Public Policy

One aspect of Christian response we have yet to consider related to the issue of out-of-wedlock births is in the arena of public policy. It has been important to establish the principle that government is not the first resort when addressing issues of family breakdown—or, for that matter, most other moral issues. We should look first to personal and civil society responses, and then see how government at various levels can both support the best of these efforts and, at times, undertake its own initiatives as well.

The use of public policy to address the issue of illegitimacy involves several possible points of entry and emphasis. Each option involves a set of presuppositions and decisions about the causes of the problem.

One option is for local, state, or federal governments to become engaged in education campaigns intended to discourage teen (or unwed) pregnancy, either on their own or in partnership with private NGO agencies. Most local school districts offers some form of sex-education program in the public schools. But few states, at least until recently, have constructed a coherent pregnancy prevention program beyond the efforts found in the schools.

A pioneering effort along these lines was undertaken by Maryland in the late 1980s. As of 1992, Maryland was the only state to have a legislated pregnancy-education program for teens. That program has involved a four-part strategy: a media campaign promoting abstinence, the establishment of teen clinics in high-risk areas, encouragement of parents to be the primary sex educators of their children, and an effort to elicit community funding support for pregnancy prevention activities. Between 1980 and 1990 the teen pregnancy rate dropped by 13 percent.[48]

The 1996 welfare reform act contained significant attention to the issue of illegitimacy. One focal point of that law was an effort to reduce the number of repeat out-of-wedlock births, and certainly to reduce the amount of federal spending to support illegitimate children. The "family cap" was the most controversial means used to accomplish this end. On the theory that the availability of welfare benefits was, perversely, encouraging women to continue having illegitimate children, a family cap on benefit amounts was passed. Women on welfare who had more children could no longer count on receiving larger benefit checks.

While it is too early to judge the impact of this provision, it is among the most controversial aspects of that law and among the least likely to find scholarly support. Analysts from across the ideological spectrum are questioning both the theory underlying this provision of the law and the projected positive consequences of that provision. As Gregory Acs has written,

> Politicians, the press, and the public have latched onto the argument that the welfare system encourages childbearing, and this argument is theoretically sound. There are real costs to raising children, however, and the support provided by the AFDC program is quite small relative to these costs. My findings suggest that variations in welfare benefit levels and the incremental benefit have no statistically significant impacts on the subsequent childbearing decisions of young mothers in general, and on the subsequent childbearing decisions of women who received welfare in particular. Furthermore, mothers who received welfare to support their first child are no more likely to have additional children in any given year through the age of 23.[49]

Besides the family cap, the welfare reform law involved the federal government much more aggressively in mandating state teen pregnancy prevention efforts. States are now required to submit plans describing the attention they will give to such efforts, and are offered the incentive of bonus grants for reductions in illegitimacy.

Given the key role of agencies of civil society in encouraging sexual responsibility, it is important that government look for opportunities to partner with and support effective pregnancy prevention programs wherever they may be found, rather than attempting to generate their own programs. The "charitable choice" provision of the welfare law provides a mechanism for government support for the most effective church-based efforts in the area of pregnancy prevention as well as other areas of need.

One final note related to government policy is called for. Rebecca Blank has argued that factors such as lack of economic opportunity and a sense of hopelessness are the critical forces contributing to teen pregnancy among the urban poor.[50] Her thesis dovetails with the well-known argument of William Julius Wilson that black male unemployment has reduced the pool of marriageable men and thus led to declining marriage rates (and consequently a higher percentage of out-of-wedlock births) among black women. Thus, the argument goes, the causal arrow points in the opposite direction: poverty causes family reconfiguration, not the other way around.[51]

Wilson's thesis continues to be hotly debated. The most recent research appears to lend only modest empirical support to Wilson's hypothesis. Wilson himself has now acknowledged the impact of non-economic forces on the rate of out-of-wedlock births.[52]

However, to the extent that economic factors contribute to the changing shape of the family, especially among the urban poor, any discussion of public policy responses to out-of-wedlock births must also include reference to the need for greater economic opportunity. To proceed further with policy proposals along those lines would take us too far afield, but we would be remiss in not mentioning this point.

Addressing the Problem of Divorce

While it is increasingly clear that out-of-wedlock birth is currently the greatest single factor affecting the structure of the American family, it remains no less important to continue to undertake efforts to slow the tide of divorce and to do what we can to mitigate its ill effects. Following our earlier pattern, we will consider individual, civil society, and public policy responses in the area of divorce.

Marital Permanence and Personal Responsibility

As with the discussion of sexual behavior, one must immediately acknowledge the irreducibly personal dimension of marital permanence and divorce prevention. The responsibility for marrying wisely, for behaving appropriately in life and towards one's spouse, for resolving conflict, for enduring hard times, for remaining sexually faithful, and for sustaining a rock-solid commitment to one's partner ultimately rests with each married individual and then, secondarily, with the entity we call the married couple.

In my own and others' research on the dynamics of marital success and failure, it seems clear that individual character is highly significant. Some mar-

riages fail simply because one or both of the partners lacks the character needed to sustain a permanent marital alliance. A wide array of character flaws can threaten a marriage: laziness, cruelty, dishonesty, impulsiveness, immaturity, tendency to addiction, irresponsibility, and selfishness are among those character traits that strain marriages to and beyond the breaking point. In such cases, the fundamental issue is not a relational one but instead, one of individual character. No government program can repair flawed character. The responsibility rests with the individual—and with those entities of civil society that help to shape the moral climate in which we all live.

There are, of course, many marriages that fail due to relational breakdowns that are not mainly related to character. By now it is clear that—at least as understood in late-twentieth-century Western society—a marriage has many of the characteristics of a living organism. Like any other living organism, a marriage needs care and tending. It needs appropriate nutrients in order to flourish. It needs a basic tool kit of survival and growth skills. And it needs mechanisms for fighting off "diseases" that threaten its existence.

The central item in the marital tool kit appears to be communication. Endless books and articles can now be found which attempt to offer principles of healthy marital communication. Advice on how to listen well, to voice one's own concerns clearly and responsibly, to move toward resolution of areas of disagreement, and so on, is readily available. These are generally little more than commonsense nostrums, but the continuing epidemic of marital breakdowns indicates the continuing need for married couples to attend to such resources.

Above all, perhaps, marital permanence requires an unshakable commitment to marital permanence itself. In cultural contexts other than our own—both at earlier times in Western history and even today in many other societies—divorce was either impossible or nearly so. In such contexts couples had to learn how to "make do" with each other. When one course of action is not an option then perforce other courses of action must be undertaken. If a couple live in a world in which divorce is not among the range of options available to them for addressing marital problems, they of necessity are required to come up with other alternatives. Of course, the fact is that today divorce is a readily available legal option, and one that in the terms of the broader society has lost any moral stigma it once had. Thus the only way in which divorce becomes an impossibility is if a married couple mentally and morally construct a world for themselves in which that is the case. To use the language of narrative for a moment, what must occur is that the couple tell themselves a story different than the story being told in the broader culture; then they must decide to inhabit that story.

Such storytelling, as the narrative theologians and philosophers tell us, is not generally something that an individual (or couple) can do on his or her own. Only communities—in particular, communities of faith—are the bearers of narratives of sufficient power that we might choose to step into them. This leads us to the next step in our discussion.

Marital Permanence: Civil Society and the Church

It is possible to propose a variety of civil society contributions to the problem of marital breakdown and divorce. One should wish for marriage enrichment and encouragement to be a part of the agenda of civic clubs and other such entities. It would be nice if public education included instruction in marriage building and divorce prevention, as is now being discussed (and has been adopted in one state, Florida). One should earnestly hope for more marriage-preserving and family-enhancing workplace policies. The entertainment industry could be—and frequently is—challenged to offer more marriage- and family-friendly music, television shows, films, and so on. There is definitely a place for all of these kinds of initiatives.

However, it seems to me unrealistic to ask what are essentially communicators and agents of contemporary culture to suddenly communicate a countercultural message. Every so often they will surprise us and do so. But most of the time these entities will reflect prevailing social values. They have no particular reason not to do so, and many reasons to do so. They are led by men and women whose own life experiences generally reflect what is going on in the society as a whole because they emerge from the society as a whole. They are cultural entities.

Thus I do not believe that a Christian civil society strategy can focus anywhere else than on the strengthening of the fundamentally countercultural religious and moral vision and practice of the churches themselves. We are beyond the time—if there was such a time—when we can coerce Sony, Disney or IBM to reflect and promote the kind of marital-permanence ethos that is one of our core Christian moral values. But we can look deep within our own faith communities and seek to renew the practice of marriage that goes on there.

Despite the increasing secularization of American society, approximately three-fourths of Americans still marry in houses of worship. With increasing but still inadequate vigor in recent years, Protestant and Catholic thinkers and leaders have begun to initiate more rigorous programs of marriage preparation and preservation. What has begun to emerge is a top-to-bottom marriage-building regime. The outlines of this regime have been most adequately profiled in Michael McManus's significant book *Marriage Savers,* and in the movement now known by the same name.[53]

McManus essentially pulled together information related to known ministries in the area of marital permanence. Arguing that the struggle for marital permanence begins in the dating years, he described teen sexual abstinence ministries such as Sex Respect, Why Wait?, and Postponing Sexual Involvement. He described an innovative program for the "seriously dating" couple called Relationship Instruction, indicating the significance of relational developments within that particular developmental stage.

One of McManus's most strenuous (and absolutely correct) claims is that no couple should marry in a church without a significant and thoughtful program of premarital preparation. He profiled the PREPARE/ENRICH and FOCCUS programs as well as Engaged Encounter, a weekend conference based on the Catholic-originated Marriage Encounter program. Other programs now exist for newlyweds. For the longer-term married couple there are suggestions for routine marriage enrichment activities as well as information concerning the linchpin Marriage Encounter program itself. Retrouvaille and Marriage Ministry are two efforts designed for the seriously troubled marriage. McManus also recommended several divorce recovery programs, which are of significant pastoral help to the divorced and can also assist such persons in preparing more adequately for another try at marriage.

McManus also suggested a solution to the problem of the "marrying Sam" minister; that is, if some churches in a community tighten and strengthen their premarital preparation requirements, those couples looking for the easy way to the altar likely can find a casual "marrying Sam" minister who will not impose such requirements. McManus proposed that congregations within particular communities initiate ecumenical "community marriage policies." These policies would establish minimal, community-wide, marital preparation and marriage ministry requirements for all of the congregations within that locality. Several dozen communities have done just that, most famously the Modesto, California area, in which the number of divorces is down considerably despite a significant rise in population. Community marriage policies, in my view, are a marvelous ecumenical venture that hold considerable promise in reducing the divorce rate—at least among those couples committed to a church wedding.

Elsewhere I have written at length concerning the theological/moral (as opposed to the programmatic) task facing the church if it is serious about building lifetime marriages.[54] My primary suggestions in this regard for the church can be summarized as follows:

- the need for a focus on Christian discipleship and character formation in order to produce more morally sound human beings whose character is of sufficient strength to sustain lifetime marriage;
- the need for a radical reclamation of the church's moral vision vis-a-vis marriage; a shift from the cultural understanding of marriage as the setting in which one can have one's relational and sexual needs met, to an understanding of marriage as the institution God established for divine purposes that extend well beyond one's own personal happiness;
- the need for much better developed relational, peacemaking, and conflict resolution skills in church life generally and in marriage in particular;

- the need for a greater emphasis on and modeling of sexual purity and fidelity and a deemphasis on personal sexual fulfillment;
- the need for nurturing a climate of relational equity and justice within marriage so that marriages don't collapse under the weight of their many injustices;
- the need to create support relationships within the church, relationships characterized by intimacy and accountability so that individuals and couples need not struggle alone;
- the need to recover and proclaim a covenantal understanding of marital permanence;
- the need to lift up models of healthy and mature marriage at each developmental stage;
- the need to develop a self-conscious and explicit countercultural ethos within our congregations related to marital permanence.

Early returns from the Marriage Savers movement and other initiatives indicate that divorce is a preventable human problem rather than a natural disaster akin to a tornado. The tools for undertaking such prevention are increasingly well understood and available. The church can offer significant and positive cultural leadership if it will take them up.

Marital Permanence: Public Policy Options

There is growing interest among policymakers and policy analysts these days in initiatives designed to encourage marital permanence. These proposals and initiatives range from the most gentle nudging of the state regulatory apparatus related to marriage and divorce to quite radical changes in the design of current laws. At the same time, opposition to such initiatives is also quite intense. Let us consider several major options.

Most states currently regulate the entry into marriage very lightly. Those seeking marriage must obtain a license by filling out a brief form and paying a small fee. There is generally a brief waiting period. Those marrying must have the legal capacity to do so, in terms of mental and psychological competence. Most states also regulate access to marriage by age, generally requiring both parties to be eighteen years old.

One reform option is to attack the problem of marital quality and divorce through more vigorous regulation of the entry into marriage. A number of different strategies have been proposed.

First, some are proposing either the requirement or the encouragement of a program of premarital preparation, including testing, counseling, and education. Such an initiative could be undertaken in tandem with another measure, the strategic use of extended waiting periods prior to granting of a marriage license. The counseling could be provided by the state itself or by others and certified by the state. In 1998, Florida became the first state in the nation to pass a law—the Marriage Preparation and Preservation Act—with precisely this approach. Couples who take a four-hour marriage preparation class can receive a license for $56 and marry with no waiting period. Those who choose not to do so must wait three days and pay $88.50.[55] Legislators in several states have introduced bills, with variations, along these lines.[56] No state thus far has mandated premarital counseling—only voluntary or incentive-based approaches are on the table.

Another strategy related to the entry into marriage is to address the age issue. States could use one or another lever of public policy to increase the age at which couples marry, reasoning from all relevant data that teen marriages are likely to be less stable. In March 1998 a Missouri legislator proposed an incentive-based law along these lines. Rep. Pat Kelley's bill would have the state offer a $1,000 bonus to any couple who delay marriage until both are at least twenty-one.[57] Close kin to this kind of approach would be a strategy aimed at encouraging or mandating *longer courtships*.[58]

Critiques of these entry-type proposals can be offered at both practical and philosophical levels. At a practical level, such policies would routinely require the state to create a new or expanded administrative apparatus for this area of the law. There is the issue of how or whether state funding would be provided for those couples unable to pay for counseling, or perhaps for all couples. A question arises concerning the possible abuse of the system through the filing of false affidavits. Finally, some argue that premarital counseling is ineffective even in the best of circumstances. It is certainly the case that coerced premarital counseling would be less likely than voluntary counseling to have a positive impact.

Philosophically, some see this kind of regulation as an intrusion of the state into what is legitimately the private sphere—the "nanny state" run amok. Indeed, this libertarian-type objection will likely doom purely mandatory measures in most states. Even those who support the basic concept here must be aware of the "iron law of unintended consequences." Given the rising rate of cohabitation in our society, it can be argued that nothing should be done to increase its frequency—but that putting "speed bumps" in the path of marriage could lead some couples simply to live together instead.

Despite these objections and concerns, I support an incentive-based approach focused on significant premarital preparation. I would broaden the difference in the way counseled and non-counseled couples are treated: a sixty-day waiting period and a $200 fee for those not receiving counseling, for example, would raise the level of incentive to undertake the premarital program. It would require experimentation to see exactly how high a fee and how long a wait should be employed.

One final note about church involvement is needed. Religious leaders could contribute mightily to the rate of participation in a state-encouraged premarital preparation process simply by offering high-quality programs themselves and refusing to marry anyone who refuses to participate in them—a policy many pastors already employ.[59] Where states move in this direction, the churches can partner with government while continuing to do what they have always done.

Current state laws regulate the conduct of marriage in three basic areas: finances, children, and domestic violence. Other than these aspects, the states remain neutral, or as Milton C. Regan puts it, "agnostic," about behavior within families.[60] Along with Sylvia Ann Hewlett and Cornel West, I believe that "government should get back into the business of fostering the value of marriage as a long-term commitment."[61]

In particular, I suggest the following modest initiative: states should use incentives to encourage couples to undertake marriage enrichment and marriage counseling activities during the course of their marriages. There would be no need for states to develop such activities or programs themselves, though they certainly would be free to do so. All they would really need to do would be to offer a modest tax incentive to couples who in any given year can certify their participation in such a program.

More broadly, policymakers need to consider a wide range of measures that, taken together, would offer public-policy support for stable and permanent marriage and family relationship. Hewlett and West, in their provocative recent work entitled *The War Against Parents,* have proposed a "parents' bill of rights"—a set of measures that would, in their view, demonstrate societal support for the honorable, sacrificial, and absolutely critical work of parents. They group their proposals under the following categories of what parents are entitled to: time for their children, economic security, a pro-family electoral system, a pro-family legal structure, a supportive external environment, and honor and dignity.[62] Other analysts and advocacy groups have for some time been constructing entire public-policy programs around the vision of strengthening families, though particular proposals vary widely—usually along ideological lines.[63]

To pursue this issue further here would take us outside the focus of this paper, but I concur with the basic claim that public policy has a legitimate role to play in offering broad support for strong and healthy marriage and family life.

Now let us consider the critical issue of how states regulate the entry into divorce. Today, most states approach this issue with the same agnostic neutrality that marks state laws related to the entry into and conduct of marriage.

All statutes specify the permissible legal grounds for divorce. Here one finds two basic but very different patterns: no-fault and fault-based grounds. Since 1985 all states have had no-fault statutes; some have fault-based grounds to go with no-fault approaches. There is an important history behind the rather strange current structure of our divorce laws.

Through most of our nation's history, divorce was available only to a husband or wife who could demonstrate that their spouse had committed an offense against marriage that was serious enough to merit the dissolution of the marriage. The presupposition of the law was that the marriage relationship was a matter of significant public interest. Marriage was viewed as a status that imposes a permanent set of obligations on all who are embedded in the relationships that marriage creates.[64] The law legitimately held people to those obligations, releasing people from them only when one partner's behavior constituted a fundamental offense against the marriage. Clearly, this legal theory was closely tied to the religious/moral legacy of the western Christian tradition.

Early in American history the list of offending behaviors, or grounds for divorce, tended to be relatively short and closely tied to a reading of biblical teaching. Over time those grounds expanded incrementally, with great variations across the fifty states.[65] But what these codes held in common was the view that the dissolution of a marriage was a grave act that should be limited to particular offenses against marriage.

Quietly and with relatively little fanfare, a revolution in divorce law was successfully undertaken in the 1970s. The first to take the plunge was the state of California in 1969. Marking a clean break with the entire history we have been outlining, non-fault-based divorce (popularized under the label "no-fault divorce") became the new benchmark for divorce law.

It is important to understand what the framers of no-fault divorce intended. They were not intending to argue that no one is ever at fault when a marriage collapses, or that the end of a marriage is not morally significant. However, they did believe that no one's interests were being served by an adversarial system in which divorcing couples had to go to court to prove to a judge that each other was to blame for a marriage's problems. As well, they were aware that as the demand for divorce began to increase in the 1960s, the strictures of then-current divorce laws were creating an environment of duplicity in the legal process. Couples genuinely and mutually wanting to divorce were having to pretend that one or the other was guilty of some particular marital offense. As well, the demand for divorce was leading some judges to stretch the permitted grounds beyond recognition.[66] The reformers' idea was to eliminate all of this duplicity by waiving the requirement of showing fault. The public interest, they believed, consisted not in keeping troubled marriages together but in enabling their dissolution to be as painless and fair as possible.[67]

The no-fault vision, if implemented in pure form, would have eliminated all fault grounds from legal codes. However, not all states were willing to go this far; a majority have retained both fault and no-fault grounds. Yet the fault grounds are at this point largely vestigial; their primary use appears to be in the post-divorce settlement process where that is permissible. Our actual divorce law regime essentially permits divorce to be initiated by either spouse for any reason at any time in the marriage. Simply by claiming "irreconcilable differences," or "marriage breakdown" and waiting a relatively brief period of time, a person can find a way of escape from his marital commitments.

Today there is much discussion about whether this thirty-year-old experiment in legal reform should be reconsidered. I believe that it should be. The argument for the abolition of no-fault divorce can be made in at least the following ways.

First, there are legal considerations. Milton Regan and others have argued that marriage was once understood as a status relationship, but now has become contractual in nature. Yet under no-fault we have a very flimsy contract. No-fault divorce allows a person to abandon the marriage relationship (with its many clearly contractual elements, including state licensure) unilaterally, without penalty, and without recourse by the offended contract partner. In legal terms, this is a "terminable-at-will" relationship. The state's continued participation in the supposed regulation and licensing of marriage is revealed as a sham, little more than "notarized dating." As Bryce J. Christensen has written, "No fault divorce put[s] the state . . . in the absurd position of requiring a license for the pronouncing of public vows which the state subsequently regards with indifference."[68]

Second, there are moral considerations. The law is a teacher, even if at times we might prefer not to notice this constitutive dimension of its impact. If it is a teacher, no-fault divorce teaches all the wrong things. It teaches men and women that marriage can be casually entered and exited. Yet it is both morally and empirically wrong to believe that this is so. It teaches that contracts—at least this one—can be violated with impunity. By its very (popular) name it teaches that no one is to be "faulted" for offenses against marriage such as adultery and abandonment where these are present. It permits gross injustices against spouses and children without penalty—indeed, by its structure no-fault divorce allies the state with the irresponsible party.[69] It teaches that marriage itself, as an institution, is not of particular social significance. It thus contributes to the weakening of personal character, relational stability, public justice, and social virtue.

Third, there are economic considerations. The ease with which anyone can obtain a divorce places the economically dependent spouse (usually the wife) in a very precarious situation. If she is abandoned, the fact that no fault is claimed tends to reduce the value of the property settlement she obtains during the divorce. Given that 90 percent of divorces leave child custody with the mother, she and her children are at risk of impoverishment, as we have seen. It is a bitter irony to note that no-fault divorce was, in part, intended to improve the financial situation for divorced women. Now it instead contributes to the very link between family breakdown and poverty that we are examining in this essay.

Despite considerable stirring and unease related to no-fault divorce laws, no state has done away with what by now is a well-established dimension of family law. As well, not every anti-divorce analyst is convinced that the return to a fault-based system would be constructive.[70] But is there something short of a rollback of no-fault divorce that we can propose related to the entry into divorce? One approach would be to toughen four particular "speed bumps" on the way to divorce: enhanced waiting periods, a more vital role for mutual consent, stronger counseling and education requirements, and modest judicial discretion in granting divorces.[71] Such changes would constitute at least an incremental reform of the no-fault divorce system.

Let us finally consider two systemic reform options. These attack the divorce problem through an overhaul of the entire marriage and divorce system. We will look first at what has come to be known as "covenant marriage."

The 1997 passage in Louisiana of the Covenant Marriage Law (and passage of a similar law in Arizona in 1998) has created considerable public attention and interest in this particular systemic reform option. Covenant marriage is best understood as an effort to create an optional fault-based marriage covenant as a supplement to the current no-fault regime.

As of August 15, 1997 married couples in Louisiana can choose voluntarily to enter into a covenant marriage. A covenant marriage contract is a different kind of arrangement than the typical current marriage, and it is to be treated as such by the legal system at every stage; this is what I mean by a systemic reform of the marriage law regime. Everything about a covenant marriage is intended to signal the heightened seriousness of this particular version of the marital relationship. Note how each aspect of the marriage law system is addressed in its provisions.

In terms of the entry into marriage, the couple must execute a formal declaration of intent to embark on such a union. This declaration must accompany an application for a marriage license. The marriage certificate itself also indicates whether this is a covenant marriage. Those seeking covenant marriage must also be able to certify by a notarized affidavit that they have received premarital counseling.

The declaration of intent to enter a covenant marriage requires the couple to seek marital counseling if they experience difficulties. Divorce or separation in a covenant marriage is fault-based; adultery, imprisonment for a felony, desertion, or physical/sexual abuse of child or spouse are the only permitted causes. Two years of continuous separation without reconciliation are required before a covenant marriage can be dissolved, though divorce can be granted somewhat sooner for the traditional fault grounds.

I view covenant marriage as an attempt to encourage rather than mandate a return to the pre–1969 *status quo* in divorce law. The mechanism it uses to offer this encouragement is solely the creation of an optional "marriage deluxe" legal structure. No incentives or disincentives, mandates or prohibitions, are employed. That is one reason why the law was passed: it could be presented in the language of choice.

Even so, a close reading of the law reveals its clear intent to encourage a reform in the way Louisianans view the permanence of marriage. The state wants to encourage couples to believe that marriage is a lifetime commitment. It is prepared to help them do so by structuring its marriage laws in a way that makes it more difficult to exit a marriage if couples contract to play by those rules from the outset. The net result, at least in the short term, is the creation of a two-tier marriage system: intentionally permanent marriages, governed by the covenant marriage laws, and other (implicitly impermanent) marriages, governed by no-fault laws. Clearly, Louisiana hopes that the number of the former will grow and the latter decline.

Criticism of this approach could come from two directions: that Louisiana is going too far, or not far enough. Already there are critics who argue that Louisiana lawmakers have no business enshrining their moral convictions about marital permanence into law. Even the vocabulary, with its clearly biblical overtones, signals the religio-moral convictions that underlie this legislation. Predictable choruses of despair concerning the growing influence of the religious right can be heard.

On the other hand, this law can be seen by serious advocates of divorce reform as not going far enough. Louisiana's law does not abolish or even modify no-fault divorce itself, but more subtly seeks to supplement it with an optional, fault-based alternative. It can be questioned whether a purely optional system is good public policy—whether it communicates public values in a sufficiently strong and vigorous manner.

More broadly, it is reasonable to ask whether a voluntary, two-tier legal system related to marriage is fundamentally coherent. Lawmakers are attempting to articulate a public valuation of marital permanence but without requiring or even using incentives to encourage anyone to act in a way that accomplishes that goal. That approach may simply be too weak to be very effective. Yet it appeals to our libertarian preference for choice making. Indeed, some are now arguing for a totally deregulated free market in marriage contracts—not just two options, but the freedom to make whatever marriage contract we want to make.[72]

My suggestion is that covenant marriage approaches be strengthened through the intentional use of incentives and disincentives, and that, despite discouraging responses thus far, this experiment should continue wherever feasible. And yet I do not consider this the most important current divorce-reform strategy.

The concept of a two-tiered divorce law system could take another form: a mandatory system hinging on the presence of children. With William Galston, I believe that this is the main direction that divorce-law reform should take.[73] The presence of children should automatically transform the legal status of marriage and raise the "guard rails" against divorce. It should also fundamentally affect decisions concerning all aspects of the post-divorce relationship, such as child support and child custody.

We have already noted the compelling evidence concerning the impact of divorce on children.[74] Society has a strong interest in supporting marriages that endure and are worth enduring, and among the most persuasive supports for this claim is what we now know about divorce's lasting impact on the lives of children. And it is children whose interests are most frequently the last to be considered in our modern culture of divorce.

If those interests were taken seriously, a strong case could be made that because roughly two-thirds of all divorces do involve children, the kinds of "entry into marriage" reforms we have already considered should not only be encouraged but ultimately mandated for all couples. At least those couples who already have children (either through out-of-wedlock birth or a prior marriage) should be required to undertake a course of premarital preparation. There should also be a meaningful waiting period prior to marriage.

The same basic principle applies when it comes to the decision to enter into divorce. Where children are involved, states should require lengthy waiting periods of perhaps as much as two years or more (with the exception of situations of abuse). Couples who have children and are considering divorce should be required to attend classes related to the impact of divorce on children, as well as to all child-related post-divorce issues. The educational process at this pivotal point should operate with a bias toward preserving the marriage. Judges should have the discretion to delay or discourage unnecessary or frivolous divorces where children are involved.

Amy Black has argued that mutual consent should be required in divorces involving children, even if it is not required for other divorces.[75] Galston would agree but would leave a five-year waiting period as an escape clause.[76] While I can see needed exceptions to this approach, I do believe that it is appropriate to modify the fault-based system for divorce where children are present. The presence of children in the home should raise the state's threshold for permitting divorce to something approaching the older fault-based standards that prevailed in American law until 1969. A unilaterally initiated divorce for purpose of personal self-fulfillment, for example, should not be permitted where children will be affected. Or, if an escape clause ultimately is required, the person seeking it should be required to pay dearly for the privilege.

Ongoing state and federal efforts to improve the financial support of children after divorce must be continued and strengthened, in tandem with other child-focused divorce-law reforms. Public policy in this area should seek the closest approximation to economic justice for children of divorce as is possible under the circumstances. The goal should be to require those who bring children into the world to continue to support them financially through childhood, even when they no longer reside together with their children, until or unless that support is no longer needed. Child-support awards need to be increased and their enforcement toughened. This was a major goal of the 1996 welfare reform law and needs continued attention. However, it must be recognized that such measures are a very poor substitute indeed for two parents and an intact family.

Conclusion: The Limits of Law

Policymakers can do much to encourage what I have called sexual character and marital permanence. Beyond the incremental and systemic proposals offered here, government can also use its "bully pulpit" and public education powers to weigh in on behalf of the public value of family stability. This year, Florida's state legislators not only passed measures intended to address marital entry and exit but also now require courses, in the public high schools, on marriage and its skills.[77] One can easily imagine many creative public education measures that could be taken along these lines if the machinery of government at every level was turned to the explicit promotion of this social value. Such measures serve the common good in a very responsible manner.

However, it is important to close with a note of realism and of admonition. The note of realism is this: law cannot produce people of good character, of sound relational skills, and of the "stuff" required to live out the meaning of the covenants they either implicitly or explicitly make. Law always has its limits and those limits are most obvious here.

Thus a word of admonition must go to individuals, couples, and churches. Ultimately the future of the family rests in our own hands. Government can encourage "the better angels of our nature" but we must be willing to live accordingly. Churches, in particular, must do much more to exercise their own leadership in this area. What government cannot mandate or prohibit for citizens, churches can—for their members. And what we mandate we can supply: character formation, relationship instruction, marriage preparation, marriage enrichment and counseling, divorce-prevention tools, and so on.

Real progress in this area of the law is most likely to result from a partnership of individuals, families, churches, government, and other spheres of society.[78] Change must begin with renewal in our hearts and lives of what once were shared values among us. These values must then find creative expression and incarnation in the preaching and programming of churches and other religious organizations. Then and only then can Christians legitimately seek to employ the limited power of government in this sphere of life to enhance public justice and serve the common good.

Notes

Chapter 1: *Economic Justice: A Biblical Paradigm*

1. We want to thank two graduate assistants, Joan and Chris Hoppe-Spink, who helped to gather materials and proofread.

2. See further Ronald J. Sider, "Toward an Evangelical Political Philosophy. *Transformation* (July–September 1997): 1–10; and for a brief discussion of the use of a biblical paradigm, Christopher J. H. Wright, "The Use of the Bible in Social Ethics," *Transformation* (January–March 1984): 10.

3. Julius Gould quoted in J. Philip Wogaman, *The Great Economic Debate: An Ethical Analysis* (Philadelphia: Westminster, 1997), 10.

4. See, for example, John Courtney Murray, *We Hold These Truths: Catholic Reflections on the American Proposition* (Kansas City: Sheed and Ward, 1960). J. Budziszewski has recently published a more popular statement: *Written on the Heart: The Case for Natural Law* (Downers Grove, Ill.: InterVarsity Press, 1997).

5. John Paul II, *Laborem exercens,* Section 13.

6. Hans Walter Wolff, *Anthropology of the Old Testament* (Philadelphia: Fortress, 1974), 29. *Flesh* here represents human beings in relationship and solidarity with others.

7. Cf. also Ecclesiastes 4:8.

8. Richard J. Mouw, *Political Evangelism* (Grand Rapids: Eerdmans, 1973), 45.

9. Thomas Aquinas, *Summa Theologiae,* 2a2ae. 66, 2, 7 in Aquinas, *Selected Political Writings,* ed. D'Entrèves (Oxford: Blackwell, 1948), 169, 171; cf. 1a2ae. 94, 5, 127.

10. *Economic Justice for All: Pastoral Letters on Catholic Social Teaching and the U.S. Economy* (Washington: National Conference of Catholic Bishops, 1986), section 64, 34.

11. Wogaman, *Great Economic Debate,* 43.

12. See, for example, James W. Skillen, *Recharging the American Experiment: Principled Pluralism for Genuine Civic Community* (Grand Rapids: Baker, 1994), especially chapter 4.

13. One should not interpret the parable to refer exclusively to material wealth. It calls people to use their gifts and resources creatively and boldly to advance God's reign— which, of course, includes material well-being.

14. See further, Stephen Charles Mott, *A Christian Perspective on Political Thought* (New York: Oxford University Press, 1993), chapter 1.

15. Max Weber, *Economy and Society: An Outline of Interpretative Sociology,* 4th ed., ed. G. Roth and C. Wittick (New York: Bedminster, 1968), II, 926.

16. For this perspective on power in the writings of Paul Tillich and James Luther Adams, cf., for example, Paul Tillich, *Love, Power and Justice: Ontological Analyses and Ethical Applications* (New York: Oxford University, 1954), esp. 35–53; Adams, "Theological Bases of Social Action," in James Luther Adams, *Taking Time Seriously* (Glencoe, Ill.: Free Press, 1957), esp. 42, 50.

17. Aristotle stated that all people do what they wish if they have the power (*Politics* 1312b3, cf. 1313b32).

18. John Calvin, *The Harmony of the Last Four Books of Moses,* 8th Commandment, on Deut. 15:1, following the translation of Harro Höpfl, *The Christian Polity of John Calvin* (Cambridge: Cambridge U., Studies in the History and Theory of Politics, 1982), 158. *Mediocrem* would seem to mean here "avoiding the extremes."

19. Rahner correctly sees this use of power as justified as the consequence of the sin to which it answers. Karl Rahner, "The Theology of Power," in Karl Rahner, *Theological Investigations* (Baltimore: Helicon, 1966), 4.395.

20. Paul Tillich, "Shadow and Substance: A Theory of Power" (1965), in Paul Tillich, *Political Expectation,* ed. J. L. Adams (New York: Harper, 1971), 118.

21. Martin Luther King, Jr., *Where Do We Go from Here: Chaos or Community?* (Boston: Beacon, 1967), 37.

22. John Goldingay, "The Man of War and the Suffering Servant," *Tyndale Bulletin* 27 (1976): 84.

23. Exodus 15:6, 12 in light of v. 9. Justice as deliverance from exploitative power is seen also in 2 Sam. 18:31: "The Lord has given you justice this day from the power of all who rose up against you." The word often translated as "deliverance" in English (e.g. the NIV in this verse) is the Hebrew word for "doing justice."

24. E. Calvin Beisner, *Prosperity and Poverty: The Compassionate Use of Resources in a World of Scarcity* (Westchester, Ill.: Crossway Books, 1988), 54.

25. Carl F. H. Henry, *Aspects of Christian Social Ethics* (Grand Rapids: Eerdmans, 1964), 160.

26. See also William Frankena, "The Concept of Social Justice," in *Social Justice,* ed. R. Brandt (Englewood Cliffs, N.J.: Prentice-Hall, 1962), pp. 18–21.

27. Cf. further Mott, *A Christian Perspective on Political Thought,* 77–88.

28. Our translation.

29. See also Isa. 30:18; Jer. 9:24; Hos. 2:19; 12:6; Mic. 6:8.

30. Our translation. Cf. also Ps. 40:10; 43:1-2; 65:6; 71:1–2, 24; 72:1–4; 116:5–6; 119:123; Isa. 45:8; 46:12–13; 59:11, 17; 61:10; 62:1–2; 63:7–8 (LXX); and frequently "deliver": Pss. 31:1; 37:28, 40.

31. Cf. Job 29:12, 14; Prov. 24:11.

32. "Triumphs" in the NRSV translates the word for "justice" in the plural–i.e., "acts of justice" (cf. the NIV, "righteous acts").

33. Cf. Psalms 107; 113:7–9.

34. Literally! See the collection (about two hundred pages of biblical texts) in Ronald J. Sider, *For They Shall Be Fed* (Dallas: Word, 1997).

35. Cf. Norman H. Snaith, *The Distinctive Ideas of the Old Testament* (London: Epworth, 1944), 68, 71–72; James H. Cone, *God of the*

Oppressed (New York: Seabury, 1975), pp. 70–71.

36. This is not to ignore the fact that there are many causes of poverty—including laziness and other sinful choices (see Sider, *Rich Christians in an Age of Hunger,* chap. 6). God wants people who are poor because of their own sinful choices to repent and be changed by the power of the Holy Spirit.

37. Ps. 72:1–4; Prov. 31:8–9; Isa. 1:10, 17, 23, 26; Jer. 22:2–3, 14–15; Dan. 4:27.

38. The following section is adapted from Ronald J. Sider, *Genuine Christianity* (Grand Rapids: Zondervan, 1996), pp. 137–41.

39. See further, Stephen Charles Mott, "The Partiality of Biblical Justice," *Transformation* (January–March, 1993): 24.

40. Hans Walter Wolff, *Anthropology of the Old Testament* (Philadelphia: Fortress, 1974), 68. The NIV translates: "... becomes poor and is unable to support himself. . . ."

41. Rights are the privileges of membership in the communities to which we belong; cf. Max L. Stackhouse, *Creeds, Society, and Human Rights: A Study in Three Cultures* (Grand Rapids: Eerdmans, 1984), 5, 44, 104–5.

42. C. Spicq, *Les Épîtres Pastorales, Études Bibliques* (Paris: Gabalda, 1969), 190 (on 1 Tim. 6:8).

43. See also Job 22, where injustice includes sins of omission—i.e., failure to provide drink for the weary and bread for the hungry (v. 7; cf. 31:17), as well as the exploitative use of economic power (v. 6a). In 31:19 the omission is failure to provide clothing. Cf. the important modern statement of benefit rights by Pope John Paul XXIII, in his encyclical, *Pacem in Terris,* where he says that each person has the right "to the means necessary for the proper development of life, particularly food, clothing, shelter, medical care, rest, and finally, the necessary social services." Pope John XXIII, *Pacem in Terris, 11,* in *Papal Encyclicals, Vol. 5: 1958-1981,* ed. C. Carlen (n.p., Consortium, 1981), 108.

44. See further, Stephen Mott, "The Contribution of the Bible to Economic Thought," *Transformation* (June–September/October–December, 1987): 31.

45. Walter Rauschenbusch, *Christianity and the Social Crisis* (Boston: Pilgrim, 1907), 20.

46. Those who resist the recognition of economic rights sometimes argue from a distinction of a *justice proper* from a *general jus-*

tice which is voluntary. The economic materials of the Bible are then said to belong to the latter (see, for instance, the writings of Ronald H. Nash [e.g., *Freedom, Justice and the State* (Lanham, Md.: University Press of America, 1980), 37, 75.]). The confinement of economic responsibility to a general, voluntary statement of social obligation does not hold up before the biblical materials. Distributive justice in its specific or proper sense of deciding between conflicting claims about the distribution of social benefits is involved in passages such as Jeremiah 5:28: "They judge not with justice the cause of the fatherless, to make it prosper, and they do not defend the rights (*mispat*) of the needy."

Another objection to our discussion of benefit rights comes from theonomists who argue that the kinds of texts we have used are not part of the civil law because no sanctions are provided. This objection misses the paradigmatic, and thus incomplete, nature of biblical law (Deut. 14:28). Furthermore, civil apparatus is provided for the third-year tithe in that it is to be stored in a central place, in the towns (Deut. 14:28). Micah 2:4–5, with its references to measuring and dividing the allotment of the land and casting the lot, is a prediction of a future redistribution of the land by Yahweh in which the *latifundia* of the aristocracy in Jerusalem will be ended. This new distribution will be administered by "the assembly of Yahweh" (Albrecht Alt, "Micha 2, 1–5 G's Anadasmos in Juda," in Albrecht Alt, *Kleine Schriften zur Geschichte des Volkes Israel*, Vol. 3 [Munich: Beck, 1959], 374). Theonomist theory also does not correspond to actual biblical practice (e.g., Nehemiah's enforcement of the prohibition on interest and of tithes for the Levites despite the lack of civil apparatus for these provisions in the Law [Neh. 5:7; 11:23; 12:44–47; 13:10–14]). What is decisive against the effort to remove benefit rights from justice proper is that the justice required of the ruler has the same characteristics as that required elsewhere. Justice involves deliverance. "May he defend the cause of the poor of the people, give deliverance to the needy, and crush the oppressor!" (Ps. 72:4).

47. Eryl W. Davies, *Prophecy and Ethics: Isaiah and the Ethical Traditions of Israel* (Sheffield, *Journal for the Study of the Old Testament, Supplement Series 16*, 1981), 69, 116.

48. Leslie Poles Hartley, *Facial Justice* (Hamish Hamilton, 1960).

49. See Roland de Vaux, *Ancient Israel: Its Life and Institutions*, trans. John McHugh (London: Darton, Longman and Todd, 1961), I, 164.

50. H. Eberhard von Waldow, "Social Responsibility and Social Structure in Early Israel," *Catholic Biblical Quarterly 32* (1970): 195.

51. See the discussion and the literature cited in Mott, *Biblical Ethics and Social Change*, 65–66; and Stephen Charles Mott, "Egalitarian Aspects of the Biblical Theory of Justice," in the *American Society of Christian Ethics, Selected Papers 1978*, ed. Max Stackhouse (Newton, Mass.: American Society of Christian Ethics, 1978), 8–26.

52. Elie Munk, *La Justice sociale en Israël* (Boudry, Switzerland: Baconnière, 1948), 75.

53. Albrecht Alt, "Micah 2:1-5 G's Anadasmos in Juda," *Kleine Schriften zur Geschichte des Volkes Israel* III, (Munich: C.H. Beck, 1959), 374.

54. In his study of early Israel, Norman Gottwald concluded that Israel was "an egalitarian, extended-family, segmentary tribal society with an agricultural-pastoral economic base . . . characterized by profound resistance and opposition to the forms of political domination and social stratification that had become normative in the chief cultural and political centers of the ancient Near East." *The Tribes of Yahweh: A Sociology of the Religion of Liberated Israel* 1250–1050 B.C.E. (London: SCM Press, 1979), 10.

55. For a survey of the literature on Leviticus 25, see R. Gnuse, "Jubilee Legislation in Leviticus: Israel's Vision of Social Reform," *Biblical Theological Bulletin 15* (1983): 43–48.

56. See the excellent book edited by Loren Wilkinson, *Earthkeeping: Christian Stewardship of Natural Resources*, 2nd ed. (Grand Rapids: Eerdmans, 1980), esp. 232–37.

57. See in this connection the fine article by Paul G. Schrotenboer, "The Return of Jubilee," *International Reformed Bulletin* (fall 1973): 19ff., esp. pp. 23–24.

58. See also Eph. 2:13–18. Marc H. Tanenbaum points out the significance of the day of atonement in "Holy Year 1975 and Its Origins in the Jewish Jubilee Year," *Jubilaeum* (1974): 64.

59. For the meaning of the word *liberty* in Lev. 25:10, see Martin Noth, *Leviticus*

(Philadelphia: Westminster, 1965), 187: "Deror, a 'liberation' . . . is a feudal word from the Accadian (an)duraru—'freeing from burdens.'"

60. The only other certain references to it are in Lev. 27:16-25; Num. 36:4: and Ezek. 46:17. It would be exceedingly significant if one could show that Isa. 61:1–2 (which Jesus cited to outline his mission in Luke 4:18–19) also refers to the year of Jubilee. De Vaux doubts that Isa. 61:1 refers to the Jubilee (*Ancient Israel*, 1:176). The same word, however, is used in Isa. 61:1 and Lev. 25:10. See John H. Yoder's argument in *Politics of Jesus* (Grand Rapids: Eerdmans, 1972), 64–77; see also Robert Sloan, *The Acceptable Year of the Lord* (Austin: Scholar Press, 1977); and Donald W. Blosser, "Jesus and the Jubilee" (Ph.D. diss., University of St. Andrews, 1979). Sharon H. Ringe, *Jesus, Liberation, and the Biblical Jubilee* (Philadelphia: Fortress, 1985), 36–45, supports Luke 4:18–19 as a Jubilee text.

61. On the centrality of the land in Israel's self-understanding, see further Christopher J. H. Wright, *An Eye for an Eye: The Place of Old Testament Ethics Today* (Downers Grove, Ill.: InterVarsity Press, 1983), esp. chaps. 3 and 4. Walter Brueggemann's *The Land* (Philadelphia: Fortress Press, 1977), is also a particularly important work on this topic.

62. De Vaux, *Ancient Israel*, 1:173–75.

63. Leviticus 25 seems to provide for emancipation of slaves only every fiftieth year.

64. See Jeremiah 34 for a fascinating account of God's anger at Israel for their failure to obey this command.

65. Some modern commentators think that Deuteronomy 15:1–11 provides for a one-year suspension of repayment of loans rather than an outright remission of them. See, for example, C. J. H. Wright, *God's People in God's Land* (Grand Rapids: Eerdmans, 1990), 148, and S. R. Driver, *Deuteronomy*, International Critical Commentary, 3rd ed. (Edinburgh: T. and T. Clark, 1895), 179–80. But Driver's argument is basically that remission would have been *impractical*. He admits that verse 9 seems to point toward remission of loans. So too Gerhard von Rad, *Deuteronomy* (Philadelphia: Westminster, 1966), 106.

66. See de Vaux, *Ancient Israel* 1:174–75, for discussion of the law's implementation. In the Hellenistic period, there is clear evidence that it was put into effect.

67. See especially John Mason's excellent article, "Assisting the Poor: Assistance Programmes in the Bible," *Transformation* (April–June, 1987): 1–14.

68. Ibid., 7.

69. See *Ibid.*, 8, for some examples; cf. also the earlier discussion of Beisner and Henry.

70. Ibid., 9.

71. Mason (p. 14, n. 39) comments: "Two Hebrew words are used for 'rights' or 'cause': the predominant word is *mishpat*, which is used elsewhere to refer to the laws and judgments of God; at Ps. 140:12 (with *mishpat*), Prov. 29:7, 31:9, and Jer. 22:16 the word is *dîn* and means most likely 'righteous judgment' or 'legal claim'" (TDOT v. III, pp. 190–91; TWOT v. 11, pp. 752–55, 947–49).

72. Ibid., 9.

73. For a much longer discussion of both the passages in Acts and Paul's collection, see Sider, *Rich Christians in an Age of Hunger*, 79–89.

74. Other chapters will deal at greater length with this question. Here we want only to address the question as it relates directly to economic justice.

75. Ronald H. Nash, *Freedom, Justice and the State* (Lanham, Md.: University Press of America, 1980), 27.

76. John Calvin, *Institutes of the Christian Religion*, ed. J. McNeill (Philadelphia: Westminster, 1960), 4.20.3, 4, 22 (pp. 1488, 1490, 1510); cf. Höpfl, *The Christian Polity of John Calvin*, 44–46. Similarly for Luther, government is an inestimable blessing of God and one of God's best gifts; cf. W. D. J. Cargill Thompson, *The Political Thought of Martin Luther*, ed. P. Broadhead (Sussex: Harvester, 1984), 66.

77. The state molds the process of mutual support among the groups; Reinhold Niebuhr, *The Nature and Destiny of Man. Vol 2: Human Destiny* (New York: Scribner's, 1964), 266.

78. Meredith G. Kline, *Kingdom Prologue* (Hamilton, Mass.: Meredith G. Kline, 1983), 34, citing Daniel 4:27 in support.

79. We insist, of course, as the previous discussion shows and the next two paragraphs indicate, on important qualifications to "distribution according to need." The able-bodied must work to earn their own way and bad choices rightly have negative economic consequences. At the same time, of course, we recognize that bad choices are frequently

rooted both in unfair structures and emotional and spiritual needs.

Chapter 2: *Poverty, Civil Society and the Public Policy Impasse*

1. See William Julius Wilson, *When Work Disappears: The World of the New Urban Poor* (New York: Random House, 1997).

2. U.S. Bureau of the Census, *March 1997 Current Population Survey*, Table A, p. vii.

3. U.S. Bureau of the Census, *The Official Statistics* (at www.census.gov/ hhes/income/income96/in96med2.html).

4. U.S. Bureau of the Census, *Statistical Abstract of the United States: 1997*, 117th ed. (Washington, D.C., 1997), 479.

5. This and the following figures are taken from Ronald Brownstein, "Promise of Reducing Poverty May Be Found inside Marriage Vows," *Los Angeles Times*, 6 October 1997, A5.

6. See Charles Murray, *Losing Ground* (New York: Basic Books, 1984); Marvin Olasky, *The Tragedy of American Compassion* (New York: Regnery Gateway, 1992); and Michael J. Horowitz, "Law and the Welfare State," in Peter L. Berger and Richard John Neuhaus, *To Empower People: From State to Civil Society*, 2nd ed., Michael Novak, ed. (Washington: AEI Press, 1996), 67–84.

7. Jean Bethke Elshtain, *Democracy on Trial* (New York: Basic Books, 1995), 5.

8. Gertrude Himmelfarb, "The Trouble with Civil Society," in *Unum Conversation*, no. 4 (Washington: Ethics and Public Policy Center): 1.

9. Alan Wolfe, "Is Civil Society Obsolete?" *The Brookings Review* 15 (fall 1997): 9.

10. Richard John Neuhaus and Peter L. Berger early on emphasized the importance of intermediary structures. See their *To Empower People* (Washington, D.C.: American Enterprise Institute, 1977) and its reissue in *To Empower People: From State to Civil Society*, 2nd ed.

11. Franz H. Mueller, "The Principle of Subsidiarity in the Christian Tradition," *The American Catholic Sociological Review* 4 (1943): 147. For a more complete consideration of intermediate social structures in Christian social thought see Stephen V. Monsma, *Positive Neutrality* (Grand Rapids, Mich.: Baker Book House, 1995), chap. 4.

12. Jacques Maritain, *Man and the State* (Chicago: University of Chicago Press, 1951), 11.

13. John N. Figgis, *Churches in the Modern State*, 2nd ed. (New York: Russell and Russell, 1914), 87.

14. Kenneth L. Woodward, "The New Holy War," *Newsweek*, 1 June 1998, 27.

15. Alexis de Tocqueville, *Democracy in America*, vol. 2 (New York: Vintage Classics, 1990), 106.

16. David Blankenhorn, "The Possibility of Civil Society," in Mary Ann Glendon and David Blankenhorn, eds., *Seedbeds of Virtue* (Lanham, Md.: Madison Books, 1995), 275.

17. Ibid., 276.

18. Mary Ann Glendon, "Forgotten Questions," in Glendon and Blankenhorn, eds., *Seedbeds of Virtue*, 13.

19. Clinton Rossiter, *Seedbed of the Republic* (New York: Harcourt Brace, 1953), 447.

20. Robert D. Putnam, "Bowling Alone: America's Declining Social Capital," *The Journal of Democracy* 6 (January 1995): 65–78.

21. See ibid., 69–70.

22. Ibid., 70.

23. Michael J. Sandel, "Making Nice is Not the Same as Doing Good," *New York Times*, 29 December 1996, E9.

24. See William J. Bennett, *The Index of Leading Cultural Indicators* (New York: Simon & Schuster, 1994).

25. See ibid. The following figures are taken from chapter 2.

26. These figures on divorce rates are from U. S. Bureau of the Census, *Statistical Abstract of the United States* (Washington, D.C., 1997), 74.

27. Ibid., 106.

28. Ibid., 67.

29. Himmelfarb, "The Trouble with Civil Society," 1–2.

30. Wolfe, "Is Civil Society Obsolete?" 11.

31. Nancy T. Ammerman, "Bowling Together: Congregations and the American Civic Order." Seventeenth Annual University Lecture in Religion, Arizona State University (February 26, 1996), 4. Also see her book-length report of this study: Nancy T. Ammerman, *Congregation and Community* (New Brunswick, N.J.: Rutgers University Press, 1997).

32. These and the following statistics are from "Spiritual America," *U.S. News and World Report*, 4 April 1994, 48–59.

33. Ibid., 50

34. Robert Wuthnow, *Christianity and Civil Society: The Contemporary Debate* (Valley Forge, Pa.: Trinity Press, 1996), 20.

35. Ibid., 38. Also see Robert Wuthnow, *I Come Away Stronger: How Small Groups Are Shaping American Religion* (Grand Rapids, Mich.: Eerdmans, 1994) and Robert Wuthnow, *Sharing the Journey: Support Groups and America's New Quest for Community* (New York: Free Press, 1994).

36. John J. DiIulio, Jr., "The Lord's Work: The Church and the 'Civil Society Sector,'" *The Brookings Review* 15 (fall 1997): 27–31.

37. William A. Galston and Peter Levine, "America's Civic Condition: A Glance at the Evidence," *The Brookings Review* 15 (fall 1997): 25.

38. See Sidney Verba, Kay Lehman Schlozman, and Henry E. Brady, *Voice and Equality: Civic Voluntarism in American Politics* (Cambridge, Mass.: Harvard University Press, 1995), 197–201, 384–388, and elsewhere.

39. See the fine summary of a number of studies showing these tendencies in Amy E. Black, *For the Sake of the Children: Reconstructing American Divorce Policy* (Wynnewood, Pa.: Crossroads, 1995), 22–31. Also see David Blankenhorn, *Fatherless America: Confronting Our Most Urgent Social Problem* (New York: Basic Books, 1995); Eric F. Dubow and Tom Lester, "Adjustment of Children Born to Teenage Mothers: The Contribution of Risk and Protective Factors," *Journal of Marriage and the Family* 52 (1990): 393–404; Richard Gill, "For the Sake of the Children," *Public Interest* (summer 1992): 81–96; Sara McLanahan and Gary Sandefur, *Growing Up with a Single Parent: What Hurts, What Helps* (Cambridge, Mass.: Harvard University Press, 1994); Judith S. Wallerstein and Sandra Blakeslee, *Second Chances: Men, Women, and Children a Decade After Divorce* (New York: Ticknor and Fields, 1989); Barbara Dafoe Whitehead, "Dan Quayle Was Right," *The Atlantic Monthly*, April 1993, 47–84; and Nicholas Zill, Donna Morrison, and Mary Jo Coiro, "Long-Term Effects of Parental Divorce on Parent-Child Relationships, Adjustment, and Achievement in Young Adulthood," *Journal of Family Psychology* (1993): 91–103.

40. Whitehead, "Dan Quayle Was Right," 66.

41. Gill, "For the Sake of the Children," 83–84.

42. Quoted in Joe Klein, "In God They Trust," *The New Yorker*, 16 June 1997, 41.

43. Allen E. Bergin, "Values and Religious Issues in Psychotherapy and Mental Health," *The American Psychologist* 46 (1991): 401.

44. See DiIulio, "The Lord's Work," 28, and Klein, "In God They Trust," 41.

45. Quoted in DiIulio, "The Lord's Work," 28.

46. Quoted in Klein, "In God They Trust," 42.

47. Sandel, "Making Nice is Not the Same as Doing Good."

48. Robert Bellah, "Community Properly Understood: A Defense of 'Democratic Communitarianism,'" *The Responsive Community* 6 (winter 1995–96): 51.

49. Ibid.

50. Ibid., 51–52.

51. David Blankenhorn, "The Possibility of Civil Society," 278–281. Also see David Kuo, "Poverty 101: What Liberals and Conservatives Can Learn from Each Other," *Brookings Review* 15 (fall 1997): 36–38.

52. Dan Coats, "Can Congress Revive Civil Society?" *Policy Review* (Jan./Feb. 1996): 27.

53. Governor's Advisory Task Force on Faith-Based Community Service Groups, *Faith in Action: A New Vision for Church-State Cooperation in Texas* (December 1996), vii.

54. William J. Bennett, "Introduction," in *The Project for American Renewal* (an undated booklet apparently put out by the office of Senator Dan Coats), i and ii.

55. See Paul Gigot, "Clinton Consults his Republican Think Tank," *Wall Street Journal*, 22 December 1995.

56. William A. Galston, "The View from the White House—Individual and Community Empowerment," in Berger and Neuhaus, *To Empower People: From State to Civil Society*, 2nd ed., 62.

57. Bill Bradley, "Civil Society and the Rebirth of our National Community," *The Responsive Community* 5 (spring 1995): 4.

58. Joe Klein, "In God They Trust," 46.

59. For an excellent description of the charitable choice provision see *A Guide to Charitable Choice: The Rules of Section 104 of the 1996 Federal Welfare Law Governing State Cooperation with Faith-based Social-service Providers* (Washington, D.C. and Annandale, Va.: Center for Public Justice and Center for Law and Religious Freedom, 1997).

60. See Klein, "In God They Trust," 46.

61. See, for example, Marvin Olasky, "The Corruption of Religious Charities," in Berger and Neuhaus, *To Empower People: From State to Civil Society*, 2nd ed., 94–104.

62. "Can Churches Save America?" *U.S. News & World Report*, 9 September 1996, 50. This conclusion is based on research by Richard Freeman of Harvard University.

63. John J. DiIulio, Jr., "The Lord's Work," 27. Also see Klein, "In God They Trust," 40–48; John Leland, "Savior of the Streets," *Newsweek* 1 June 1998, 20–25; and Kenneth L. Woodward, "The New Holy War," *Newsweek* 1 June 1998, 26–29.

64. Quoted in Wuthnow, *Christianity and Civil Society*, 17.

65. Quoted in Klein, "In God They Trust," 46.

66. Thomas Maier, "Learning in Fortress Bronx," *Newsday*, 17 May 1993, 17. Emphasis added. There are numerous similar journalistic accounts. See, for example, Jean Merl, "Inner-city Students Find Success at Catholic Schools," *Los Angeles Times*, 31 March 1992, A12, A18–A19.

67. See David J. Post, "African-Americans Turning to Christian Academies," *New York Times*, 4 August 1996, Education Life section, 28.

68. Ibid.

69. James S. Colemen and Thomas Hoffer, *Public and Private High Schools* (New York: Basic Books, 1987), 213. Also see the formal study by John E. Chubb and Terry M. Moe, "Politics, Markets, and Equality in Schools" (paper delivered at the annual meeting of the American Political Science Association, September 3–6, 1992).

70. Post, "African-Americans Turning to Christian Academies," 27.

71. James Brooke, "Minorities Flock to Cause of Vouchers for Schools," *New York Times*, 27 December 1997, A1 and A6.

72. Jacques Steinberg, "Voucher Program for Inner-City Children," *New York Times*, 10 June 1998, A 27.

73. Rene Sanchez, "Cleveland Charts New Educational Course," *Washington Post*, 10 September 1996, A1.

74. Berger and Neuhaus, *To Empower People*, 6.

75. See George F. Will, "A GI Bill for Mothers," *Newsweek*, 22 December 1997, 88.

76. Quoted in Klein, "In God They Trust," 46.

77. The case for doing so has been made by Ronald Sider and Heidi Rolland in their "Correcting the Welfare Tragedy: Toward a New Model for Church-State Partnership," in Carlson-Thies and Skillen, eds., *Welfare in America*, 454–479 and Stephen V. Monsma, "Overcoming Poverty: The Role of Religiously Based Nonprofit Organizations," in Carlson-Thies and Skillen, eds., *Welfare in America*, 426–453.

78. Quoted in Klein, "In God They Trust," 44.

79. June 1, 1998, pp. 20–29. *U.S. News & World Report* recently carried a similar cover story. See "Can Churches Save America?" *U.S. News & World Report*, 9 September 1996, 46–53.

80. Klein, "In God They Trust," 40–48. This article was substantially reprinted in *The Responsive Community*, under the title, "Can Faith-Based Groups Save Us?" followed by a symposium composed of responses by six scholars. See *The Responsive Community* 8 (winter 1997–98): 25–52.

81. Verba, Schlozman, and Brady, *Voice and Equality*.

82. Bill Bradley, "Civil Society and the Rebirth of Our National Community," *The Responsive Community* 5 (spring 1995): 8.

Chapter 3: *The Market System, the Poor, and Economic Theory*

1. Barend A. de Vries, *Champions of the Poor* (Washington, D.C.: Georgetown University Press, 1998), 5.

2. *Chicago Tribune*, 31 May 1998, Business section, 1. Excerpted from Richard C. Longworth, *Global Squeeze: The Coming Crisis for First-World Nations* (Chicago: NTC Contemporary Publishing Co., 1998).

3. Jonathan Mills, "The End of Property Rights and the Future of Social Justice Prophecy," *Christian Scholar's Review* (spring 1998): 299.

4. David Wessel and John Harwood, "Capitalism is Giddy With Triumph; Is It Possible to Overdo It?" *The Wall Street Journal*, 14 May 1998, 10.

5. Jerry Z. Muller, *Adam Smith in His Time and Ours* (New York: The Free Press, 1993), 46.

6. Albert O. Hirschman, *The Passions and the Interests* (Princeton, N.J.: The Princeton University Press, 1997), 14.

7. Hunt, 50.

8. For a more extensive treatment of income distribution in Adam Smith's writing see *Economics as a Moral Science: The Political Economy of Adam Smith* (Cheltenham, U.K.: Edward Elgar Publishing Co., 1997), ch. 6.

9. Oliver Williamson, Mancur Olson, and North are examples of the new institutionalists who have performed a valuable service by showing that institutions matter. They have not seriously contested the rational choice way of approaching economic analysis, however.

10. De Vries, 32.

11. Adam Smith, *Wealth of Nations*, ed. by R.H. Campbell and A.S. Skinner (Indianapolis: Liberty Press, 1976), 22.

12. Robert H. Frank, *Microeconomics and Behavior*, 3rd ed. (New York: McGraw-Hill, 1997), 21.

13. Wessel and Harwood, 10.

14. Browning and Browning, *Public Finance* (Englewood Cliffs, N.J.: Prentice Hall, 1995), 87.

15. Robert L. Heilbroner, "Modern Economics as a Chapter in the History of Economic Thought" (Paper presented at a joint session of the History of Economic Thought and American Economic Association, 1975).

16. Robert H. Nelson, *Reaching for Heaven on Earth* (Savage, Md.: Rowman & Littlefield Publishers Inc., 1991), xiv.

17. Israel M. Kirzner, "The 'Austrian' Perspective on the Crisis," in *The Crisis in Economic Theory*, edited by Dan Bell and Irving Kristol (New York: Basic Books Inc., 1981), 112.

18. Kirzner, 115.

19. Friedrich A. Hayek, "The Use of Knowledge in Society," in *Perspectives in Economic Thought*, edited by Martin C. Speckler (New York: McGraw-Hill, 1990), 193.

20. Norman Barry, *Hayek's Social and Economic Philosophy* (London: MacMillan, 1979), 10.

21. Geoffrey M. Hodgson, "Institutional Economic Theory: The Old Versus the New," in *Why Economists Disagree*, ed. by David L. Prychitko (New York: State University of New York Press, 1998), 157.

22. David L. Prychitko, *Why Economists Disagree* (New York: State University of New York Press, 1998), 153.

23. Gary Becker, "The Economic Approach to Human Behavior," in *Rational Choice*, edited by Jon Elston (Oxford: Blackwell Press, 1986), 119.

24. Lewis E. Hill, "The Philosophical Foundations of Institutional Economics" (Paper presented at the Association for Social Economics, St. Louis, April 2, 1977), 11.

Chapter 4: *Christian Economic Justice and the Impasse in Political Theory*

1. Ronald Beiner, *What's the Matter with Liberalism?* (Berkeley: University of California, 1992), 2.

2. Ibid.

3. The brief itself can be found in the March 27, 1997 *New York Review of Books;* for a criticism of it see J. Bottum's article, "Debriefing the Philosophers," *First Things* (June/July 1997): 26–30.

4. Michael Sandel, *Democracy's Discontent: America in Search of a Public Philosophy* (Cambridge: Harvard University Press, 1998), 4.

5. While Sandel does an adequate job of describing the classical republican perspective in his book, for a fuller and more comprehensive account of classical republicanism as a tradition, see J.G.A. Pocock, *The Machiavellian Moment* (Princeton: Princeton University Press, 1975).

6. Pierre Manent, *An Intellectual History of Liberalism* (Princeton: Princeton, 1995), 4; emphasis in the original.

7. For a provocative rejection of the standard account of modern history (which typically culminates in the celebration of the modern nation-state as the *solution* to the problem of contentious religions), see William T. Cavanaugh, "'A Fire Strong Enough to Consume the House:' The Wars of Religion and the Rise of the State," *Modern Theology* (October 1995), 397–420.

8. John Milbank, *Theology and Social Theory: Beyond Secular Reason* (Oxford: Blackwell, 1990), 17.

9. I develop at more length and in more detail this exclusionary nature of liberalism in a paper, "Rawls, Religion, and Liberalism." For other accounts see Milbank, Cavanaugh, and Stanley Hauerwas, "The Democratic Policing of Christianity," *Pro Ecclesia* (spring 1994): 215–231; and Barry Harvey, "Insanity, Theocracy, and the Public Realm: Public Theology, the Church, and the Politics of Liberal

Democracy," *Modern Theology* (January 1994): 27–57.

10. E. J. Dionne, *Why Americans Hate Politics* (New York: Touchstone, 1992), 116–118.

11. See John Rawls, *A Theory of Justice* (Harvard University Press, 1971), 3–4, and again at 14. The literature surrounding *A Theory of Justice* is simply too vast to cite. For an early extension of Rawlsian liberalism into the area of constitutional law see Ronald Dworkin, *Taking Rights Seriously* (Duckworth, 1977). Much, of course has happened since *A Theory of Justice* in the defense of liberalism. Included in this is the fact that Rawls himself has shifted his ground somewhat, apparently in response to his communitarian critics. See his *Political Liberalism* (Columbia University, 1993). I cite this change, the controversy surrounding it, and how various voices within the Christian community have interpreted this shift (as well as the argument of *Political Liberalism* itself) in my paper, "Rawls, Religion, and Liberalism."

12. Sandel, 290.

13. William Galston, "Defending Liberalism," *American Political Science Review* (December 1982): 621–629.

14. Michael Perry, *Love & Power: The Role of Religion and Morality in American Politics* (Oxford University Press, 1991), 138.

15. Margaret Moore, *The Foundations of Liberalism* (Oxford University Press, 1993), 193.

16. William Galston, *Liberal Purposes: Goods, Virtues and Diversity in the Liberal State* (Cambridge University Press, 1991), 292.

17. Galston, *Liberal Purposes,* 261.

18. Ibid., 278 and 258 respectively.

19. Ibid., 279.

20. Perry, *Love & Power,* 81 and 88. Another, and well-known, account of just this sort of argument is Stephen Carter's *The Culture of Disbelief.*

21. Galston, *Liberal Purposes,* 258, 293, and 294 respectively.

22. Stephen Macedo, *Liberal Virtues: Citizenship, Virtue and Community in Liberal Constitutionalism* (Oxford, 1990), 52 and 63 respectively.

23. Stephen Macedo, "Liberal Civic Education and Religious Fundamentalism: The Case of God v. John Rawls?" *Ethics* (April 1995): 485 and 496. In case you have not read this fine and illuminating article, Macedo rules in the decision. God loses.

24. Moore, *Foundations,* 177.

25. Beiner, *What's the Matter with Liberalism?,* 24 and 25.

26. Moore, *Foundations,* 178.

27. Harvey, "Insanity, Theocracy, and the Public Realm," 30.

28. See Alasdair MacIntyre, *After Virtue* (University of Notre Dame, 1981); Michael Sandel, *Liberalism and the Limits of Justice* (Cambridge University Press, 1982); Michael Walzer, *Spheres of Justice: A Defense of Pluralism and Equality* (Basic Books, 1983); and Charles Taylor, *Sources of the Self: The Making of the Modern Identity* (Harvard University Press, 1989). What is problematic about this attribution is that while these thinkers and their works are almost universally recognized as the initial assault of communitarian thought upon the liberal bastion, *none* of these philosophers in fact claim to be communitarian. Indeed in an article in 1995, MacIntyre explicitly repudiated the title. See his, "The Spectre of Communitarianism," *Radical Philosophy* (March/April 1995): 35.

29. Ronald Beiner, "Liberalism: What's Missing?" *Society* 32, no. 5 (July/August 1995): 18–22.

30. Amitai Etzioni, "Introduction," in *The Essential Communitarian Reader* (New York: Rowman & Littlefield, 1998), xvii. All the following citations in this section come from this text unless otherwise noted.

31. Stanley Hauerwas, *In Good Company: The Church as Polis* (Notre Dame, 1995), 25. See also the comments attached to footnote #16 at that site.

32. Steven Lukes, "The Responsive Community," *Dissent* (spring 1998): 87–89.

33. My citations of Dahrendorf's article come from Etzioni's edited volume, *The Essential Communitarian Reader.*

34. Lukes (1998), 88.

35. Lukes (1998), 89.

36. Ibid.

37. Quoted in Lukes (1998), 87.

38. Beiner, *What's the Matter With Liberalism?,* 15–16.

39. Ibid., 29.

40. Ibid.

41. While I have not discussed communitarian thought with respect to whether it excludes or includes the voice of the church (which was my focus in the sections on liberalism), I think two points can be made here: 1) the fact that communitarianism cannot

escape liberalism's description of reality leads to the conclusion that ultimately communitarianism, too, must "police" the Christian voice; and 2) the presence of William Galston, a leading Neo-Aristotelian liberal, as co-editor of *Responsive Community* and frequent articulator of communitarian policy proposals, both confirms some of the close affinities between liberalism and communitarianism as well as indicating the type of policing communitarian thought must take. We might be able to distinguish between the "hard" policing of liberal neutralists, and the "soft" policing of Neo-Aristotelians and communitarians. I consider the two options as both fraught with problems for the church, which in its practices does economic justice for the poor. It strikes me that the former culminates in a callous, secular society such as we presently experience, while the latter tempts the church to a civil religion (liberal or conservative) which simply baptizes the power of the state.

42. Despite the controversy surrounding his thesis, it strikes me that there is no better text to understand the historical roots of this crisis than Alasdair MacIntyre's *After Virtue* (University of Notre Dame: 1981).

43. For an especially moving and trenchant account of just how the modern state goes about the destruction of rural areas and all sources of tradition and meaning, see the numerous collected essays of Wendell Berry.

44. Beiner, *What's the Matter with Liberalism?*, 173.

45. For a sampling of such voices, see Stanley Hauerwas, *In Good Company: The Church as Polis* (University of Notre Dame, 1995); John Milbank, *Theology and Social Theory: Beyond Secular Reason* (Basil, 1990); and my own, "Do We Really Need a Public Philosophy?," *Books & Culture* (January/February 1997); and "Ecclesiocentrism," *Books & Culture* (November 1997).

46. Hauerwas, "The Democratic Policing of Christianity," 229.

47. Beiner, *What's the Matter With Liberalism?*, 171.

48. John Dunn, *Rethinking Modern Political Theory* (Cambridge University Press, 1985), 189.

49. For some titles see Beiner, *Political Judgment* (University of Chicago Press, 1983) and more recently, *Philosophy In a Time of Lost Spirit: Essays on Contemporary Theory*

(Toronto: University of Toronto Press, 1997); Peter Steinberger, *The Concept of Political Judgment* (University of Chicago Press, 1993); N.J. Rengger, *Political Theory, Modernity and Postmodernity* (Blackwell, 1995); two articles of note are, Richard S. Ruderman. "Aristotle and the Recovery of Political Judgment," *American Political Science Review* (June 1997): 409–420; and Larence Biskowski, "Practical Foundations for Political Judgment: Arendt on Action and World," *Journal of Politics* (November 1993): 867–877.

50. For Beiner's full discussion, see *Political Judgment* (1983): 129–152. While Beiner's definition has been criticized as too Aristotelian for complex pluralist societies, I do not enter this debate here. But I do think that this or some similar account of political judgment can serve well the practical needs of communities at whatever level, both in terms of their internal relations, and as it applies to their relations with other communities.

51. Sandel, *Democracy's Discontent*, 350.

52. However, the recovery of *phronesis* is itself problematic. Paul Stern, in his treatment of the topic, speaks of how *"phronesis* has assumed great importance among political theorists." But current accounts of *phronesis* seem to be stuck between the twin perils of appeals to nature (which threaten to rob judgment of its historical quality) and contingency (which cuts judgment adrift from any standard beyond the local and particular). Acknowledges Stern: "The available alternatives both seem problematic." See Paul Stern, "The Rule of Wisdom and the Rule of Law in Plato's *Statesman,*" *American Political Science Review* (June 1997): 264–267. It is just the Christian overcoming of this problem that forms the basis of my present scholarly efforts. Good work has already begun. See, for example, Stanley Hauerwas and Charles Pinches, *Christians Among the Virtues* (University of Notre Dame Press, 1997).

53. See my "Ecclesiocentrism," in *Books & Culture* (November 1997).

54. Milbank, *Theology & Social Theory*, 389. But for a fuller discussion of the centrality of *Civitas Dei* as a source for Christian thought, see the entirety of chapter 12, 380–434.

55. Ibid., 406.

56. Ibid., 388.

57. For a popular account of this perspective, see Rodney Clapp's *A Peculiar People* (InterVarsity Press, 1997).

58. Hauerwas, *In Good Company,* 22; emphasis in the original.

59. Hauerwas, *In Good Company,* 26.

Chapter 5: *The Privatizing of Compassion: A Critical Engagement with Marvin Olasky*

1. Craig M. Gay, *With Liberty and Justice for Whom? The Recent Evangelical Debate Over Capitalism* (Grand Rapids: Eerdmans, 1991).

2. Marvin Olasky, *The Tragedy of American Compassion* (Washington, D.C.: Regnery, 1992). Henceforth cited as "Olasky."

3. Olasky, 4.

4. Olasky, 18.

5. Olasky, 11.

6. Olasky, 13.

7. Olasky, 8.

8. Olasky, 20.

9. Olasky, 21.

10. Olasky, 11.

11. Olasky, 17.

12. Olasky, 21.

13. Olasky, 28.

14. Olasky, 29.

15. Olasky, 32.

16. Olasky, 32.

17. Olasky, 32.

18. Olasky, 62ff.

19. Olasky quoting Greeley, 52.

20. Olasky quoting Greeley, 54.

21. Greeley quoted by Olasky, 61.

22. Olasky, 107.

23. Olasky, 109.

24. Olasky, 110.

25. Olasky, 111.

26. Olasky, 120.

27. Olasky, 125.

28. Olasky, 127.

29. Olasky, 128.

30. Olasky, 116–17 for example.

31. Olasky, 143–146.

32. Olasky, 149.

33. Olasky, 163–165.

34. Olasky, 167.

35. Olasky, 168.

36. Olasky, 174.

37. Olasky, 175.

38. Olasky, 169.

39. Olasky, 169.

40. Olasky, 170–72, 174.

41. Olasky, 176.

42. Olasky, 181-82.

43. Olasky, 173.

44. Olasky, 178.

45. Olasky, 183.

46. Olasky, 183.

47. Robert Moffitt, "Incentive Effects of the U.S. Welfare System: A Review," *Journal of Economic Literature* (March 1992): 1–61.

48. Moffitt (1992), 7.

49. There is a slight break in continuity for the real benefit sum before 1975 because data on real benefits in Food Stamps and Medicaid are unavailable from 1965 through 1974, but this does not affect the result.

50. Olasky, 168.

51. Robert Moffitt, "An Economic Model of Welfare Stigma," *American Economic Review* 73 (December 1983): 1023. Moffitt's work finds significant evidence of stigma in 1975 data, and my own work finds no significant change in stigma from that time through the mid-1990s; there are no studies of stigma by economists before 1975, mainly due to the unavailability of data.

52. Because support for the individual statements that follow is scattered throughout the 122 references in Moffitt and is sometimes the result of splices of several different sources, I will not attempt to directly cite support for each claim that follows. The reader is directed to Moffitt (1992) for full citations.

53. Moffitt, 1992, 28.

54. Moffitt, 29.

Chapter 6: *Income Distribution in the United States*

1. U.S. Census Bureau. "Historical Income Tables—Families, (Table) F-2. Share of Aggregate Income Received by Each Fifth and Top 5 Percent of Families (all Races): 1947 to 1996" (published 29 September 1997); available from http://www.census.gov/hhes/income/histinc/f02.html.

2. U.S. Census Bureau. "Historical Income Tables—Families, (Table) F-3. Mean Income Received by Each Fifth and Top 5 Percent of Families (all Races): 1966 to 1996" (published 29 September 1997); available from http://www.census.gov/hhes/income/histinc/f03.html.

3. U.S. Census Bureau. "Historical Income Tables—Families, (Table) F-18. Average Income-to-Poverty Ratios for Families, by Income Quintile, Race, and Hispanic Origin:

1967 to 1996" (published 29 September 1997); available from http://www.census.gov/hhes/income/histinc/f18.html.

4. Policies to aid those in the lowest part of the income distribution will be discussed in more detail in later chapters.

5. The biblical passages cited in this section are indicative rather than exhaustive.

6. See also Isa. 5:8–10; Jer. 34:8–22; Mic. 2:1–4; 3:1–4.

7. For more regarding the biblical teachings in this area, see: George Monsma, Jr., "Biblical Principles Important for Economic Theory and Practice," in *On Moral Business*, edited by Max Stackhouse, Dennis McCann, and Shirley Roels (Grand Rapids, Mich.: Wm. B. Eerdmans, 1995), 38–45. For a good collection of relevant biblical passages see: Ronald Sider, *Cry Justice* (New York: Paulist Press, 1980).

8. One important area in which relative levels of income and wealth are important is in the competition for jobs, particularly for better-paying jobs. Relative, as well as absolute, levels and qualities of education and training are important in the competition for employment. As the level of income in a society rises, so does the average level of education and training, so a person must acquire more and more to maintain the same absolute ability to obtain a job of a certain level. Changes in laws and in the context of life also raise the level of necessary income. For example, it is now illegal in many cities to live in a housing unit without both electricity and functioning indoor plumbing, although living without these is common in many other nations and was common 100 years ago in the United States. And with the increase in average income, which has resulted in widespread ownership of automobiles, the nation has developed in ways that make access to many jobs very difficult unless one has an automobile available. Twenty years ago the lack of a computer in their home would have had little or no impact on the ability of children to prepare for a career. But soon children without regular access to computers will be at a serious disadvantage in getting an education and preparing for a career. And health care advances have brought higher costs as well as many benefits.

9. 1996 was chosen as the end point because this was the last year for which data were available when the analysis was done.

Since the unemployment rate and the stage of the business cycle can influence the distribution of income, 1974 was chosen as the beginning point because it was the year in the mid-1970s which had the closest unemployment rate to that of 1996, and, like those years, was neither at the peak nor the trough of the business cycle. The unemployment rate in 1974 was 5.6 percent; in 1996 it was 5.4 percent. The choice of another beginning year in the same period would not change the substance of the results, although the increase in inequality would be a bit smaller if an earlier year was chosen. The share of the lowest-income fifth of families ranged from 5.5 to 5.7 percent during the period 1971 to 1977, and the share of the highest fifth ranged from 40.6 to 41.4 during those years. The size of the absolute change in income for the various fifths would also be a bit different if a different starting year had been selected, but the general pattern would be the same.

10. The incomes in 1974 were adjusted to the 1996 prices using the CPI-U-X1, a modified Consumer Price Index that the Bureau of Labor Statistics believes more accurately reflects changes in housing costs before 1983 than the standard CPI. If the standard CPI had been used, the income figures for all fifths in 1974 would have been higher in relation to 1996, and the data would show a greater decline in real income for the bottom fifth, and declines in real income for the second and third fifths as well. Many economists think even the CPI-U-X1 has overstated the rate of inflation. This may well be true, but there is no consensus regarding the exact degree of overstatement. If the overstatement is as large as some think, even the lowest fifth may not have lost real income, on average. But these possible problems with the adjustment for inflation do not affect the data on the percent of income going to each fifth. That has clearly become less equal.

11. Both the number of poor persons and the poverty rate have fluctuated with the business cycle, but the trend has been upwards.

12. U.S. Department of Commerce, Bureau of the Census, *Poverty in the United States: 1996*, by Leatha Lamison-White, Current Population Reports, Series P60–198 (Washington, D.C.: U.S. Government Printing Office, 1997), 1.

13. The sharp decrease for black married-couple families occurred mainly in one year,

1994, which causes me to wonder if perhaps it resulted at least in part from some change in the statistical procedure rather than from a real decrease of that magnitude. The significant drop in the rate for black families with no husband present occurred more gradually during the economic expansion of the 1990s.

14. The rates for families with no wife present, a much smaller category overall, are between these two figures, but closer to the married-couple figures.

15. Bureau of the Census, *Poverty in the United States: 1996*, by Leatha Lamison-White, 24–27, C-14.

16. Isabel Sawhill and Daniel McMurrer, *Economic Mobility in the United States* (Washington, D.C.: The Urban Institute, 1996), Table 2; available from http://www.urban.org/oppor/opp_031b.html; accessed 16 July 1998.

17. Peter Gottschalk, "Inequality, Income Growth, and Mobility: The Basic Facts," *Journal of Economic Perspectives*, 11, no. 2 (spring 1997): 37.

18. Ibid., 38.

19. Peter Gottschalk and Timothy Smeeding, "Cross-National Comparisons of Earnings and Income Inequality," *Journal of Economic Literature* 35 (June 1997): 661. This is based on data from the Luxembourg Income Study, a major attempt to get comparable data from a variety of countries. The data are for the latest years available for the various countries, generally years in the early 1990s.

20. Ibid., 663. The five countries with median incomes below 70 percent of that of the United States were not included in this comparison.

21. Ibid., 667.

22. Edward Wolff, *Economics of Poverty, Inequality, and Discrimination* (Cincinnati: South-Western College Publishing, 1977), 76–80.

23. Gottschalk, "Inequality, Income Growth, and Mobility," 38.

24. John Weicher, *The Distribution of Wealth* (Washington, D.C.: AEI Press, 1996), 13.

25. Edward Wolff, *Economics of Poverty, Inequality, and Discrimination* (Cincinnati: South-Western College Publishing, 1977), 372–373.

26. Erik Hurst, Ming Ching Luoh, and Frank Stafford, *Wealth Dynamics of American Families, 1984–1994* (Ann Arbor, Mich: Department of Economics and Institute for Social Research, University of Michigan, 1996), 29; also available as PDF file from http://www.isr.umich.edu/src/psid/pdf.html.

27. John Weicher, "Wealth and Its Distribution, 1983–1992: Secular Growth, Cyclical Stability," *Review* 79, no. 1 (Federal Reserve Bank of St. Louis, 1997): 3–23. In this article he also presents some data from the SCF for 1992, which follow the same general pattern as the data for 1989.

28. Hurst, Luoh, and Stafford, 33.

29. *Economic Report of the President, 1998* (Washington, D.C.: GPO, 1998), 320.

30. See the articles in a symposium on discrimination in the *Journal of Economic Perspectives* 12, no. 2 (spring 1998): 23–126, especially the article by William Darity and Patrick Mason, "Evidence on Discrimination in Employment: Codes of Color, Codes of Gender," 63–90, for evidence on this. One of the commentators, James Heckman, disagrees with the conclusion that the evidence shows discrimination in labor markets.

31. For statistics regarding this see: *Economic Report*, 330.

32. Glenn Loury, "Discrimination in the Post-Civil Rights Era: Beyond Market Interactions," *Journal of Economic Perspectives* 12, no. 2 (spring 1998): 117–126.

33. Actually Solon used the male head of the household in which the "son" was raised.

34. I.e., 95 percent of the population had a higher income.

35. Gary Solon, "Intergenerational Income Mobility in the United States," *American Economic Review* 82, no. 3 (June 1992): 403–4. If the correlation is actually 0.5, the probabilities would be 49, 17, and 3 percent respectively.

36. Daniel McMurrer, Mark Condon, and Isabel Sawhill, *Intergenerational Mobility In the United States* (Washington, D.C.: The Urban Institute, 1997); available from http://www.urban.org/oppor/opp_04b.htm; accessed 26 September 1998.

37. Ibid. The association implied by a 0.5 correlation is about 6 times greater.

38. For a summary of information from a number of studies of conditions of poor persons, see: Maya Federman et al., "What Does it Mean to be Poor in America?" *Monthly Labor Review* 119, no. 5 (May 1996): 3–17.

39. Much of what Glenn Loury says about the importance of social networks as deter-

minants of economic opportunity for minorities is applicable to others growing up in poor neighborhoods as well. See: Loury.

40. The data reported in this section will not always be for the exact period 1974–1996 used in most cases above, because various relevant studies have used different starting and ending years.

41. If the CPI-U-X1 overstates inflation sufficiently, it is possible that no groups, except perhaps the lowest three deciles of males, actually had declines in real wages, but the relative changes would be unaffected by errors in the CPI.

42. Gottschalk, "Inequality, Income Growth, and Mobility," 25. He adjusts for inflation using the Personal Consumption Expenditure deflator to avoid the possible overstatement of the CPI.

43. Ibid., 26–27.

44. Ibid., 28–29.

45. If the CPI-U-X1 has overstated the amount of inflation the reductions may be less than those indicated, or may even be increases for some groups, but the relative changes would not be affected.

46. Gottschalk, "Inequality, Income Growth, and Mobility," 30. Since he uses the Personal Consumption Expenditure deflator rather than the CPI to adjust for inflation, his figures are not subject to the possible biases of the CPI.

47. *Economic Report of the President,* 332.

48. Yolanda Kodrzycki, "Labor Markets and Earnings Inequality: A Status Report," *New England Economic Review* (May/June 1996): 21.

49. See, for example: Gottschalk and Smeeding, 646–651; and George Johnson, "Changes in Earnings Inequality: The Role of Demand Shifts," *Journal of Economic Perspectives* 11, no. 2 (spring 1997).

50. Robert Topel, "Factor Proportions and Relative Wages: The Supply-Side Determinants of Wage Inequality," *Journal of Economic Perspectives* 11, no. 2 (spring 1997): 65.

51. See, for example: Gottschalk and Smeeding, 646–650; Johnson, 46–49.

52. Gottschalk and Smeeding, 648–649.

53. Ibid., 649. Similar points are made by Johnson, 47; and Topel, 61.

54. Gottschalk and Smeeding, 680.

55. Ibid., 647; Kodrzycki, 14.

56. Robert Feenstra, "Integration of Trade and Disintegration of Production," *Journal of Economic Perspectives,* forthcoming.

57. Gottschalk and Smeeding, 649.

58. Gottschalk, "Inequality, Income Growth, and Mobility," 32; Kodrzycki, 19.

59. Gottschalk, "Inequality, Income Growth, and Mobility," 33; Gottschalk and Smeeding, 650–651.

60. Topel, 62–64.

61. For discussions of institutional factors in wage setting see: David Howell, *Institutional Failure and the American Worker,* Public Policy Brief No. 29 (Annandale-on-Hudson, N.Y.: Jerome Levy Economics Institute, 1997); James Galbraith, *Unemployment, Inflation and the Job Structure,* Working Paper No. 154 (Annandale-on-Hudson, N.Y.: Jerome Levy Economics Institute, 1996); Francine Blau and Lawrence Kahn, *Wage Inequality: International Comparisons of Its Sources* (Washington, D.C.: AEI Press, 1996).

62. Gottschalk, "Inequality, Income Growth, and Mobility," 34; Gottschalk and Smeeding, 651–653.

63. Richard Freeman, "Labor Market Institutions and Earnings Inequality," *New England Economic Review* (May/June 1996): 158–160.

64. Richard Freeman, "How Much Has De-Unionization Contributed to the Rise in Male Earnings Inequality?" in *Uneven Tides: Rising Inequality in America,* ed. Sheldon Danziger and Peter Gottschalk (New York: Russell Sage Foundation, 1993), 137.

65. Ibid., 153; Nicole Fortin and Thomas Lemieux, "Institutional Changes and Rising Wage Inequality: Is There a Linkage?" *Journal of Economic Perspectives* 11, no. 2 (spring 1997): 89; Freeman, "Labor Market Institutions and Earnings Inequality," 163–165; and Gottschalk and Smeeding, 647.

66. Fortin and Lemieux, 79.

67. Ronald Ehernberg and Robert Smith, *Modern Labor Economics: Theory and Public Policy* (Reading, Mass.: Addison-Wesley, 1997), 118.

68. Economic Policy Institute, The Datazone, "Value of the Minimum Wage, 1960-97"; available from http://www.epinet.org/test/datazone/minimumwage.html; accessed 27 September 1998. Values were adjusted for inflation using the CPI-U-X1.

69. Barry Bluestone and Teresa Ghilarducci, *Making Work Pay,* Public Policy Brief

No. 28 (Annandale-on-Hudson, N.Y.: Jerome Levy Economics Institute, 1996), 15. Data from source updated for 1997.

70. Fortin and Lemieux, 88–89.

71. Freeman, "Labor Market Institutions and Earnings Inequality," 166.

72. Michael Horrigan and Ronald Mincy, "The Minimum Wage and Earnings and Income Inequality," in *Uneven Tides: Rising Inequality in America*, edited by Sheldon Danziger and Peter Gottschalk (New York: Russell Sage Foundation, 1993), 264.

73. Bluestone and Ghilarducci, *Making Work Pay*, 16.

74. Horrigan and Mincy, "The Minimum Wage and Earnings and Income Inequality," 269.

75. Bluestone and Ghilarducci, *Making Work Pay*, 16–20.

76. Sheldon Danziger and Peter Gottschalk, *America Unequal* (Cambridge: Harvard University Press, 1995), 25.

77. Bureau of the Census, *Poverty in the United States: 1996*, by Leatha Lamison-White, pp. C-8 to C-13.

78. Ibid., pp. C-2, C-8, & C-9.

79. These differences are also substantial for white, black, and Hispanic families considered separately. Ibid., pp. C-8 to C-13.

80. Danziger and Peter Gottschalk, *America Unequal*, 102–10. Some of the combined effects of these factors on the increase in poverty were offset by the growth in mean income over this period, since the poverty line in the United States is not adjusted for growth in average incomes.

81. Maria Cancian, Sheldon Danziger, and Peter Gottschalk, *The Changing Contributions of Men and Women to the Level and Distribution of Family Income, 1968–1988*, Working Paper No. 62 (Annandale-on-Hudson, N.Y.: Jerome Levy Economics Institute, 1991), 26–30; similar results are reported for black and white married couples in Maria Cancian, Sheldon Danziger, and Peter Gottschalk, "Working Wives and Family Income Inequality Among Married Couples," in *Uneven Tides: Rising Inequality in America*, edited by Sheldon Danziger and Peter Gottschalk (New York: Russell Sage Foundation, 1993), 195–221; but this source does not contain data for Hispanics or all families considered together.

82. House Committee on Ways and Means, *1998 Green Book*, 105th Cong., 2d sess., 1998, Committee Print 105–7, 402.

83. Edward Gramlich, Richard Kasten, and Frank Sammartino, "Growing Inequality in the 1980s: The Role of Federal Taxes and Cash Transfers," in *Uneven Tides: Rising Inequality in America*, edited by Sheldon Danziger and Peter Gottschalk (New York: Russell Sage Foundation, 1993), 239.

84. Ibid., 237.

85. Gottschalk, "Inequality, Income Growth, and Mobility," 35.

86. Bluestone and Ghilarducci, *Making Work Pay*, 14–20.

87. Ibid., 20–25.

88. Food stamp information based on data in: House Committee on Ways and Means, *1998 Green Book*, 923–936. If the family had child care expenses caused by work or training, or very high housing costs, the food stamp payment would be higher.

89. This analysis follows the pattern of a study by Robert Greenstein reported in: Bluestone and Ghilarducci, *Making Work Pay*, 26–27.

90. House Committee on Ways and Means, *1998 Green Book*, 928–931.

91. Oren Levin-Waldman, *A New Path from Welfare to Work*, Public Policy Brief No. 31 (Annandale-on-Hudson, N.Y.: Jerome Levy Economics Institute, 1997).

92. Marlene Kim, *The Working Poor: Lousy Jobs or Lazy Workers?* Working Paper No. 154 (Annandale-on-Hudson, N.Y.: Jerome Levy Economics Institute, 1996).

Chapter 7: *Redefining Progress: Economic Indicators and the Shalom of God*

1. Clifford Cobb, Ted Halstead and Jonathan Rowe, "If the GDP is up, why is America down?" *The Atlantic Monthly*, October 1995, 59–78.

2. Economists use the term "welfare" when discussing social well-being and utility. But, given that welfare is usually associated with income support programs of the government, "welfare" is not used here. Progress and well-being are related, but distinct, categories. "Well-being" is used here to describe a subjective state influenced by level of goods, services, and the fullness of life one enjoys. Progress is associated with movement toward some norm, for example, toward higher edu-

cation, longer life expectancy, and a higher level of consumption. It is considered *good* when life expectancy increases, when literacy and productivity increase, when infant mortality declines, when people participate in the body politic, and when the environment is healthy. Progress toward a properly defined norm will increase well-being, but the two concepts are not the same.

3. Mervyn A. King, "Economic Growth and Social Development: A Statistical Investigation," *Review of Income and Wealth* 20 (1974): 251–272.

4. Irma Adelman and Cynthia Taft Morris, *Economic Growth and Social Equity in Developing Countries* (Stanford: Stanford University Press, 1973).

5. James Tobin and William Nordhaus, "Is Growth Obsolete?" in *Economic Growth* (New York: National Bureau of Economic Research, 1972).

6. M.V.S. Rao, Krzystof Prowit, and Nancy Baster, *Indicators of Human and Social Development: Report on the State of the Art* (Tokyo: United Nations University, 1978).

7. Other recent efforts have been Herman Daly and John B. Cobb, Jr., *For the Common Good* (Boston: Beacon Press, 1989) and Clifford W. Cobb and John B. Cobb, Jr., *The Green National Product: A Proposed Index of Sustainable Economic Welfare* (Lanham, Md.: University Press of America, 1994).

8. Jonathan Rowe, "Down Among the Economists," copied from Internet, http://www.adbusters.org/Articles/rowe.html, April 18, 1997.

9. Judith Eleanor Innes, *Knowledge and Public Policy: The Search for Meaningful Indicators*, 2d ed. (New Brunswick, N.J.: Transaction Publishers, 1990), 120.

10. OECD, *Measuring Social Well-Being: A Progress Report on the Development of Social Indicators* (Paris: OECD, 1976), 13.

11. Robert V. Horn, *Statistical Indicators for the Economic and Social Sciences* (Cambridge: Cambridge University Press, 1993), 152.

12. Ian Miles, *Social Indicators for Human Development* (London: United Nations University, 1985), 47.

13. Ibid., 46.

14. Hazel Henderson shares the mission of Cobb, Halstead, and Rowe to dethrone GDP as a measure of progress, but she advocates the use of several indicators rather than a single comprehensive one. Hazel Henderson, *Paradigms in Progress: Life Beyond Economics* (Indianapolis: Knowledge Systems Inc., 1991), 187.

15. Judith Eleanor Innes, 177.

16. One cannot but be disheartened by the reception economists gave the redefining progress proposal. Cobb, Halstead, and Rowe invited economists to the table to discuss issues of vital interest to the body politic. Rather than accepting and engaging Cobb, Halstead, and Rowe in substantive debate, economists arrogantly dismissed the redefining progress proposal and either missed the main points of the proposal or decided to ignore them. See Jonathan Rowe, 1997.

17. Temple also warns against the notion of a "Christian solution" to social problems and economic ills. Revelation does not suggest such solutions. But the Bible does reveal that Christians are to respond to a diseased society. Temple wisely notes that the church will likely be attacked from two sides as a result of this. It will be labeled as political when it merely articulates the principles, and attacked by advocates of particular policies who will say that the church is impotent if it does not support their agenda. William Temple, *Christianity and Social Order* (New York: Seabury, 1977).

18. For a complete and detailed discussion of poverty indicators, see Amartya Sen, *On Economic Inequality*, enlarged edition with a substantial annex "*On Economic Inequality* after a Quarter Century," by Amartya Sen and James Foster (Oxford: Oxford University Press, 1997).

19. This argument is sound if one accepts that the marginal utility of each dollar of additional income is the same for all people. This is an assumption that economists, as a rule, don't like making.

20. John Rawls, *A Theory of Justice* (Oxford: Clarendon Press, 1972).

21. For example, H. S. Chenery, et al., *Redistribution with Growth* (New York: Oxford University Press, 1974).

22. Robert V. Horn, 88.

23. For a discussion of the measure and the desirable characteristics of such a measure, see Sen, 1997.

24. E. J. Mishan, "Is a Welfare Index Possible?" in *The Green National Product: A Proposed Index of Sustainable Economic Welfare*, eds. Clifford W. Cobb and John B. Cobb, Jr.

(Lanham, Md.: University Press of America, 1994), 172.

25. For a detailed discussion of the ethical issues surrounding the morality of the market, see Alan Hamlin in "The Morality of the Market," in *Market Capitalism and Moral Values: Proceedings of Section F (Economics) of the British Association for the Advancement of Science Sussex 1993*, ed. Samuel Brittan and Alan Hamlim (Aldershot: Edward Elgar Publishing Limited, 1995).

26. Dasgupta suggests that it is not so much differences in ethical views that cause division among social scientists and are the heart of political debates, but differences of opinion about how the world works. "It is all well and good to talk about hypothetical cases in which two people agree on the facts and disagree about the values, but they tend to be only hypothetical cases." Partha Dasgupta, *An Inquiry into Well-being and Destitution* (Oxford: Oxford University Press, 1993), 6. One can also see how significant one's understanding of how the world works is in determining what gets measured and why. What isn't considered important in one's understanding of the world doesn't register as a fact.

27. Michael J. Sandel, "America's Search for a New Public Philosophy," *The Atlantic Monthly*, March 1996, 66.

28. Kenneth E. Boulding, "Puzzles over Distribution," *Challenge* 28, no. 5 (November/December 1985): 4–10.

29. Adam Smith, *The Theory of Moral Sentiments* (New York: Augustus M. Kelly Publishers, 1966) and *The Wealth of Nations* (New York: Random House, 1937).

30. For example, Margaret Levi, "Social and Unsocial Capital: A Review Essay of Robert W. Putnam's *Making Democracy Work*," *Politics & Society* 24, no. 1 (March 1996): 45–55; and Michael W. Foley and Bob Edwards, "Escape from Politics? Social Theory and the Social Capital Debate," *American Behavioral Scientist* 40 (March/April 1997): 550–561.

31. Robert P. Putnam, "The Prosperous Community: Social Capital and Economic Growth," *Current* 356 (October 1993): 4–9. See also Robert P. Putnam, "Bowling Alone: America's Declining Social Capital," *Journal of Democracy* 6, no. 1 (January 1995): 65–78; and Robert P. Putnam, "Tuning in, Tuning out: The Strange Disappearance of Social

Capital in America," *Political Science and Politics* 28, no. 4 (December 1995): 664–683.

32. See also Michael Foley and Bob Edwards, "Social Capital and the Political Economy of Our Discontent," *American Behavioral Scientist* 40 (March/April 1997): 669–678.

33. James S. Coleman, "Social Capital in the Creation of Human Capital," *American Journal of Sociology* 94, supplement (1988): S95–S120. See also Coleman, 1990.

34. Ibid., S96.

35. John Brehm and Wendy Rahn, "Individual-Level Evidence for the Causes and Consequences of Social Capital," *American Journal of Political Science* 41, no. 3 (July 1997): 999–1023.

36. Edwards and Foley, 674–675. Heying also sees this getting worse before it gets better. He considers the effect of economic restructuring and globalization on the capacity to affect society and concludes that as companies turn their attention from local to national to transnational interests and markets, so do their local commitments wither. The net result is a shift from local community organizations to a diffuse set of economic interests. Charles H. Heying, "Civic Elites and Corporate Delocalization: An Alternative Explanation for Declining Civic Engagement," *American Behavioral Scientist* 40 (March/April, 1997): 656–667.

37. Coleman, 1988, S117.

38. Andrew Greeley, "Coleman Revisited: Religious Structures as a Source of Social Capital," *American Behavioral Scientist* 40 (March/April 1997): 587–594.

39. Smith, *Theory of Moral Sentiments*.

Chapter 8: *Health Policy and the Poverty Trap*

1. One reason that public assistance rolls dropped following 1996 passage of welfare reform legislation is that it guaranteed Medicaid to former public assistance recipients for at least one year after they found work. Some studies have documented this effect. See Kathleen Thiede Call, et al., "Who is Still Uninsured in Minnesota? Lessons from State Reform Efforts," *Journal of the American Medical Association* 278 (October 8, 1997): 1191–1195.

2. I focus here on adults of working age and their children. There are connections also between age, disability, and poor health that

merit attention. However, the focus of this project is on "empowering the poor." Those with chronic conditions preventing work or those past their working years present a different ensemble of issues to the health care system and the Christian community.

3. Robert G. Evans, "Sharing the Burden, Containing the Cost: Fundamental Conflicts in Health Care Finance," in *Health Politics and Policy,* 3rd ed., edited by Theodor J. Litman and Leonard S. Robins (Albany, N.Y.: Delmar, 1997), pp. 278ff.

4. Paula M. Lantz, et al., "Socioeconomic Factors, Health Behaviors, and Mortality: Results from a Nationally Representative Prospective Study of U.S. Adults," *Journal of the American Medical Association* 279 (June 1998): 1703–1708; Gregory Pappas, et al., "The Increasing Disparity in Mortality Between Socioeconomic Groups in the United States, 1960 and 1986," *New England Journal of Medicine* 329 (July 1993): 103–109. This disparity is not limited to the United States, though it may be wider here. Income and health are linked in all countries, developed and underdeveloped. See, for example, Chris Power and Sharon Matthews, "More Equal than Others?" *The Lancet* 350 (November 1997): 1584–1589, and Jan Sundquist and Sven-Erik Johansson, "Indicators of Socio-economic Position and the Relation to Mortality in Sweden," *Social Science & Medicine* 45, no. 12 (1997): 1757–1766. But see Ken Judge, et al., "Income Inequality and Population Health," *Social Science & Medicine* 46, nos. 4–5 (1998): 567–579.

5. Karen Donelan, et al., "Whatever Happened to the Health Insurance Crisis in the United States? Voices From a National Survey," *Journal of the American Medical Association* 276 (October 1996): 1346–1350; Paula Braveman, et al., "Insurance-Related Difference in the Risk of Ruptured Appendix," *New England Journal of Medicine* 331 (August 1994): 444–449. There is a voluminous literature on insurance, medical care, and health status.

6. David Hilfiker, *Not All of Us are Saints: A Doctor's Journey with the Poor* (New York: Hill and Wang, 1994), 52.

7. J. Hadley, E.P. Steinberg, and J. Feder, "Comparison of Uninsured and Privately Insured Hospital Patients: Condition on Admission, Resource Use, and Outcome," *Journal of the American Medical Association* 265 (January 1991): 374–379; "Hospital Emer-

gency Rooms and Patient Dumping," (http://www.citizen.org/public_citizen/hrg/dumping.html).

8. Paul W. Newacheck, et al., "Health Insurance and Access to Primary Care for Children," *New England Journal of Medicine* 338 (February 1998): 513–519; Families USA Special Report, "Unmet Needs: The Large Differences in Health Care Between Uninsured and Insured Children" (http://epn.org/families/unmet.html; accessed June 6, 1997).

9. These data come from the March 1997 Census Bureau Current Population Survey. See http://www.census.gov/hhes/hlthins/cover96.html.

10. David Falcone and Robert Broyles, "Access to Long-Term Care: Race as a Barrier," *Journal of Health Politics, Policy, and Law* 19 (Fall 1994): 583–595. For a review of literature, application to managed care, and suggestions for reform, see Sara Rosenbaum, et al., "Civil Rights in a Changing Health Care System," *Health Affairs* 16 (January/February 1997): 90–105.

11. Marian E. Gornick, et al., "Effects of Race and Income on Mortality and Use of Services among Medicare Beneficiaries," *New England Journal of Medicine* 335 (September 1996): 791–799.

12. For example, Ron Shinkman, "Latino Kinds Underinsured," *Modern Healthcare* (10 March 1997): 36.

13. Keith J. Mueller, "Rural Health Care Delivery and Finance: Policy and Politics," in *Health Politics and Policy,* edited by Litman and Robins, 402–418.

14. The best discussions of this phenomenon are Deborah Chollet, "Employer-Based Health Insurance in a Changing Work Force," *Health Affairs* 13 (spring I 1994): 315–326; and John Holahan, et al., "A Shifting Picture of Health Insurance Coverage," *Health Affairs* 14 (winter 1995): 253–264.

15. These data are from "The Medicaid Program at a Glance," The Kaiser Commission on the Future of Medicaid (April 1997).

16. "Medicaid's Role for Children," The Kaiser Commission on the Future of Medicaid (May 1997).

17. The ideas and language in this section draw heavily from Clarke E. Cochran, *Health Care Policy: Where Do We Go From Here?* (Wynnewood, Pa.: Crossroads Monograph #17, 1997), 5–26.

18. Julianna Casey, IHM, *Food for the Journey: Theological Foundations for the Catholic Healthcare Ministry* (St. Louis: Catholic Health Association, 1991), 16.

19. "Address to the Catholic Health Care Ministry," Phoenix, Ariz., September 14, 1987. There is now renewed attention even among secular health care professionals to the spiritual dimensions of healing and even to the connection of prayer to healing.

20. Scripture quotations are from the Revised Standard Version.

21. Karen Lebacqz, *Justice in an Unjust World* (Minneapolis: Augsburg, 1987), 62.

22. See Clarke E. Cochran, "Religious Traditions and Health Care Policy: Potential for Democratic Discourse?" *Journal of Church and State* 39 (winter 1997): 15–35.

23. Helpful works are: Hessel Bouma, et al., *Christian Faith, Health, and Medical Practice* (Grand Rapids, Mich.: Eerdmans, 1989), and Casey, *Food for the Journey*.

24. Bouma, et al., *Christian Faith*, 23.

25. See Michael Walzer, *Spheres of Justice: A Defense of Pluralism and Equality* (New York: Basic Books, 1983), chap. 3. The discussion of justice below also draws upon Walzer.

26. See Cochran, *Health Care Policy*, 16–17.

27. David Hilfiker, in his struggle to minister to the poorest of the poor, describes the tension between personal, professional, and social responsibility. See *Not All of Us are Saints*, esp. chap. 8.

28. For a Christian perspective on differentiated responsibilities for health, including the church, see United States Catholic Conference, "Health and Health Care: A Pastoral Letter of the American Catholic Bishops," November 19, 1981. The best policy discussion of risk, risk transfer, and principles of justice is Deborah A. Stone, "The Struggle for the Soul of Health Insurance," in *The Politics of Health Care Reform: Lessons from the Past, Prospects for the Future*, ed. James A. Morone and Gary S. Belkin (Durham, N.C.: Duke University Press, 1994), 26–56.

29. On the central, Christian, political importance of liberty, see Glenn Tinder, *The Political Meaning of Christianity: An Interpretation* (Baton Rouge: Louisiana State University Press, 1989).

30. Daniel Callahan, *What Kind of Life? The Limits of Medical Progress* (New York: Simon & Schuster, 1990), 151.

31. Bouma, et al., *Christian Faith*, chap. 6.

32. Stanley Hauerwas's many works on health care and theology promote the politics of Christian witness. See the recent works: *After Christendom?* (Nashville: Abingdon, 1991) and *Dispatches from the Front* (Durham: Duke University Press, 1994).

33. See Cochran, *Health Care Policy*, 45–57; among other accounts, see Theda Skocpol, *Boomerang: Clinton's Health Security Effort and the Turn Against Government in U.S. Politics* (New York: Norton, 1996).

34. Uwe Reinhardt, "Wanted: A Clearly Articulated Social Ethic for American Health Care," *Journal of the American Medical Association* 278 (November 1997): 1446–1447. Some reject the principle of health care justice. See three responses to this article: *Journal of the American Medical Association* 279 (March 1998): 745–746.

35. My description will draw upon Daniel Callahan, *What Kind of Life?* (New York: Simon & Schuster, 1990), especially chapter 7. See also David M. Eddy, "What Care is 'Essential'? What Services are 'Basic'?" *Journal of the American Medical Association* 265 (February 1991): 782, 786–788.

36. Callahan, *What Kind of Life?*, 191. Description of the third level depends on a variety of factors related to age, social functioning, bodily needs, and the efficacy of individual curative treatments (see pp. 180–181 for a summary).

37. One could also take the level of benefits covered by standard public or private employment-based insurance, though these policies generally cover many procedures besides truly basic services.

38. I will not discuss the long-term financing problems in Medicare, or the various proposals to reform its payment and other structures in order to ensure its future financial viability. An excellent, brief guide to Medicare options is *Medicare Reform: A Twentieth Century Fund Guide to the Issues* (New York: Twentieth Century Fund, 1995).

39. Enrollments to date have almost exclusively involved adults and children. There is far less experience nationally with managed care for elderly and disabled persons, especially Medicaid recipients residing in nursing homes. I omit in this account many details of managed care plans and features. The early history of Medicaid-managed care is summarized conveniently in "Medicaid and Man-

aged Care," Kaiser Commission on the Future of Medicaid, Policy Brief (April 1995).

40. The best short summary is "Provisions in the Balanced Budget Act of 1997 Relating to Children," Children's Defense Fund, October 16, 1997, accessed November 6, 1997 at http://www.childrensdefense.org/fairstart _provisions1.html.

41. Catholic Health Association Health Policy Issue Brief, "Managed Care for Persons Dually Eligible for Medicare and Medicaid," December 1997, accessed December 28, 1997 at http:www.chausa.org/pubs/ pubscont.asp ?issue=ib9712.

42. Geraldine Dallek addresses a number of these concerns, "A Consumer Advocate on Medicaid-Managed Care," *Health Affairs* 15 (fall 1996): 174–177; also Colleen M. Grogan, "The Medicaid-Managed Care Policy Consensus for Welfare Recipients: A Reflection of Traditional Welfare Concerns — Deservingness, Need and Empowerment," unpublished paper, January 1997; and Harvey Bograd, et al., "Extending Health Maintenance Organization Insurance to the Uninsured: A Controlled Measure of Health Care Utilization," *Journal of the American Medical Association* 277 (April 1997): 1067–1072.

43. Bruce E. Landon, et al., "Quality Management by State Medicaid Agencies Converting to Managed Care: Plans and Current Practice," *Journal of the American Medical Association* 279 (January 1998): 211–216.

44. There is some evidence of exclusion of such providers from ordinary managed care contracts; Andrew B. Bindman, et al., "Selection and Exclusion of Primary Care Physicians by Managed Care Organizations," *Journal of the American Medical Association* 279 (March 1998): 675–679.

45. See Cara Lesser, et al., "Care for the Uninsured and Underserved in the Age of Managed Care," http://www.cmwf.org/ health_care/lesser.html, accessed January 26, 1998.

46. See Robert Langreth, "After Seeing Profits from the Poor, Some HMOs Abandon Them," *Wall Street Journal*, 7 April 1998, B1 & B4; Michael Moss and Chris Adams, "For Medicaid Patients, Doors Slam Closed," *Wall Street Journal*, 7 April 1998, B1 & B4.

47. This description draws upon Cindy Mann and Jocelyn Guyer, "Overview of the New Child Health Block Grant," Center on Budget and Policy Priorities, August 6, 1997, accessed on August 8, 1997, http://www .cbpp.org/chhlth.htm.

48. On Maine's program, see Louise Kertesz, "Welfare Goes to Work," *Modern Healthcare* (1 December 1997): 33; on Minnesota, see Call, et al., "Who is Still Uninsured in Minnesota?" For an early assessment of CHIP implementation, see Trish Riley, Cynthia Pernice, and Robert Mollica, "How Will States Implement Children's Health Insurance Programs?" *Health Affairs* 17 (May/June 1998): 260–263.

49. Laura Summer, et al., "Millions of Uninsured and Underinsured Children are Eligible for Medicaid," Center on Budget and Policy Priorities, December 10, 1996, accessed February 13, 1997; http://www.cbpp.org/ mcaidprt.htm; "Outreach to Medicaid-eligible Children More Critical Now, but Few Efforts So Far," *State Health Watch* 4 (January 1997): 1, 8.

50. Kenneth E. Thorpe, "Incremental Strategies for Providing Health Insurance for the Uninsured: Projected Federal Costs and Number of Newly Insured," *Journal of the American Medical Association* 278 (July 1997): 329–333.

51. As David Hilfiker points out, it is important not to be glib in holding the poor responsible. For many mere daily survival is heroic. See *Not All of Us are Saints,* esp. pp. 143–144. Recent research indicates that "irresponsible" smoking, drinking or other bad health habits account for only a small percentage of the difference in death rates between the poor and non-poor. In fact, alcohol consumption increases with income. See Lantz, et al., "Socioeconomic Factors."

52. Steven A. Schroeder, "Doctors and Diversity: Improving the Health of Poor and Minority People," *Chronicle of Higher Education,* 1 November 1996, B5.

53. See Stephen V. Monsma's chapter in this volume. For the communal context of health care specifically, see Ezekiel J. Emanuel and Linda L. Emanuel, "Preserving Community in Health Care," *Journal of Health Politics, Policy, and Law* 22 (February 1997): 147–184; Gary Gunderson, *Deeply Woven Roots: Improving the Quality of Life in Your Community* (Minneapolis: Fortress Press, 1997); and various essays in the January/February 1998 issue of *Health Progress.*

54. There is a parallel here with the potential new role of religious institutions

under welfare reform's "Charitable Choice" provisions.

55. Amy Goldstein, "Clinics on the Critical List," *Washington Post National Weekly Edition,* 12 January 1998, pp. 31–32. The fault is not always greedy managed-care companies or inept Medicaid administrators; sometimes community health center operators have not taken advantage of their opportunities under managed care.

56. See Gary J. Young, et al., "Does the Sale of Nonprofit Hospitals Threaten Health Care for the Poor?" *Health Affairs* 22 (January/February 1997): 137–141, and J. Weissman, "Uncompensated Hospital Care: Will it be There if We Need It?" *Journal of the American Medical Association* 276 (September 1996): 823–828.

57. St. Mary's program is cited, not because it is groundbreaking, but because it is typical of a well-developed, hospital-grounded, outreach effort. Not all religious hospitals, however, support these kinds of efforts to the extent possible or necessary in their communities. Information on St. Mary's program comes from hospital publications and interviews in early 1998 with Ms. Judi Blakey, Health Communities and Advocacy Coordinator, and Sr. Mary Kathleen Small, CSJ, Director of Community Health Outreach.

58. Hilfiker, *Not All of Us are Saints,* esp. chapter 11.

59. Statement of purpose in CCHF's quarterly journal, *Health and Development.* CCHF can be contacted at P.O. Box 23429, Chicago, IL 60623. Phone: 773-843-2700. Http://www.cchf.org.

60. The following ideas and examples draw substantially upon, *Strong Partners: Realigning Religious Health Assets for Community Health* (Atlanta, Ga.: The Carter Center, 1998).

61. William Foege, "Foreword," in *Strong Partners,* 4.

62. *Strong Partners* provides a number of examples of such foundations and the issues that they face. The Catholic Health Association journal, *Health Progress,* also regularly features examples of these kinds of efforts.

63. Donald W. Light, "The Rhetoric and the Realities of Community Health Care: The Limits of Countervailing Powers to Meet the Health Needs of the Twenty-first Century," *Journal of Health Politics, Policy, and Law* 22 (February 1997): 105–145.

Chapter 9: *Taxation and Economic Justice*

1. John E. Anderson, "Biblical Principles Applied to Federal, State, and Local Taxation Policy," in *Biblical Principles and Public Policy: The Practice,* edited by Richard C. Chewning (Colorado Springs: Navpress, 1991), 127–142. See also John E. Anderson and George Langelett, "Economics and the Evangelical Mind," *Bulletin of the Association of Christian Economists* 28 (1996), 5–24.

2. Matthew 2:22 records that Joseph was afraid to return to this region with Mary and Jesus when they returned from Egypt.

3. Judas the Galilean is considered the author of this view .

4. That is, the redemption price of those who had devoted themselves, a child, or another possession to the Lord. See Leviticus 27:1–8.

5. James Gwartney, "Human Freedom and the Bible," paper presented at the Consultation on the Mixed Market Economy, Wheaton College, September 18–20, 1987.

6. Stephen Charles Mott, "How Should Christians Use the Bible?" *Bulletin of the Association of Christian Economists* 13: 7–19.

7. John Mason, "Biblical Teaching and Assisting the Poor," *Transformation* 4: 1–14.

8. Christopher Wright, *An Eye for an Eye: the Place of Old Testament Ethics Today* (Downers Grove, Ill.: Intervarsity, 1983), 147.

9. I am indebted to Bruce A. Gregg for his careful exposition of the Epistle of James and a number of helpful discussions on the rich and poor in Scripture.

10. Carl F.H. Henry, "Linking the Bible to Public Policy," in *Biblical Principles and Public Policy: The Practice,* edited by Richard C. Chewning (Colorado Springs: Navpress, 1991), 26–27.

11. National Commission on Restructuring the Internal Revenue Service, *A New Vision for a New IRS* (Washington, D.C.: 1997).

12. Robert I. Lerman and Shlomo Yitzhaki, "A Note on the Calculation and Interpretation of the Gini Index," *Economic Letters* 15: 363–368.

13. Lynn Karoly, "Trends in Income Inequality: The Impact of, and Implications for, Tax Policy," in *Tax Progressivity and Income Inequality,* edited by Joel Slemrod (New York: Cambridge Univ. Press, 1996), 127.

14. The material in this section is adapted from A.B. Atkinson, *Public Economics in Action: The Basic Income/Flat Tax Proposal* (New York: Oxford Univ. Press, 1995).

15. The optimal tax rate can be written so that the first term on the right-hand- side is the efficiency component and the second term in brackets is the equity component.

16. Edgar K. Browning and William R. Johnson, "The Trade-Off Between Equality and Efficiency," *Journal of Political Economy* 92 (1984): 175–203.

17. Ibid., 201.

18. This basic outline of material in this section is adapted from Atkinson, *Public Economics in Action,* 12–13, with extensions of his arguments.

19. Jerry A. Hausman, "Labor Supply," in *How Taxes Affect Economic Activity,* edited by Henry Aaron and Joseph Pechman (Washington, D.C.: Brookings Institution, 1981).

20. Robert K. Triest, "The Efficiency Cost of Increased Progressivity," in *Tax Progressivity and Income Inequality.*

21. Barry Bosworth and Gary Burtless, "The Effects of Tax Reform on Labor Supply, Investment, and Saving," *Journal of Economic Perspectives* 6 (1990): 3–26.

22. This section is based on Joel Slemrod, "On the High Income Laffer Curve," in *Tax Progressivity and Income Inequality.*

23. Ibid., 208–209.

24. Robert E. Hall and Alvin Rabushka, *The Flat Tax,* 2nd ed. (Stanford, Calif.: Hoover Institution Press, 1995). See also Hall, Rabushka, et. al., *Fairness and Efficiency in the Flat Tax* (Washington, D.C.: AEI Press, 1996).

25. Joseph Pechman, "The Future of the Income Tax," *American Economic Review* 80 (1990): 1–20.

26. Henry J. Aaron and William G. Gale, eds, *Economic Effects of Fundamental Tax Reform* (Washington, D.C.: Brookings Institution, 1996).

27. Alan J. Auerbach, "Tax Reform, Capital Allocation, Efficiency, and Growth," *Economic Effects of Fundamental Tax Reform.*

28. William M. Gentry and R. Glenn Hubbard, "Distributional Implications of Introducing a Broad-Based Consumption Tax," unpublished paper.

29. Eugene Steuerle, "Policy Watch: Tax Credits for Low-Income Workers with Children," *Journal of Economic Perspectives* 4 (1996): 201–211.

30. This point has been made in the public debate over federal safety net programs by Wendell Primus, *The Safety Net Delivers* (Washington, D.C.: Center on Budget and Policy Priorities, 1996).

Chapter 10: *Just Schools*

1. Thomas P. Carter and Michael L. Chatfield, "Effective Schools for Language Minority Students," *American Journal of Education* 97 (1986): 200–233.

2. John E. Chubb & Terry M. Moe, *Politics, Markets and America's Schools* (Washington, D.C.: The Brookings Institution, 1990); their book-in-progress makes this point even more explicitly.

3. Reginald M. Clark, *Family Life and School Achievement: Why Poor Black Children Succeed or Fail* (Chicago: University of Chicago Press, 1983), 120; see also Susan Mayer, *What Money Can't Buy: Family Income and Children's Life Chances* (Cambridge: Harvard University Press, 1997).

4. Claire Smrekar, *The Impact of School Choice and Community* (Albany: SUNY Press, 1996).

5. Susan P. Choy, *Public and Private Schools: How Do They Differ?* (Washington, D.C.: National Center for Education Statistics, NCES 97–983, 1997), 21.

6. James S. Coleman & Thomas Hoffer, *Public and Private High Schools: The Impact of Communities* (New York: Basic Books, 1987), 213.

7. James G. Cibulka, Timothy J. O'Brien, & Donald Zewe, *Inner City Private Elementary Schools: A Study* (Milwaukee: Marquette University Press, 1982), 136–142.

8. Anthony S. Bryk, Valerie G. Lee, & Peter B. Holland, *Catholic Schools and the Common Good* (Cambridge: Harvard University Press, 1995), 57, 247.

9. See a splendid collection of papers on this topic in the *Journal of Education* 175, no. 2 (1993); see also Edward A. Wynne & Kevin Ryan, *Reclaiming Our Schools: A Handbook on Teaching Character, Academics, and Discipline,* 2nd ed. (New York: Macmillan, 1996); Thomas Lickona, *Educating for Character* (New York: Bantam Books, 1991); William Kilpatrick, *Why Johnny Can't Tell Right From Wrong* (New York: Touchstone, 1993).

10. Charles L. Glenn, "Religion, Textbooks, and the Common School," *The Public Interest* 88 (summer 1987).

11. See Charles L. Glenn, "Effective Schools . . . and Beyond," in *Commissions, Reports, Reforms, and Educational Policy*, edited by Rick Ginsberg and David N. Plank (New York: Praeger, 1995).

12. *The Educational Progress of Hispanic Students*, NCES 95–787 (Washington, D.C.: U.S. Department of Education: National Center for Education Statistics, 1995), 12.

13. *The Educational Progress of Black Students*, NCES 95–765 (Washington, D.C.: U.S. Department of Education: National Center for Education Statistics, 1995), 12.

14. *The Educational Progress of Black Students*, 13–17.

15. E. D. Hirsch, Jr., *The Schools We Need . . . and Why We Don't Have Them* (New York: Doubleday, 1996), 5, quoting R. F. Ferguson, "Shifting Challenges: Fifty Years of Economic Change Towards Black White Earnings Equality," *Daedalus 124* (winter 1995): 1, 37–76.

16. *The Educational Progress of Hispanic Students*, 21.

17. *The Educational Progress of Black Students*, 19.

18. Maureen Stone, *The Education of the Black Child: The Myth of Multiracial Education* (London: Fontana, 1981), 25–26.

19. Stone, 100, 147.

20. Stone, 6.

21. Hirsch, 7.

22. Alain Seksig, "Que peut l'école contre le racisme?" *Face au racisme, 1: Les moyens d'agir*, edited by Pierre-André Taguieff (Paris: Éditions La Découverte, 1992), 90.

23. Lisa Delpit, *Other People's Children: Cultural Conflict in the Classroom* (New York: The New Press, 1995), 29.

24. Quoted by Arturo Tosi, *Immigration and Bilingual Education* (Oxford: Pergamon Press, 1984), 167.

25. Hirsch, 25.

26. Hirsch, 33, 41–42.

27. Hirsch, 90–91.

28. Charles L. Glenn with Ester J. de Jong, *Educating Immigrant Children: Schools and Language Minorities in Twelve Nations* (New York: Garland, 1996).

29. John Edwards, "The Context of Bilingual Education," *Journal of Multilingual and Multicultural Development 2* (1981): 25–44, 37.

30. Gary Orfield, "Hispanic Education: Challenges, Research, and Policies," *American Journal of Education 95*, 1 (November 1986): 11.

31. Albert Benderson, "Educating the New Americans," *Focus 17* (Princeton, N.J.: Educational Testing Service, 1986), 9.

32. Joan Baratz-Snowden, D. Rock, D. J. Pollack, & Gita Wilder, *Parent Preference Study* (Princeton: Educational Testing Service, 1988).

33. Bernard Spolsky, "Bilingual Education in the United States," in *International Dimensions of Bilingual Education*, edited by James E. Alatis (Washington, D.C.: Georgetown University, 1978), 277.

34. Peter Skerry, *Mexican Americans: The Ambivalent Minority* (New York: Free Press, 1993), 289.

35. Louis Porcher, "Introduction," in *La scolarisation des enfants étrangers en France*, edited by Porcher (Paris: CREDIF, 1978), 13–14.

36. Joan Baratz-Snowden, D. Rock, D. J. Pollack, & Gita Wilder, *The Educational Progress of Language Minority Students: Findings from the NAEP 1985–86 Special Study* (Princeton: Educational Testing Service, 1988), iii.

37. Bureau for Refugee Programs, *The PASS Tracking Study: Final Report* (Washington, D.C.: U.S. Department of State, July 1987), 3.

38. John H. Bishop, "Signaling, Incentives, and School Organization in France, the Netherlands, Britain, and the United States," in *Improving America's Schools: The Role of Incentives*, edited by Eric A Hanushek and Dale W. Jorgenson (Washington, D.C.: National Academy Press, 1996), 131, 134.

39. Eric A. Hanushek, "Outcomes, Costs, and Incentives in Schools," in *Improving America's Schools: The Role of Incentives*, edited by Eric A Hanushek and Dale W. Jorgenson (Washington, D.C.: National Academy Press, 1996), 30.

40. Hanushek, 38.

41. Susan P. Choy, *Public and Private Schools: How Do They Differ?* (Washington, D.C.: National Center for Education Statistics, NCES 97–983, 1997), 5–6.

42. Millicent Lawton, "Discrimination Charged in Texas Exit-Exam Lawsuit," *Education Week*, 22 October 1997, 3.

43. Hirsch, 213–14.

44. Hirsch, 179, quoting Christopher Jencks, "What's Behind the Drop in Test

Scores?" Working Papers, Department of Sociology, Harvard University, Cambridge, Mass., July–August, 1975.

45. Harold W. Stevenson, "The Asian Advantage: The Case of Mathematics," *American Educator 11* (summer 1987); Harold W. Stevenson and James W. Stigler, *The Learning Gap: Why Our Schools Are Failing and What We Can Learn from Japanese and Chinese Education* (New York: Summit Books, 1992).

46. Chester E. Finn, Jr., *We Must Take Charge: Our Schools and Our Future* (New York: Free Press, 105).

47. Finn, 110.

48. See, for example, Jim Cummins, "Four Misconceptions about Language Proficiency in Bilingual Education," *NABE Journal V*, 3 (spring 1981); "The Entry and Exit Fallacy in Bilingual Education," *NABE Journal IV*, 3 (spring 1980).

49. Alice Perez Peters, *Self-Esteem as it Relates to Reading Facility and Bilingual Schooling of Puerto Rican Students*, dissertation, Loyola University of Chicago, 1979.

50. Julian T. Lopez, *Self-concept and Academic Achievement of Mexican-American Children in Bilingual Bicultural Programs*, dissertation, United States International University, 1980.

51. Anne G. Seligson, *Study of the Self-concept of Mexican-American Children in a Bilingual Program*, dissertation, United States International University, 1979.

52. Maykel Verkuyten, *Zelfbeleving en identiteit van jongeren uit etnische minderheden* (Arnhem: Gouda Quint, 1988).

53. J. R. Porter and R. E. Washington, "Black Identity and Self-Esteem: A Review of Studies of Black Self-Concept, 1968–1978," *Annual Review of Sociology 5* (1979).

54. *The Economist*, 28 July 1990, 11.

55. Carole Tavris, "Chasing Self-Esteem's Shadow," *Education Week*, 16 October 1991.

56. Hirsch, 181, citing various studies of pass-fail grading.

57. Hirsch, 184.

58. Hirsch, 210, 212.

59. Robert H. Meyer, "Value-Added Indicators of School Performance," in *Improving America's Schools: The Role of Incentives*, edited by Eric A Hanushek and Dale W. Jorgenson (Washington, D.C.: National Academy Press, 1996), 219.

60. Meyer, 213–14.

61. *The Educational Progress of Hispanic Students*, 5.

62. *The Educational Progress of Black Students*, 4.

63. James S. Catterall, "Standards and School Dropouts: A National Study of Tests Required for High School Graduation," *American Journal of Education 98*, no. 1 (November 1989): 1–34.

64. Eric A. Hanushek, "Outcomes, Costs, and Incentives in Schools," in *Improving America's Schools: The Role of Incentives*, edited by Eric A Hanushek and Dale W. Jorgenson (Washington, D.C.: National Academy Press, 1996), 33.

65. Hanushek, 30.

66. Diane August and Kenji Hakuta, eds., *Improving Schooling for Language-Minority Children: A Research Agenda* (Washington, D.C.: National Academy Press, 1997), 58.

67. August and Hakuta, 59, 70.

68. August and Hakuta, 60 (emphasis added).

69. August and Hakuta, 179.

70. August and Hakuta, 70.

71. For a characteristic statement, see Jim Cummins, "The Role of Primary Language Development in Promoting Educational Success for Language Minority Students," in *Schooling and Language Minority Students* (Sacramento: Office of Bilingual Education, California State Department of Education, 1982).

72. August and Hakuta, 94.

73. August and Hakuta, 177–78.

74. August and Hakuta, 189.

75. August and Hakuta, 178.

76. Hanushek, 39.

77. Peter Mortimore, et al., *School Matters* (Berkeley: University of California Press, 1988).

78. P. Concha, L. Garcia, and A. Perez, "Cooperation versus Competition: A Comparison of Anglo-American and Cuban-American Youngsters in Miami," *Social Psychology 95* (1975): 273–74.

79. I. S. Stewart, "Cultural Differences Between Anglos and Chicanos," *Integrated Education 13*, no. 6 (1975): 21–23.

80. Quoted by Sandra Lee McKay, in "Weighing Educational Alternatives," in *Language Diversity: Problem or Resource?* edited by S.L. McKay and Sau-ling Cynthia Wong (Cambridge: Newbury House, 1988), 350.

81. J. Kleinfeld, "Positive Stereotyping: The Cultural Relativist in the Classroom," *Human Organization* 34 (1975): 269–74.

82. Laura Lippman, Shelley Burns, and Edith McArthur, *Urban Schools: The Challenge of Location and Poverty*, NCES 96–194 (Washington, D.C.: U.S. Department of Education: National Center for Education Statistics, 1996), 2–3, quoting James S. Coleman and others in *Equality of Educational Opportunity* (1966).

83. Lippman, Burns, and McArthur, 3, quoting studies by Anderson and others (1992) and Jencks and Mayer (1990).

84. Lippman, Burns, and McArthur, 29 and *passim*.

85. Lippman, Burns, and McArthur, 39.

86. For an extensive discussion of the instructional integration of LEP children, see Ester J. de Jong, "Integrated Education for Language Minority Children," in *Educating Immigrant Children: Schools and Language Minorities in Twelve Nations*, by Charles L. Glenn with Ester J. de Jong (New York: Garland, 1996).

87. See Charles L. Glenn, "'Bussing' in Boston: What We Could Have Done Better," in *Forty Years After the Brown Decision: Implications of School Desegregation for U.S. Education, Readings on Equal Education 13*, edited by Kofi Lomotey and Charles Teddlie (New York: AMS Press, 1996).

88. Charles L. Glenn, "The New Common School," in *Creating the New Common School* (Quincy, Mass.: Massachusetts Department of Education, 1987), 11.

89. See Charles L. Glenn, "Controlled Choice in Massachusetts Public Schools," *The Public Interest 103* (April 1991).

90. Charles L. Glenn, "Do Parents Get the Schools They Choose?" *Equity and Choice 9*, no. 1 (fall 1992).

91. Charles L. Glenn, et al., *Choice and School Distinctiveness* (Baltimore, Md.: Center on Families, Communities, Schools, and Children's Learning, Johns Hopkins University, 1996).

92. "Student Strategies to Avoid Harm at School," NCES 95–203 (U.S. Department of Education: National Center for Education Statistics, 1995), 1.

93. "How Safe Are the Public Schools: What Do Teachers Say?" NCES 96–842 (U.S. Department of Education: National Center for Education Statistics, 1996), 1–2.

94. *The Educational Progress of Hispanic Students*, 8–9.

95. *The Educational Progress of Black Students*, 9.

96. Martha M. McCarthy, Nelda H. Cambron-McCabe, and Stephen B. Thomas, *Public School Law: Teachers' and Students' Rights*, 4th ed. (Boston: Allyn and Bacon, 1996), 236.

97. Robert L. Hampel, *The Last Little Citadel: American High Schools Since 1940* (Boston: Houghton Mifflin, 1986), 94.

98. Gerald Grant, *The World We Created at Hamilton High* (Cambridge: Harvard University Press, 1986), 173–74.

99. Lippman, Burns, and McArthur, 3, quoting studies by Hoffer (1992) and Glazer (1992).

100. John E. Chubb and Terry M. Moe, *Politics, Markets and America's Schools* (Washington, D.C.: The Brookings Institution, 1990), 19, 187.

101. Lippman, Burns, and McArthur, 81.

102. Choy, 10–13, 16.

103. Choy, 8, 14, 18.

104. Choy, 19.

105. Choy, 21.

106. Lippman, Burns, and McArthur, 5.

107. I attended the meetings of one city-wide parent advisory council for about a year. It was dominated by "professional parents," some of whom had served for twenty years and more, and the only contention with the school system administration was over the latter's attempt to reduce the budget for the lavish, annual, parent advisory council banquet at a downtown hotel.

108. Robert Ballion, *Les Consommateurs d'école* (Paris: Stock, 1982).

109. See the account in G. Alfred Hess, Jr., *Restructuring Urban Schools: A Chicago Perspective* (New York: Teachers College Press, 1995); more critical views have been expressed by Chester Finn and others.

110. Charles L. Glenn, "Letting Poor Parents Act Responsibly, *Journal of Family and Culture 2*, no. 3 (1986): 1–18.

111. Gary Natriello, Edward L. McDill, and Aaron M. Pallas, *Schooling Disadvantaged Children: Racing Against Catastrophe* (New York: Teachers College Press, 1990), 15–32.

112. Jonathan Kozol, *Savage Inequalities* (New York: Harper Perennial, 1992), 123.

113. Eric A. Hanushek, "Outcomes, Costs, and Incentives in Schools," in *Improving America's Schools : The Role of Incentives,*

edited by Eric A Hanushek and Dale W. Jorgenson (Washington, D.C.: National Academy Press, 1996), 40–41.

114. August and Hakuta, 128.

115. James S. Coleman et al., "Equality of Educational Opportunity," excerpted in James S. Coleman, *Equality and Achievement in Education* (Boulder: Westview Press, 1990), 119.

116. Lisbeth B. Schorr with Daniel Schorr, *Within Our Reach: Breaking the Cycle of Disadvantage* (New York: Doubleday Anchor, 1989), 259.

117. James S. Coleman, "Families and Schools," *Educational Researcher 16*, no. 6 (August/September 1987): 32–38.

118. Thomas Snyder and Linda Shafer, *Youth Indicators, 1996,* NCES 96–027 (U.S. Department of Education: National Center for Education Statistics, 1996), 5.

119. David Osborne and Ted Gaebler, *Reinventing Government* (Reading, Mass.: Addison-Wesley, 1992), 45–46.

120. James S. Coleman, "Quality and Equality in American Education: Public and Catholic Schools," reprinted in *Equality and Achievement in Education* (Boulder: Westview Press, 1990), 247.

121. Coleman, 1987.

122. Schorr, xxii; a fine example of such an approach is the "intergenerational literacy program" implemented in Chelsea, Massachusetts, as part of Boston University's efforts to turn around a very needy school system.

123. Lawrence M. Mead, *Beyond Entitlement: The Social Obligations of Citizenship* (New York: Free Press, 1986), 3.

124. Kozol, 4.

125. Jomills Henry Braddock II, Robert L. Crain, and James M. McPartland, "A Long-Term View of School Desegregation: Some Recent Studies of Graduates as Adults," *Phi Delta Kappan 66* (December 1984): 259–64.

126. James S. Coleman, "Toward Open Schools," *The Public Interest 9* (fall 1967): 20–27.

127. Charles L. Glenn, "Controlled Choice in Massachusetts Public Schools," *The Public Interest 103* (spring 1991): 88–105.

128. Richard John Neuhaus, *America Against Itself: Moral Vision and the Public Order* (Notre Dame, Ind.: University of Notre Dame Press, 1992), 185, 111.

129. William Julius Wilson, *The Truly Disadvantaged* (Chicago: University of Chicago Press, 1987), 138.

130. Charles L. Glenn, "Common Standards and Educational Diversity," in *Subsidiarity and Education: Aspects of Comparative Educational Law,* edited by Jan De Groof (Leuven, Belgium: Acco, 1994).

Chapter 11: *The Good City*

1. Our use of "inner city" refers to the *pockets of concentrated poverty* in or near the central cities of many of our major metropolitan regions. Most neighborhoods within our metropolitan regions (including our central cities) are not "inner-city" as we are using that term here, even though many from outside those neighborhoods may consider them as such.

2. M. Marty, *The One & the Many: America's Struggle for the Common Good* (Cambridge, Mass.: Harvard Univ. Press, 1997), 17.

3. A twentieth anniversary revisiting of the Kerner Commission's work spoke of "quiet riots" to reflect the continuing damage within our inner-city communities; see F. Harris & R. Wilkins, eds., *Quiet Riots: Race & Poverty in the U.S.* (New York: Pantheon, 1988).

4. See several recent analyses which speak to this: M. Weir, "Central Cities Loss of Power in State Politics," *Cityscape* 2:23–40 (May 1996); R. Cook, "Cities: Decidedly Democratic, Declining in Population," *Congressional Quarterly* (12 July 1997): 1645–1653; D. Muniak/D. Auger, "The National Government & U.S. Cities in the Post-Reagan/Bush Era," *Regional Studies* 29(1995): 737–744.

5. See M. Rich, *Federal Policy-making & the Poor: National Goals, Local Choices, & Distributional Outcomes* (Princeton: Princeton Univ. Press, 1993), which observes that the most troubled areas of our inner cities often did not fare as well as better-off central city neighborhoods and suburban communities in the administration of block grant programs initiated in the 1960s.

6. See M. Orfield, *Metropolitics: A Regional Agenda for Community & Stability* (Washington, D.C.: Brookings Institution Press, 1997), which reports on developments in this direction in the Minneapolis-St. Paul metropolitan region.

7. I am pleased to see a substantial outpouring of interest in this question of late. During his tenure as Secretary of Housing and

Urban Development, Henry Cisneros offered commendable leadership towards both a moral and policy response to the problems of our inner cities within their metropolitan regions; see a number of his addresses in this regard: "Regionalism: The New Geography of Opportunity" (March 1995), "Higher Ground: Faith Communities & Community Building" (February 1996), "Urban Entrepreneurialism & National Economic Growth" (September 1995).

8. We include in this commentary authoritative "tradition" within the Roman Catholic Church, as well as work over the millennia from the faithful Jewish communities; our appeal is to the longstanding tradition within those communities which find the Bible authoritative, which continually rehearse the biblical materials for insight into contemporary problems.

9. C.J.H. Wright, *God's People in God's Land: Family, Land, & Property in the Old Testament* (Grand Rapids, Mich.: Eerdmans Publishing Co., 1990), 175–176, xviii, respectively.

10. See in this regard the works of Stephen Innes, *Creating the Commonwealth: The Economic Culture of Puritan New England* (New York: W.W. Norton & Co., 1995); and Barry Shain, *The Myth of American Individualism: The Protestant Origins of American Political Thought* (Princeton: Princeton Univ. Press, 1994).

11. See Richard John Neuhaus, *Doing Well & Doing Good* (New York: Doubleday, 1992), wherein he writes: "At least in America, the ideas of democracy must be in conversation with the moral intuitions sustained and articulated by religion. Tocqueville said religion is the first political institution in American democracy. That is even more true today than it was in the 1930s. . . . In sum, in 1992 as in 1776, the Judeo-Christian tradition provides the "meaning system" or the "plausibility structure" of American moral discourse, personal and public" (4–5). Stephen Carter's, *The Culture of Disbelief* (New York: Anchor Books, 1993) in effect argues a similar position.

12. See several of the essays in Glenn Loury's *One by One from the Inside Out* (New York: The Free Press, 1995), as well as much of the recent work of John DiIulio, such as "The Lord's Work: The Church & the 'Civil Society Sector'" in *The Brookings Review* 15:27 (fall 1997).

13. *Sources:* Bureau of the Census, *Census of the Population (1970, 1980, 1990): General Social & Economic Characteristics;* Bureau of the Census, *Current Population Reports,* P60–198 "Poverty in the U.S.: 1996."

14. Labels carry significance. I use "inner city" to describe only those neighborhoods within or near the central cities of many of our major metropolitan regions which are characterized by *concentrated poverty*. A better term might be the older notion of "slums," but we fear most residents of these areas would find this characterization offensive. Wilson, Jargowsky, and Glaeser all speak of "ghettos," an unwelcome description for those we know who live in such settings; see W.J. Wilson, *The Truly Disadvantaged* (Chicago: Univ. of Chicago Press, 1987); E. Glaeser, "Ghettos: The Changing Consequences of Ethnic Isolation," *Regional Review* 7:18–24 (spring 1997). Long-standing and acrimonious debate surrounds the use of "culture of poverty" and "underclass" to describe those who are at issue here. In their review article, E. Mills and L. Lubuele make "inner cities" synonymous with the central city of a metropolitan region; see Mills and Lubuele, "Inner Cities," *Journal of Econ. Literature* XXXV (1997): 727–756. Anthony Downs uses "core area" to include both the central cities and inner-ring suburbs; see Anthony Downs, "The Challenge of Our Declining Big Cities," *Housing Policy Debate* 8 (1997): 359–408. Our use of "inner city" comes closest to the geographic spread of Downs's core area, albeit not inclusive of the entire area of either central city or inner-ring suburbs, nor aligned tightly with the 40 percent poverty rate tipping point used by Jargowsky.

15. One encounters major problems working with census information by race. How should Hispanics be recorded: as white, black, or Hispanic (or in all three categories)? The 1980 census does not list Hispanics separately by metropolitan region. In both 1970 and 1990 the census lists Hispanics by metropolitan region, but in different ways (lumping a number of Hispanics at least with the white count in 1970, and breaking-out white Hispanics in 1990). In table 2 we seek to offer as consistent a rendering as we can of the racial composition of central city poverty for 1969 and 1989. The racial composition of metropolitan regions is not published in popular form for non-census years.

16. Source: Bureau of the Census, Census of the Population (1970, 1990): General Social & Economic Characteristics.

17. P. Jargowsky, *Poverty and Place: Ghettos, Barrios, and the American City* (New York: Russell Sage Foundation, 1997), chapter 2. The 40 percent figure is selected in part because "experienced observers" call such neighborhoods ghettos (if primarily black), barrios (if primarily Hispanic), or slums (if primarily white). He describes them as having "a threatening appearance, marked by dilapidated housing, vacant units with broken or boarded-up windows, abandoned and burned-out cars, and men "hanging out" on street corners" (p. 11). In terms of ethnic type (using a two-thirds-non-white of overall neighborhood population for making the assignment) 42.4 percent of high-poverty neighborhoods in 1990 were black, 26.9 percent were mixed ethnic, 17.1 percent were Hispanic, and 13.7 percent were white.

18. Jargowsky, *op.cit.*, 30f.

19. Source: *1990 Census of Population,* Summary Tape File 3A; *1980 Census of Population,* Summary Tape File 3A; *1970 Census of Population,* Fourth Count machine-readable file.

20. J. Kasarda, "Inner City Concentrated Poverty & Neighborhood Distress: 1970 to 1990," *Housing Policy Debate* 4 (1993): 253–302; reproducing his table 1 (p. 258). See in this regard as well J. Madden, "Changes in the Distribution of Poverty Across & Within the U.S. Metropolitan Areas, 1979–89," *Urban Studies* 33 (1996): 1581–1600.

21. Calculated as the central city percentage of families in a given income quintile divided by the central city percentage of all families. *Source:* Current Population Survey data, 1964 to 1994, except 1969 and 1988, which are interpolated.

22. C. Mayer, "Does Location Matter?" *New England Economic Review,* "Special Issue: Earnings Inequality" (May/June 1996): 26–40, quoting p. 28.

23. D. Cutler and E. Glaeser, "Are Ghettos Good or Bad?" *Quarterly Journal of Economics* CXII (1997): 827–872.

24. Jargowsky, *op.cit.,* drawing particularly from pp. 38ff.

25. We must remind ourselves that Kasarda examines only the 100 largest central cities, whereas Jargowsky canvassed all metropolitan statistical areas; and neither studied areas outside metropolitan regions. Jargowsky argues the nature of non-metropolitan poverty is substantively different. We harbor a suspicion, however, that there could be a growing concentration of rural poverty within small pockets as well, in regional enclaves like northwest Mississippi and the upper peninsula of Michigan, as well as small towns throughout the country.

26. *Source:* Current Population Reports (P–60–198), *Poverty in the U.S.: 1996.*

27. D. Massey, "The Age of Extremes: Concentrated Affluence & Poverty in the Twenty-First Century," along with reactions to his address in *Demography* 33 (1996): 395–428; quotations noted here are from p. 395. Massey's argument gains support from J. Kasarda, et al., "Central-City and Suburban Migration Patterns: Is a Turnaround on the Horizon?" *Housing Policy Debate* 8 (1997): 307–357; see also R. Fernandez and R. Rogerson, "Income Distribution, Communities, & the Quality of Public Education," *Quarterly Journal of Economics* CXI (1996): 135–164. For an assessment questioning the implications of growing economic stratification, see M. Kremer, "How Much Does Sorting Increase Inequality?" *Quarterly Journal of Economics* CXII (1997): 115–139.

28. Massey, ibid., 402f.

29. Massey, 403–409.

30. S. Kuznets, *Modern Economic Growth* (New Haven: Yale Univ. Press, 1966).

31. Jargowsky, *op.cit.,* 1.

32. The quotations in this and the previous paragraph come from chapter 4 of Jargowsky's work.

33. See William Julius Wilson, *The Truly Disadvantaged.* Wilson responded to his critics and generally reaffirmed the arguments of the earlier work in *When Work Disappears: The World of the New Urban Poor* (New York: Alfred A. Knopf, 1996).

34. We choose the term "regularized" work to allow for the fact that those in the inner city generally do have contact with the work world, but typically not the types of jobs that offer sufficient wages and benefits to lift oneself and one's family out of poverty status. See, in this regard, K. Edin and L. Lein, *Making Ends Meet: How Single Mothers Survive Welfare & Low-Wage Work* (New York: Russell Sage Foundation, 1997).

35. Wilson, 57.

36. Cutler and Glaeser, "Are Ghettos Good or Bad?"

37. E. Glaeser, 20, 22, 24. For an affirming view, see L. Krivo, et. al., "Race, Segregation, and the Concentration of Disadvantage: 1980–1990," *Social Problems* 45 (February 1998): 61–80.

38. E. Mills and L. Lubele, quoting in this paragraph 741, 749, 751.

39. It would be hard to offer a representative selection of this work. See the Mills and Lubele review article (ibid.) for portions of this. See also: M. Corcoran, "Rags to Rags: Poverty & Mobility in the U.S.," *Annual Rev. of Sociology* 21 (1995): 237–267; L. Tigges, et al., "Social Isolation of the Urban Poor: Race, Class, & Neighborhood Effects on Social Resources," *Sociological Quarterly* 39 (winter 1998): 53–78; T. Vartanian, "Neighborhood Effects on AFDC Exits: Examining the Social Isolation, Relative Deprivation, & Epidemic Theories," *Social Services Review* 71 (December 1997): 548–573.

40. See P. Gleason and G. Cain, "Earnings of Black & White Youth & Their Relation to Poverty" (Institute for Research on Poverty, Discussion Paper #1138–97, August 1997).

41. J. Kain, "Housing Segregation, Negro Employment & Metropolitan Decentralization," *Quarterly Journal of Economics* 82, #2 (1968): 175–192. See also his revisiting of this debate in "The Spatial Mismatch Hypothesis: Three Decades Later," *Housing Policy Debate* 3, #2 (1992): 371–460.

42. Mills and Lubele, p. 733f.

43. See R. Freeman, "Who Escapes? The Relation of Church-Going & Other Background Factors to the Socio-Economic Performance of Black Male Youths from Inner city Poverty Tracts," in R. Freeman and H. Holzer, eds., *The Black Youth Employment Crisis* (Chicago: Univ. of Chicago Press, 1986), 353–376.

44. See in this regard the arguments of Glenn Loury: "Discrimination in the Post-Civil Rights Era: Beyond Market Interactions," *Journal of Economic Perspectives* 12 (spring 1998): 117–126; "An American Tragedy: The Legacy of Slavery Lingers in our Cities' Ghettos," *Brookings Review* 16 (spring 1998): 38–43.

45. See the papers in the "wage inequality" symposium presented in the *Journal of Economic Perspectives* 11 (spring 1997), as well as the special issue of the *New England Econ. Rev.* (May/June 1996) entitled "Earnings Inequality: Spatial & Labor Market Contributions to Earnings Inequality." For a more recent report see I. Sawhill and D. McMurrer, *Getting Ahead: Economic & Social Mobility in America* (Washington, D.C.: Urban Institute Press, 1998).

46. Considerable anecdotal evidence exists to support this dismal assessment. See, for example, Moynihan's remembrances of New York City in the years of his youth compared to what he perceives today as New York's senior senator: Daniel P. Moynihan, "Toward a New Intolerance," *Public Interest* #112 (summer 1993): 119–122. And his is but one of many accounts arguing that a number of inner city school systems struggle today, too often unsuccessfully, to overcome the conditions of the streets and homes: an outcome clearly not helped by so many families removing their children from these schools, whether by moving to other school districts within the metropolitan region or by placing their children in private schools.

47. See: D. Ellwood, "The Spatial Mismatch Hypothesis: Are There Teenage Jobs Missing in the Ghetto?" in *The Black Youth Employment Crisis*, edited by R. Freeman & H. Holzer (Chicago: Univ. of Chicago Press, 1986); C. Jencks, *Rethinking Social Policy: Race, Poverty, & the Underclass* (Cambridge: Harvard Univ. Press, 1992); especially ch. 4, "The Ghetto"; L. Mead, *The New Politics of Poverty* (New York: Basic Books, 1992).

48. See: C. Rogers, "Job Search & Unemployment Duration: Implications for the Spatial Mismatch Hypothesis," *Journal of Urban Economics* 42 (July 1997): 109–132; H. Holzer, "Black Employment Problems: New Evidence, Old Questions," *Journal of Policy & Management* 13 (fall 1994): 699–722; K. Ihlanfeldt & M. Young, "Intrametropolitan Variation in Wage Rates: The Case of Atlanta Fast-Food Restaurant Workers," *Review of Economics & Statistics* LXXVI (August 1994): 425–33; H. Holzer, et al., "Work, Search, & Travel among White & Black Youth," *Journal of Urban Economics* 35 (May 1994): 320–345; J. Kain, "The Spatial Mismatch Hypothesis: Three Decades Later," *Housing Policy Debate* 3 (1992): 371–460.

49. In addition to the citations noted in the previous note we mention here more of the studies that lead us to this assessments: H. Holzer, *What Employers Want: Job*

Prospects for Less-Educated Workers (New York: Russell Sage Foundation, 1996); K. O'Regan and J. Quigley, "Teenage Employment & the Spatial Isolation of Minority & Poverty Households," *Journal of Human Resources* 31 (summer 1996): 692–702; K. Ihlanfeldt and M. Young, "The Spatial Distribution of Black Employment Between the Central City & the Suburbs," *Economic Inquiry* 34 (October 1996): 693–707. K. Ihlanfeldt, "Information on the Spatial Distribution of Job Opportunities within Metropolitan Areas," *Journal of Urban Economics* 41 (March 1997): 218–242; S. Raphael, "Inter- & Intra-Ethnic Comparisons of the Central City-Suburban Youth Employment Differential: Evidence from the Oakland Metropolitan Area," *Industrial & Labor Relations Rev.* 51 (April 1998): 505–524.

50. See Wilson's *When Work Disappears,* note 19 or section I above, where he finds evidence of this among employers of all races. See also P. Kasinitz and J. Rosenberg, "Missing the Connection: Social Isolation & Employment on the Brooklyn Waterfront," *Social Problems* 43 (May 1996): 170–197; and two working papers by H. Holzer: "Why Do Small Establishments Hire Fewer Blacks than Large Ones?" Institute for Research on Poverty, Discussion Paper #1119–97 (January 1997); and "Employer Hiring Decisions & Antidiscrimination Policy," Institute for Research on Poverty, Discussion Paper #1085–96 (April 1996).

51. See: K. Jackson, *Crabgrass Frontier: The Suburbanization of the United States* (New York: Oxford Univ. Press, 1985); J. Teaford, *City & Suburb: The Political Fragmentation of Metropolitan America, 1950–1970* (Baltimore: Johns Hopkins Univ. Press, 1979); S. Warner, Jr., *Streetcar Suburbs: The Process of Growth in Boston, 1870–1900* (Cambridge: Harvard & MIT Presses, 1962); R. Vernon, *The Myth & Reality of Our Urban Problems* (Cambridge: Harvard Univ. Press, 1966).

52. See M. Schill & S. Wachter, "The Spatial Bias of Federal Housing Programs," *Research Impact Paper #3* (Philadelphia: Wharton Real Estate Center, The Wharton School, Univ. of Pennsylvania, December 1994).

53. See E. Mills, "Non-Urban Policies as Urban Policies," *Urban Studies* 24 (December 1987): 561–69.

54. Charles Tiebout, "A Pure Theory of Local Expenditures," *Journal of Political Economy* 64 (October 1956): 418.

55. I am not aware of solid evidence of economic-class-based real-estate discrimination, but such evidence does exist for race-based discrimination. See J. Yinger, "Evidence on Discrimination in Consumer Markets," *Journal of Economic Perspectives* 12 (spring 1998): 23–40 and H. Ladd, "Evidence on Discrimination in Mortgage Lending," *Journal of Economic Perspectives* 12 (spring 1998): 41–62.

56. This process of non-poor flight has been observed by a number of others. Mills and Lubele, 734, dub it—somewhat inaccurately they note—the "flight-from-blight" model. See also P. Salins, "Cities, Suburbs, & the Urban Crisis," *The Public Interest* #113 (fall 1993): 91–104. For something of a counterview, see D. Bradford and W. Oates, "Suburban Exploitation of Central Cities & Governmental Structure" in H. Hochman/G. Peterson (eds.), *Redistribution through Public Choice* (New York: Columbia Univ. Press, 1974), pp. 43–90.

57. For a compelling case study of this, see J. Rabinovitz, "Fighting Poverty Programs: Hartford Faces Vote to Bar New Nonprofit Services," *New York Times,* 24 March 1996, A41.

58. Mills and Lubele, 137.

59. See C. Brown and W. Oates, "Assistance to the Poor in a Federal System," *Journal of Public Economics* 32 (April 1987): 307–330.

60. M. Porter, "The Competitive Advantage of the Inner City," *Harvard Business Rev.* 73 (May/June 1995): 55. For follow-up assessments of Porter's argument, see the articles in *The Review of Black Political Economy* 24 (fall/winter 1995), as well as Porter's "New Strategies for Inner City Economic Development," *Economic Development Quarterly* 11 (February 1997): 11–28.

61. "The inescapable fact is that businesses operating in the inner city face greater obstacles than those based elsewhere. Many of those obstacles are needlessly inflicted by government. Unless the disadvantages are addressed directly, instead of indirectly through subsidies or mandates, the inner city's competitive advantages will continue to erode." 62.

62. See "Rebuilding Inner City Communities: A New Approach to the Nation's Urban

Crisis," a statement by the Research & Policy Committee of the Committee for Economic Development, 1995.

63. See ninety-first American Assembly, "Community Capitalism: Rediscovering the Markets of America's Urban Neighborhoods," lifted from the web-site of the Brookings Institution at <http//www.brook.edu/es/urbancen/commune.htm>. See also a special issue of the *New England Econ. Rev.* (March/April 1997) on "The Effects of State & Local Public Policies on Economic Development," assessing what we do and don't know about strategies to revive our inner cities.

64. These initiatives are contemporary versions of a venerable tradition of organizing the residents of poor neighborhoods to gain some control over their communities. See "Heleneace & Human Capital," *Amer. Econ. Rev.* 74 (September 1984): 685–688.

65. A longstanding concern surrounding inner city investment has been the worry that lending agencies discriminate against certain geographic areas (drawing literal or figurative "red-lines" around such areas as guidelines in making loans). Sorting through whether in fact geographic regions are used in this way has not been an easy task. See in this regard G. Tootell, "Redlining in Boston: Do Mortgage Lenders Discriminate Against Neighborhoods,?" *Quarterly Journal of Economics* CXI (November 1996): 1049–1080.

66. In support of this cautious assessment see L. Papke, "What Do We Know about Enterprise Zones?" National Bureau of Economic Research Working Paper #4251 (January 1993); and P. Kasinitz and J. Rosenberg, "Why Enterprise Zones Will Not Work," *City Journal* 3 (autumn 1993): 63–69.

67. See: G. Loury and L. Loury, "Not by Bread Alone: The Role of the African-American Church in Inner city Development," *The Brookings Rev.* 15 (winter 1997): 10–13; J. Klein, "In God They Trust," *New Yorker*, 16 June 1997, 40–48; J. DiIulio, "In America's Cities: The Church & the 'Civil Society Sector,'" *The Brookings Rev.* 15 (fall 1997): 27–35.

68. See P. Boyer, *Urban Masses & Moral Order in America, 1820–1920* (Cambridge, Mass.: Harvard Univ. Press, 1978) and M. Olasky, *The Tragedy of American Compassion* (Wheaton, Ill.: Crossway Books, 1992).

69. N. Lemann, "The Myth of Community Development" *New York Times Magazine*, 9 January 1994, 28.

70. The best known of these is in Mt. Laurel, New Jersey (a community near Camden), which, after twenty-six years of legal entanglements, allowed the construction of 140 town houses for low- and moderate-income families in the spring of 1997.

71. See, for example, S. Popkin, et al., "Labor Market Experiences of Low-Income Black Women in Middle-Class Suburbs: Evidence from a Survey of Gautreaux Program Participants," *Journal of Policy Analysis & Management* 12 (summer 1993): 556–573. For a more cautionary assessment see X. Briggs, "Moving Up versus Moving Out: Neighborhood Effects in Housing Mobility Programs," *Housing Policy Debate* 8, #1 (1997): 195–234.

72. For the best current analysis of these programs see R. Blank, *It Takes a Nation: A New Agenda for Fighting Poverty* (Princeton, N.J.: Princeton Univ. Press, 1997). We plumb the biblical tradition to inform this issue in J. Mason, "Biblical Teaching & the Objectives of Welfare Policy in the U.S.," in *Welfare in America: Christian Perspectives on a Policy in Crisis*, edited by S. Carlson-Thies and J. Skillen (Grand Rapids, Mich.: Eerdmans Publishing Co., 1996), 145–185.

73. See H. Holzer and K. Ihlanfeldt, "Customer Discrimination & Employment Outcomes for Minority Workers," Institute for Research on Poverty, Discussion Paper #1122–97 (February 1997), where they present evidence that customer-based discrimination finds greatest expression among blacks and may be growing more important over time. See also Joseph Macariello's chapter in this volume concerning economic empowerment of the poor through targeted employment and management practices.

74. For an exception, see John DiIulio, "The Coming of the Super-Predators," *The Weekly Standard*, 27 November 1996, 23–28.

75. See G. Duncan, et al., *Years of Poverty, Years of Plenty: The Changing Fortunes of American Workers & Families* (Ann Arbor, Mich.: Univ. of Michigan Press, 1984), 26f.; J. Smith, "Race & Human Capital," *Amer. Econ. Rev.* 74 (September 1984): 685–688.

76. See C. Rouse, "Private School Vouchers & Student Achievement: An Evaluation of the Milwaukee Parental Choice Program," *Quarterly Journal of Economics* CXIII (May 1998): 553–602, and D. Neal, "Measuring Catholic School Performance," *The Public Interest* #127 (spring 1997): 81–87. See

M. Winerip, "Schools for Sale," *New York Times Magazine,* 14 June 1998, 42–49 for a more cautious assessment. See also the essay by Charles Glenn in this volume.

77. See his *New Visions for Metropolitan America* (Washington, D.C.: The Brookings Institution, 1994).

78. Several students of our metropolitan regions argue that suburban economic health turns directly on the economic health of the central city, such that attempts at regional cooperation can appeal to the self-interest of the suburban communities. See in this regard R. Voith, "Central City Decline: Regional or Neighborhood Solutions?" *Business Rev.,* publication of the Federal Reserve Bank of Philadelphia (March/April 1996): 3–16. We suspect the socioeconomic well-being of suburban communities is linked with that of the central city, but only in the long-term. The short-term relationship will represent costs and not benefits to the suburban communities.

79. See M. Orfield, *Metropolitics: A Regional Agenda for Community & Stability* (Washington, D.C.: Brookings Institution Press, 1997). See also A. Downs, 401ff.; K. Reardon, "State & Local Revitalization Efforts in East St. Louis, Illinois," *Annals, AAPSS* #551 (May 1997): 235–247.

80. In addition to the citations in note 4 of the introduction see D. Caraley, "Washington Abandons the Cities," *Political Science Quarterly* 107 (spring 1992): 1–30 and W. Duncombe and J. Yinger, "Why Is It So Hard to Help Central City Schools?" *Journal of Policy Analysis & Management* 16 (winter 1997): 85–113.

81. Mills and Lubele, 753. See also Kasarda, et al., "Central-City & Suburban Migration Patterns: Is a Turnaround on the Horizon?," *Housing Policy Debate,* 8, #2 (1997): 346.

82. Glaeser, 24.

83. A. Downs, 388.

84. Drawing on the labors for his *Theologische Ethik des Alten Testaments,* Eckart Otto writes: "I maintain that the text of the Hebrew Bible can still address our entire society and not solely the Christian or Jewish communities." Otto, "Of Aims & Methods in Hebrew Bible Ethics," *Semeia* 66 (1995): 161. Speaking of the (sapiential) teaching of Proverbs, he writes: "Where a certain action leads again and again to a positive or negative outcome, one could expect that there exists something like a structure. Sapiential ethics tries to recognize these structures, to adjust human actions to them, and so to lay ground for a positive and successful life. This kind of 'natural law' . . . is deeply theological. The structures ordering nature and society have their ontological basis in the creation of the world. Human beings possess knowledge of them not by revelation but by observation of the world. . . . Sapiential ethics aimed at an accord between the natural order and moral conduct because for the wise it was obvious that there was no other chance for a good life. In the final analysis, life cannot succeed against God's creation." Ibid., 167.

85. We are quite aware of the assertion that many of the pentateuchal provisions have counterparts in the law codes of other early Near Eastern societies—which for some observers suggest that these laws were not given by God through Moses, but were dictated by the ordinary circumstances of life in that region. We embrace the traditional view, that in ways which may not be clear to us today, God delivered through Moses at least the foundations for (Exodus 19 and 20), if not the totality of, all of the legal and extralegal provisions in the Pentateuch that were to instruct early Israel. Regarding this debate see E. Otto, "Town & Rural Countryside in Ancient Israelite Law: Reception & Redaction in Cuneiform & Israelite Law," *Journal for the Study of the Old Testament* 57 (March 1993): 3–22.

86. C.J.H. Wright, *God's People in God's Land: Family, Land, & Property in the Old Testament* (Grand Rapids, Mich.: Eerdmans Publishing Co., 1990), 175–176, xviii, respectively.

87. We borrow heavily here from two earlier attempts to systematize this material; see J. Mason, "Biblical Teaching & Assisting the Poor," *Transformation* 4 (April/June 1987): 1–14 and "Biblical Teaching & the Objectives of Welfare Policy in the U.S.," in *Welfare in America: Christian Perspectives on a Policy in Crisis,* edited by S. Carlson-Thies and J. Skillen (Grand Rapids: Eerdmans Publishing Co., 1996), 145–185.

88. Gottwald describes early Israel as ". . . an egalitarian, extended-family, segmentary tribal society with an agricultural-pastoral economic base." N. Gottwald, *Tribes of Yahweh* (Maryknoll, N.Y.: Orbis Books, 1979), 389.

89. Ibid., ch. 28.

90. In addition to Gottwald's account see: C. H. J. DeGeus, *Tribes of Israel* (Amsterdam: Van Gorcum, 1976); L. Stager, "The Archaeology of the Family in Ancient Israel" *Bulletin of the Amer. Schools of Oriental Research* 260 (1985): 1–35; D. Hopkins, "Life on the Land: The Subsistence Struggles of Early Israel," *Biblical Archaeologist* 50 (1987): 178–191.

91. Ibid., 144.

92. Wolff gives the number twenty and Gottwald, fifty. See H. Wolff, *Anthropology of the Old Testament* (Philadelphia: Fortress Press, 1976), 215; Gottwald, 267ff.

93. Though the larger share of the output would have been consumed by the *beth'ab* producing it, the existence of laws regulating market activity (Lev. 19:35f.) attests to some exchange of goods and services. Israel was located on the main trading route between Egypt and nations to the north and east, and market activity beyond subsistence farming would have developed early in the history of this general region of the world.

94. See Ruth 4:1ff., where Boaz convenes with other elders at the town gate to transact legal proceedings. A number of studies have established that the "elders at the gate" provided political oversight of the community and handled any disputes. See in this regard: R. Wilson, "Enforcing the Covenant: The Mechanisms of Judicial Authority in Early Israel," in *The Quest for the Kingdom of God*, edited by H. Huffmon, et al. (Winona Lake, Ind.: Eisenbrauns, 1983), 59–75; H. Boecker, *Law & the Administration of Justice in the Old Testament & Ancient East* (Minneapolis: Augsburg Publishing House, 1980).

95. We see no other way to interpret 1 Samuel 8; an earthly kingship was not God's preference for Israel. See in this regard R. Hendel, "The Social Origins of the Aniconic Tradition in Early Israel," *Catholic Biblical Quarterly* 50 (July 1988): 365–382. In opposition to this view, see D. Howard, "The Case for Kingship in Deuteronomy & the Former Prophets," *Westminster Theol. Jrnl.* 52 (1990): 101–115.

96. See in this regard M. Greenberg, "Biblical Attitudes toward Power: Ideal & Reality in Law & Prophets," in *Religion & Law: Biblical-Judaic & Islamic Perspectives*, edited by E. Firmage, et al. (Winona Lake, Ind.: Eisenbrauns, 1990), 102–125.

97. The compelling story of Ruth offers us a number of examples of how the less vulnerable should provide special care for the more vulnerable.

98. From the textual account (Deut. 14:28–29—"store in your towns"), along with the application of this teaching in Jewish communities, it seems more than likely that the administration of the third-year tithe involved local governmental oversight of the produce submitted. See M. Katz, *Protection of the Weak in the Talmud* (New York: Columbia Univ. Press, 1925) and A. Levine, *Free Enterprise & Jewish Law* (New York: KTAV Publishing House, Yeshiva Univ. Press, 1980), especially ch. 9 on "The Role of Government in the Free Enterprise Economy."

99. The narrative both compels and troubles me, so much so that I sought systematically to explore it; see J. Mason, "Centralization & Decentralization in Social Arrangements: Explorations into Biblical Social Ethics," *Journal of the Association of Christian Economists* (U.K.) #13 (fall 1992): 3–47.

100. We have summarized this standard as follows: "Assistance to the poor was intended to maintain each family unit as an economically viable and contributing component of the community, such that the family would have the confidence that if it worked as fully as it should, and otherwise remained a faithful member of the community, then the community would not allow economic difficulties to debilitate the family so that it could not continue to be viable and contributing." See Mason, ". . . Assisting the Poor," 8.

101. F. Frick, *The City in Ancient Israel* (Missoula, Mont.: Scholars Press, 1977); V. Fritz, *The City in Ancient Israel* (Sheffield, England: Sheffield Academic Press, 1995).

102. Gottwald, 253.

103. Frick, 29, 32, 39.

104. Ibid., 58.

105. Ibid., 16f. and p. 13 here.

106. Ibid., 81.

107. Ibid., 95.

108. Fritz, 51.

109. Frick does allow for greater social differentiation in the cities of the monarchies, especially as Canaanite cities are absorbed into Israel. Even so, the Israelite cities did not know the levels of social differentiation found elsewhere. See Frick, especially around p. 99.

110. Fritz, 53 and 55f.; the two sites noted are Tell Qiri and Ai.

111. Ibid., 84 re Kinneret, and 93 re Megiddo.

112. Ibid., 176.

113. Ibid., 183.

114. The content of these last two paragraphs has been informed primarily by the valuable studies of Hopkins and Stager.

115. H. Williamson, *Ezra-Nehemiah* (Waco, Tex.: Word Books, 1985), 202.

116. Frick, 92.

117. The picture we gather from the biblical documents is of a form of justice and local governmental administration far more popular than what has evolved in most countries in the modern era. The elder/heads of the city or village *beth'avoth* would convene near the main city gate and engage the issue before them in the presence of other citizens gathered there, with give and take among the elders and others.

118. For a much darker theological view of the city, see J. Ellul, *The Meaning of the City* (Grand Rapids, Mich.: Eerdmans Publishing Co., 1970).

119. An additional example to that of Nehemiah is the watchman of Ezekiel's chapters 3 and 33, who is commanded to read the signs of the times and then warn the people of the dangers faced by pursuing present paths.

120. R. Goodin, *Protecting the Vulnerable* (Chicago: Univ. of Chicago Press, 1985), 44.

121. See A. Ryan, "Liberalism" in *A Companion to Contemporary Political Philosophy,* edited by R. Goodin and P. Tettit (Cambridge, Mass.: Blackwell, 1995), 291–311.

Chapter 12: *Organizing the Poor*

1. My thanks go to members of Christians Supporting Community Organizing network for their assistance on this project, especially to Marilyn Stranske, Mike Miller, and Robert Linthicum. I owe a special debt to Mike Miller, Kim Bobo, and Tom Lenz for their review of this manuscript, and to my student assistants, Beth DenBleyker and Nicole Woodward. Thanks to all of you!

2. Robert Linthicum, *Empowering the Poor: Community Organizing Among the City's 'Rag, Tag, and Bobtail'* (Monrovia, Calif.: MARC, a division of World Vision International, 1991), 25.

3. Rebecca Blank, *It Takes a Nation: A New Agenda for Fighting Poverty* (Princeton, N.J.: Princeton University Press, 1997), 56.

4. Dean Baker and Lawrence Mishel, "Profits Up, Wages Down, Workers' Losses Yield Big Gains for Business" (Washington Economic Policy Institute, 1995), *http://epn .org/epi/eppuwd/html.*

5. "Poverty Deepening in the United States: Children and the Elderly Hit the Hardest," *Human Development Report, 1997* (Press release from the United Nations Development Programme, 12 June 1997).

6. Jacob M. Schlesinger, "U.S. Economy Shows Foreign Nations Ways to Grow Much Faster," *The Wall Street Journal,* 6/19/97, A1.

7. Margery Austin Turner, Michael Fix, and Raymond J. Struyk, *Opportunities Denied, Opportunities Diminished* (Washington: Urban Institute, 1991), 9.

8. William Julius Wilson. *When Work Disappears: The World of the New Urban Poor* (New York: Alfred A. Knopf, 1996), 14.

9. Peter Edelman, speech at the Hull House Association Board Retreat, Chicago, Ill., 10 January 1998.

10. Bill Powell, "Days of Rage in Paris," *Newsweek,* 11 December 1995, 51.

11. Personal interview with Madeleine Talbott, Director of ACORN in Chicago, 1 July 1998.

12. Nina Wallerstein, "Powerlessness, Empowerment, and Health: Implications for Health Promotion Programs," *American Journal of Health Promotion* 6, no. 3 (Jan./Feb. 1992): 198.

13. Martin Luther King, *Why We Can't Wait* (New York: Harper & Row, 1964), 27–40.

14. William Schneider, "The Suburban Century Begins," *The Atlantic Monthly,* July 1992, 33.

15. It should be noted that there are some exceptions to this: the early CIO in the 1930s, which influenced the National Labor Relations Act, SNCC's work in the South, which led to voting rights legislation; and the National Welfare Rights Organization of the early 1970s.

16. Michael Lipsky, "Protest as a Political Resource," *American Political Science Review,* 62 (December 1968): 1144–1158.

17. Thomas Aquinas, *On Politics and Ethics* (New York: W.W. Norton, 1988), 15.

18. For a more detailed discussion of power and justice see Paul Tillich, *Love,*

Power, and Justice (Oxford: Oxford University Press, 1954).

19. All quotes from the Bible are drawn from the New Living Translation.

20. Howard Thurman, *Jesus and the Disinherited* (Boston, Mass.: Beacon Press, 1996), 17.

21. Albert Nolan, *Jesus Before Christianity* (Maryknoll, N.Y.: Orbis Books, 1992), 40.

22. Shelby Steele, *The Content of Our Character* (New York: St. Martin's Press, 1988), 15.

23. Barbara Leslie Epstein, *The Politics of Domesticity, Women, Evangelism, and Temperance in Nineteenth Century America* (Middletown, Conn.: Wesleyan University Press, 1981), 25.

24. Ibid.

25. Ibid., 68–9.

26. George Marsden, *Understanding Fundamentalism and Evangelicalism* (Grand Rapids, Mich.: William Eerdmans Publishing Co., 1994), 27–29.

27. Ibid., 30.

28. Bob Lupton, Peggy Lupton, and Gloria Yancey, "Relocation: Living in the Community," in *Restoring at Risk Communities*, edited by John Perkins (Grand Rapids, Mich.: Baker Book House, 1995), 82.

29. Linthicum, *Empowering the Poor*, 23.

30. Personal interview with Mike Miller, 5 January 1998.

31. Barack Obama, "Why Organize/Problems and Promise in the Inner City," in *After Alinsky: Community Organizing in Illinois*, edited by Peg Knoepfle (Springfield Ill.: Illinois Issues, 1990), 38.

32. Linthicum, *Empowering the Poor*, 23.

33. Ibid., 211.

34. See Taylor Branch, *A Pillar of Fire: America in the King Years, 1963–65* (New York: Simon & Schuster, 1998) for a description of these organizing efforts.

35. Personal interview with Greg Galluzo, 6 May 1998.

36. William Droel, "Community Organizing—Empowerment for Human Rights," *Blueprint for Social Justice*, Vol. LI, no. 2, (October 1997).

37. Personal interview with Father Michael Jacques of Saint Peter Claver Church, New Orleans, 25 June 1998.

38. Pacific Institute for Community Organizations, *Reweaving the Fabric of America's Communities*, PICO 25th Anniversary book, (1997), 20.

39. Personal interview with Father Michael Jacques, 25 June 1998.

40. Steven Kloehn, "Activists Powered by Faith, Not Plans," *Chicago Tribune*, 20 October 1997.

41. Personal Interview with Reverend Dennis Jacobson, pastor of Incarnation Lutheran Church, Milwaukee, 26 May 1998.

42. Ed Chambers, speech at the Hillenbrand lecture, Chicago, 22 May 1998.

43. Industrial Areas Foundation, *IAF: 50 Years Organizing for Change*, 1990, 17.

44. Personal interview with Ed Chambers, Executive Director of the Industrial Areas Foundation, 8 June 1998.

45. Industrial Areas Foundation, *Organizing for Family and Congregation*, 1978, 22–23.

46. David Moberg, "All Together Now," *The Reader*, 10/17/97, 20.

47. Personal interview with Dennis Jacobson, 26 May 1998.

48. Personal interview with Reverend Joseph Ellwanger, Cross Lutheran Church, 26 May 1998.

49. PICO, *Reweaving the Fabric*.

50. Christians Supporting Community Organizing, "A Proclamation and Call to Our Churches" (Denver, Colo.: CSCO, 1997).

51. Personal interview with Johnnie Ray Youngblood, pastor of St. Paul Community Church, East Brooklyn, New York, 21 May 1998.

52. Ibid.

53. Samuel G. Freedman, *Upon This Rock: The Miracles of a Black Church* (New York: Harper Collins, 1993), 334.

54. Ibid., 338.

55. Personal interview with Johnnie Ray Youngblood, 21 May 1998.

56. Personal interview with Jonathan Lange, BUILD organizer, 29 June 1998.

57. http://www.cpn.org/sections/topics/community/stories/e_brooklyn.html, 18.

58. Ibid.

59. http://www.cpn.org/sections/topics/religion/religion.html, 2.

60. http://www.cpn.org/sections/topics/you...es-studies/baltimore_commonwealth.html

61. Mike Miller, notes from a presentation by Jonathan Lange at the Campaign for

Human development twenty-fifth anniversary, 26 August 1995.

62. Personal interview with Jonathan Lange, 29 June 1998.

63. Ibid.

64. Mike Miller notes, 26 August 1995.

65. Personal interview with Jonathan Lange, 29 June 1998.

66. Mike Miller notes, 26 August 1995.

67. Personal interview with Jonathan Lange, 29 June 1998.

68. New Orleans Sponsoring Committee, *All Congregations Together (ACT): 1997 Annual Report.*

69. Gregg Soll and Fritz Wagner, "The Role of Faith-Based Organizations in Improving the Quality of Life of Cities: The New Orleans Experience," (Paper presented at the annual meeting of the Association of Collegiate Schools of Planning, Ft. Lauderdale, Fla., No.v 6–9, 1997), 9.

70. Personal interview with Father Michael Jacques, S.S.E., pastor of St. Peter Clavers Church, 26 June 1998.

71. Ibid.

72. Gregg Soll and Fritz Wagner, "The Role of Faith-Based Organizations in Improving the Quality of Life of Cities: The New Orleans Experience," 11.

73. Personal interview with Father Michael Jacques, S.S.E., 26 June 1998.

74. Gregg Soll and Fritz Wagner, "The Role of Faith-Based Organizations in Improving the Quality of Life of Cities: The New Orleans Experience," 10.

75. Personal interview with Father Michael Jacques, 26 June 1998.

76. Personal interview with Reverend Ellwanger.

77. Personal interview with Reverend Dennis Jacobson.

78. Personal interview with Reverend Ellwanger.

79. Ibid.

80. Personal interview with Reverend Dennis Jacobson.

81. Personal interview with John Donahue, Executive Director of the Chicago Coalition for the Homeless, 23 June 1998.

82. Ibid.

83. Personal interview with Madeleine Talbott, Director of ACORN Chicago chapter, 1 July 1998.

84. Jack Newfield, "Rivera Rules," *Tikkun,* 6, no. 12 (November/December 1997).

85. Christian Tenbrock, "Dreaming of Joe Hill," *Die Zeit,* 16 August 1996; reprinted, in English, in the *World Press Review,* December 1996.

86. Jack Newfield, "Rivera Rules."

87. Steven Greenhouse, "Deeper Shade of Blue Collar: Unions Concentrating on the Lower Rungs of the Economic Ladder" *New York Times,* 10 August 1997, Sec. 1, 26.

88. Sara Mosley, "At Hotel-Casino, Triumphant Shouts of 'Union,'" *New York Times,* 5 February 1998, A12.

89. Steven Greenhouse, "Deeper Shade of Blue Collar."

90. Personal interview with Kim Bobo, Director of the National Interfaith Committee for Worker Justice, 7 May 1998.

91. Ibid.

92. Personal interview with Reverend Peter Laarmann, pastor of Judson Memorial Church, 19 May 1998.

Chapter 13: *Business and Empowerment*

1. This idea has been treated extensively by both Max Weber and Michael Novak. See Max Weber, *The Protestant Ethic and the Spirit of Capitalism,* trans. Talcott Parsons (New York: Charles Scribner's Sons, 1958); Michael Novak, *The Spirit of Democratic Capitalism* (New York: Simon and Schuster, 1982); and Michael Novak, *The Catholic Ethic and the Spirit of Capitalism* (New York: Free Press, 1993).

2. Richard John Neuhaus, *Doing Well & Doing Good* (New York: Doubleday, 1992), 5–6.

3. Psalm 8:4–6. All scriptural quotations are taken from the New Revised Standard Version.

4. C.S. Lewis, *Mere Christianity* (New York: Macmillan Publishing Company, 1952), 79.

5. From correspondence with the author in 1995. See also Pollard's expression of his views on management in C. W. Pollard, *The Soul of the Firm* (Grand Rapids: Harper Business, 1996). In much the same vein, Kenneth Lay, Chairman and Chief Executive Officer of Enron Corporation, states: "I was and am a strong believer that one of the most satisfying things in life is to create a highly moral and ethical environment in which every individual is allowed to reach their God-given potential. There are few things more satisfying than to see individuals reach levels of performance

that they would have thought was virtually impossible for themselves." Quoted in Michael Novak, *Business as a Calling* (New York: Free Press, 1996), 22.

6. In addition to the direct biblical texts, the following four sources have been instrumental in my thinking about the development of godly qualities in humankind at work: J.I. Packer, *Knowing Man* (New York: Cornerstone Books, 1978); Michael Novak, *The Spirit of Democratic Capitalism* (New York: Simon and Schuster, 1981); R.C. Sproul, *In Search of Significance* (New York: Regal Books, 1991); and Michael Novak, *Business as a Calling* (New York: The Free Press, 1996).

7. Lester C. Thurow, "Companies Merge; Families Break Up," *New York Times*, 3 September 1995, Sec. 4, p. 11.

8. Joseph A. Schumpeter, *Capitalism, Socialism and Democracy* (New York: Harper and Row Publishers, 1950), 82–83.

9. An excellent source of material on management succession is Richard F. Vancil, *Passing the Baton: Managing the Process of CEO Succession* (Boston, Mass.: Harvard Business School Press, 1987).

10. Douglas McGregor, *The Human Side of Enterprise* (New York: McGraw-Hill, 1960).

11. Here I cite three prominent secular authors and three works which, in whole or in part, support the view of human nature contained in the Bible: Chester I. Barnard, *The Functions of the Executive* (Cambridge, Mass.: Harvard University Press, 1938); Peter F. Drucker, *The Practice of Management* (New York: Harper and Row Publishers, 1954); and Douglas McGregor, *The Human Side of Enterprise* (New York: McGraw Hill, 1960).

12. Michael Novak, *The Spirit of Democratic Capitalism* (New York: Simon and Schuster, 1982), 16, 186.

13. This section, and especially exhibits 2 and 3, reflect the overall approach to the design of management systems taken in Joseph A. Maciariello and Calvin J. Kirby, *Management Control Systems: Using Adaptive Systems to Attain Control* (Englewood Cliffs, N.J.: Prentice-Hall, 1994). The general approach is repeated in Calvin J. Kirby and Joseph A. Maciariello, "Integrated Product Development and Adaptive Management Systems," *Drucker Management* (fall 1994); in Joseph A. Maciariello, "Management Systems at ServiceMaster: A Theocentric Approach," *Drucker Management* (spring 1996); and in

"Management Systems at Lincoln Electric: A Century of Agility," *Journal of Agility and Global Competition* 1, no. 4 (November 1997): 46–61.

14. Chester I. Barnard, *The Functions of the Executive* (Cambridge, Mass.: Harvard University Press, 1938), 115.

15. See footnote 13 for numerous references regarding the detailed design of management systems.

16. See Matthew 18:1–4, especially verse 4; 20:20–28, esp. 25–28, 23:1–12, esp. 11–12; Mark 10:35–45, esp. 42–45; Luke 9:46–48; 22:24–27, esp. 26–27; John 5:19–20; 13:1–17, esp. 14–17; Philippians 2:3–11, esp. verse 7. An example of the opposite of servant leadership is 3 John 9–10.

17. Mark 10:42–45.

18. This list of attributes of servant leaders draws on Charles R. Swindoll, *Improving Your Serve* (Waco, Tex.: Word Books, 1981).

19. Peter Senge, *The Fifth Discipline* (New York: Doubleday/Currency, 1990).

20. Peter Senge, et al., *The Fifth Discipline Fieldbook* (New York: Doubleday/Currency, 1994).

21. I would like to thank the following people for their assistance on the following section: Bill Pollard, chairman of The ServiceMaster Company, and many members of his team; Richard S. Sabo, long-time assistant to the chief executive officer at Lincoln Electric Company; J. Kermit Campbell, former chief executive officer and chairman of Herman Miller, Inc.; Paul Doyle, manager of organizational development and training at Donnelly Corporation; and William Raymond, executive director of Good Samaritan Ministries.

22. ServiceMaster refers to their four overall values as objectives. Because these objectives form the basis of the culture of ServiceMaster, and because this chapter is interested in tracing the influence of the culture of an organization upon the design of its management systems, I shall treat these objectives as values. In the models presented here, values serve two purposes: they influence the behavior of the members of the organization and they become variables whose status we seek to assess periodically within the management systems. Values thus define the culture and become objectives whose status we seek to assess. So for the purposes of the discussion of the ServiceMaster example, this analysis

will use the terms "objectives" and "values" interchangeably.

23. *1997 Annual Report, The ServiceMaster Company* (Downers Grove, Ill.: The ServiceMaster Company, March 1998), 3.

24. Drug screening is conducted for all new recruits. In addition, random screening of all service workers is conducted continuously.

25. Robert Greenleaf, *Servant Leadership* (New York: Paulist Press, 1977), 13–14.

26. *1997 Annual Report,* The ServiceMaster Company, 2.

27. The management systems at Lincoln Electric are described in detail by the author in "Management Systems at Lincoln Electric: A Century of Agility," *Journal of Agility and Global Competition,* I, no. 4 (November 1997): 46–61.

28. James F. Lincoln, *A New Approach to Industrial Economics* (New York: The Devon-Adir Company, 1961).

29. Matthew 7:12.

30. In order to organize these management systems issues, each of the seven issues is followed by a citation of where each issue is classified within the management systems of the company, according to the classifications in figures 2 and 3 of the chapter.

31. This diagram is practically identical to figure 13 on page 132 of *Changing Forever: The Well-Kept Secret of America's Leading Companies,* by Carl F. Frost (East Lansing, Mich.: Michigan State University Press, 1996). It is adapted and used here by permission of Carl F. Frost.

32. As in the Lincoln Electric example, each of the seven principles and processes is followed by a citation of where it is classified within the management systems of the company, according to the classifications in figures 3 and 4 of the chapter.

33. Taken from the homepage of the Herman Miller, Inc. website, <http://www.hermanmiller.com/>.

34. *A Different Kind of Company* (Zeeland, Mich.: Herman Miller, Inc., 1997).

35. Max DePree has written three books in which he describes aspects of the values and management systems which have guided the growth and development of Herman Miller. These books are: *Leadership Is an Art* (New York: Bantam Doubleday Dell Publishing Group, Inc., 1989); *Leadership Jazz* (New York: Bantam Doubleday Dell Publishing

Group, Inc., 1992); and *Leading Without Power* (San Francisco: Jossey-Bass Publishers, 1997).

36. J. Kermit Campbell, "Changing the Meaning of Management," *Drucker Management* (fall 1994): 7.

37. The revised edition of Robert Levering and Milton Moskowitz, *The 100 Best Companies to Work for in America* (New York: Penguin Group, 1993), lists Donnelly Corporation as one of the ten best companies to work for in America. Lincoln Electric and Herman Miller also made their list of the hundred best companies to work for in America.

38. Paul Doyle and Carol Kaplan, "The Greatest Reward for a Person's Work" (paper presented at the Work in America Institute, New York, September 12, 1997), 4, 5.

39. Robert J. Doyle, "The Legacy of John F. Donnelly" (address delivered at the College of Business Administration, University of Notre Dame, Notre Dame, Indiana, October 4, 1996), 11, 12, and 5. Quoted by permission.

40. Changes in the composition of work and the growing importance of knowledge are the principal themes of two recent and important books: Peter Drucker, *The Post-Capitalist Society* (New York: HarperCollins, 1993), and Robert B. Reich, *The Work of Nations* (New York: Vintage Books, Random House, 1992).

41. B.F. Skinner, *Beyond Freedom and Dignity* (New York: A. Knopf. Inc., 1971).

42. R.C. Sproul, *In Search of Significance* (New York: Regal Books, 1991), 17.

43. Pope John Paul II, *Centesimus Annus* (May 1, 1991, social encyclical on the 100th Anniversary of *Rerum Novarum*).

44. Jonathan Boswell, *Community and the Economy: The Theory of Public Cooperation* (London: Routledge, 1990), 201, quoted in Robert N. Bellah, et al., *Habits of the Heart Updated Edition* (Berkeley, Calif.: University of California Press, 1996), xxix.

45. Rosabeth Moss Kanter, "Upsize, Downsize," *The New York Times,* 27 September 1995.

46. William Raymond, in a personal communication with the author on April 9, 1998, reports that he and his staff at Good Samaritan Ministries have had "conversations with people working in urban areas around the United States—and there is a hopefulness [in these cities] that often belies

the seemingly insurmountable problems" that currently exist.

Chapter 14: *Transforming American Welfare*

1. Pope John Paul II, *Centesimus Annus*, para. 34, as reprinted in George Weigel, ed., *A New Worldly Order: John Paul II and Human Freedom* (Washington, D.C.: Ethics and Public Policy Center, 1992), 45.

2. Amy L. Sherman, "Establishing A Church-based Welfare-to-Work Mentoring Ministry: A Practical 'How-To' Manual" (MS, available from Trinity Presbyterian Church-Urban Ministry, Charlottesville, Virginia, n.d. [1998]), 2. A helpful compilation of the verses is Ronald J. Sider, ed., *Cry Justice: The Bible Speaks on Hunger & Poverty* (Downers Grove, Ill.: InterVarsity, 1980).

3. John D. Mason, "Biblical Teaching and the Objectives of Welfare Policy in the United States," in *Welfare in America: Christian Perspectives on a Policy in Crisis*, edited by Stanley W. Carlson-Thies and James W. Skillen (Grand Rapids, Mich.: Eerdmans, 1996), 159–60.

4. See "A New Vision for Welfare Reform," reprinted as the appendix to Carlson-Thies and Skillen, eds., *Welfare in America*.

5. Mason, "Biblical Teaching," 160–61.

6. See Mason, "Biblical Teaching," and Luis Lugo, *Equal Partners: The Welfare Responsibility of Governments & Churches* (Washington, D.C.: Center for Public Justice, 1998).

7. On the importance of a governmental role, see Mason, "Biblical Teaching"; Lugo, *Equal Partners;* Stephen Charles Mott, "Foundations of the Welfare Responsibility of the Government," in *Welfare in America*, edited by Carlson-Thies and Skillen, 186–208; and Stanley Carlson-Thies, "Welfare Reform's Challenge to the Evangelical Church," in the book resulting from the conference, "Christian Faith & Public Policy: Where Do We Go From Here?" (Union University, October 1998).

8. Quoted in Mott, "Foundations of the Welfare Responsibility," 193–94.

9. "New Vision for Welfare Reform," 577.

10. "New Vision for Welfare Reform," 578.

11. See, e.g., Charles Noble, *Welfare As We Knew It: A Political History of the American Welfare State* (New York: Oxford Univ. Press, 1997), 7–10.

12. See, e.g., Lester M. Salamon and Helmut K. Anheier, *The Emerging Nonprofit Sector: An Overview* (Manchester: Manchester Univ. Press, 1996).

13. Marvin Olasky, *The Tragedy of American Compassion* (Washington, D.C.: Regnery Gateway, 1992); James L. Payne, *Overcoming Welfare: Expecting More from the Poor—and from Ourselves* (New York: Basic Books, 1998).

14. Olasky notes some of these trends in his *Tragedy of American Compassion*. See also John Mason's critique of Olasky's account, in Mason, "Biblical Teaching," 181–85; and Paul Boyer, *Urban Masses and Moral Order in America, 1820–1920* (Cambridge: Harvard Univ. Press, 1992).

15. For a summary of the New Deal innovations, see Robert H. Bremner, "The New Deal and Social Welfare," in *Fifty Years Later: The New Deal Evaluated*, edited by Harvard Sitkoff (New York: Alfred A. Knopf, 1985), 69–92. On the New Deal period and later, see, e.g., James T. Patterson, *America's Struggle Against Poverty, 1900–1985* (Cambridge: Harvard Univ. Press, 1986); Noble, *Welfare As We Knew It;* and Robert Morris and John E. Hansan, "A Decade-Long Drift to Public 'Conservatism' Redefining the Federal Roles in Social Welfare: Anticipating the Future and Preparing for It," in *The National Government and Social Welfare: What Should Be the Federal Role?* edited by John E. Hansan and Robert Morris (Westport, Conn.: Auburn House, 1997), 1–16.

16. Gareth Davies argues that the no-questions asked, entitlement concept was an aberration in the Great Society idea; see his *From Opportunity to Entitlement: The Transformation and Decline of Great Society Liberalism* (Lawrence: Univ. Press of Kansas, 1996). For a more critical view of Great Society welfare ideas, see Lawrence M. Mead, *Beyond Entitlement: The Social Obligations of Citizenship* (New York: Free Press, 1986).

17. See Steven Rathgeb Smith and Michael Lipsky, *Nonprofits for Hire: The Welfare State in the Age of Contracting* (Cambridge: Harvard Univ. Press, 1993).

18. Mary Jo Bane and David T. Ellwood, *Welfare Realities: From Rhetoric to Reform* (Cambridge: Harvard Univ. Press, 1994).

19. Bremner, "New Deal and Social Welfare," 69ff.

20. Mead, *Beyond Entitlement;* Lawrence M. Mead, *The New Politics of Poverty:*

The Nonworking Poor in America (New York: Basic Books, 1992).

21. For summaries, see *Congressional Quarterly 1996 Almanac* (Washington, D.C.: Congressional Quarterly, 1997), 6–13 to 6–21; *Congressional Quarterly 1997 Almanac* (Washington, D.C.: Congressional Quarterly, 1998), 2–57 to 2–58, 6–31 to 6–36; Anne Marie Cammisa, *From Rhetoric to Reform? Welfare Policy in American Politics* (Boulder, Colo.: Westview Press, 1998).

22. United States General Accounting Office, *Welfare Reform: States Are Restructuring Programs to Reduce Welfare Dependence*, GAO/HEHS-98-109 (Washington, D.C.: GAO, June 1998).

23. Lawrence M. Mead, "Welfare Employment," in *The New Paternalism: Supervisory Approaches to Poverty*, edited by Lawrence M. Mead (Washington, D.C.: Brookings Institution Press, 1997), 61–63.

24. See, e.g., Government Accounting Office, *Welfare Reform.*

25. For a detailed explanation of the provision, see *A Guide to Charitable Choice: The Rules of Section 104 of the 1996 Federal Welfare Law Governing State Cooperation with Faith-based Social-Service Providers* (Washington, D.C.: Center for Public Justice, and Annandale, Va: Center for Law and Religious Freedom of the Christian Legal Society, January 1997). On the significance of the provision, see Stanley W. Carlson-Thies, "Faith-based Institutions Cooperating with Public Welfare: The Promise of the Charitable Choice Provision, " in *Welfare Reform and Faith-based Organizations*, edited by Derek H. Davis (Waco, Texas: J. M. Dawson Institute of Church-State Studies, Baylor University, forthcoming). For a quick introduction to the provision and to the controversy over it, see Stanley W. Carlson-Thies and Melissa Rogers, "Charitable Choice: Two Views," *Sojourners* 27, no. 4 (July/August 1998): 28–30.

26. Government Accounting Office, *Welfare Reform;* Richard P. Nathan and Thomas L. Gais, "Overview Report: Implementation of the Personal Responsibility Act of 1996," Federalism Research Group of the Rockefeller Institute of Government, State University of New York (accessed at http://rockinst.org/appam.html on 28 October 1998.

27. William Julius Wilson, *When Work Disappears: The World of the New Urban Poor* (New York: Alfred A. Knopf, 1996).

28. For an eloquent statement, see Lugo, *Equal Partners* .

29. Sheila Zedlewski, et al., "Potential Effects of Congressional Welfare Reform Legislation on Family Incomes," The Urban Institute, 26 July 1996.

30. See, e.g., LaDonna Pavetti, "New Welfare Reform: One Size Fits All?" *Forum for Applied Research and Public Policy* 12, no. 4 (winter 1997): 20.

31. On the Community-Directed Assistance Program, see Amy L. Sherman, *Fruitful Collaboration between Government and Christian Social Ministries: Lessons from Virginia and Maryland* (Washington, D.C.: Center for Public Justice, January 1998).

32. Julie Strawn, "Beyond Job Search or Basic Education: Rethinking the Role of Skills in Welfare Reform," *Policy & Practice* 56, no. 2 (August 1998): 48–55; Mark Elliott, Don Spangler, and Kathy Yorkievitz, *What's Next After Work First*, Field Report series (Philadelphia: Public/Private Ventures, 1998).

33. Mead, "Welfare Employment," 57f.

34. Elliott, et al., "What's Next," 12ff.

35. Stacey Hawkins Adams, "Welfare Reform Still Challenge, Report Says; Some Who Leave System Still Needy," *Richmond Times Dispatch*, 15 December 1998, p. B-1 (accessed via Lexis-Nexis, 18 December 1998).

36. Strawn, "Beyond Job Search," 50.

37. Pavetti, "New Welfare Reform," 20.

38. Ronald B. Mincy and Hillard Pouncy, "Paternalism, Child Support Enforcement, and Fragile Families," in Mead, ed., *The New Paternalism*, 130–160. See also "Reinvesting Welfare Savings: Aiding Needy Families and Strengthening State Welfare Reform," Center on Budget and Public Priorities (30 March 1998), 10–11.

39. Bruce Katz and Kate Carnevale, "The State of Welfare Caseloads in America's Cities," Brookings Institution Center on Urban and Metropolitan Policy (May 1998), Appendix A.

40. On "address discrimination," see Joleen Kirschenman and Kathryn M. Neckerman, "'We'd Love to Hire Them, But . . . : The Meaning of Race for Employers," in *The Urban Underclass*, edited by Christopher

Jencks and Paul E. Peterson (Washington, D.C.: Brookings Institution, 1991), 203–32.

41. Katz and Carnevale, "State of Welfare Caseloads."

42. One particularly creative approach to revitalizing cities to create new opportunities for the poor is the American Community Renewal Act promoted in the House of Representatives by J. C. Watts (R-Oklahoma) and Jim Talent (R-Missouri). Although introduced with significant support in both the 104th and 105th Congresses, it has never been made a sufficiently high priority by the Republican leadership to make headway.

43. Jason DeParle, "Wisconsin Welfare Experiment: Easy to Say, Not So Easy to Do," *New York Times*, 18 October 1998, A1.

44. Elaine M. Ryan, "The Unfinished Agenda: Two Years after TANF," *Policy & Practice* 56, no. 3 (December 1998): 9f.

45. See, e.g., "A Conversation with Ron Haskins," *Policy & Practice* 56, no. 2 (August 1998): 36–46.

46. In late 1998 officials in both Pennsylvania and Maryland, for instance, proclaimed that as long as the families had fulfilled their part of the bargain, they would not be cut off the rolls even if they went past the two-year limit without securing employment or being in approved "work activities."

47. Technically there never was an individual entitlement to federal/state assistance, but AFDC functioned as a federal guarantee of aid in the case of families with dependent children.

48. Paul Marshall, "Rights Talk and Welfare Policy," in *Welfare in America*, edited by Carlson-Thies and Skillen, 290. See also Mary Ann Glendon, "What's Wrong with Welfare Rights?" in the same volume.

49. See Mead, *Beyond Entitlement*.

50. Cori E. Uccello and L. Jerome Gallagher, "General Assistance Programs: The State-Based Part of the Safety Net," *New Federalism: Issues and Options for States*, no. A-4 (Urban Institute, Assessing the New Federalism project, January 1997).

51. Rebecca M. Blank, *It Takes a Nation: A New Agenda for Fighting Poverty* (New York: Russell Sage Foundation and Princeton: Princeton Univ. Press, 1997). ch. 2.

52. Glenn C. Loury, "Welfare Pair," *The New Republic*, 5 & 12 January 1998, 9.

53. These points are emphasized in Nathan and Gais, "Overview Report."

54. On variations in state programs, see, e.g., Government Accounting Office, *Welfare Reform;* and L. Jerome Gallagher, et al., *One Year After Federal Welfare Reform: A Description of State Temporary Assistance for Needy Families (TANF) Decisions as of October 1997* (Washington, D.C.: Urban Institute, May 1998).

55. On the fear, see Paul E. Peterson, *The Price of Federalism* (Washington, D.C.: Brookings Institution, 1995), ch. 5. In fact, there has been some competitive benefits cutting, e.g., in the Washington metropolitan area.

56. In May 1999, the U.S. Supreme Court struck down a California law restricting welfare benefits for new residents to the level they would receive in the state they left.

57. Mead, *Beyond Entitlement*, ch. 11.

58. In 1998 Sen. Paul Wellstone (D-Minn.) introduced, but did not win passage of, a measure to enable recipients to get additional vocational and higher education.

59. Wayne Vroman, "Effects of Welfare Reform on Unemployment Insurance," *New Federalism: Issues and Options for States*, no. A-22 (Urban Institute, Assessing the New Federalism project, May 1998).

60. On "Faith and Families," see Amy L. Sherman, Mississippi's "Faith and Families" Congregational Mentoring Program (Washington, D.C.: Center for Public Justice, January 1998).

61. Judith M. Gueron and Amy Brown, "Work After Welfare," *Washington Post*, 13 August 1998, A21.

62. On the constitutional issues, see Carl H. Esbeck, "A Constitutional Case for Governmental Cooperation with Faith-based Social Service Providers," *Emory Law Journal* 46, no. 1 (winter 1997): 1–41, with supportive responses by Douglas Laycock and John Garvey; and Stephen V. Monsma and J. Christopher Soper, eds., *Equal Treatment of Religion in a Pluralistic Society* (Grand Rapids, Mich.: William B. Eerdmans, 1998).

63. Americans United for Separation of Church and State has threatened litigation. It is noteworthy, however, that despite similar threats, no legal challenge has actually ever been made to the similar rules governing child-care certificates under the Child Care and Development Block Grant program, which was first adopted in 1990.

64. Stanley W. Carlson-Thies, "'Don't Look to Us': The Negative Responses of the

Churches to Welfare Reform," *Notre Dame Journal of Law, Ethics & Public Policy* 11, no. 2, "Entitlements" special issue (1997): 667–689.

65. A notable instance of the nonprofit intermediary idea is the role played by Good Samaritan Ministries, Holland, Michigan, in the Project Zero experimental welfare reform.

66. Senate Bill 778, as signed into law in May 1996.

67. A creative collection of legislative measures was first proposed by Sen. Dan Coats (R-Indiana) in 1995 under the title "A Project for American Renewal." See *Mending Fences: Renewing Justice between Government and Civil Society*, ed. James W. Skillen (Washington, D.C.: Center for Public Justice; Grand Rapids, Mich.: Baker Books, 1998). See also *To Empower People: From State to Civil Society*, ed. Michael Novak, 2nd ed. (Washington, D.C.: AEI Press, 1996).

68. See, e.g., Marvin Olasky, *Renewing American Compassion* (New York: Free Press, 1996), 182–85. For a skeptical comment on such schemes, see Stanley W. Carlson-Thies, "There is No Substitute for Government's Special Role in Fighting Poverty," in the *Policy Review* symposium "Charity Tax Credits and Debits," no. 87 (Jan./Feb., 1998): 33–41.

69. See, e.g., Donald W. Dayton, *Discovering an Evangelical Heritage* (New York: Harper & Row, 1976); Norris Magnuson, *Salvation in the Slums: Evangelical Social Work, 1865–1920* (Grand Rapids, Mich.: Baker Book House, 1990); and Olasky, *Tragedy of American Compassion*.

70. David O. Moberg, *The Great Reversal: Evangelism and Social Concern*, rev. ed. (Philadelphia: J. B. Lippincott, 1977).

71. For an introduction to the CCDA, see John M. Perkins, ed., *Restoring At-Risk Communities: Doing It Together and Doing It Right* (Grand Rapids, Mich.: Baker Books, 1995).

72. Stephen V. Monsma, *When Sacred and Secular Mix: Religious Nonprofit Organizations and Public Money* (Lanham, Md.: Rowman & Littlefield, 1996).

73. Lugo, *Equal Partners*, 17ff.; Charles L. Glenn, *The Ambiguous Embrace: Government and Faith-based Schools and Social Agencies* (unpublished MS, April 1998).

74. Some of this language is borrowed from Carlson-Thies, "Welfare Reform's Challenge to the Evangelical Church."

Chapter 15: *Rebuilding Marriage and the Family*

*The author gratefully acknowledges the considerable assistance of Jessica Pritchett in preparing this chapter.

1. Pre-1980 statistics: William J. Bennett, *Index of Leading Cultural Indicators* (New York: Simon & Schuster, 1994), 46; post-1890 statistics: Chart 97, *Statistical Abstract of the United States 1997* (Washington, D.C.: U.S. Department of Commerce, 1997), 79. A recent check of 1996 statistics (the freshest number available) reveals that the rate is holding steady at 32 percent. See the data summary from the Annie E. Casey Foundation at www.aecf.org/kc1997.

2. Chart 96, *Statistical Abstract of the United States 1997* (Washington, D.C.: U.S. Department of Commerce, 1997), 78.

3. Chart 97, *Statistical Abstract of the United States 1997* (Washington, D.C.: U.S. Department of Commerce, 1997), 78.

4. Suzanne M. Bianchi and Daphne Spain, "Women, Work, and Family in America," *Population Bulletin* 51, no. 3 (December 1996): 39.

5. As reported by the National Center for Health Statistics, accessed at www.cdc.gov/nchswww/fastats/divorce.htm. See also Chart 145, *Statistical Abstract of the United States 1997* (Washington, D.C.: U.S. Department of Commerce, 1997), 105.

6. Chart 149, *Statistical Abstract of the United States 1997* (Washington, D.C.: U.S. Department of Commerce, 1997), 106.

7. Charles S. Clark, "Marriage and Divorce," *CQ Researcher* 6, no. 18 (10 May 1996): 423.

8. William A. Galston, "Divorce American Style," *The Public Interest* (Summer 1996): 14.

9. U.S. Department of Education, National Center for Education Statistics, *Youth Indicators 1996*, accessed at www.nces.ed.gov.

10. Chart 75, *Statistical Abstract of the United States 1997* (Washington, D.C.: U.S. Department of Commerce, 1997), 63.

11. Nancy Dreher, "Divorce and the American Family," *Current Health* 2 (November 1996): 6.

12. Maggie Gallagher, "Washington Encourages Teenage Pregnancy," *Forbes*, 23 September 1996, 152.

13. Daniel R. Meyer, "Supporting Children Born Outside of Marriage: Do Child Support Awards Keep Pace with Changes in Fathers'

Incomes?" *Social Science Quarterly* 76, no. 3 (September 1995): 577.

14. Bianchi and Spain, "Women, Work, and Family in America," 36.

15. Quoted in Michael Wentzel and Sherrie Negrea, "How Did It Happen? The Roots of Poverty in Rochester," *Rochester Democrat and Chronicle*, 7 November 1993.

16. Bianchi and Spain, "Women, Work, and Family in America," 29.

17. Ibid., 36.

18. Ibid.

19. Annie E. Casey Foundation, *KIDS COUNT* Data Online, accessed at www.aecf.org/kc1997.

20. Ibid.

21. Gallagher, "Washington Encourages Teenage Pregnancy," 152.

22. Richard R. Peterson, "A Re-evaluation of the Economic Consequences of Divorce," *American Sociological Review* 61 (June 1996): 528–36.

23. Galston, "Divorce American Style," *The Public Interest* (Summer 1996): 16.

24. Bianchi and Spain, "Women, Work, and Family in America," 12.

25. Ibid.

26. Atlee L. Stroup and Gene E. Pollock, "Economic Consequences of Marital Dissolution," *Journal of Divorce and Remarriage* 22, nos. 1–2 (1994): 52.

27. Timothy J. Biblarz and Adrian D. Raftery, "The Effects of Family Disruption on Social Mobility," *American Sociological Review* 58 (1993): 97–109.

28. Celvia Stovall Dixon and Kathryn D. Rettig, "An Examination of Income Adequacy for Single Women Two Years After Divorce," *Journal of Divorce and Remarriage* 22, nos. 1–2 (1994): 56.

29. Judith Wallerstein and Sandra Blakeslee, *Second Chances* (Boston: Houghton Mifflin, 1996), 8.

30. Teresa A. Mauldin, "Women Who Remain Above the Poverty Level in Divorce: Implications for Family Policy," *Family Relations* 39 (April 1990): 141–46.

31. Chart 606, *Statistical Abstract of the United States 1997* (Washington, D.C.: U.S. Department of Commerce, 1997), 387.

32. Quoted on Americans for Divorce Reform website, accessed at www.divorcereform.org/pov.html.

33. William A. Galston, "Putting Children First," *American Educator* (summer 1992): 13.

34. Sara McLanahan and Gary Sandefur, *Growing Up With a Single Parent: What Hurts, What Helps* (Cambridge, Mass.: Harvard University Press, 1994), 24.

35. Timothy J. Biblarz and Adrian D. Raftery, "The Effects of Family Disruption on Social Mobility," *American Sociological Review* 58 (1993): 97.

36. Perhaps the best recent works documenting these consequences are Judith Wallerstein and Sandra Bladeslee, *Second Chances: Men, Women and Children a Decade After Divorce* (Boston: Houghton Mifflin, 1996); David B. Larson, et al., *The Costly Consequences of Divorce: Assessing the Clinical, Economic, and Public Health Impact of Marital Disruption in the United States* (Rockville, Md.: National Institute for HealthCare Research, n.d.); Paul R. Amato and Alan Booth, *A Generation At Risk: Growing Up in an Era of Family Upheaval* (Cambridge, Mass.: Harvard University Press, 1998).

37. Wallerstein and Blakeslee, *Second Chances*, 18.

38. Barbara DaFoe Whitehead, *The Divorce Culture* (New York: Knopf, 1997), 183.

39. David Popenoe, "The Controversial Truth," *New York Times*, 26 December 1992.

40. Carol J. DeVita, "The United States at Mid-Decade," *Population Bulletin* 50, no. 4 (March 1996): 38.

41. Quoted in Galston, "Putting Children First," *The American Educator*, 12.

42. Ibid.

43. Frank F. Furstenberg, Jr., "The Future of Marriage," *American Demographics* (June 1996): 39.

44. Alan Guttmacher Institute, accessed at www.info-sys.hom.vix.com/men/nofather/guttmacher.html.

45. Rebecca Blank, *It Takes a Nation* (New York: Russell Sage Foundation, 1997), 37–38.

46. Maggie Gallagher, "Washington Encourages Teenage Pregnancy," 152.

47. William Bennett, *Index of Leading Cultural Indicators*, 104.

48. M. David Goodwin, "Maryland Bucking Teen-birth Trend," *Louisville Courier-Journal*, 16 June 1992.

49. Gregory Acs, "The Impact of Welfare on Young Mothers' Subsequent Childbearing Decisions," *Human Resources* (fall 1996): accessed at proquest.com.

50. Blank, *It Takes a Nation*, 38.

51. See William Julius Wilson, *When Work Disappears* (New York: Knopf, 1996), especially ch. 4.

52. See the discussion in Robert D. Mare and Christopher Winship, "Socio-economic Change and the Decline of Marriage for Blacks and Whites," in *The Urban Underclass*, edited by Christopher Jencks and Paul Paterson (Washington, D.C.: The Brookings Institution, 1991).

53. Michael McManus, *Marriage Savers* (Grand Rapids: Zondervan, 1993).

54. See Glen Stassen and David P. Gushee, *Christian Ethics as Following Jesus* (Downers Grove, Ill.: InterVarsity, 1999), ch. 9.

55. Reported in http://archives.his.com/smartmarriages/0201/html.

56. Ann Scott Tyson, "States Put Speed Bumps in Divorce Path," *Christian Science Monitor*, 10 September 1996; See also Pia Nordlinger, "The Anti-Divorce Revolution," *Weekly Standard*, 2 March 1998, 26.

57. *Kansas City Star*, 12 March 1998, in http://archives.his.com/smartmarriages/0113/html. To receive the money couples would also have to certify that they had never had a child, an abortion, or a sexually transmitted disease. These extra provisions are unhelpful, in my view.

58. Carl E. Schneider, "The Law and the Stability of Marriage: The Family as a Social Institution," in *Promises to Keep*, edited by David Popenoe, et al. (Lanham, Md.: Rowman & Littlefield, 1996), 196.

59. See McManus, *Marriage Savers*, ch. 7.

60. Regan, "Postmodern Family Law," in Popenoe, *Promises to Keep*, 166.

61. Sylvia Ann Hewlett and Cornel West, *The War Against Parents* (New York: Houghton Mifflin, 1998), 242.

62. Ibid., ch. 9.

63. For a discussion of some of the starkly different approaches that go by the name of "pro-family" politics, see David P. Gushee, "Family Values?" *Prism* 3, no. 4 (May/June 1996): 15–17.

64. For the concept of marriage as a status relationship, see Regan, "Postmodern Family Law," in Popenoe, *Promises to Keep*, 147–71.

65. Among the most common fault grounds among the dozens that appear in state laws are adultery, physical and mental cruelty, attempted murder, desertion, habitual drunkenness, use of addictive drugs, insanity, impotence, and infection of one's spouse with a venereal disease. American Bar Association, *Guide to Family Law* (New York: Random House, 1996), 68–69.

66. For this analysis, see Mary Ann Glendon, *Abortion and Divorce in Western Law* (Cambridge, Mass.: Harvard University Press, 1987), 65.

67. Ibid., 66.

68. Bryce J. Christensen, "Taking Stock: Assessing Twenty Years of 'No Fault' Divorce," *The Family in America* 5, no. 9 (September 1991): 3.

69. Ibid., 4.

70. See Barbara DaFoe Whitehead, "The Divorce Trap," *New York Times*, 13 January 1997, A22.

71. For an extended discussion of these proposals, see my forthcoming "The Divorce Epidemic: Evaluating Policy Responses That Can Reduce Divorce," in David P. Gushee, ed., *Christian Faith and Public Policy: Where Do We Go from Here?* (Anticipated publication, 2000).

72. See Christopher Wolfe, "The Marriage of Your Choice," *First Things* 50 (February 1995): 37–41.

73. Galston, "The Reinstitutionalization of Marriage," in Popenoe, *Promises to Keep*, 285–87.

74. This is the case even where there has been profound marital and family difficulty prior to the divorce—but especially where there has not, which is the case roughly 70 percent of the time according to one authoritative recent study. See Amato and Booth, *A Generation At Risk*, 220.

75. Amy Black, "For the Sake of the Children: Reconstructing American Divorce Policy," *Crossroads Monograph Series on Faith and Public Policy* 1, no. 2, (Wynnewood, Pa.: 1995) 40.

76. Galston, "The Reinstitutionalization of Marriage," 286.

77. Reported in http://archives.his.com/smartmarriages/0201.html.

78. The best available statement calling for just such a partnership is "Marriage in America: A Report to the Nation," authored by the Council on Families in America. See Popenoe, *Promises to Keep*, 293–318.